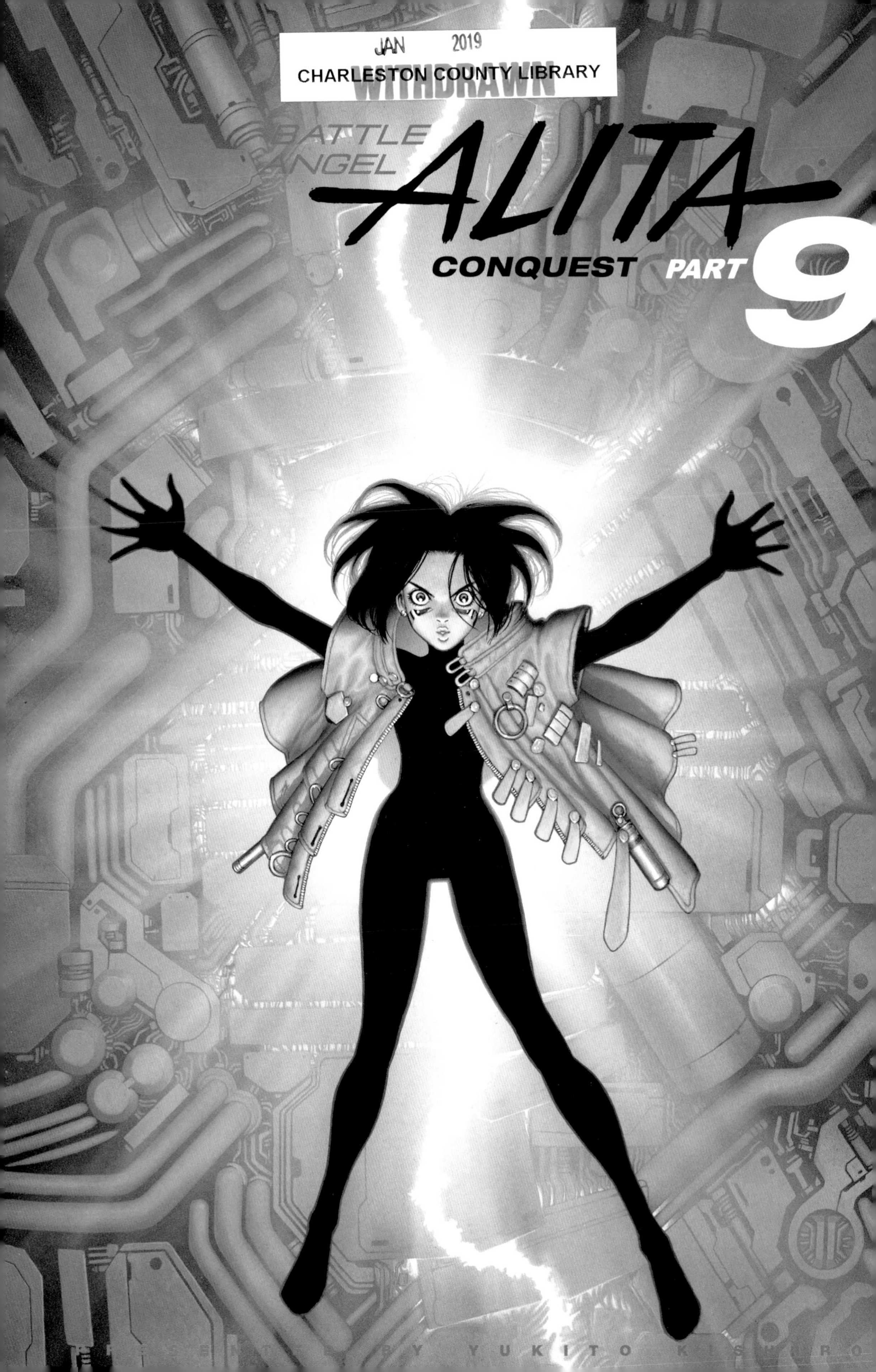
BATTLE ANGEL
ALITA
CONQUEST PART 9
BY YUKITO

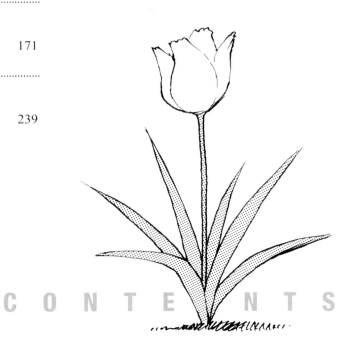

C O N T E N T S

FIGHT_048 No Brainer

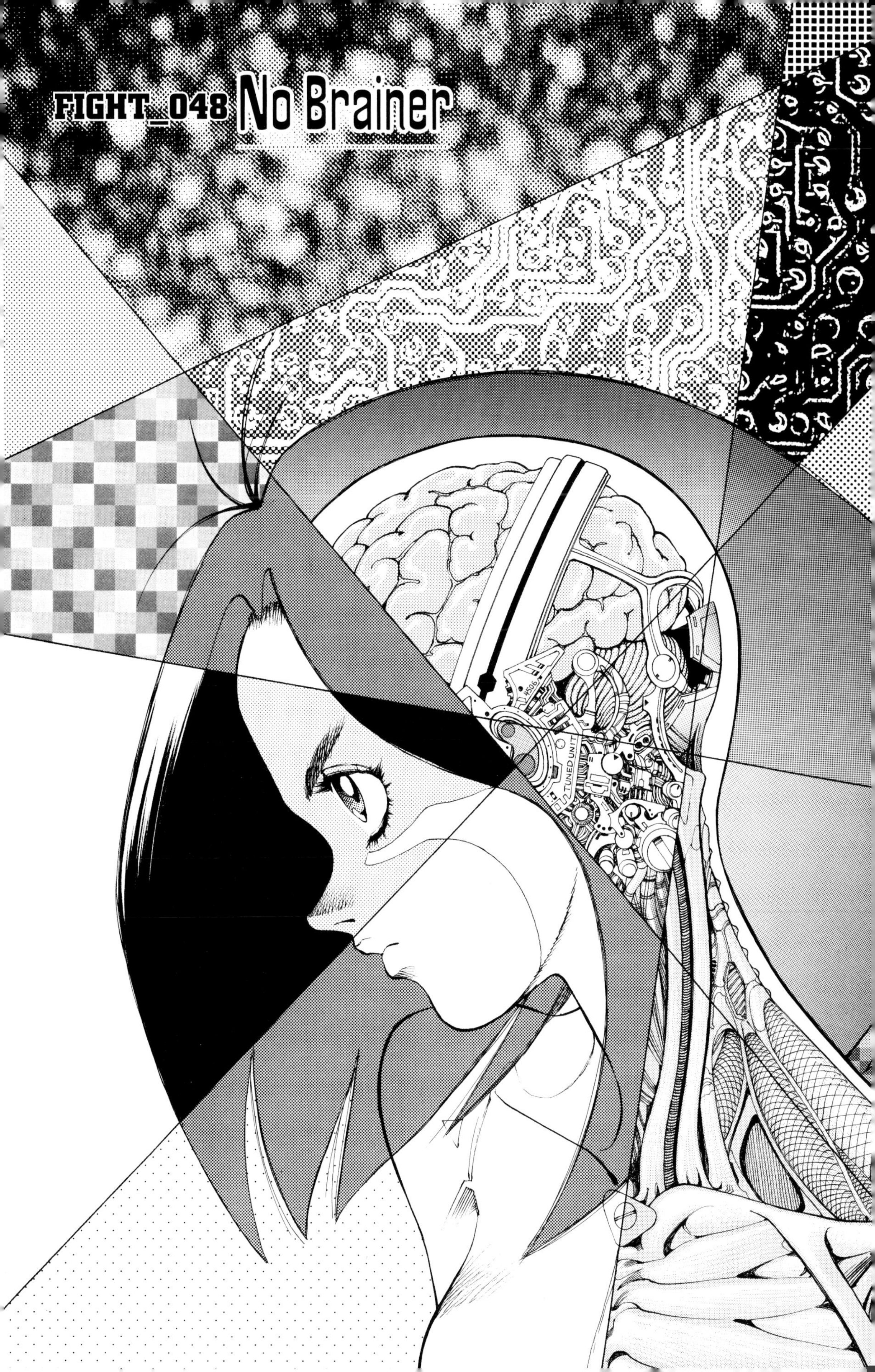
TUNED UNIT

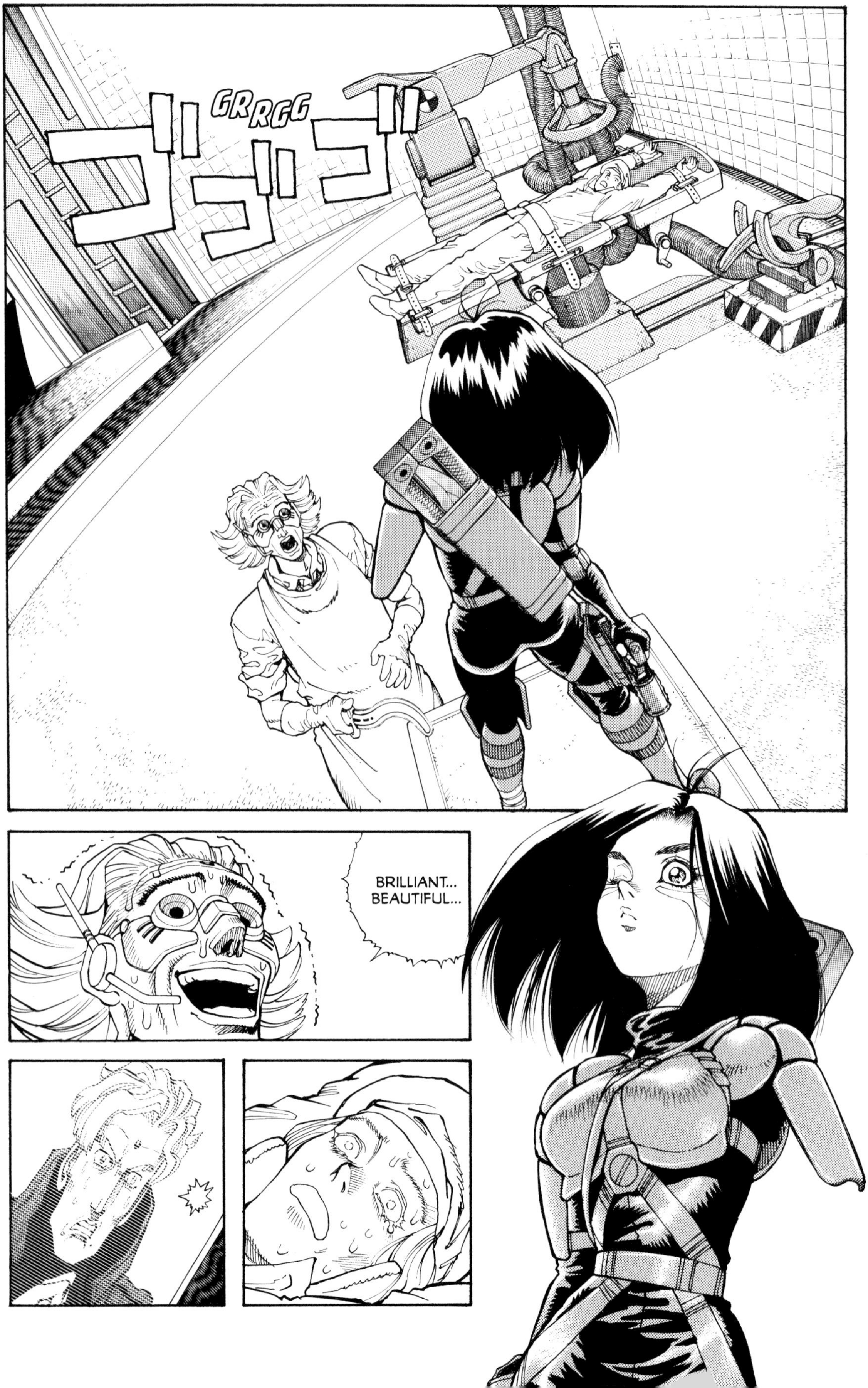
GRRGG
BRILLIANT...
BEAUTIFUL...

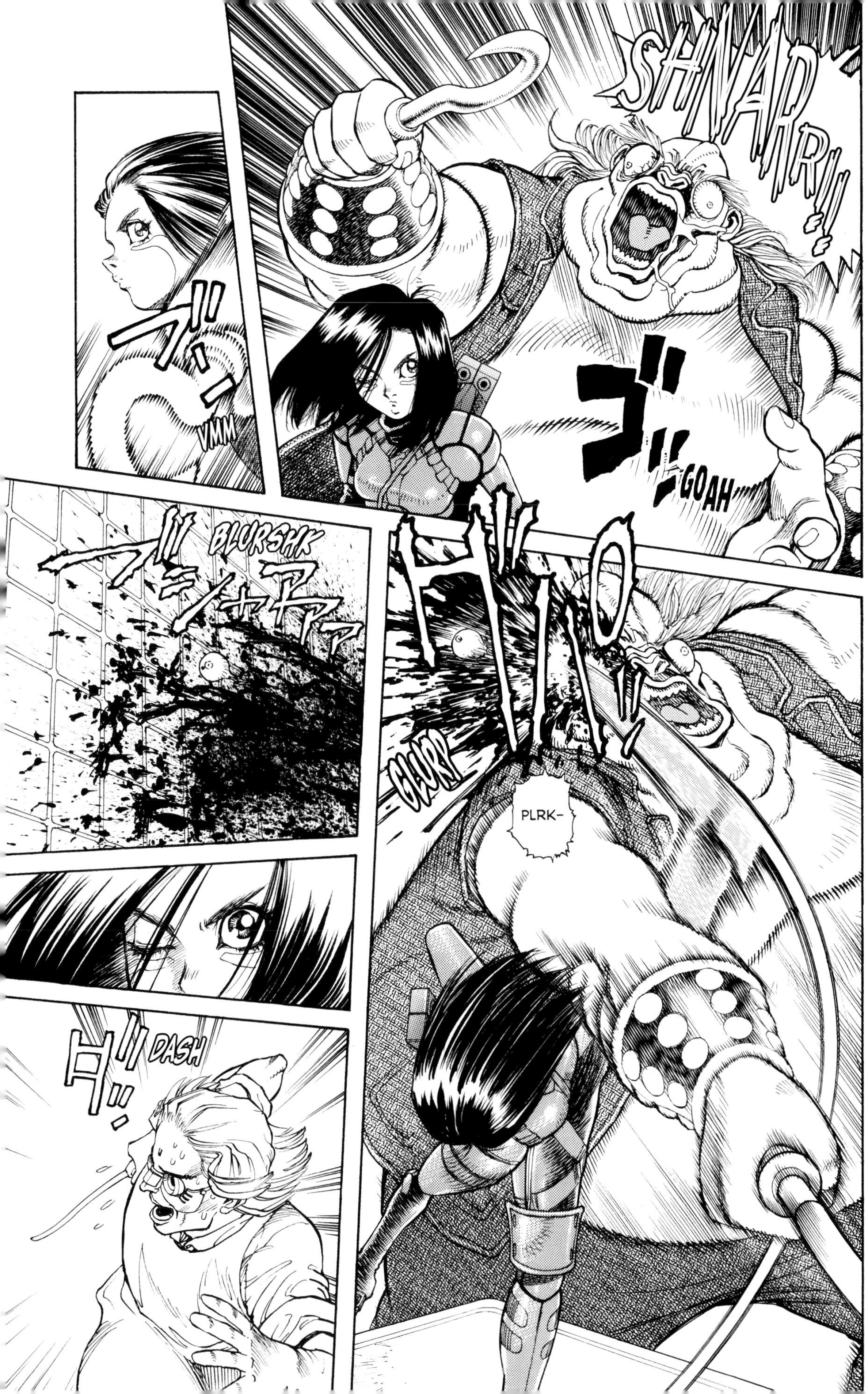

SHNARRR!!
GOAH
VMM
GLORP
PLRK-
BLURSHK
DASH

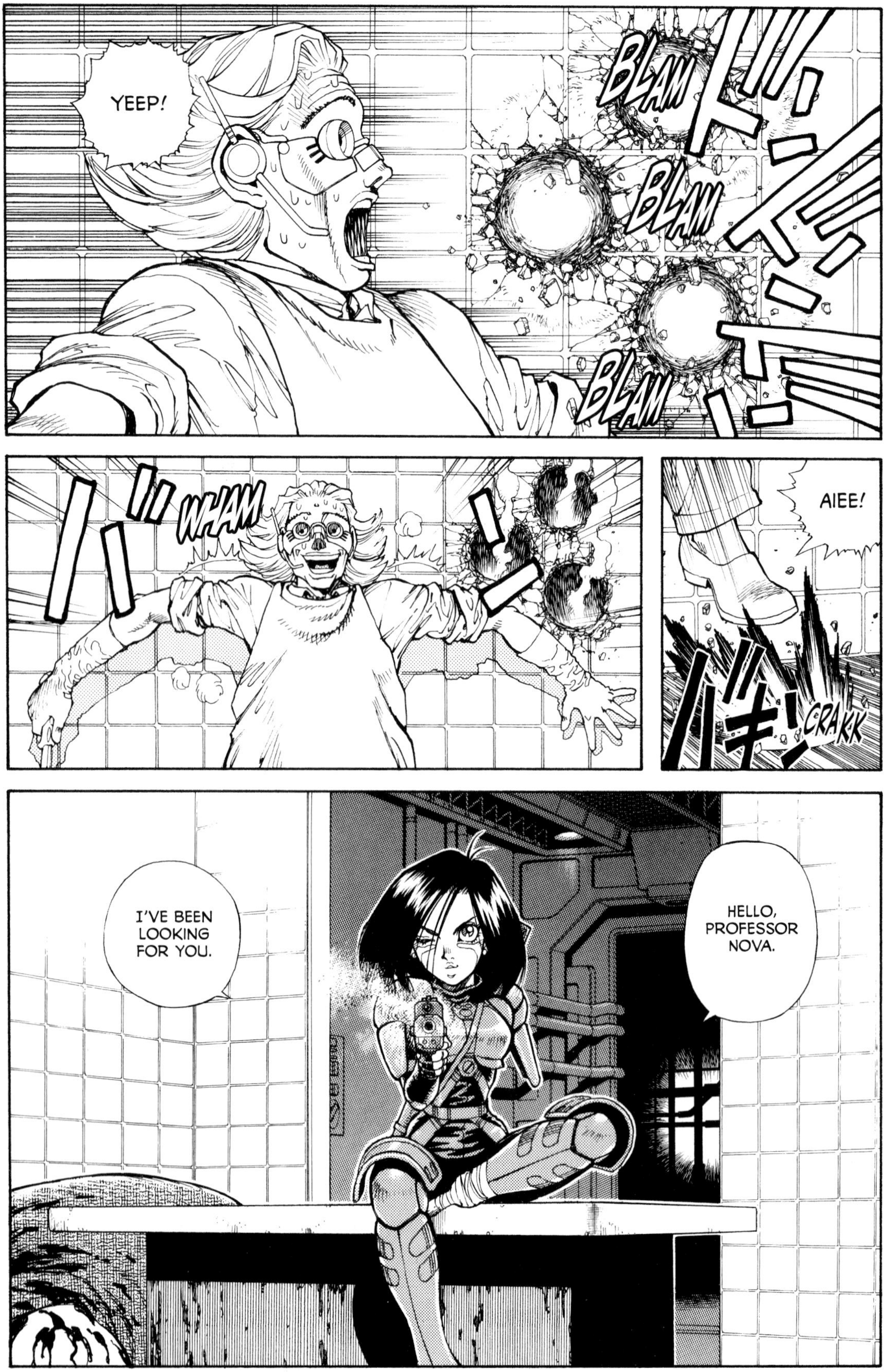
BLAM
YEEP!
BLAM
BLAM
AIEE!
CRAKK
WHAM
HELLO, PROFESSOR NOVA.
I'VE BEEN LOOKING FOR YOU.

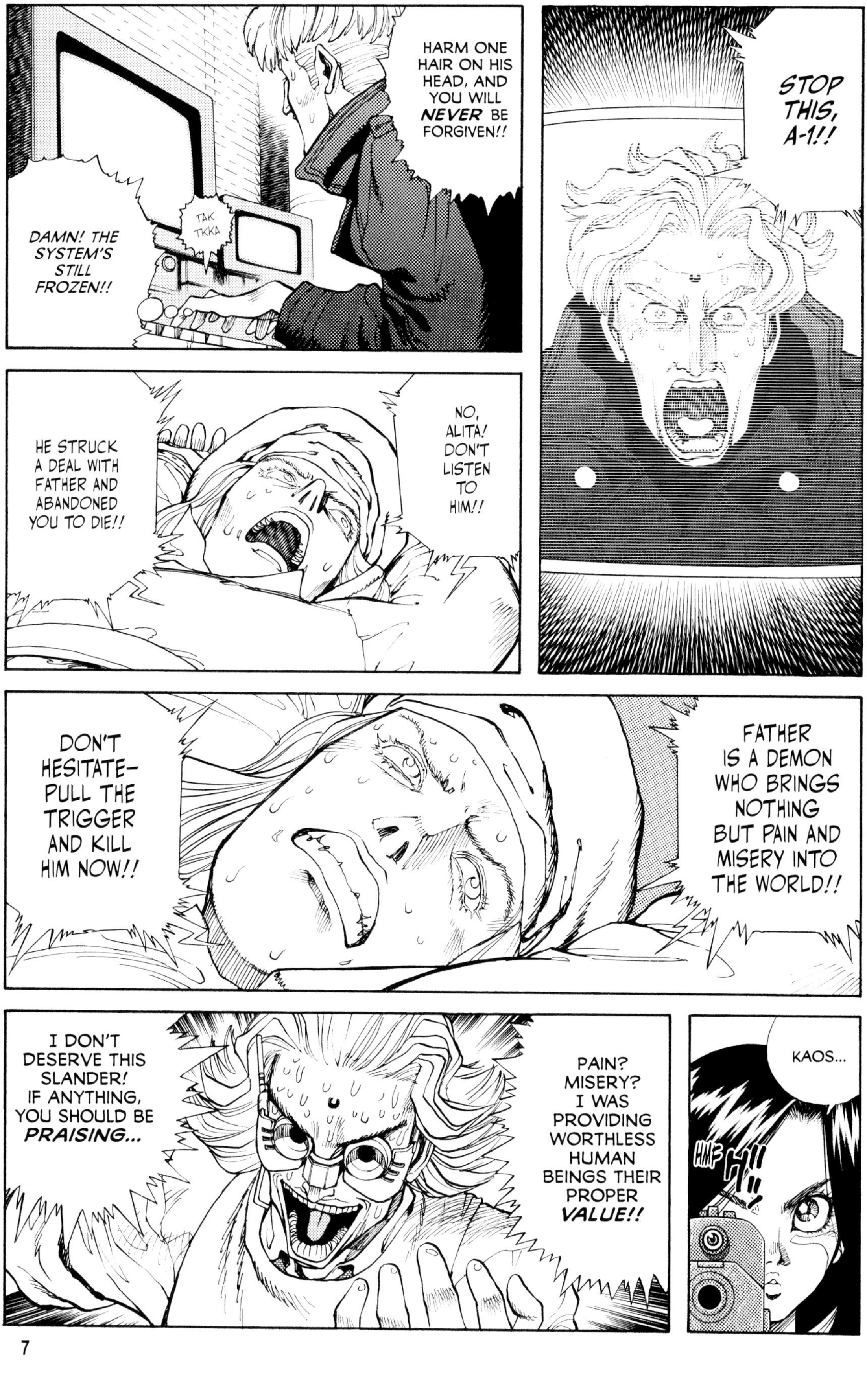
STOP THIS, A-1!!
HARM ONE HAIR ON HIS HEAD, AND YOU WILL NEVER BE FORGIVEN!!
TAK TKKA
DAMN! THE SYSTEM'S STILL FROZEN!!
NO, ALITA! DON'T LISTEN TO HIM!!
HE STRUCK A DEAL WITH FATHER AND ABANDONED YOU TO DIE!!
FATHER IS A DEMON WHO BRINGS NOTHING BUT PAIN AND MISERY INTO THE WORLD!!
DON'T HESITATE–PULL THE TRIGGER AND KILL HIM NOW!!
KAOS...
HMF
PAIN? MISERY? I WAS PROVIDING WORTHLESS HUMAN BEINGS THEIR PROPER VALUE!!
I DON'T DESERVE THIS SLANDER! IF ANYTHING, YOU SHOULD BE PRAISING...

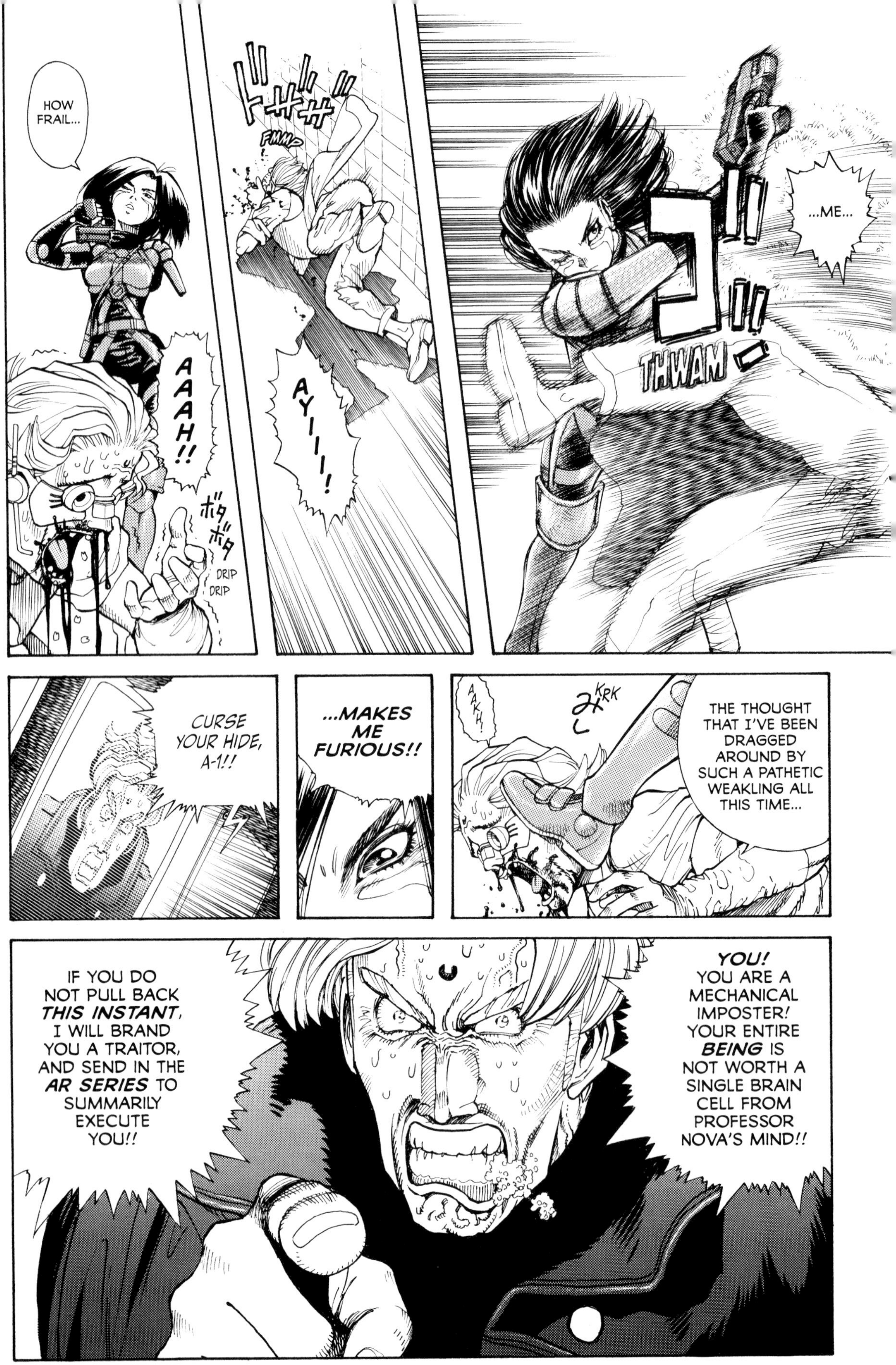
...ME...
THWAM
FMMP
AYIIIII!
HOW FRAIL...
AAAAH!!
ボタボタ
DRIP DRIP
AAKH!
KRK
THE THOUGHT THAT I'VE BEEN DRAGGED AROUND BY SUCH A PATHETIC WEAKLING ALL THIS TIME...
...MAKES ME FURIOUS!!
CURSE YOUR HIDE, A-1!!
YOU! YOU ARE A MECHANICAL IMPOSTER! YOUR ENTIRE BEING IS NOT WORTH A SINGLE BRAIN CELL FROM PROFESSOR NOVA'S MIND!!
IF YOU DO NOT PULL BACK THIS INSTANT, I WILL BRAND YOU A TRAITOR, AND SEND IN THE AR SERIES TO SUMMARILY EXECUTE YOU!!

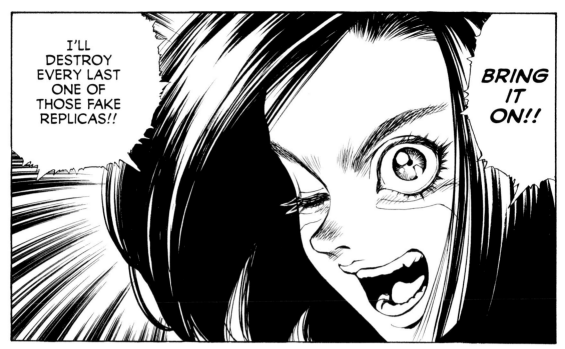

BRING IT ON!!
I'LL DESTROY EVERY LAST ONE OF THOSE FAKE REPLICAS!!
...!!
SHE'S STRONGER!!
WHATEVER HAPPENED... SHE'S NOT THE SAME ALITA AS YESTERDAY!
HMPH!
EEEP!
BEG FOR YOUR LIFE, IF YOU MUST!!
BUT I WILL NOT SPARE IT.
NO... I CAN'T STAND THE THOUGHT OF NEVER TASTING FLAN AGAIN!

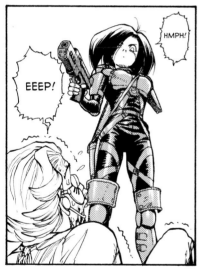

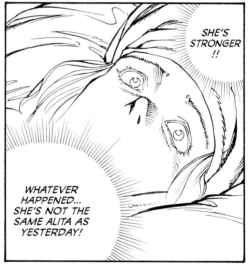

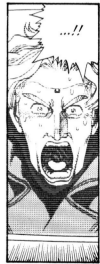

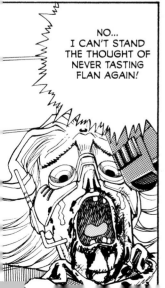

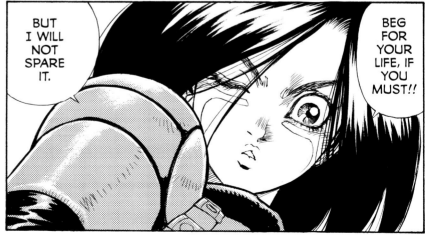

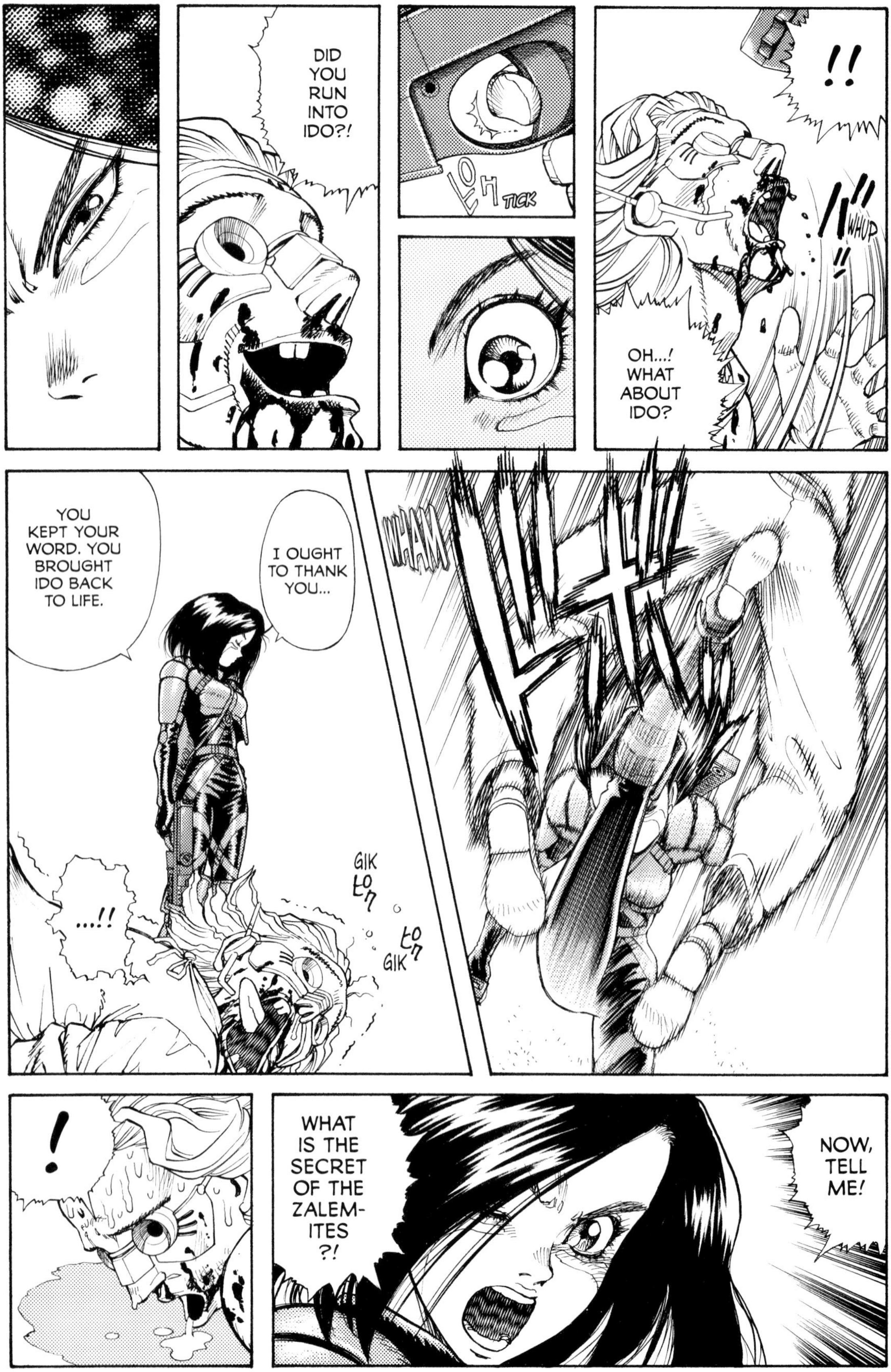
!!
WHUD
OH...! WHAT ABOUT IDO?
TICK
DID YOU RUN INTO IDO?!
WHAM
I OUGHT TO THANK YOU...
YOU KEPT YOUR WORD. YOU BROUGHT IDO BACK TO LIFE.
GIK
GIK
...!!
NOW, TELL ME!
WHAT IS THE SECRET OF THE ZALEM-ITES?!
!

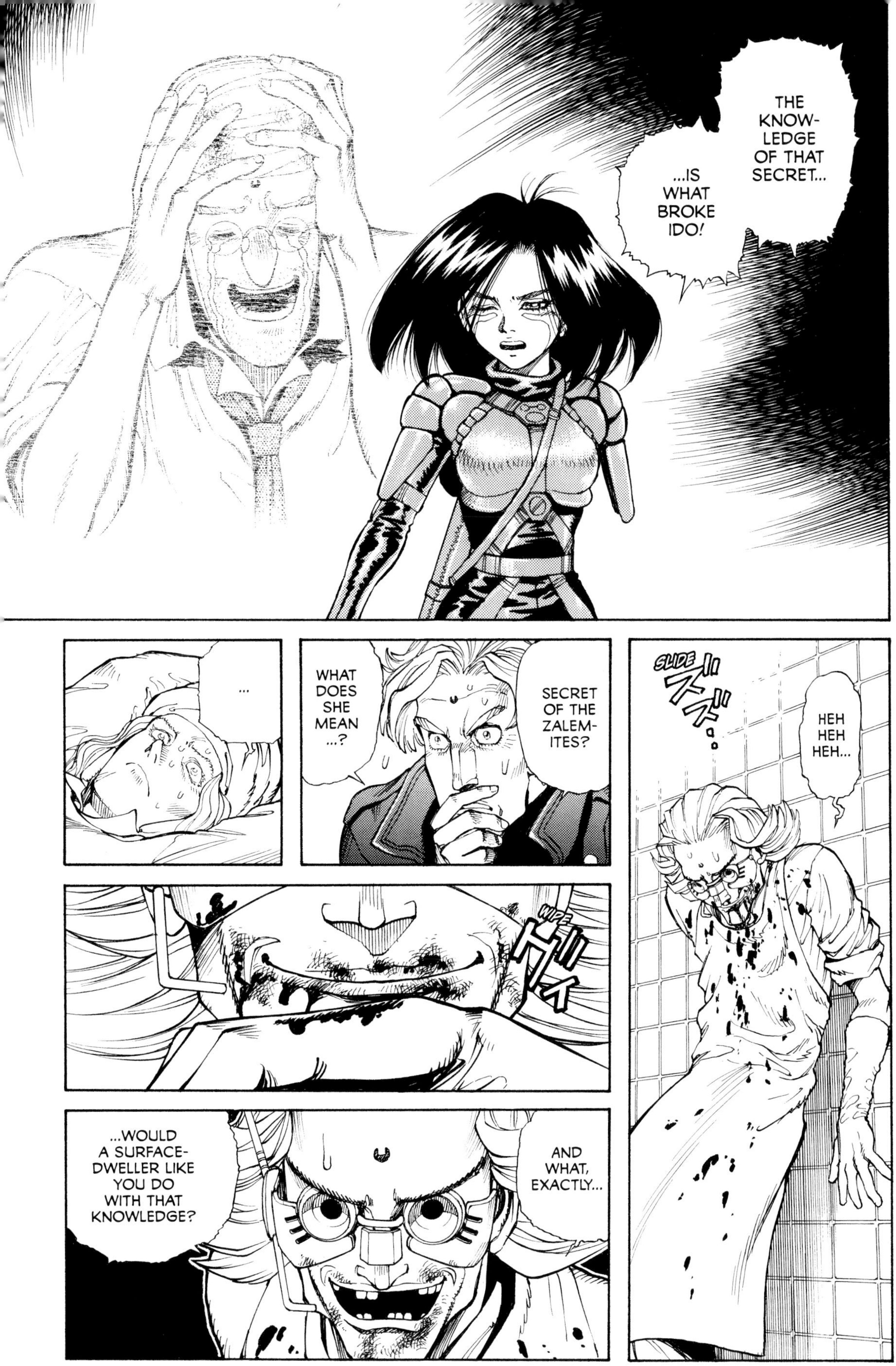
THE KNOW-LEDGE OF THAT SECRET...
...IS WHAT BROKE IDO!
SLIDE
HEH HEH HEH...
SECRET OF THE ZALEM-ITES?
WHAT DOES SHE MEAN ...?
...
WIPE
AND WHAT, EXACTLY...
...WOULD A SURFACE-DWELLER LIKE YOU DO WITH THAT KNOWLEDGE?

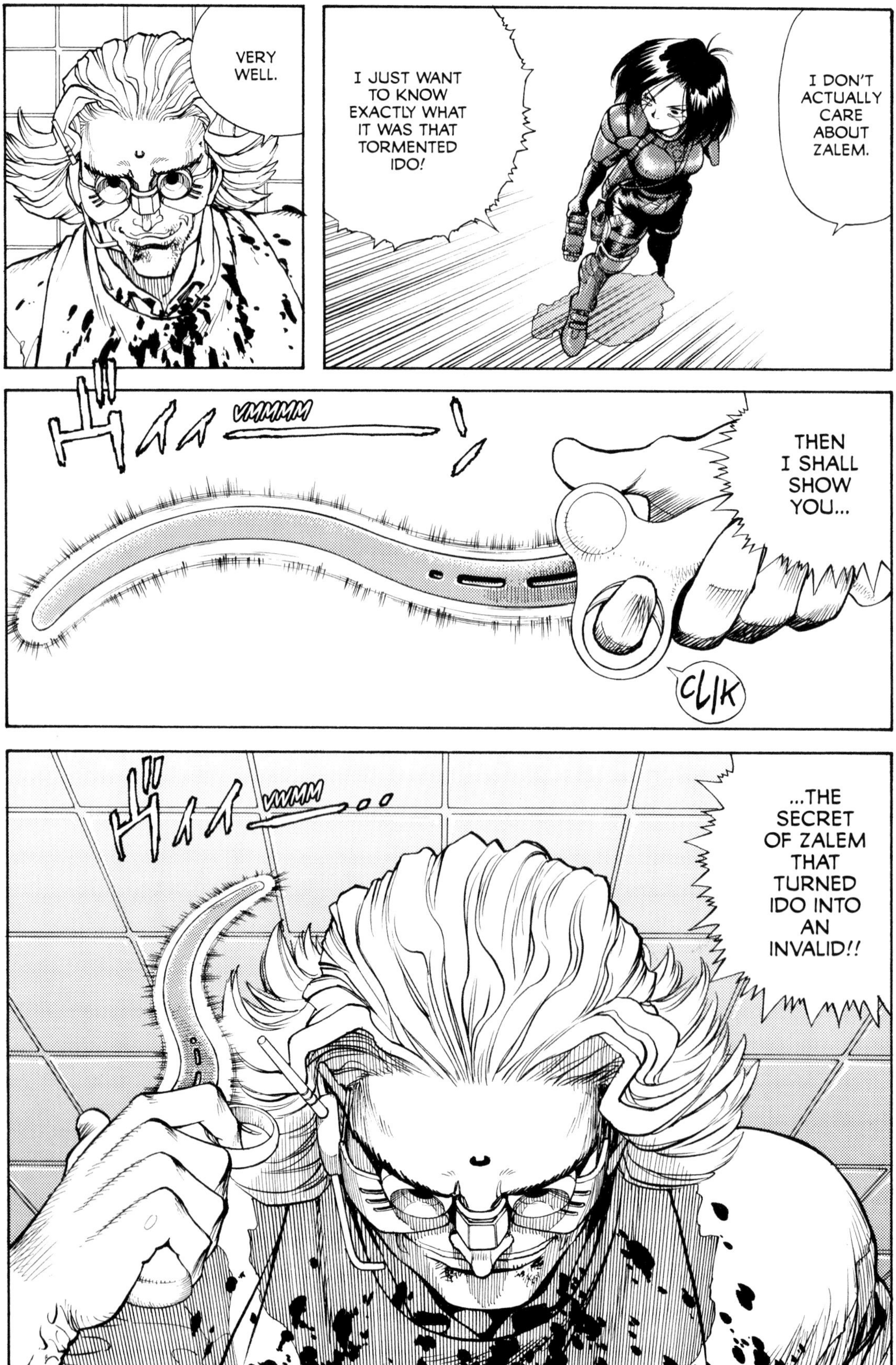
I DON'T ACTUALLY CARE ABOUT ZALEM.
I JUST WANT TO KNOW EXACTLY WHAT IT WAS THAT TORMENTED IDO!
VERY WELL.
THEN I SHALL SHOW YOU...
VMMMM
CLIK
...THE SECRET OF ZALEM THAT TURNED IDO INTO AN INVALID!!
VMMM

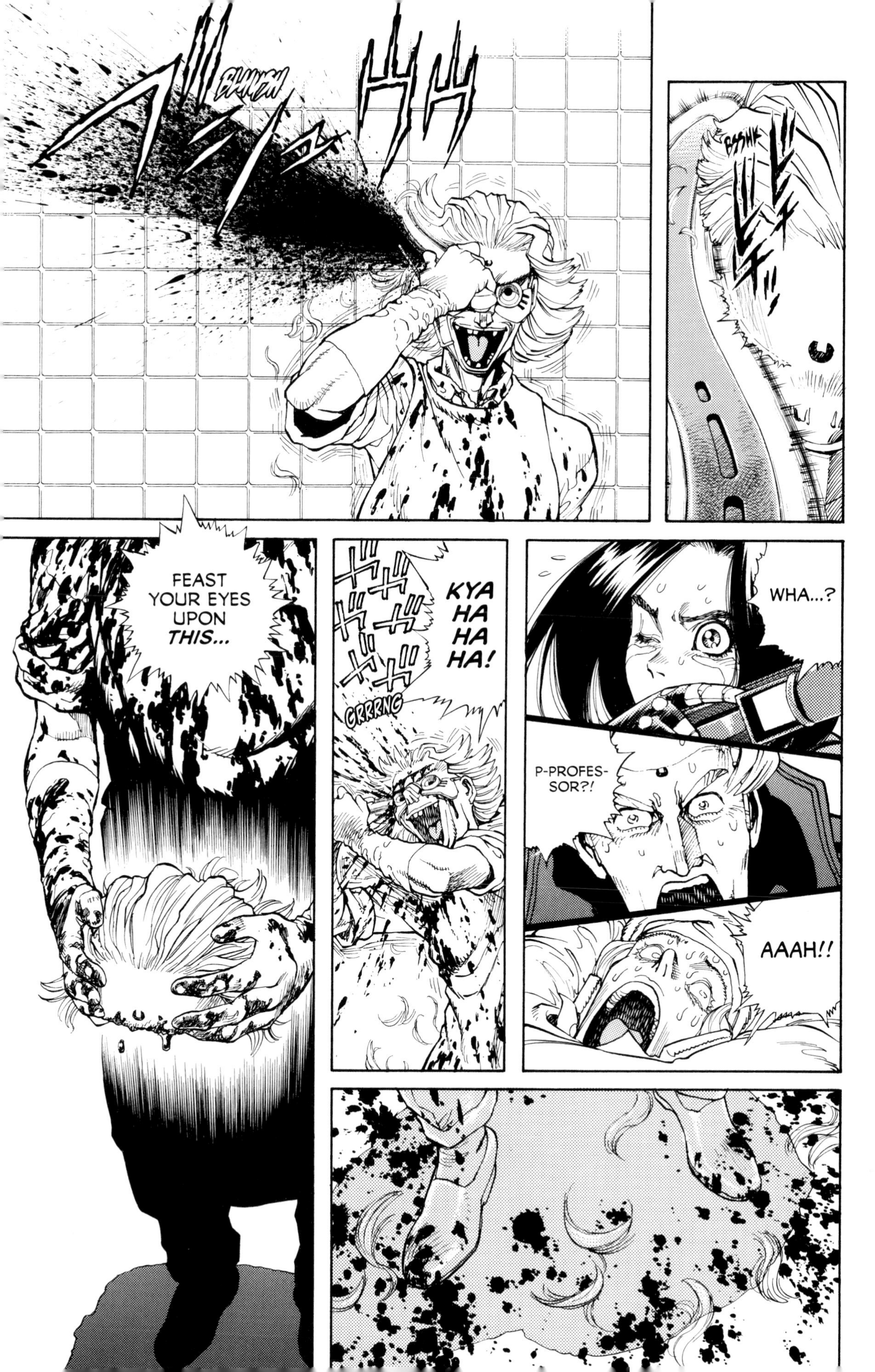
BSSHK
BHHSH
WHA...?
P-PROFES-
SOR?!
AAAH!!
KYA
HA
HA
HA!
CRRRNG
FEAST
YOUR EYES
UPON
THIS...

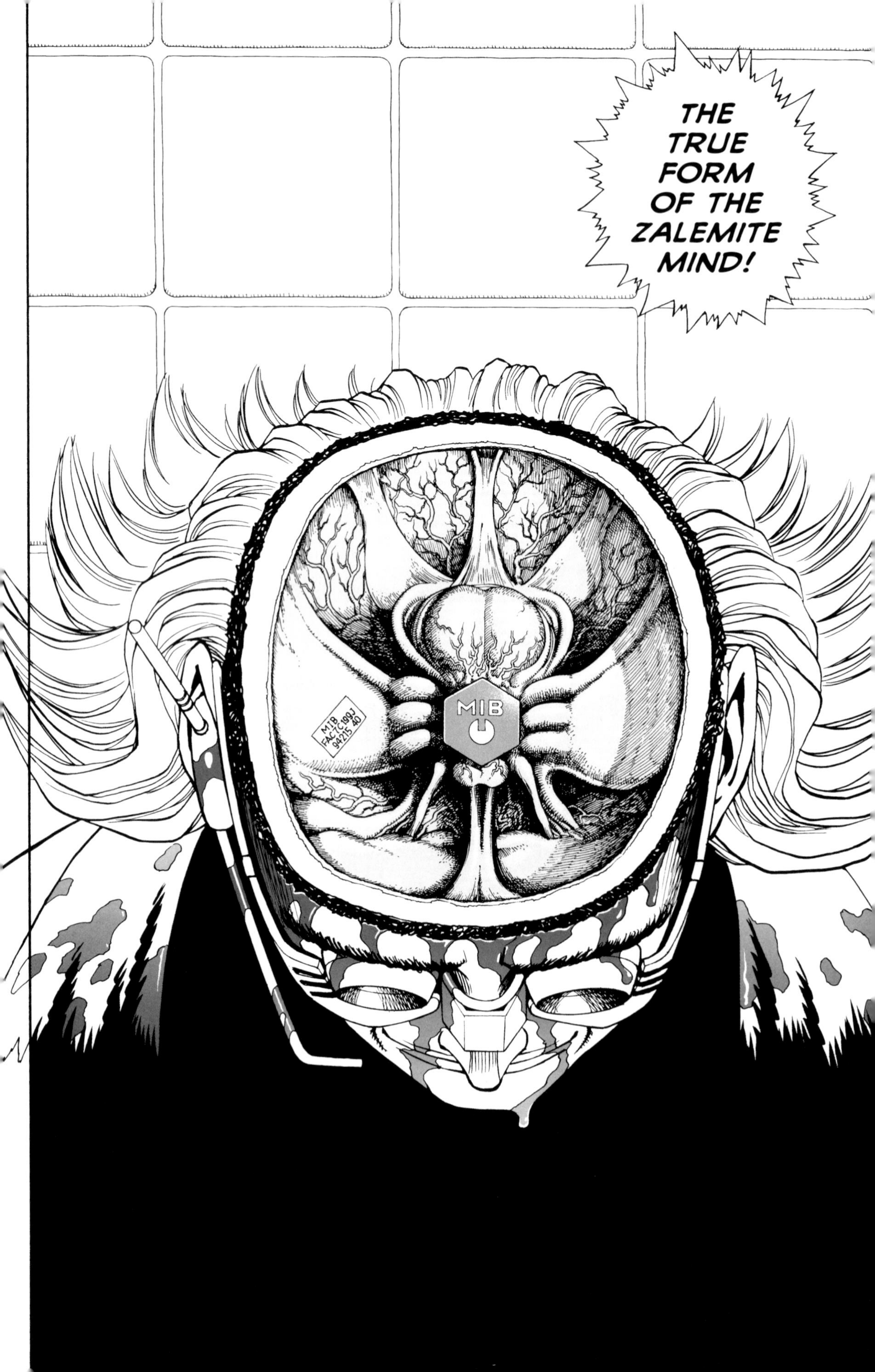
THE TRUE FORM OF THE ZALEMITE MIND!
MIB

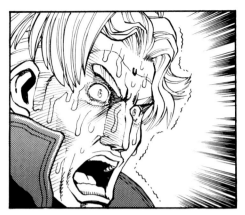

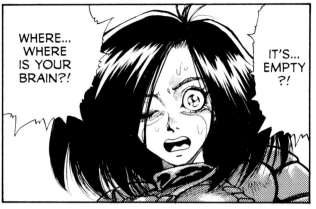

IT'S... EMPTY ?!
WHERE... WHERE IS YOUR BRAIN?!
CAN YOU SEE THAT TINY BIOCHIP IN THE CENTER?
MIB
MIB FACTC199J 94215 40
IT IS HANDLING ALL OF THE FUNCTIONS OF THE BRAIN.
ZALEM'S CHILDREN ARE BORN THROUGH A STRICT EUGENICS* PROGRAM. THEY UNDERGO MANY TESTS (INTELLIGENCE, MENTALITY, PERSONALITY, PHYSICAL, ETC.) BEFORE AGE 19, WHEN THEY HAVE THEIR "INITIATION" AND RECEIVE THE MARK OF ZALEM CITIZENSHIP ON THEIR FOREHEADS!
THAT INITIATION PROCESS IS A SURGERY THAT REMOVES THE BRAIN AND EMBEDS A CHIP WITH ALL OF THE SUBJECT'S MEMORIES COPIED ONTO IT!!

***Eugenics:** An area of science dedicated to improving human genetics. It is designed to remove unwanted genetic structures and preserve superior ones.

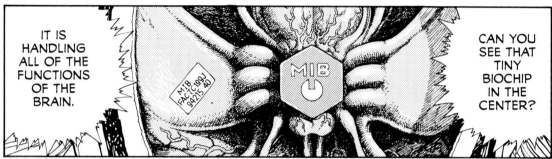

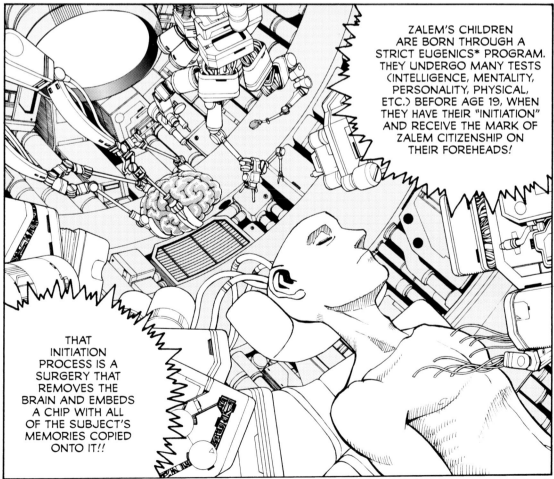

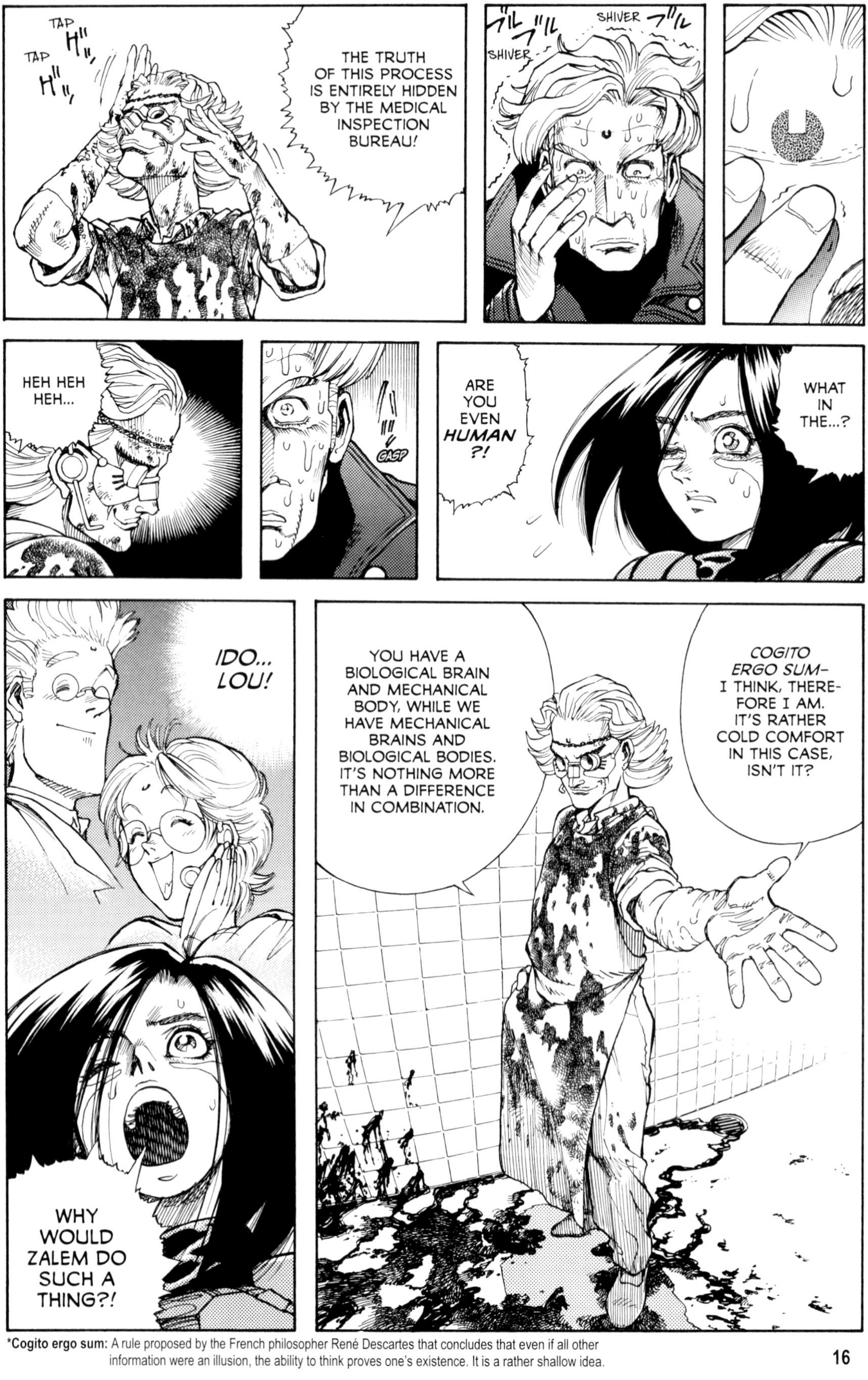
SHIVER
SHIVER
TAP
TAP
THE TRUTH OF THIS PROCESS IS ENTIRELY HIDDEN BY THE MEDICAL INSPECTION BUREAU!
WHAT IN THE...?
ARE YOU EVEN *HUMAN* ?!
GASP
HEH HEH HEH...
COGITO ERGO SUM– I THINK, THEREFORE I AM. IT'S RATHER COLD COMFORT IN THIS CASE, ISN'T IT?
YOU HAVE A BIOLOGICAL BRAIN AND MECHANICAL BODY, WHILE WE HAVE MECHANICAL BRAINS AND BIOLOGICAL BODIES. IT'S NOTHING MORE THAN A DIFFERENCE IN COMBINATION.
IDO... LOU!
WHY WOULD ZALEM DO SUCH A THING?!

***Cogito ergo sum:** A rule proposed by the French philosopher René Descartes that concludes that even if all other information were an illusion, the ability to think proves one's existence. It is a rather shallow idea.

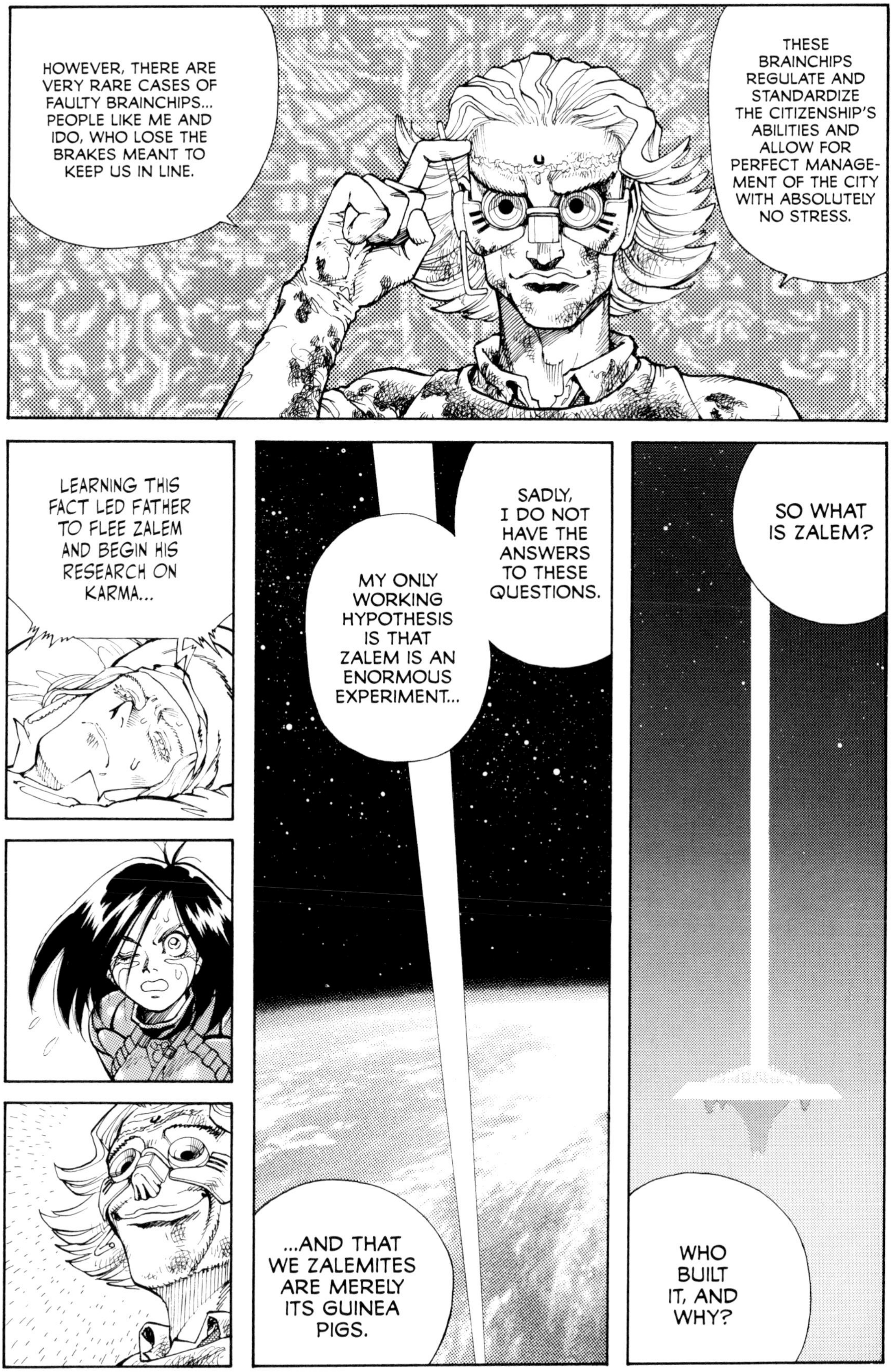
THESE BRAINCHIPS REGULATE AND STANDARDIZE THE CITIZENSHIP'S ABILITIES AND ALLOW FOR PERFECT MANAGEMENT OF THE CITY WITH ABSOLUTELY NO STRESS.
HOWEVER, THERE ARE VERY RARE CASES OF FAULTY BRAINCHIPS... PEOPLE LIKE ME AND IDO, WHO LOSE THE BRAKES MEANT TO KEEP US IN LINE.
SO WHAT IS ZALEM?
WHO BUILT IT, AND WHY?
SADLY, I DO NOT HAVE THE ANSWERS TO THESE QUESTIONS.
MY ONLY WORKING HYPOTHESIS IS THAT ZALEM IS AN ENORMOUS EXPERIMENT...
...AND THAT WE ZALEMITES ARE MERELY ITS GUINEA PIGS.
LEARNING THIS FACT LED FATHER TO FLEE ZALEM AND BEGIN HIS RESEARCH ON KARMA...

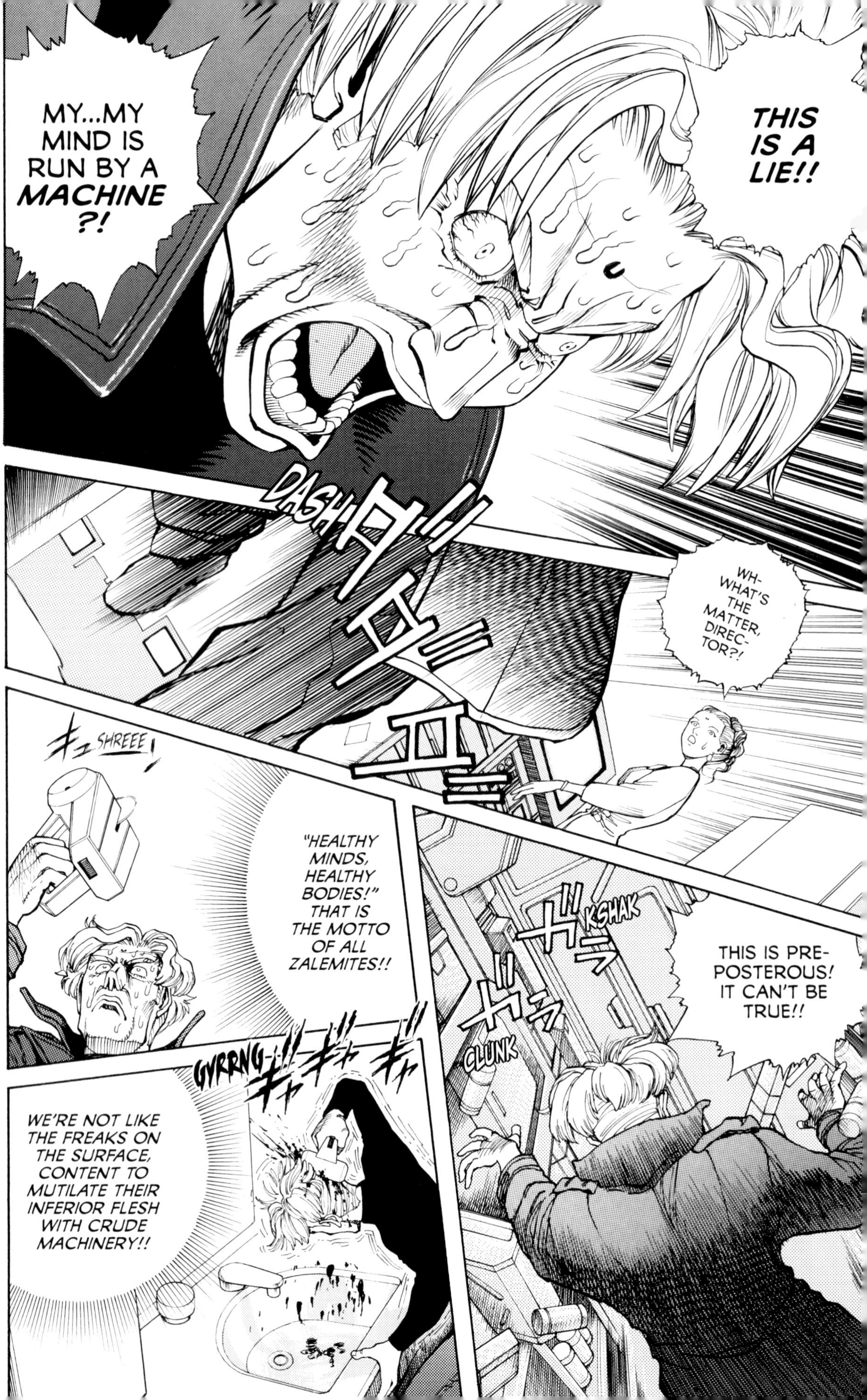
THIS IS A LIE!!
MY...MY MIND IS RUN BY A MACHINE ?!
DASH
WH-WHAT'S THE MATTER, DIRECTOR?!
KSHAK
THIS IS PRE-POSTEROUS! IT CAN'T BE TRUE!!
CLUNK
SHREEE
"HEALTHY MINDS, HEALTHY BODIES!" THAT IS THE MOTTO OF ALL ZALEMITES!!
GYRRNG
WE'RE NOT LIKE THE FREAKS ON THE SURFACE, CONTENT TO MUTILATE THEIR INFERIOR FLESH WITH CRUDE MACHINERY!!

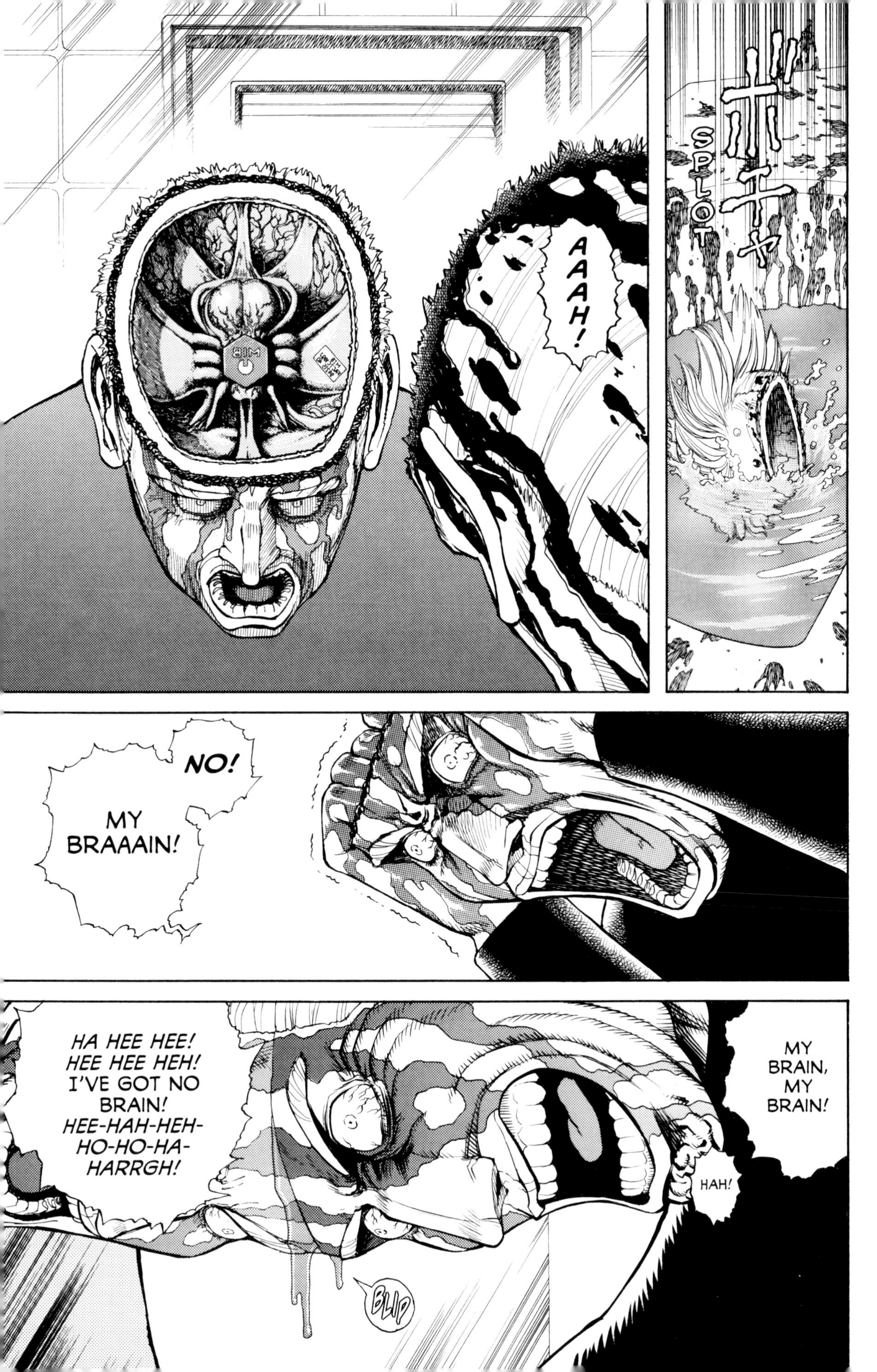
SPLOT
AAAH!
NO!
MY BRAAAIN!
MY BRAIN, MY BRAIN!
HAH!
HA HEE HEE! HEE HEE HEH! I'VE GOT NO BRAIN! HEE-HAH-HEH-HO-HO-HA-HARRGH!
BLIP

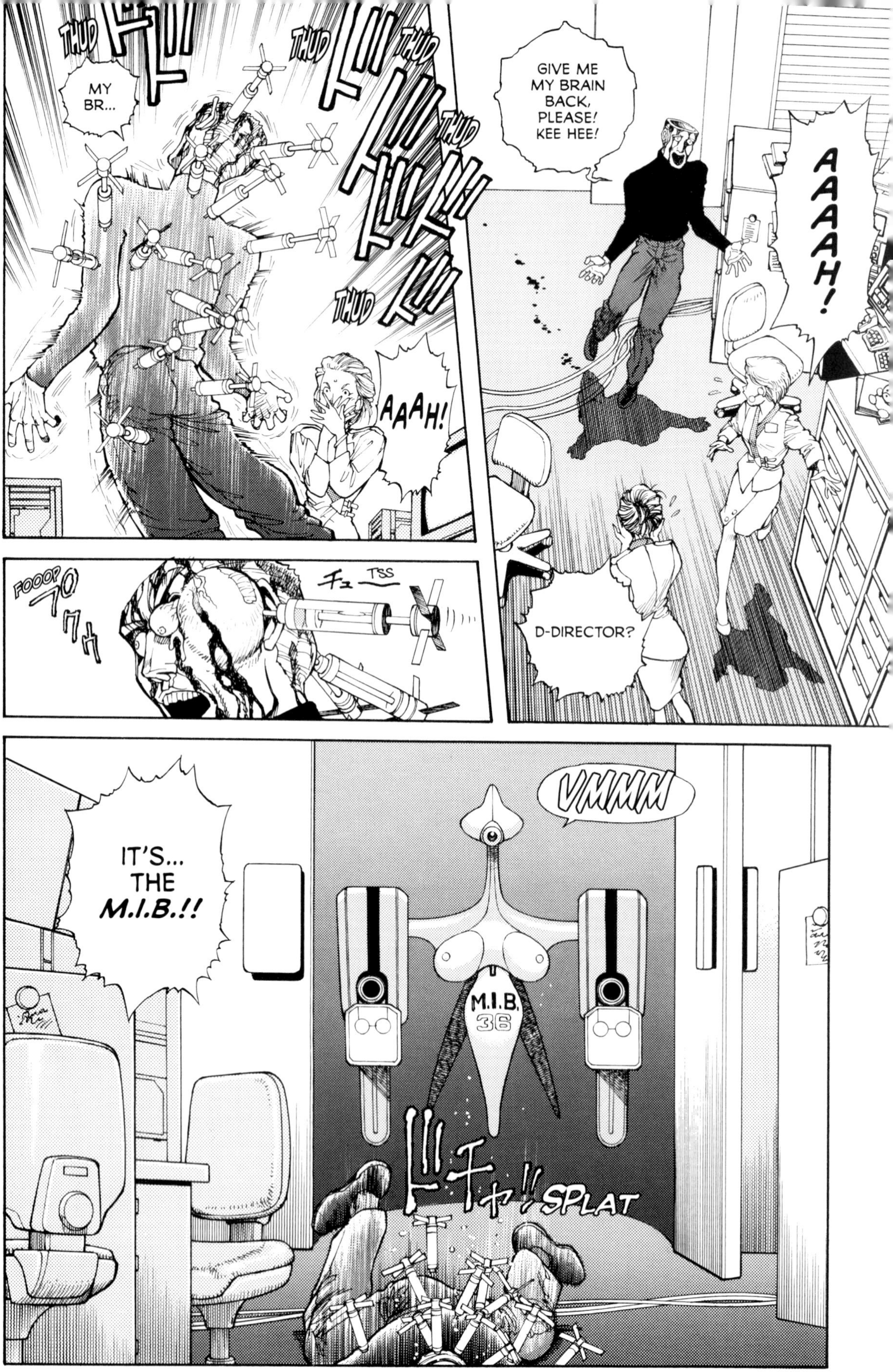
GIVE ME MY BRAIN BACK, PLEASE! KEE HEE!
AAAAAH!
D-DIRECTOR?
THUD
THUD
THUD
THUD
THUD
MY BR...
AAAH!
TSS
FOOOP
VMMMM
IT'S... THE M.I.B.!!
M.I.B. 36
SPLAT

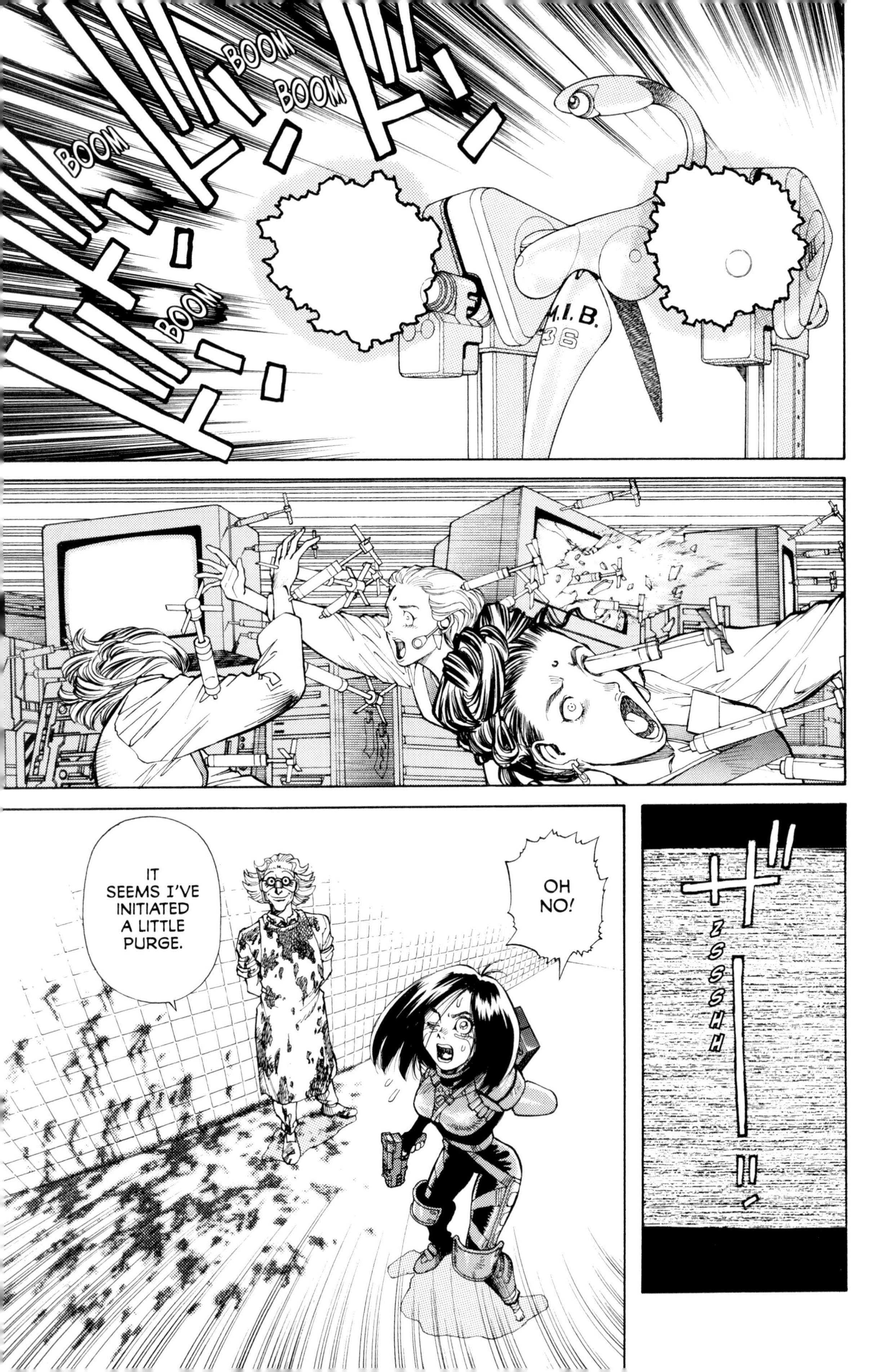
BOOM
BOOM
BOOM
BOOM
ZSSSHH
OH NO!
IT SEEMS I'VE INITIATED A LITTLE PURGE.

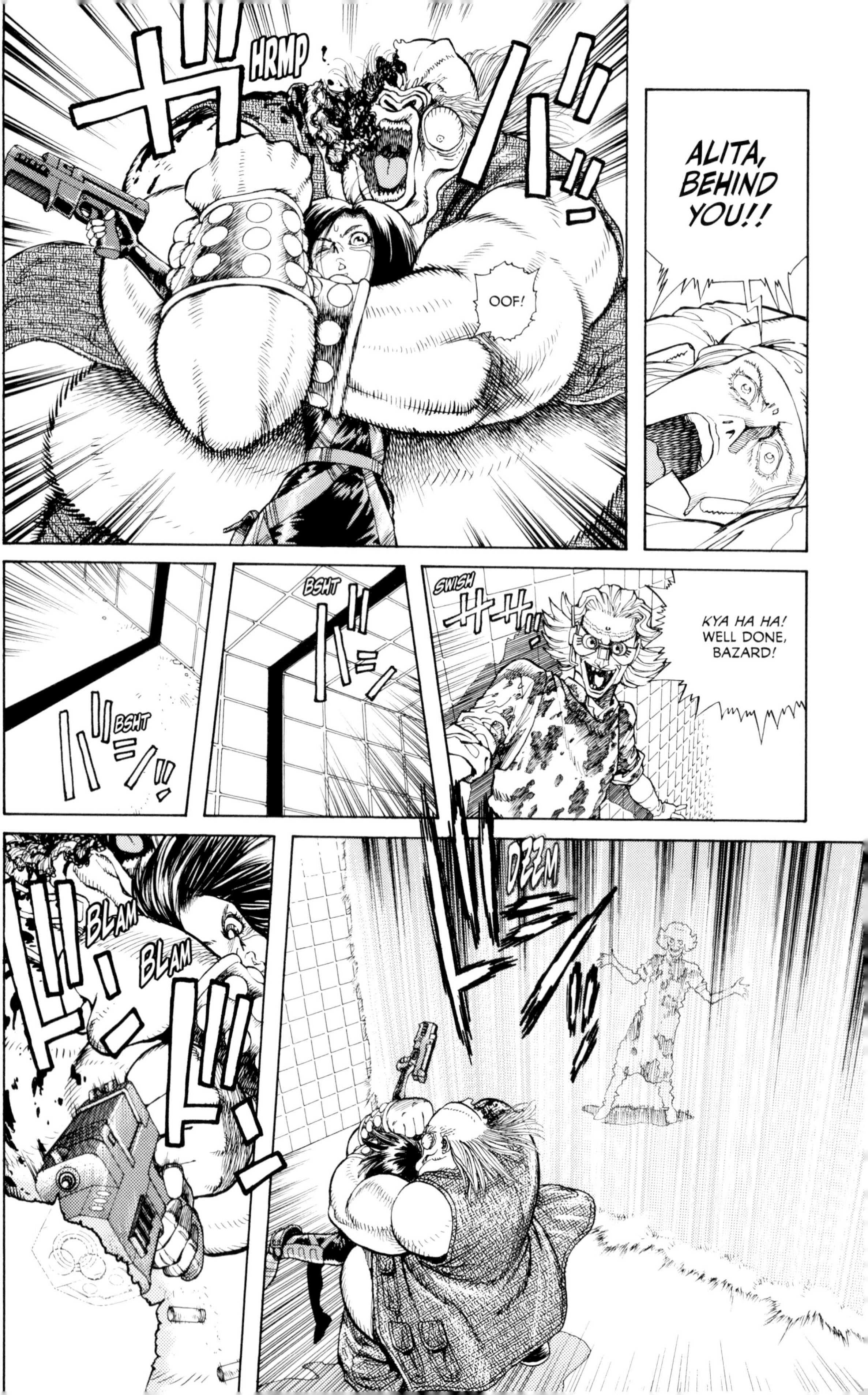
ALITA, BEHIND YOU!!
HRMP
OOF!
SWISH
KYA HA HA! WELL DONE, BAZARD!
BSHT
BSHT
DZZM
BLAM
BLAM

GANK

FWUR

MERE PISTOLS CANNOT BREACH THIS WALL OF ULTRA-PRESSURIZED WATER!

KYA HA HA HA!

I'VE LIVED TOO LONG TO MEET MY END IN A PLACE LIKE *THIS!*

SO LONG!

CHWANG

CHWANG

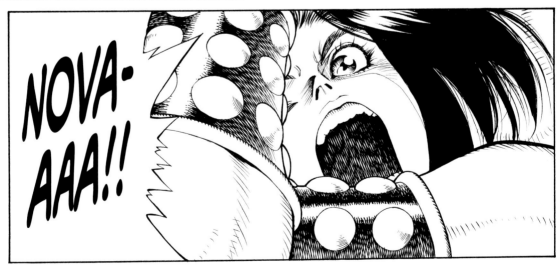

NOVA-AAA!!

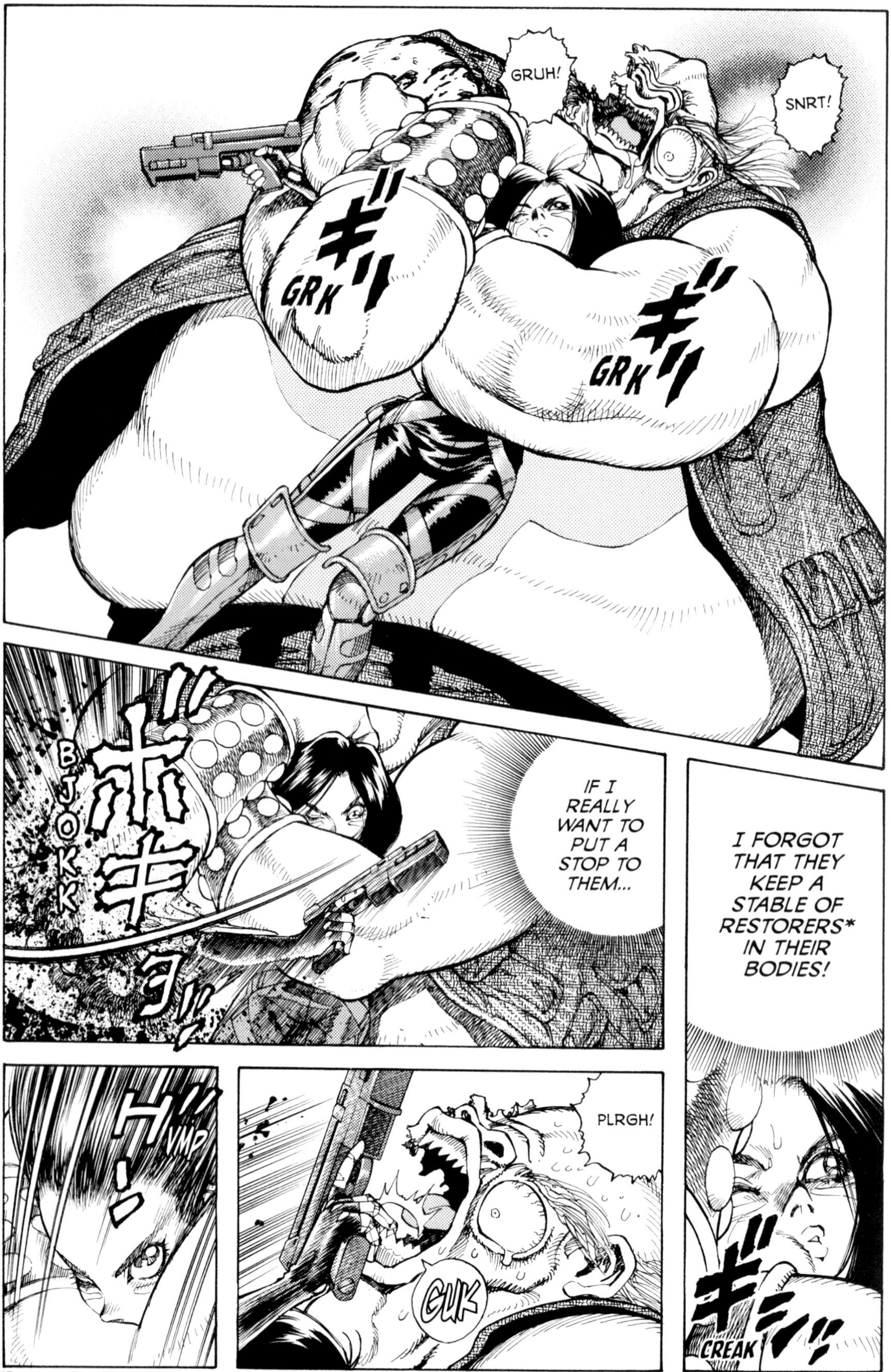
SNRT!
GRUH!
GRK
GRK
I FORGOT THAT THEY KEEP A STABLE OF RESTORERS* IN THEIR BODIES!
CREAK
IF I REALLY WANT TO PUT A STOP TO THEM...
BJOKK
PLRGH!
GUK
VMP

*Restorers: One of Nova's line of nanomachines. It repairs bodily damage on the cellular level. (See Fight 25.)

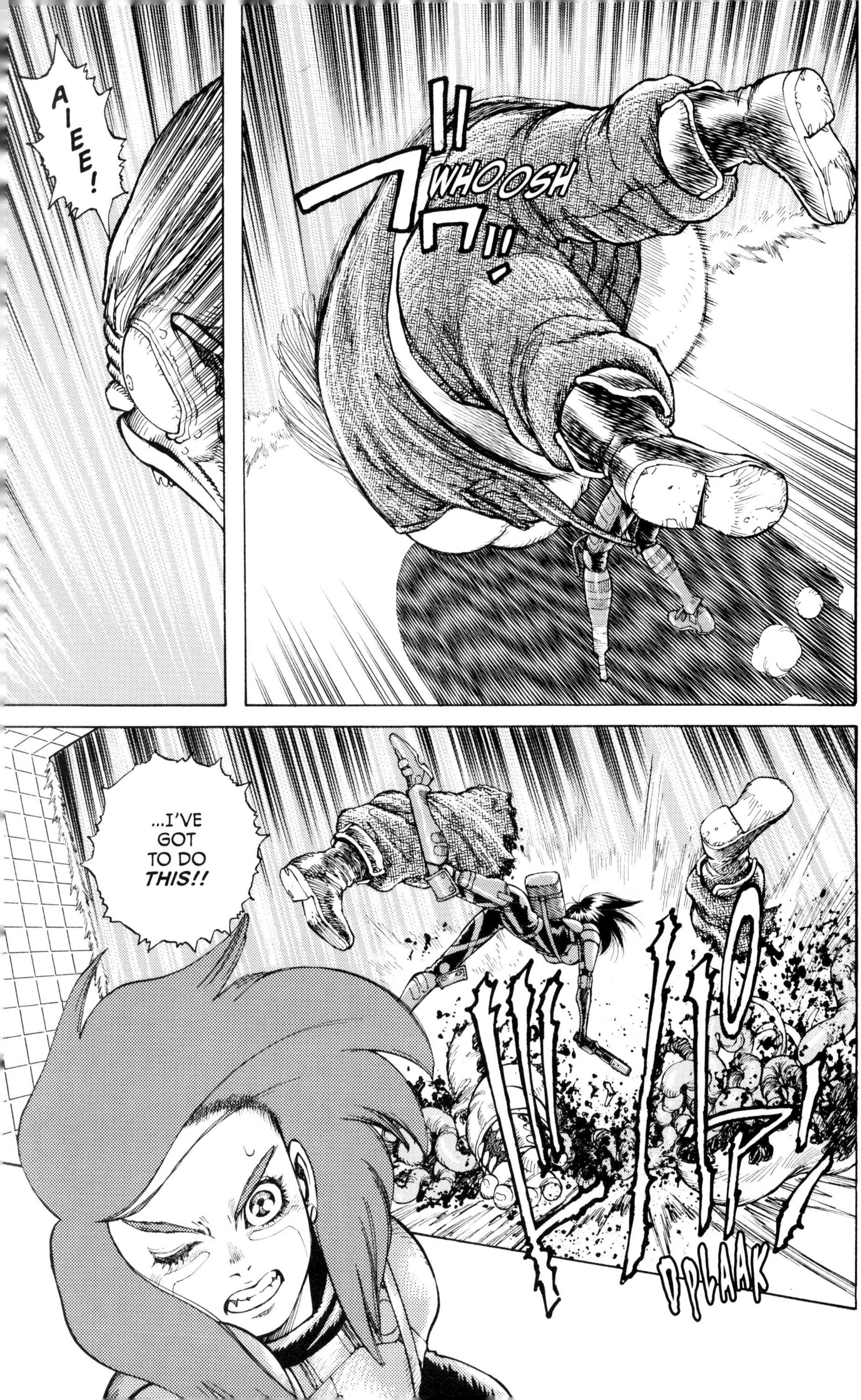
WHOOSH
AIEEE!
...I'VE GOT TO DO *THIS!!*
DPLAAK

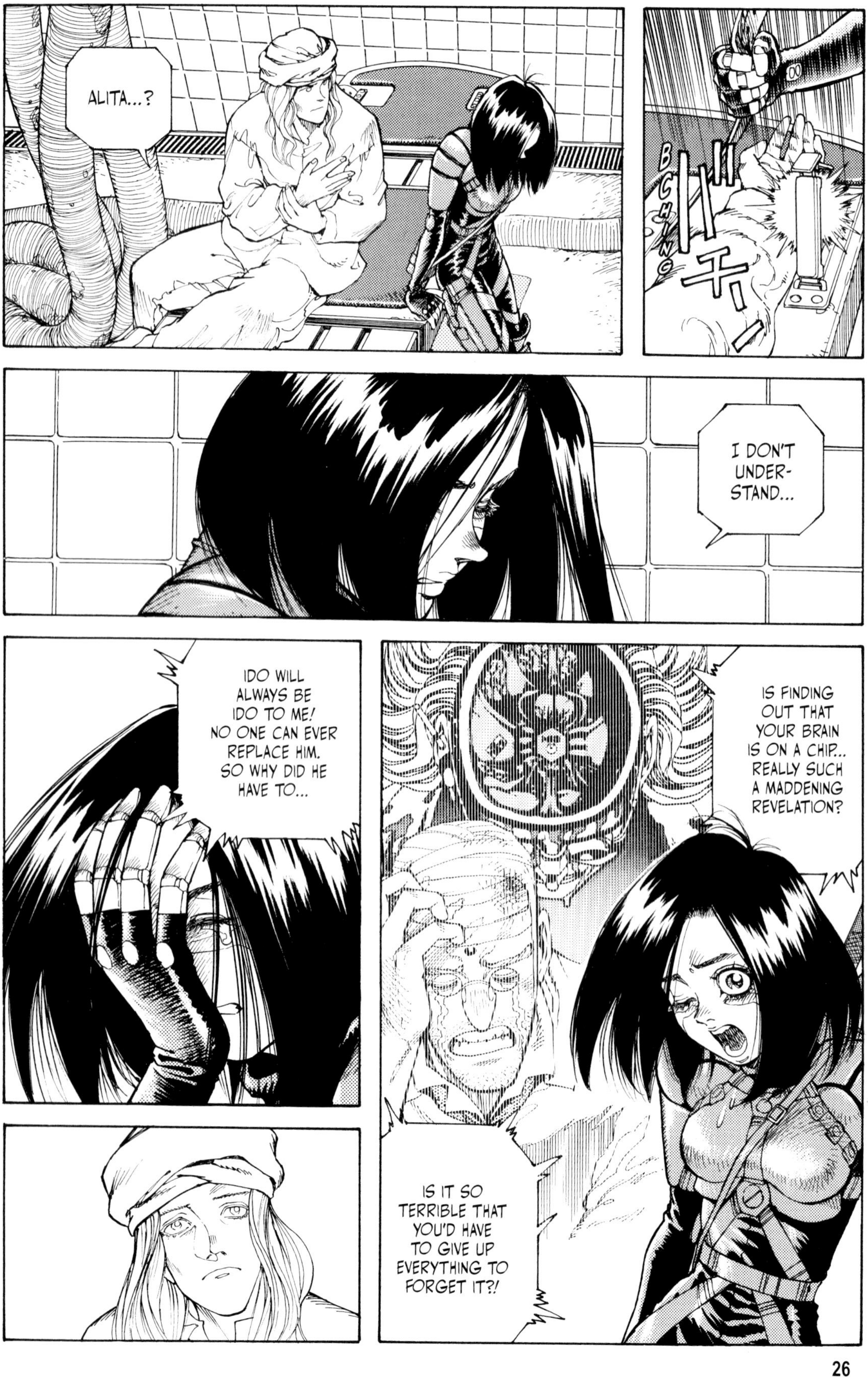
BCHING
ALITA...?
I DON'T UNDER-STAND...
IS FINDING OUT THAT YOUR BRAIN IS ON A CHIP... REALLY SUCH A MADDENING REVELATION?
IS IT SO TERRIBLE THAT YOU'D HAVE TO GIVE UP EVERYTHING TO FORGET IT?!
IDO WILL ALWAYS BE IDO TO ME! NO ONE CAN EVER REPLACE HIM. SO WHY DID HE HAVE TO...

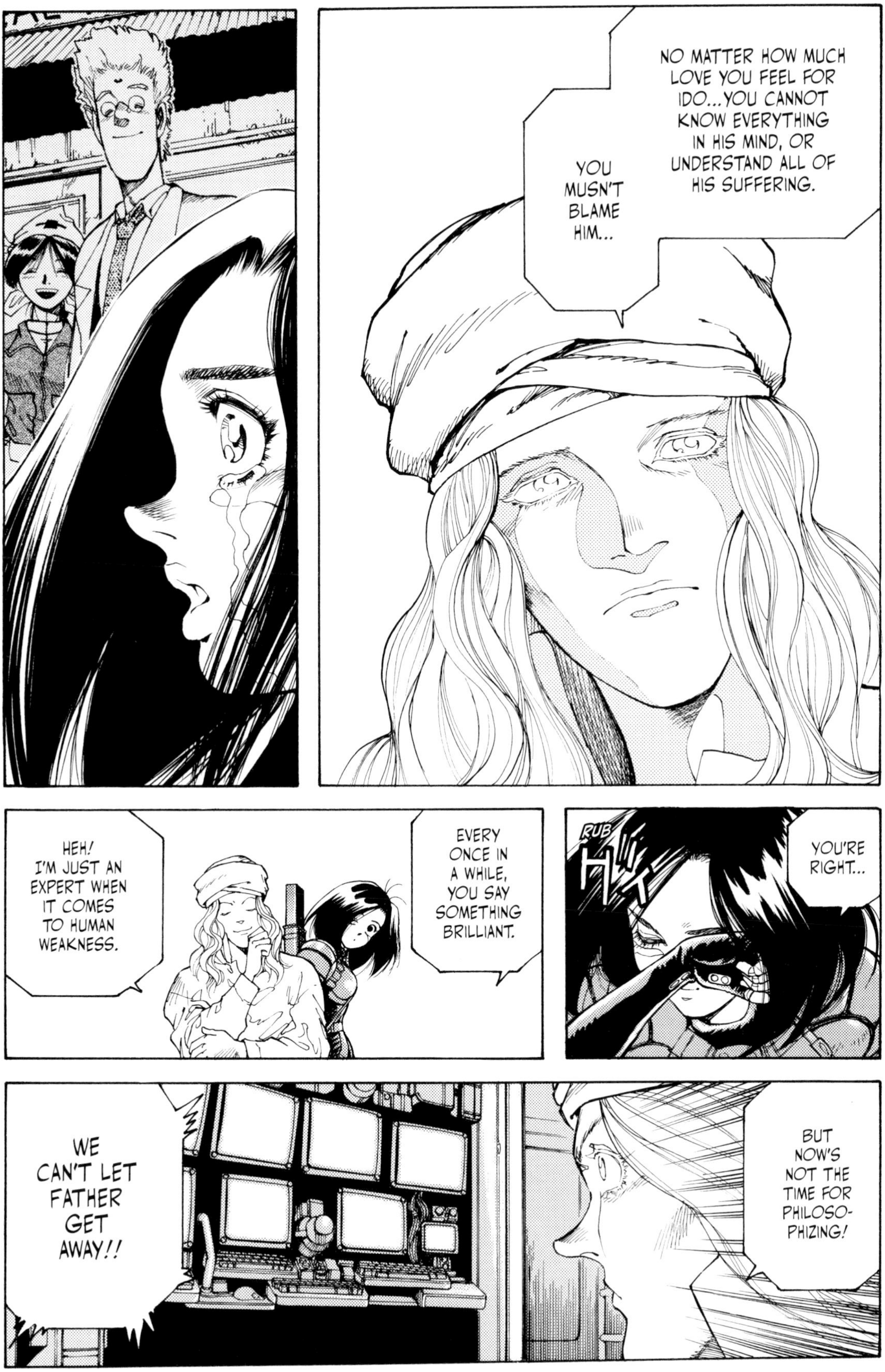
NO MATTER HOW MUCH LOVE YOU FEEL FOR IDO...YOU CANNOT KNOW EVERYTHING IN HIS MIND, OR UNDERSTAND ALL OF HIS SUFFERING.
YOU MUSN'T BLAME HIM...
RUB
YOU'RE RIGHT...
EVERY ONCE IN A WHILE, YOU SAY SOMETHING BRILLIANT.
HEH! I'M JUST AN EXPERT WHEN IT COMES TO HUMAN WEAKNESS.
BUT NOW'S NOT THE TIME FOR PHILOSO-PHIZING!
WE CAN'T LET FATHER GET AWAY!!

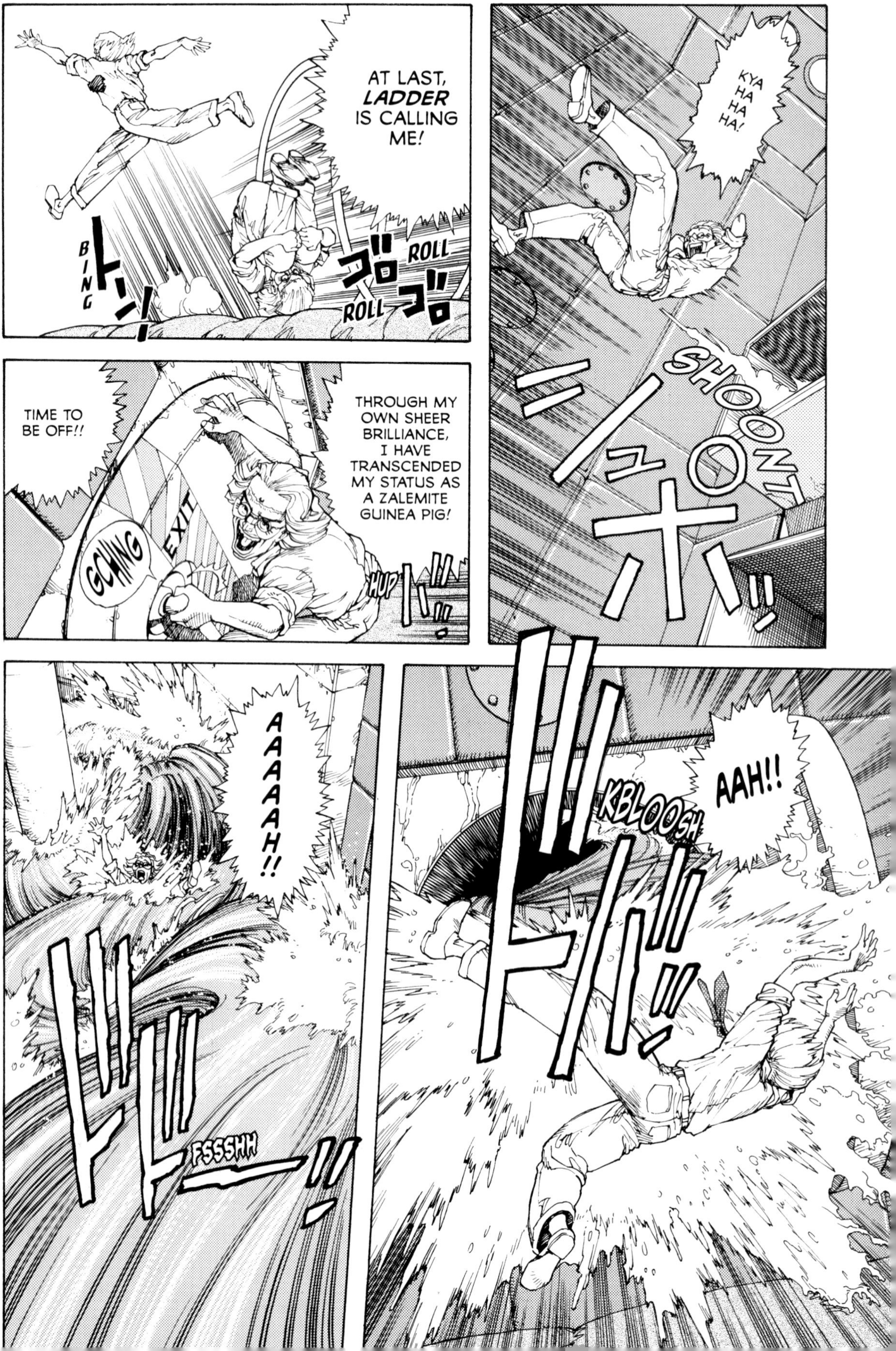
KYA HA HA HA!
SHOONT
AT LAST, LADDER IS CALLING ME!
ROLL
ROLL
BING
THROUGH MY OWN SHEER BRILLIANCE, I HAVE TRANSCENDED MY STATUS AS A ZALEMITE GUINEA PIG!
TIME TO BE OFF!!
HUP
GCHNG
EXIT
AAH!!
KBLOOSH
AAAAAAH!!
FSSSHH

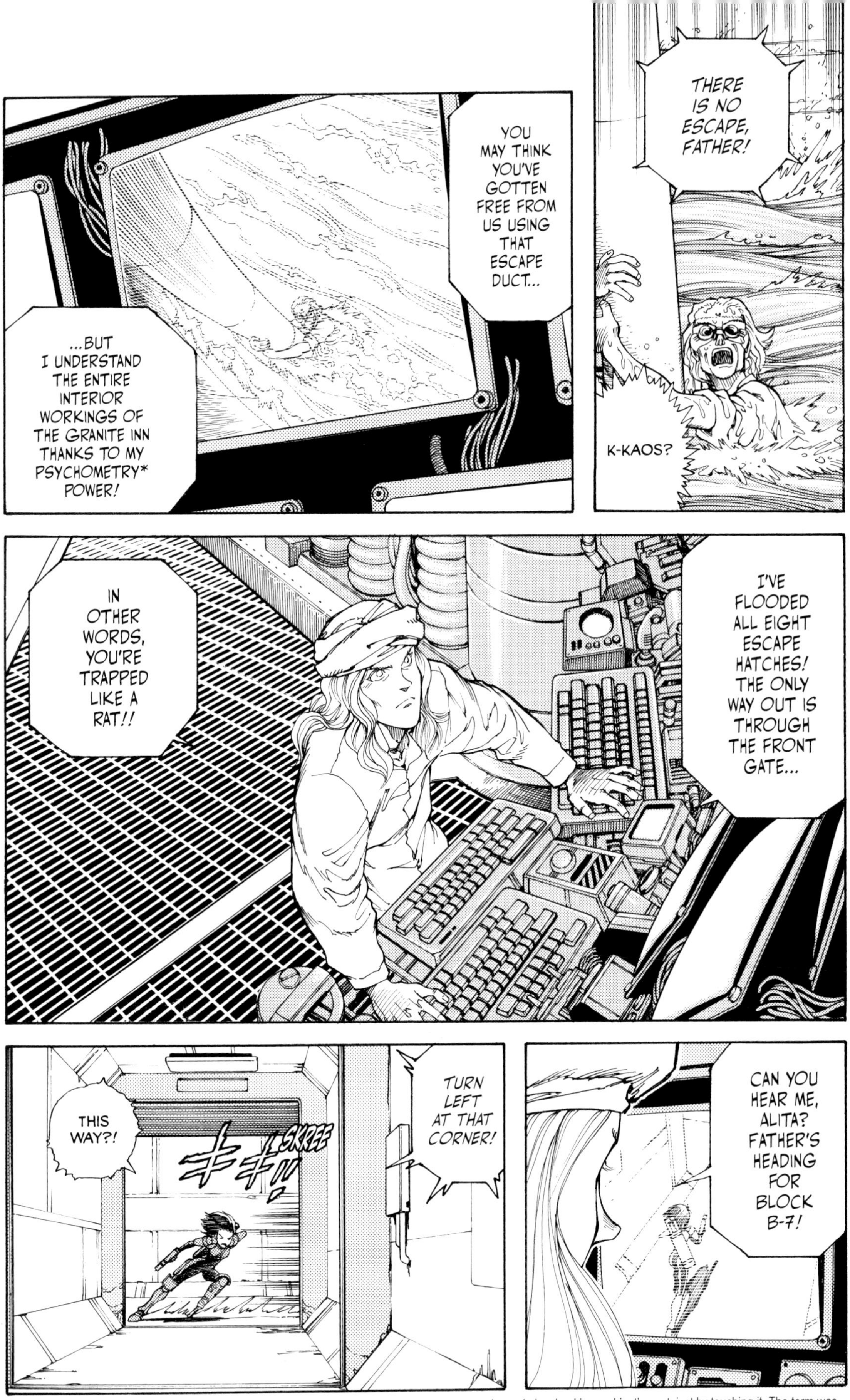
THERE IS NO ESCAPE, FATHER!
K-KAOS?
YOU MAY THINK YOU'VE GOTTEN FREE FROM US USING THAT ESCAPE DUCT...
...BUT I UNDERSTAND THE ENTIRE INTERIOR WORKINGS OF THE GRANITE INN THANKS TO MY PSYCHOMETRY* POWER!
I'VE FLOODED ALL EIGHT ESCAPE HATCHES! THE ONLY WAY OUT IS THROUGH THE FRONT GATE...
IN OTHER WORDS, YOU'RE TRAPPED LIKE A RAT!!
CAN YOU HEAR ME, ALITA? FATHER'S HEADING FOR BLOCK B-7!
TURN LEFT AT THAT CORNER!
THIS WAY?!
SKREE

***Psychometry:** The ability to glean information about events and people involved in an object's past, just by touching it. The term was coined by American spiritual researcher J.R. Buchanan (1814-1899). (See Fight 38.)

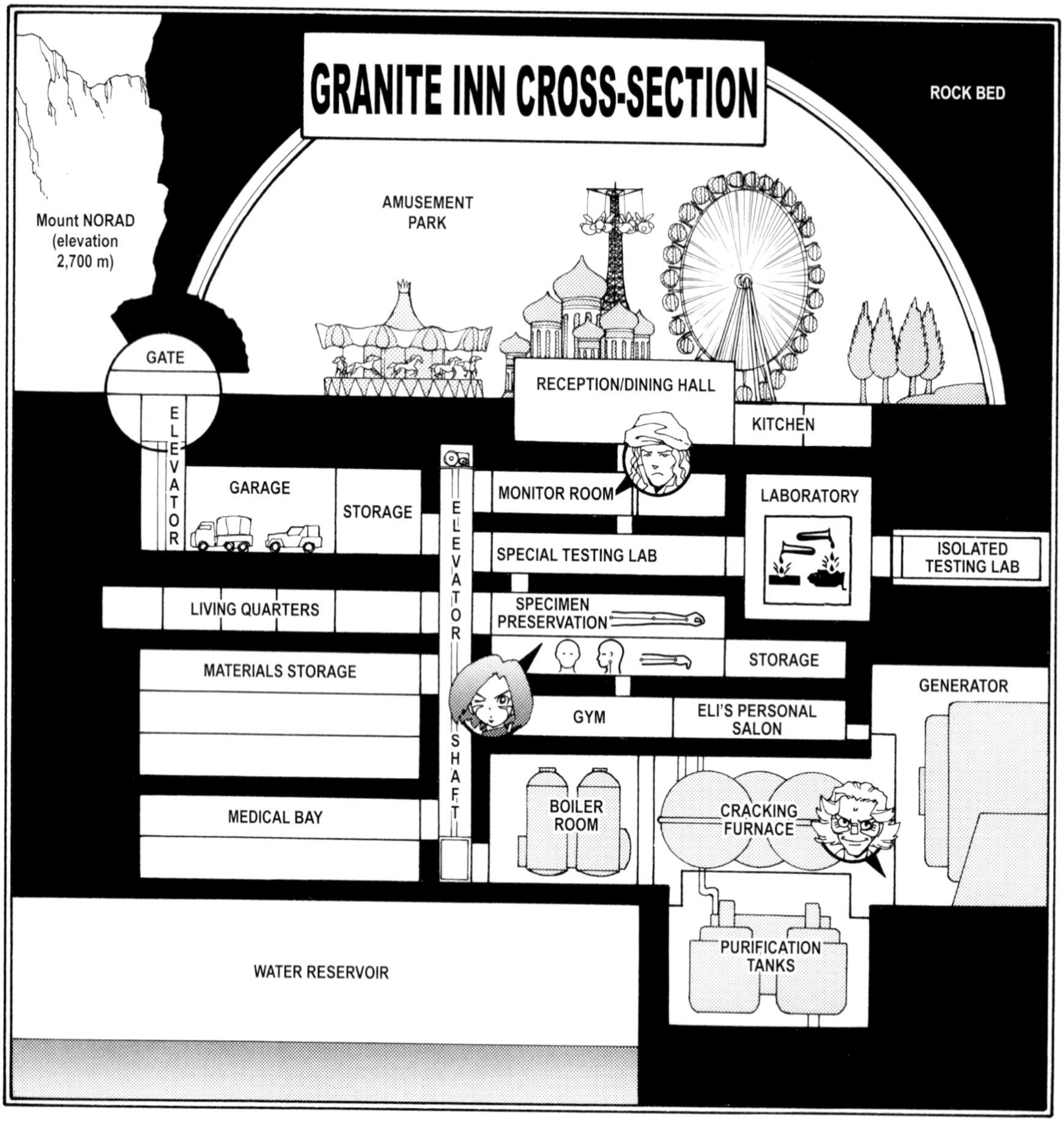
GRANITE INN CROSS-SECTION
ROCK BED
Mount NORAD (elevation 2,700 m)
AMUSEMENT PARK
GATE
RECEPTION/DINING HALL
KITCHEN
ELEVATOR
GARAGE
STORAGE
ELEVATOR SHAFT
MONITOR ROOM
LABORATORY
SPECIAL TESTING LAB
ISOLATED TESTING LAB
LIVING QUARTERS
SPECIMEN PRESERVATION
STORAGE
MATERIALS STORAGE
GENERATOR
GYM
ELI'S PERSONAL SALON
BOILER ROOM
CRACKING FURNACE
MEDICAL BAY
PURIFICATION TANKS
WATER RESERVOIR

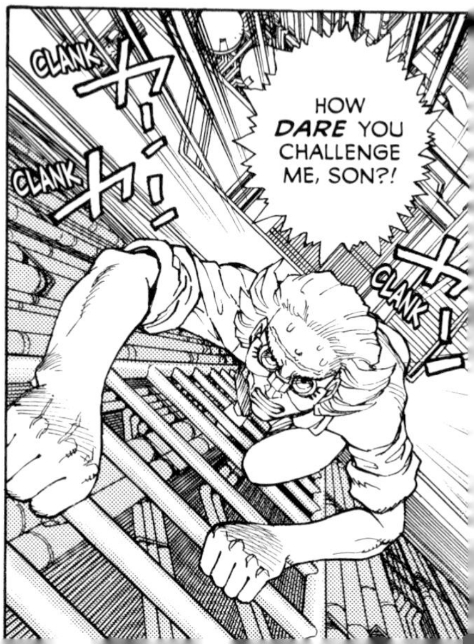
CLANK
CLANK
HOW *DARE* YOU CHALLENGE ME, SON?!
CLANK

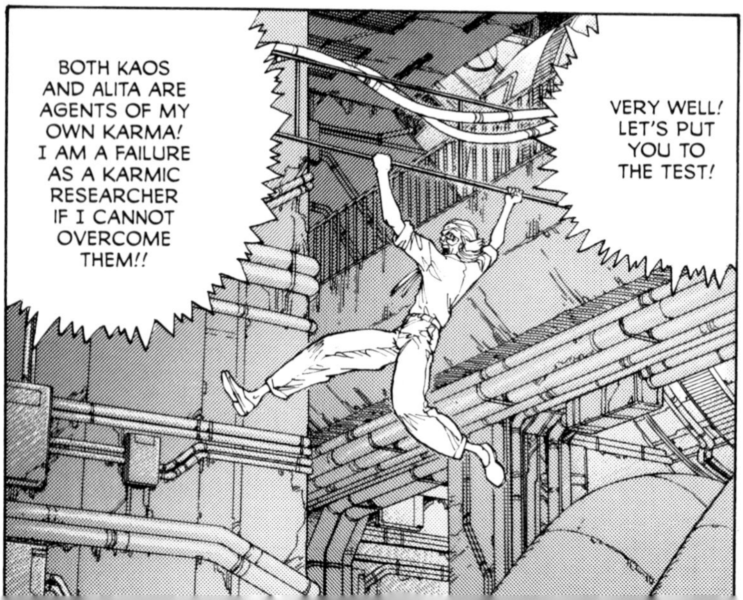
BOTH KAOS AND ALITA ARE AGENTS OF MY OWN KARMA! I AM A FAILURE AS A KARMIC RESEARCHER IF I CANNOT OVERCOME THEM!!
VERY WELL! LET'S PUT YOU TO THE TEST!

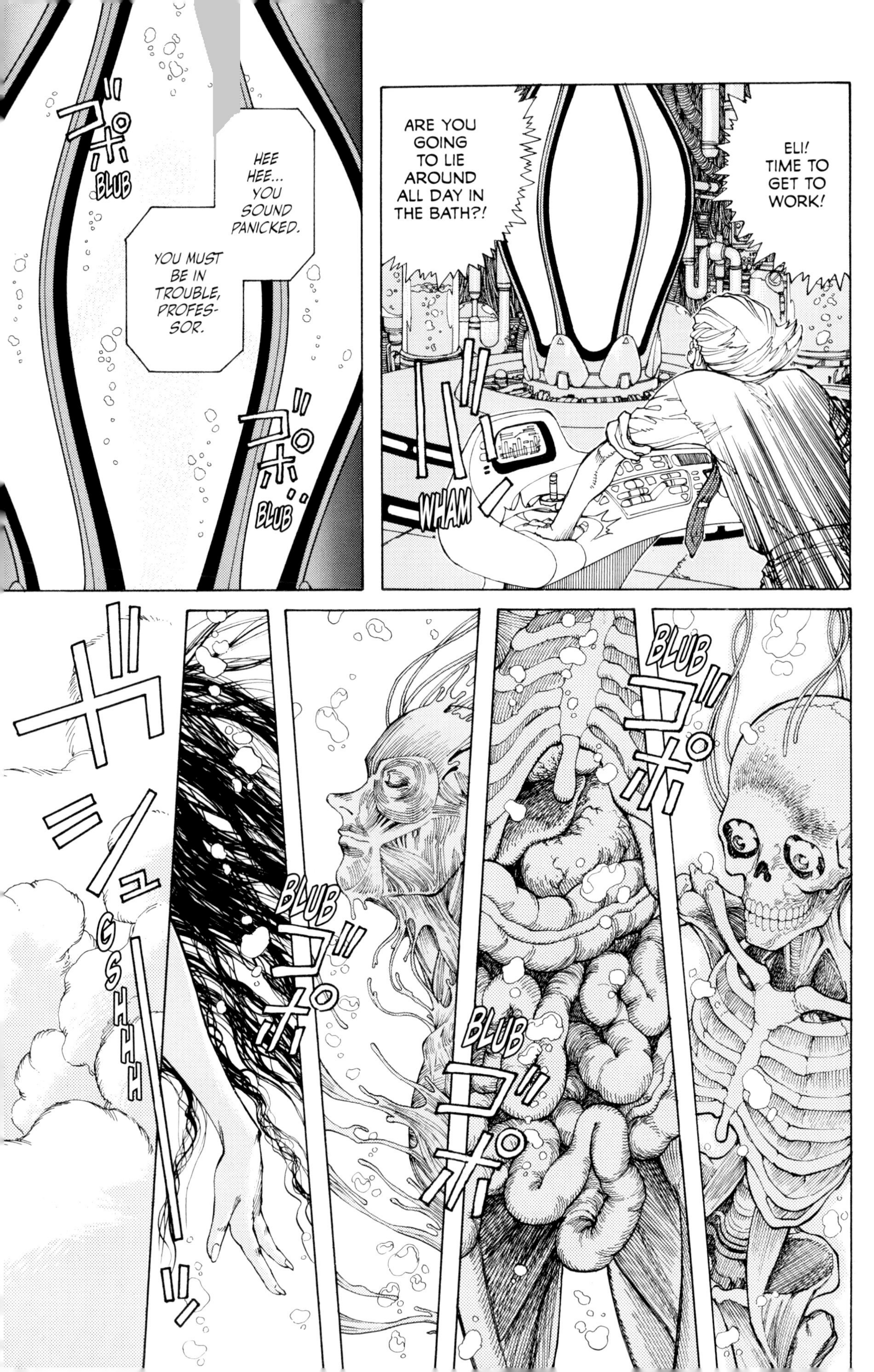

ELI! TIME TO GET TO WORK!
ARE YOU GOING TO LIE AROUND ALL DAY IN THE BATH?!
WHAM
HEE HEE... YOU SOUND PANICKED.
BLUB
YOU MUST BE IN TROUBLE, PROFES-SOR.
BLUB
BLUB
BLUB
BLUB
GSHHHH

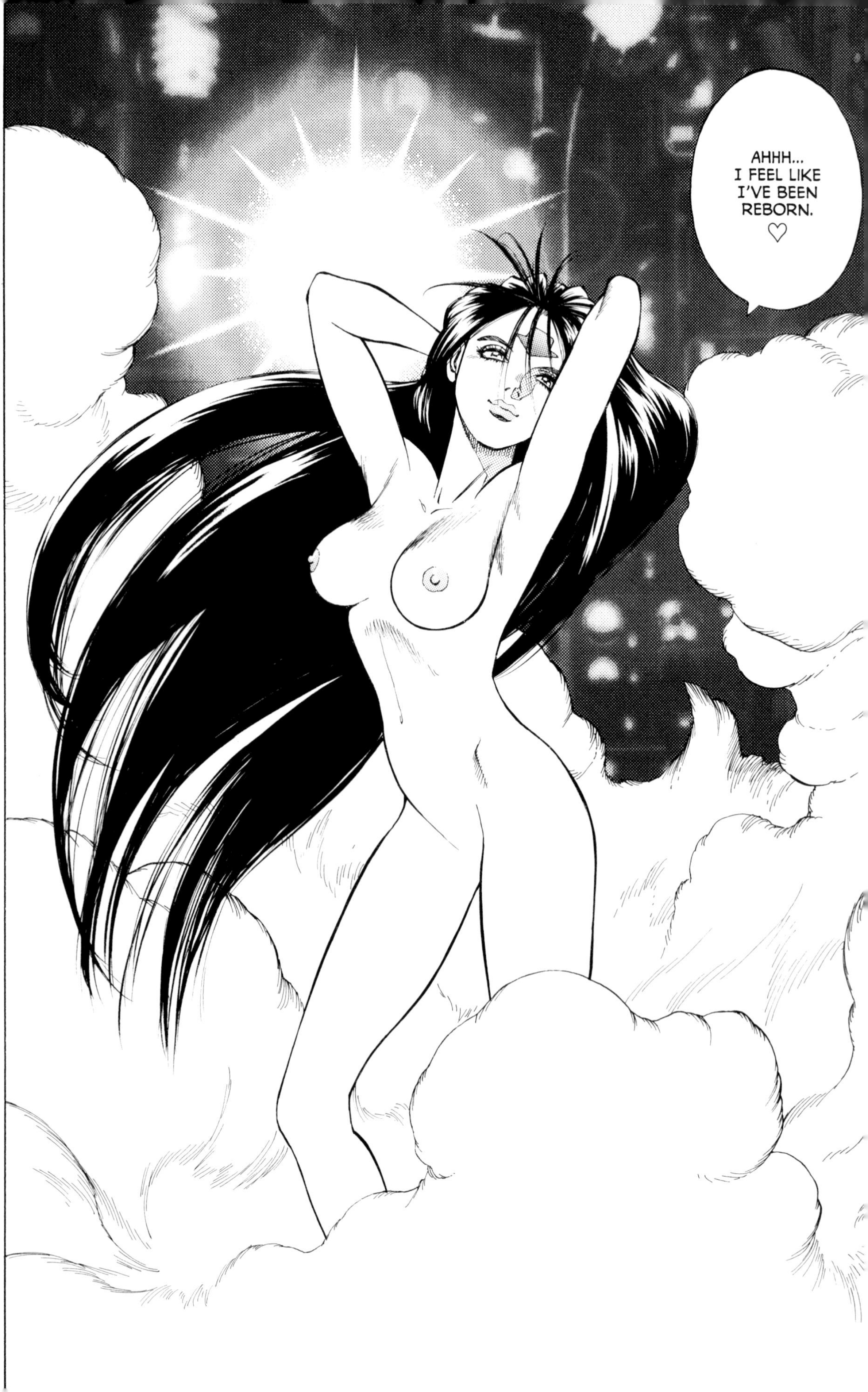
AHHH... I FEEL LIKE I'VE BEEN REBORN. ♡

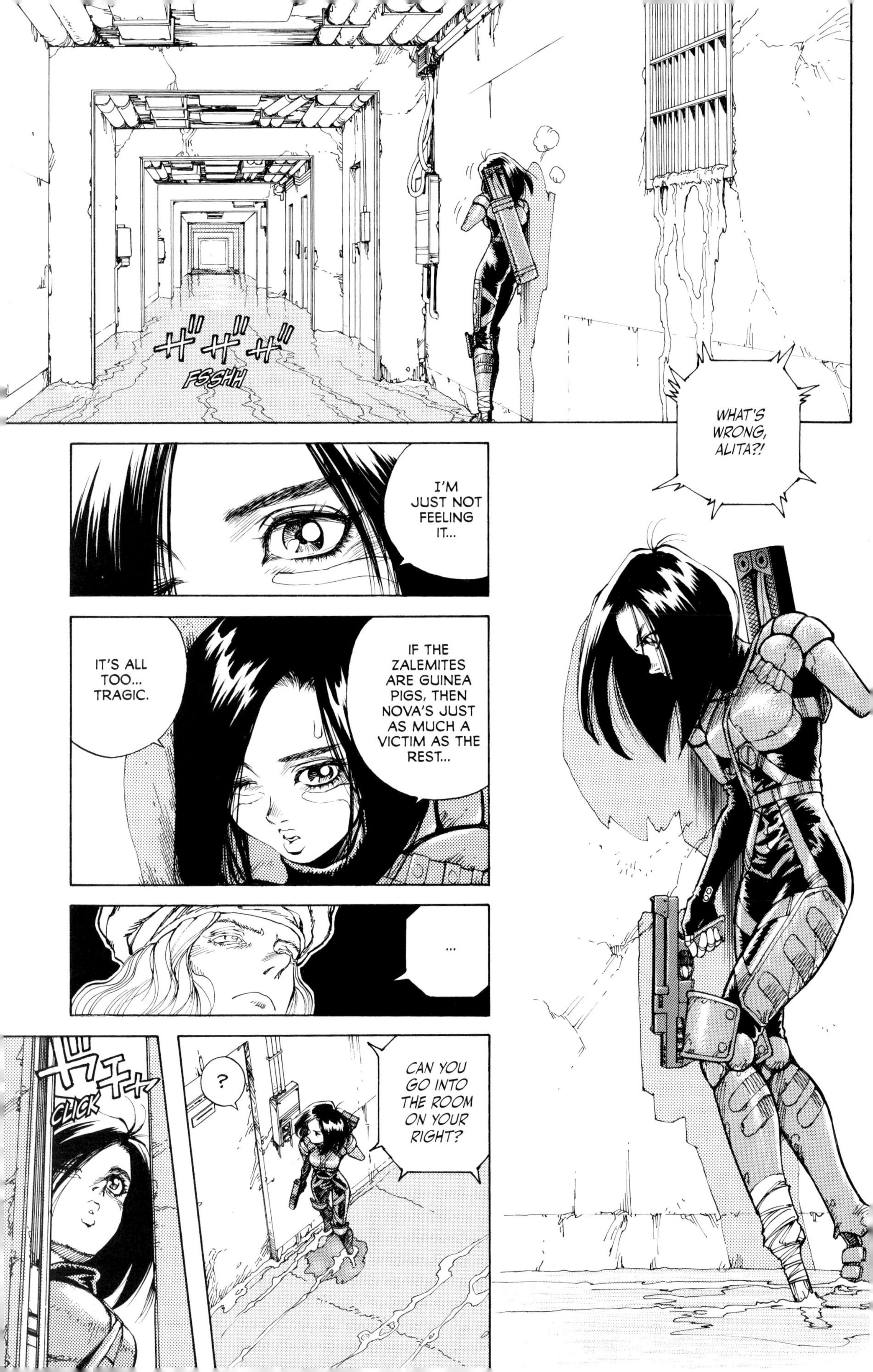
ザザザ
FSSHH
WHAT'S WRONG, ALITA?!
I'M JUST NOT FEELING IT...
IF THE ZALEMITES ARE GUINEA PIGS, THEN NOVA'S JUST AS MUCH A VICTIM AS THE REST...
IT'S ALL TOO... TRAGIC.
...
CAN YOU GO INTO THE ROOM ON YOUR RIGHT?
?
ガチャ
CLICK

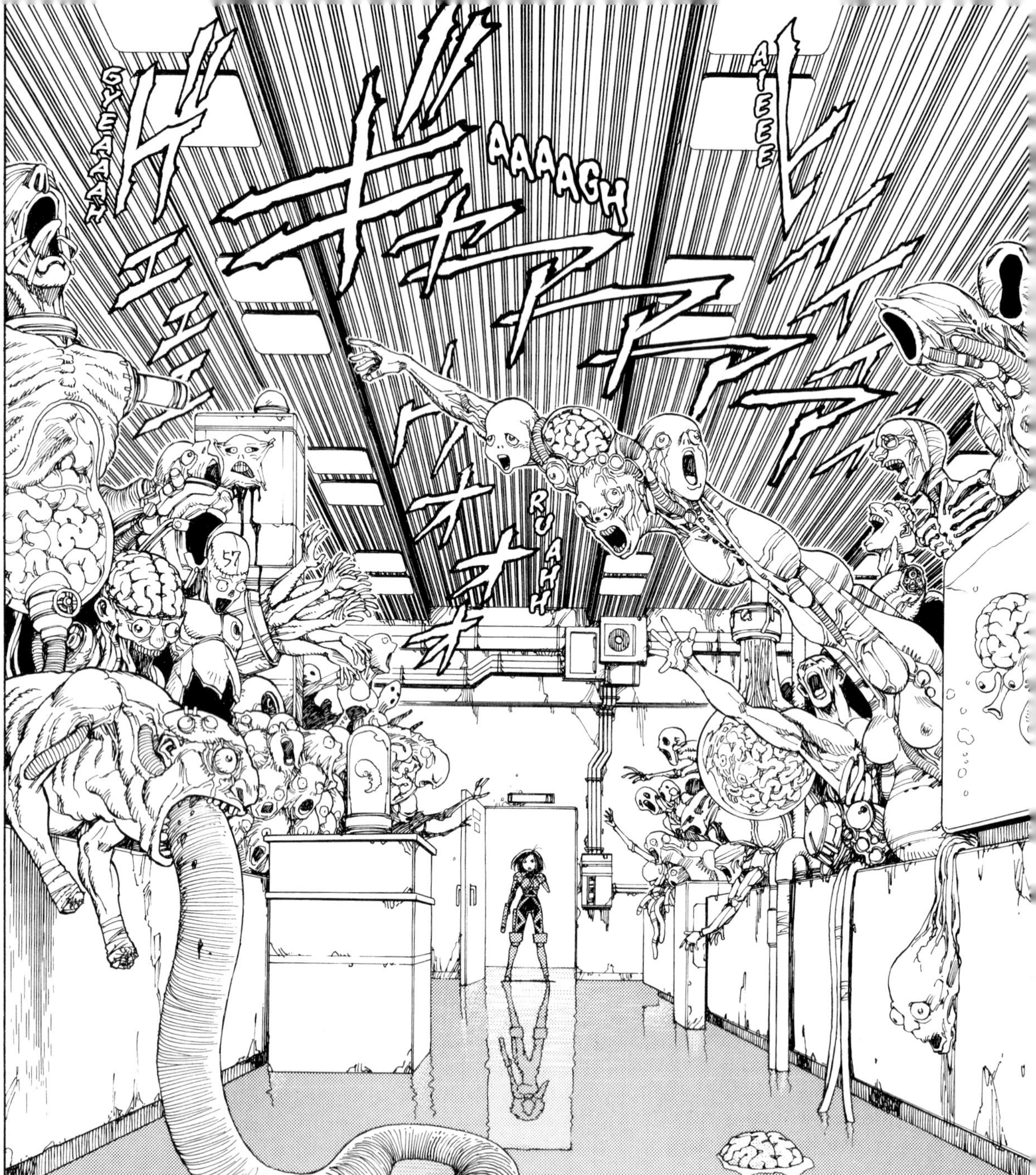
AIEEE
AAAAGH
RUAHH
GYEAAAH
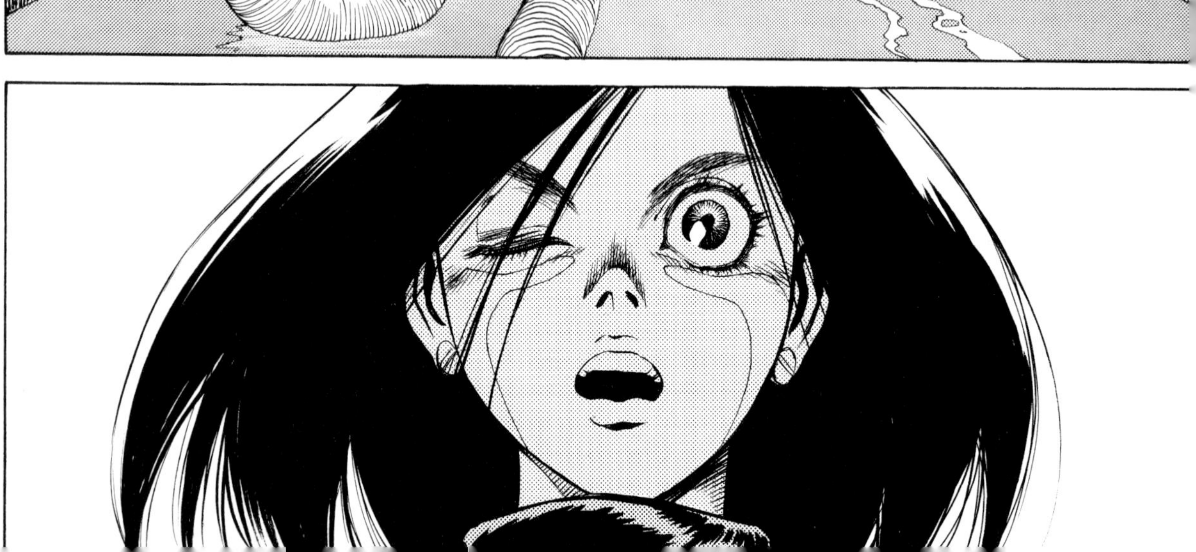

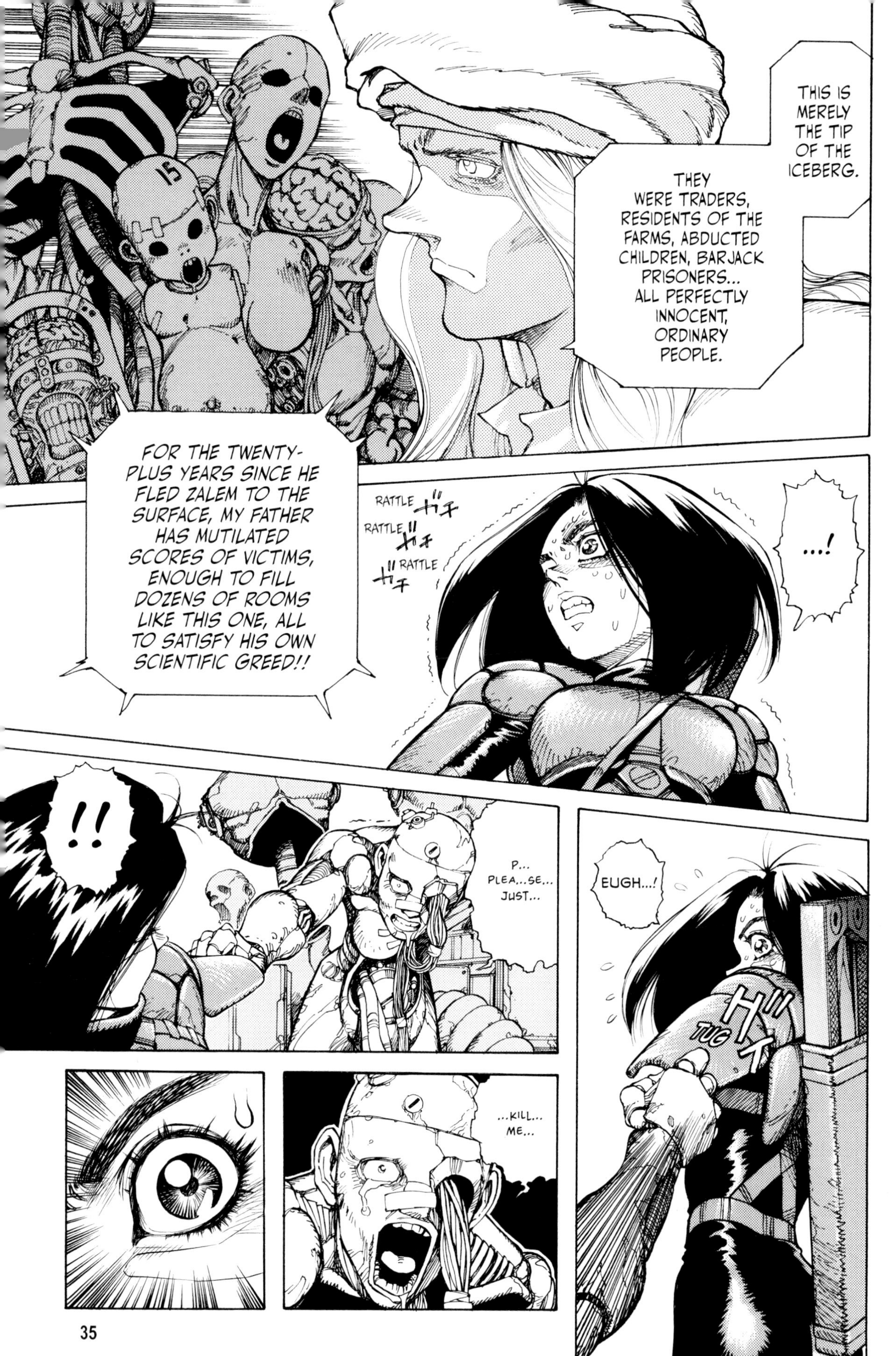
THIS IS MERELY THE TIP OF THE ICEBERG.
THEY WERE TRADERS, RESIDENTS OF THE FARMS, ABDUCTED CHILDREN, BARJACK PRISONERS... ALL PERFECTLY INNOCENT, ORDINARY PEOPLE.
FOR THE TWENTY-PLUS YEARS SINCE HE FLED ZALEM TO THE SURFACE, MY FATHER HAS MUTILATED SCORES OF VICTIMS, ENOUGH TO FILL DOZENS OF ROOMS LIKE THIS ONE, ALL TO SATISFY HIS OWN SCIENTIFIC GREED!!
...!
RATTLE
RATTLE
RATTLE
EUGH...!
TUG
!!
P... PLEA...SE... JUST...
...KILL... ME...

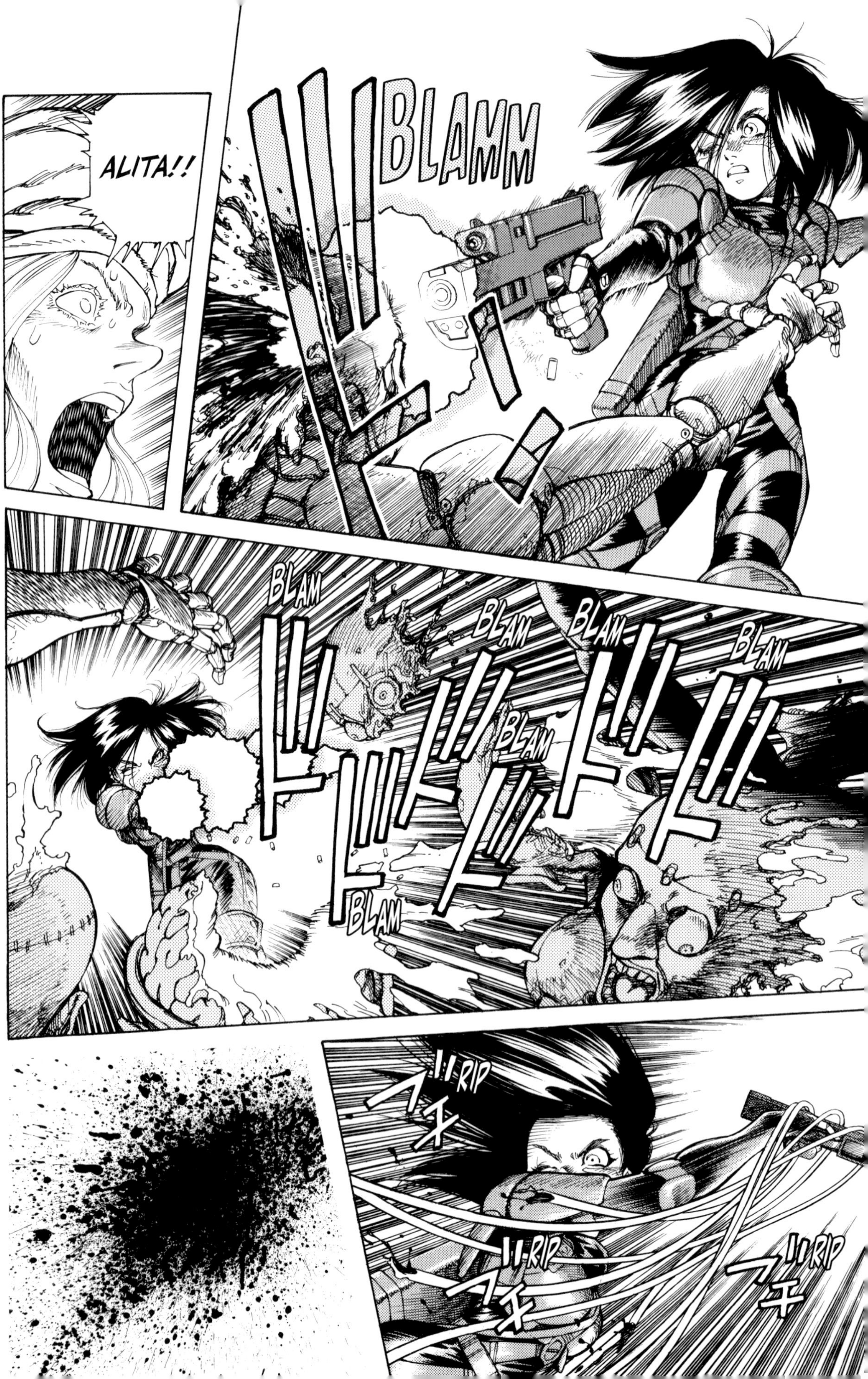

BLAMM
ALITA!!
BLAM
BLAM
BLAM
BLAM
BLAM
BLAM
RIP
RIP
RIP

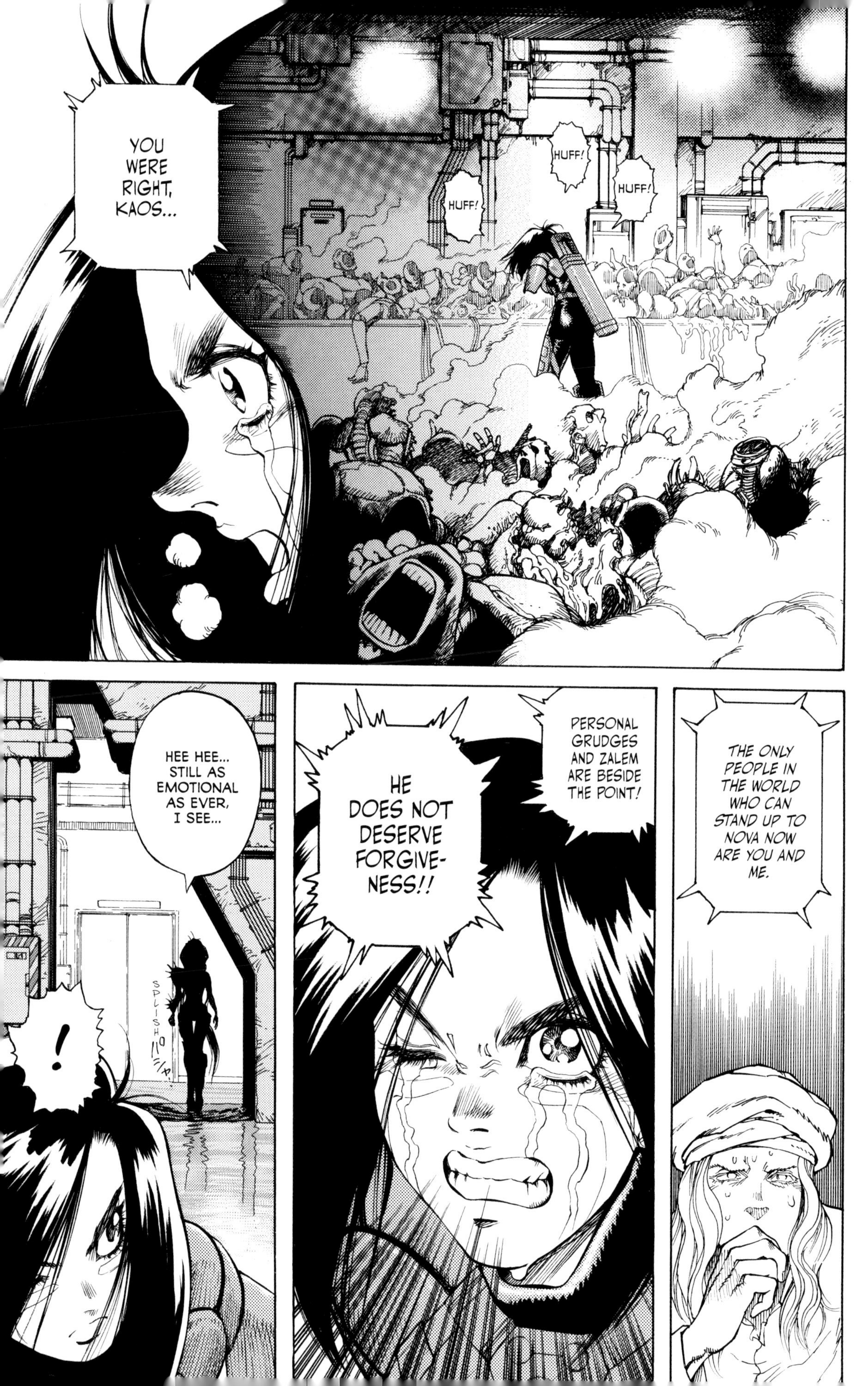
HUFF!
HUFF!
HUFF!
YOU WERE RIGHT, KAOS...
THE ONLY PEOPLE IN THE WORLD WHO CAN STAND UP TO NOVA NOW ARE YOU AND ME.
PERSONAL GRUDGES AND ZALEM ARE BESIDE THE POINT!
HE DOES NOT DESERVE FORGIVENESS!!
HEE HEE... STILL AS EMOTIONAL AS EVER, I SEE...
SPLISH
!

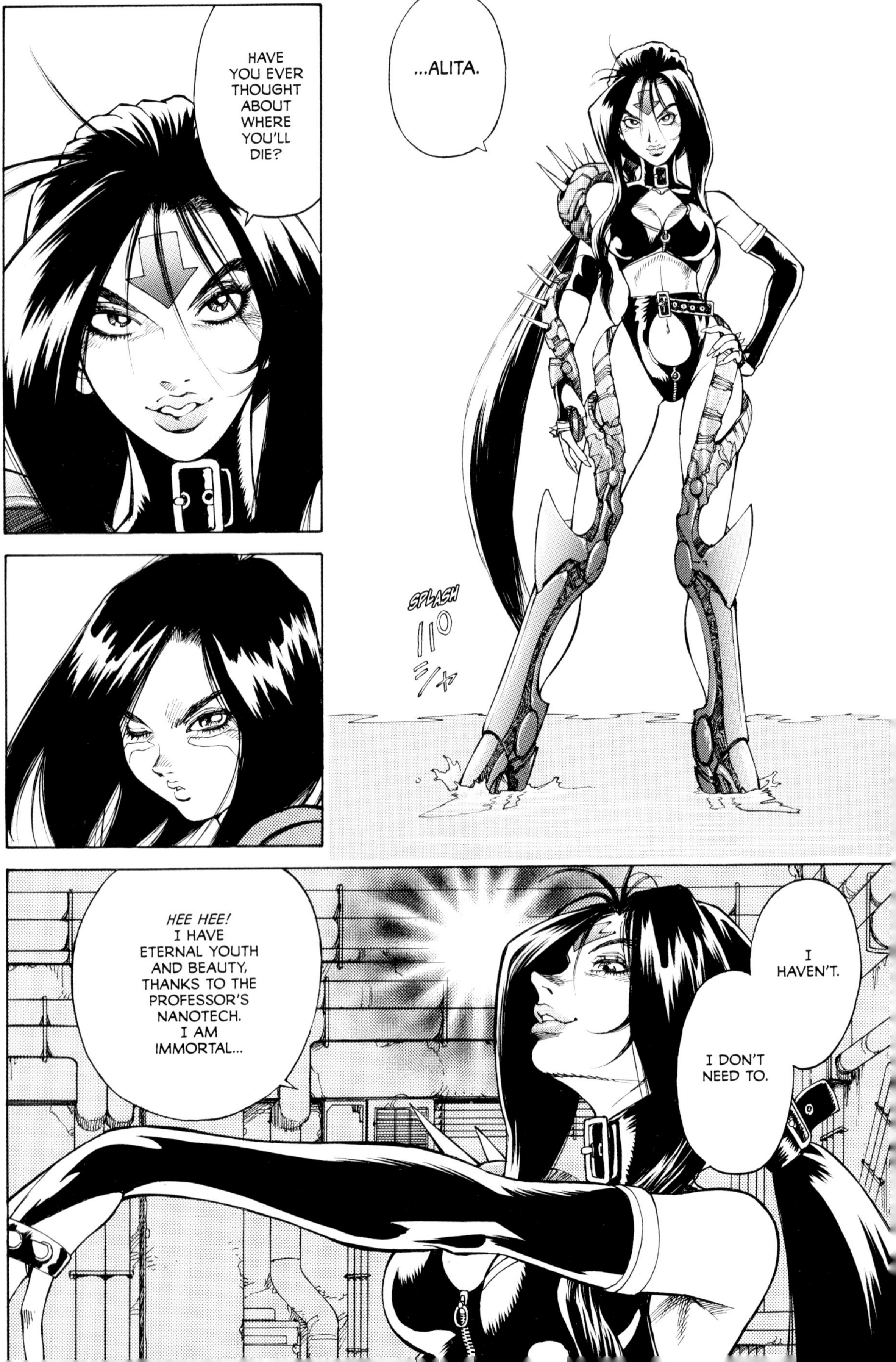
...ALITA.
SPLASH
HAVE YOU EVER THOUGHT ABOUT WHERE YOU'LL DIE?
I HAVEN'T.
I DON'T NEED TO.
HEE HEE! I HAVE ETERNAL YOUTH AND BEAUTY, THANKS TO THE PROFESSOR'S NANOTECH. I AM IMMORTAL...

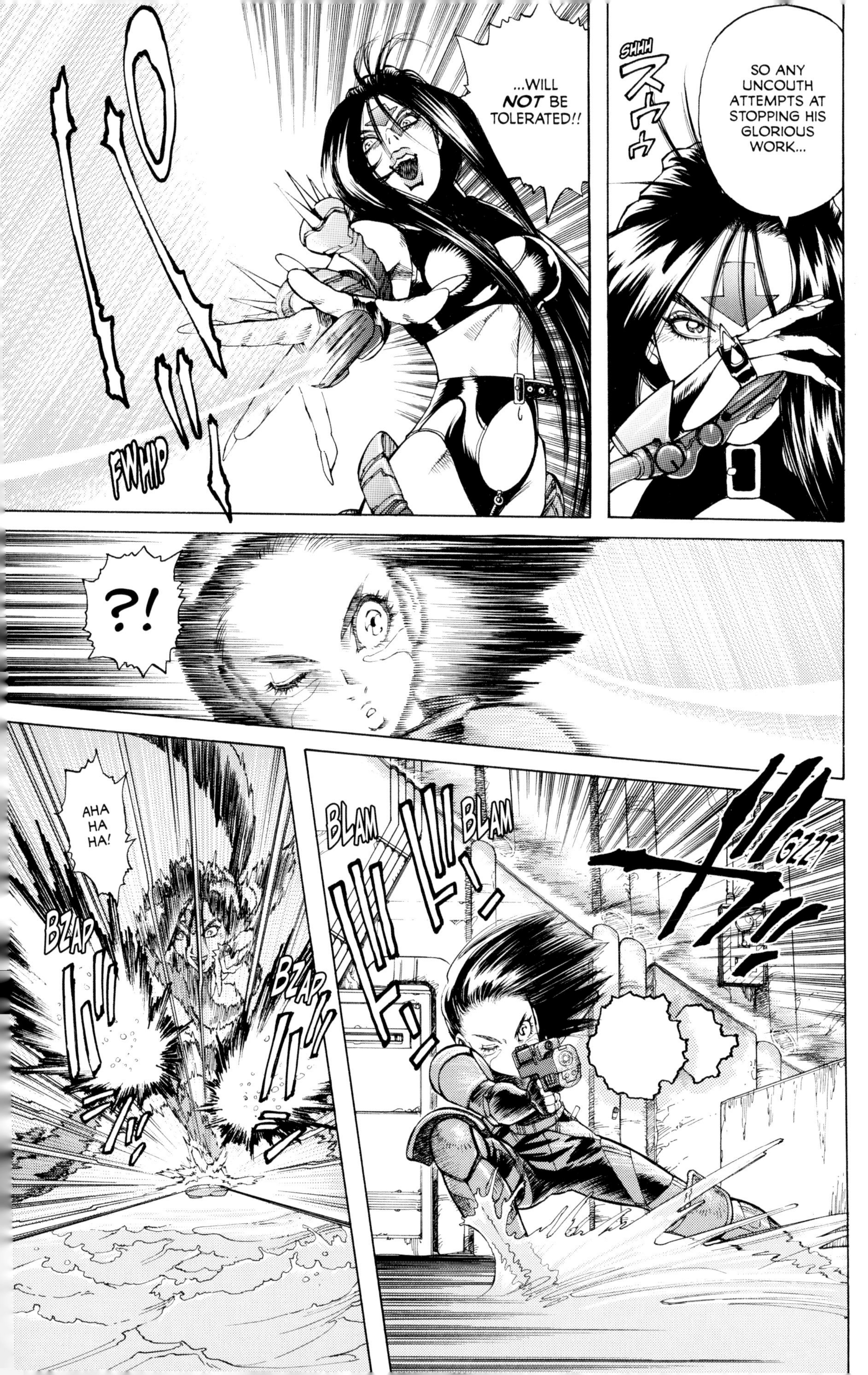
SHHH
SO ANY UNCOUTH ATTEMPTS AT STOPPING HIS GLORIOUS WORK...
...WILL ***NOT*** BE TOLERATED!!
FWHIP
?!
BLAM
BLAM
GZZT
AHA HA HA!
BZAP
BZAP

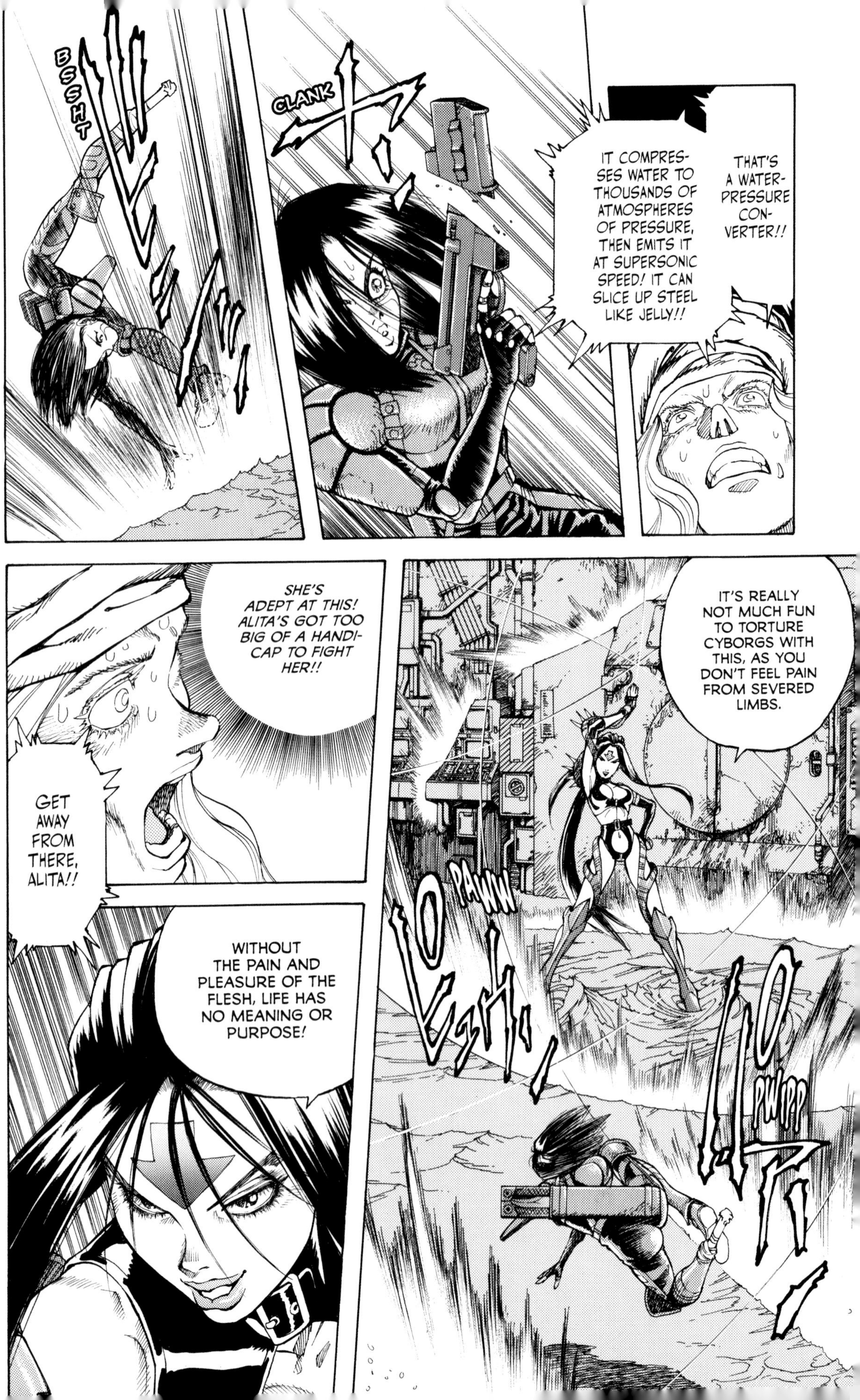
THAT'S A WATER-PRESSURE CON-VERTER!!
IT COMPRES-SES WATER TO THOUSANDS OF ATMOSPHERES OF PRESSURE, THEN EMITS IT AT SUPERSONIC SPEED! IT CAN SLICE UP STEEL LIKE JELLY!!
CLANK
BSSHT
IT'S REALLY NOT MUCH FUN TO TORTURE CYBORGS WITH THIS, AS YOU DON'T FEEL PAIN FROM SEVERED LIMBS.
PWIPP
PAWW
SHE'S ADEPT AT THIS! ALITA'S GOT TOO BIG OF A HANDI-CAP TO FIGHT HER!!
GET AWAY FROM THERE, ALITA!!
WITHOUT THE PAIN AND PLEASURE OF THE FLESH, LIFE HAS NO MEANING OR PURPOSE!

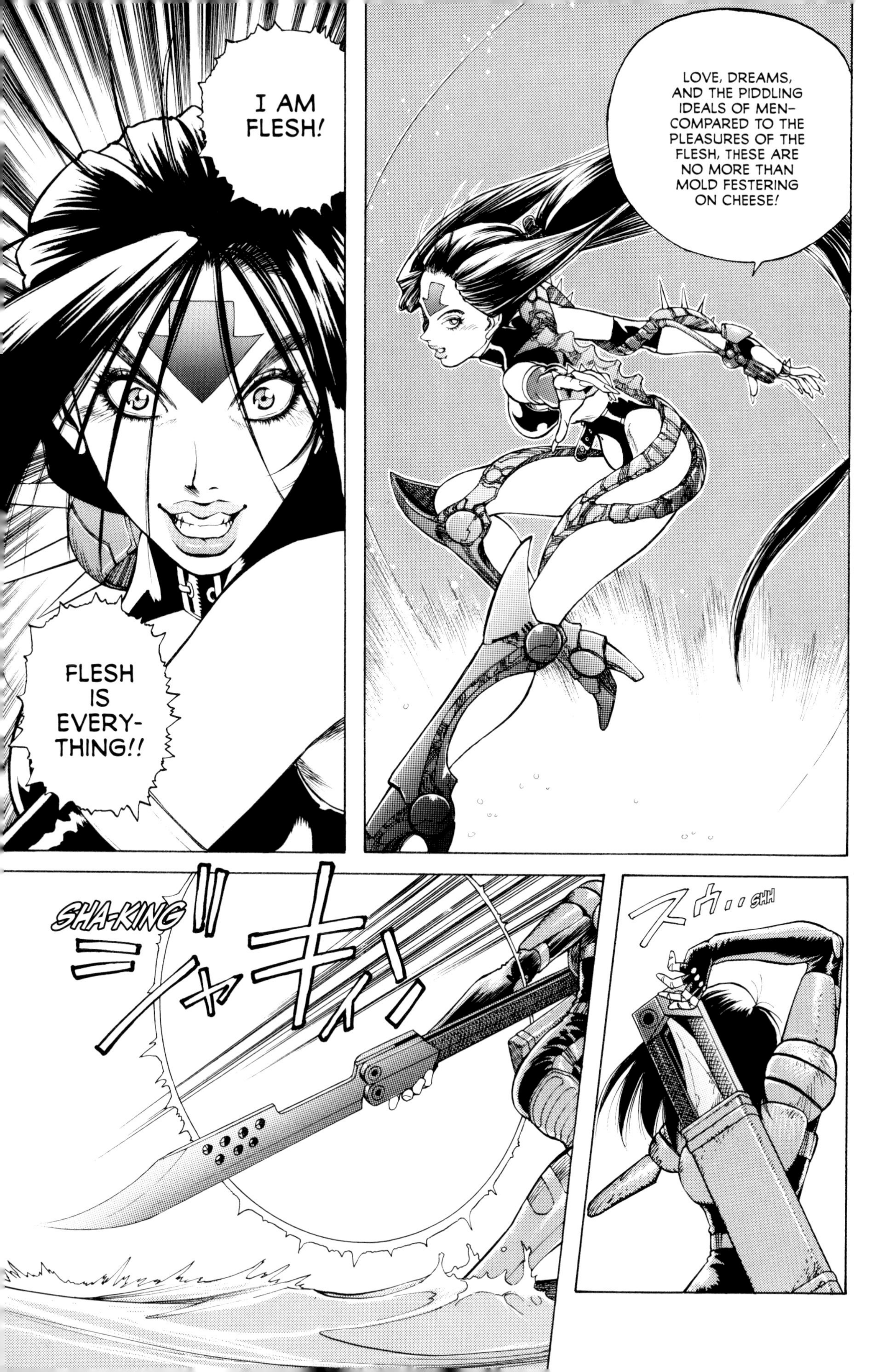
LOVE, DREAMS, AND THE PIDDLING IDEALS OF MEN— COMPARED TO THE PLEASURES OF THE FLESH, THESE ARE NO MORE THAN MOLD FESTERING ON CHEESE!
I AM FLESH!
FLESH IS EVERY-THING!!
スゥ・・ SHH
SHA-KING!!
シャキィン

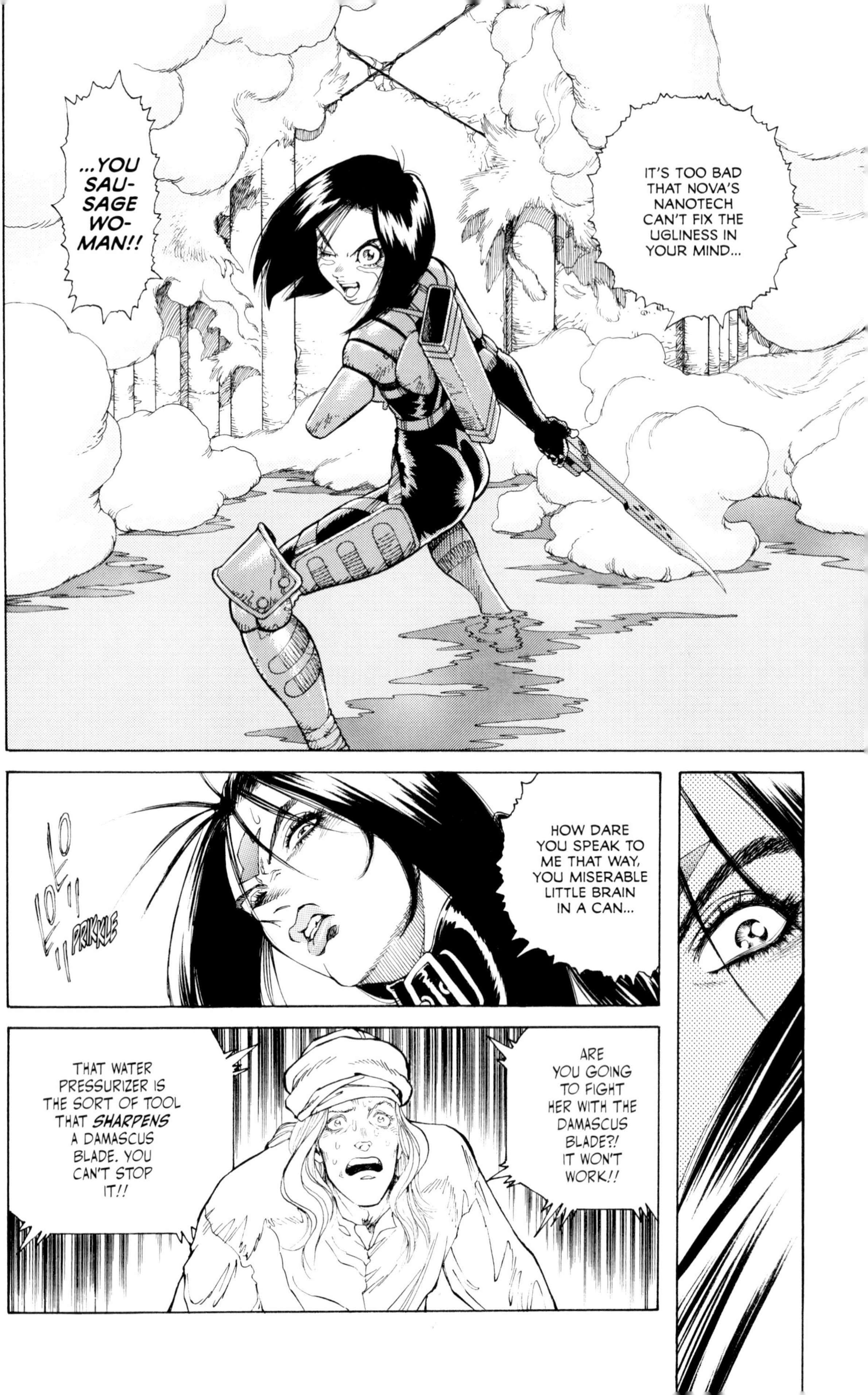
IT'S TOO BAD THAT NOVA'S NANOTECH CAN'T FIX THE UGLINESS IN YOUR MIND...
...YOU SAU-SAGE WO-MAN!!
HOW DARE YOU SPEAK TO ME THAT WAY, YOU MISERABLE LITTLE BRAIN IN A CAN...
PRIKKLE
ARE YOU GOING TO FIGHT HER WITH THE DAMASCUS BLADE?! IT WON'T WORK!!
THAT WATER PRESSURIZER IS THE SORT OF TOOL THAT *SHARPENS* A DAMASCUS BLADE. YOU CAN'T STOP IT!!

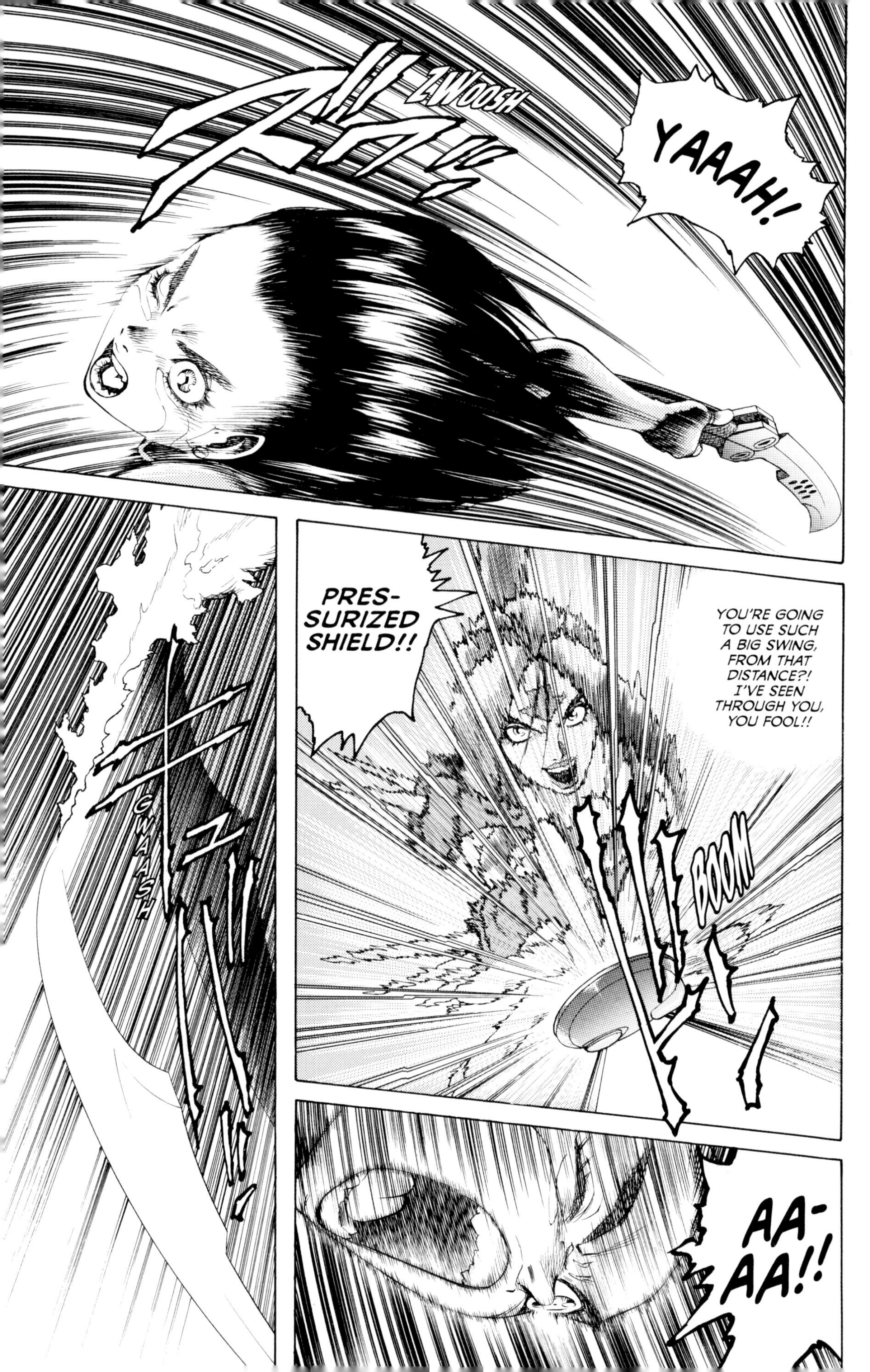
YAAAH!
ZWOOSH
YOU'RE GOING TO USE SUCH A BIG SWING, FROM THAT DISTANCE?! I'VE SEEN THROUGH YOU, YOU FOOL!!
PRES-SURIZED SHIELD!!
BOOM
AA-AA!!
GWAASH

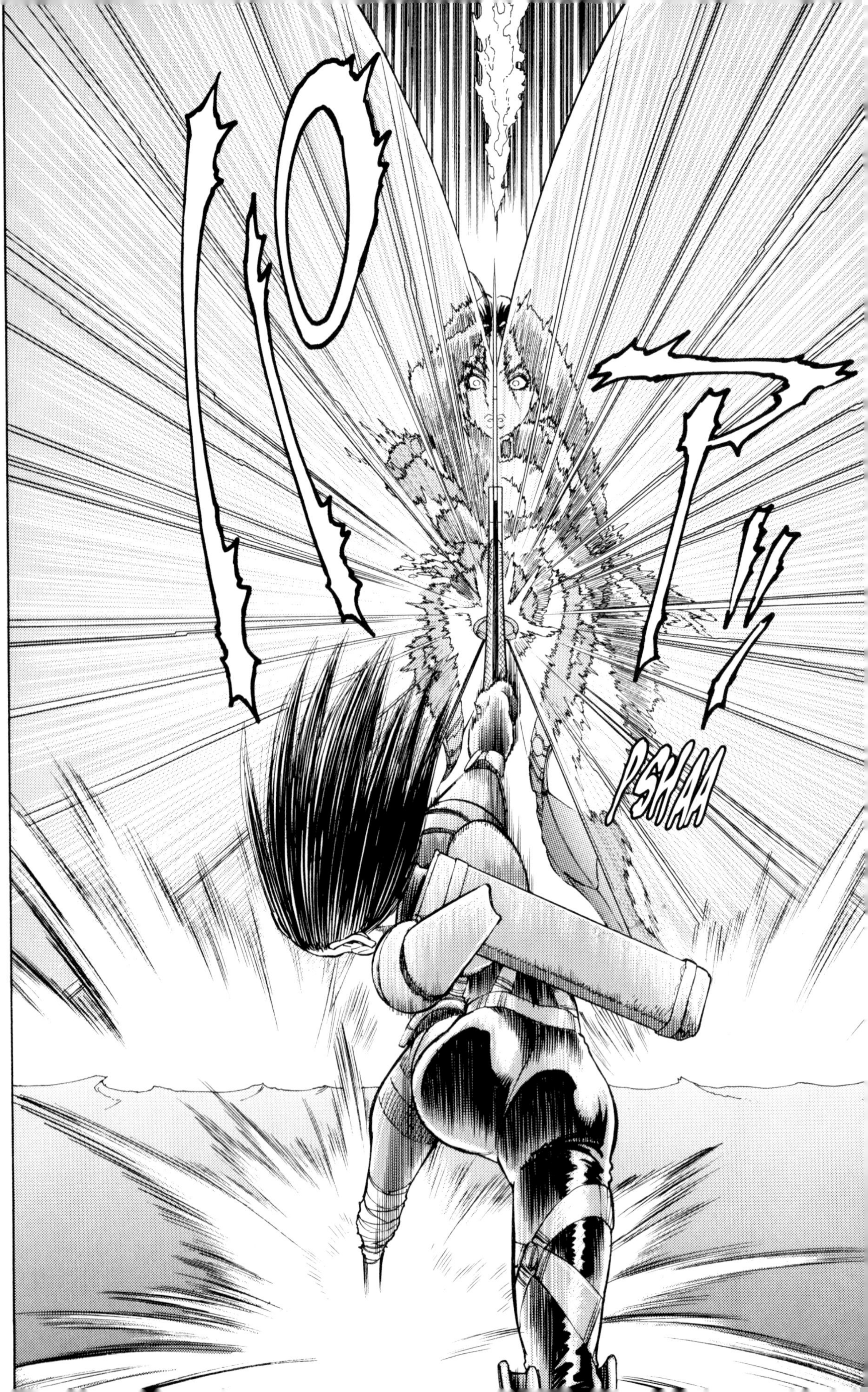
PSHAA

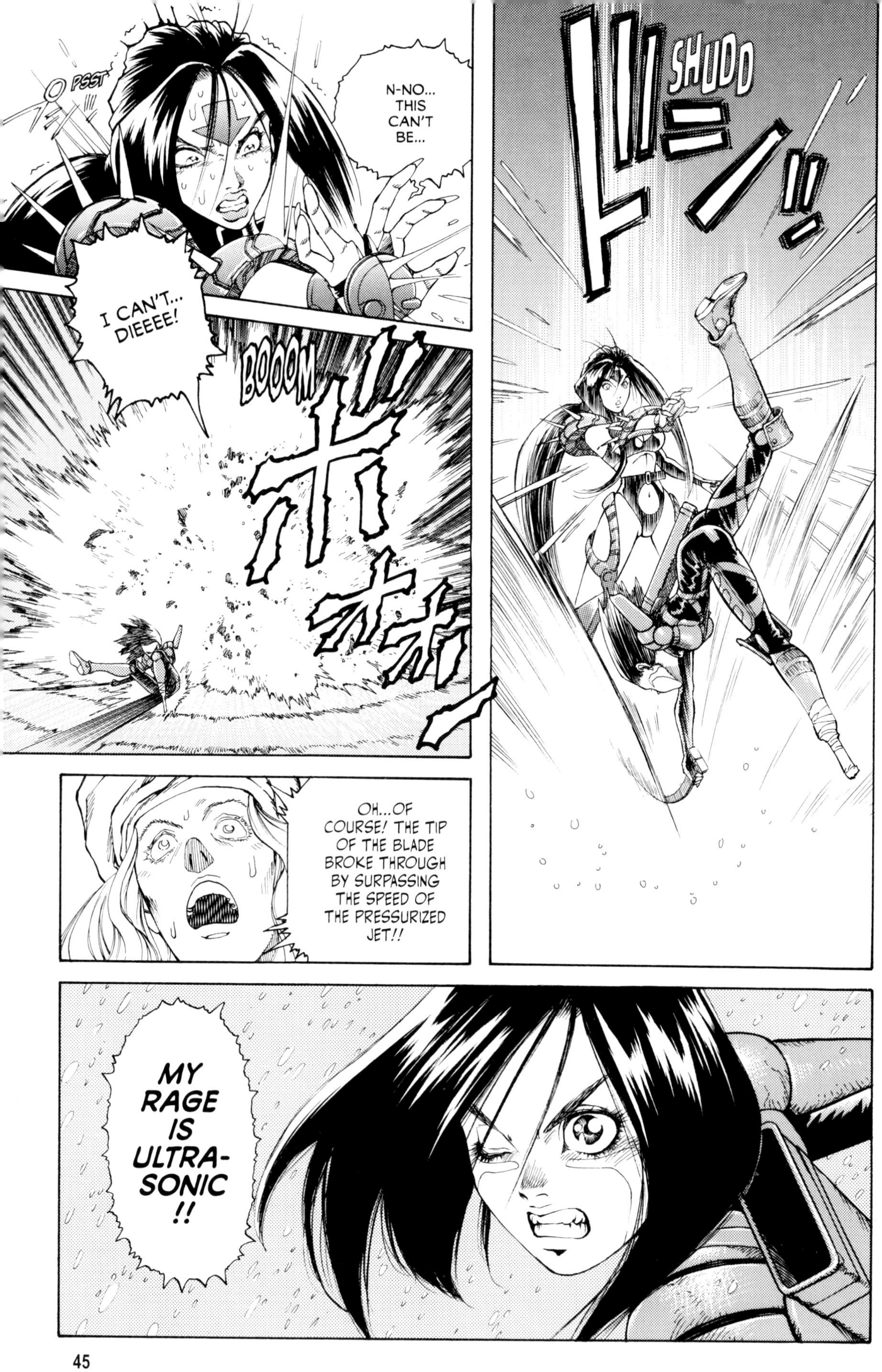
SHUDD
PSST
N-NO... THIS CAN'T BE...
I CAN'T... DIEEEE!
BOOM
OH...OF COURSE! THE TIP OF THE BLADE BROKE THROUGH BY SURPASSING THE SPEED OF THE PRESSURIZED JET!!
MY RAGE IS ULTRA-SONIC!!

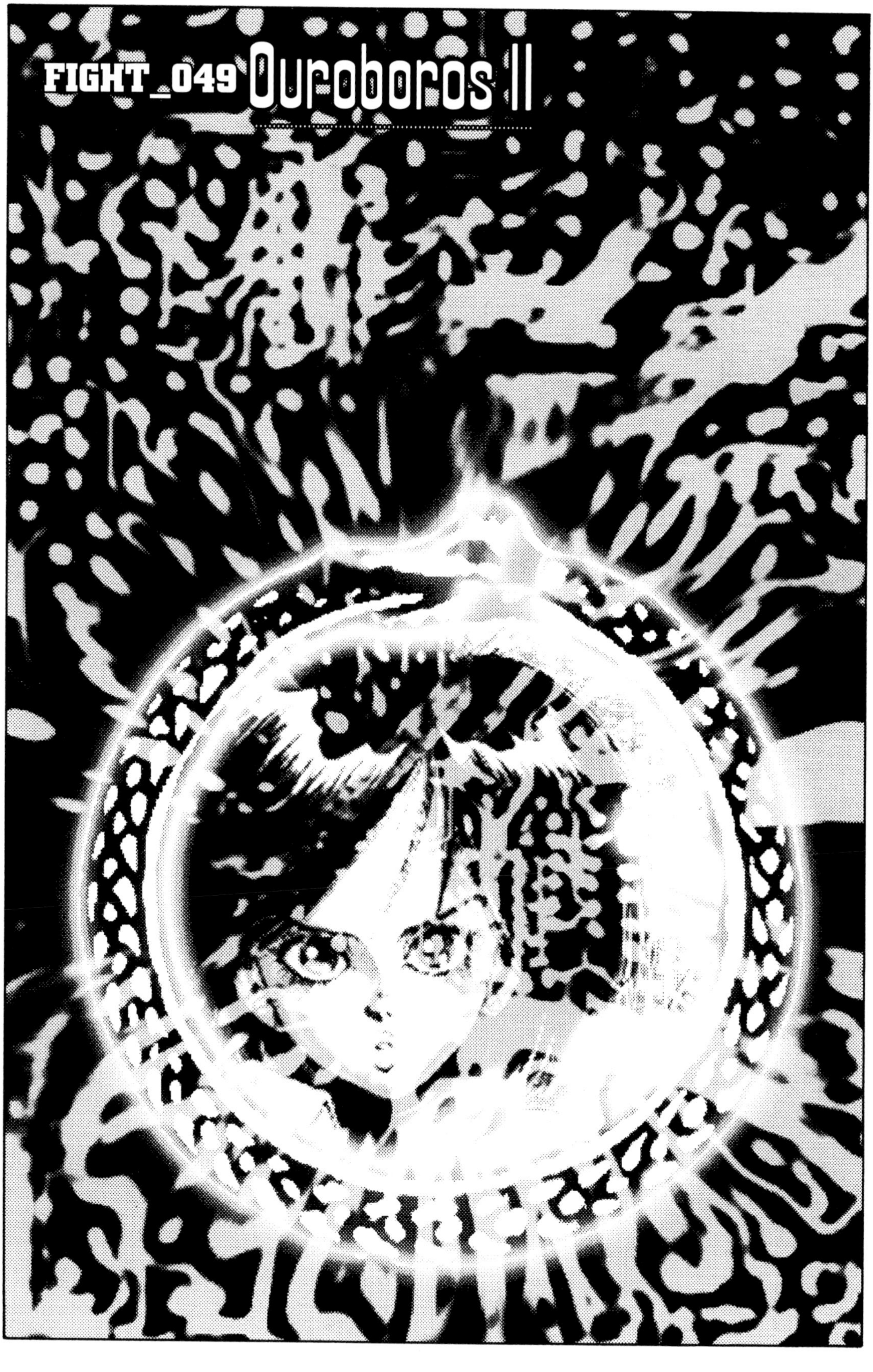
FIGHT_049 Ouroboros II

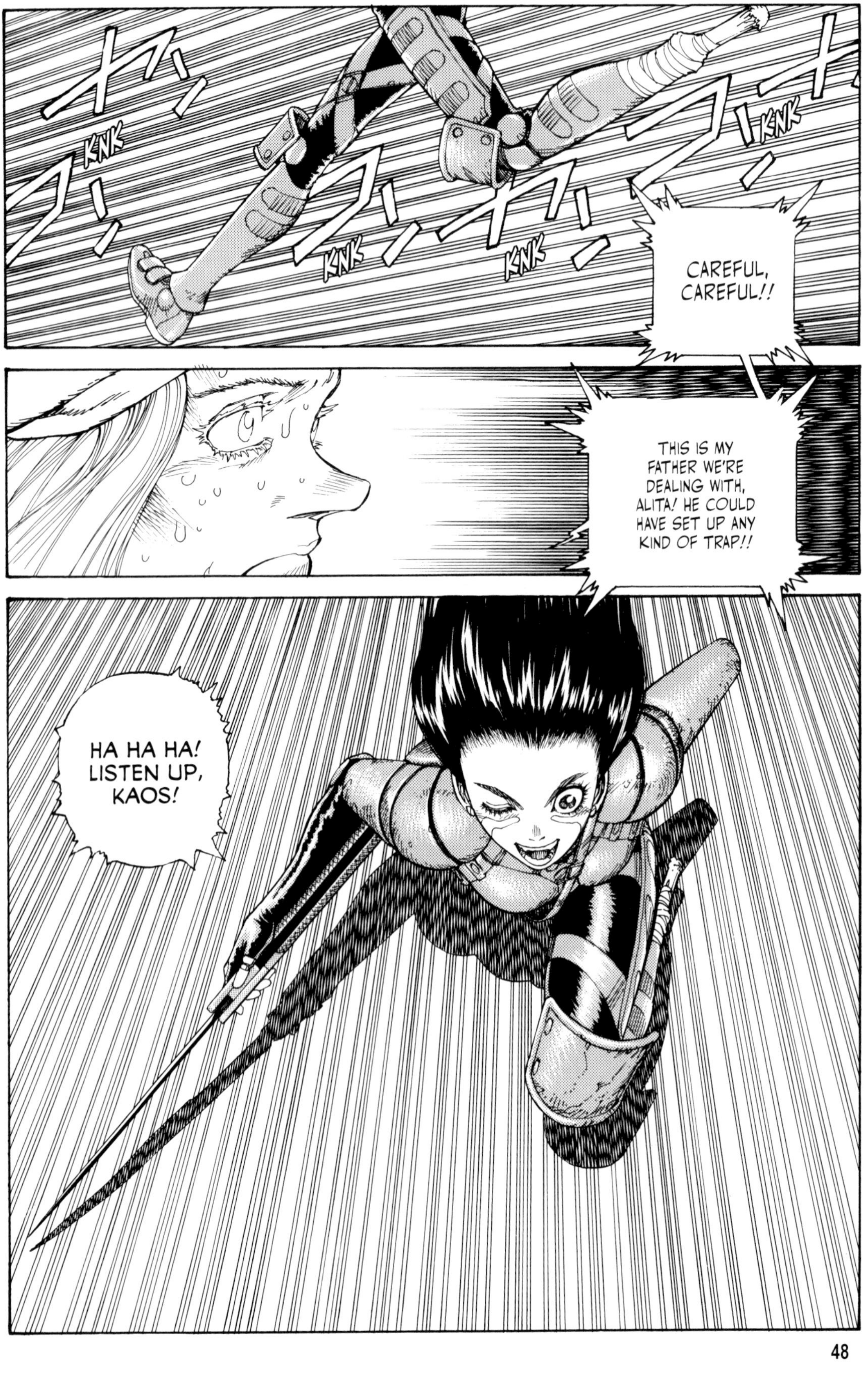
KNK
KNK
KNK
KNK
CAREFUL, CAREFUL!!
THIS IS MY FATHER WE'RE DEALING WITH, ALITA! HE COULD HAVE SET UP ANY KIND OF TRAP!!
HA HA HA! LISTEN UP, KAOS!

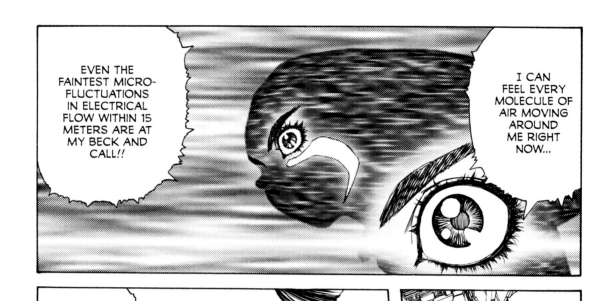

I CAN FEEL EVERY MOLECULE OF AIR MOVING AROUND ME RIGHT NOW...
EVEN THE FAINTEST MICRO-FLUCTUATIONS IN ELECTRICAL FLOW WITHIN 15 METERS ARE AT MY BECK AND CALL!!
I'VE NEVER FELT SUCH A TRIUMPHANT SURGE IN *KI!!*
I'LL DESTROY HIM!!
NO MATTER WHAT TRAPS OR OBSTACLES HE THROWS IN MY WAY...
...I CANNOT BE STOPPED!!

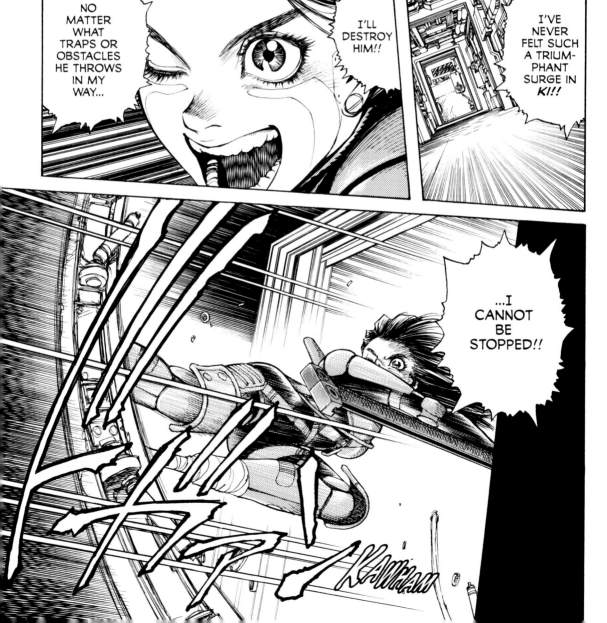

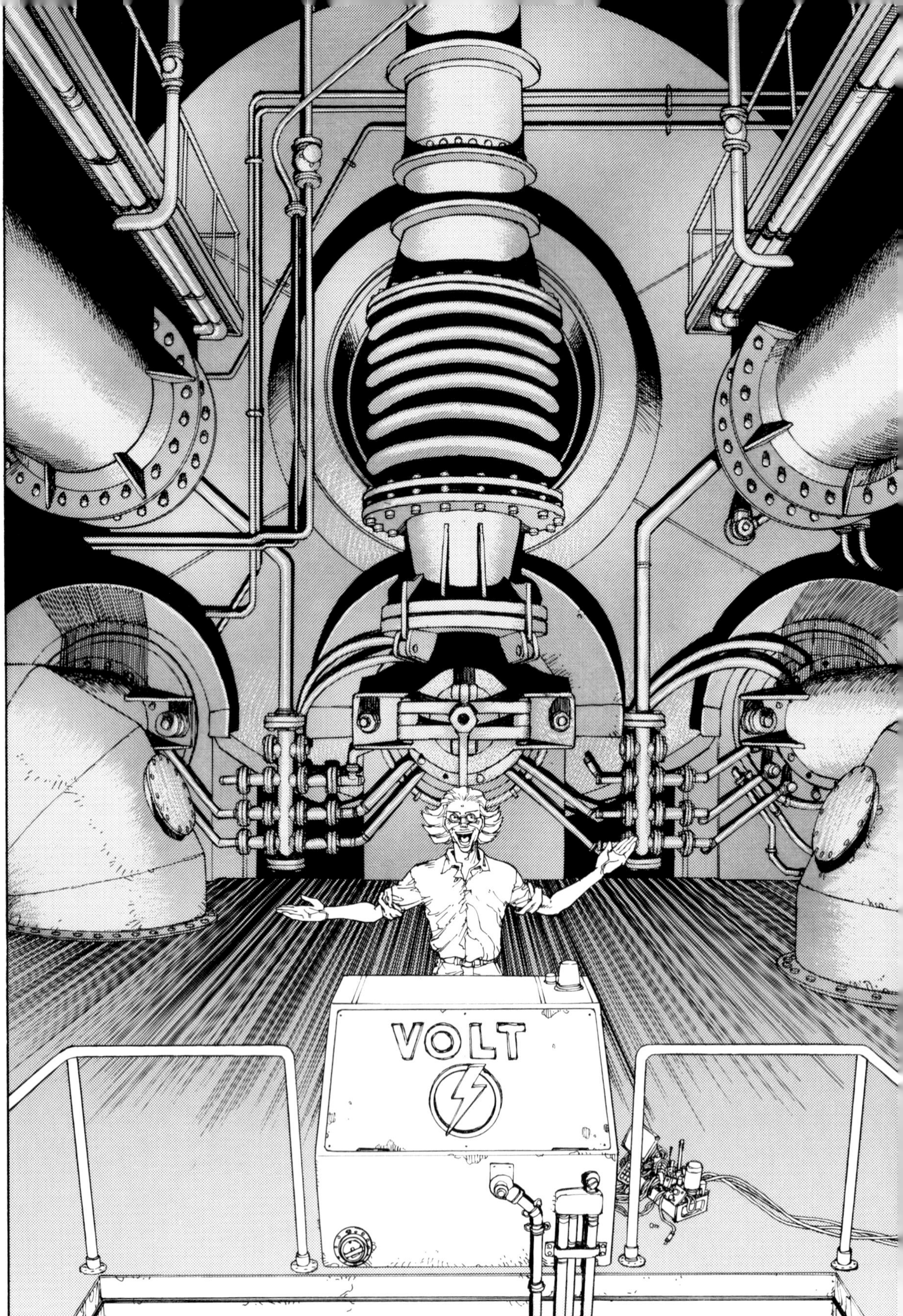
VOLT

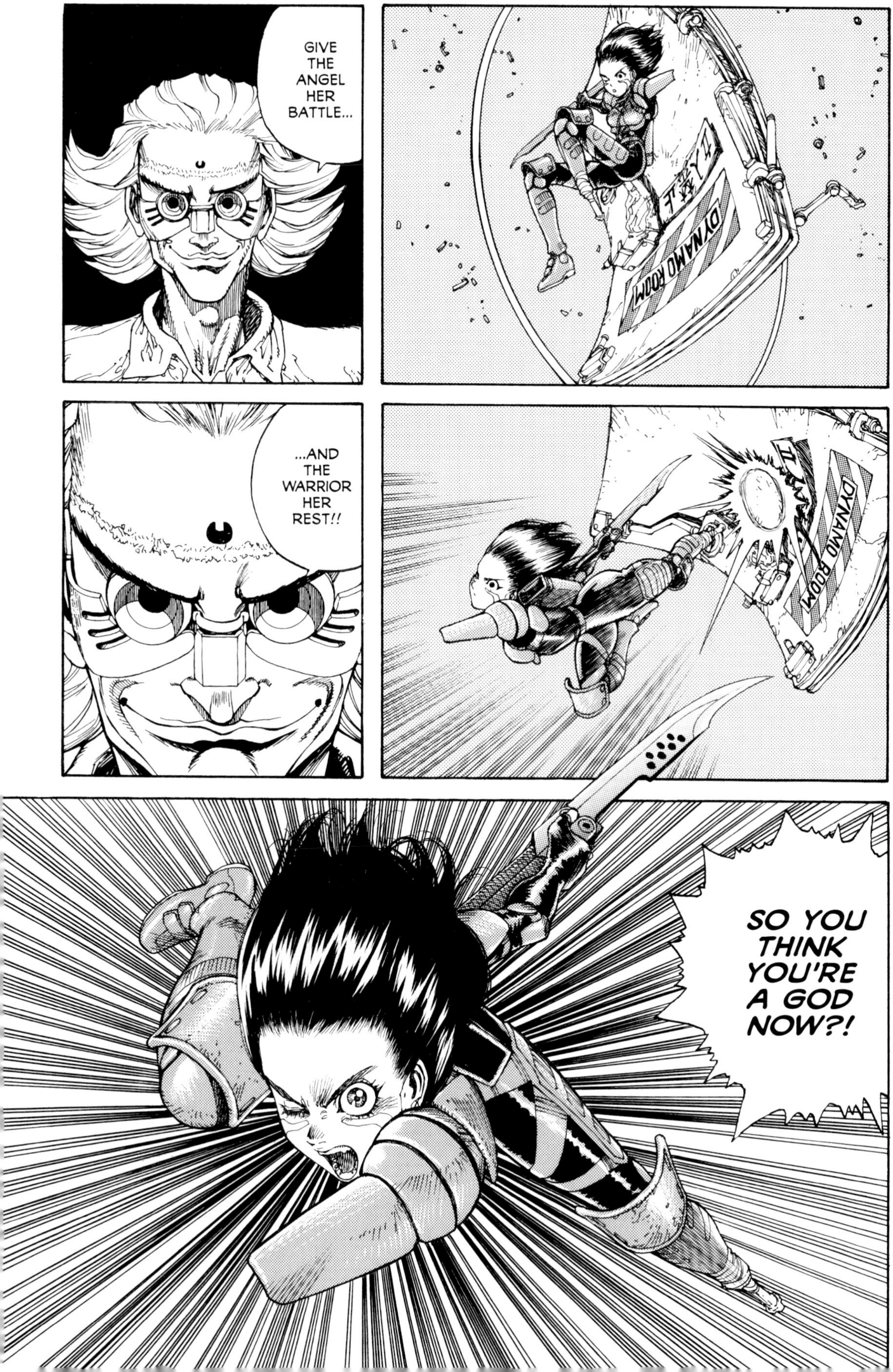
DYNAMO ROOM
GIVE THE ANGEL HER BATTLE...
DYNAMO ROOM
...AND THE WARRIOR HER REST!!
SO YOU THINK YOU'RE A GOD NOW?!

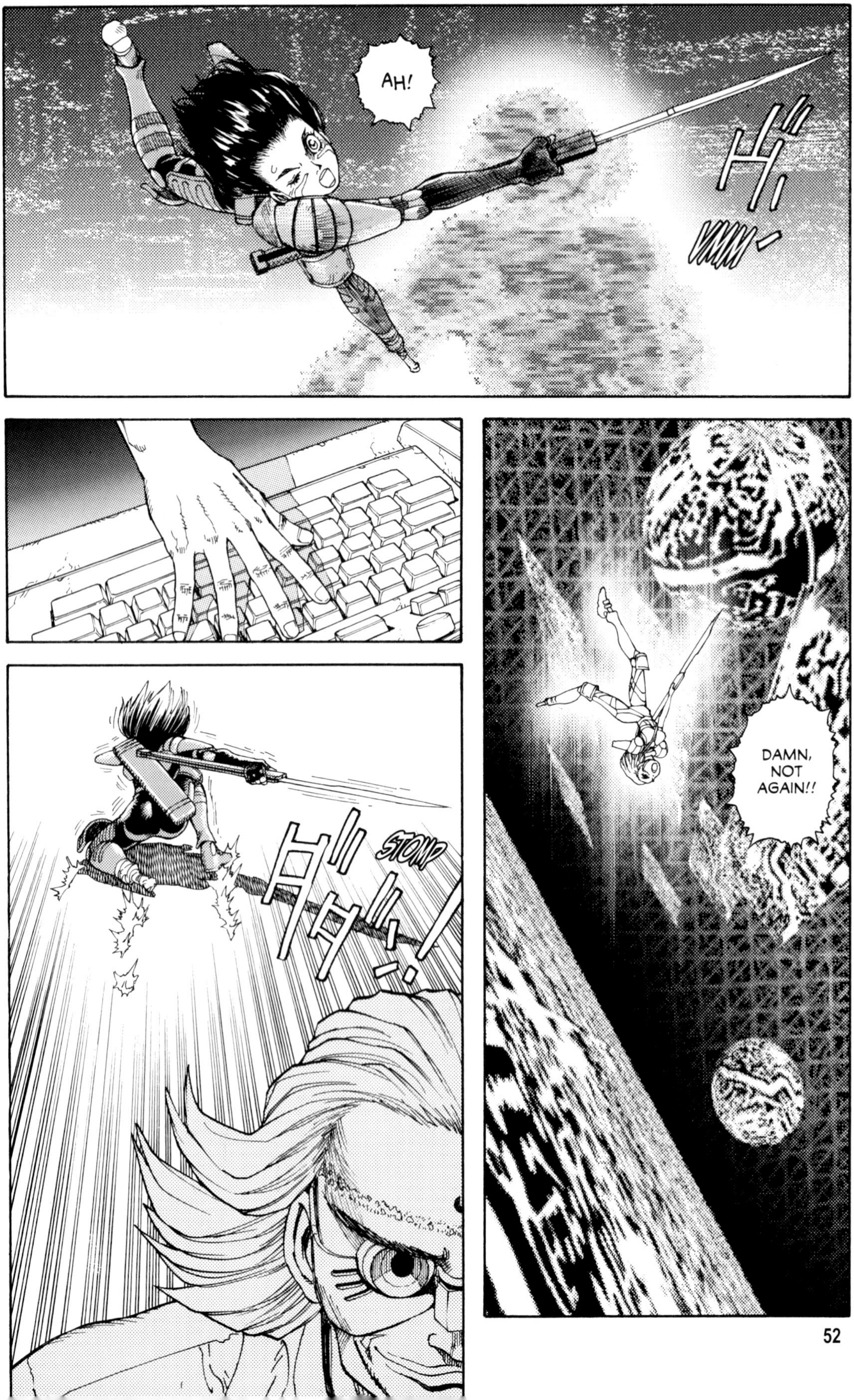
AH!
DAMN, NOT AGAIN!!
STOMP

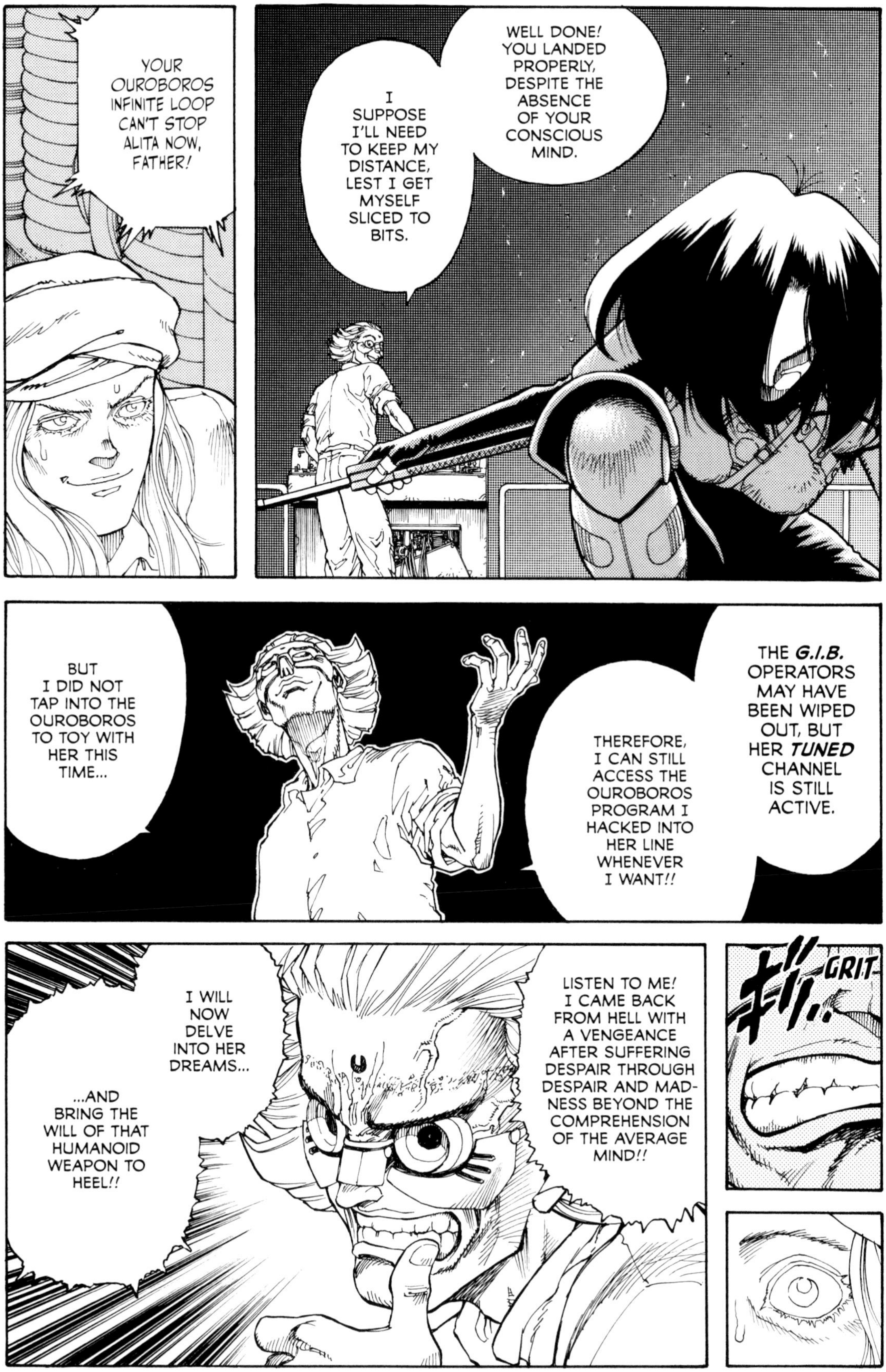
WELL DONE! YOU LANDED PROPERLY, DESPITE THE ABSENCE OF YOUR CONSCIOUS MIND.
I SUPPOSE I'LL NEED TO KEEP MY DISTANCE, LEST I GET MYSELF SLICED TO BITS.
YOUR OUROBOROS INFINITE LOOP CAN'T STOP ALITA NOW, FATHER!
THE *G.I.B.* OPERATORS MAY HAVE BEEN WIPED OUT, BUT HER *TUNED* CHANNEL IS STILL ACTIVE.
THEREFORE, I CAN STILL ACCESS THE OUROBOROS PROGRAM I HACKED INTO HER LINE WHENEVER I WANT!!
BUT I DID NOT TAP INTO THE OUROBOROS TO TOY WITH HER THIS TIME...
GRIT
LISTEN TO ME! I CAME BACK FROM HELL WITH A VENGEANCE AFTER SUFFERING DESPAIR THROUGH DESPAIR AND MADNESS BEYOND THE COMPREHENSION OF THE AVERAGE MIND!!
I WILL NOW DELVE INTO HER DREAMS...
...AND BRING THE WILL OF THAT HUMANOID WEAPON TO HEEL!!

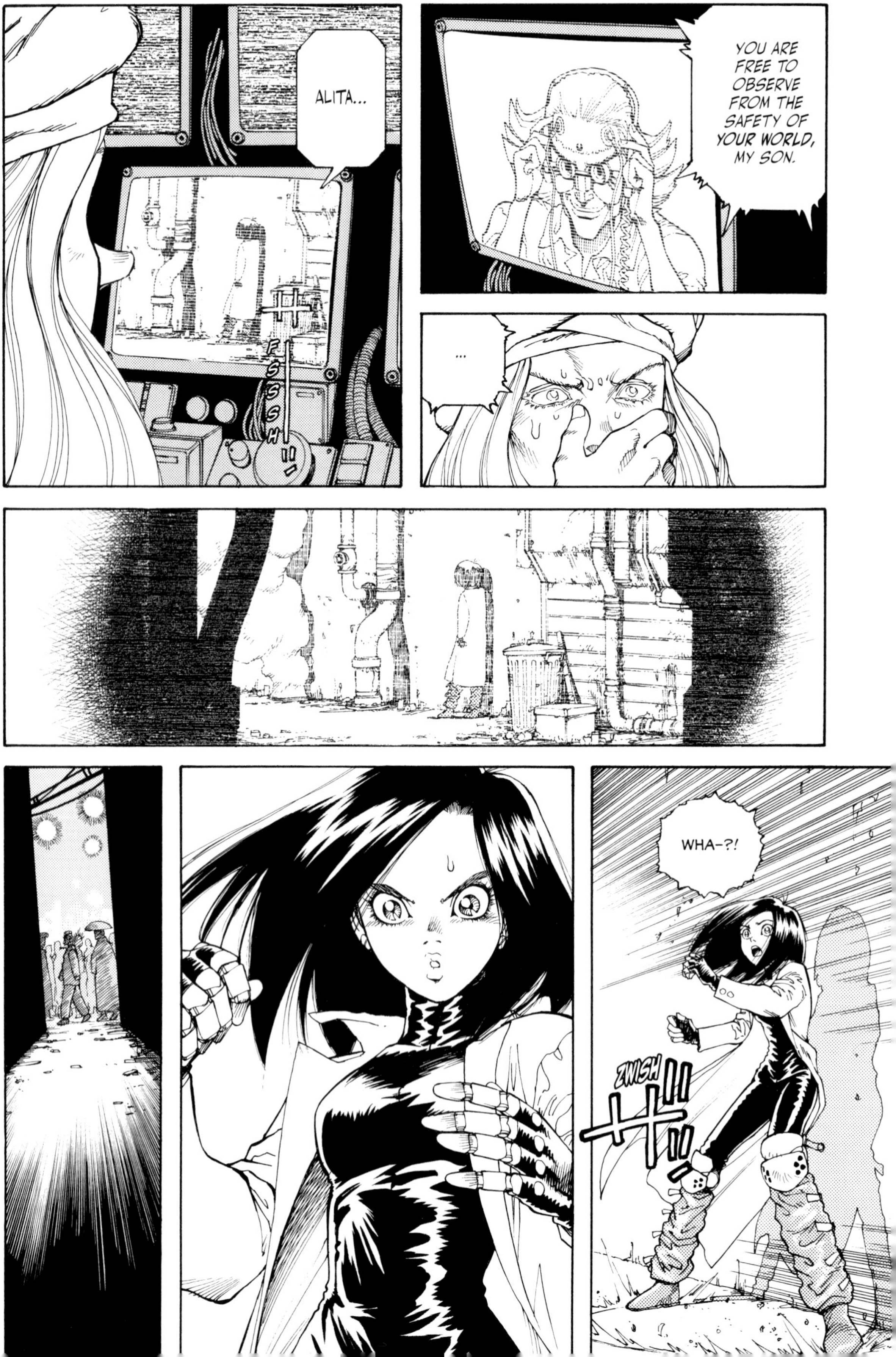
YOU ARE FREE TO OBSERVE FROM THE SAFETY OF YOUR WORLD, MY SON.
...
ALITA...
FSSSH!!
WHA-?!
ZWISH!!

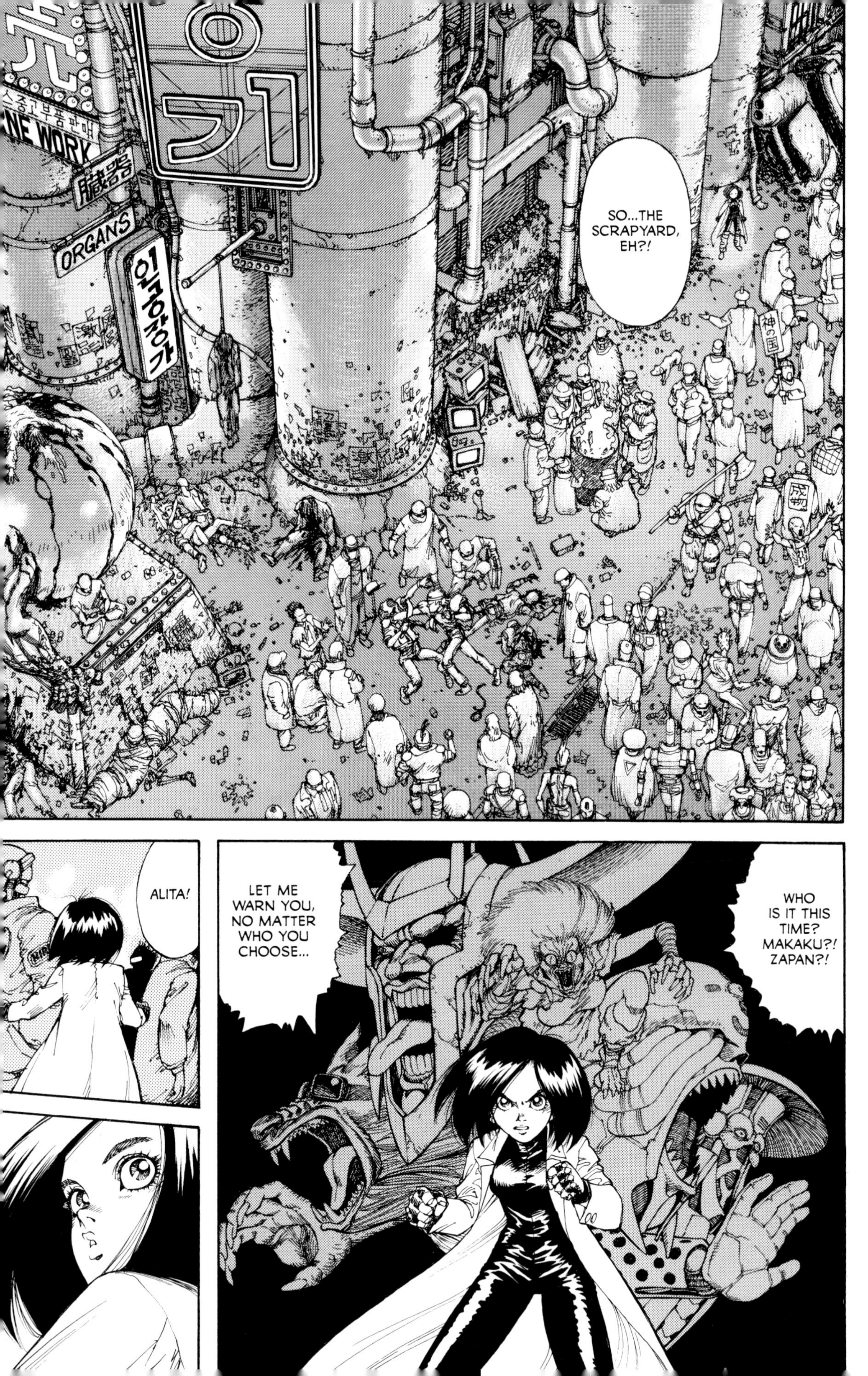
ORGANS
臓器
SO...THE SCRAPYARD, EH?!
WHO IS IT THIS TIME? MAKAKU?! ZAPAN?!
LET ME WARN YOU, NO MATTER WHO YOU CHOOSE...
ALITA!

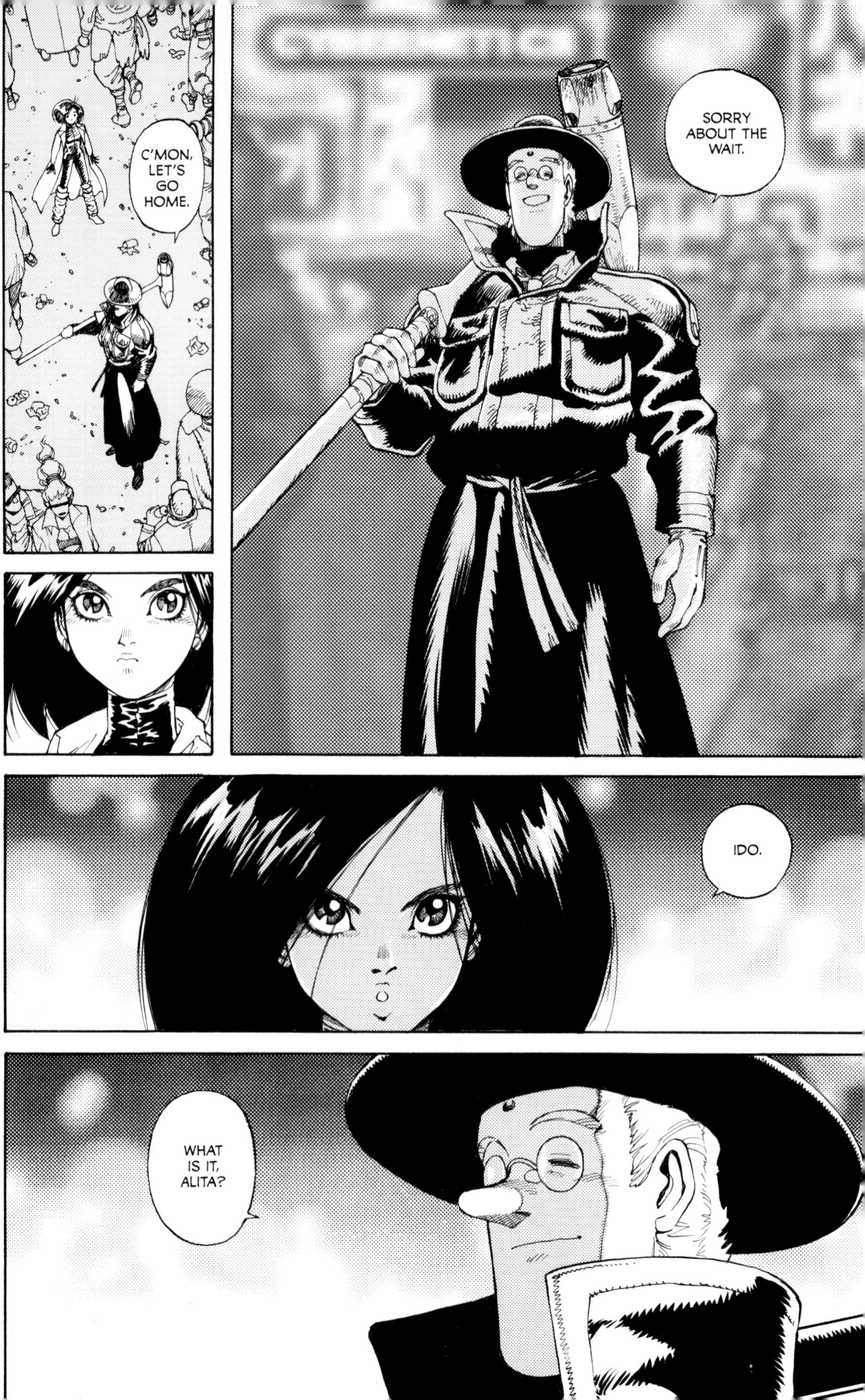
SORRY ABOUT THE WAIT.
C'MON, LET'S GO HOME.
IDO.
WHAT IS IT, ALITA?

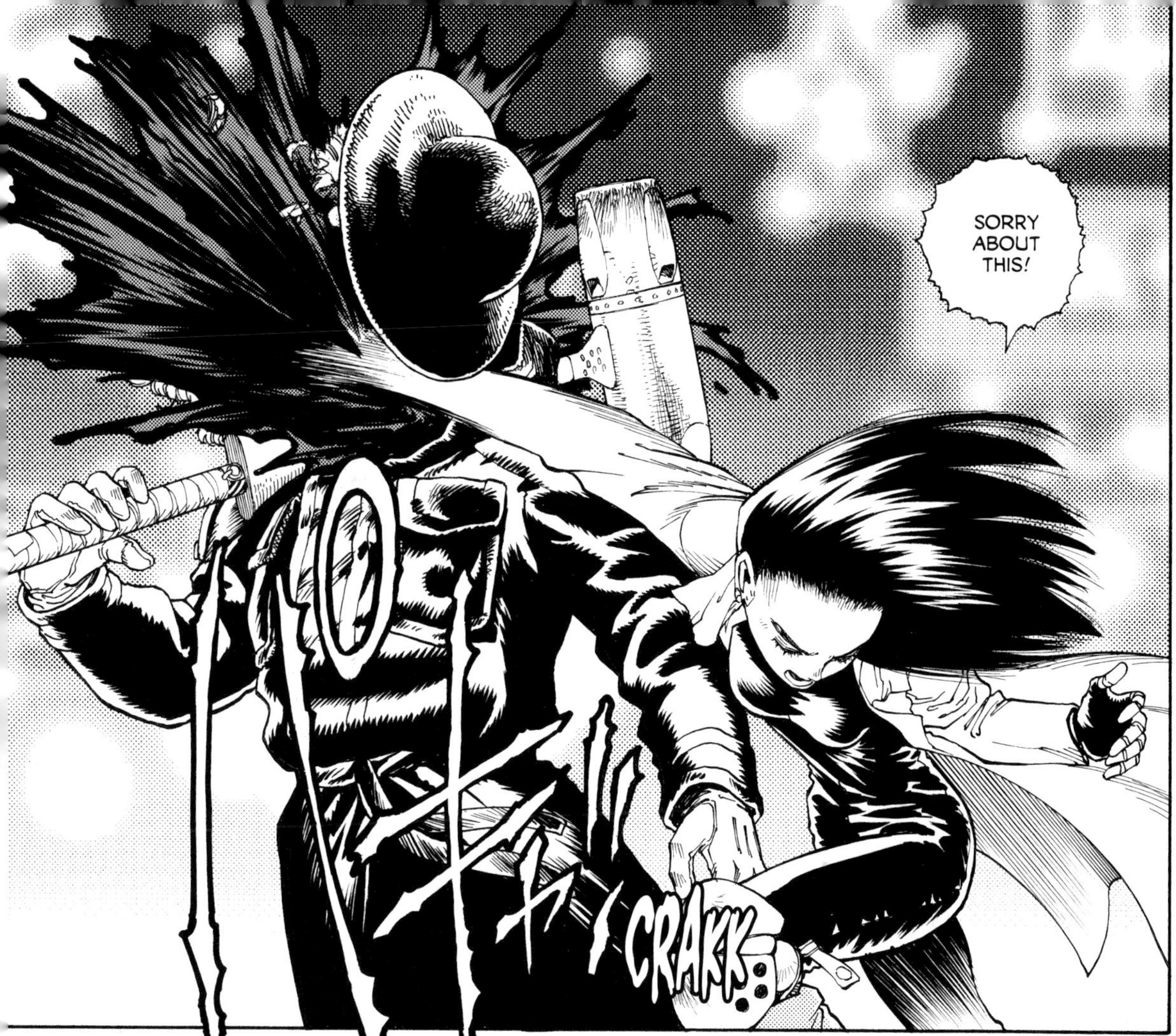
SORRY ABOUT THIS!
CRAKK

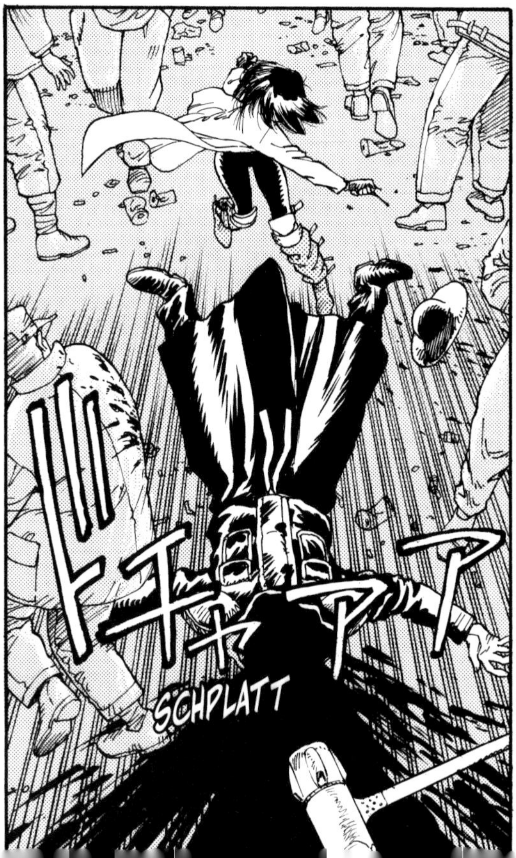
SCHPLATT

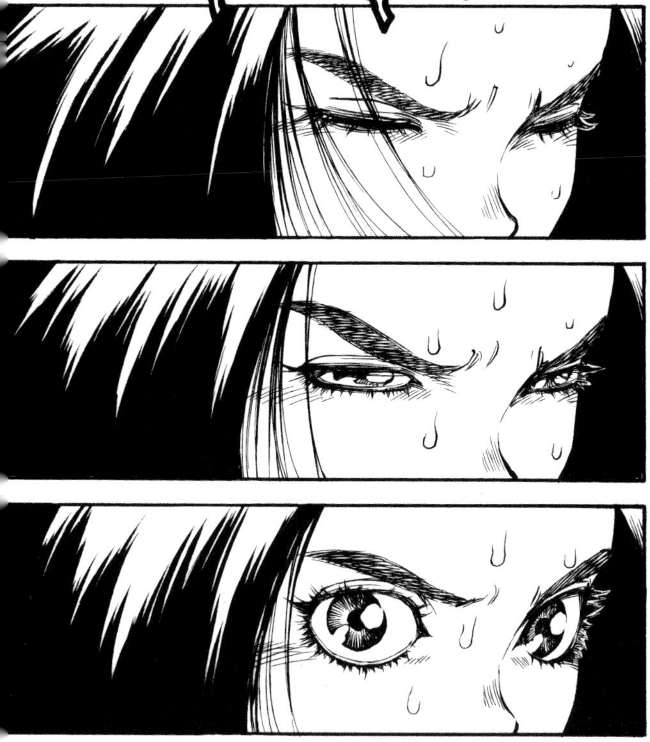

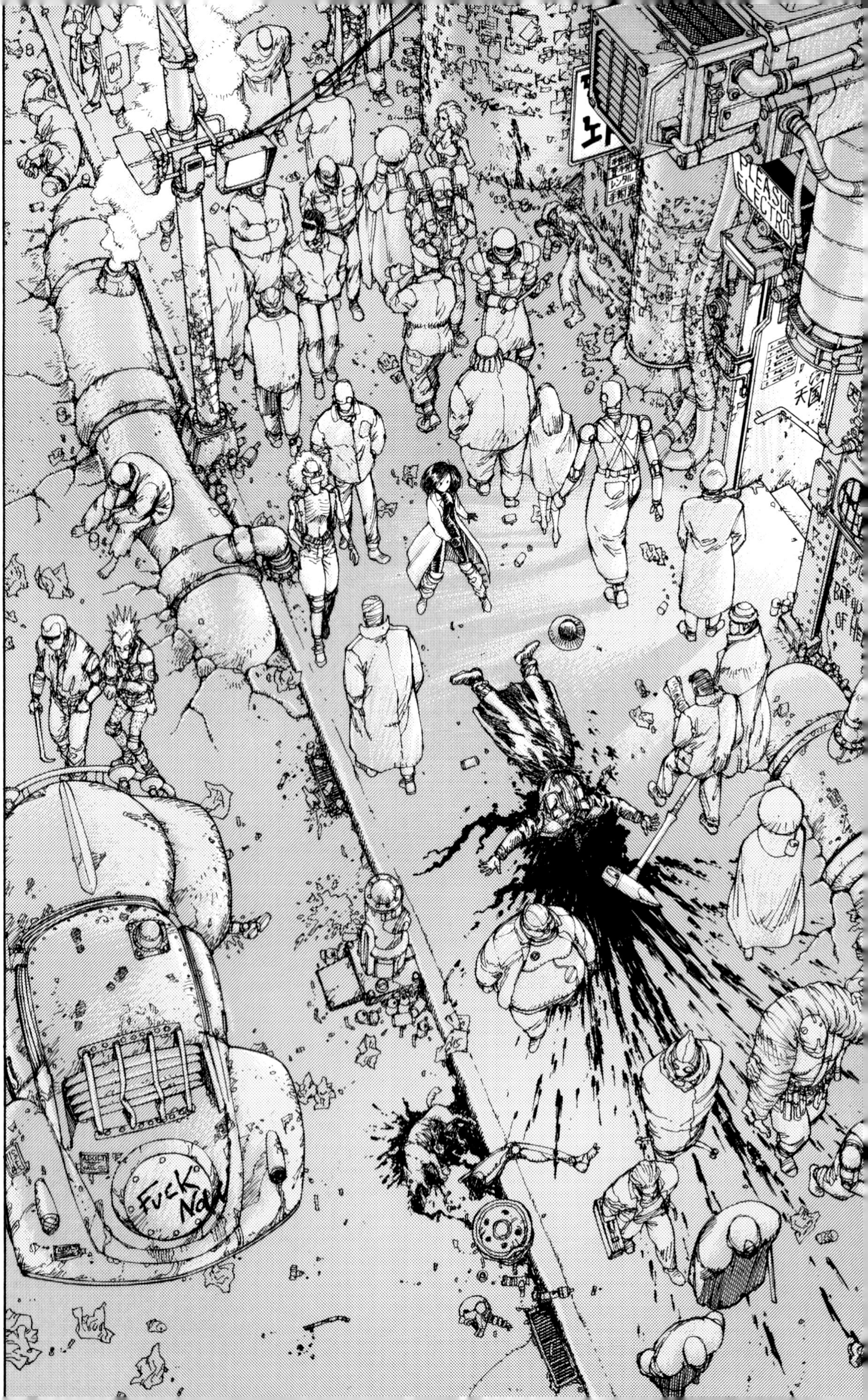
Fuck Now

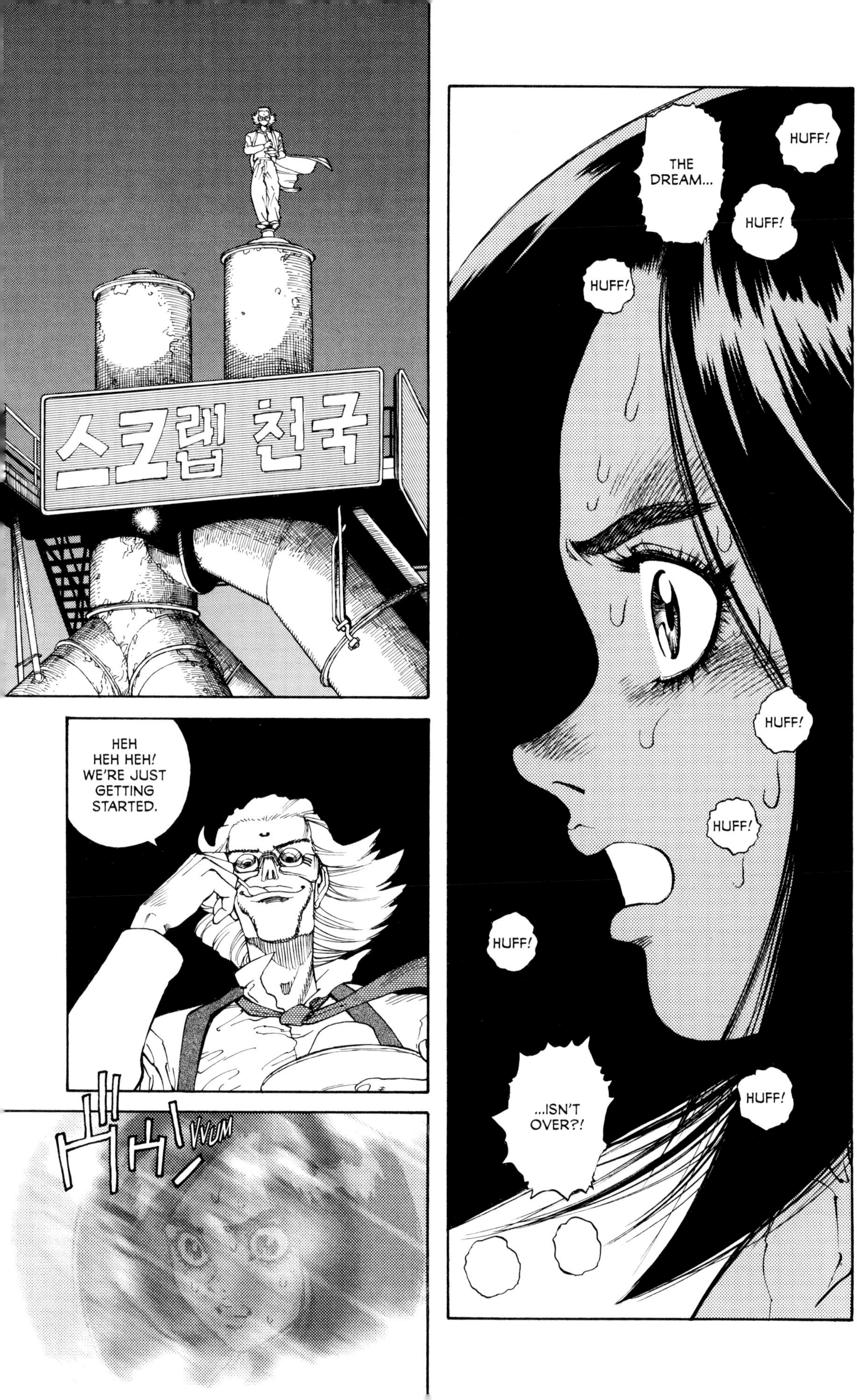
HUFF!
THE DREAM...
HUFF!
HUFF!
HUFF!
HUFF!
HUFF!
...ISN'T OVER?!
HUFF!
스크랩 천국
HEH HEH HEH! WE'RE JUST GETTING STARTED.
VVUM

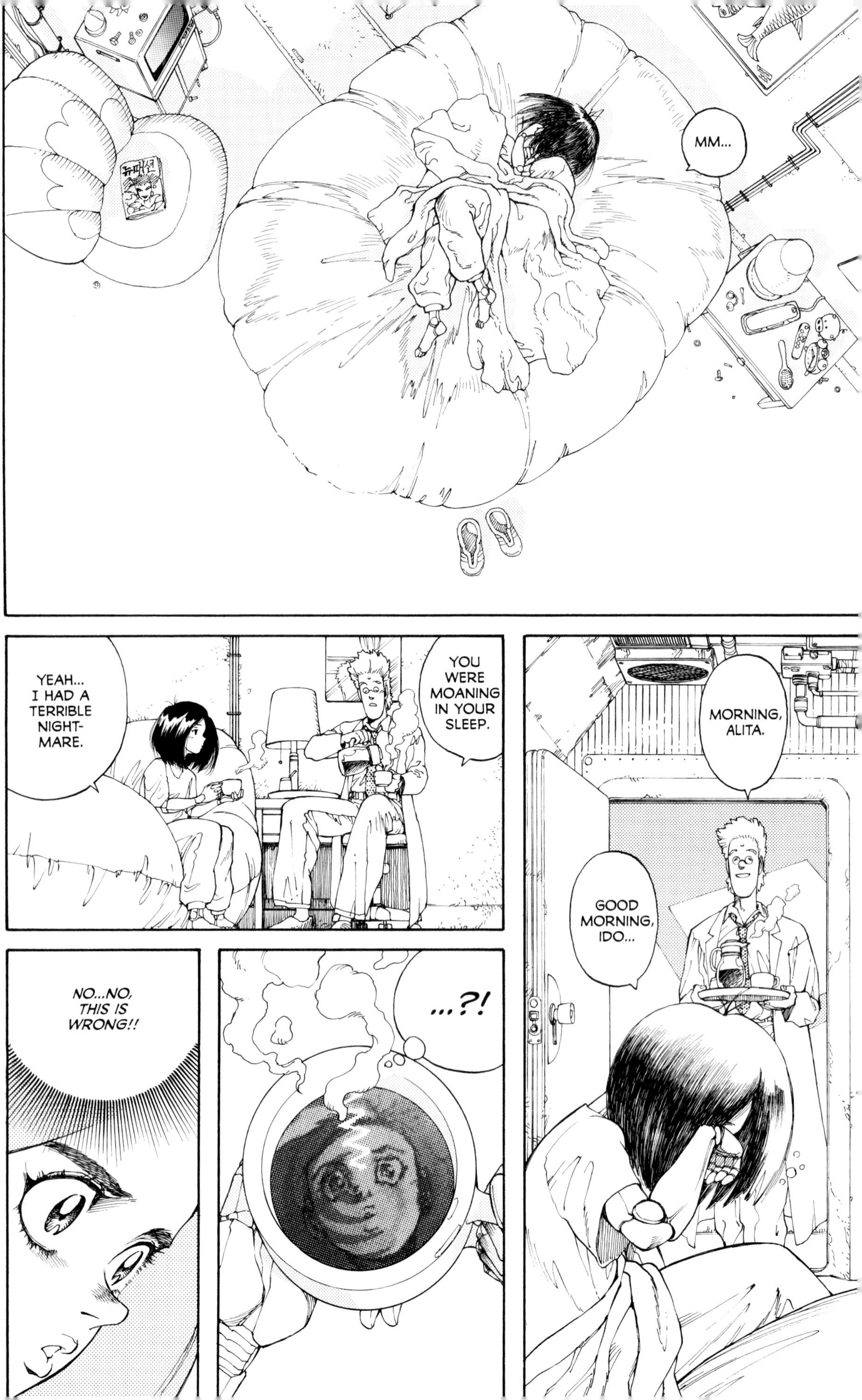
MM...
MORNING, ALITA.
GOOD MORNING, IDO...
YOU WERE MOANING IN YOUR SLEEP.
YEAH... I HAD A TERRIBLE NIGHT-MARE.
...?!
NO...NO, THIS IS WRONG!!

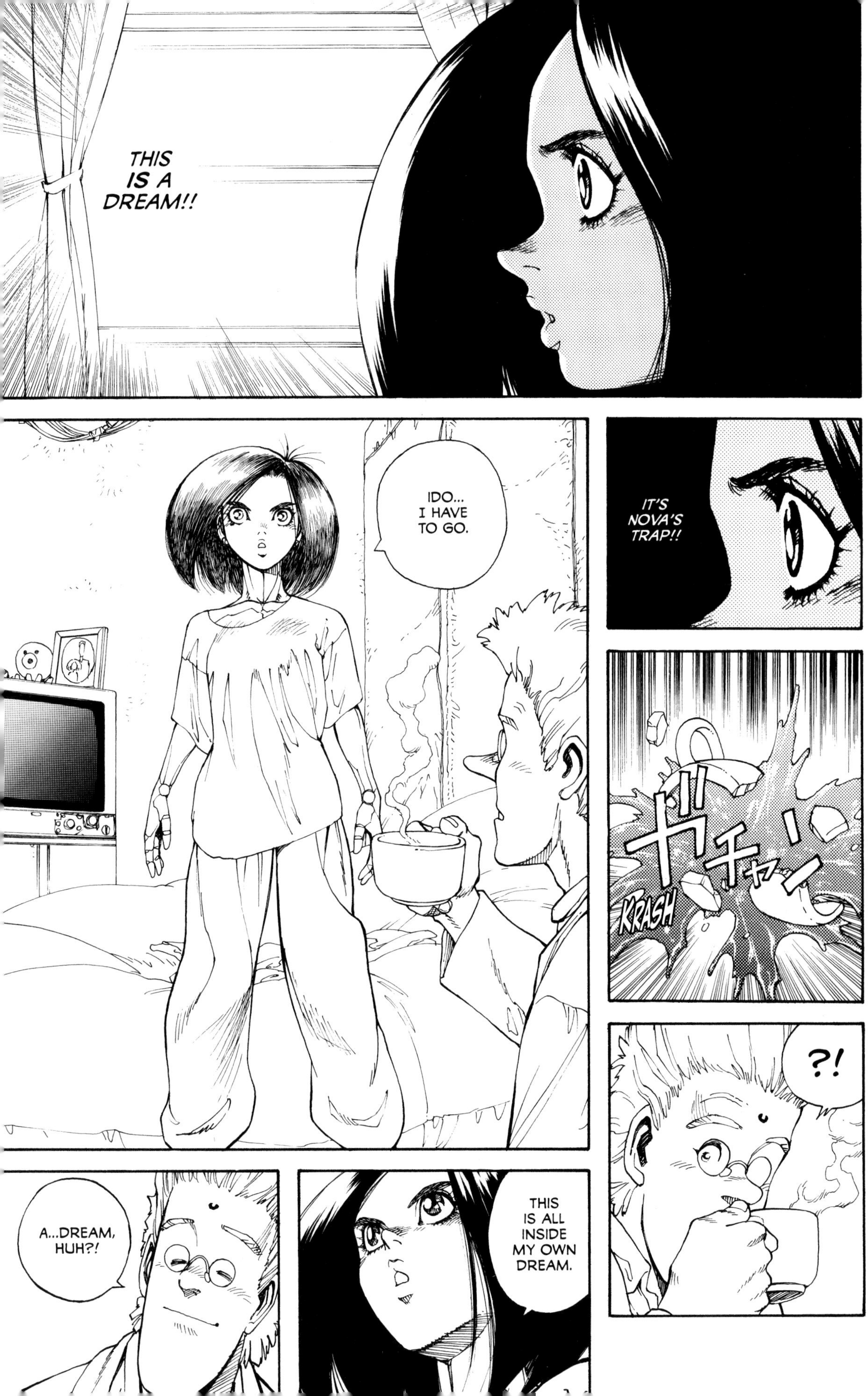
THIS IS A DREAM!!
IT'S NOVA'S TRAP!!
ガチャーン
KRASH
?!
IDO... I HAVE TO GO.
THIS IS ALL INSIDE MY OWN DREAM.
A...DREAM, HUH?!

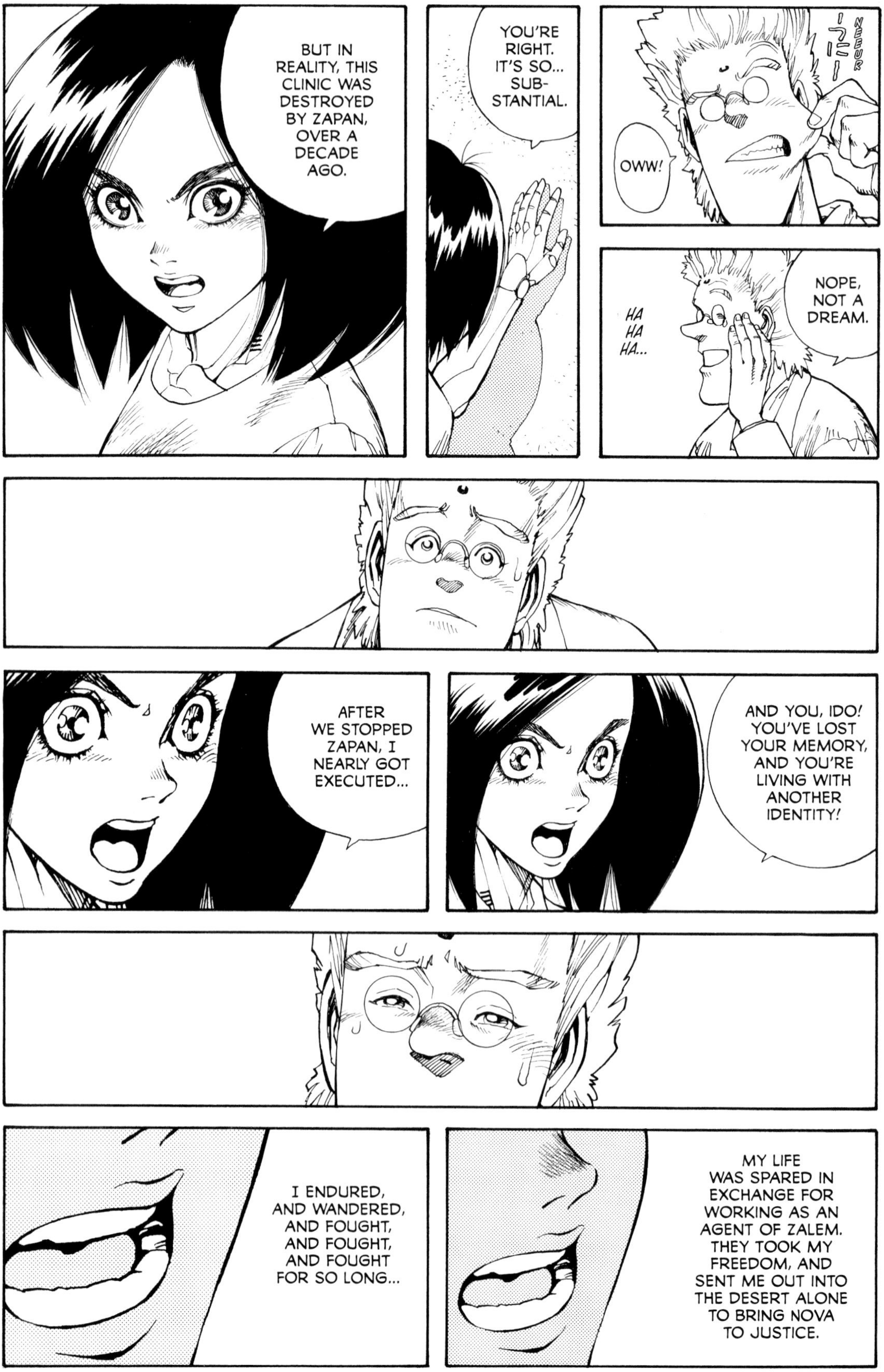
NEEUR
OWW!
NOPE, NOT A DREAM.
HA HA HA...
YOU'RE RIGHT. IT'S SO... SUB-STANTIAL.
BUT IN REALITY, THIS CLINIC WAS DESTROYED BY ZAPAN, OVER A DECADE AGO.
AND YOU, IDO! YOU'VE LOST YOUR MEMORY, AND YOU'RE LIVING WITH ANOTHER IDENTITY!
AFTER WE STOPPED ZAPAN, I NEARLY GOT EXECUTED...
MY LIFE WAS SPARED IN EXCHANGE FOR WORKING AS AN AGENT OF ZALEM. THEY TOOK MY FREEDOM, AND SENT ME OUT INTO THE DESERT ALONE TO BRING NOVA TO JUSTICE.
I ENDURED, AND WANDERED, AND FOUGHT, AND FOUGHT, AND FOUGHT FOR SO LONG...

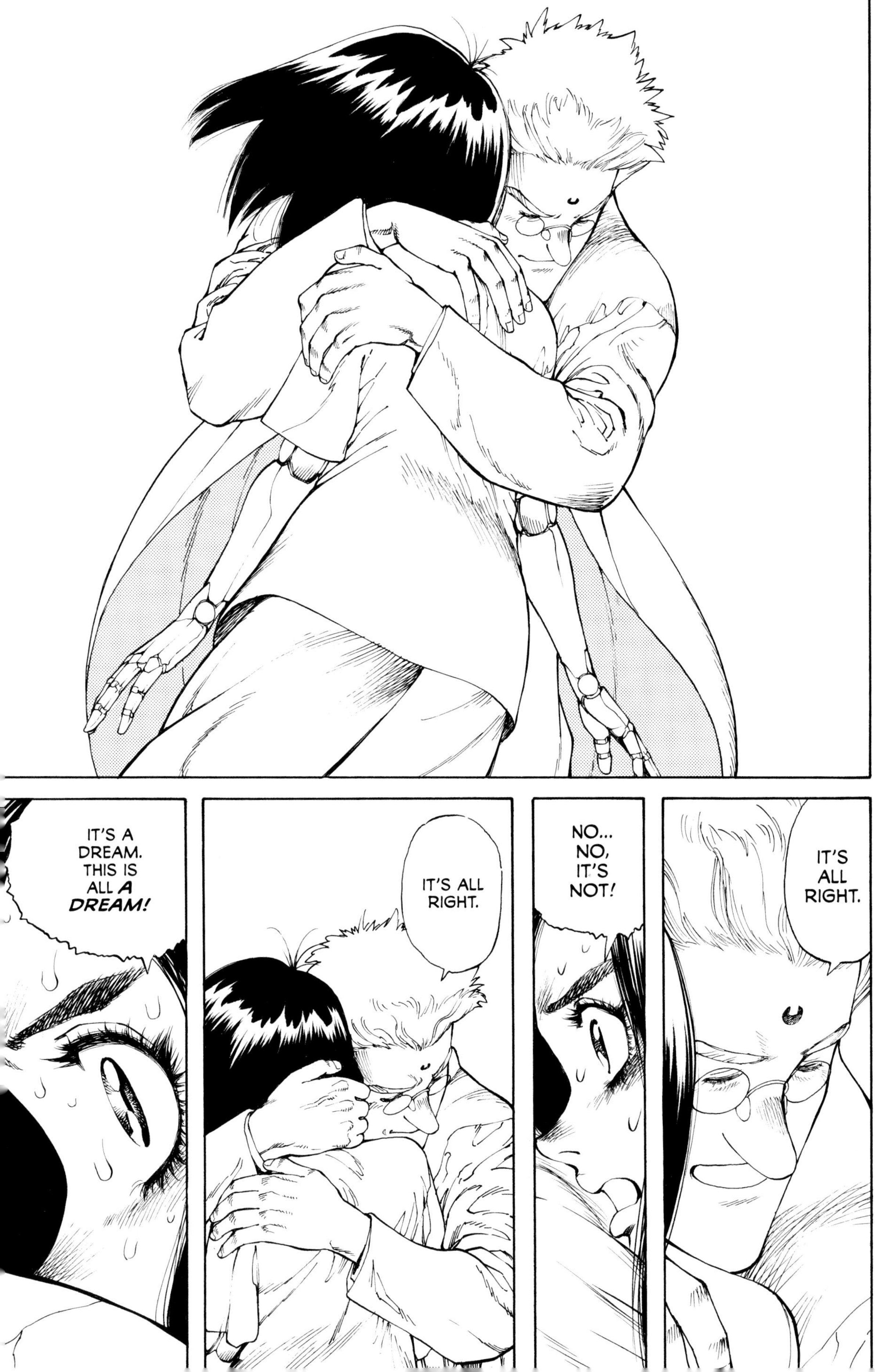
IT'S ALL RIGHT.
NO... NO, IT'S NOT!
IT'S ALL RIGHT.
IT'S A DREAM. THIS IS ALL ***A DREAM!***

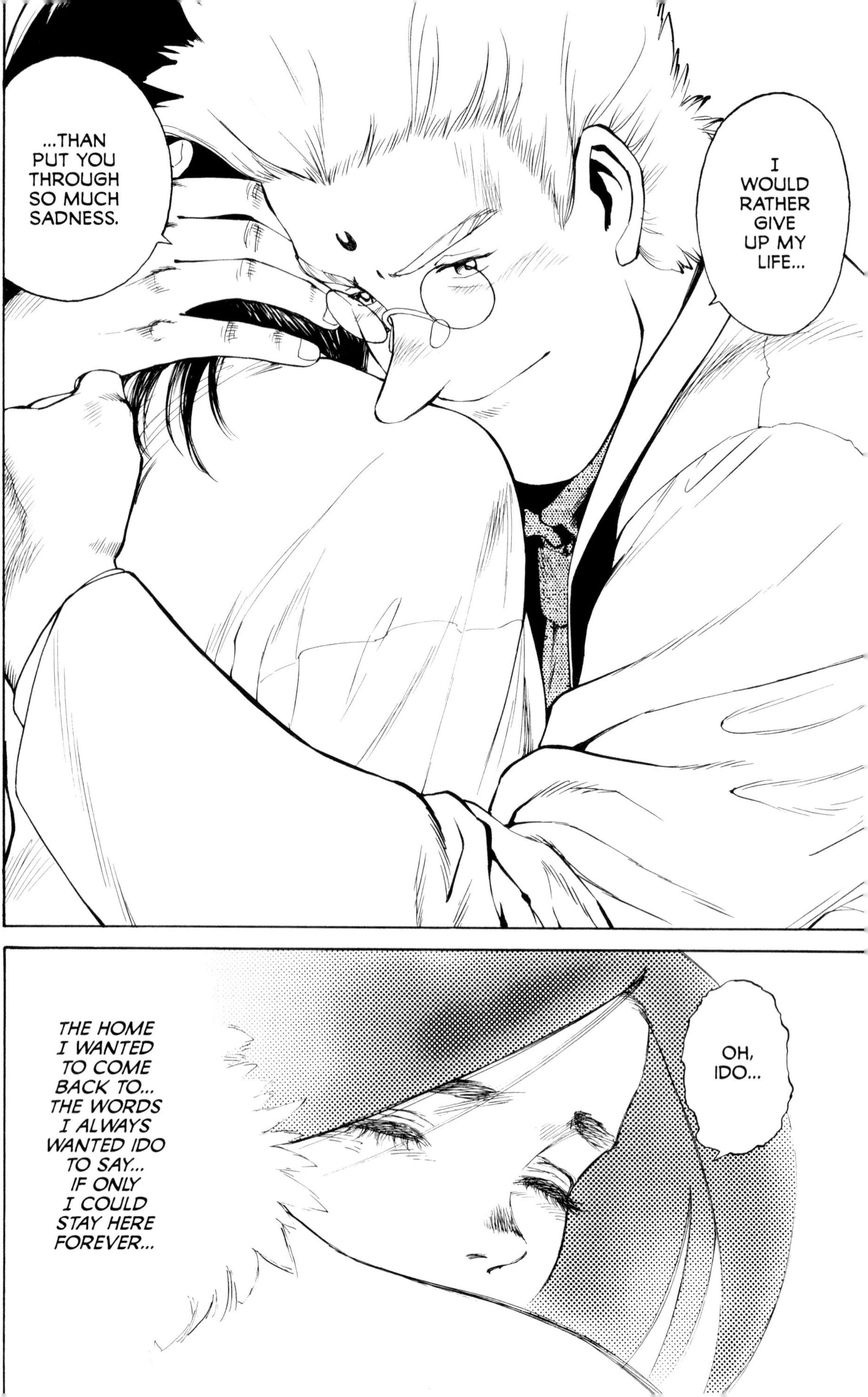
I WOULD RATHER GIVE UP MY LIFE...
...THAN PUT YOU THROUGH SO MUCH SADNESS.
OH, IDO...
THE HOME I WANTED TO COME BACK TO... THE WORDS I ALWAYS WANTED IDO TO SAY... IF ONLY I COULD STAY HERE FOREVER...

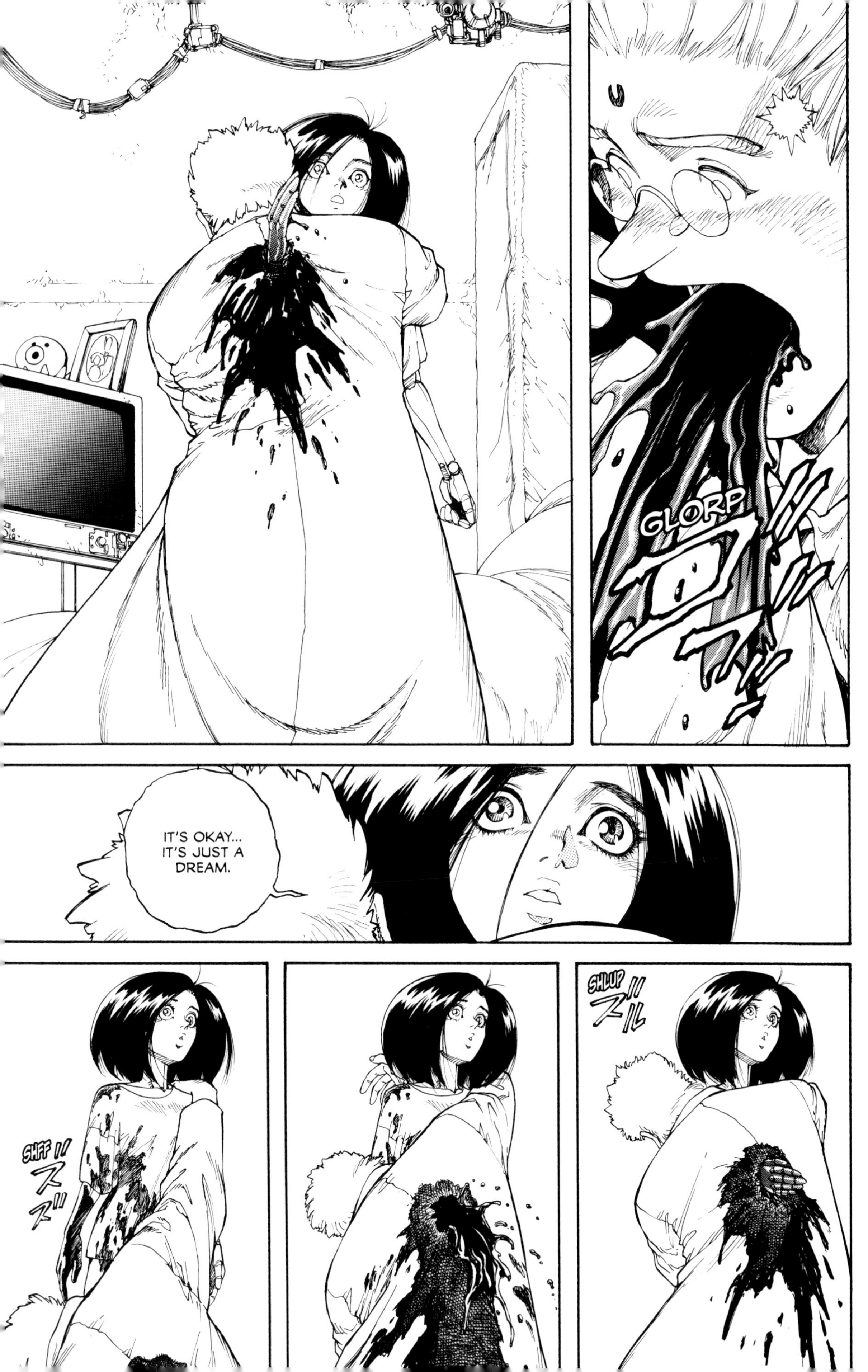
GLORP
IT'S OKAY... IT'S JUST A DREAM.
SHLUP
ズル
SHFF
ズズ

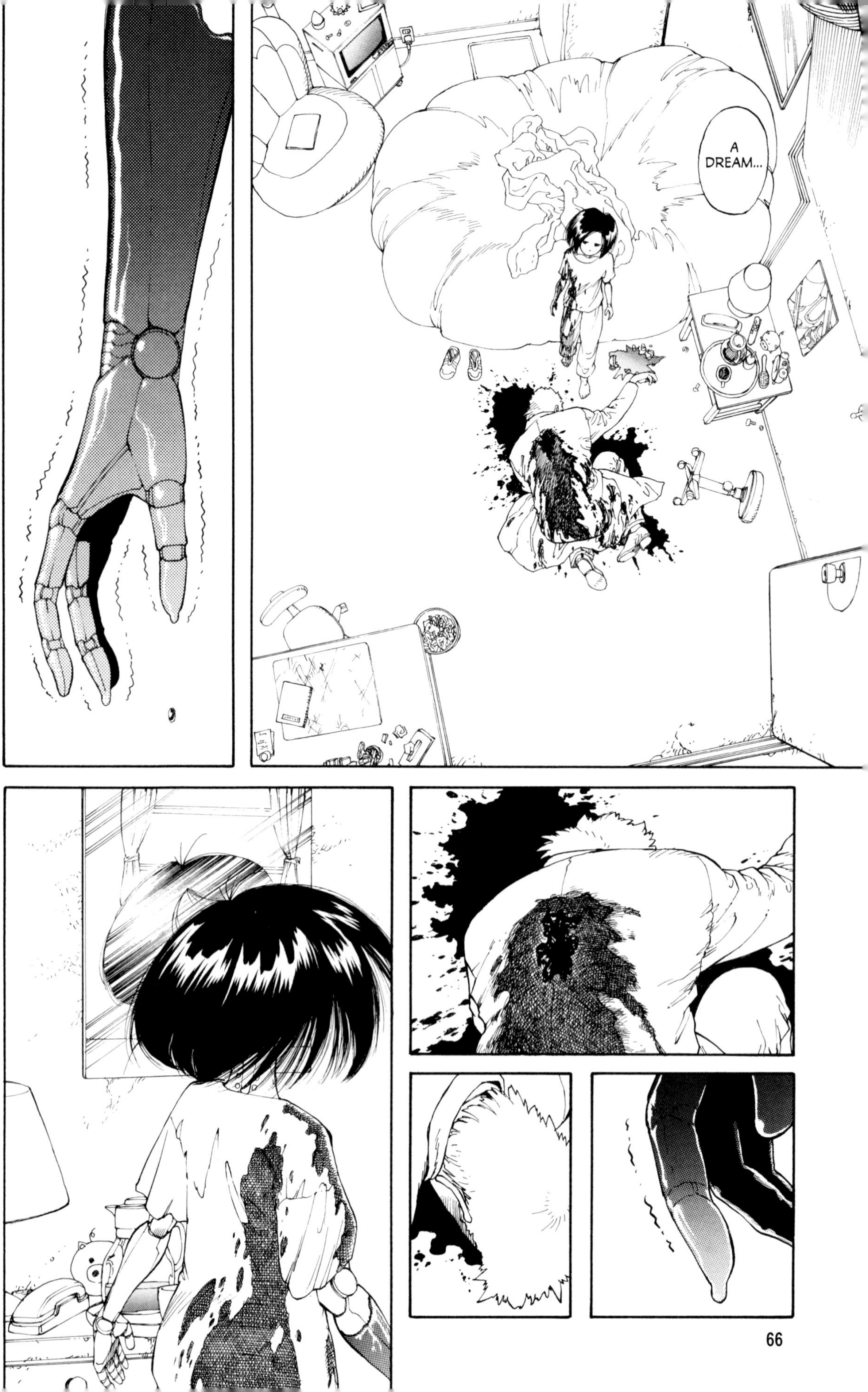
A DREAM...

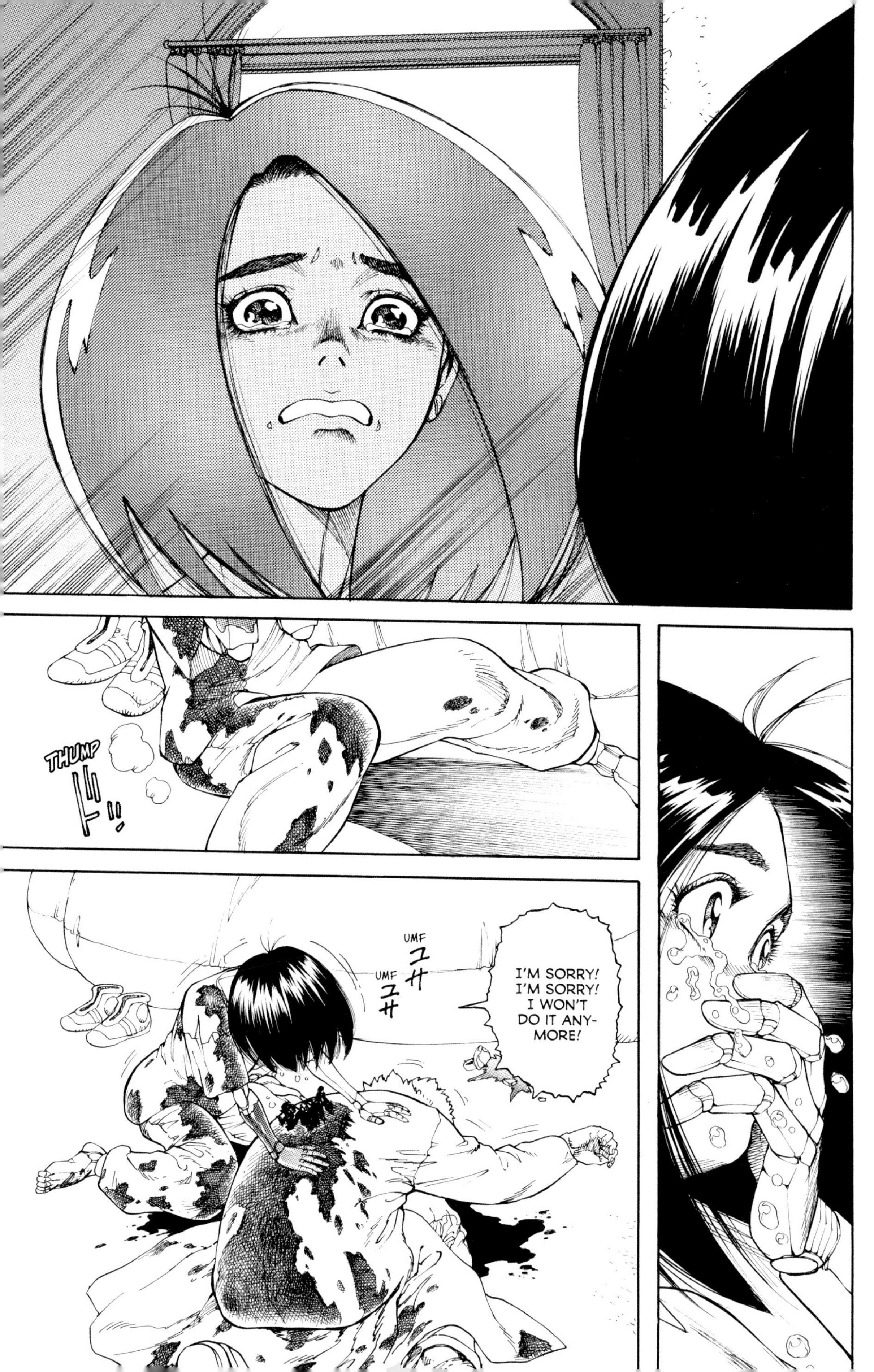
THUMP
ドッ!!
I'M SORRY! I'M SORRY! I WON'T DO IT ANYMORE!
UMF
ユサ
UMF
ユサ

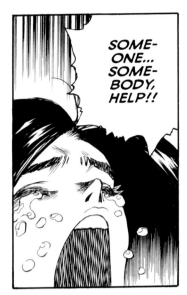

I WON'T DISOBEY YOU ANYMORE...
PLEASE... COME BACK...
SOME-ONE... SOME-BODY, HELP!!
HEH HEH! JUST ONE MORE PUSH!
VVUM

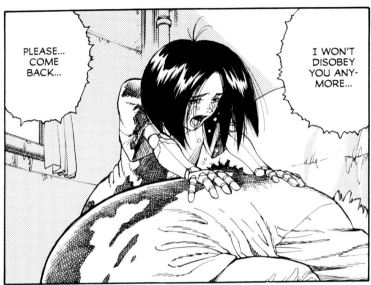

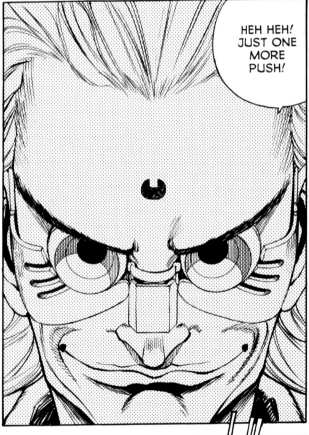

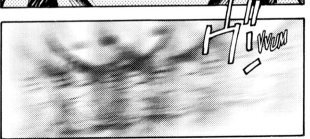

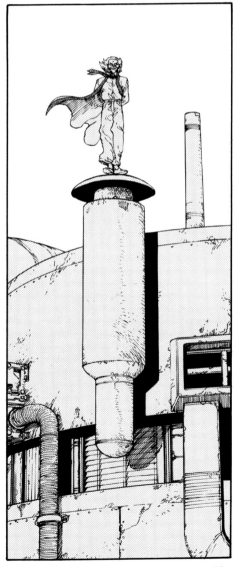

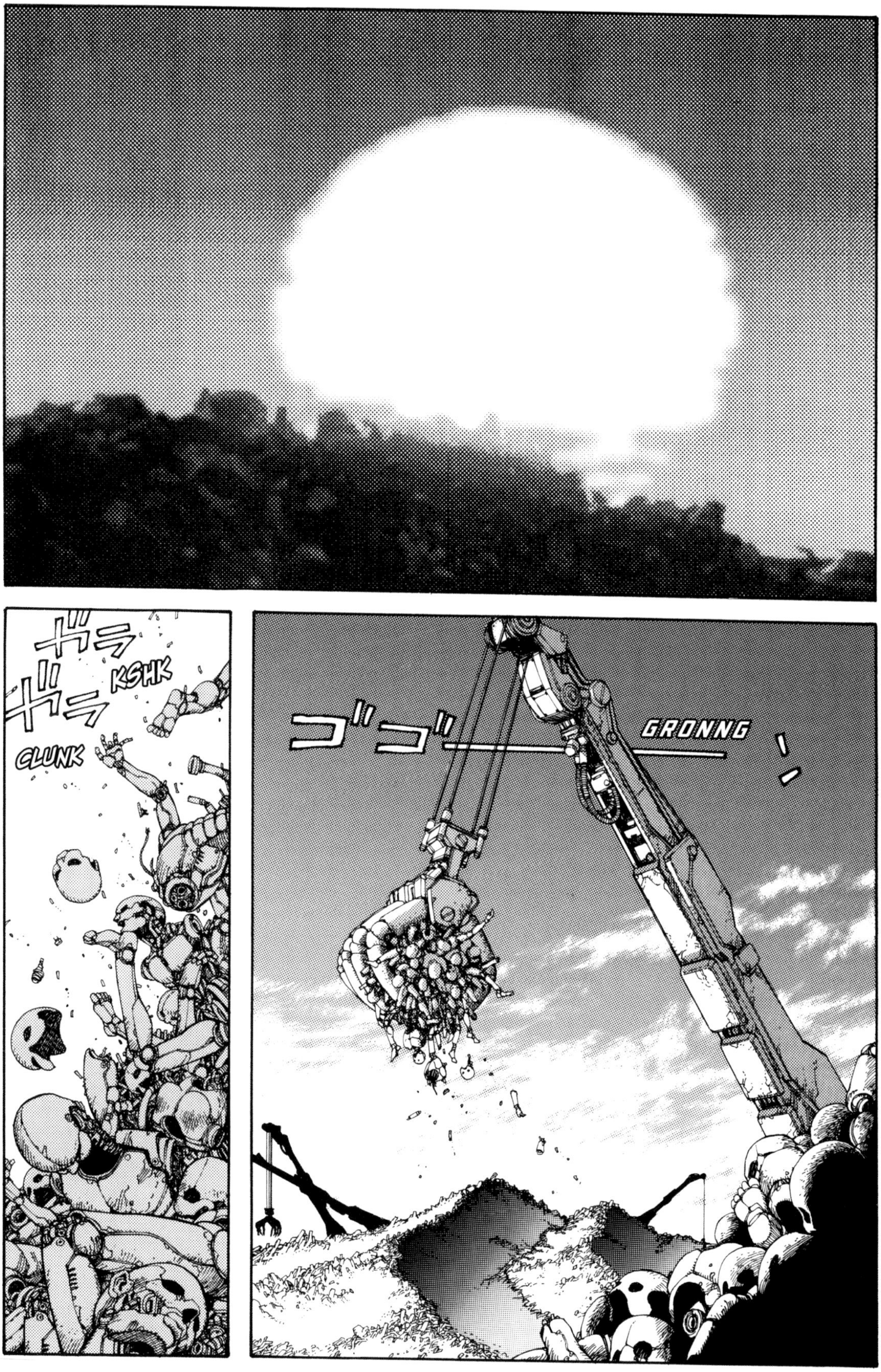
ゴゴ
GRONNG
ガラ
ガラ
KSHK
CLUNK

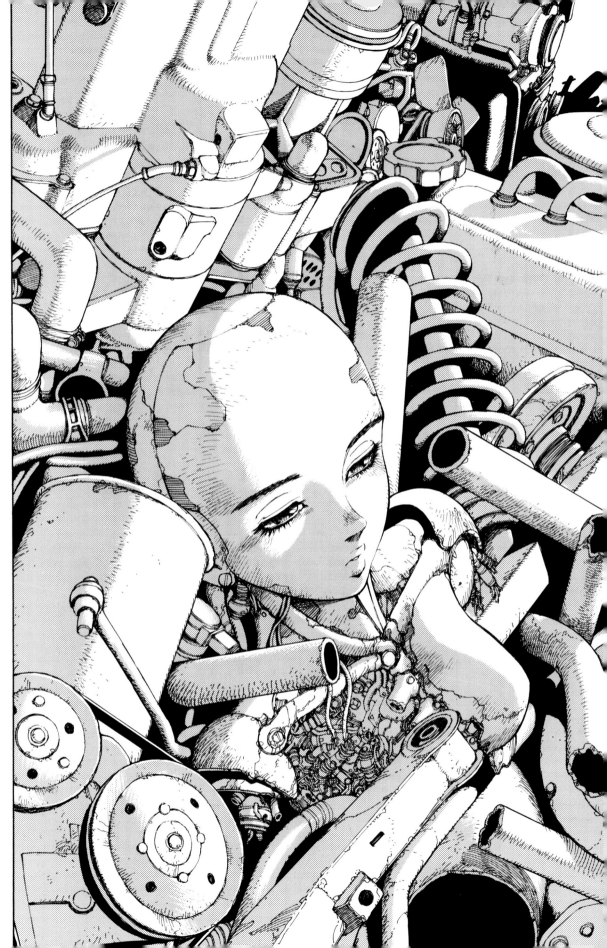

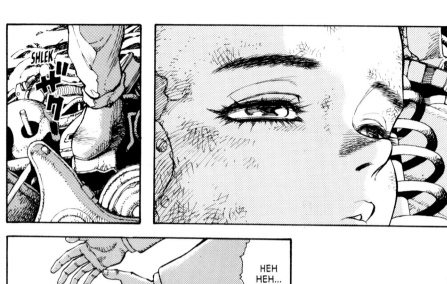

SHLEK

HEH
HEH...

HEH
HEH HEH!
NOW THIS IS
A BIT MORE
LIKE IT.

KYA
HA
HA
HA!

WHO...

...IS
THAT
...?

HE'S
SCARY...

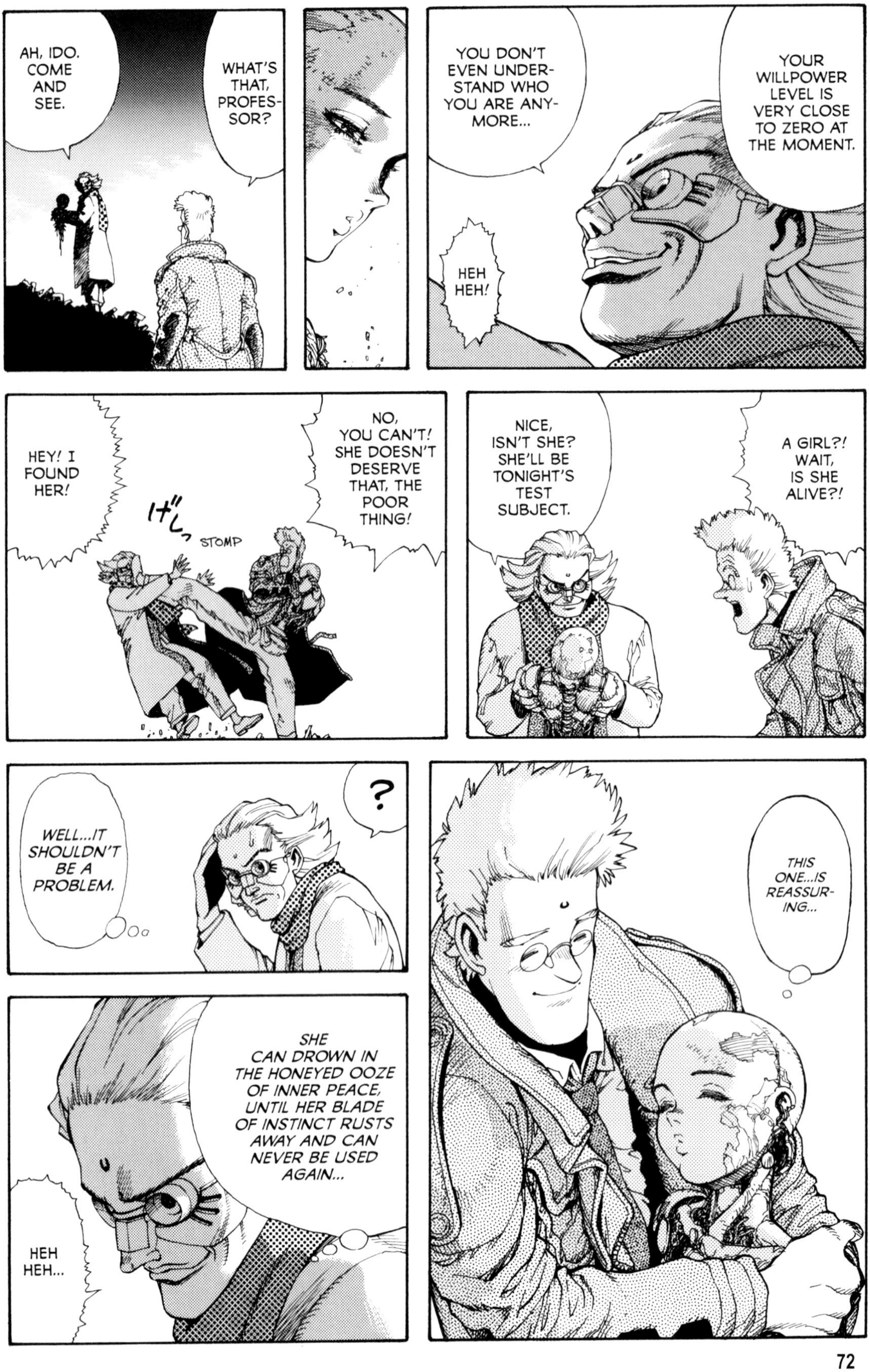
YOUR WILLPOWER LEVEL IS VERY CLOSE TO ZERO AT THE MOMENT.
YOU DON'T EVEN UNDERSTAND WHO YOU ARE ANYMORE...
HEH HEH!
WHAT'S THAT, PROFESSOR?
AH, IDO. COME AND SEE.
A GIRL?! WAIT, IS SHE ALIVE?!
NICE, ISN'T SHE? SHE'LL BE TONIGHT'S TEST SUBJECT.
NO, YOU CAN'T! SHE DOESN'T DESERVE THAT, THE POOR THING!
HEY! I FOUND HER!
げしっ
STOMP
THIS ONE...IS REASSURING...
?
WELL...IT SHOULDN'T BE A PROBLEM.
SHE CAN DROWN IN THE HONEYED OOZE OF INNER PEACE, UNTIL HER BLADE OF INSTINCT RUSTS AWAY AND CAN NEVER BE USED AGAIN...
HEH HEH...

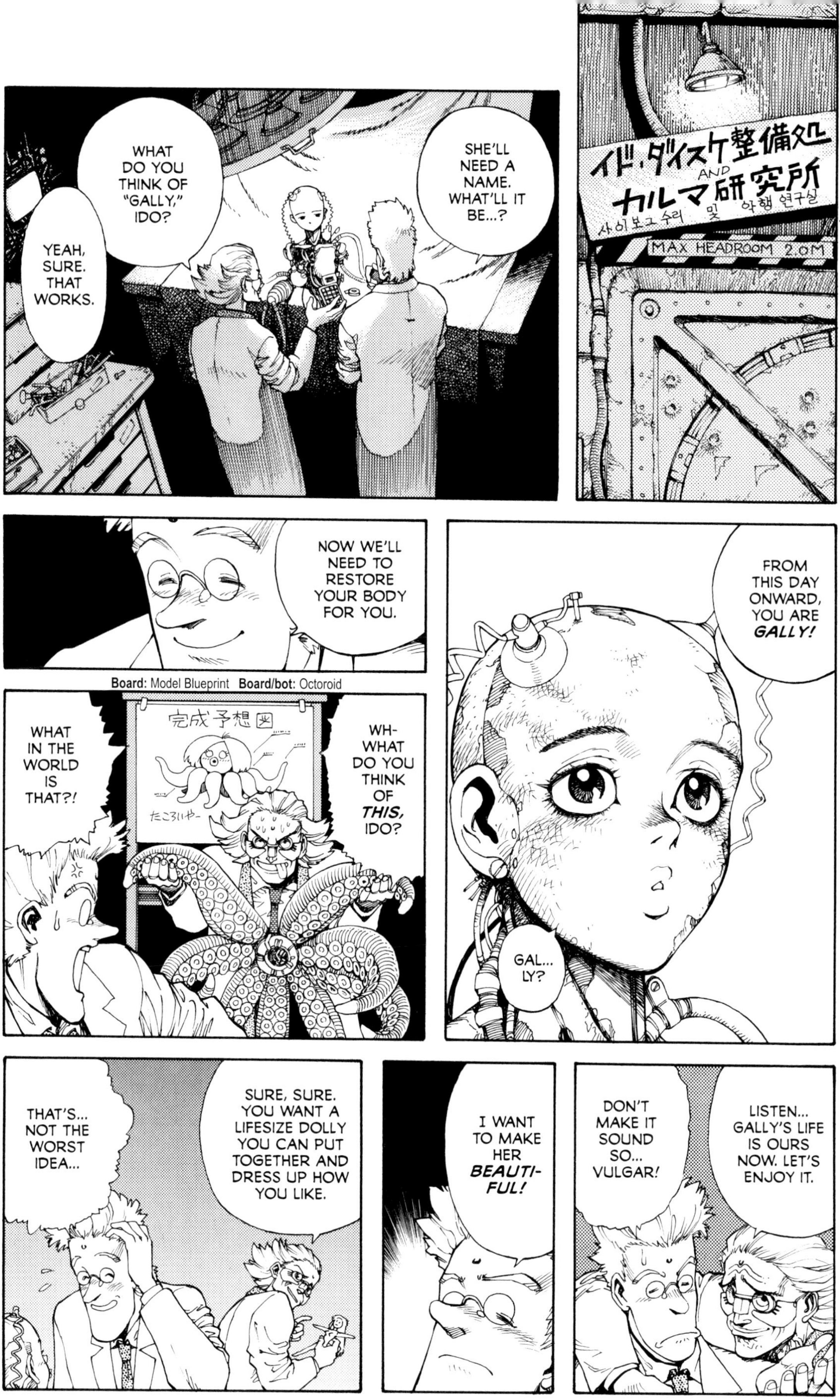
イド・ダイスケ整備処
AND
カルマ研究所
사이보그 수리 및 악행 연구실
MAX HEADROOM 2.0M
and Karmic Laboratory
SHE'LL NEED A NAME. WHAT'LL IT BE...?
WHAT DO YOU THINK OF "GALLY," IDO?
YEAH, SURE. THAT WORKS.
FROM THIS DAY ONWARD, YOU ARE *GALLY!*
GAL... LY?
NOW WE'LL NEED TO RESTORE YOUR BODY FOR YOU.
Board: Model Blueprint **Board/bot:** Octoroid
WH-WHAT DO YOU THINK OF *THIS,* IDO?
WHAT IN THE WORLD IS THAT?!
完成予想図
たころいやー
LISTEN... GALLY'S LIFE IS OURS NOW. LET'S ENJOY IT.
DON'T MAKE IT SOUND SO... VULGAR!
I WANT TO MAKE HER *BEAUTIFUL!*
SURE, SURE. YOU WANT A LIFESIZE DOLLY YOU CAN PUT TOGETHER AND DRESS UP HOW YOU LIKE.
THAT'S... NOT THE WORST IDEA...

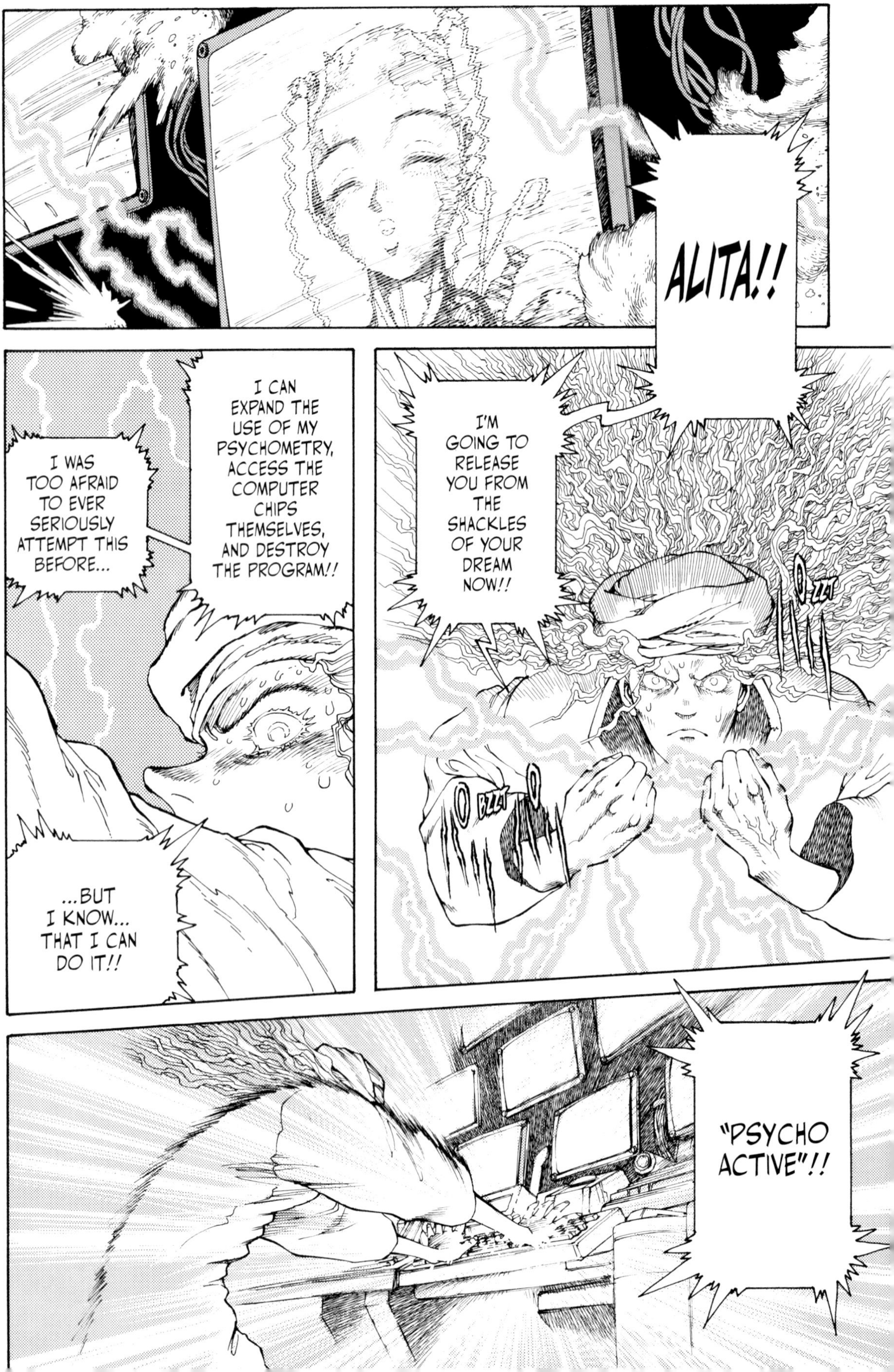
ALITA!!
I'M GOING TO RELEASE YOU FROM THE SHACKLES OF YOUR DREAM NOW!!
BZZT
I CAN EXPAND THE USE OF MY PSYCHOMETRY, ACCESS THE COMPUTER CHIPS THEMSELVES, AND DESTROY THE PROGRAM!!
I WAS TOO AFRAID TO EVER SERIOUSLY ATTEMPT THIS BEFORE...
...BUT I KNOW... THAT I CAN DO IT!!
"PSYCHO ACTIVE"!!

VWMM
THE FOOL...
RUNNING OUROBOROS THROUGH THE *TUNED* CHANNEL MEANS THAT THE PROGRAM IS UNDER *DUAL* LAYERS OF PROTECTION.
ONE BIOLOGICAL BRAIN CANNOT OVERCOME THE TWIN HYPER-COMPUTERS OF ZALEM AND GRANITE INN. IT'S NO COMPETITION.
NOW TASTE YOUR OWN POWER-LESSNESS, MY SON!

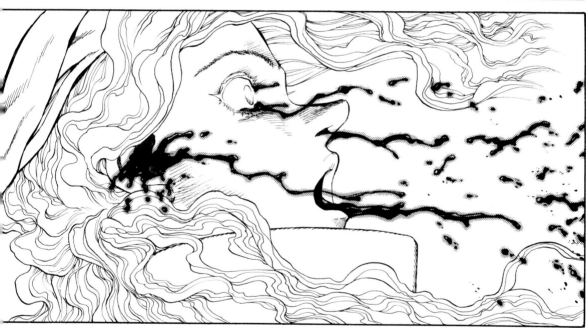

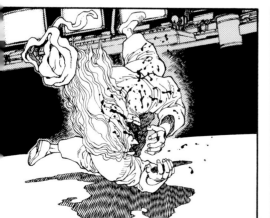

?!

UH...

UNG...

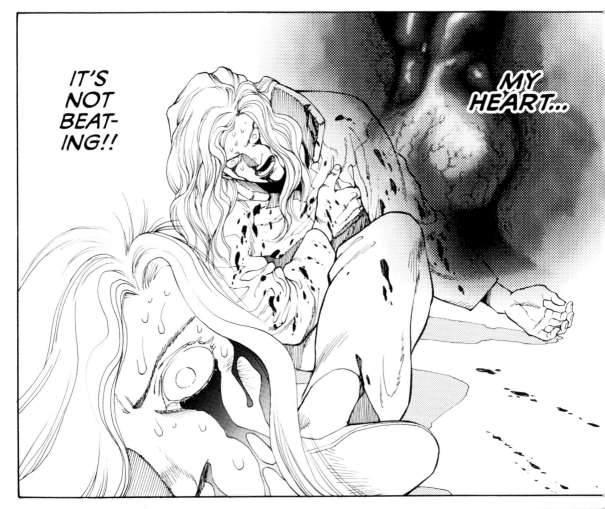

IT'S NOT BEAT- ING!!

MY HEART...

...

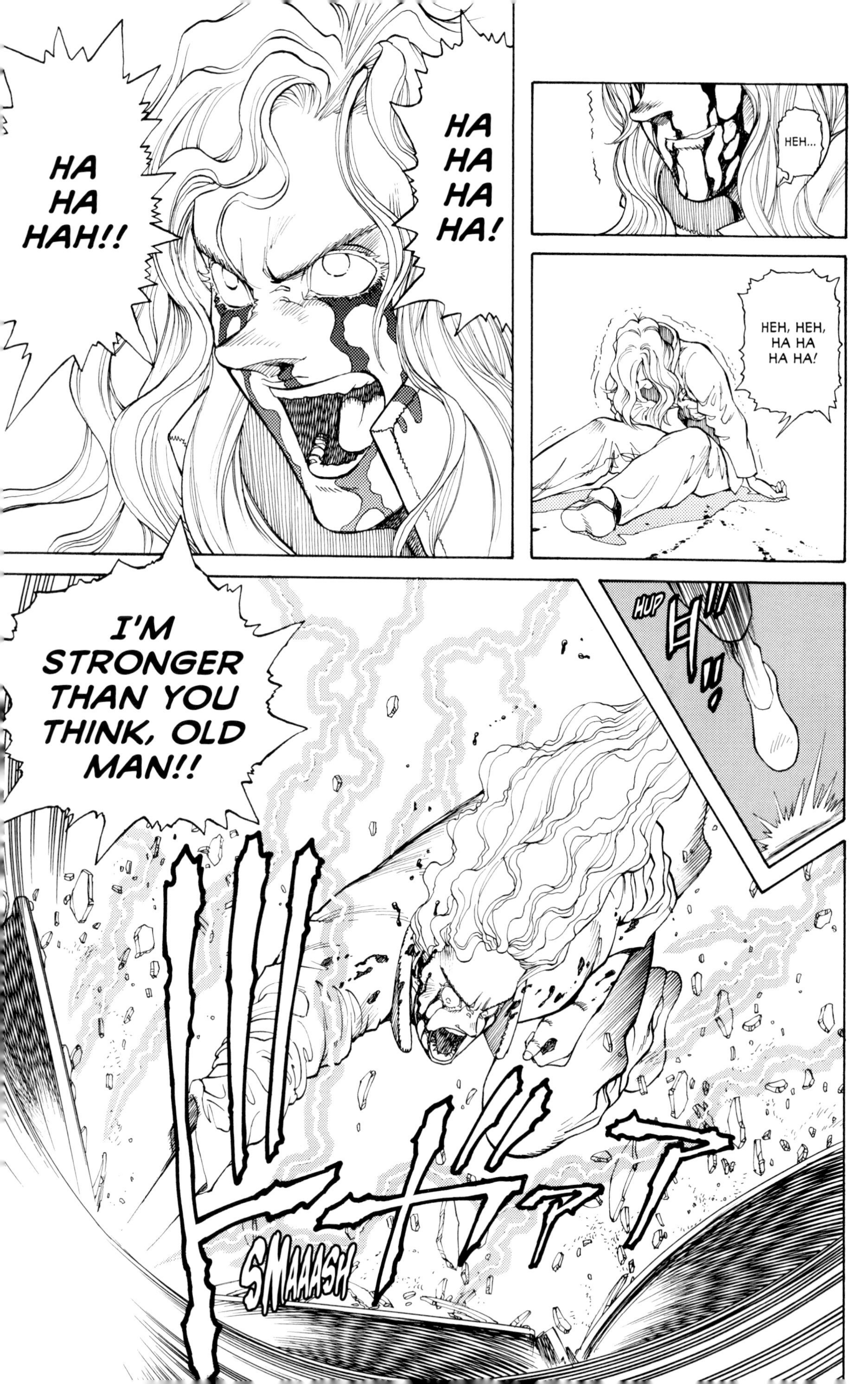
HEH...
HEH, HEH, HA HA HA HA!
HA HA HA HA!
HA HA HAH!!
HUP
I'M STRONGER THAN YOU THINK, OLD MAN!!
SMAAASH

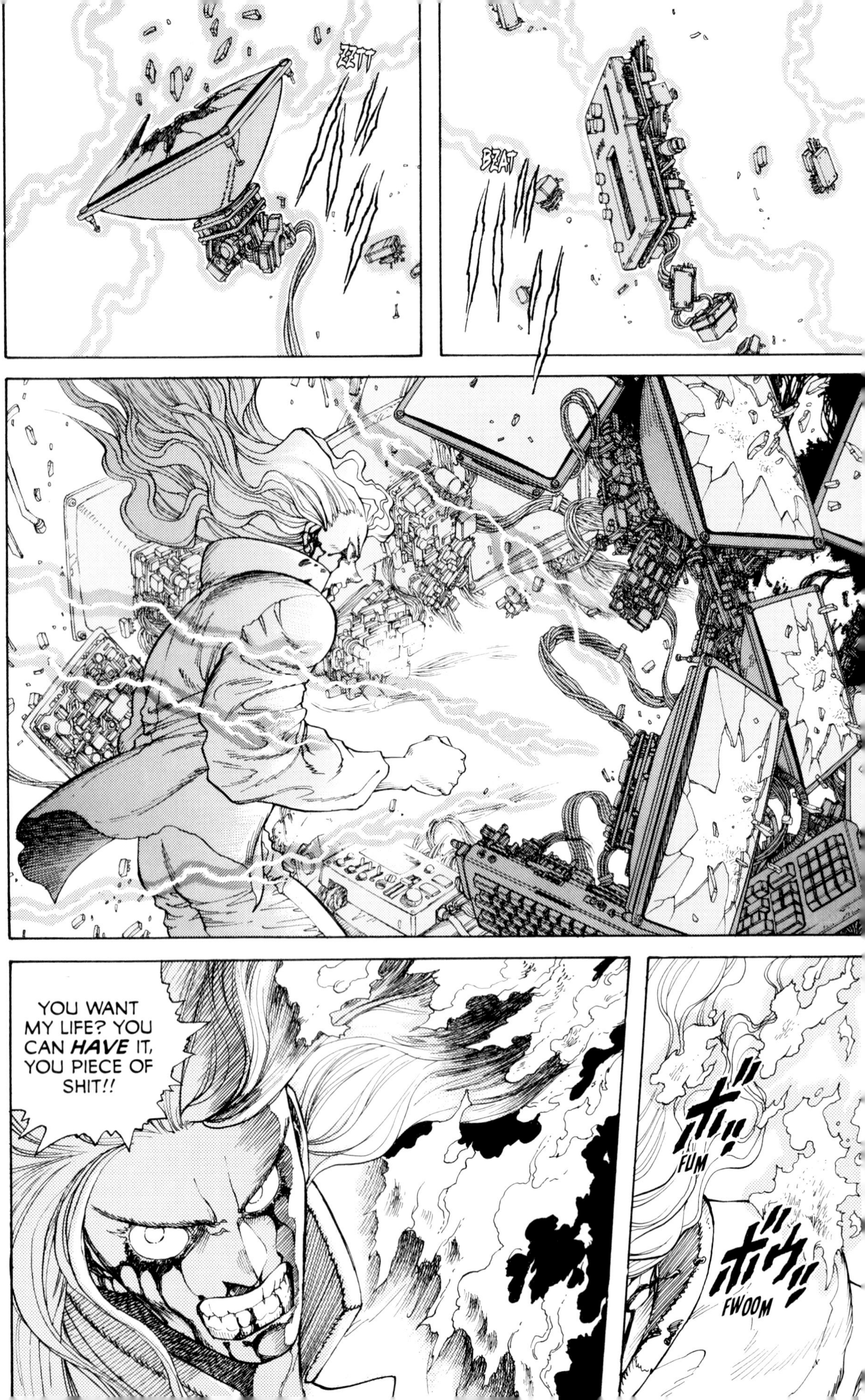
BZAT
ZZTT
ボッ!!
FUM
ボウッ!!
FWOOM
YOU WANT MY LIFE? YOU CAN *HAVE* IT, YOU PIECE OF SHIT!!

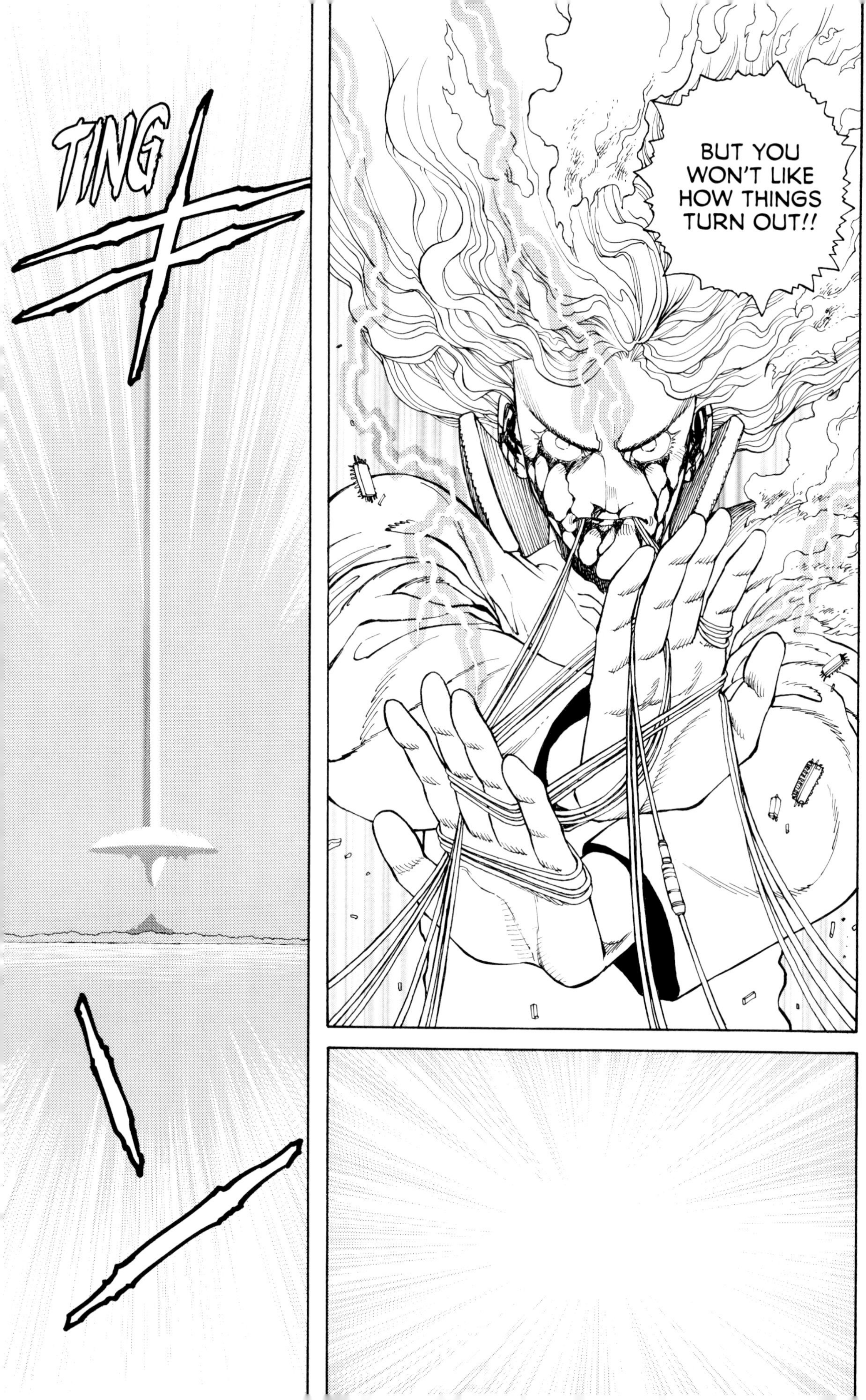
BUT YOU WON'T LIKE HOW THINGS TURN OUT!!
TING

BEEP
BEEP
Ground Inspection Bu
TIK TIK TIK
BEEP BEEP BEEP
BZZT
BZAT
PKAK

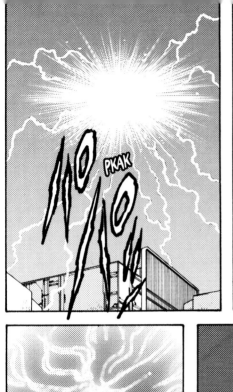

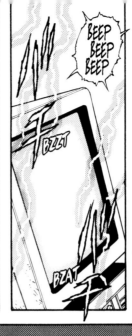

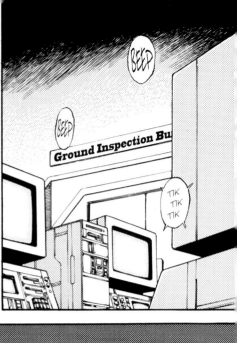

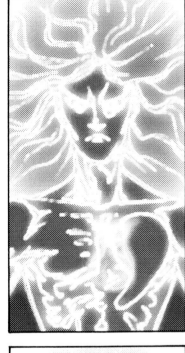

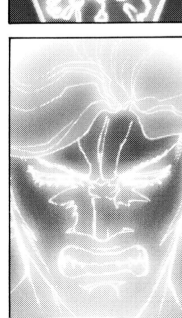

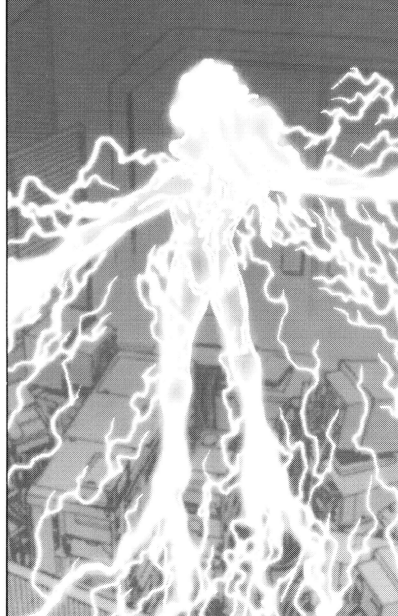

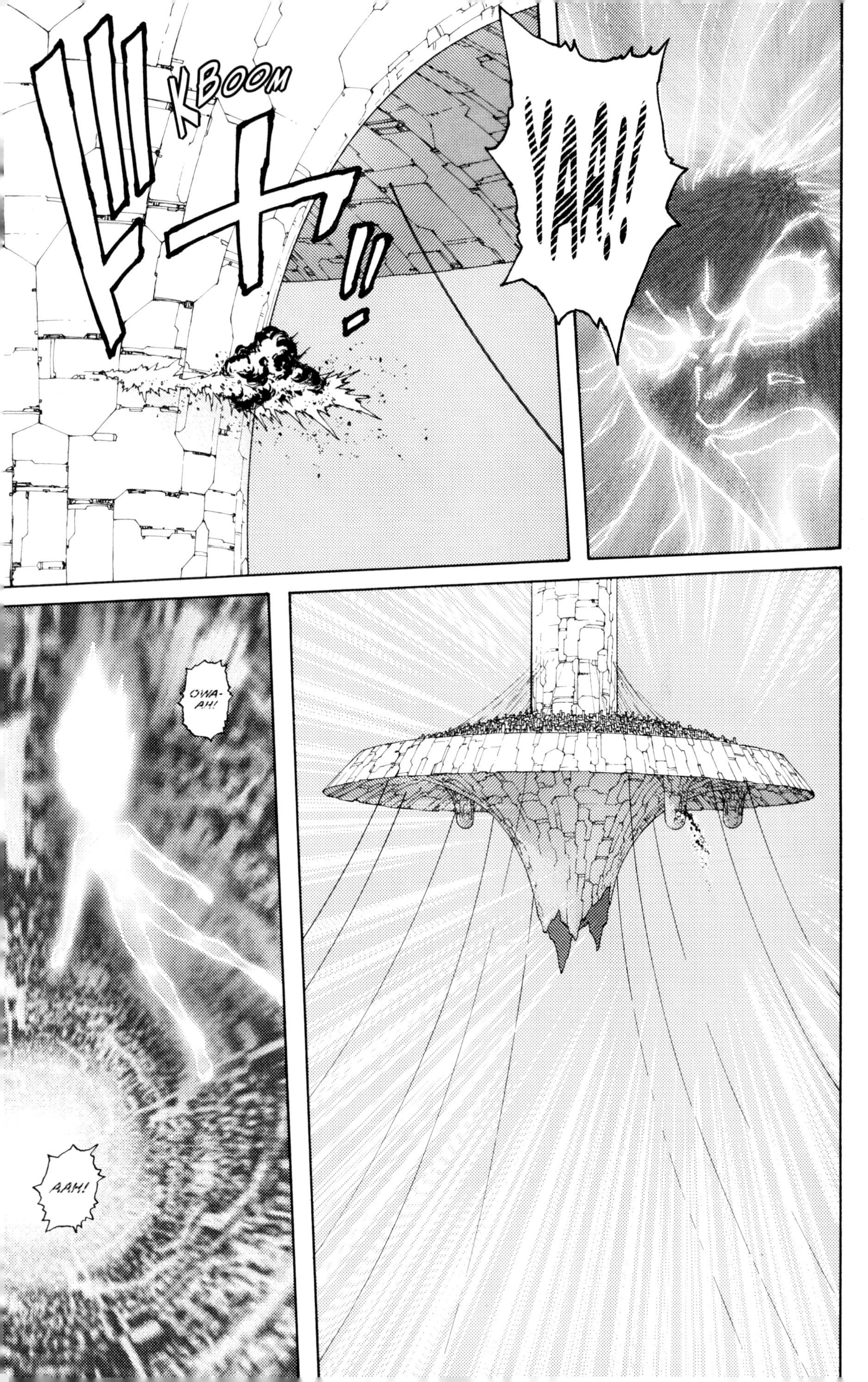
YAA!!
KBOOM
OWA-AH!
AAH!

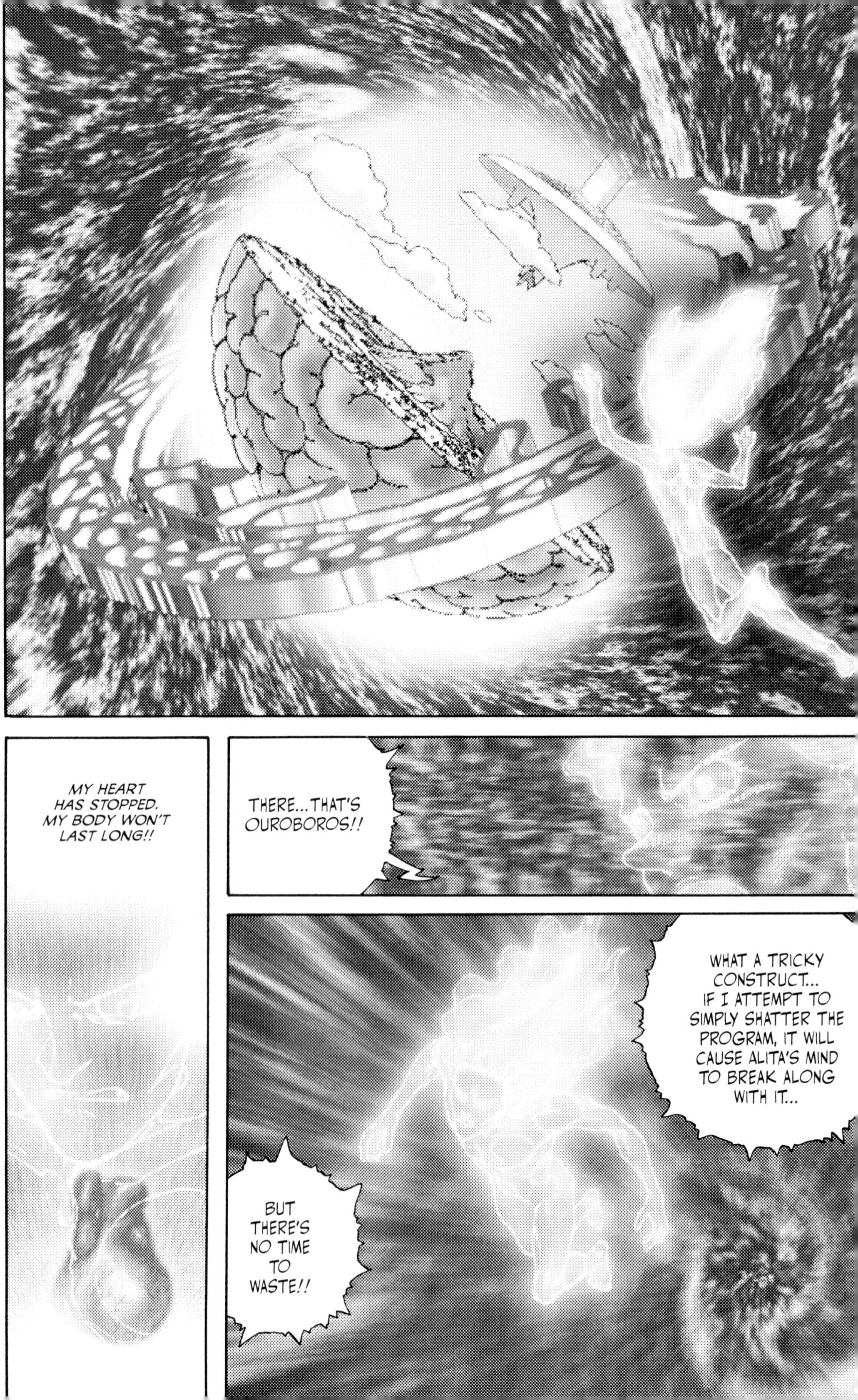
THERE...THAT'S OUROBOROS!!
WHAT A TRICKY CONSTRUCT... IF I ATTEMPT TO SIMPLY SHATTER THE PROGRAM, IT WILL CAUSE ALITA'S MIND TO BREAK ALONG WITH IT...
BUT THERE'S NO TIME TO WASTE!!
MY HEART HAS STOPPED. MY BODY WON'T LAST LONG!!

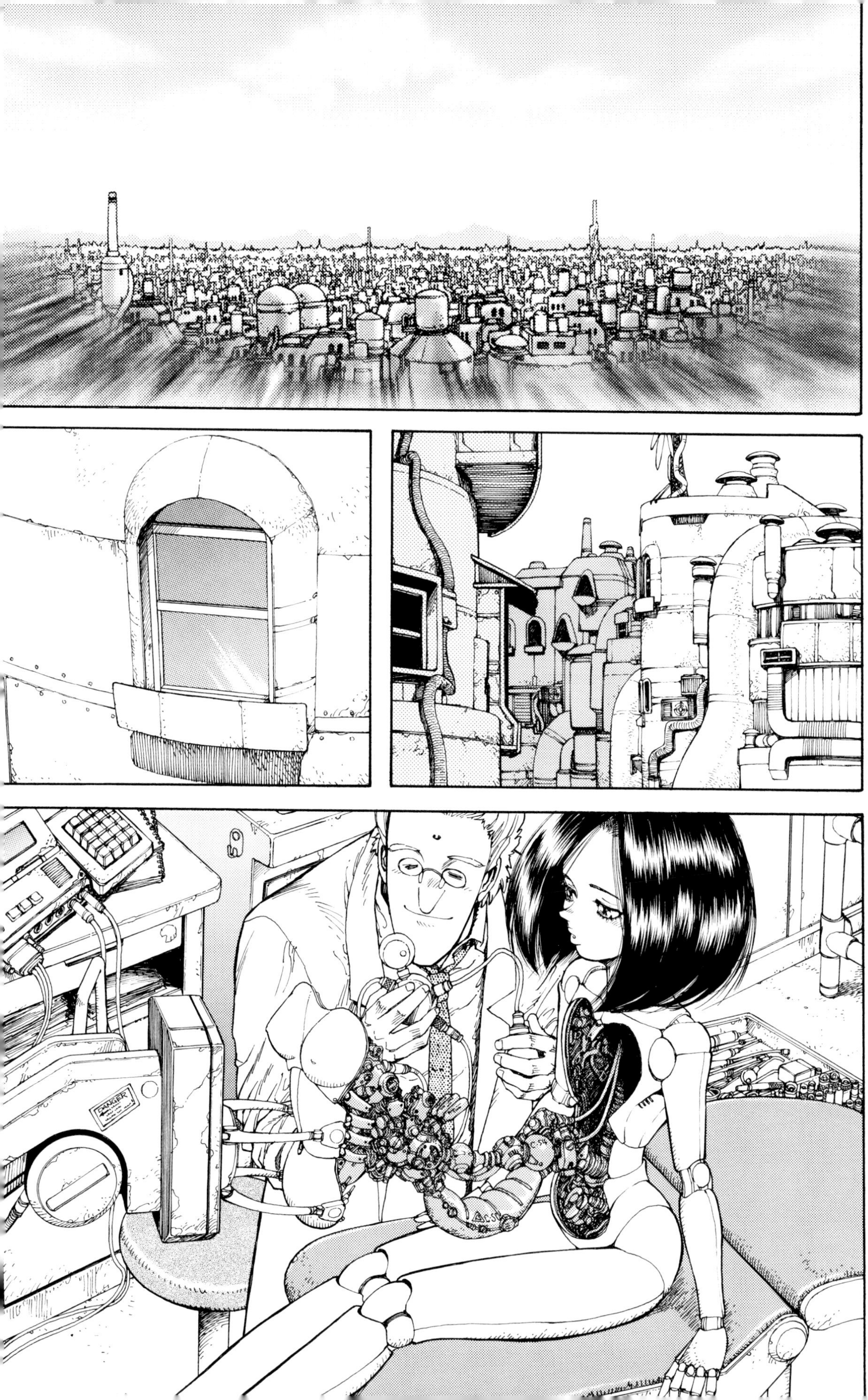
DANGER

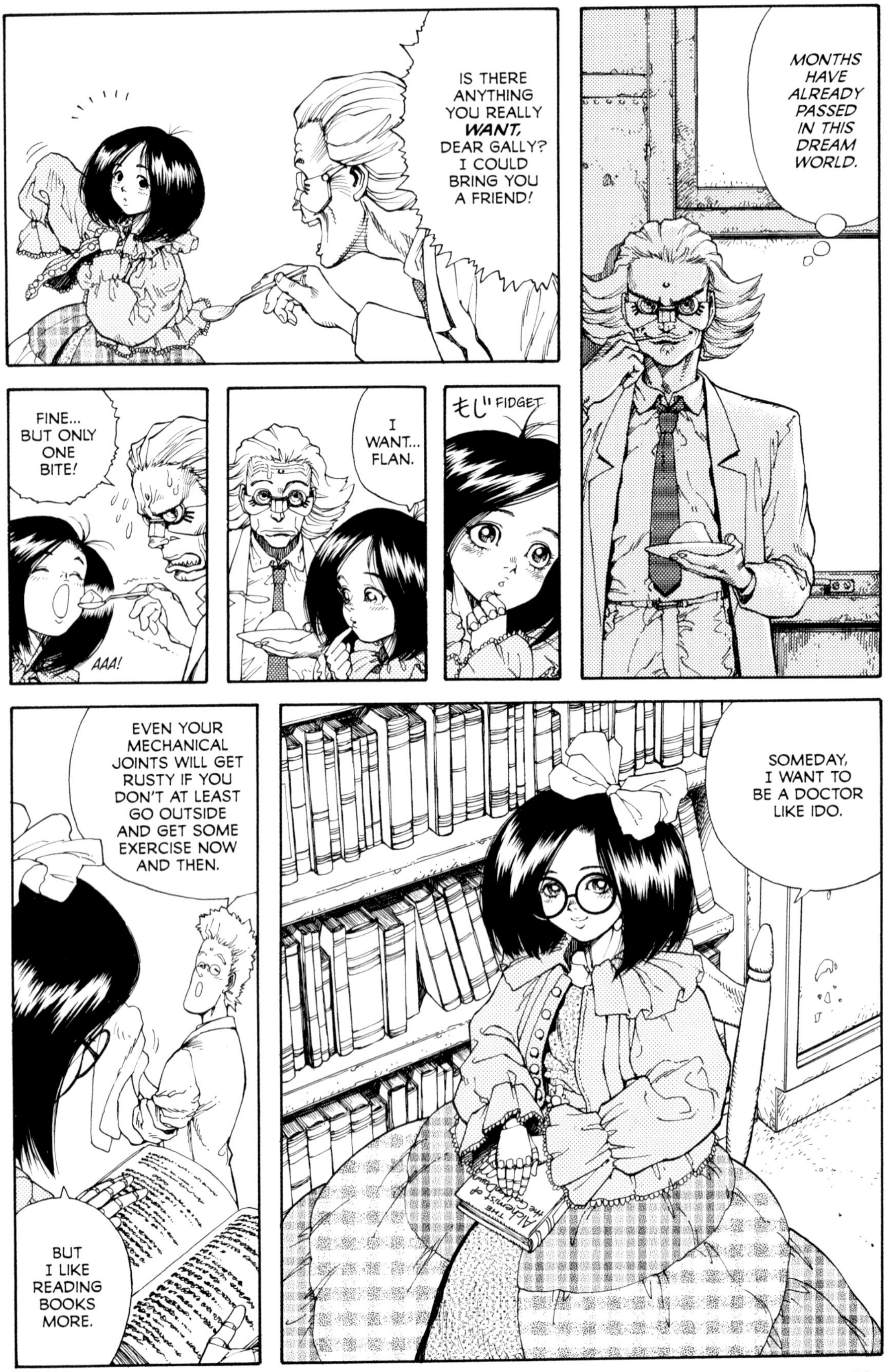
MONTHS HAVE ALREADY PASSED IN THIS DREAM WORLD.
IS THERE ANYTHING YOU REALLY *WANT,* DEAR GALLY? I COULD BRING YOU A FRIEND!
もじ FIDGET
I WANT... FLAN.
FINE... BUT ONLY ONE BITE!
AAA!
SOMEDAY, I WANT TO BE A DOCTOR LIKE IDO.
EVEN YOUR MECHANICAL JOINTS WILL GET RUSTY IF YOU DON'T AT LEAST GO OUTSIDE AND GET SOME EXERCISE NOW AND THEN.
BUT I LIKE READING BOOKS MORE.

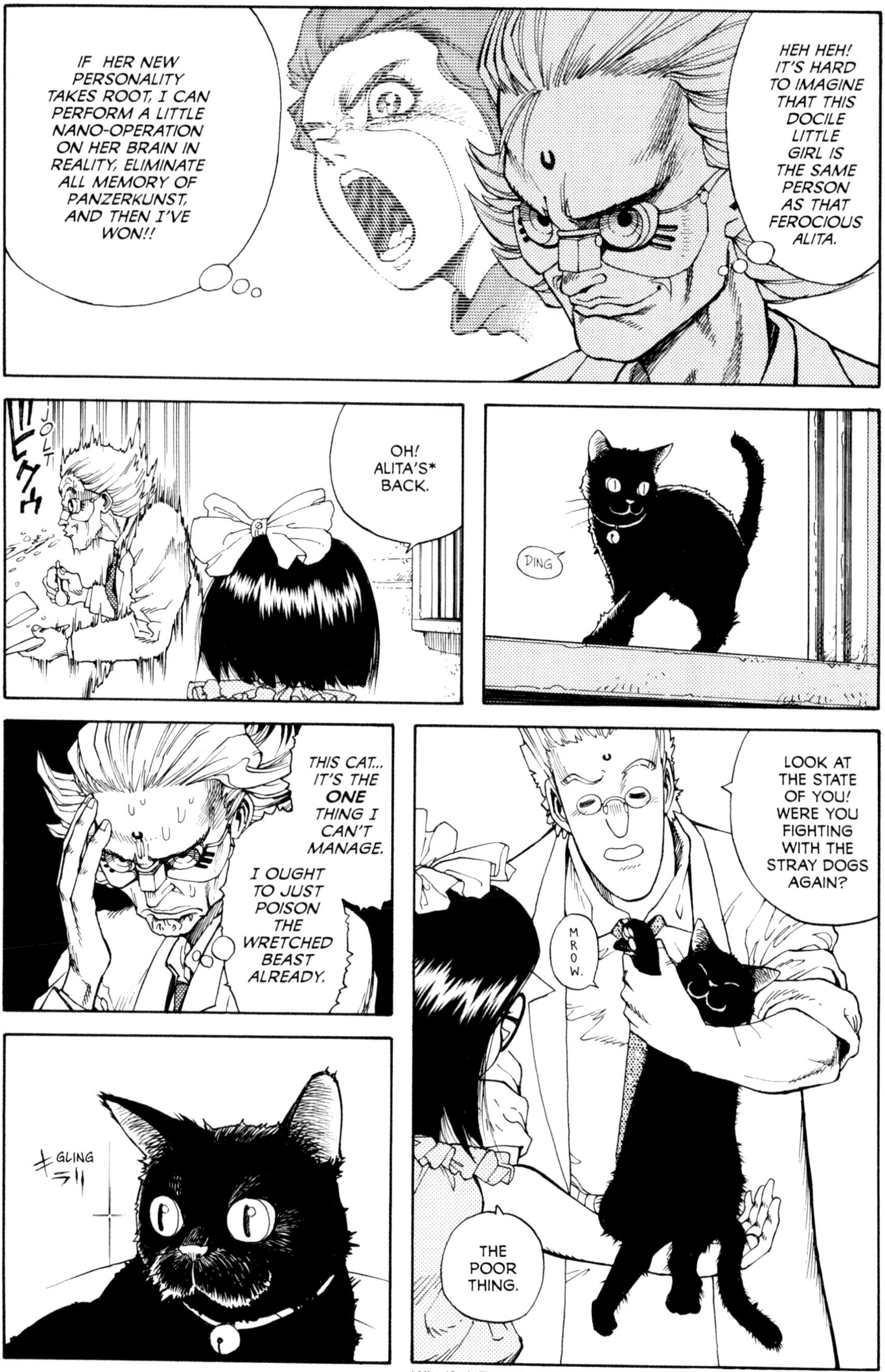
HEH HEH! IT'S HARD TO IMAGINE THAT THIS DOCILE LITTLE GIRL IS THE SAME PERSON AS THAT FEROCIOUS ALITA.
IF HER NEW PERSONALITY TAKES ROOT, I CAN PERFORM A LITTLE NANO-OPERATION ON HER BRAIN IN REALITY, ELIMINATE ALL MEMORY OF PANZERKUNST, AND THEN I'VE WON!!
DING
OH! ALITA'S* BACK.
JOLT
LOOK AT THE STATE OF YOU! WERE YOU FIGHTING WITH THE STRAY DOGS AGAIN?
MROW.
THE POOR THING.
THIS CAT... IT'S THE **ONE** THING I CAN'T MANAGE.
I OUGHT TO JUST POISON THE WRETCHED BEAST ALREADY.
GLING

***Alita (Cat):** The male cat that Ido kept years ago. (See Fight 1.)

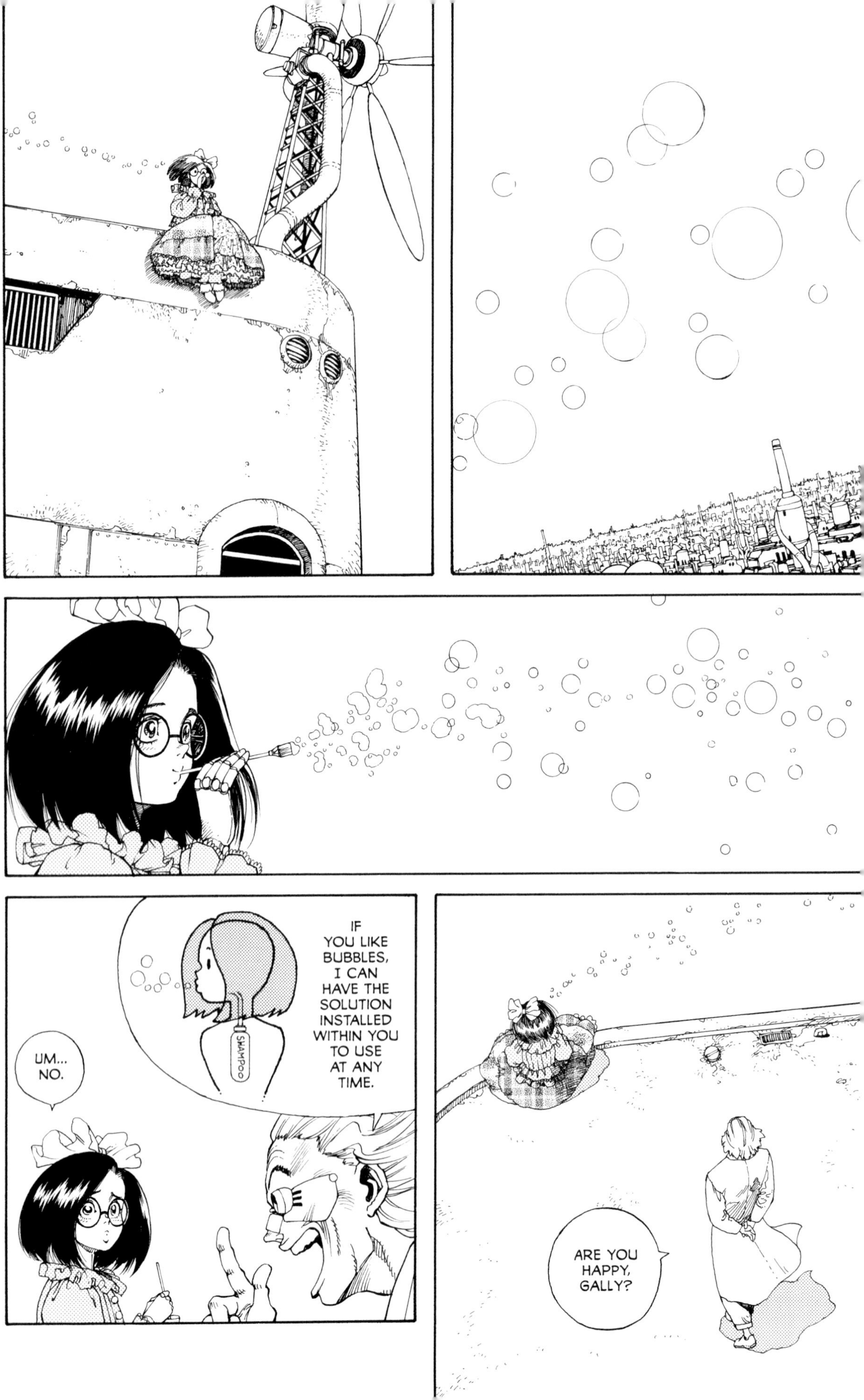
ARE YOU HAPPY, GALLY?
IF YOU LIKE BUBBLES, I CAN HAVE THE SOLUTION INSTALLED WITHIN YOU TO USE AT ANY TIME.
SHAMPOO
UM... NO.

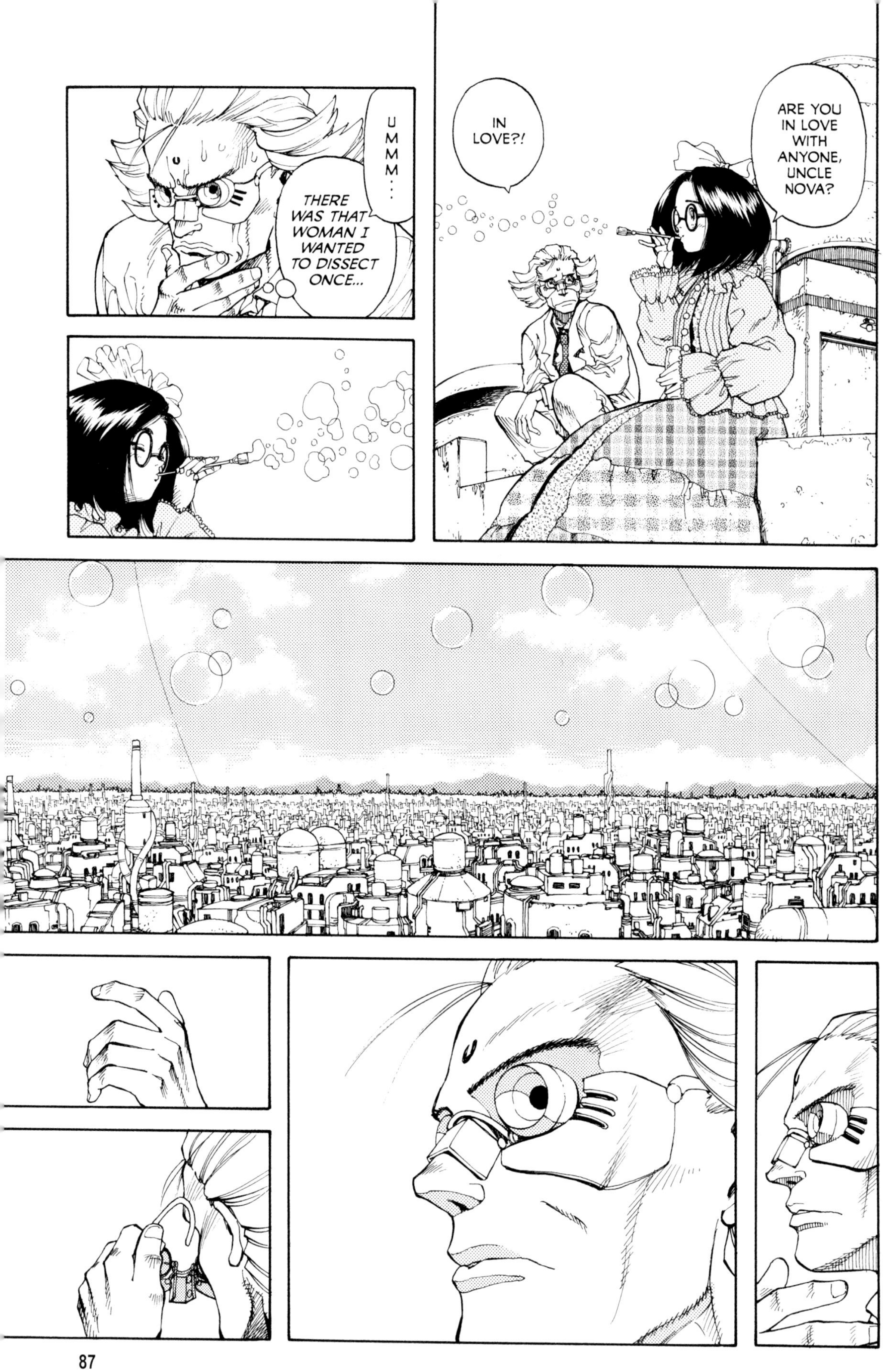
ARE YOU IN LOVE WITH ANYONE, UNCLE NOVA?
IN LOVE?!
UMMM...
THERE WAS THAT WOMAN I WANTED TO DISSECT ONCE...

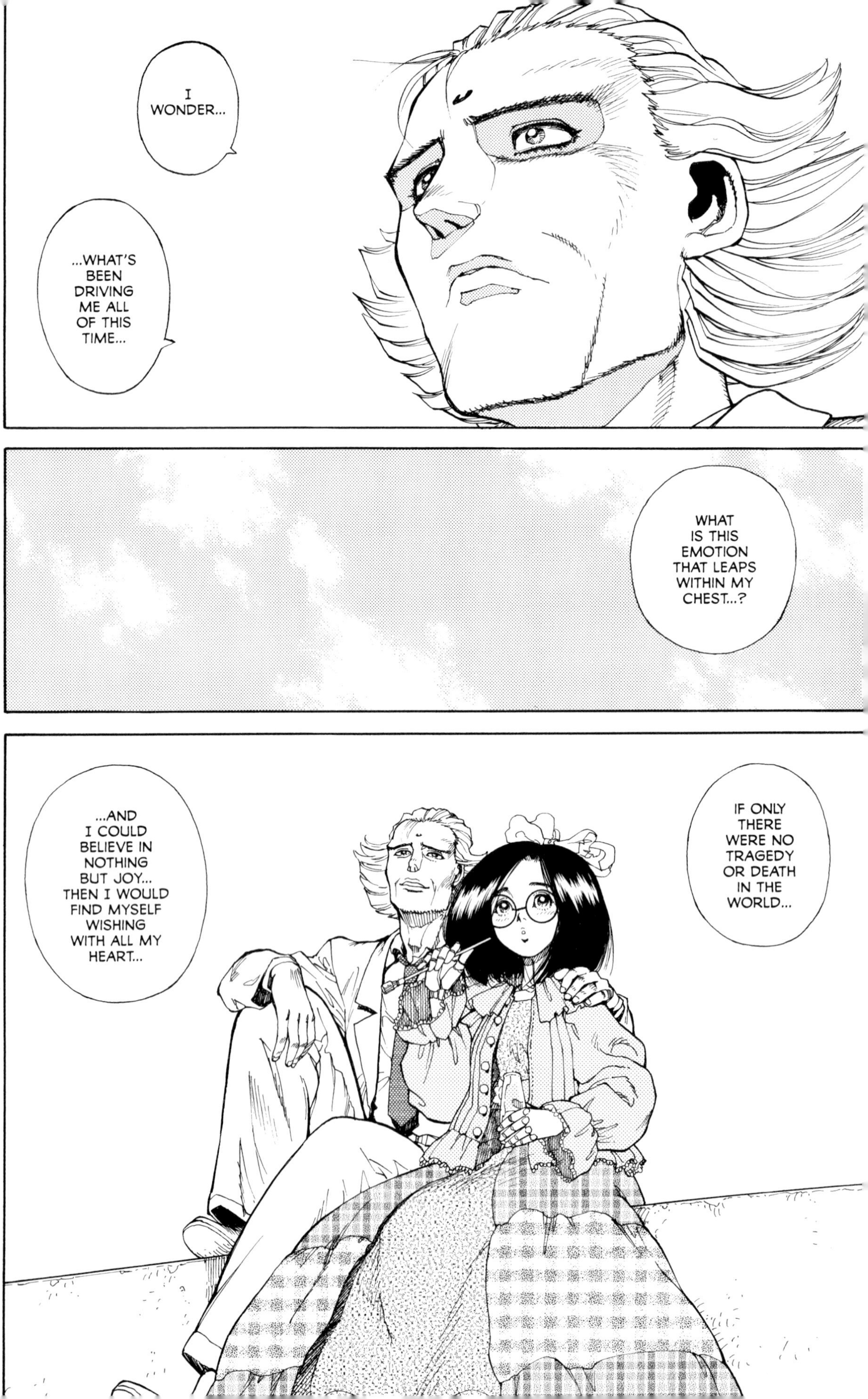
I WONDER...
...WHAT'S BEEN DRIVING ME ALL OF THIS TIME...
WHAT IS THIS EMOTION THAT LEAPS WITHIN MY CHEST...?
IF ONLY THERE WERE NO TRAGEDY OR DEATH IN THE WORLD...
...AND I COULD BELIEVE IN NOTHING BUT JOY... THEN I WOULD FIND MYSELF WISHING WITH ALL MY HEART...

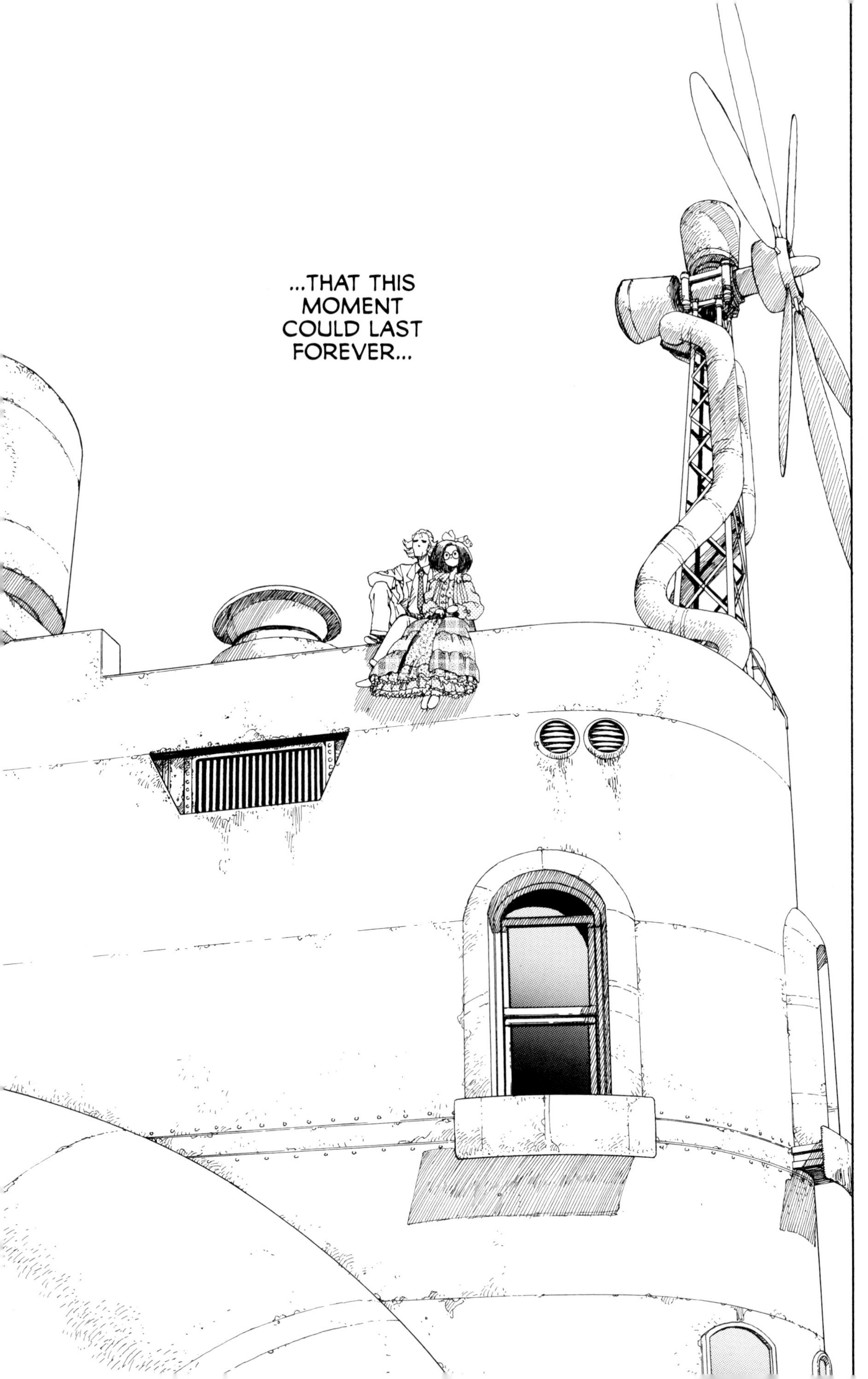
...THAT THIS MOMENT COULD LAST FOREVER...

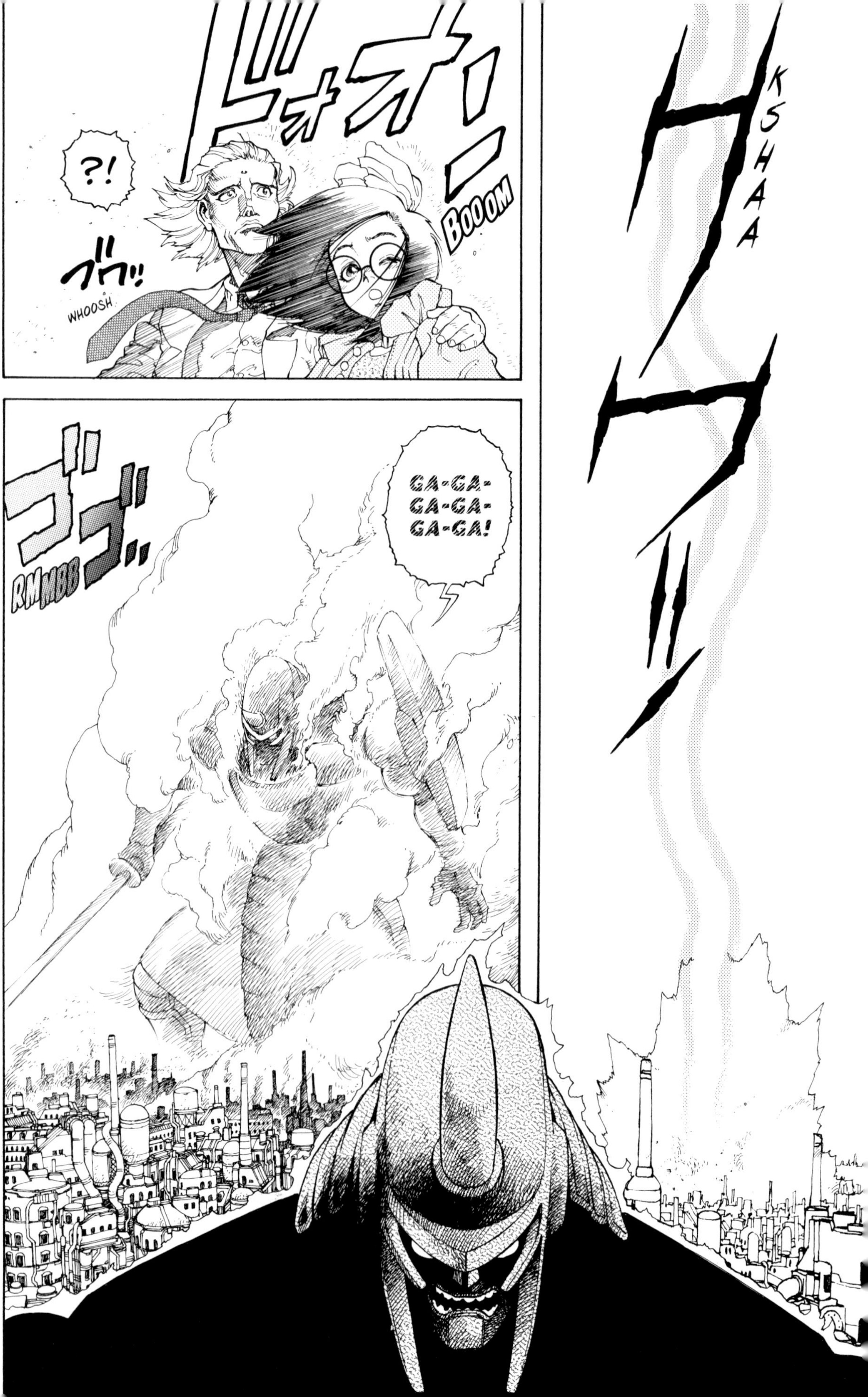
KSHAA
ドォオン
BOOOM
?!
ブワ!!
WHOOSH
GA-GA-GA-GA-GA-GA!
ゴゴ
RMMBB

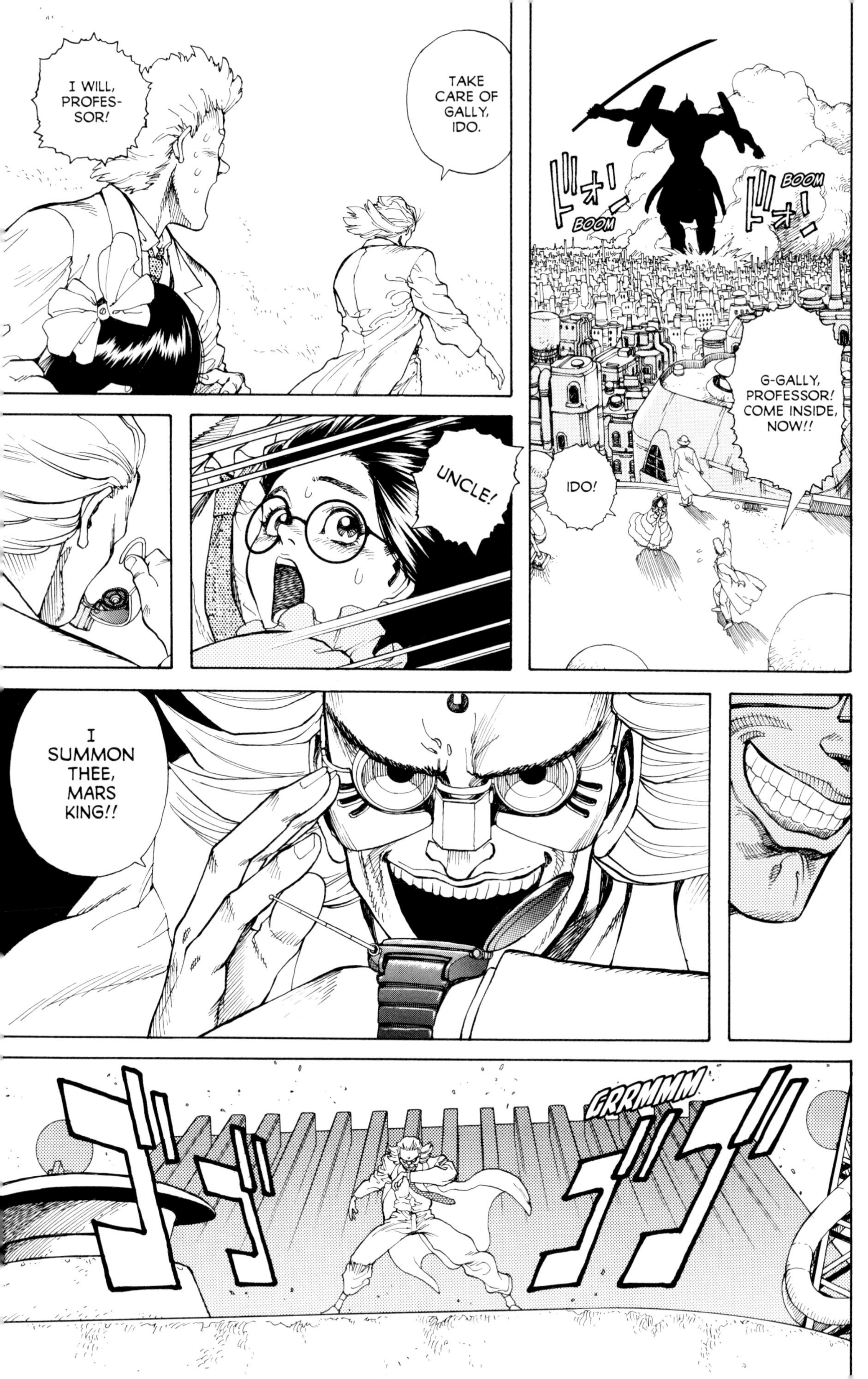
BOOM
BOOM
G-GALLY, PROFESSOR! COME INSIDE, NOW!!
IDO!
TAKE CARE OF GALLY, IDO.
I WILL, PROFES-SOR!
UNCLE!
I SUMMON THEE, MARS KING!!
GRRMMM

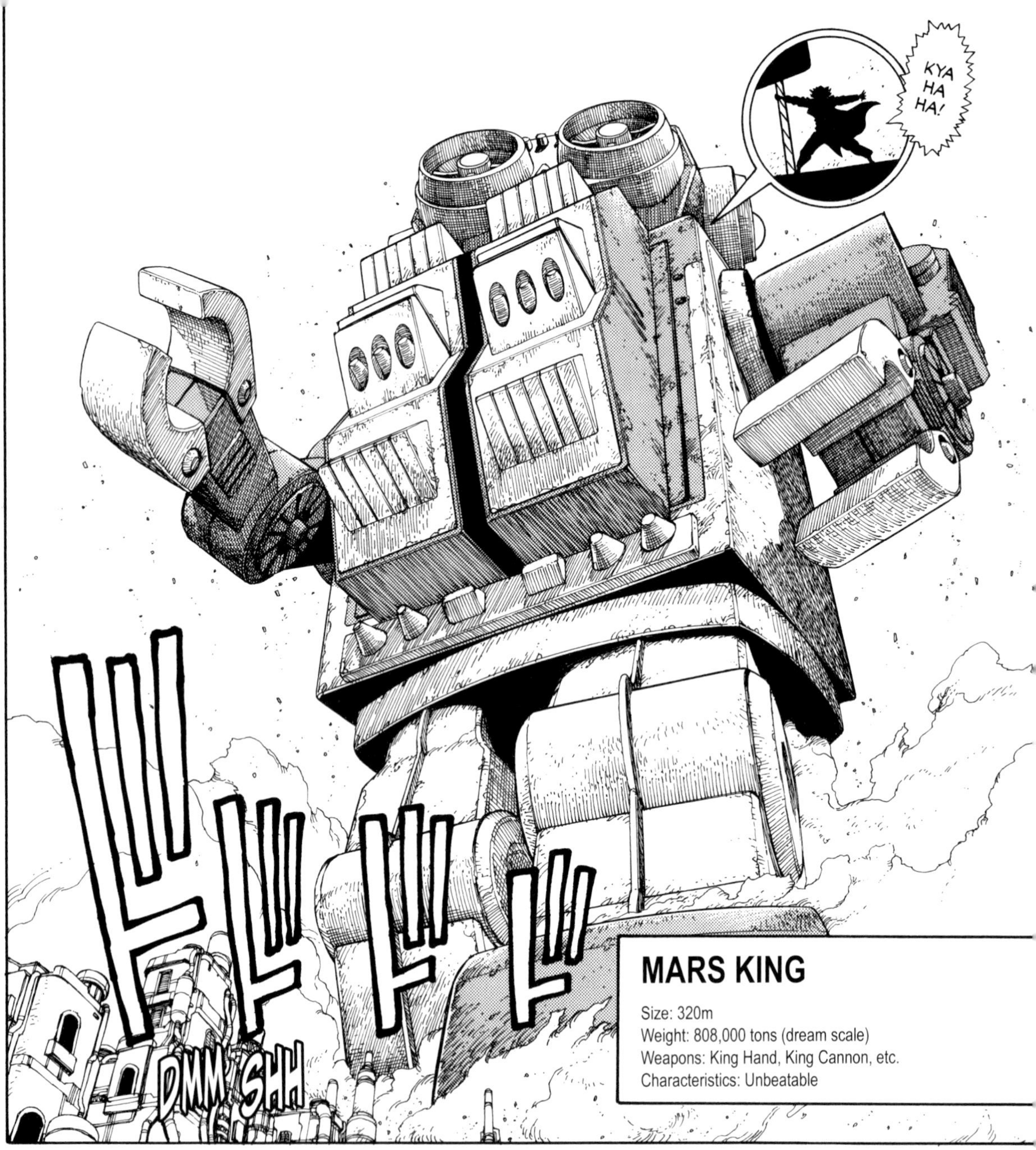
KYA HA HA!
DMM SHH
MARS KING
Size: 320m
Weight: 808,000 tons (dream scale)
Weapons: King Hand, King Cannon, etc.
Characteristics: Unbeatable

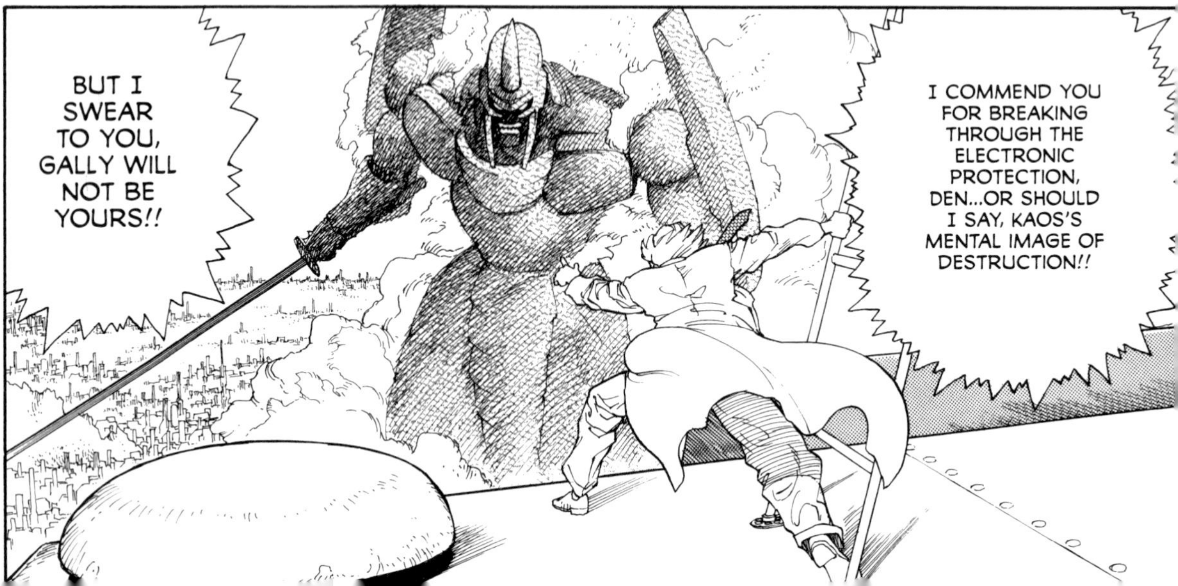
I COMMEND YOU FOR BREAKING THROUGH THE ELECTRONIC PROTECTION, DEN...OR SHOULD I SAY, KAOS'S MENTAL IMAGE OF DESTRUCTION!!
BUT I SWEAR TO YOU, GALLY WILL NOT BE YOURS!!

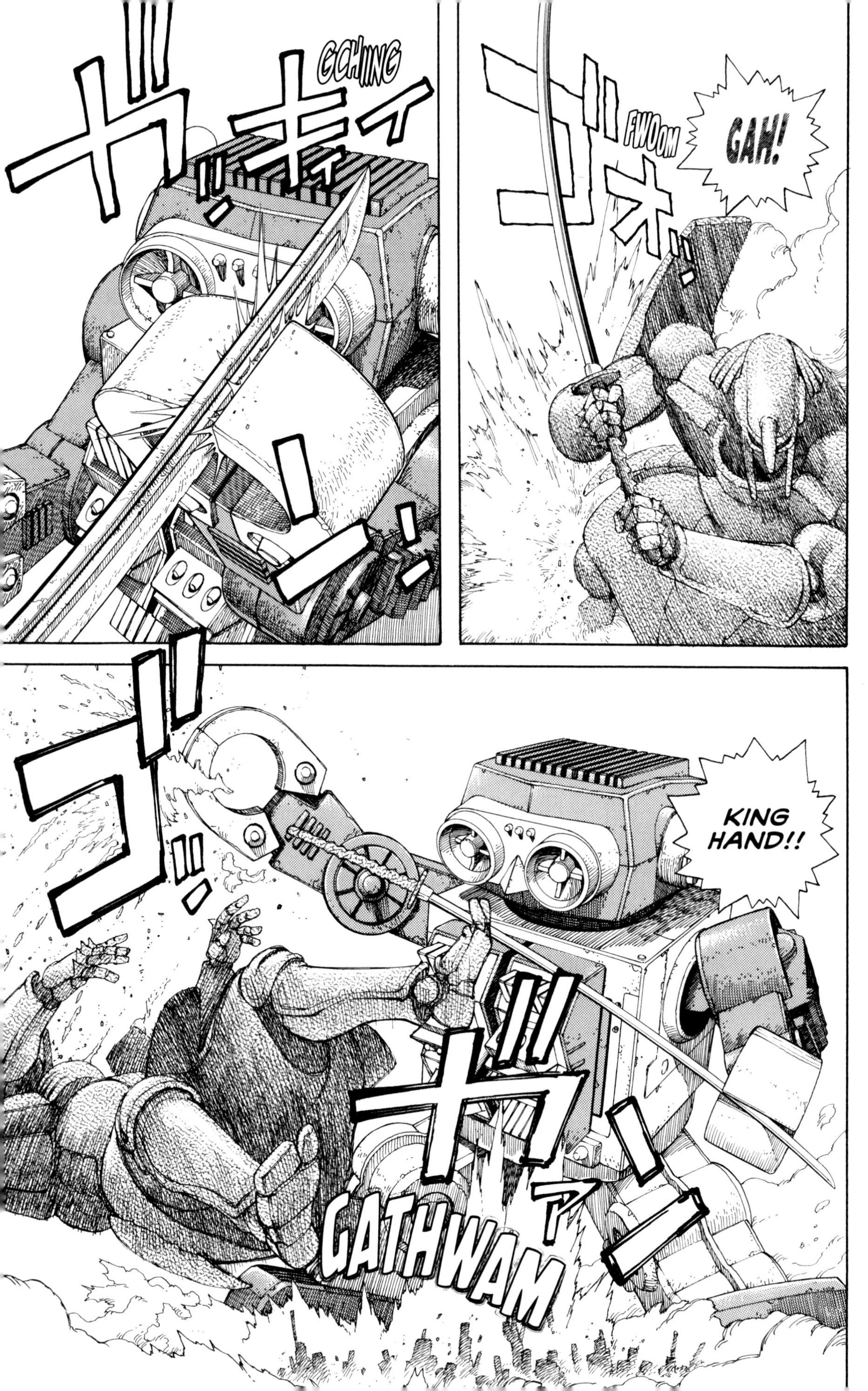
GAH!
FWOOM
GCHIING
KING HAND!!
GATHWAM

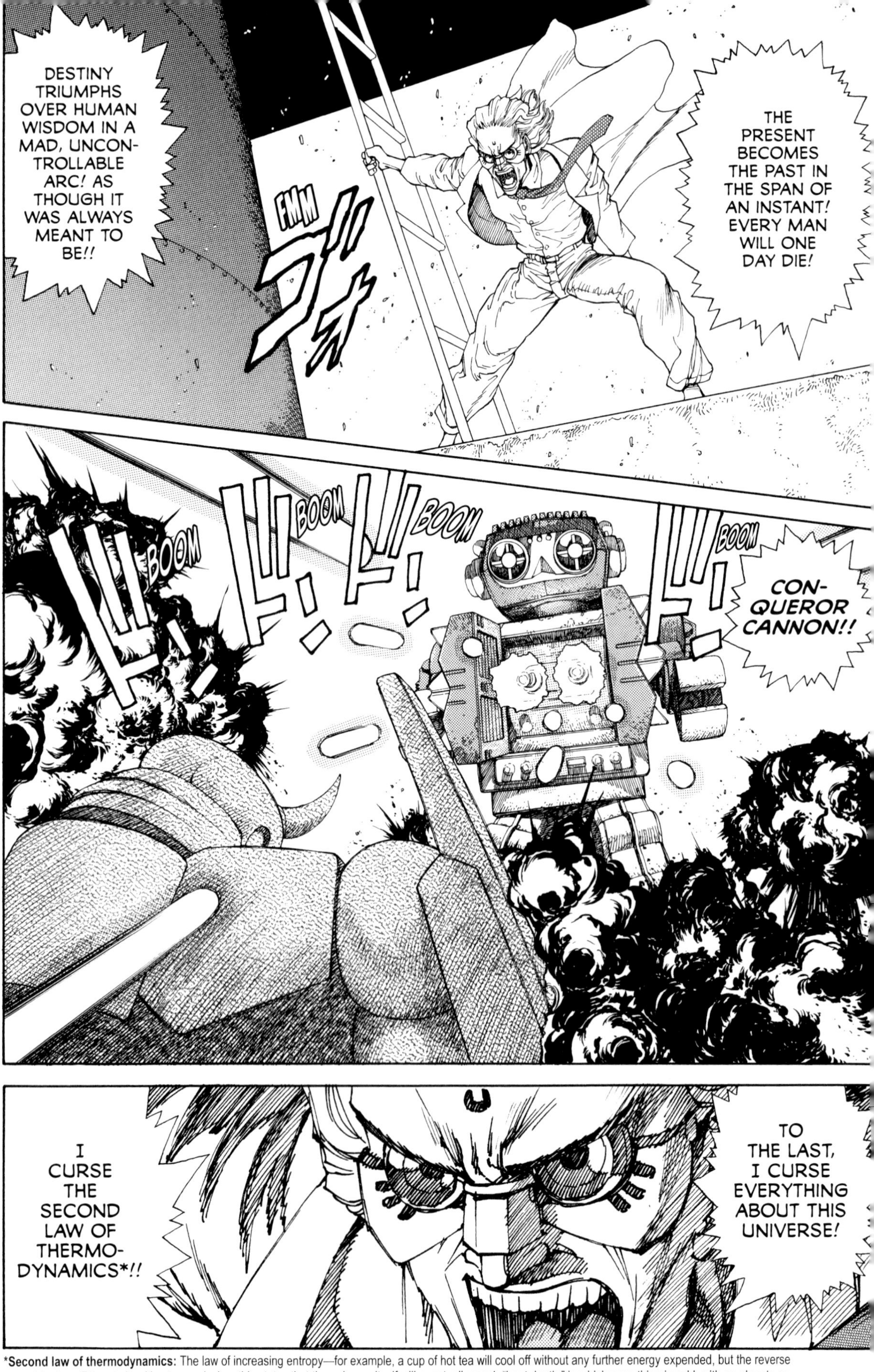
THE PRESENT BECOMES THE PAST IN THE SPAN OF AN INSTANT! EVERY MAN WILL ONE DAY DIE!
DESTINY TRIUMPHS OVER HUMAN WISDOM IN A MAD, UNCONTROLLABLE ARC! AS THOUGH IT WAS ALWAYS MEANT TO BE!!
FMM
CONQUEROR CANNON!!
BOOM
BOOM
BOOM
BOOM
TO THE LAST, I CURSE EVERYTHING ABOUT THIS UNIVERSE!
I CURSE THE SECOND LAW OF THERMODYNAMICS*!!

***Second law of thermodynamics:** The law of increasing entropy—for example, a cup of hot tea will cool off without any further energy expended, but the reverse cannot be true. Taken to its ultimate conclusion, this states that the universe itself will eventually reach "heat death," in which everything is cold, with no planets or concept of time.

ZDOUM

DON'T WORRY, WE'RE SAFE HERE.

I'M SURE THAT THE PROFESSOR WILL DRIVE THAT MONSTER AWAY.

ZDUMM

TCK

PLNK

IDO.

I NEED TO FIGHT, TOO.

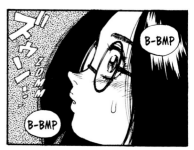

B-BMP

B-BMP

B-BMP

I FIGHT...

DING

WHY, THAT'S SILLY...

WHY WOULD YOU FIGHT?!

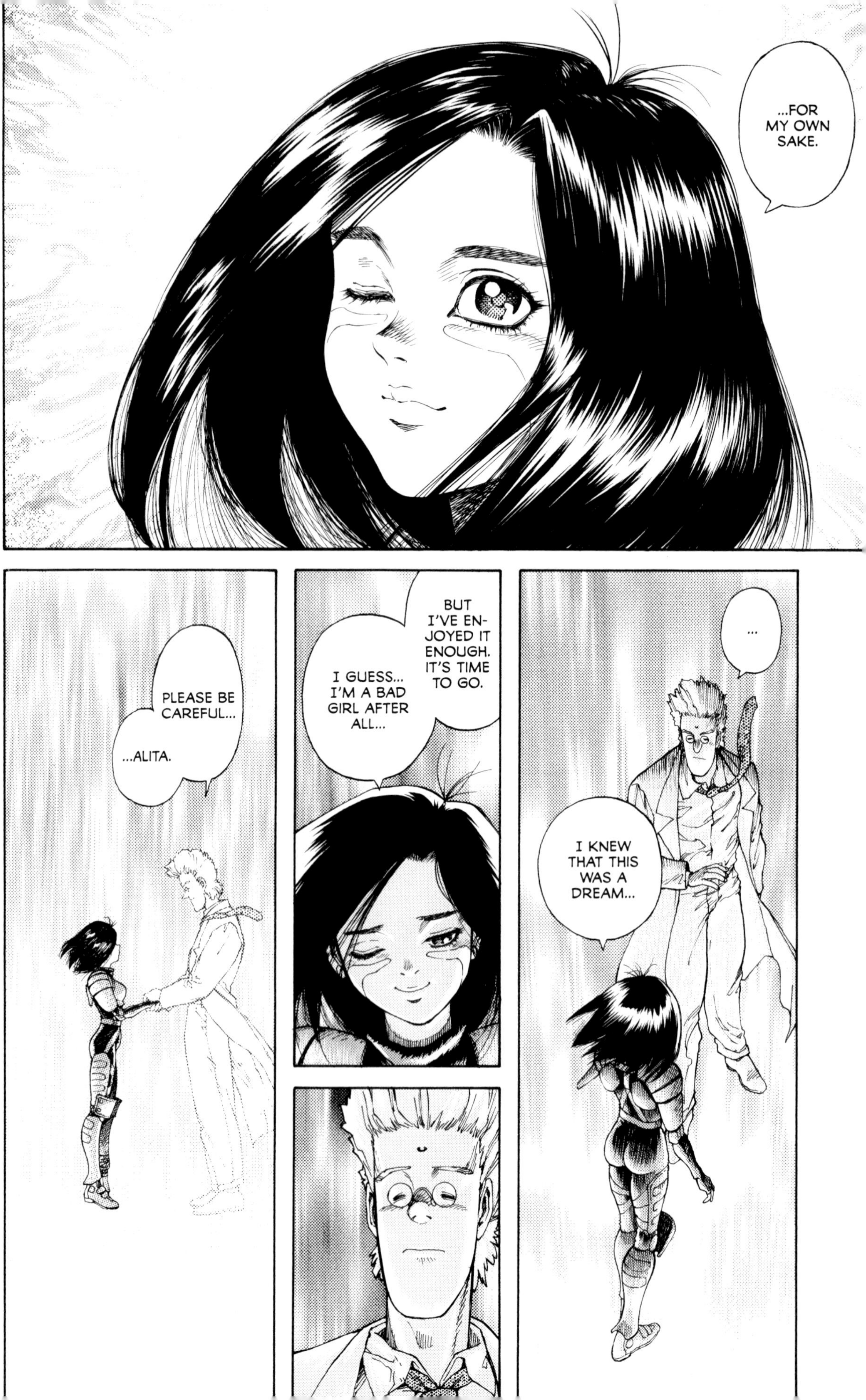
...FOR MY OWN SAKE.
...
I KNEW THAT THIS WAS A DREAM...
BUT I'VE EN-JOYED IT ENOUGH. IT'S TIME TO GO.
I GUESS... I'M A BAD GIRL AFTER ALL...
PLEASE BE CAREFUL...
...ALITA.

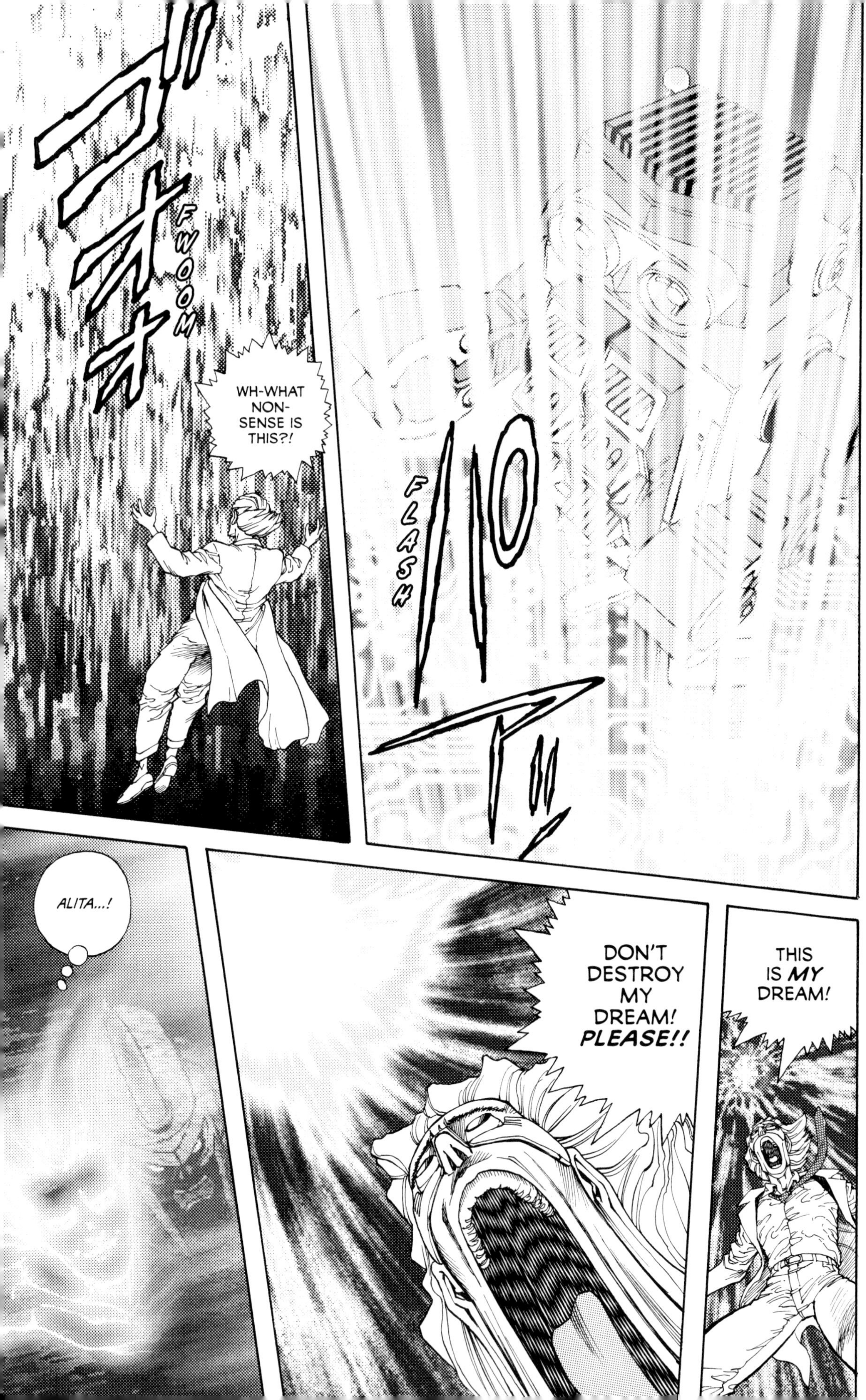
FLASH
FWOOM
WH-WHAT NON-SENSE IS THIS?!
THIS IS *MY* DREAM!
DON'T DESTROY MY DREAM! ***PLEASE!!***
ALITA...!

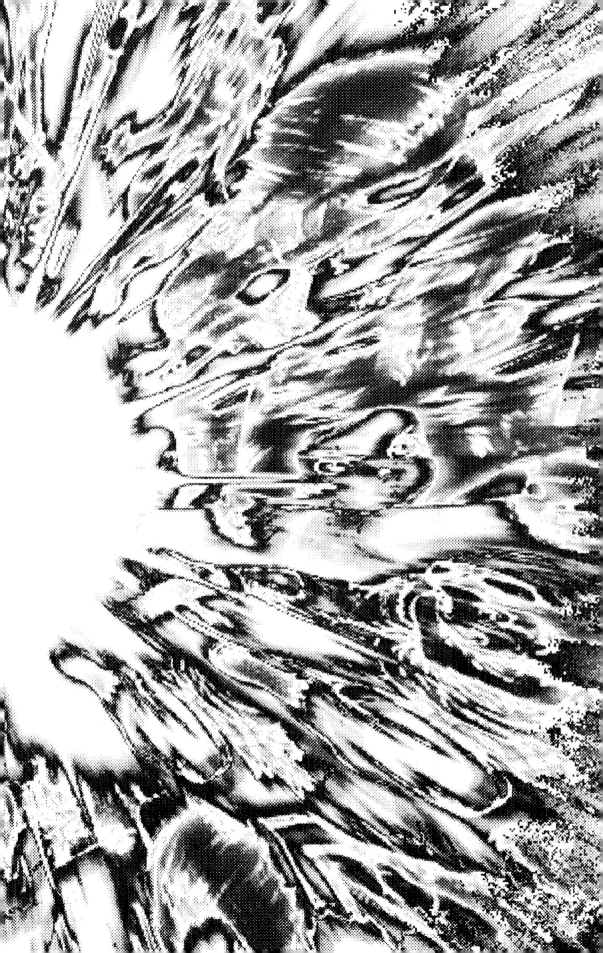

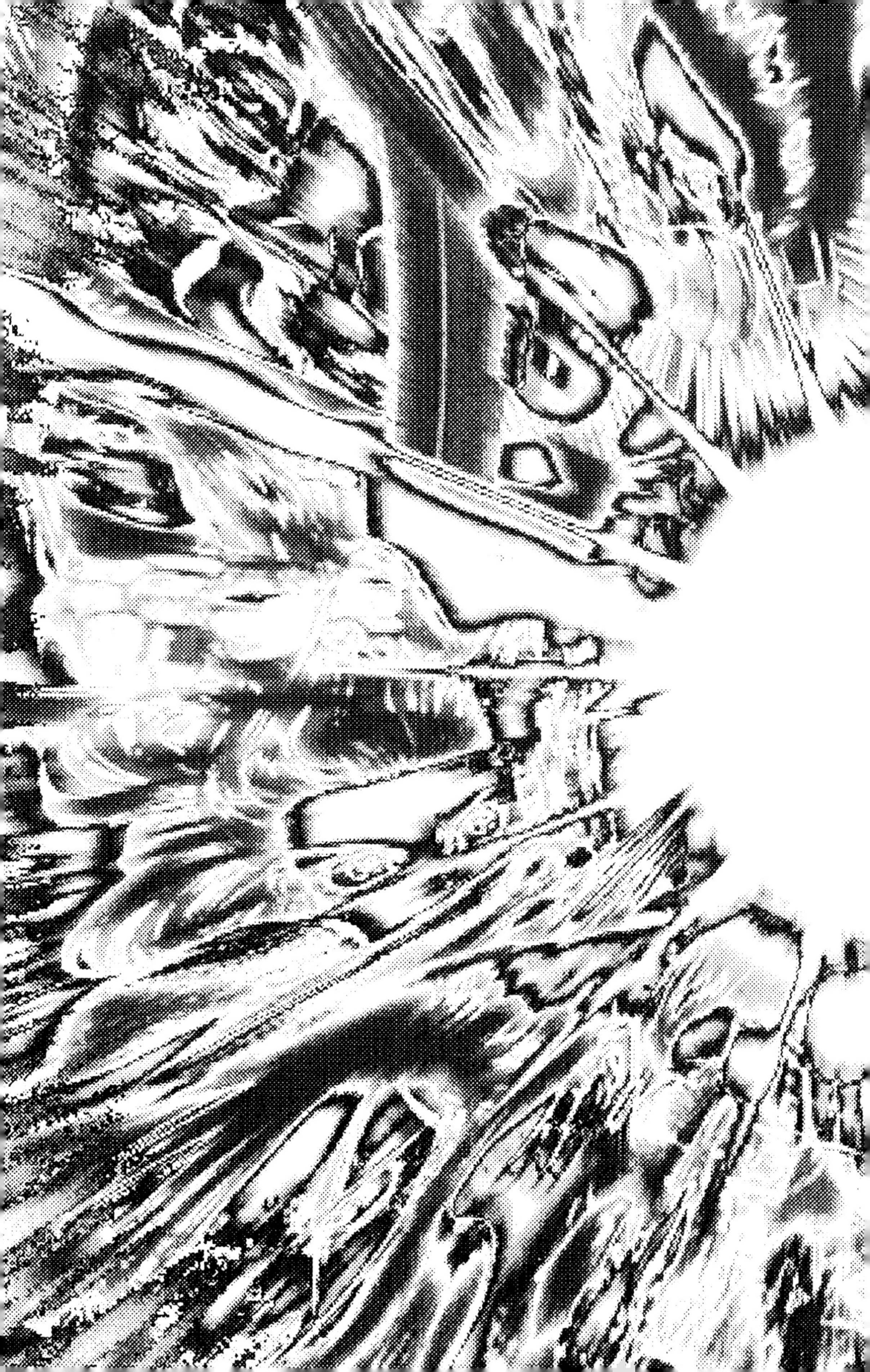

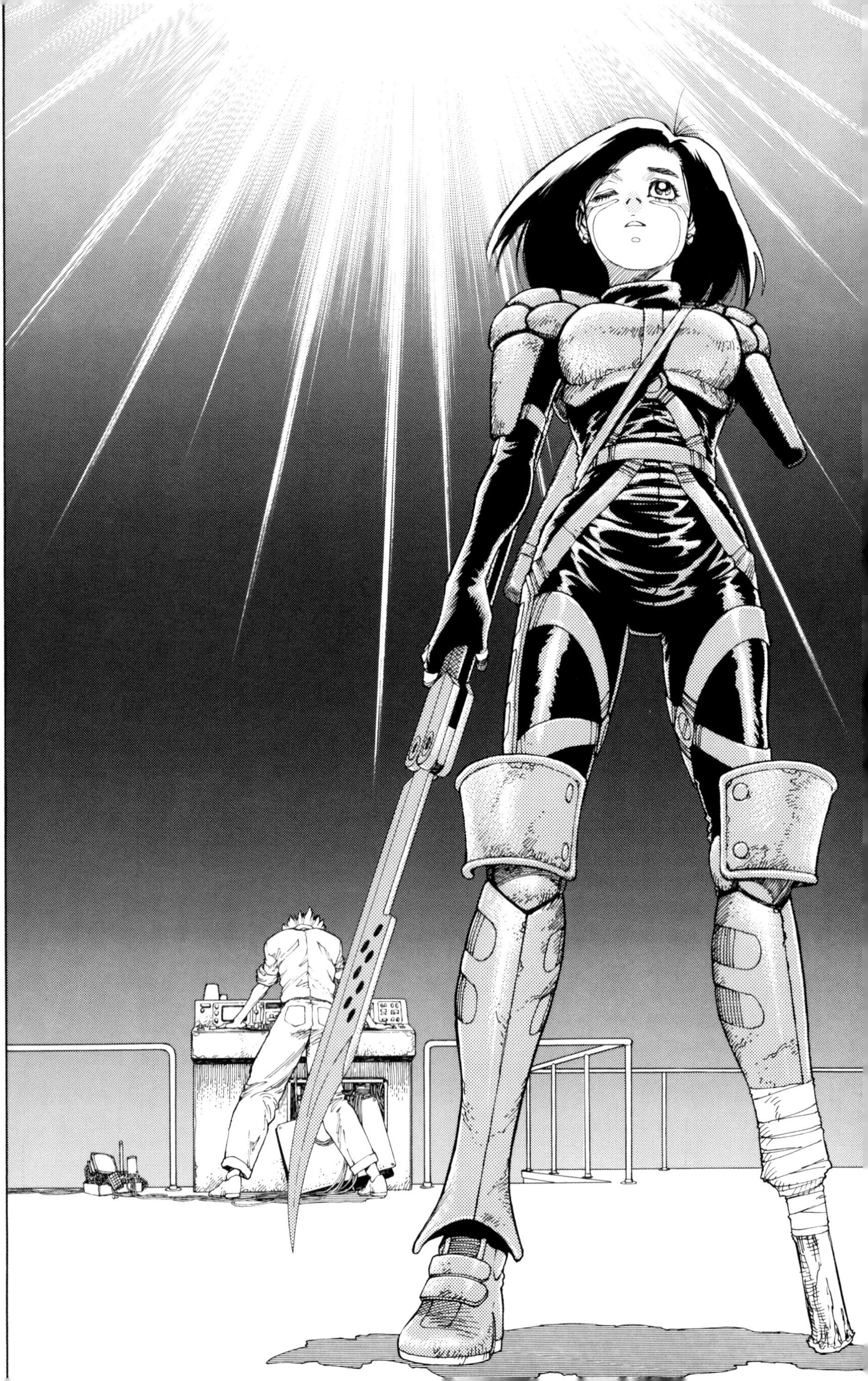

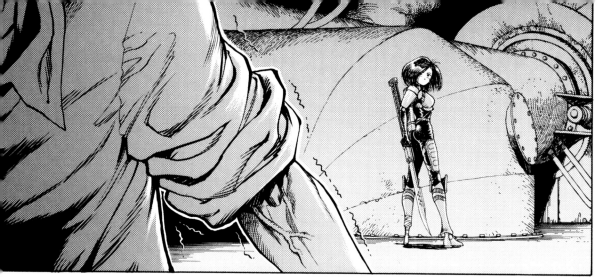

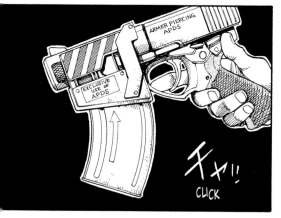

IF ONLY THIS WERE STILL MY DREAM...
ARMER PIERCING APDS
EXCLUSIVE USE OF APDS
チャ!!
CLICK
...I WOULD HAVE DONE *ANYTHING* TO KEEP YOU SAFE...

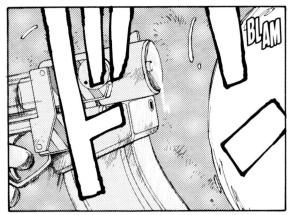

BL AM

ANYTHING
TO
PROTECT
THAT
ETERNAL
MOMENT...

BSST

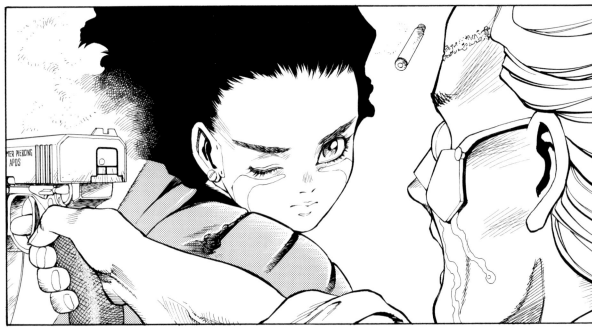

MER PIERCING
APDS

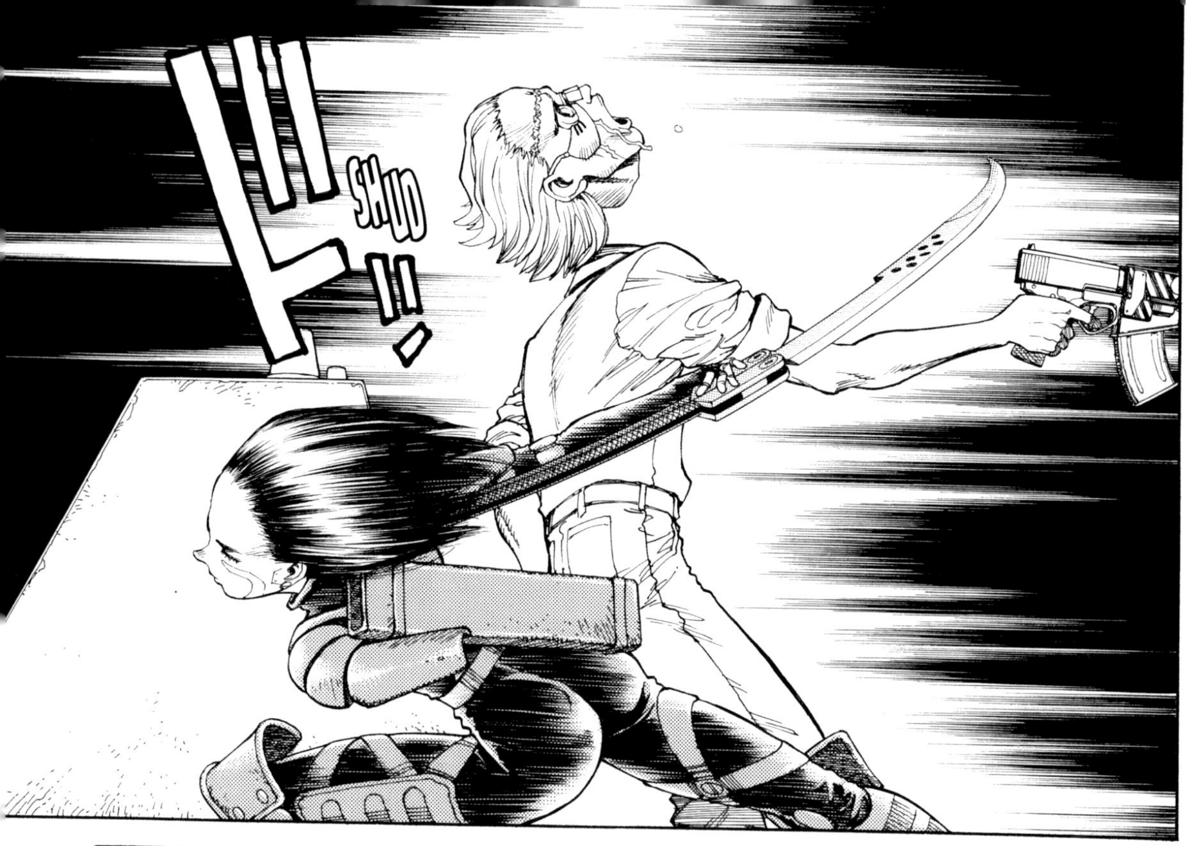
SHUD

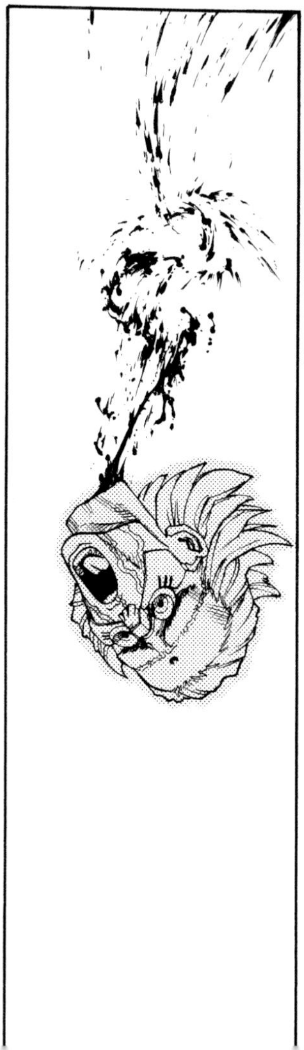

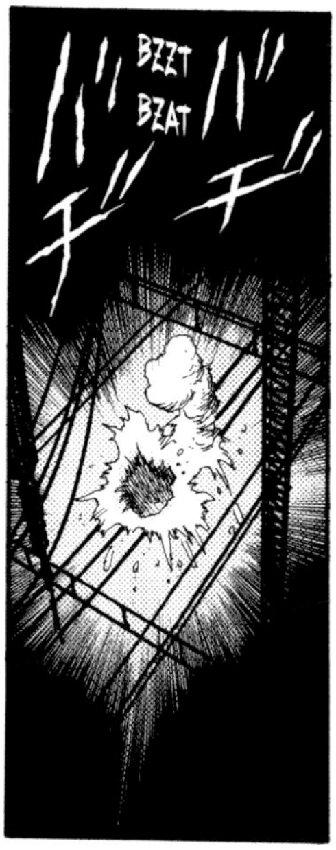
BZZT
BZAT

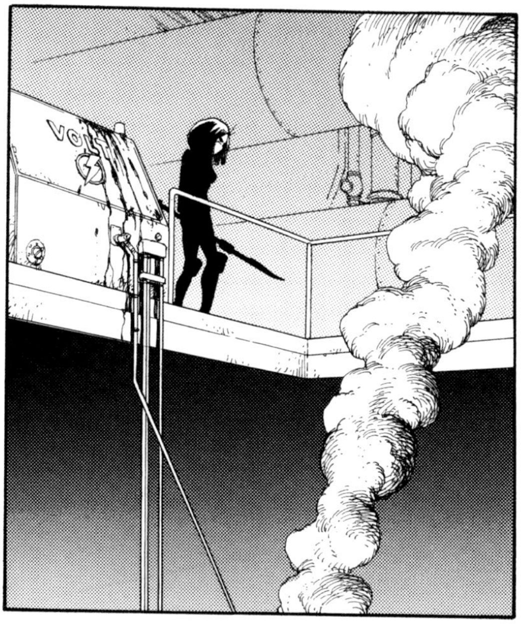

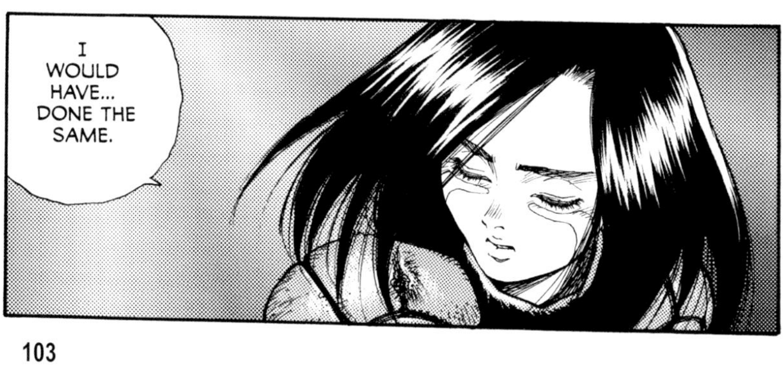
I WOULD HAVE... DONE THE SAME.

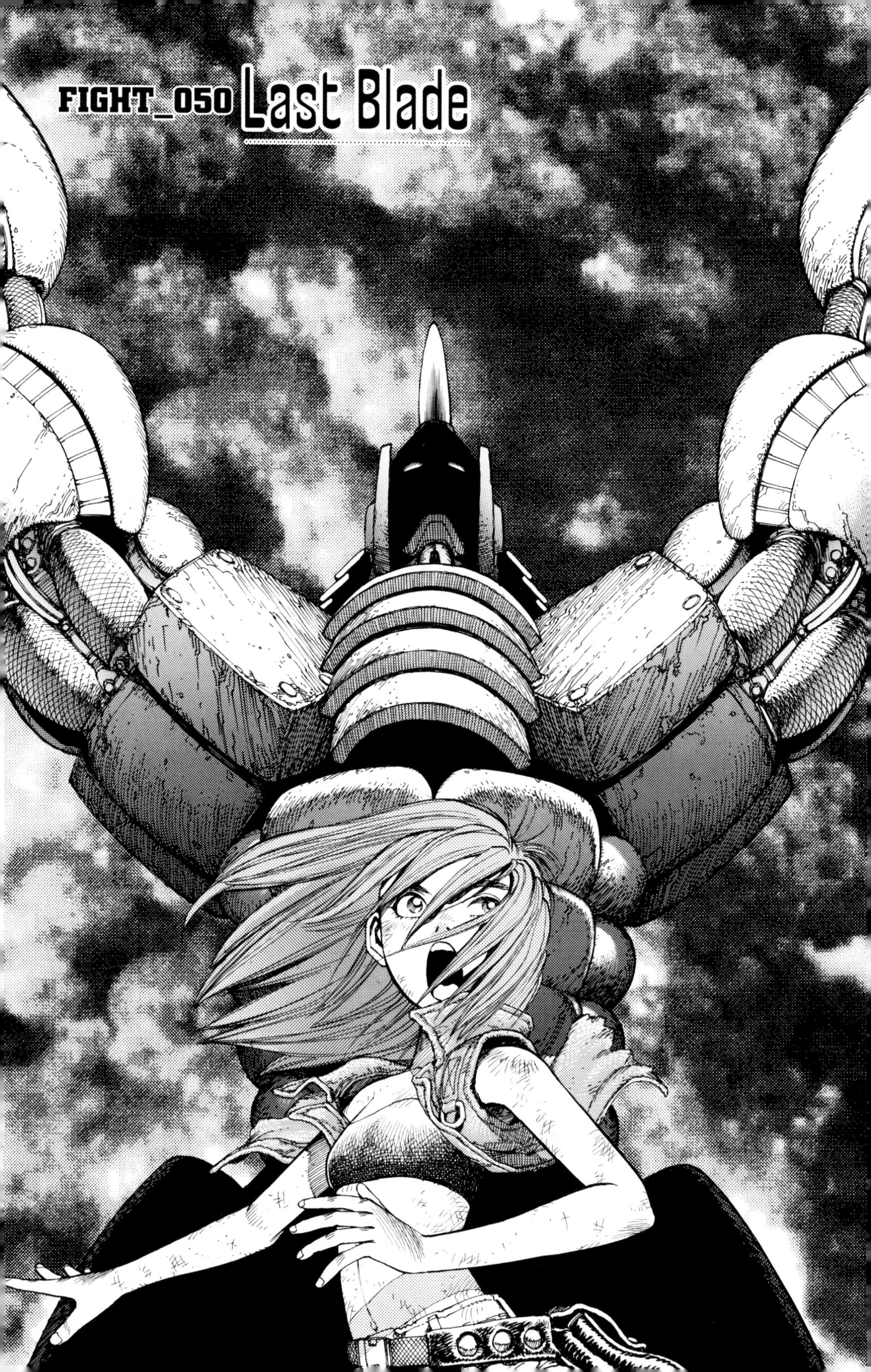
FIGHT_050 Last Blade

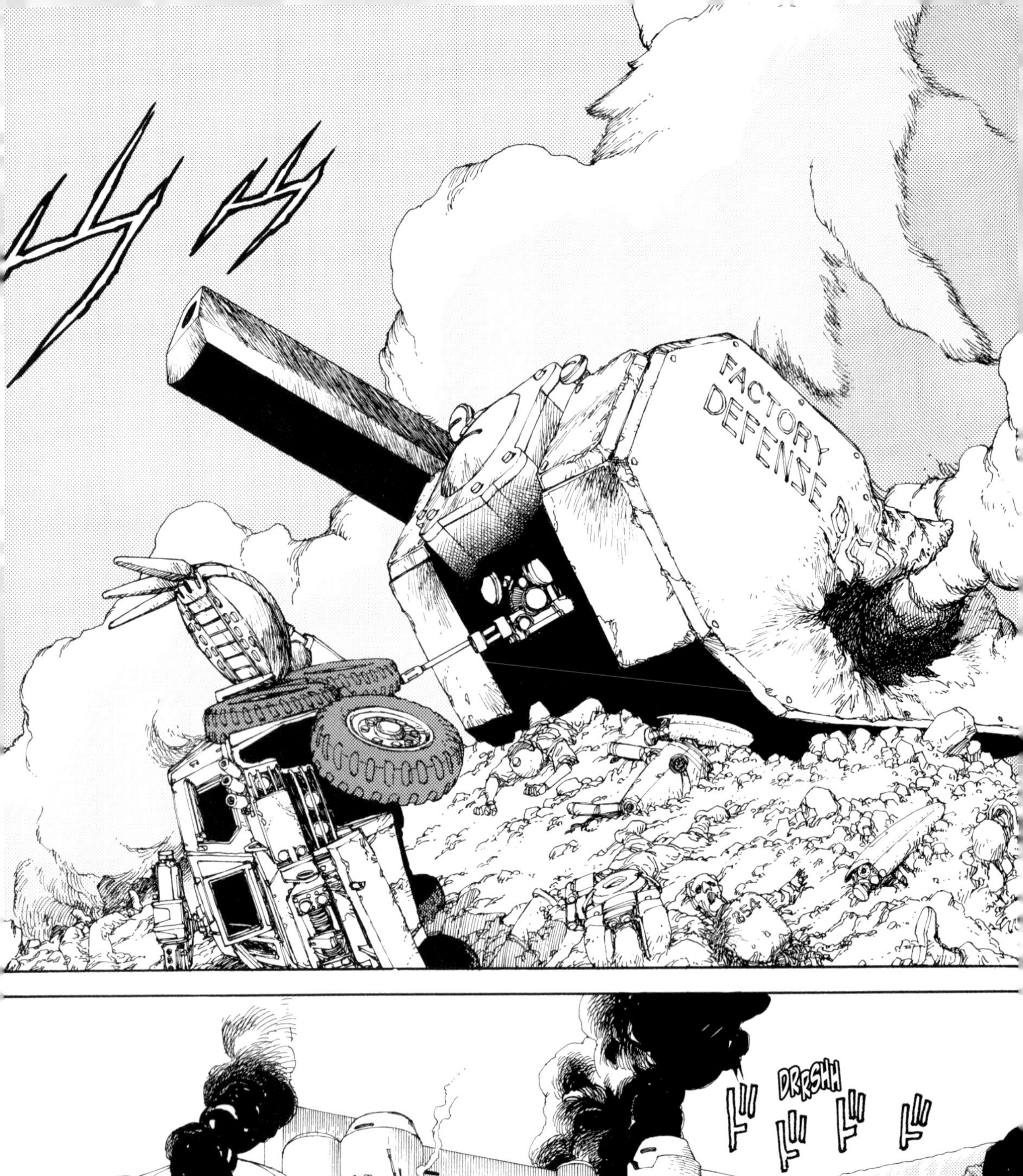
FACTORY
DEFENSE

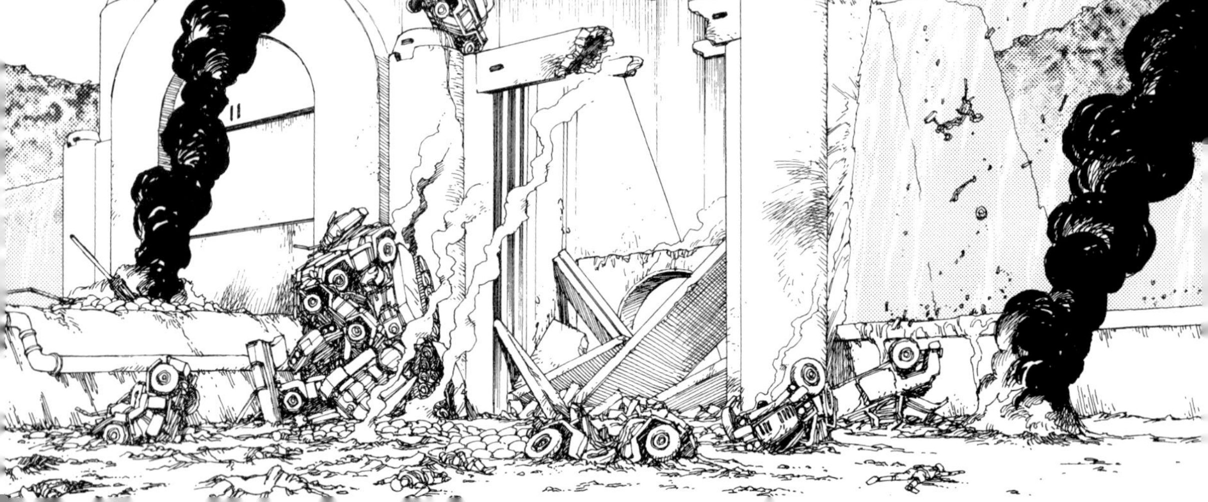
DRRSHH
ドドドド

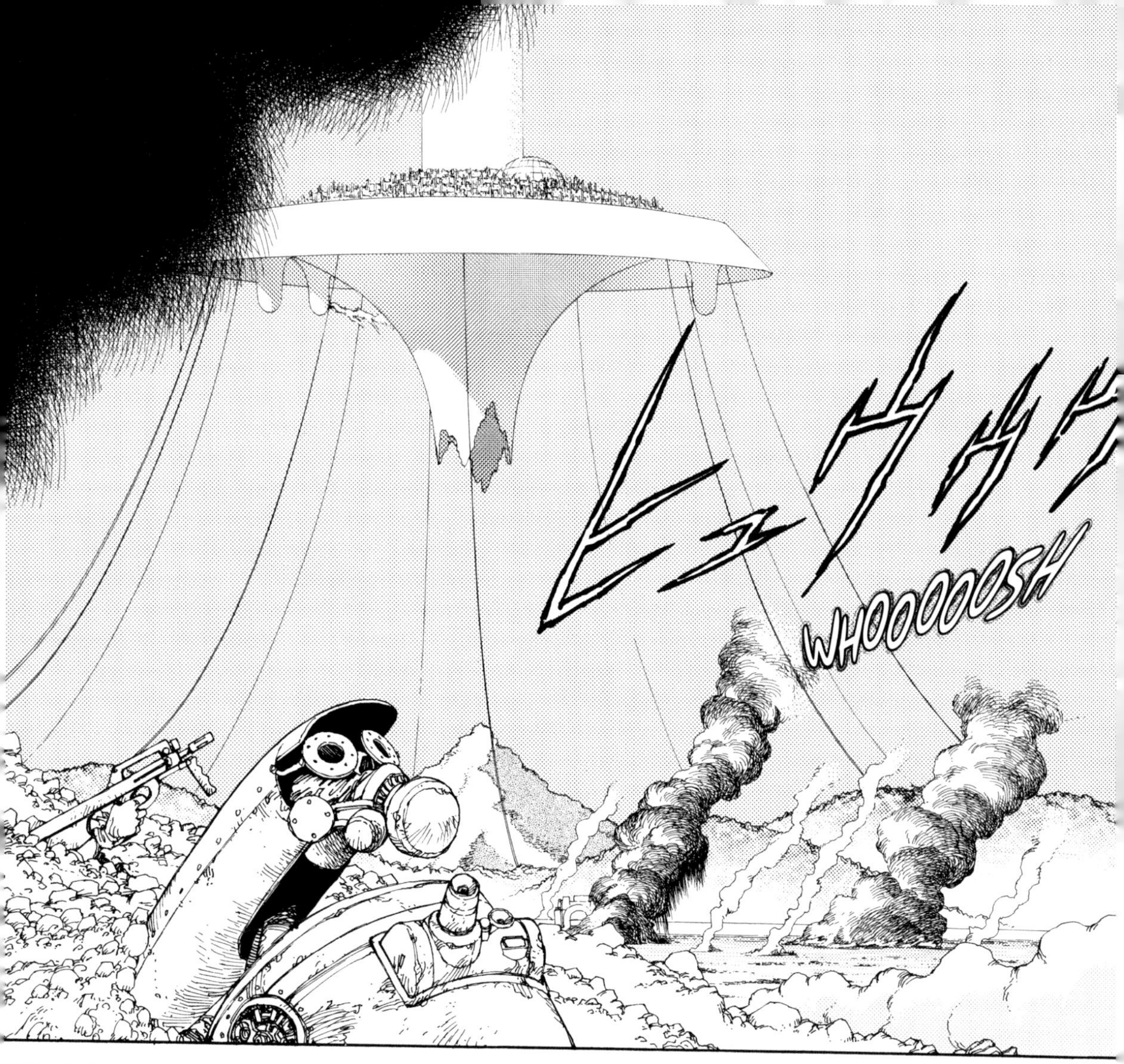
WHOOOOOOSH
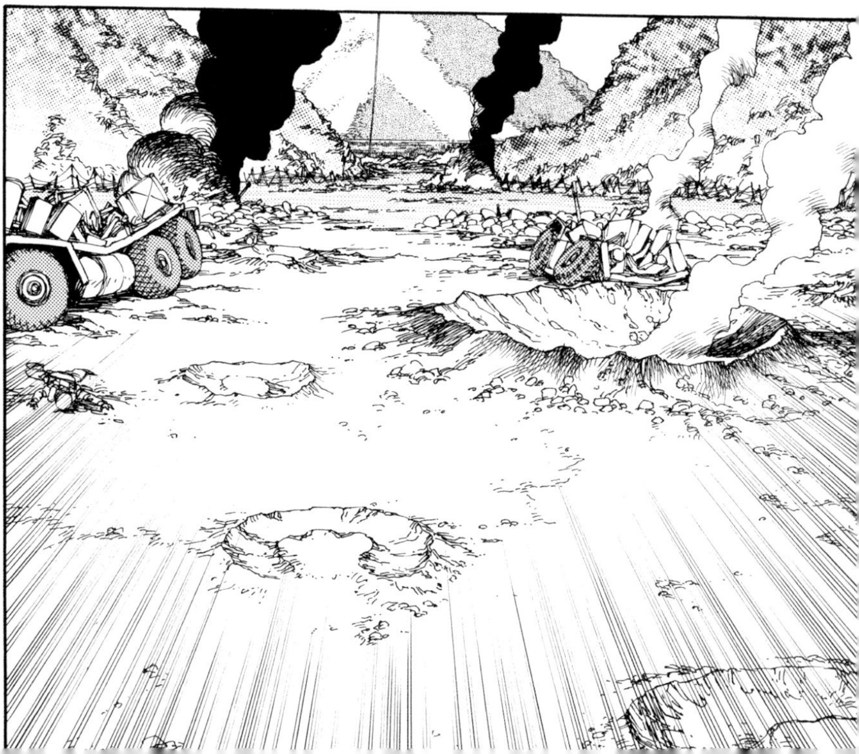
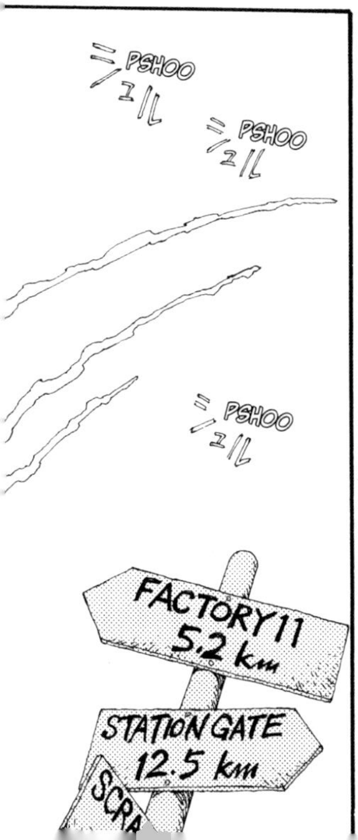
PSHOO
PSHOO
PSHOO
FACTORY 11
5.2 km
STATION GATE
12.5 km
SCRA

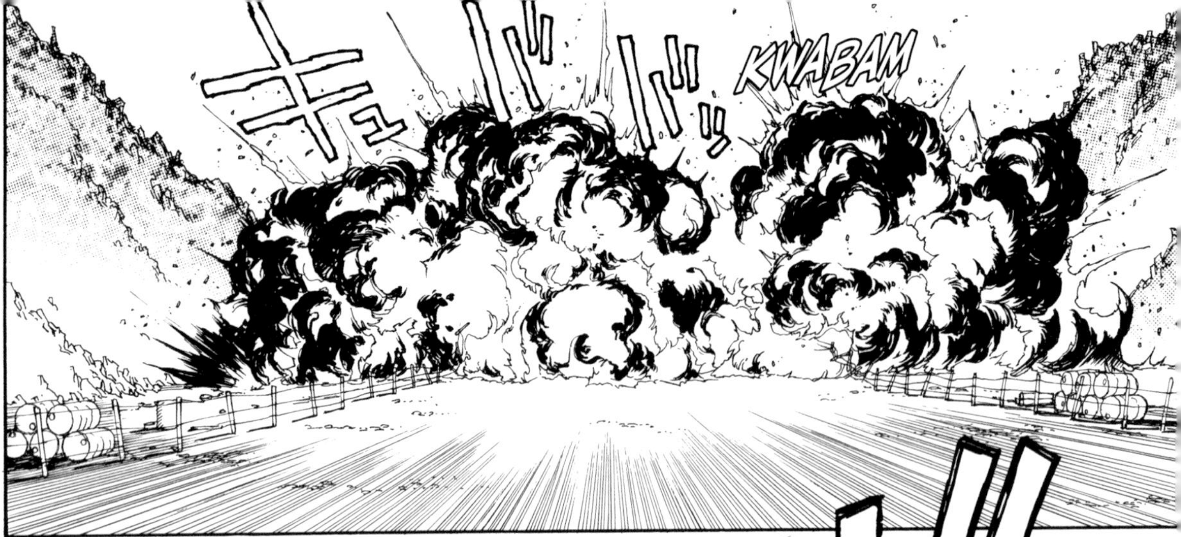
KWABAM
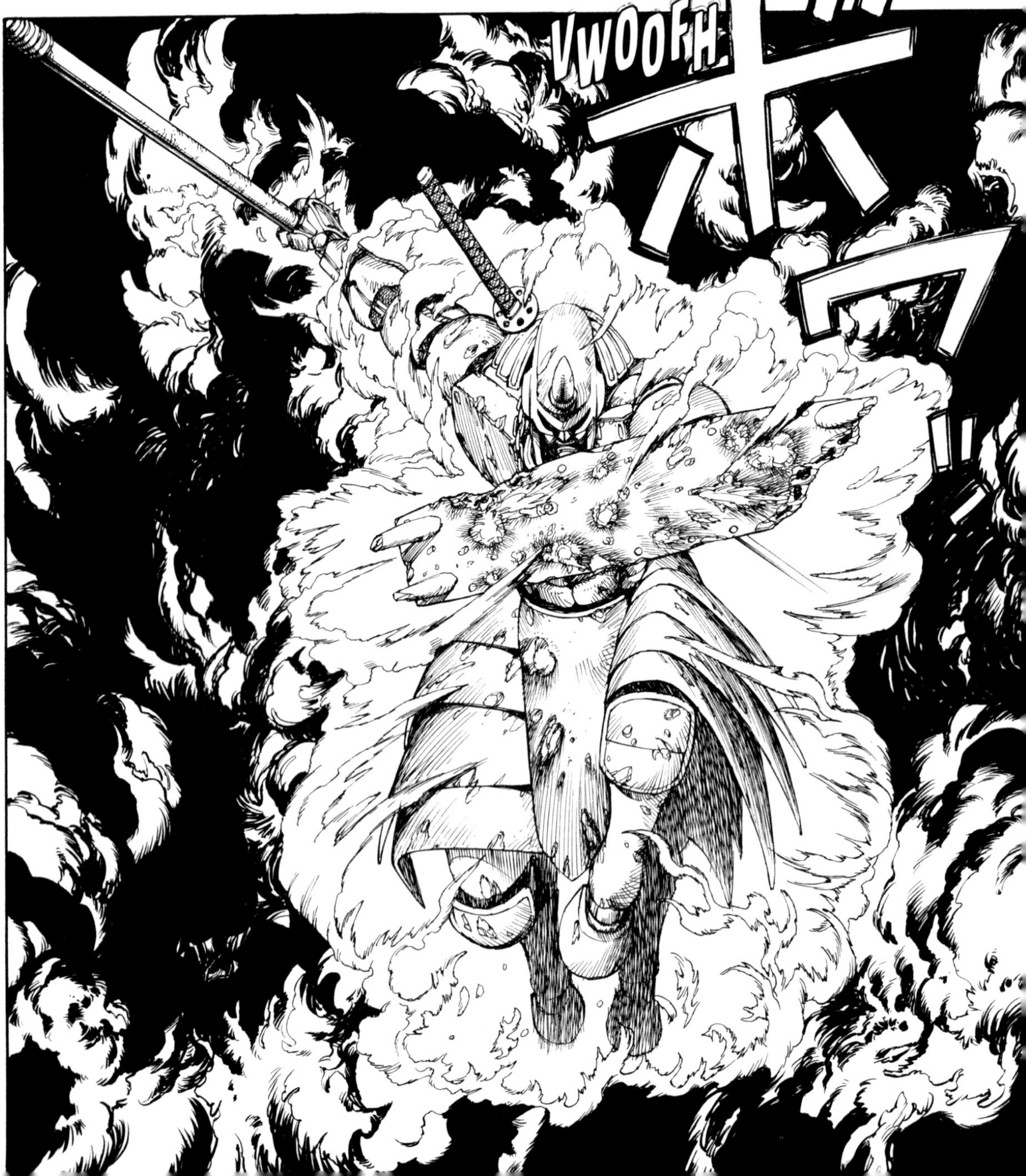
VWOOFH
ボヴ

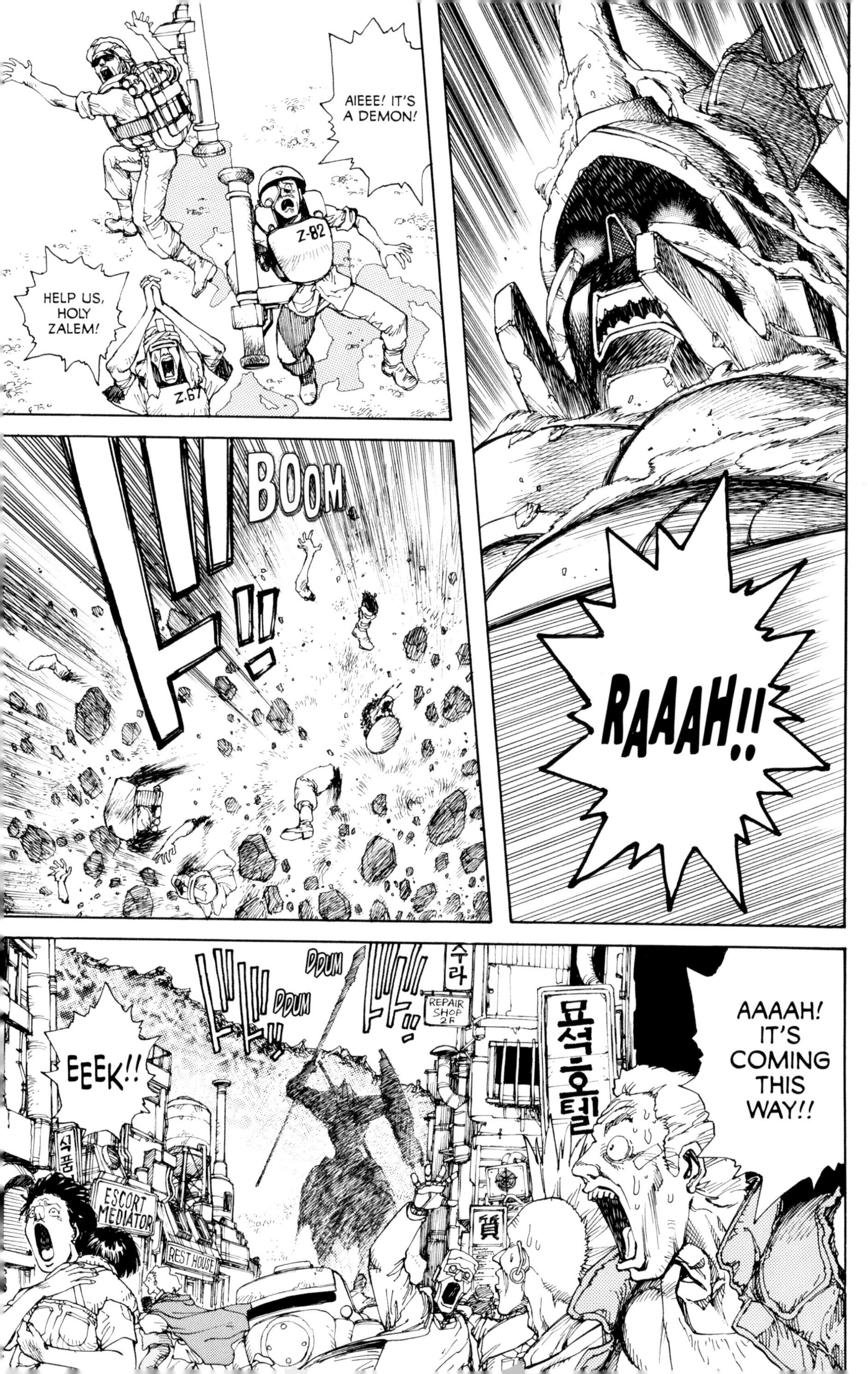
RAAAH!!
AIEEE! IT'S A DEMON!
Z-82
HELP US, HOLY ZALEM!
Z-67
BOOM
AAAAH! IT'S COMING THIS WAY!!
묘석호텔
수라
REPAIR SHOP 2F
DDUM
DDUM
EEEK!!
質
식품
ESCORT MEDIATOR
REST HOUSE

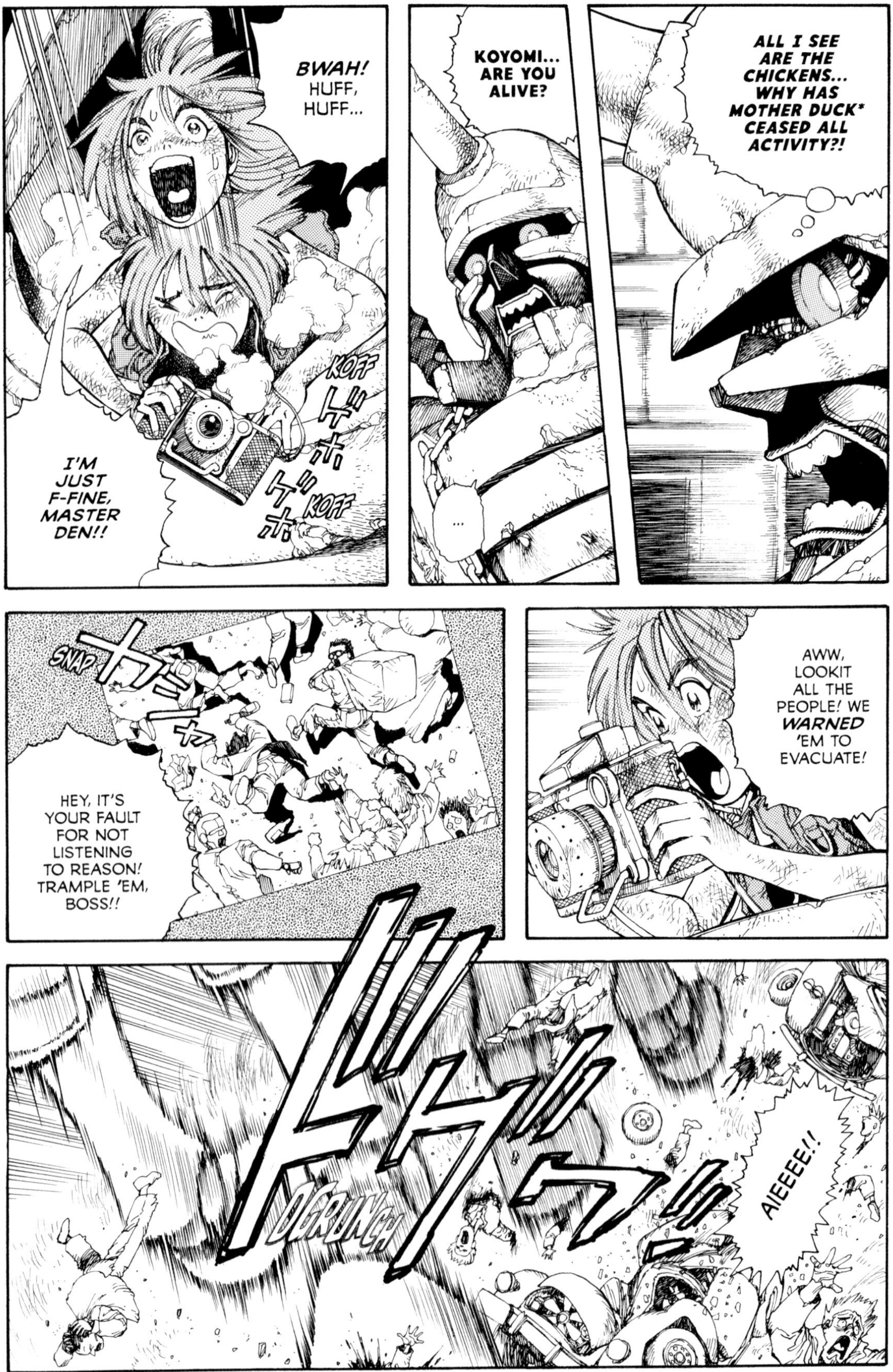
ALL I SEE ARE THE CHICKENS... WHY HAS MOTHER DUCK* CEASED ALL ACTIVITY?!
KOYOMI... ARE YOU ALIVE?
...
BWAH! HUFF, HUFF...
KOFF
KOFF
I'M JUST F-FINE, MASTER DEN!!
AWW, LOOKIT ALL THE PEOPLE! WE WARNED 'EM TO EVACUATE!
SNAP
HEY, IT'S YOUR FAULT FOR NOT LISTENING TO REASON! TRAMPLE 'EM, BOSS!!
DGRUNCH
AIEEEE!!

***Mother Duck:** In Barjack slang, this refers to the official Factory mobilized troops, made up of Deckmen and Netmen robots. These are distinguished from the Chickens, the locals hired as mercenary forces.

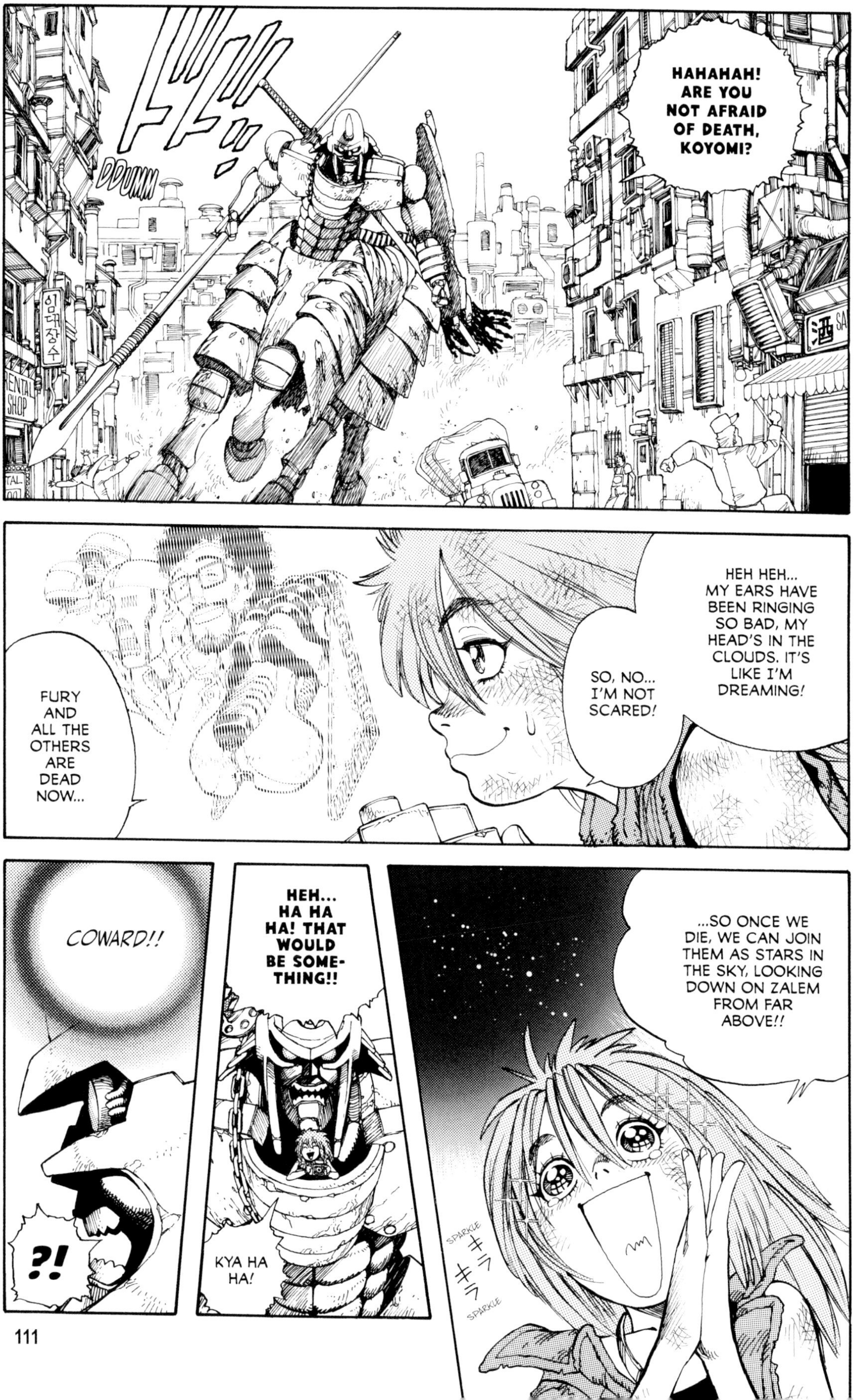
DDUMM
HAHAHAH! ARE YOU NOT AFRAID OF DEATH, KOYOMI?
RENTAL SHOP
HEH HEH... MY EARS HAVE BEEN RINGING SO BAD, MY HEAD'S IN THE CLOUDS. IT'S LIKE I'M DREAMING!
SO, NO... I'M NOT SCARED!
FURY AND ALL THE OTHERS ARE DEAD NOW...
...SO ONCE WE DIE, WE CAN JOIN THEM AS STARS IN THE SKY, LOOKING DOWN ON ZALEM FROM FAR ABOVE!!
SPARKLE キラ キラ SPARKLE
HEH... HA HA HA! THAT WOULD BE SOME-THING!!
KYA HA HA!
COWARD!!
?!

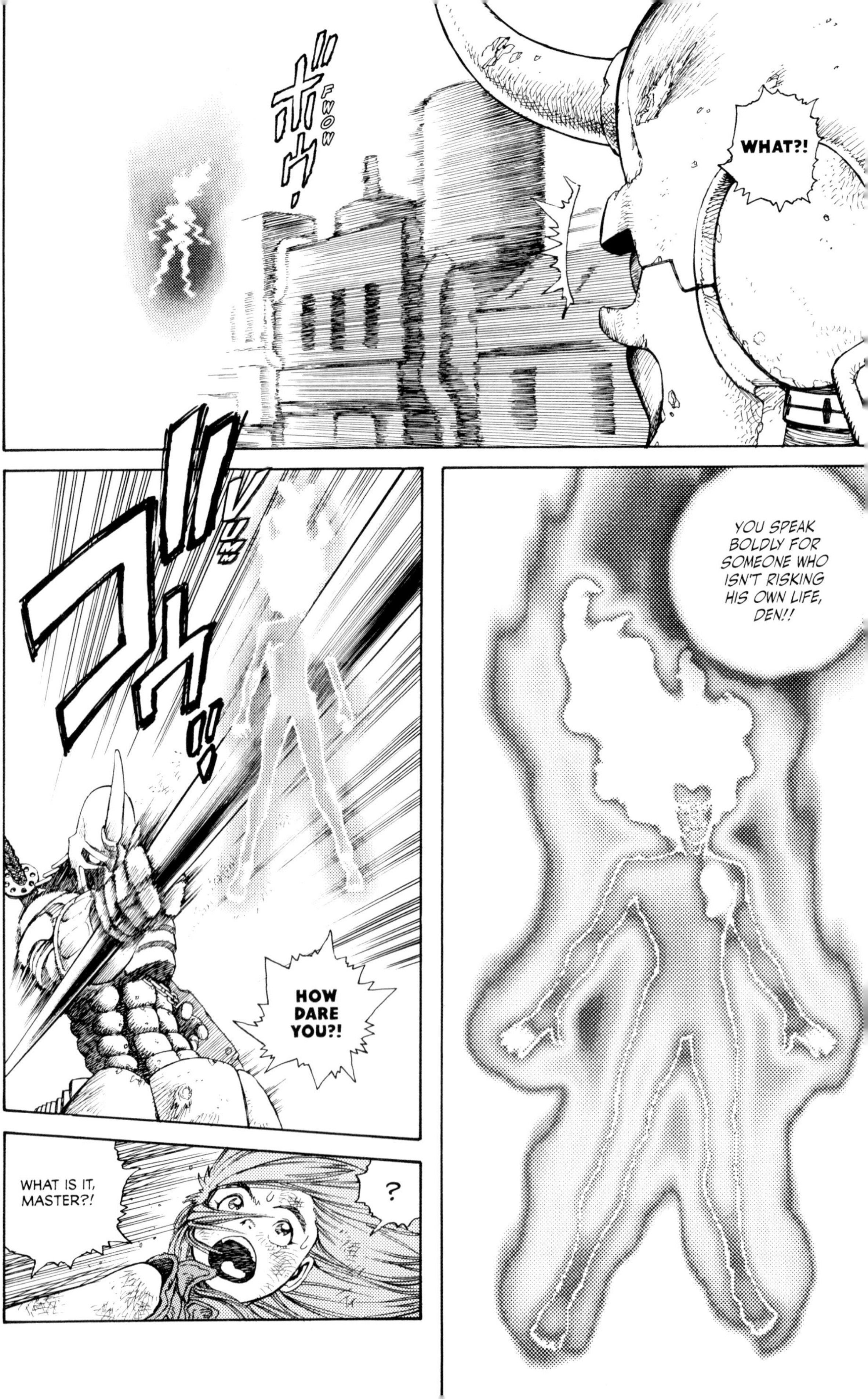
WHAT?!
FWOW
YOU SPEAK BOLDLY FOR SOMEONE WHO ISN'T RISKING HIS OWN LIFE, DEN!!
VUMM
HOW DARE YOU?!
?
WHAT IS IT, MASTER?!

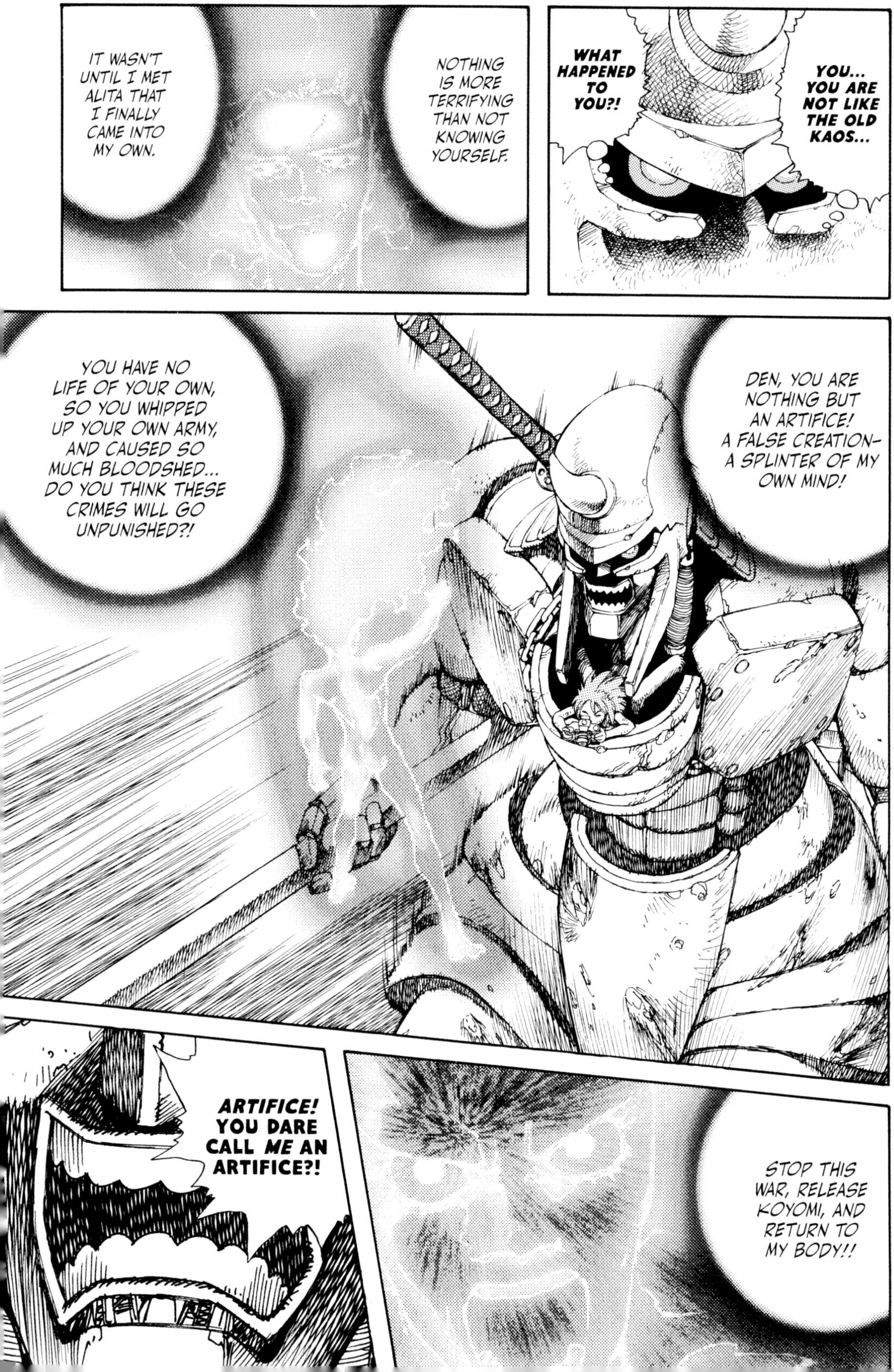
YOU... YOU ARE NOT LIKE THE OLD KAOS...
WHAT HAPPENED TO YOU?!
NOTHING IS MORE TERRIFYING THAN NOT KNOWING YOURSELF.
IT WASN'T UNTIL I MET ALITA THAT I FINALLY CAME INTO MY OWN.
DEN, YOU ARE NOTHING BUT AN ARTIFICE! A FALSE CREATION– A SPLINTER OF MY OWN MIND!
YOU HAVE NO LIFE OF YOUR OWN, SO YOU WHIPPED UP YOUR OWN ARMY, AND CAUSED SO MUCH BLOODSHED... DO YOU THINK THESE CRIMES WILL GO UNPUNISHED?!
STOP THIS WAR, RELEASE KOYOMI, AND RETURN TO MY BODY!!
ARTIFICE! YOU DARE CALL *ME* AN ARTIFICE?!

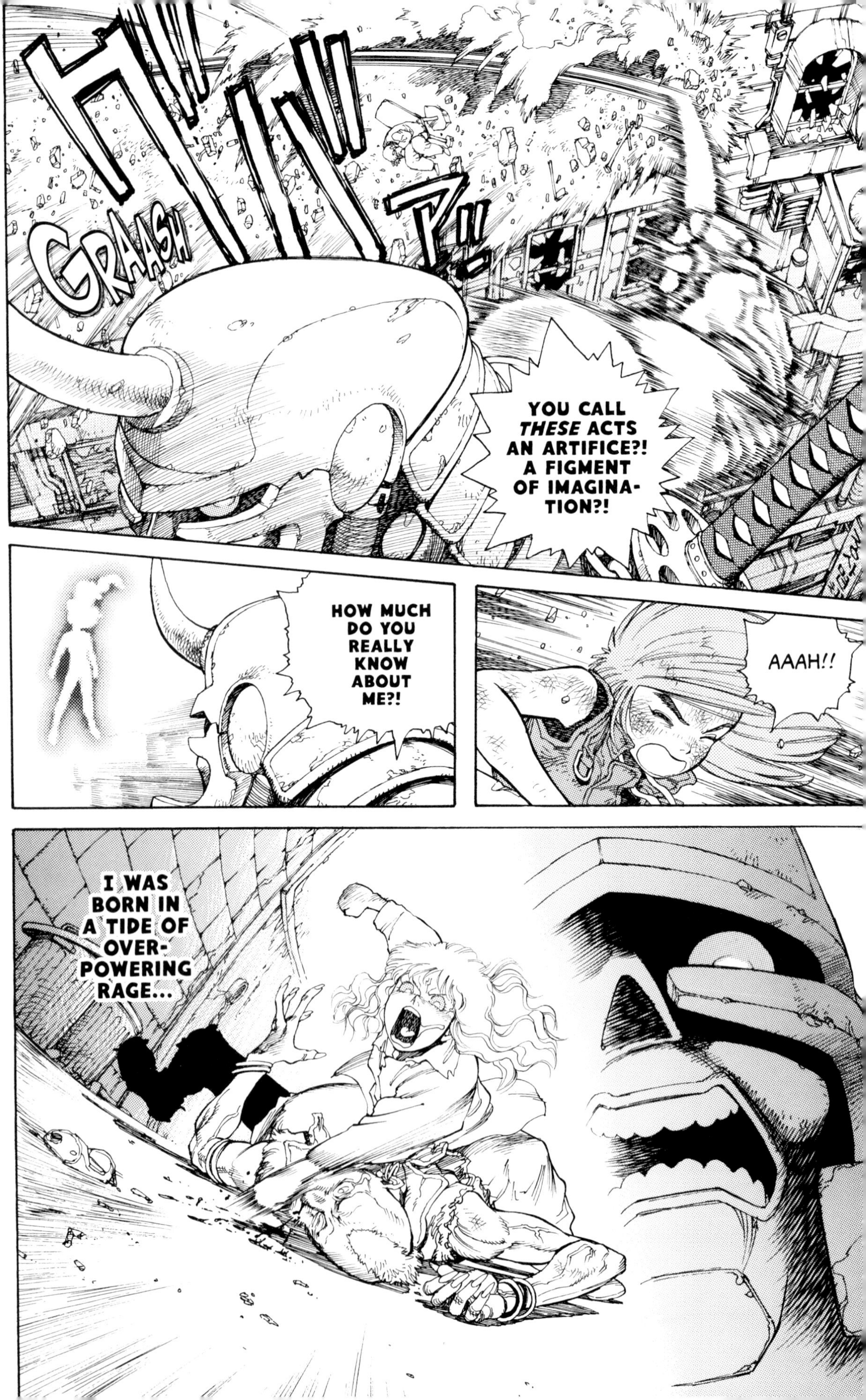
CRASH
YOU CALL *THESE* ACTS AN ARTIFICE?! A FIGMENT OF IMAGINATION?!
AAAH!!
HOW MUCH DO YOU REALLY KNOW ABOUT ME?!
I WAS BORN IN A TIDE OF OVERPOWERING RAGE...

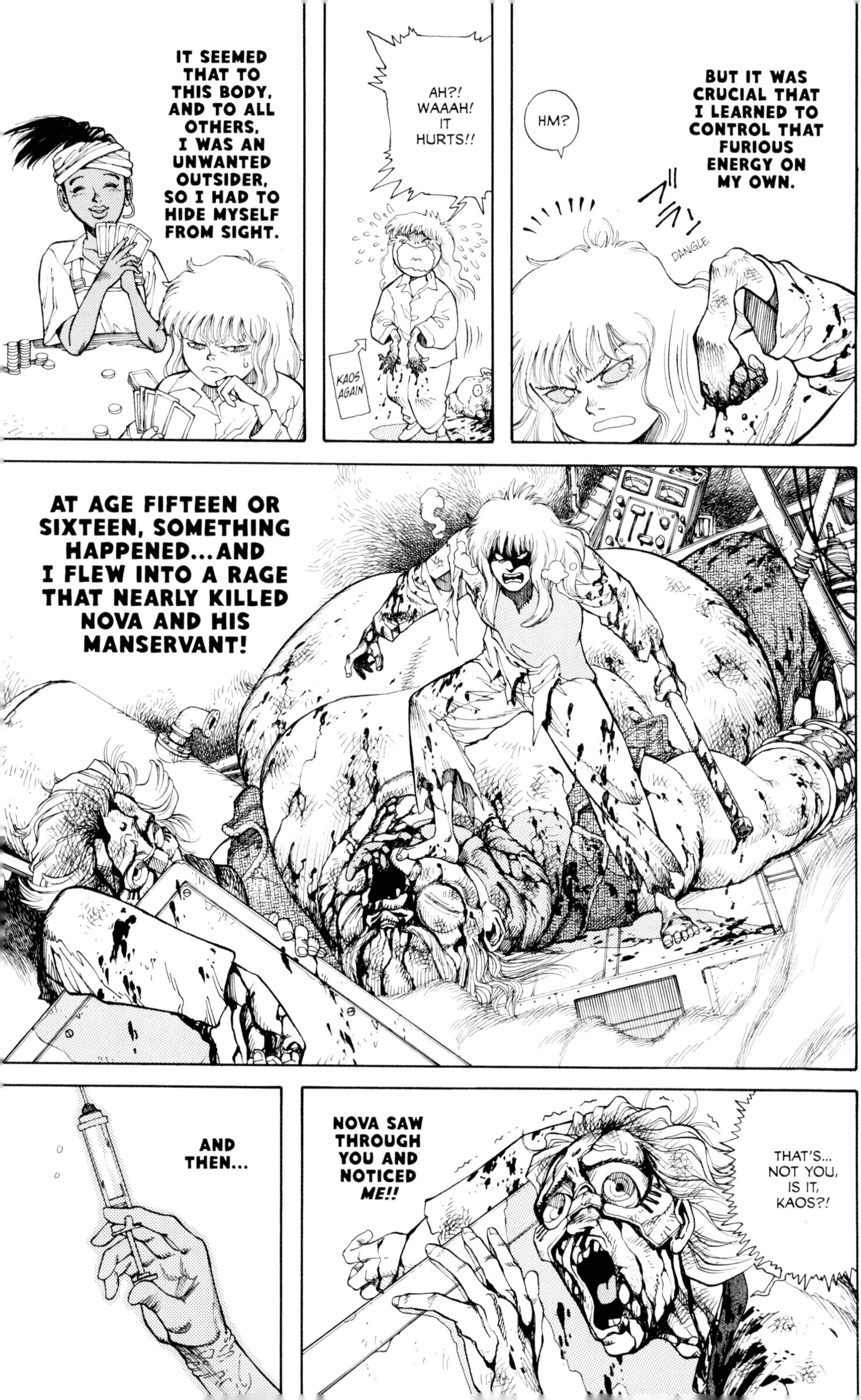
BUT IT WAS CRUCIAL THAT I LEARNED TO CONTROL THAT FURIOUS ENERGY ON MY OWN.
HM?
DANGLE
AH?! WAAAH! IT HURTS!!
KAOS AGAIN
IT SEEMED THAT TO THIS BODY, AND TO ALL OTHERS, I WAS AN UNWANTED OUTSIDER, SO I HAD TO HIDE MYSELF FROM SIGHT.
AT AGE FIFTEEN OR SIXTEEN, SOMETHING HAPPENED...AND I FLEW INTO A RAGE THAT NEARLY KILLED NOVA AND HIS MANSERVANT!
THAT'S... NOT YOU, IS IT, KAOS?!
NOVA SAW THROUGH YOU AND NOTICED *ME!!*
AND THEN...

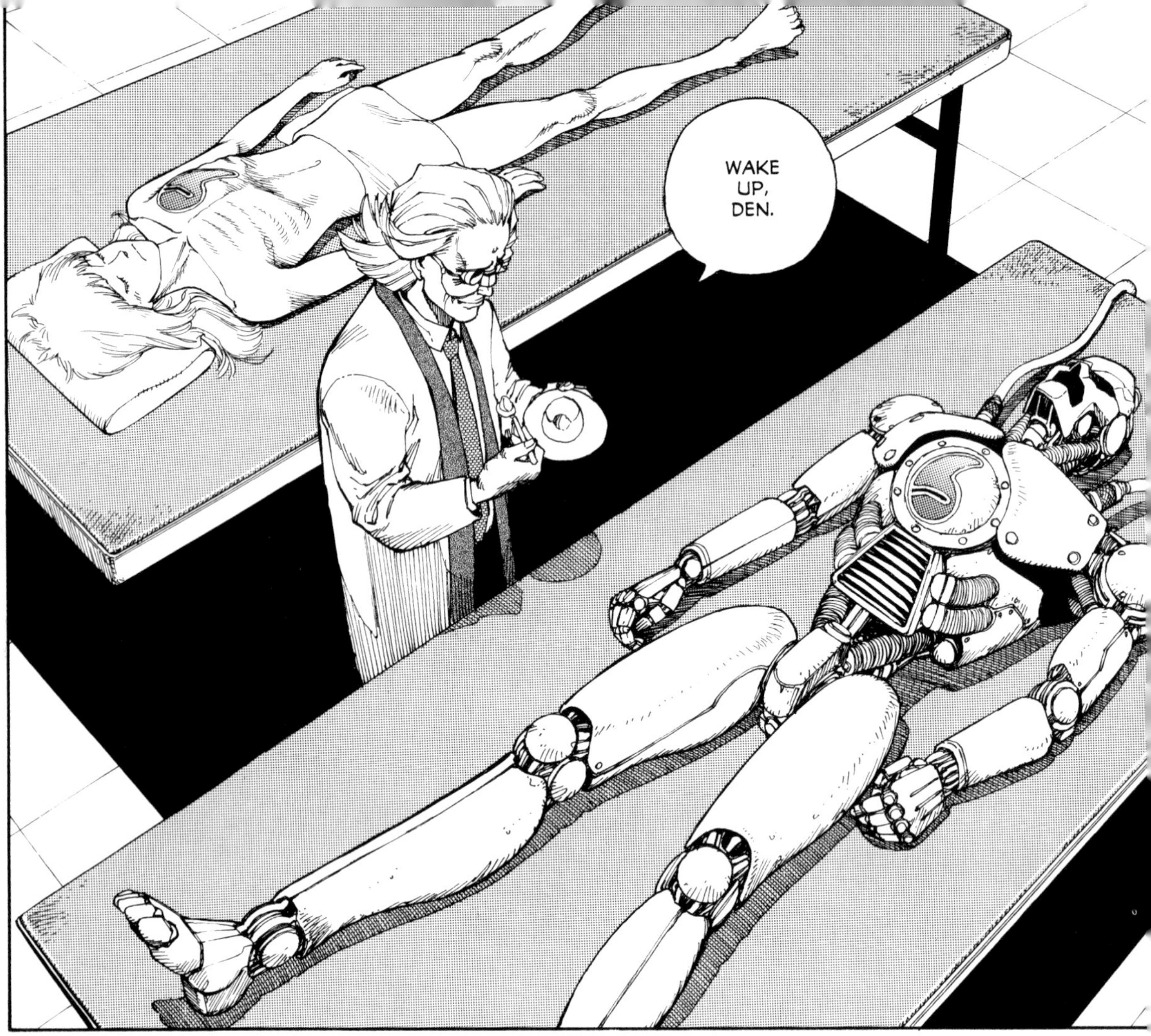
WAKE UP, DEN.

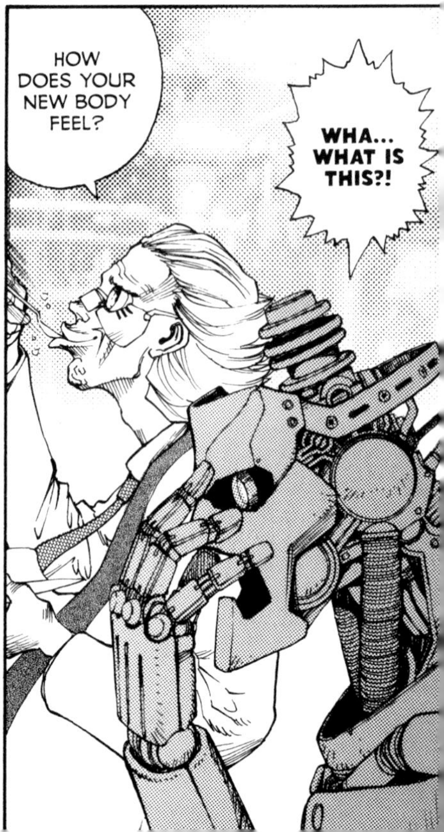
WHA... WHAT IS THIS?!
HOW DOES YOUR NEW BODY FEEL?

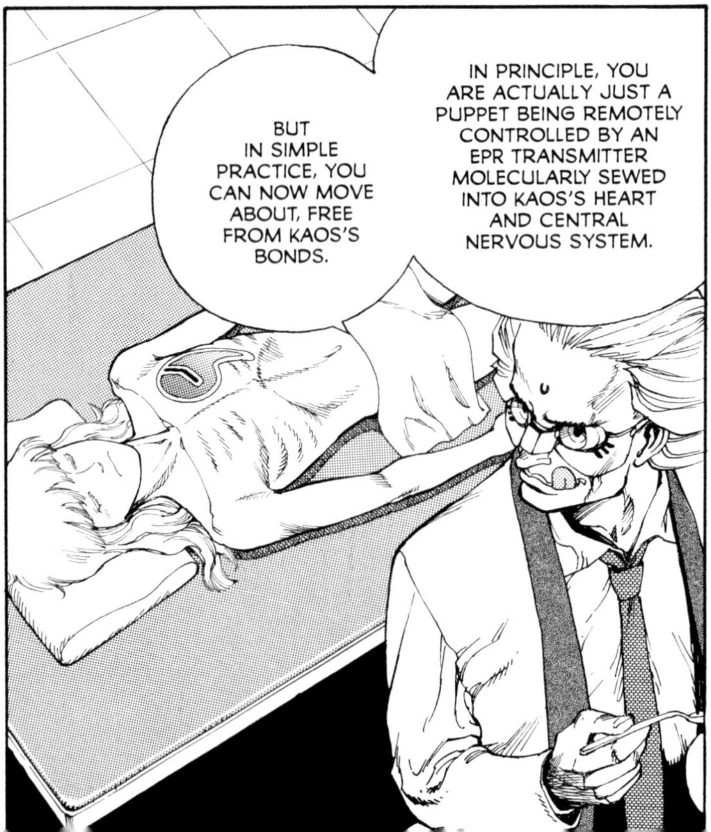
IN PRINCIPLE, YOU ARE ACTUALLY JUST A PUPPET BEING REMOTELY CONTROLLED BY AN EPR TRANSMITTER MOLECULARLY SEWED INTO KAOS'S HEART AND CENTRAL NERVOUS SYSTEM.
BUT IN SIMPLE PRACTICE, YOU CAN NOW MOVE ABOUT, FREE FROM KAOS'S BONDS.

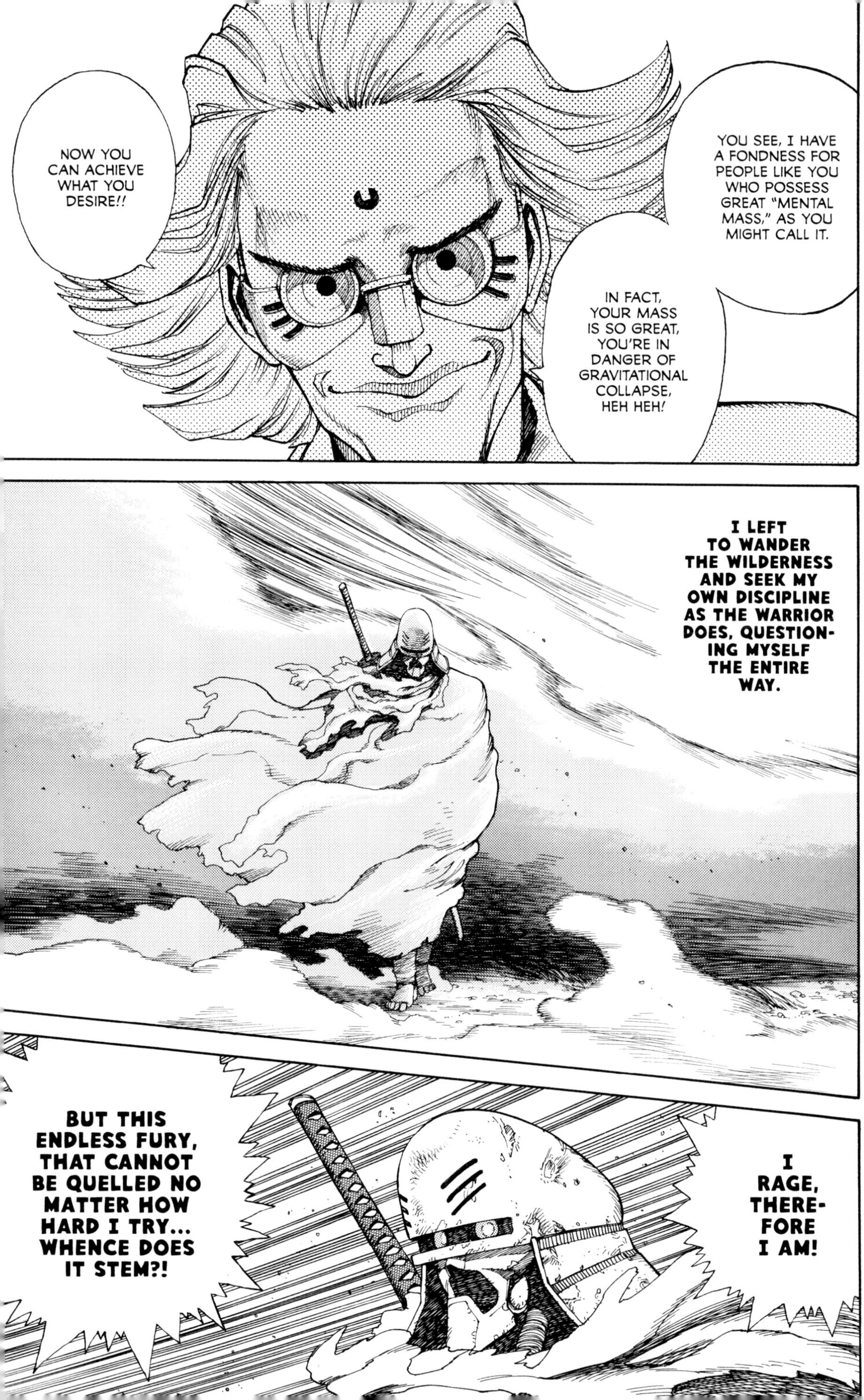
YOU SEE, I HAVE A FONDNESS FOR PEOPLE LIKE YOU WHO POSSESS GREAT "MENTAL MASS," AS YOU MIGHT CALL IT.
IN FACT, YOUR MASS IS SO GREAT, YOU'RE IN DANGER OF GRAVITATIONAL COLLAPSE, HEH HEH!
NOW YOU CAN ACHIEVE WHAT YOU DESIRE!!
I LEFT TO WANDER THE WILDERNESS AND SEEK MY OWN DISCIPLINE AS THE WARRIOR DOES, QUESTIONING MYSELF THE ENTIRE WAY.
BUT THIS ENDLESS FURY, THAT CANNOT BE QUELLED NO MATTER HOW HARD I TRY... WHENCE DOES IT STEM?!
I RAGE, THEREFORE I AM!

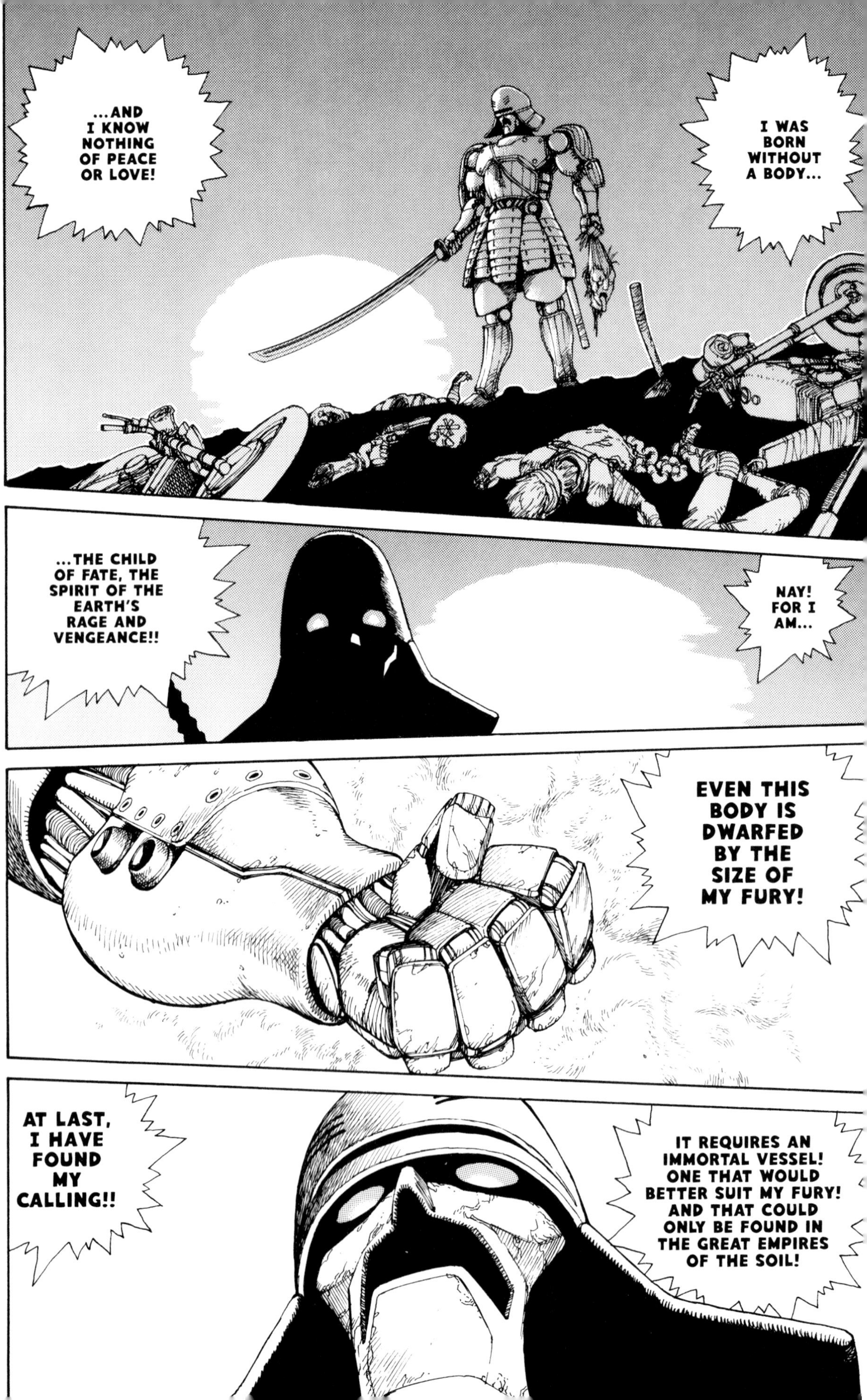
I WAS BORN WITHOUT A BODY...
...AND I KNOW NOTHING OF PEACE OR LOVE!
NAY! FOR I AM...
...THE CHILD OF FATE, THE SPIRIT OF THE EARTH'S RAGE AND VENGEANCE!!
EVEN THIS BODY IS DWARFED BY THE SIZE OF MY FURY!
IT REQUIRES AN IMMORTAL VESSEL! ONE THAT WOULD BETTER SUIT MY FURY! AND THAT COULD ONLY BE FOUND IN THE GREAT EMPIRES OF THE SOIL!
AT LAST, I HAVE FOUND MY CALLING!!

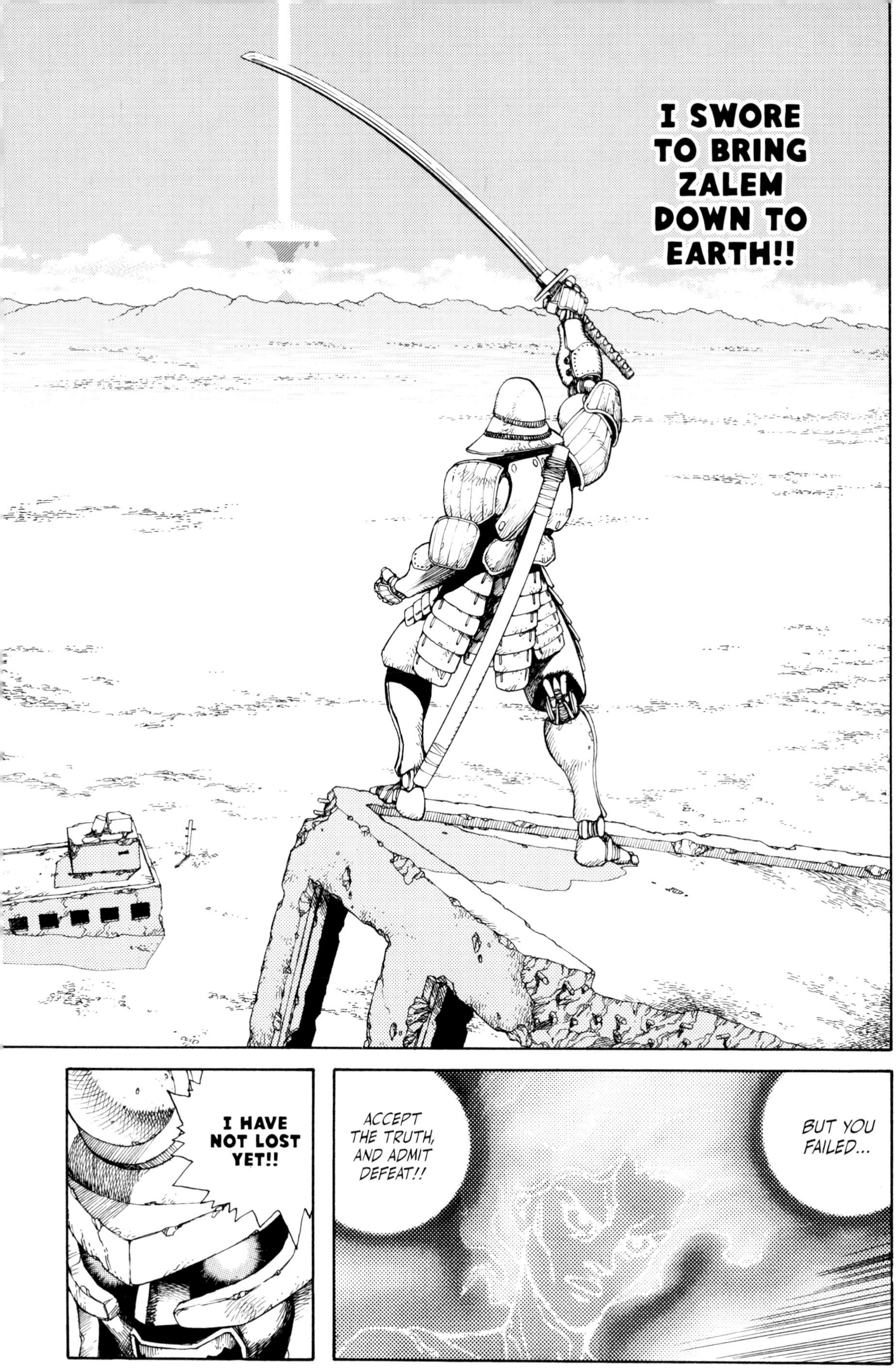
I SWORE TO BRING ZALEM DOWN TO EARTH!!
BUT YOU FAILED...
ACCEPT THE TRUTH, AND ADMIT DEFEAT!!
I HAVE NOT LOST YET!!

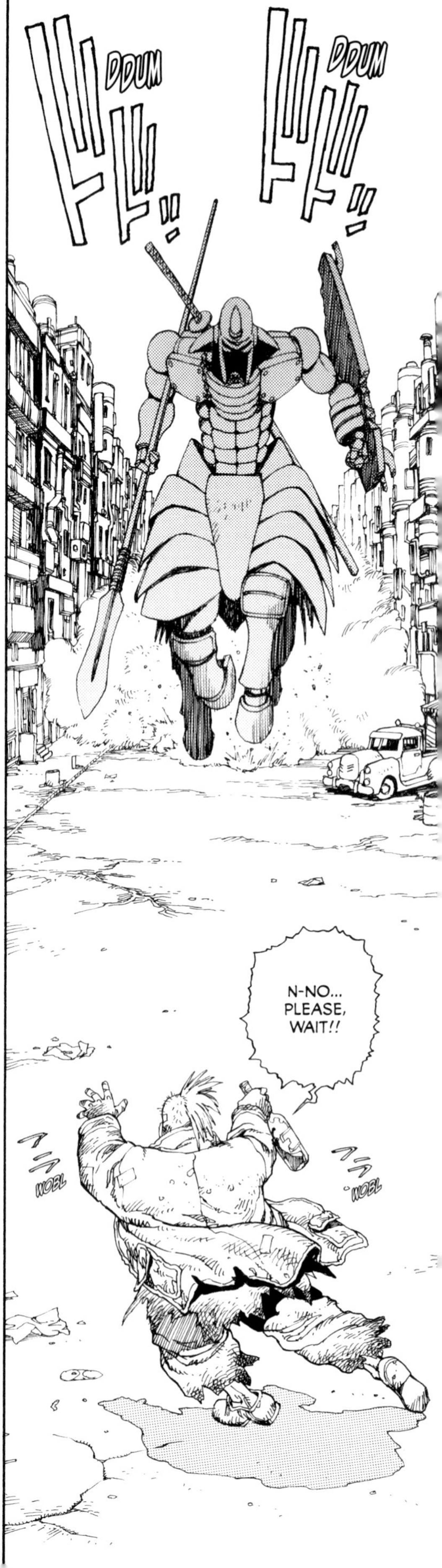
DDUM
DDUM
N-NO... PLEASE, WAIT!!
WOBL
WOBL
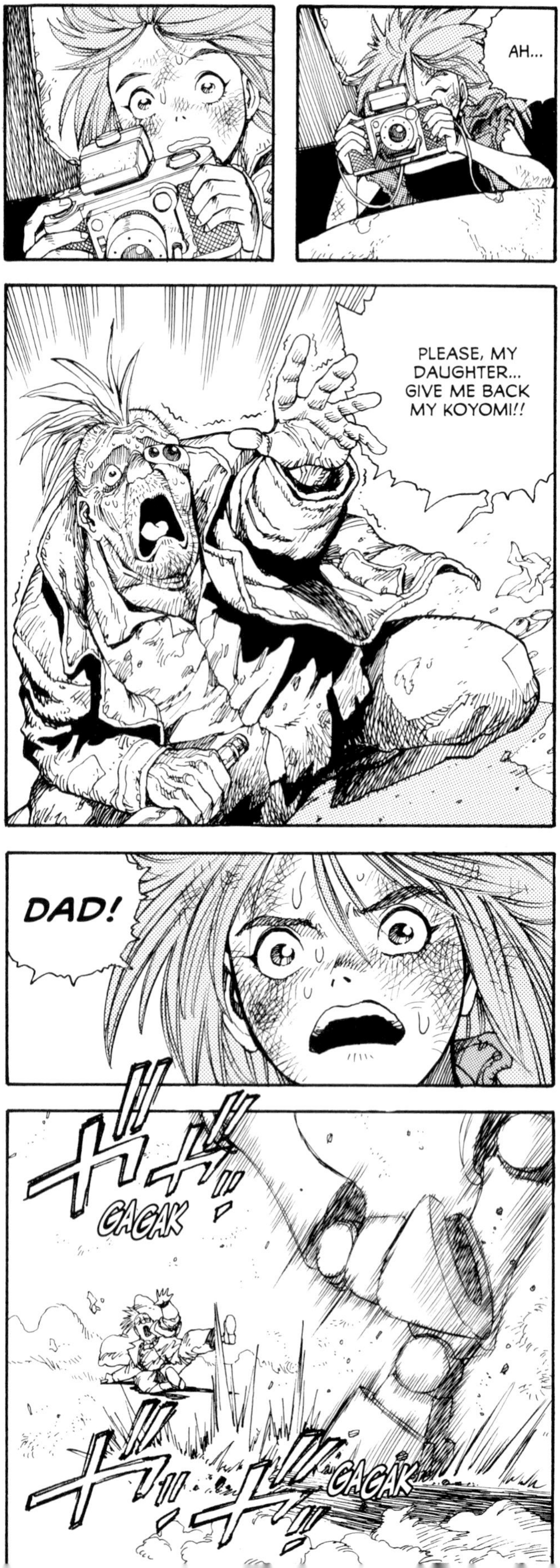
AH...
PLEASE, MY DAUGHTER... GIVE ME BACK MY KOYOMI!!
DAD!
GACAK
GACAK

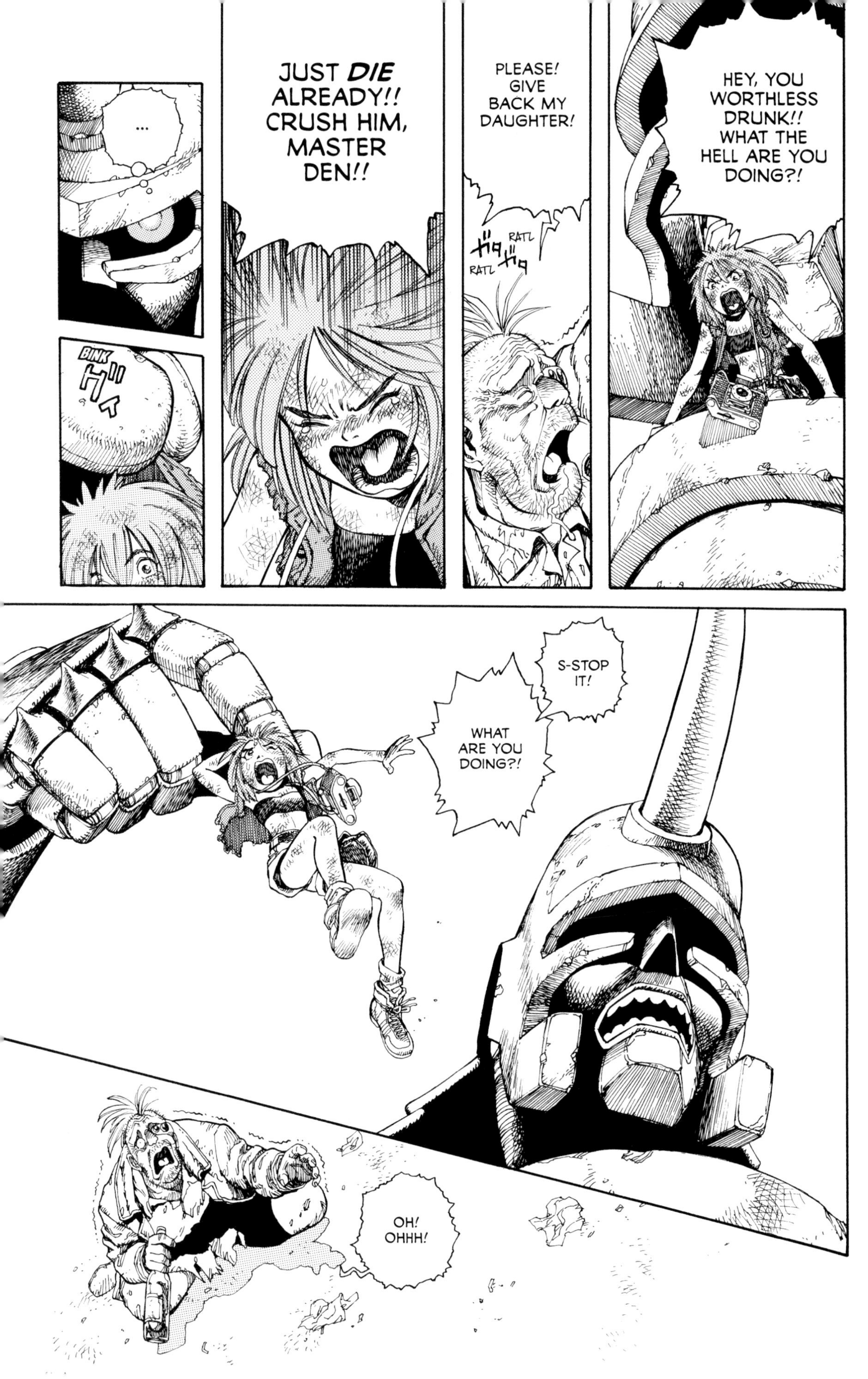
HEY, YOU WORTHLESS DRUNK!! WHAT THE HELL ARE YOU DOING?!
PLEASE! GIVE BACK MY DAUGHTER!
RATL RATL
JUST DIE ALREADY!! CRUSH HIM, MASTER DEN!!
...
BINK
S-STOP IT!
WHAT ARE YOU DOING?!
OH! OHHH!

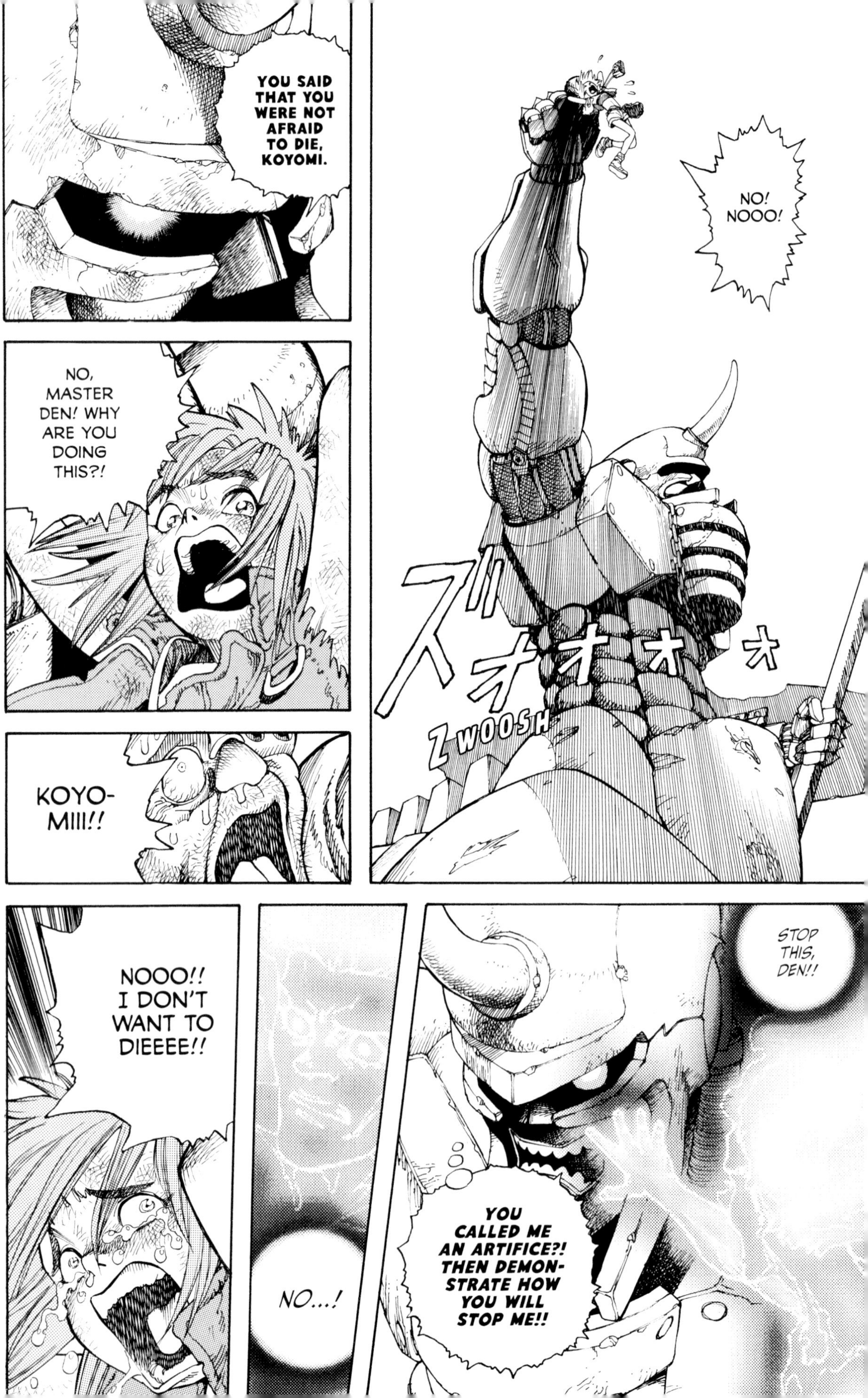
NO! NOOO!
ズオオオオ
ZWOOSH
YOU SAID THAT YOU WERE NOT AFRAID TO DIE, KOYOMI.
NO, MASTER DEN! WHY ARE YOU DOING THIS?!
KOYO-MIII!!
STOP THIS, DEN!!
YOU CALLED ME AN ARTIFICE?! THEN DEMON-STRATE HOW YOU WILL STOP ME!!
NO...!
NOOO!! I DON'T WANT TO DIEEEE!!

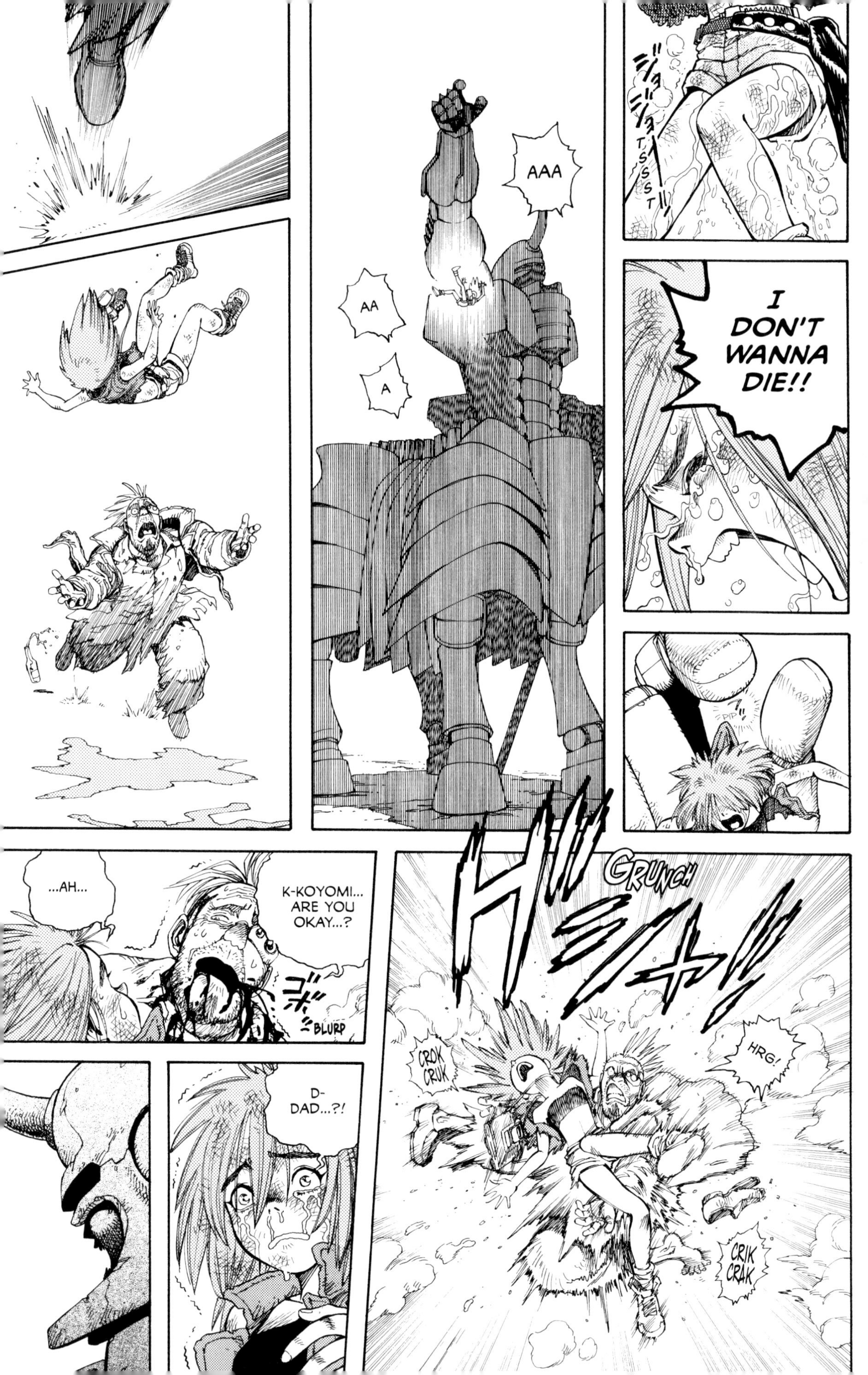
TSSST
I DON'T WANNA DIE!!
PIP
AAA
AA
A
GRUNCH
HRG!
CROK CRUK
CRIK CRAK
K-KOYOMI... ARE YOU OKAY...?
...AH...
BLURP
D-DAD...?!

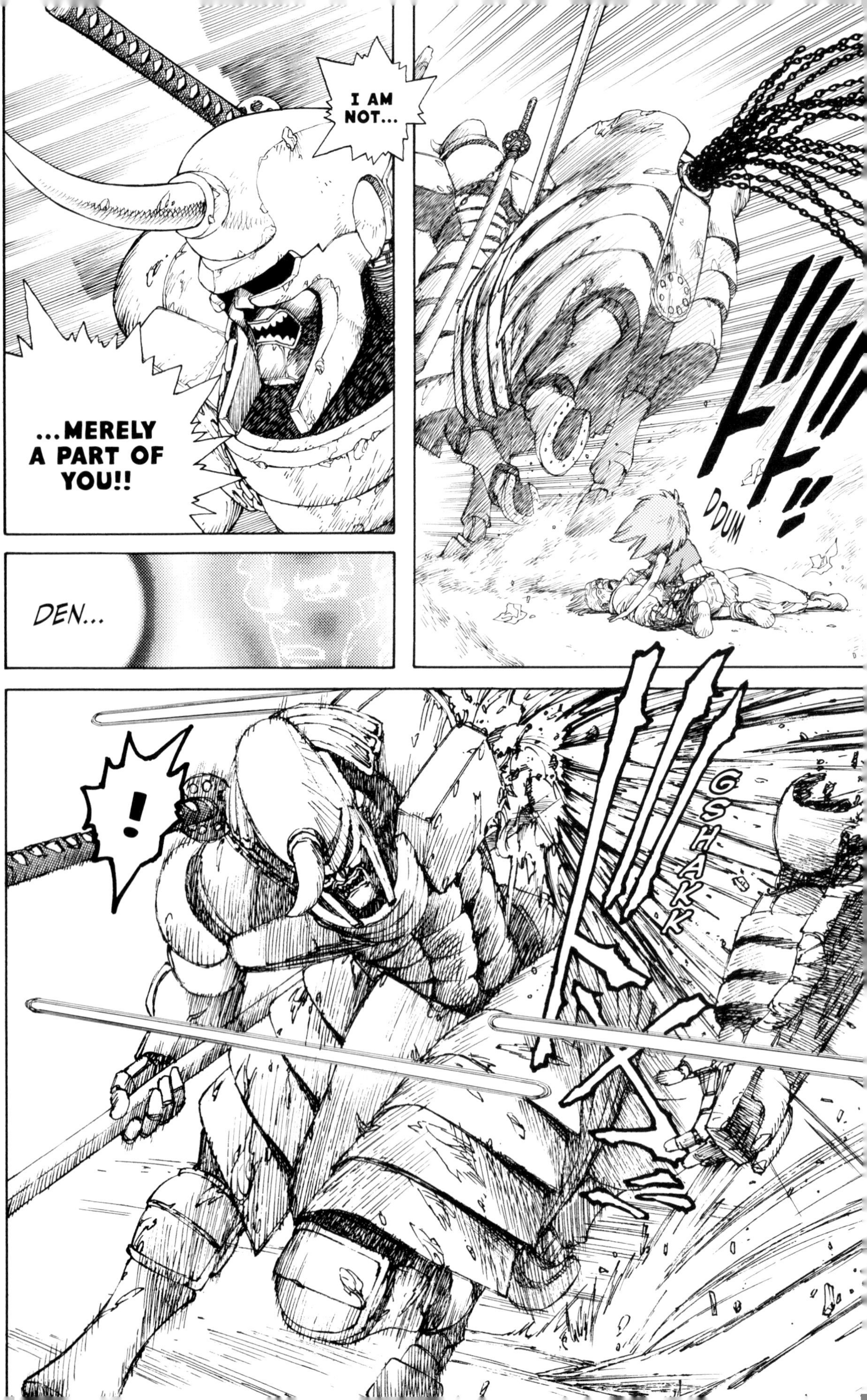
DDUM
I AM NOT...
...MERELY A PART OF YOU!!
DEN...
GSHAKK
!

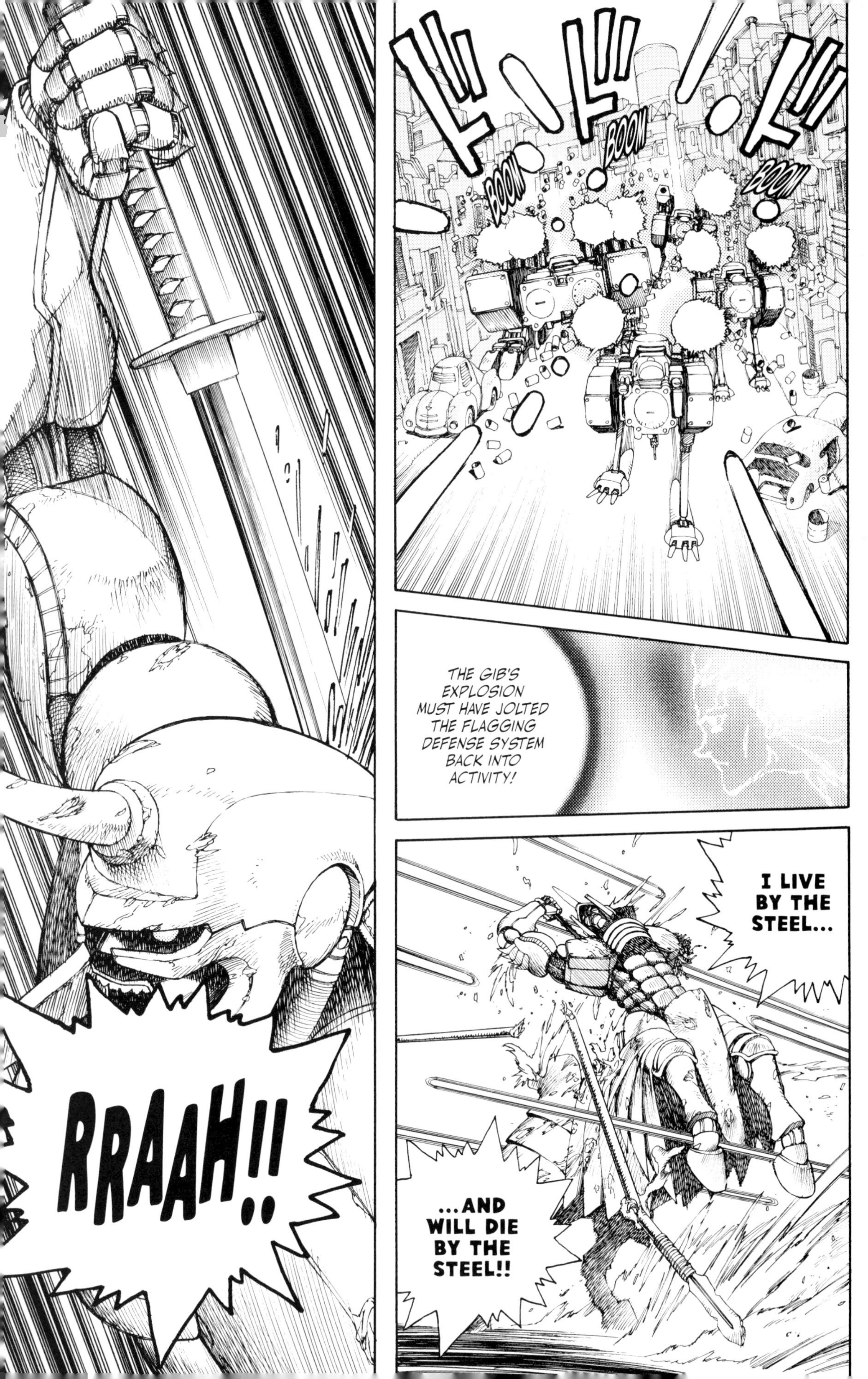
ド
BOOM
ド
BOOM
ド
BOOM
THE GIB'S EXPLOSION MUST HAVE JOLTED THE FLAGGING DEFENSE SYSTEM BACK INTO ACTIVITY!
I LIVE BY THE STEEL...
...AND WILL DIE BY THE STEEL!!
RRAAH!!

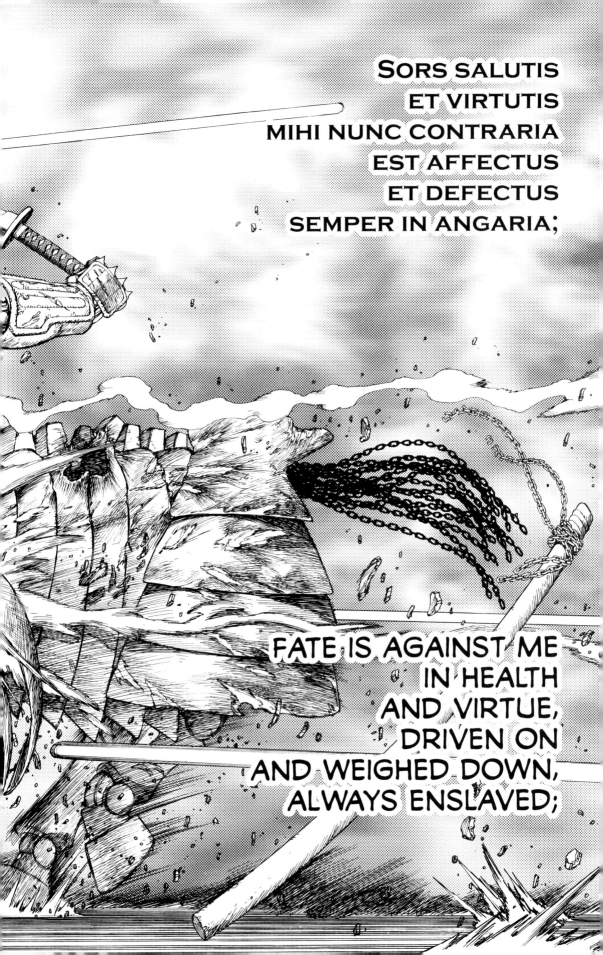

SORS SALUTIS
ET VIRTUTIS
MIHI NUNC CONTRARIA
EST AFFECTUS
ET DEFECTUS
SEMPER IN ANGARIA;

FATE IS AGAINST ME
IN HEALTH
AND VIRTUE,
DRIVEN ON
AND WEIGHED DOWN,
ALWAYS ENSLAVED;

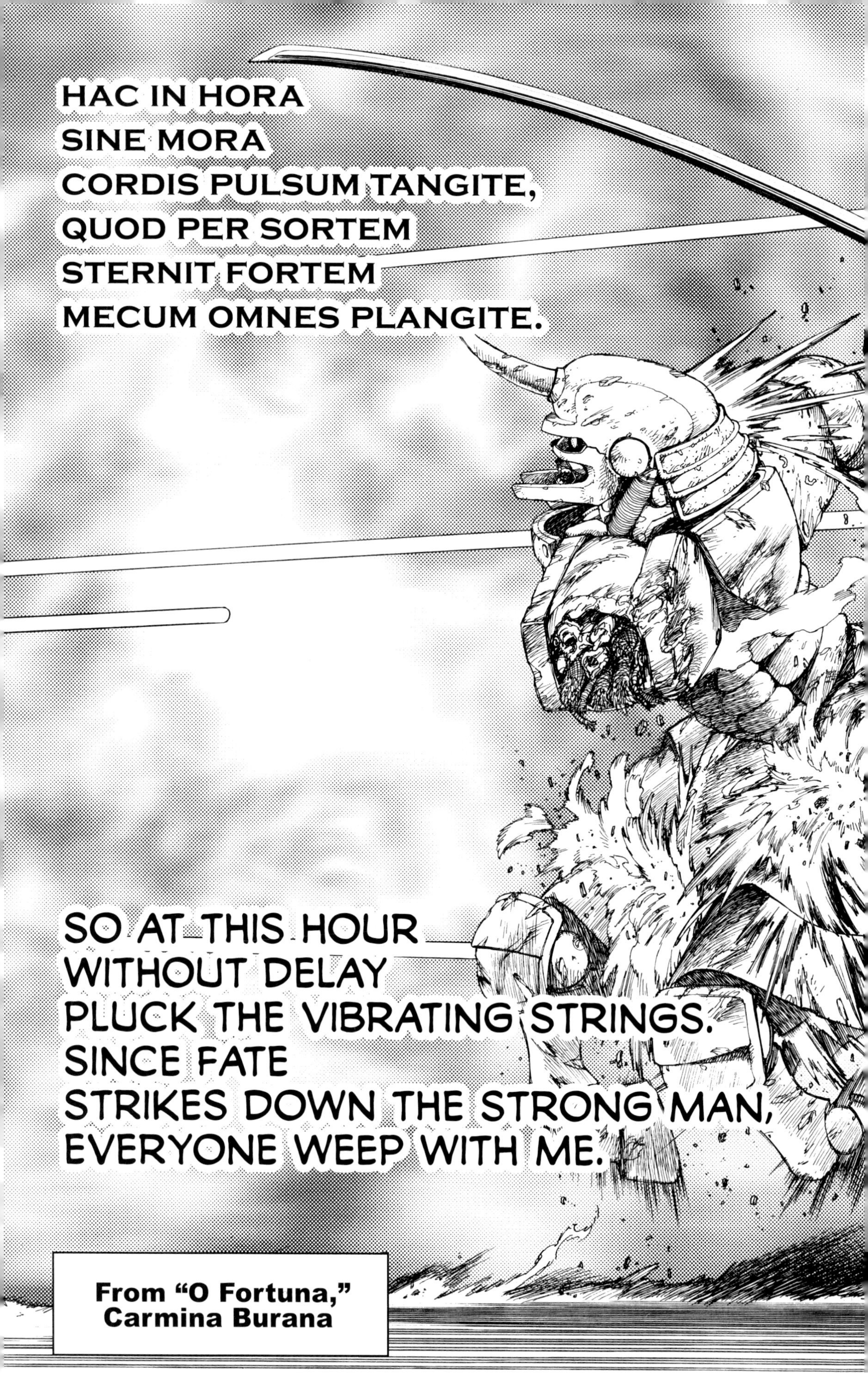
HAC IN HORA
SINE MORA
CORDIS PULSUM TANGITE,
QUOD PER SORTEM
STERNIT FORTEM
MECUM OMNES PLANGITE.
SO AT THIS HOUR
WITHOUT DELAY
PLUCK THE VIBRATING STRINGS.
SINCE FATE
STRIKES DOWN THE STRONG MAN,
EVERYONE WEEP WITH ME.
From "O Fortuna,"
Carmina Burana

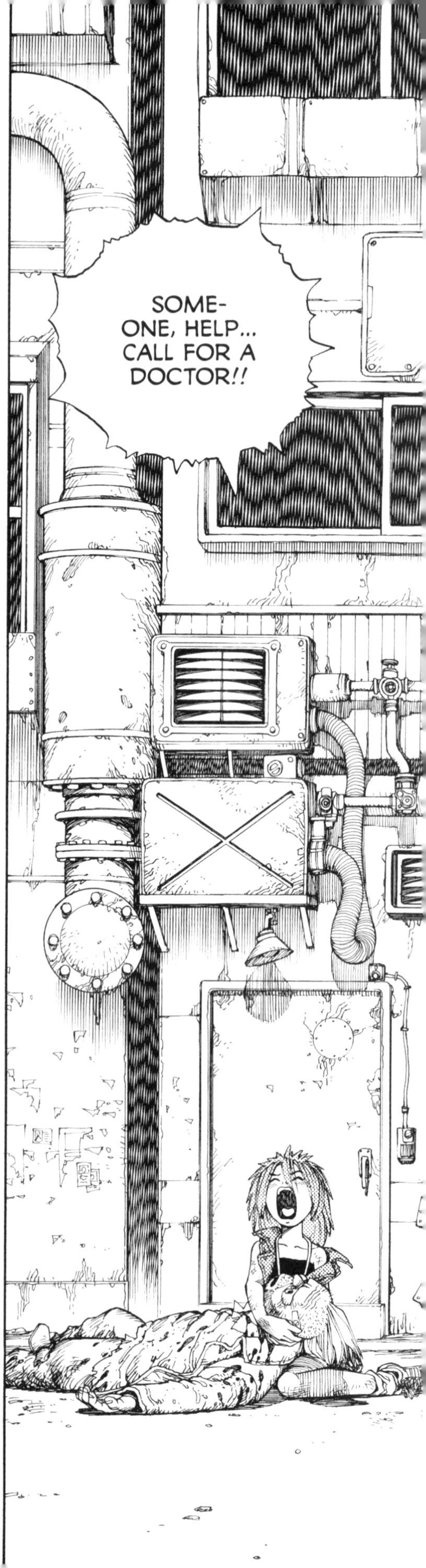
SOME-ONE, HELP... CALL FOR A DOCTOR!!

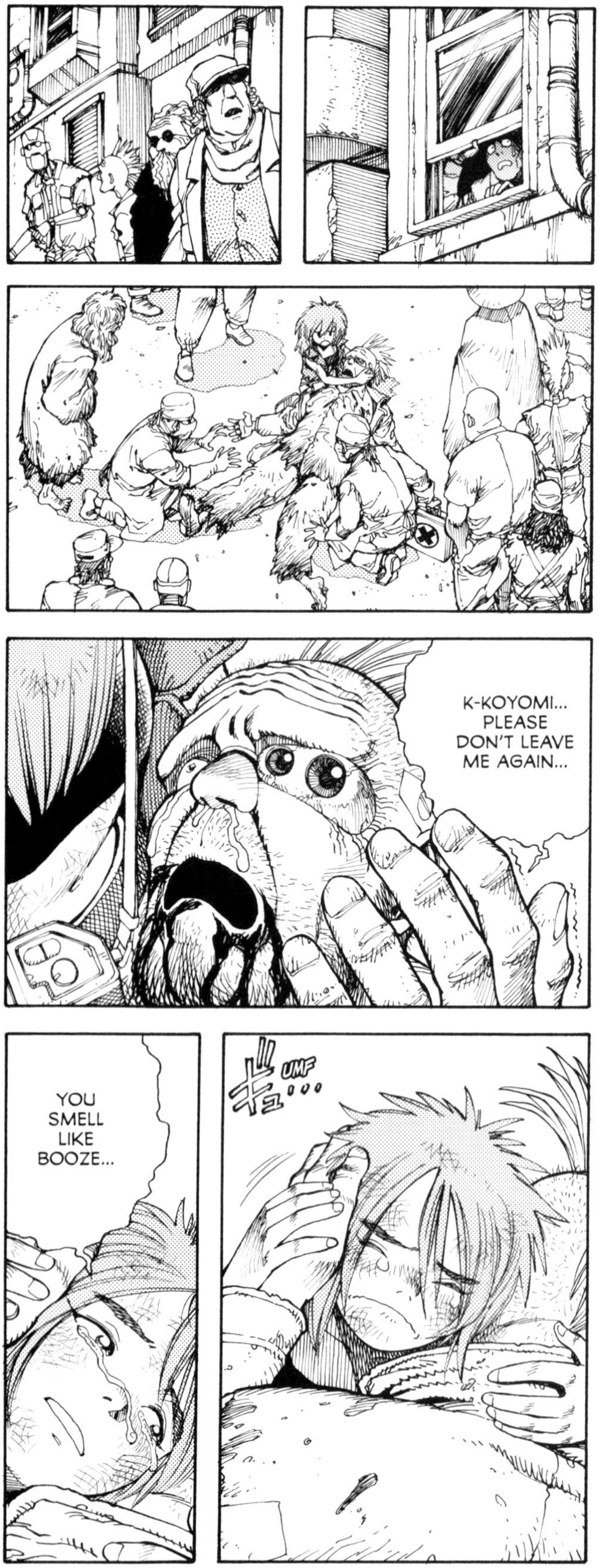
K-KOYOMI... PLEASE DON'T LEAVE ME AGAIN...
UMF
YOU SMELL LIKE BOOZE...

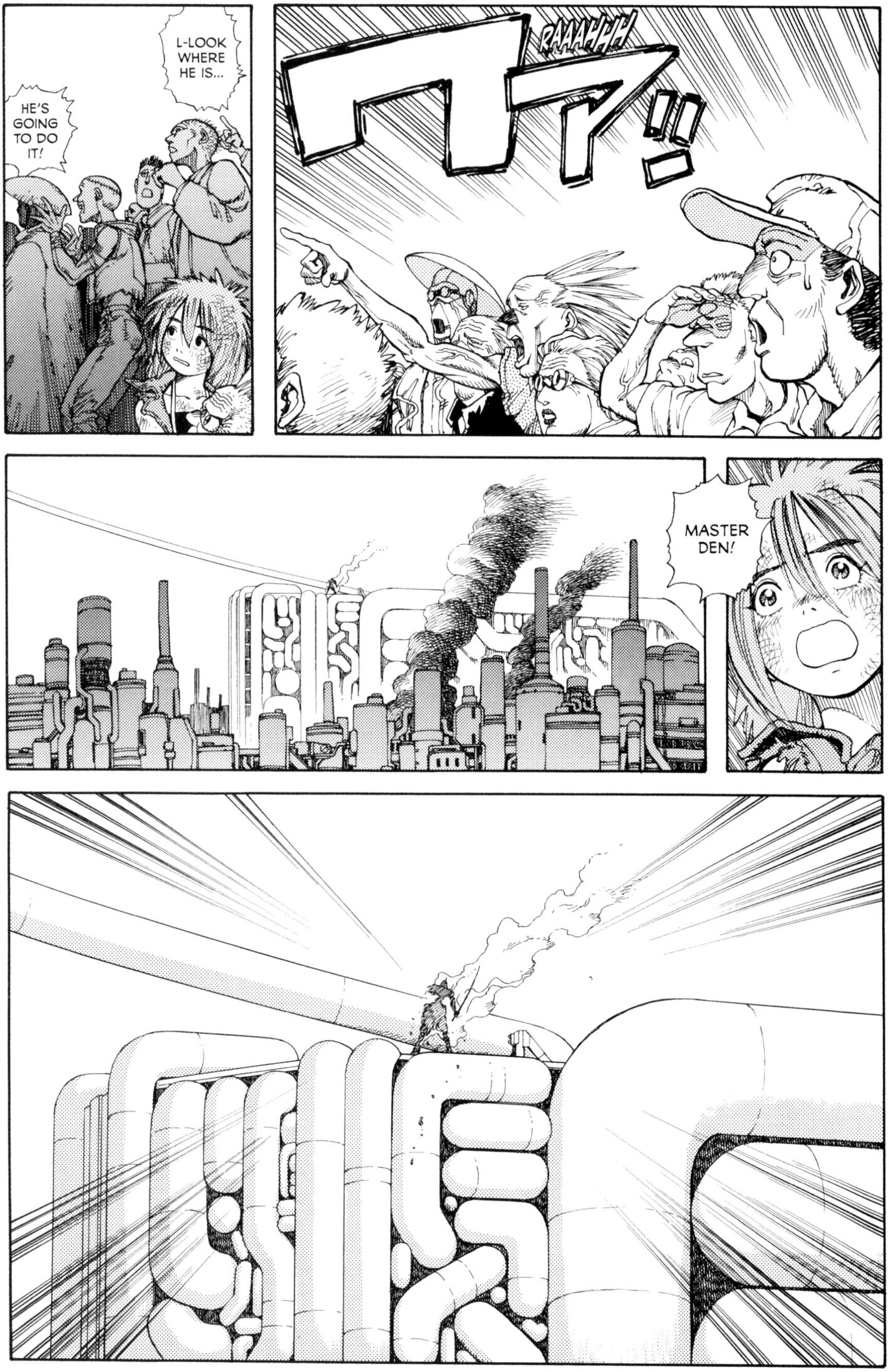
RAAAHHH
L-LOOK WHERE HE IS...
HE'S GOING TO DO IT!
MASTER DEN!

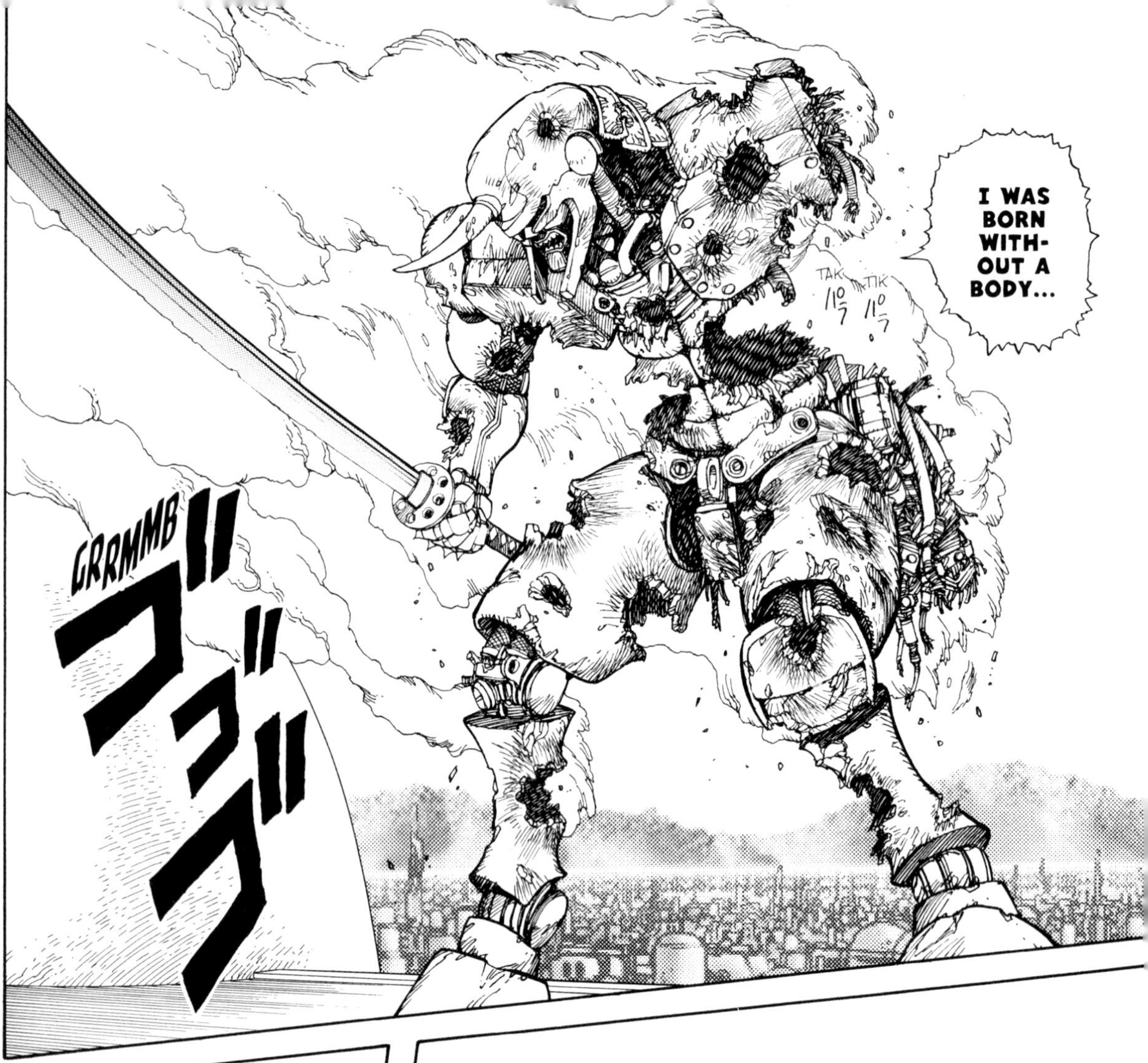
I WAS BORN WITH-OUT A BODY...
TAK TIK
GRRMMB
ゴゴゴ

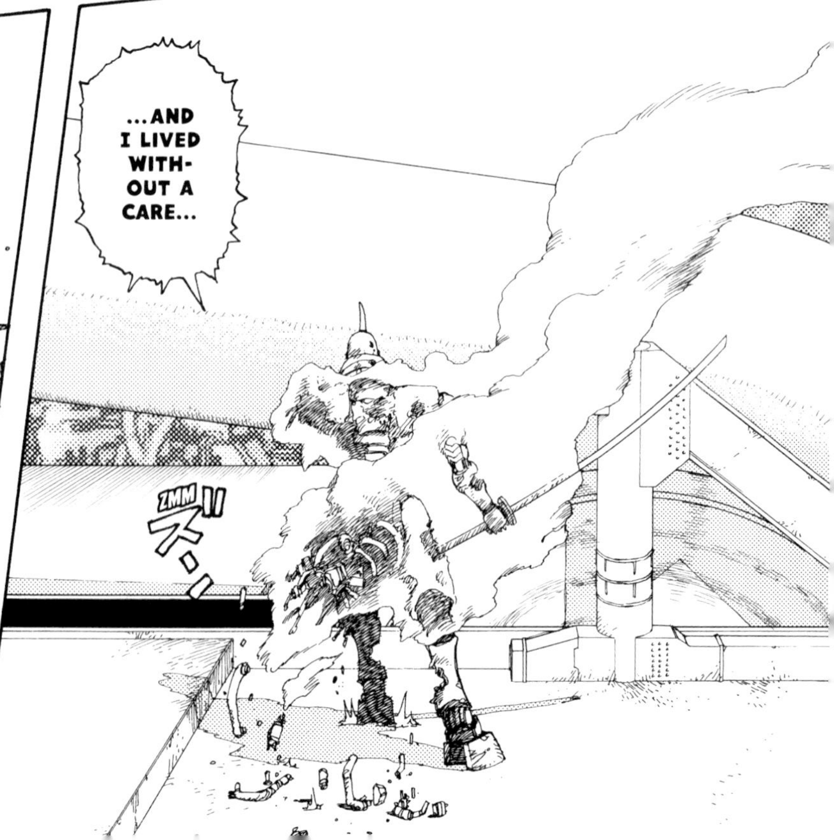
...AND I LIVED WITH-OUT A CARE...
ZMM
ズ

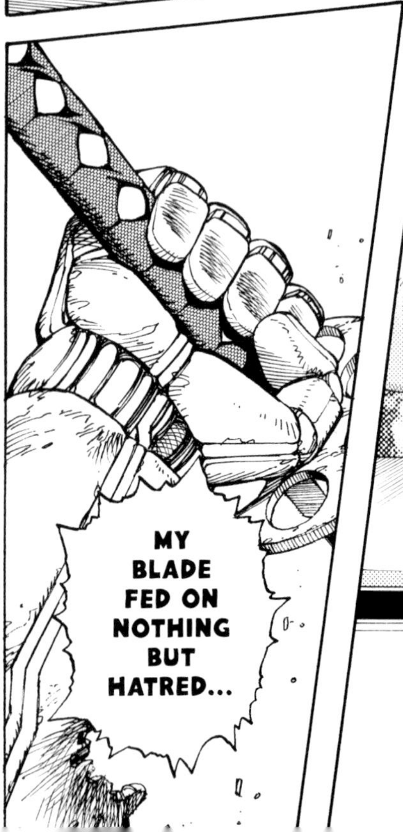
MY BLADE FED ON NOTHING BUT HATRED...

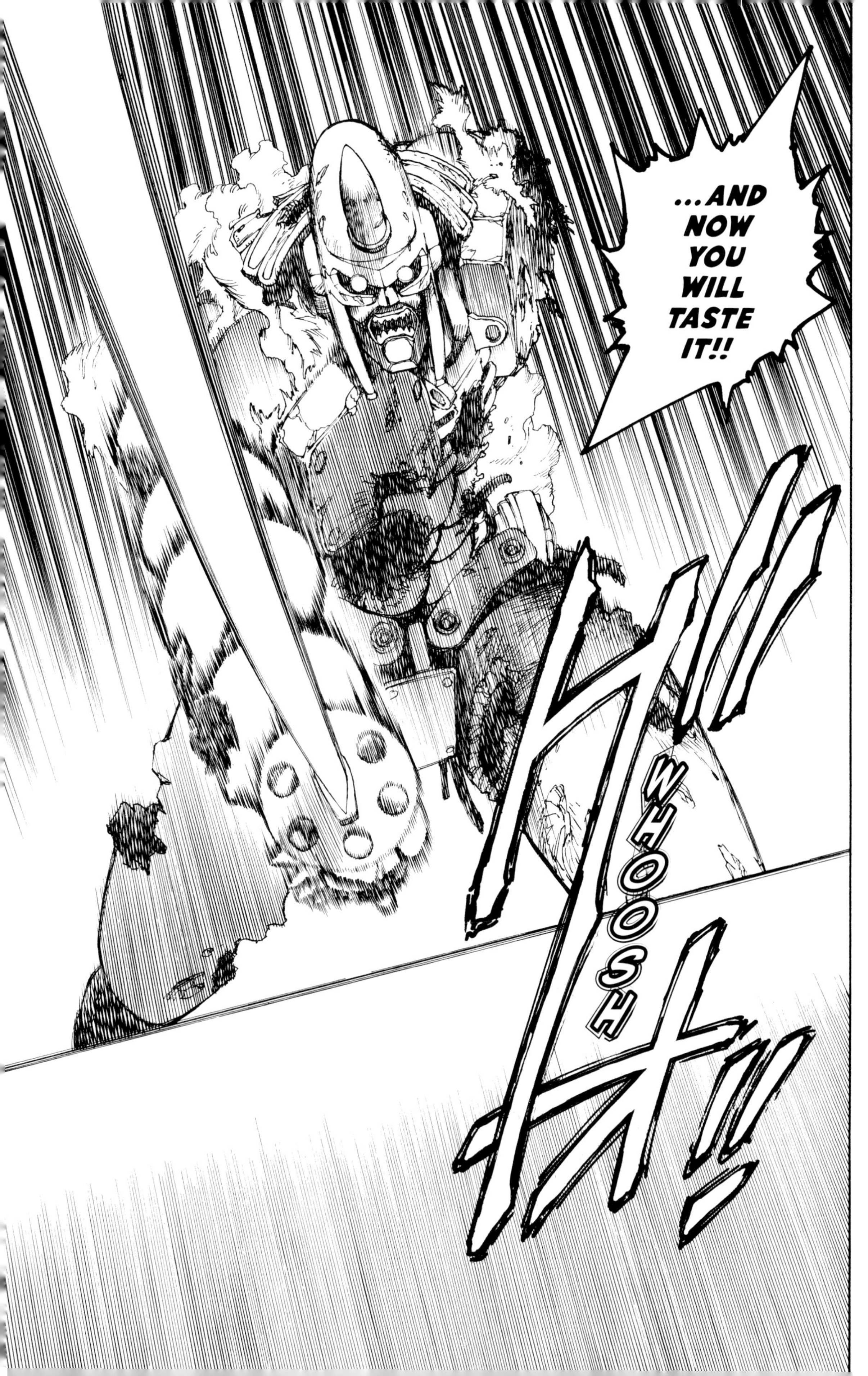
...AND NOW YOU WILL TASTE IT!!
WHOOSH

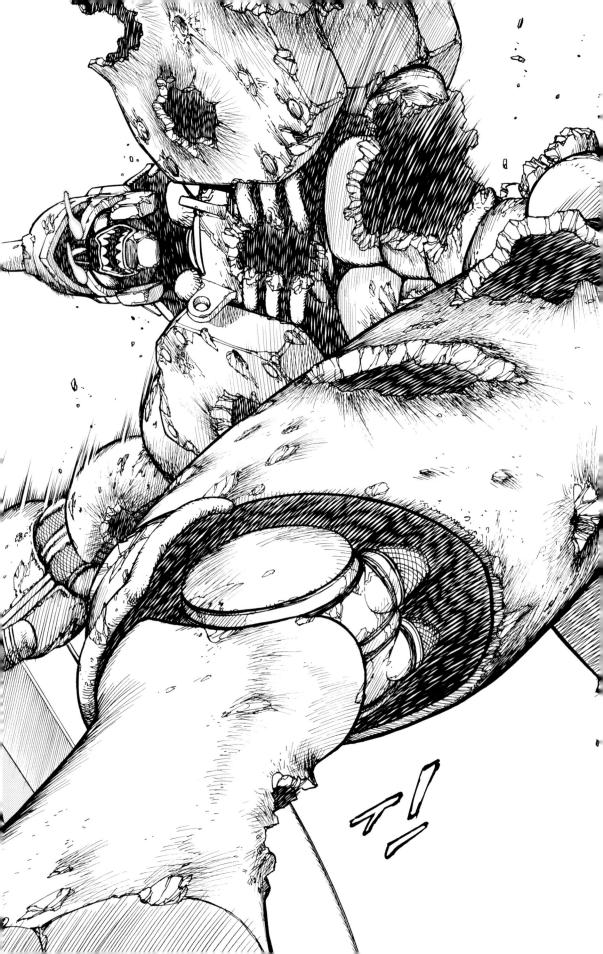

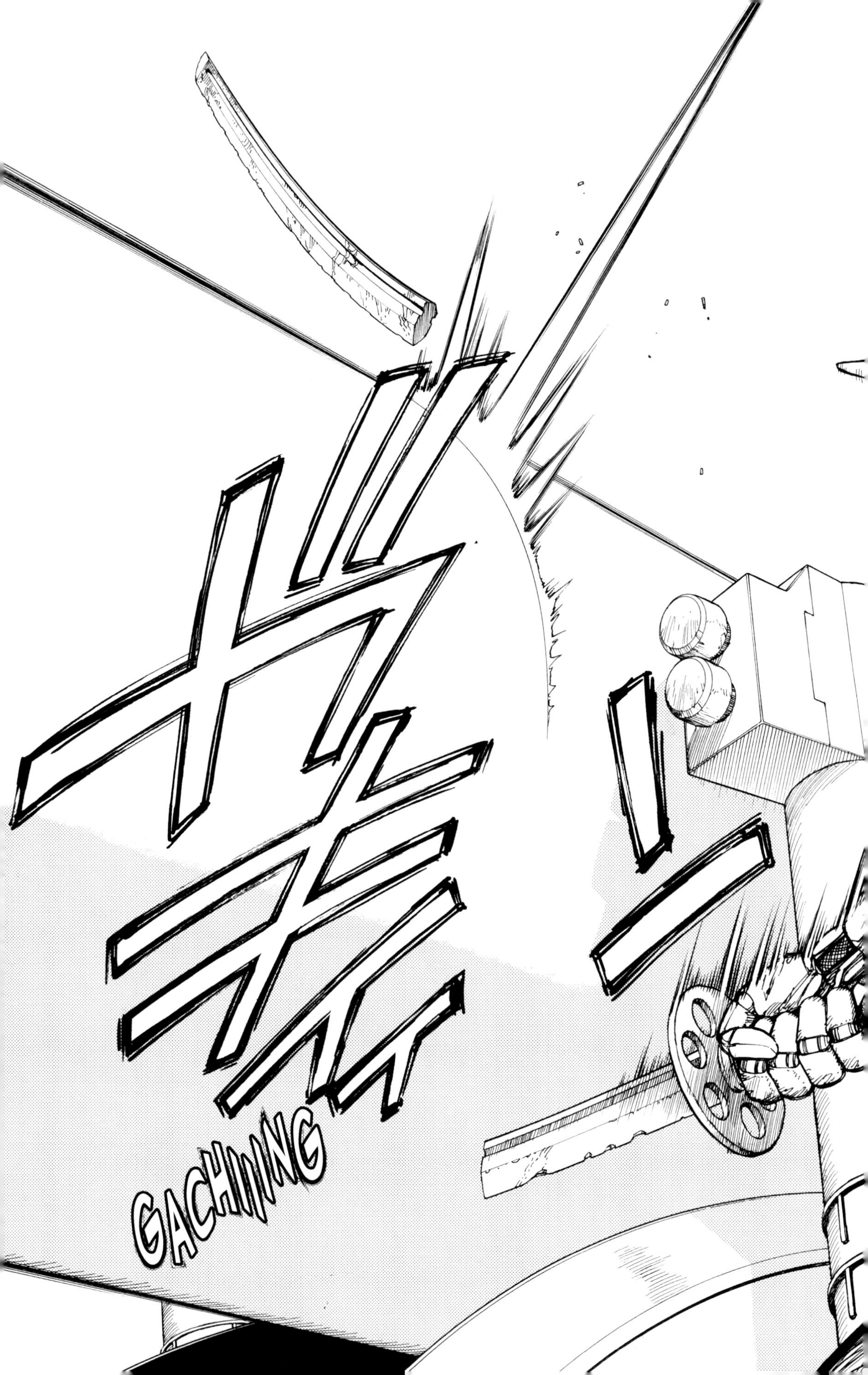
GACHIIING

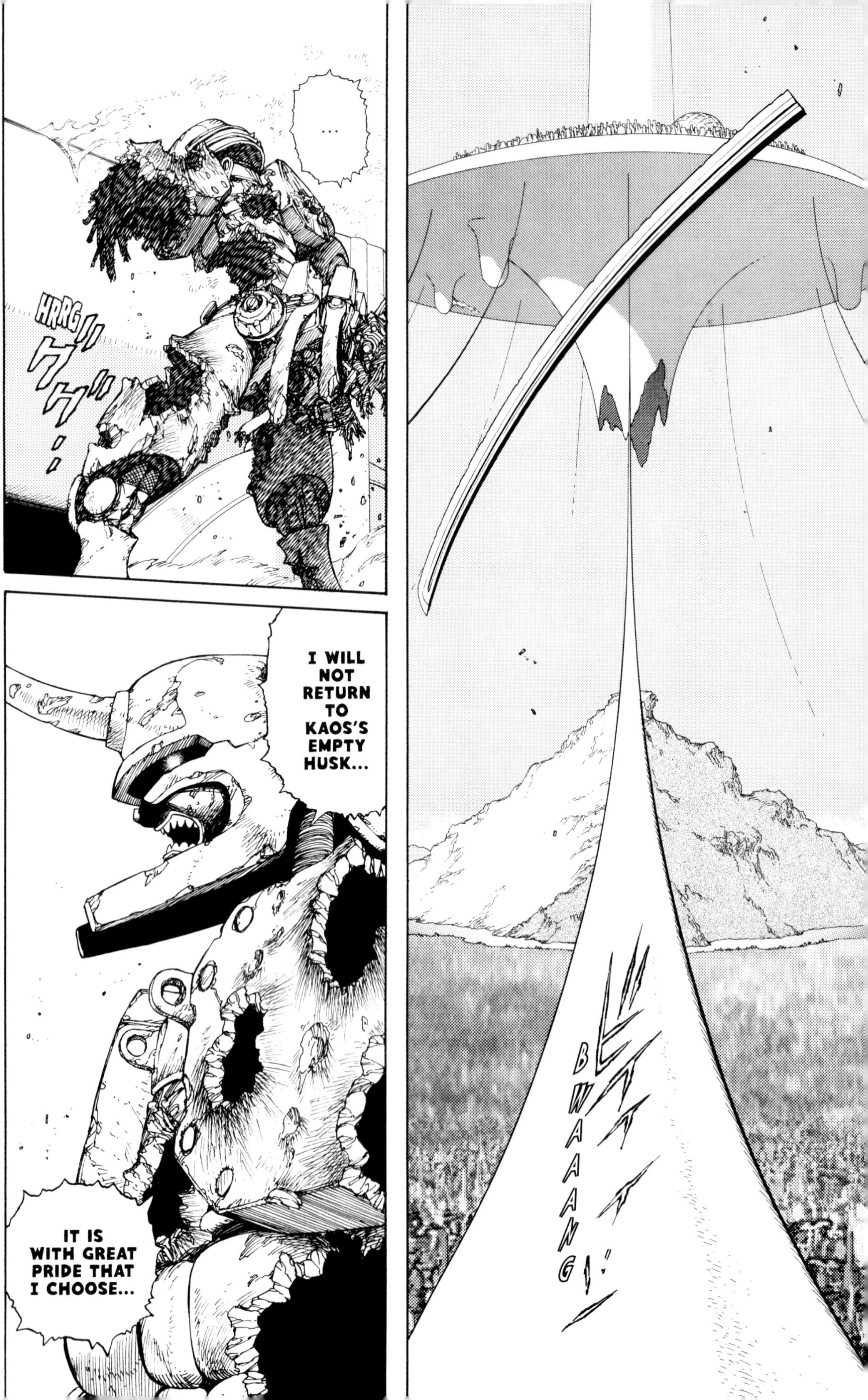
BWAAAANG!!
...
HRRG!!
I WILL NOT RETURN TO KAOS'S EMPTY HUSK...
IT IS WITH GREAT PRIDE THAT I CHOOSE...

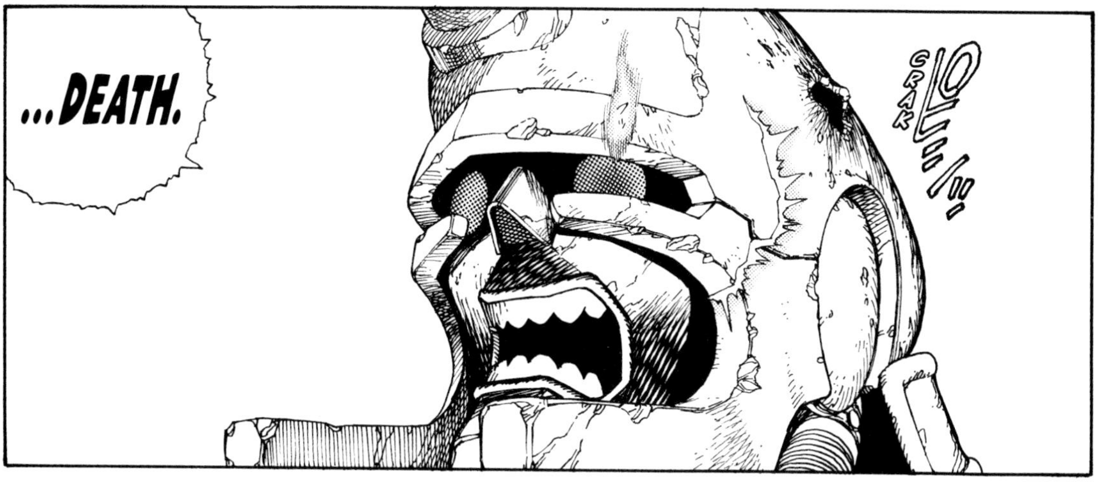
...DEATH.
GRAK
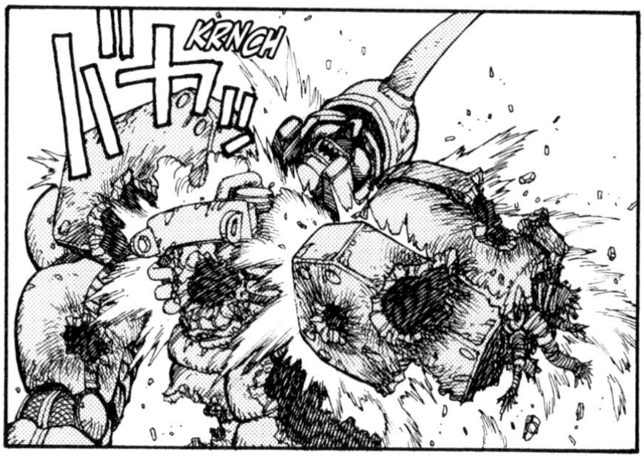
KRNCH
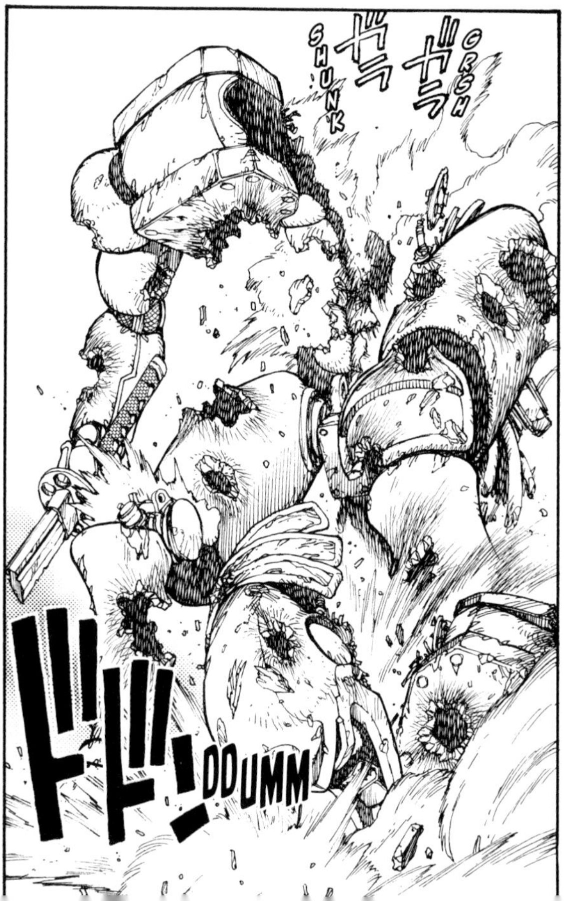
CRSH
SHUNK
DDUMM
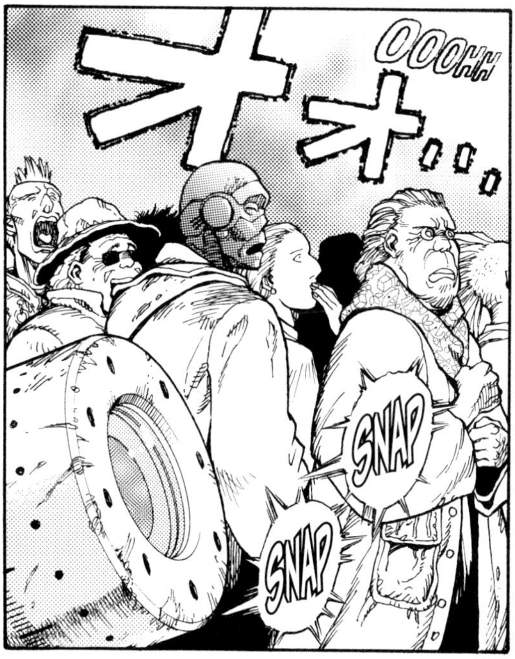
OOOHH
SNAP
SNAP
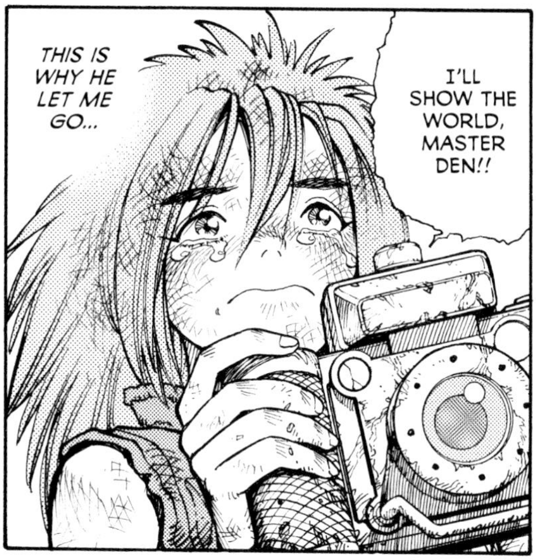
I'LL SHOW THE WORLD, MASTER DEN!!
THIS IS WHY HE LET ME GO...

FIGHT_051 Epitaph

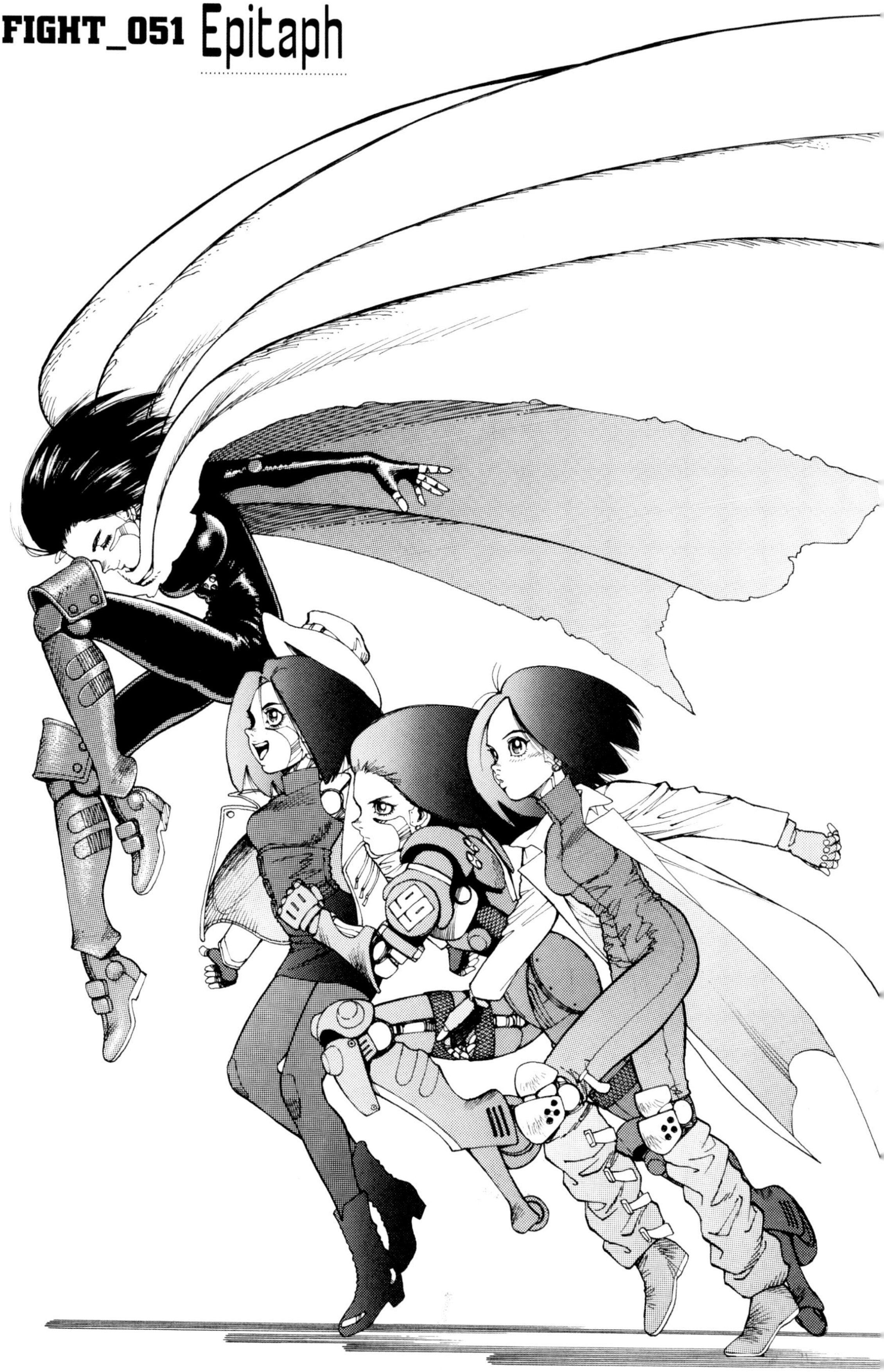

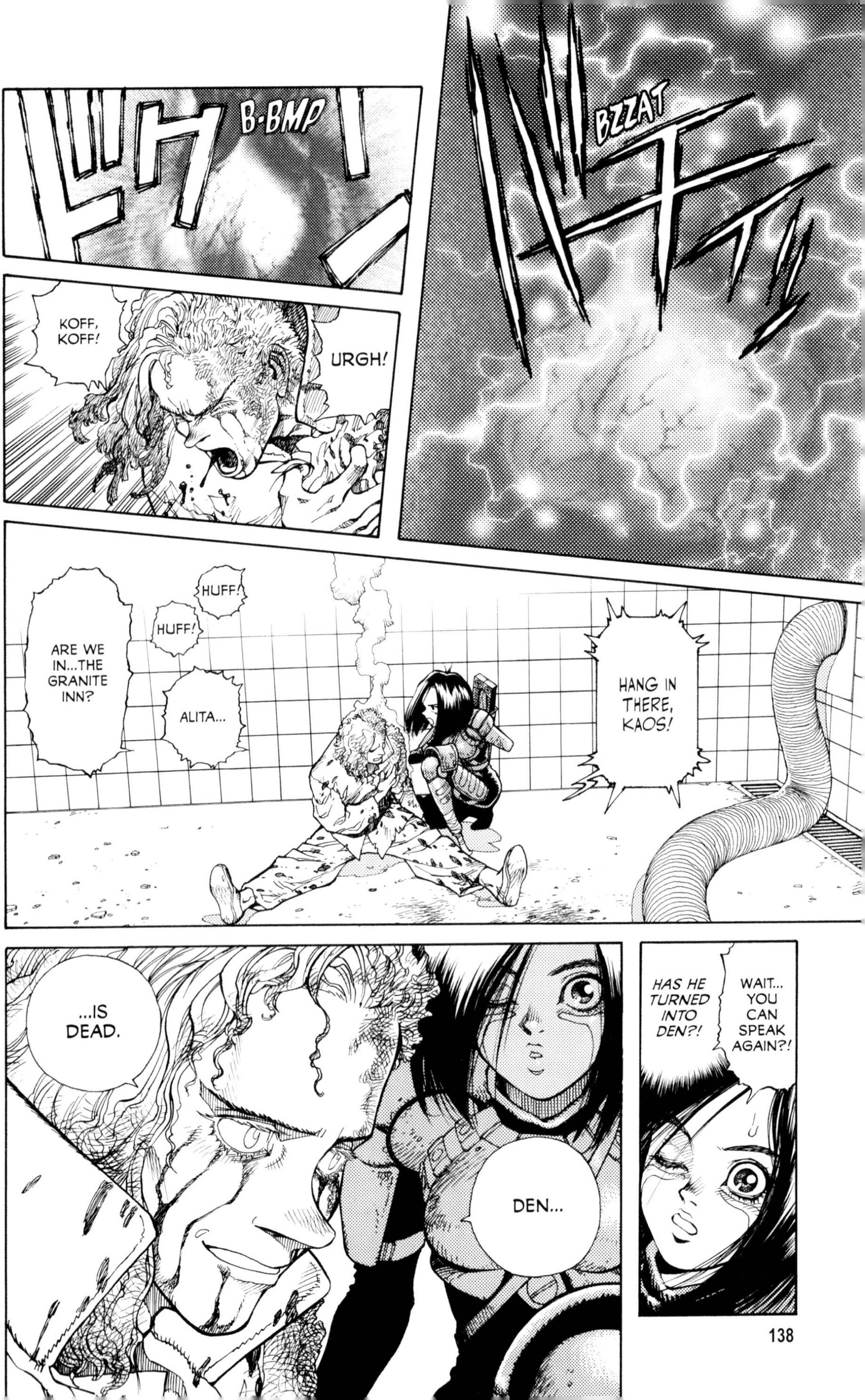
BZZAT
B-BMP
KOFF, KOFF!
URGH!
HANG IN THERE, KAOS!
HUFF!
HUFF!
ALITA...
ARE WE IN...THE GRANITE INN?
WAIT... YOU CAN SPEAK AGAIN?!
HAS HE TURNED INTO DEN?!
DEN...
...IS DEAD.

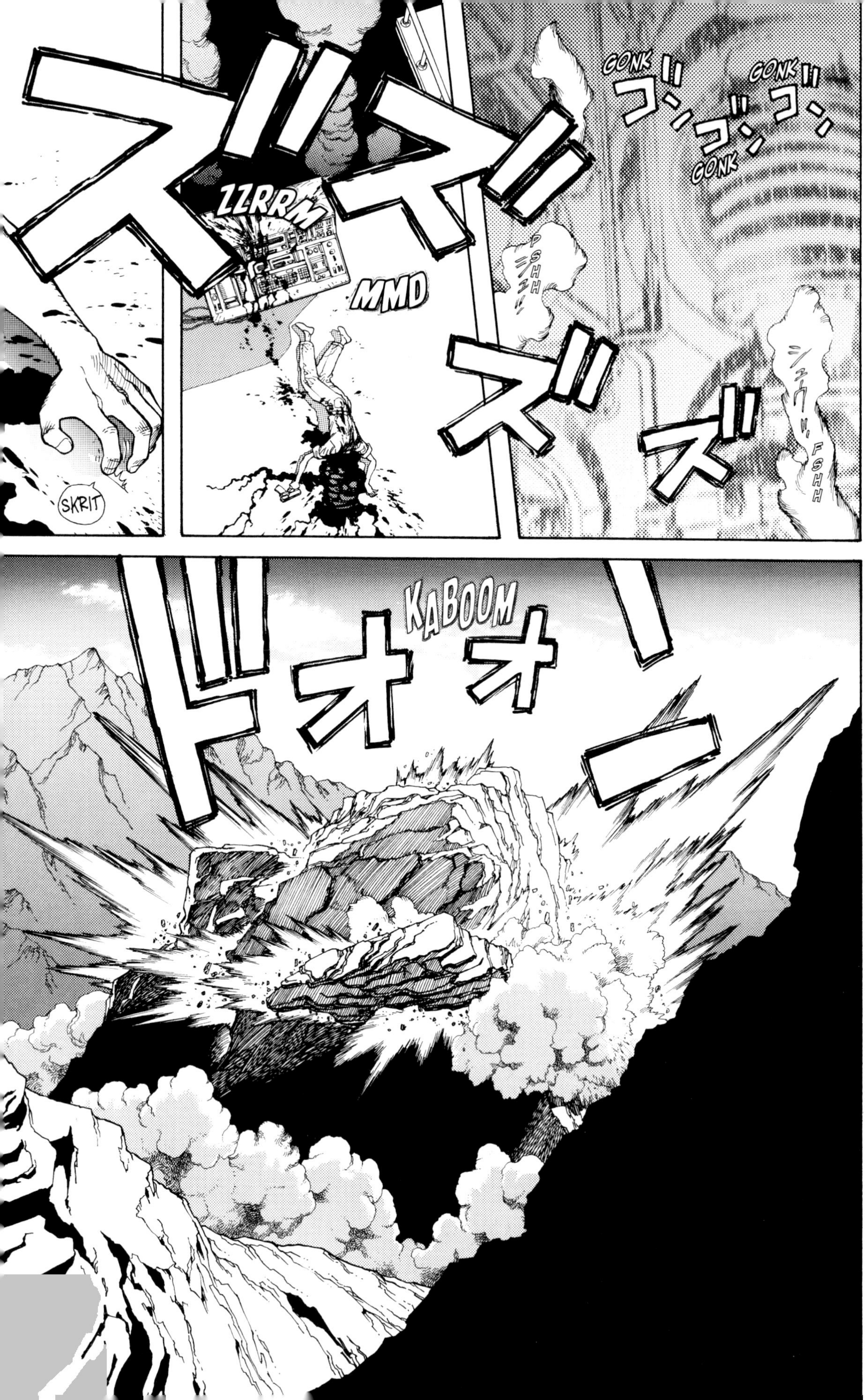

ゴン!! GONK!!
ゴン!! GONK!!
ゴン GONK
PSHH
FSHH
ズズ
ZZRRM
MMD
SKRIT
ドオオーン
KABOOM

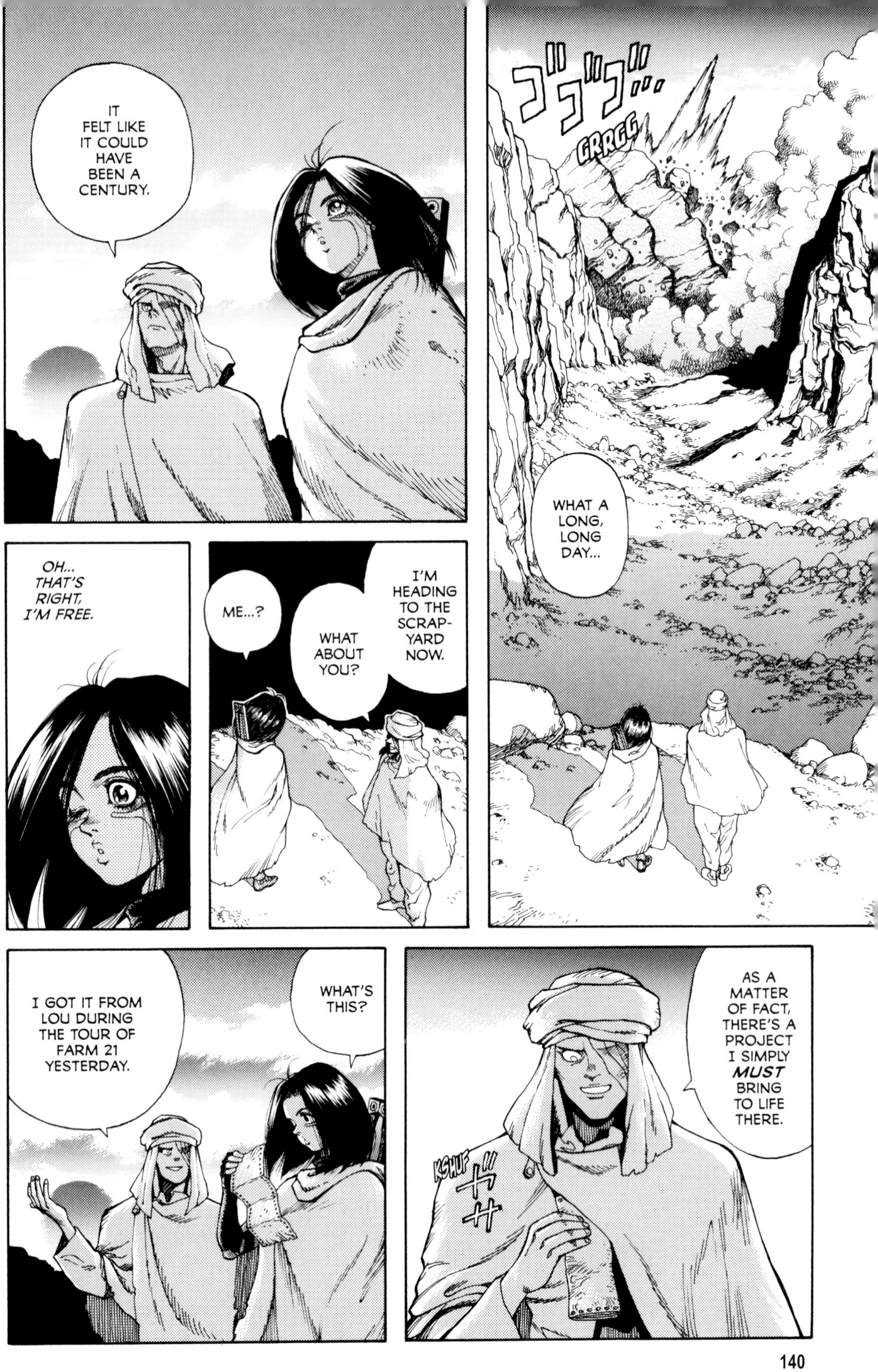
ゴゴゴ
GRRGG
WHAT A LONG, LONG DAY...
IT FELT LIKE IT COULD HAVE BEEN A CENTURY.
I'M HEADING TO THE SCRAP-YARD NOW.
WHAT ABOUT YOU?
ME...?
OH... THAT'S RIGHT, I'M FREE.
AS A MATTER OF FACT, THERE'S A PROJECT I SIMPLY **MUST** BRING TO LIFE THERE.
KSHUF
WHAT'S THIS?
I GOT IT FROM LOU DURING THE TOUR OF FARM 21 YESTERDAY.

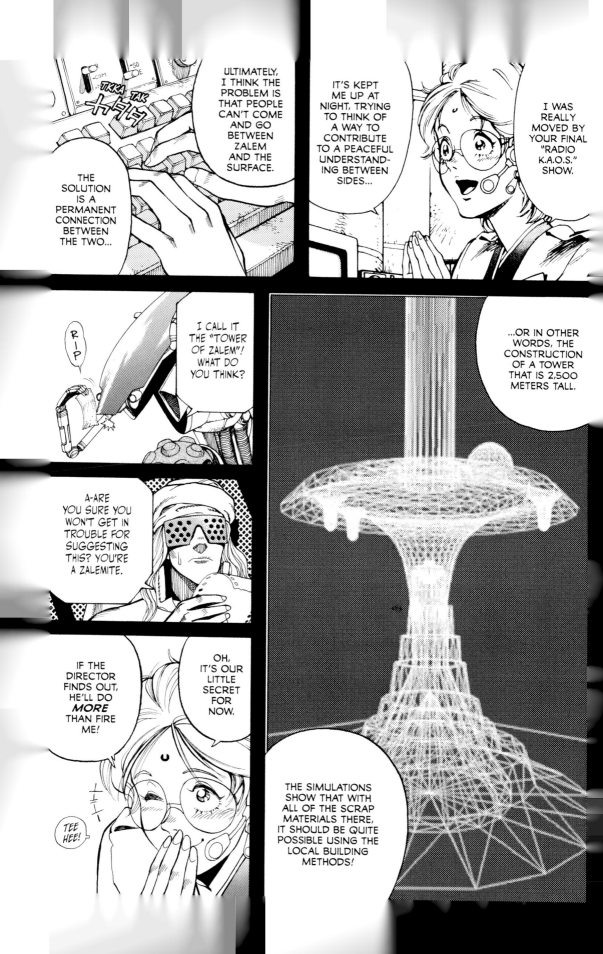

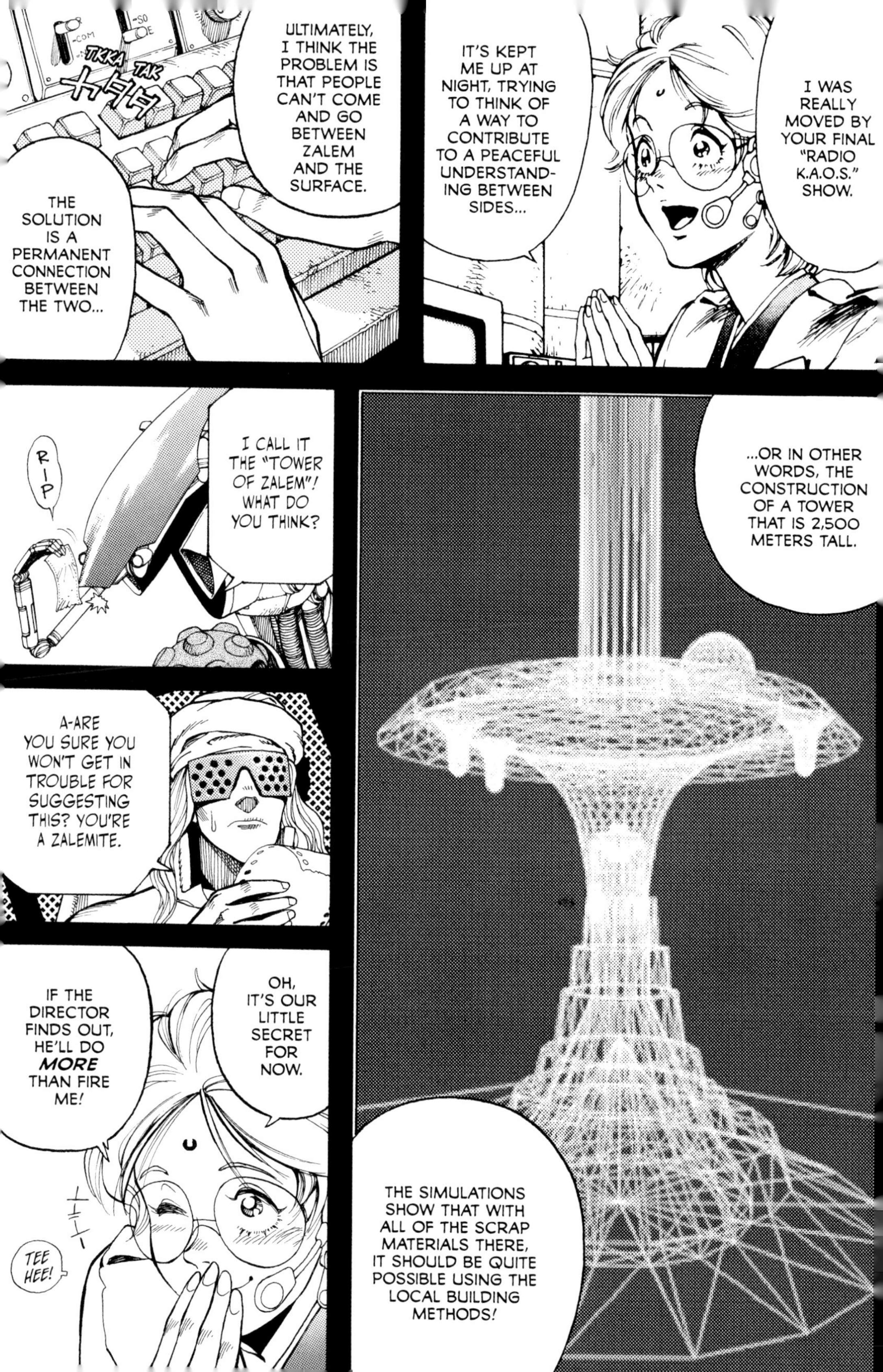
I WAS REALLY MOVED BY YOUR FINAL "RADIO K.A.O.S." SHOW.
IT'S KEPT ME UP AT NIGHT, TRYING TO THINK OF A WAY TO CONTRIBUTE TO A PEACEFUL UNDERSTAND-ING BETWEEN SIDES...
ULTIMATELY, I THINK THE PROBLEM IS THAT PEOPLE CAN'T COME AND GO BETWEEN ZALEM AND THE SURFACE.
TKKA TAK
THE SOLUTION IS A PERMANENT CONNECTION BETWEEN THE TWO...
...OR IN OTHER WORDS, THE CONSTRUCTION OF A TOWER THAT IS 2,500 METERS TALL.
THE SIMULATIONS SHOW THAT WITH ALL OF THE SCRAP MATERIALS THERE, IT SHOULD BE QUITE POSSIBLE USING THE LOCAL BUILDING METHODS!
I CALL IT THE "TOWER OF ZALEM"! WHAT DO YOU THINK?
R I P
A-ARE YOU SURE YOU WON'T GET IN TROUBLE FOR SUGGESTING THIS? YOU'RE A ZALEMITE.
OH, IT'S OUR LITTLE SECRET FOR NOW.
IF THE DIRECTOR FINDS OUT, HE'LL DO ***MORE*** THAN FIRE ME!
TEE HEE!

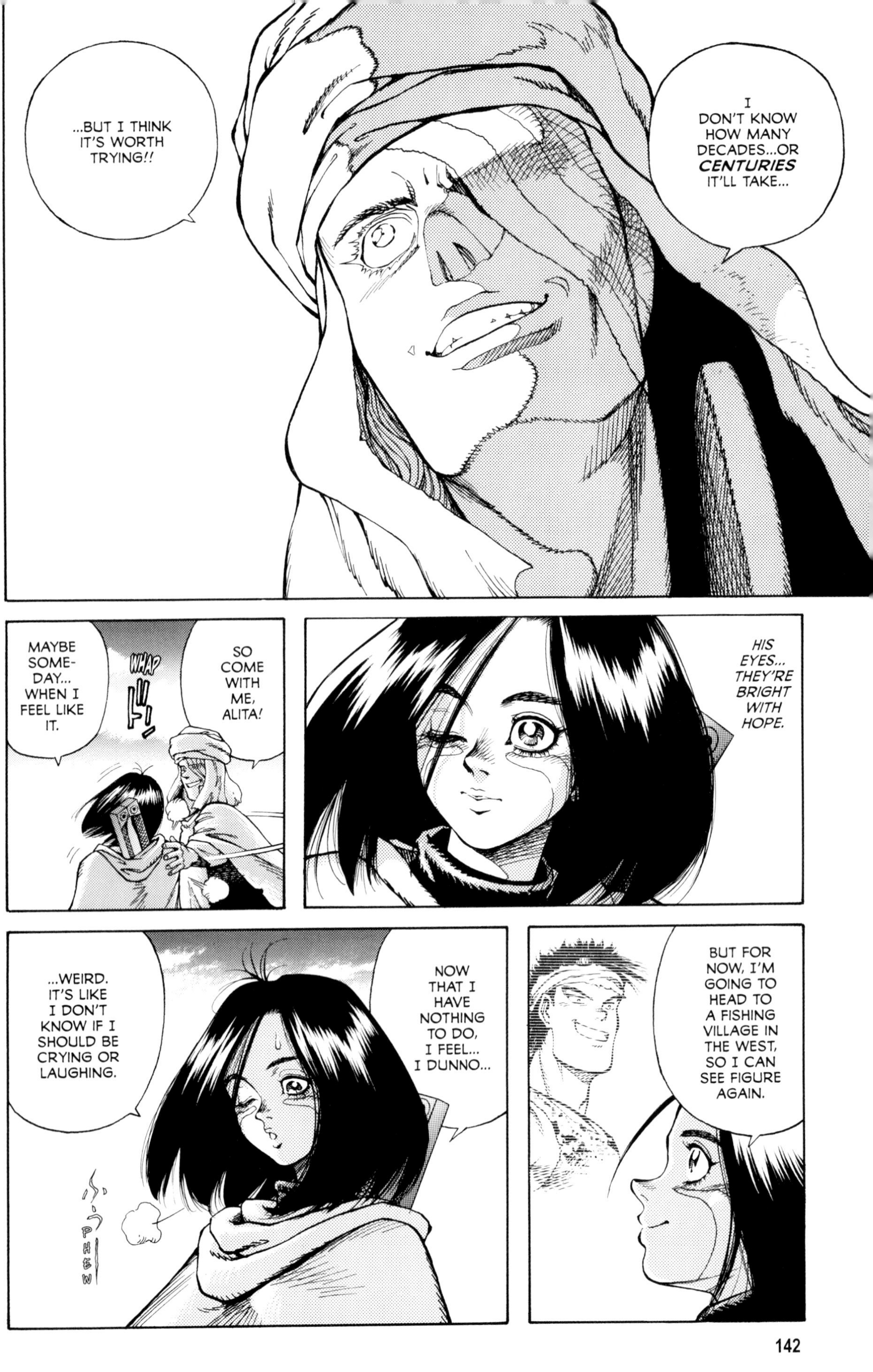
I DON'T KNOW HOW MANY DECADES...OR ***CENTURIES*** IT'LL TAKE...
...BUT I THINK IT'S WORTH TRYING!!
HIS EYES... THEY'RE BRIGHT WITH HOPE.
SO COME WITH ME, ALITA!
WHAP
MAYBE SOME-DAY... WHEN I FEEL LIKE IT.
BUT FOR NOW, I'M GOING TO HEAD TO A FISHING VILLAGE IN THE WEST, SO I CAN SEE FIGURE AGAIN.
NOW THAT I HAVE NOTHING TO DO, I FEEL... I DUNNO...
...WEIRD. IT'S LIKE I DON'T KNOW IF I SHOULD BE CRYING OR LAUGHING.
PHEW

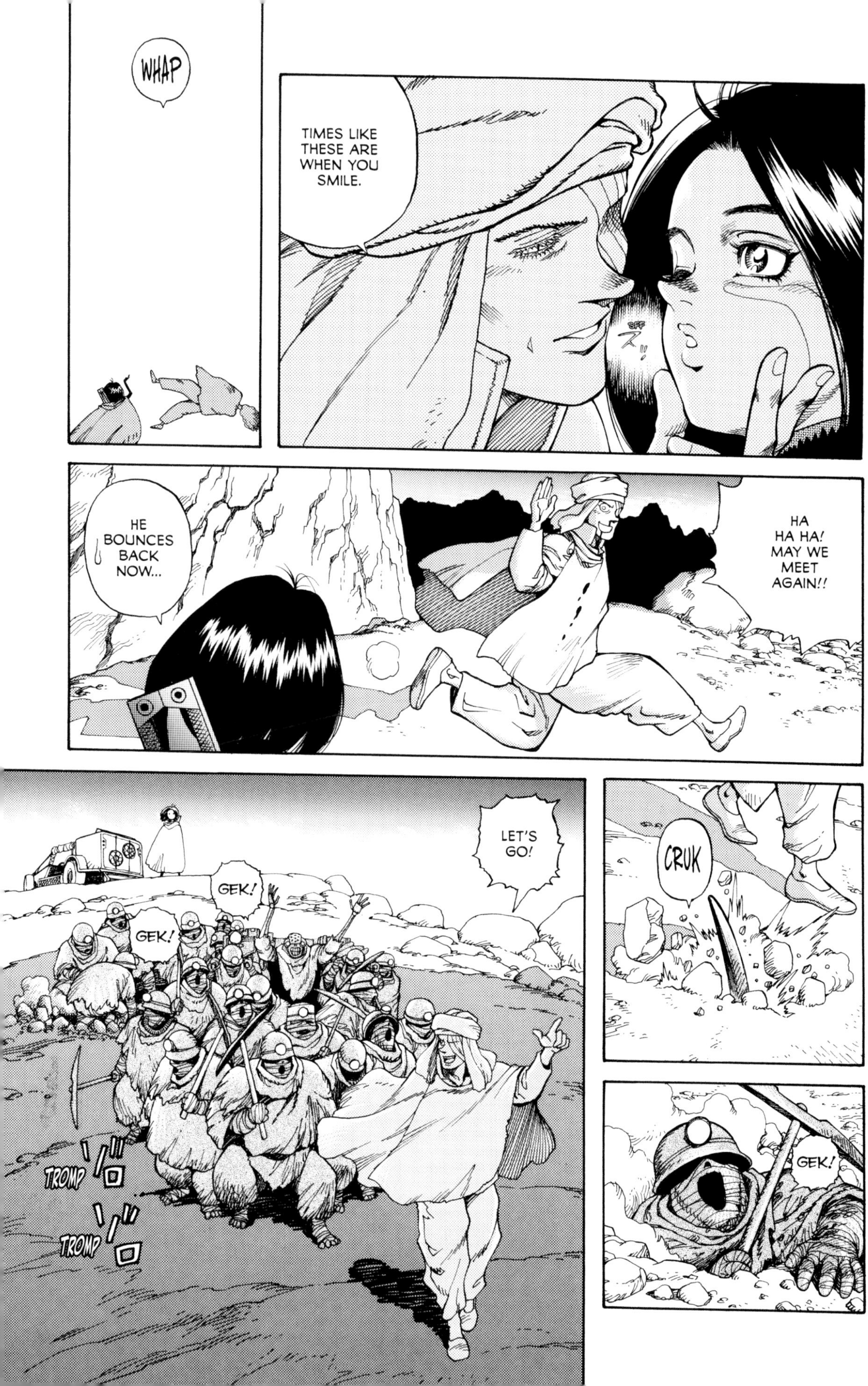
TIMES LIKE THESE ARE WHEN YOU SMILE.
SFF
WHAP
HA HA HA! MAY WE MEET AGAIN!!
HE BOUNCES BACK NOW...
CRUK
GEK!
LET'S GO!
GEK!
GEK!
TROMP
TROMP

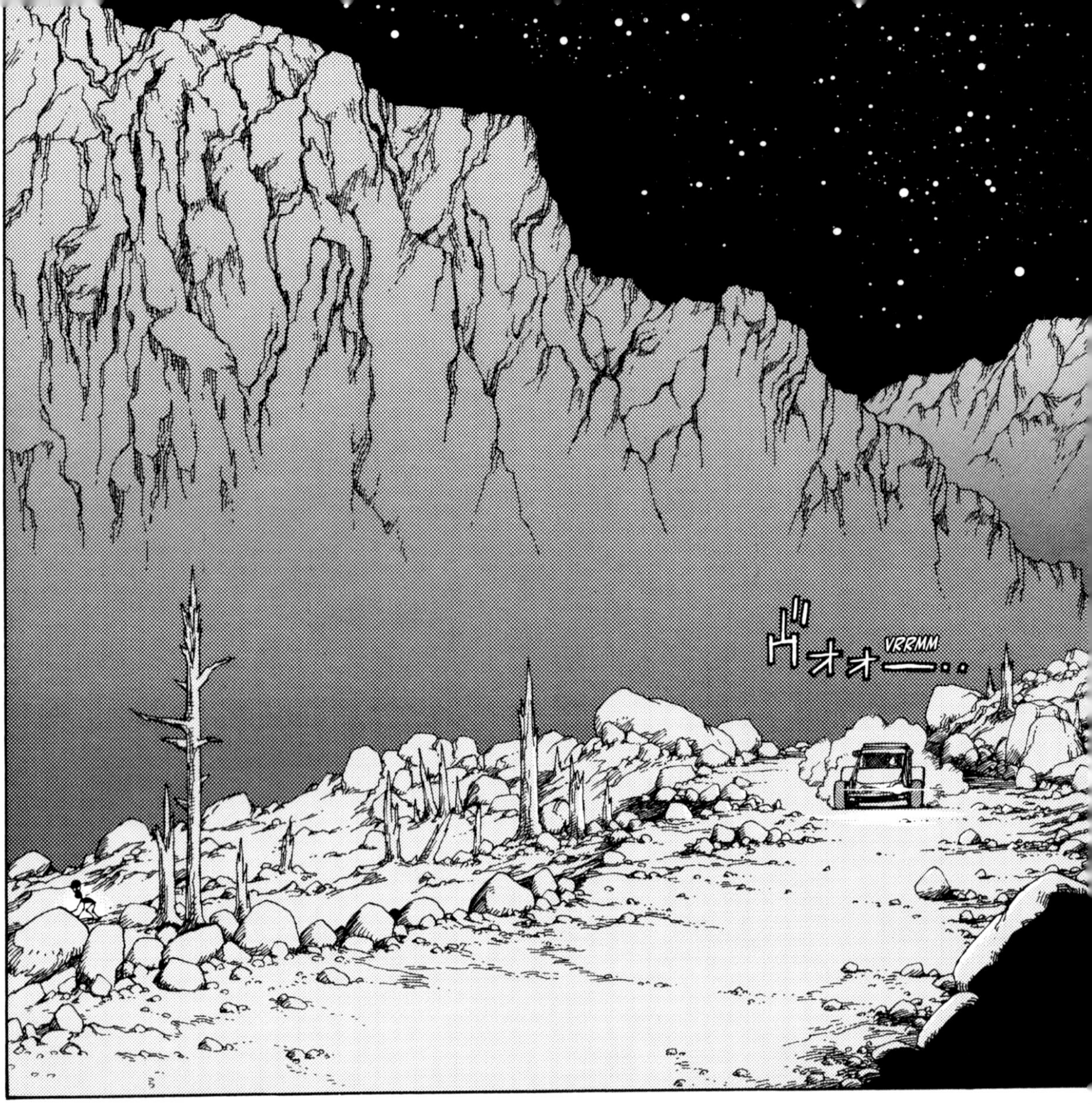
ヴオオー・・
VRRMM
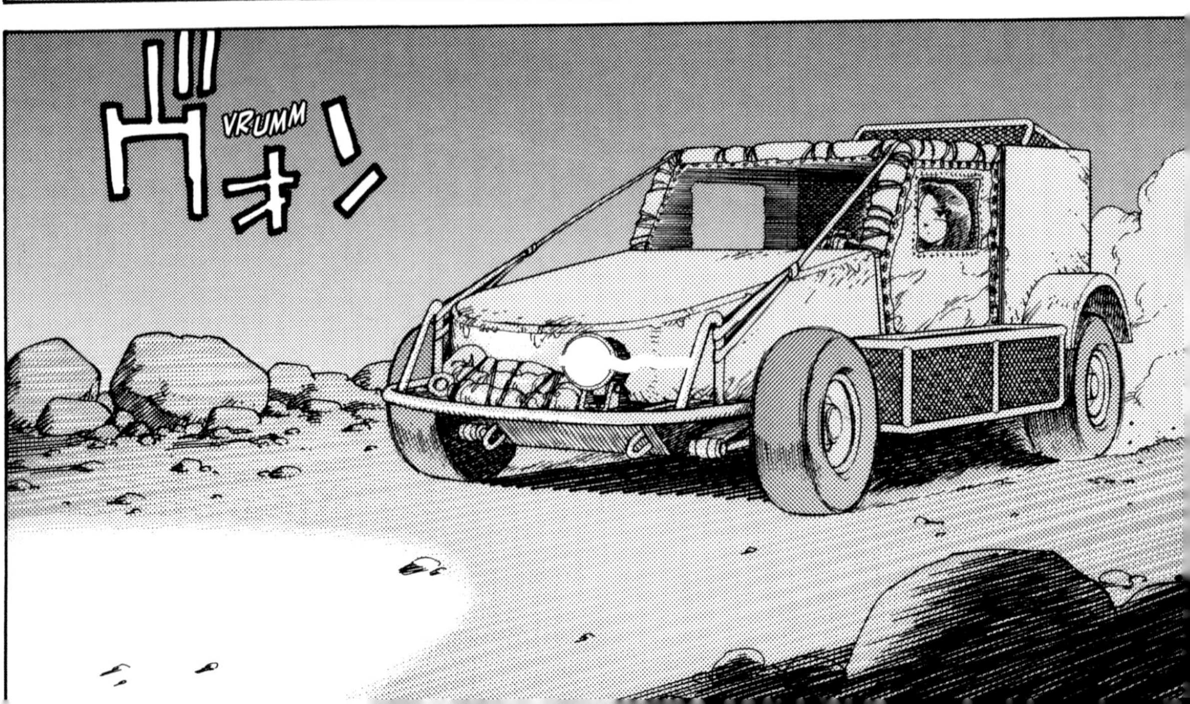
ヴオン
VRUMM

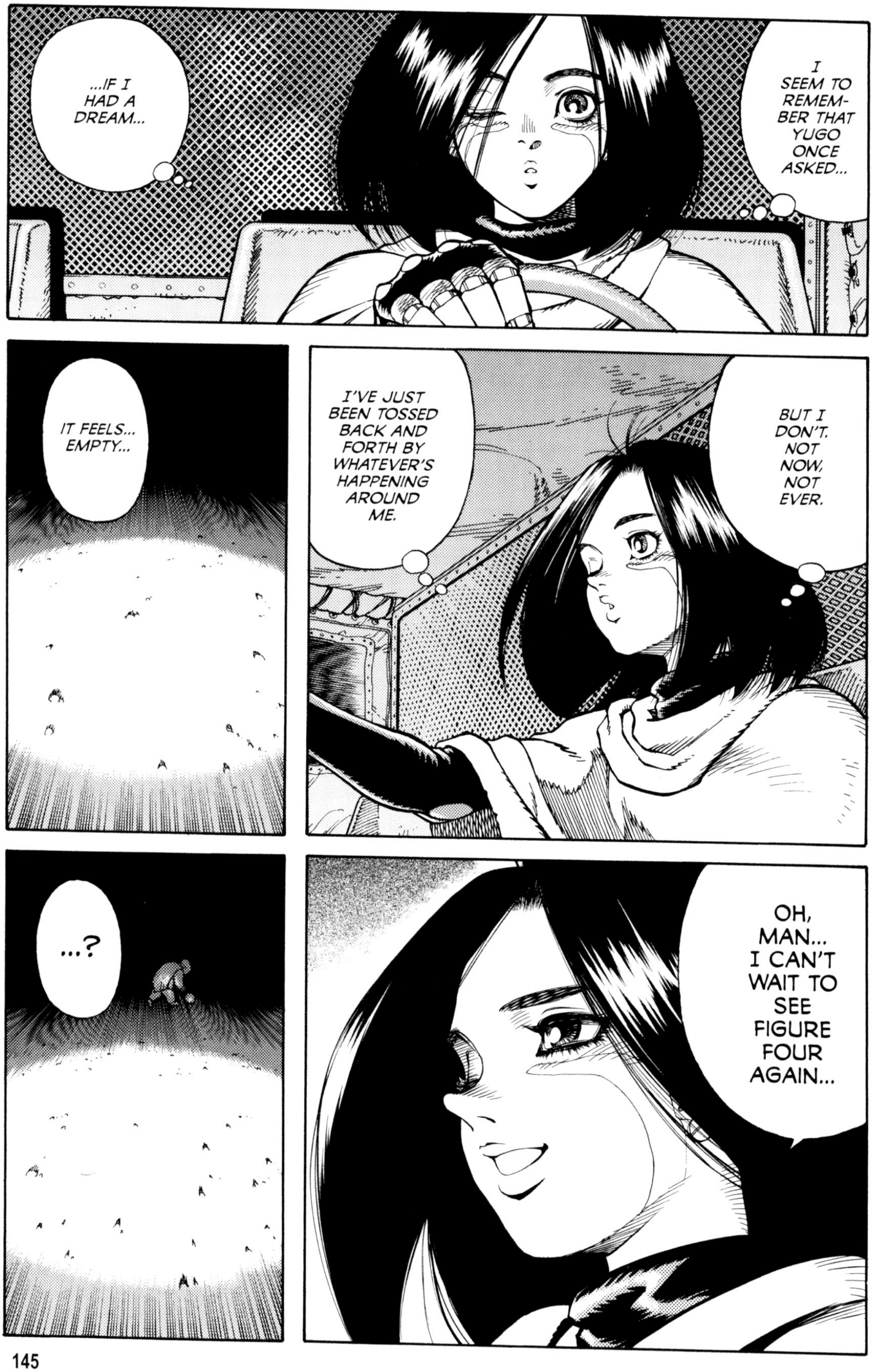
I SEEM TO REMEMBER THAT YUGO ONCE ASKED...
...IF I HAD A DREAM...
BUT I DON'T. NOT NOW, NOT EVER.
I'VE JUST BEEN TOSSED BACK AND FORTH BY WHATEVER'S HAPPENING AROUND ME.
IT FEELS... EMPTY...
OH, MAN... I CAN'T WAIT TO SEE FIGURE FOUR AGAIN...
...?

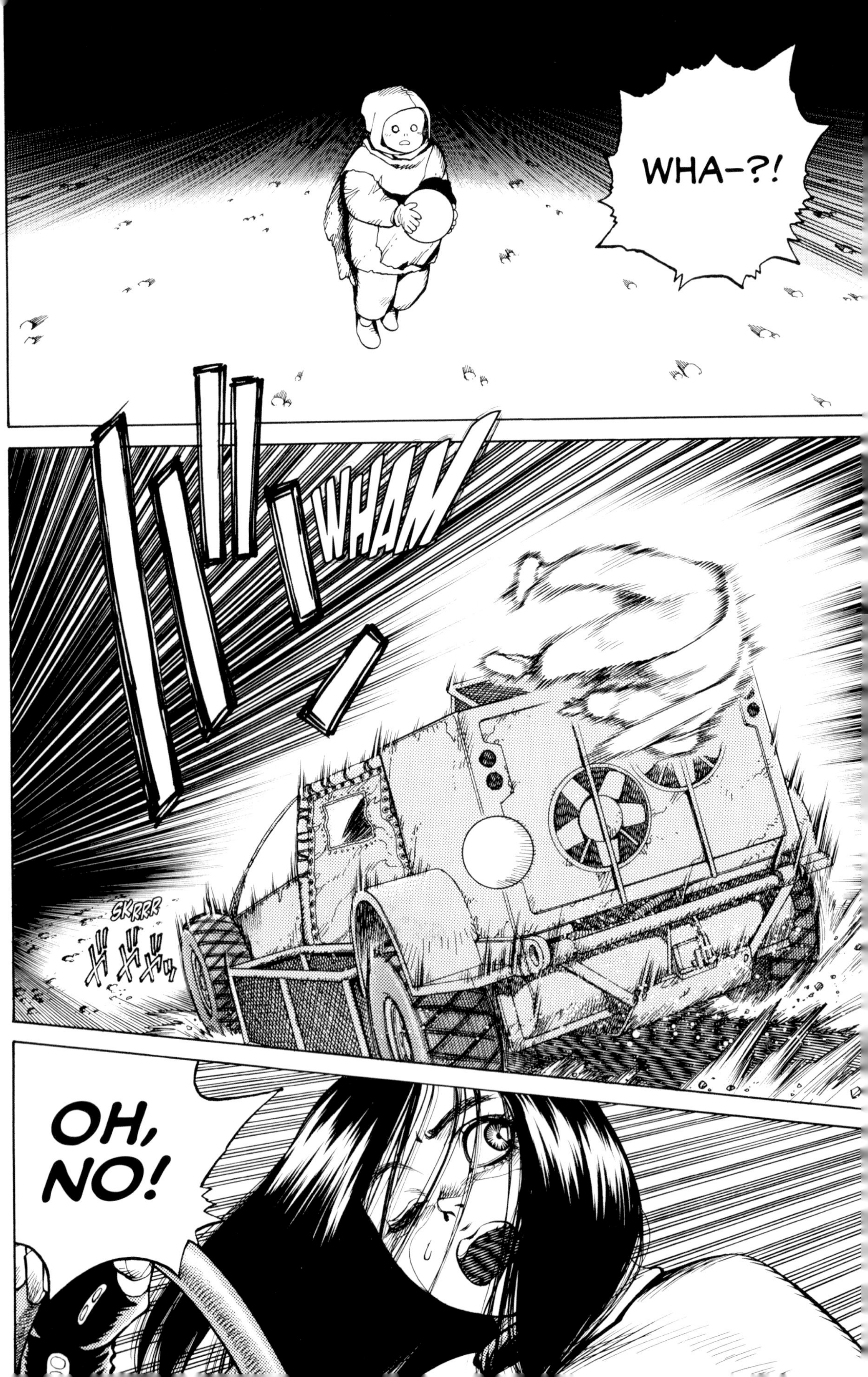
WHA-?!
WHAM
SKRRR
ザザザッ
OH, NO!

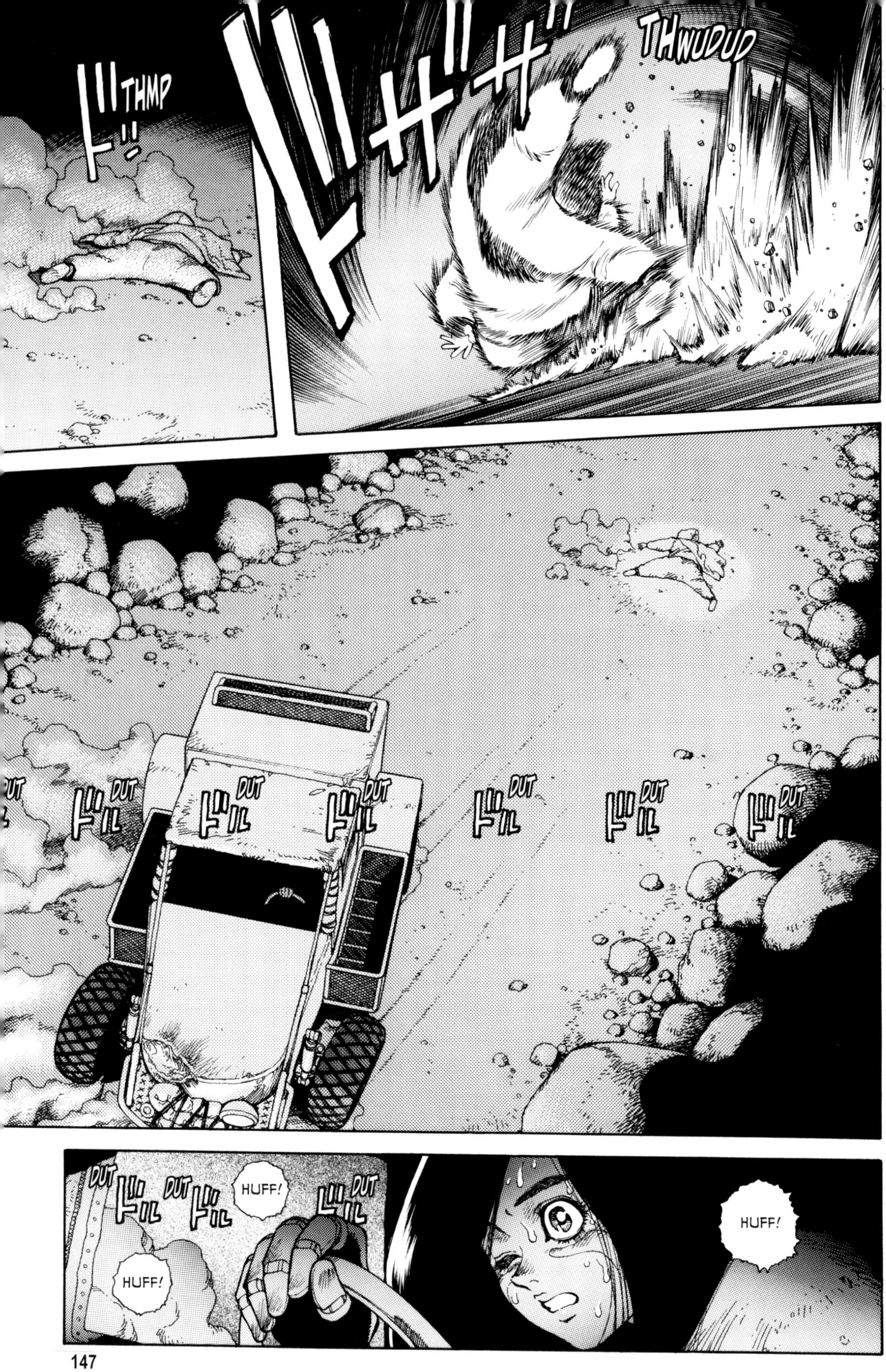
THWUDUD
THMP
DUT
DUT
DUT
DUT
DUT
DUT
DUT
HUFF!
DUT
HUFF!
DUT
DUT
HUFF!

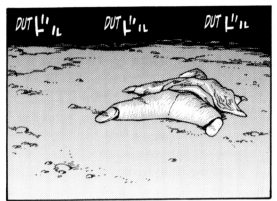

THAT'S IT... I'M NOT CUT OUT FOR DRIVING.
NO MORE VEHICLES!
DUT ドル
DUT ドル
DUT ドル
DUT ドル
DUT ドル
DUT ドル
DUT ドル
I-I NEED TO HELP HIM...
DUT ドル
DUT ドル
DUT ドル
B-BUT...
WHAT WAS THIS LITTLE CHILD DOING OUT HERE...?

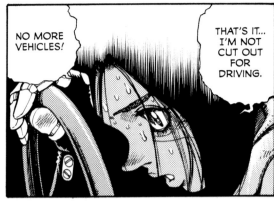

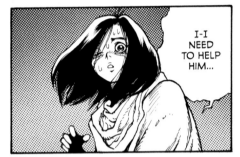

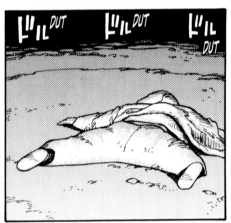

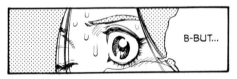

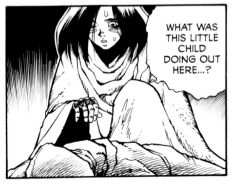

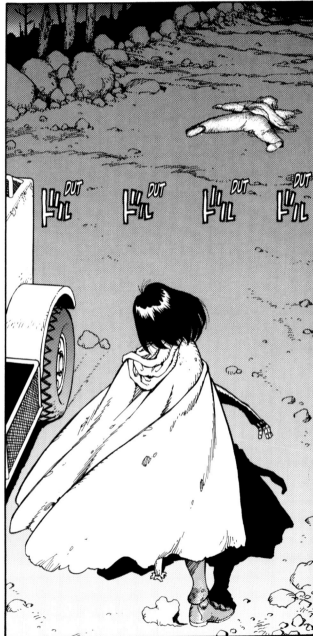

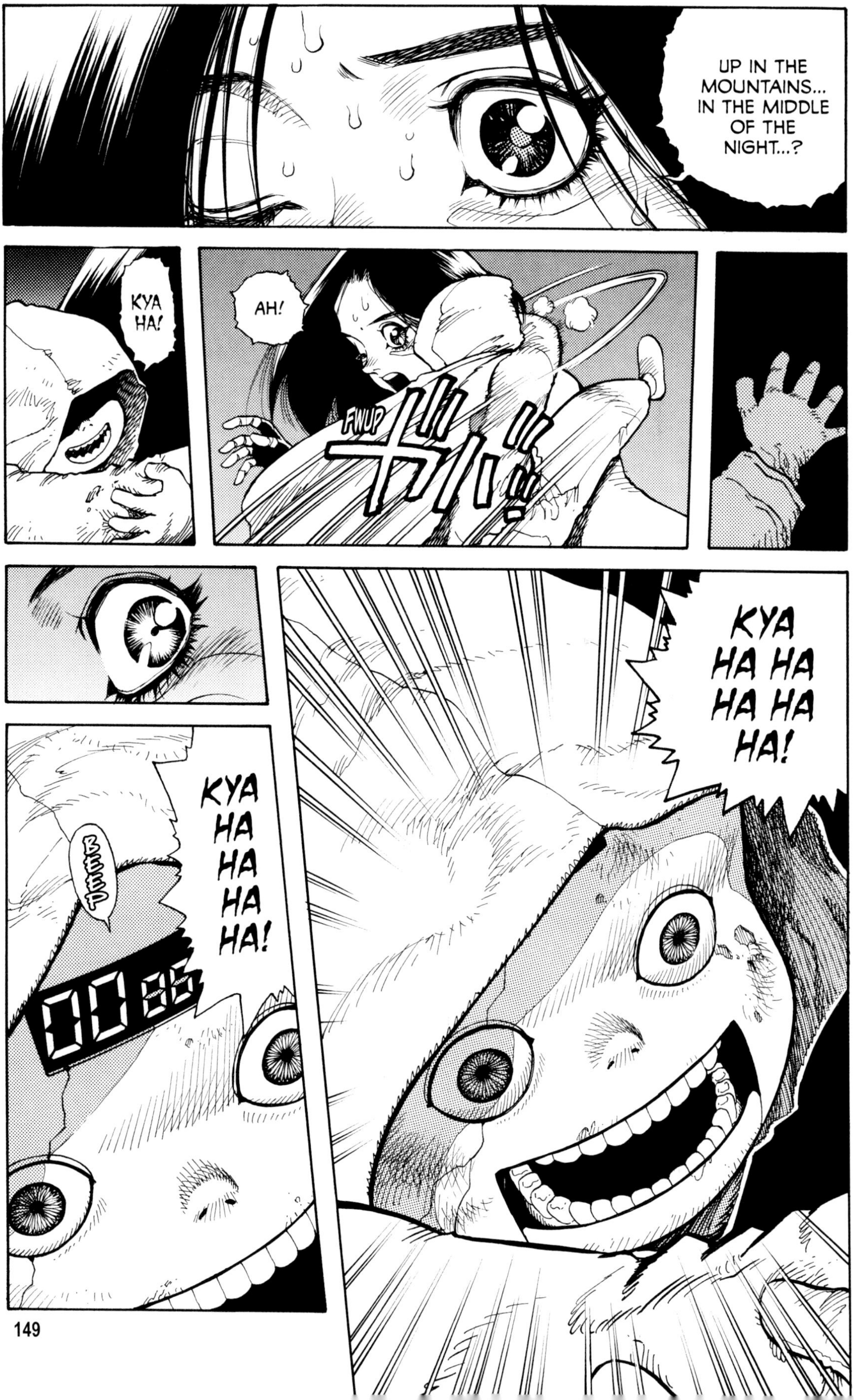
UP IN THE MOUNTAINS... IN THE MIDDLE OF THE NIGHT...?
AH!
FWUP
KYA HA!
KYA HA HA HA HA HA!
KYA HA HA HA HA HA!
BEEP

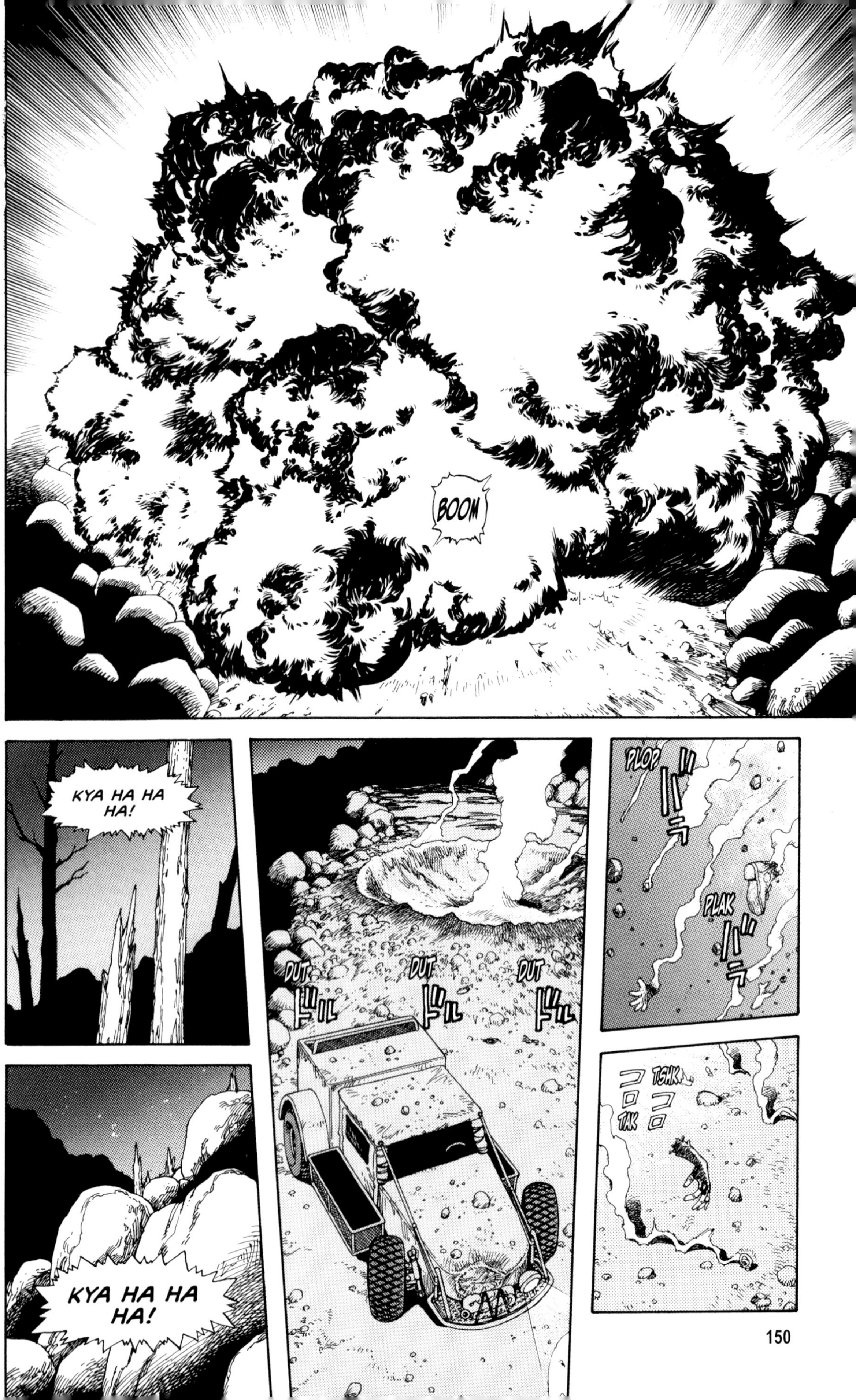
BOOM
PLOP
バラ
PLAK
バラ
TSHK
コロ
コロ
TAK
DUT
ドル
DUT
ドル
DUT
ドル
KYA HA HA HA!
KYA HA HA HA!

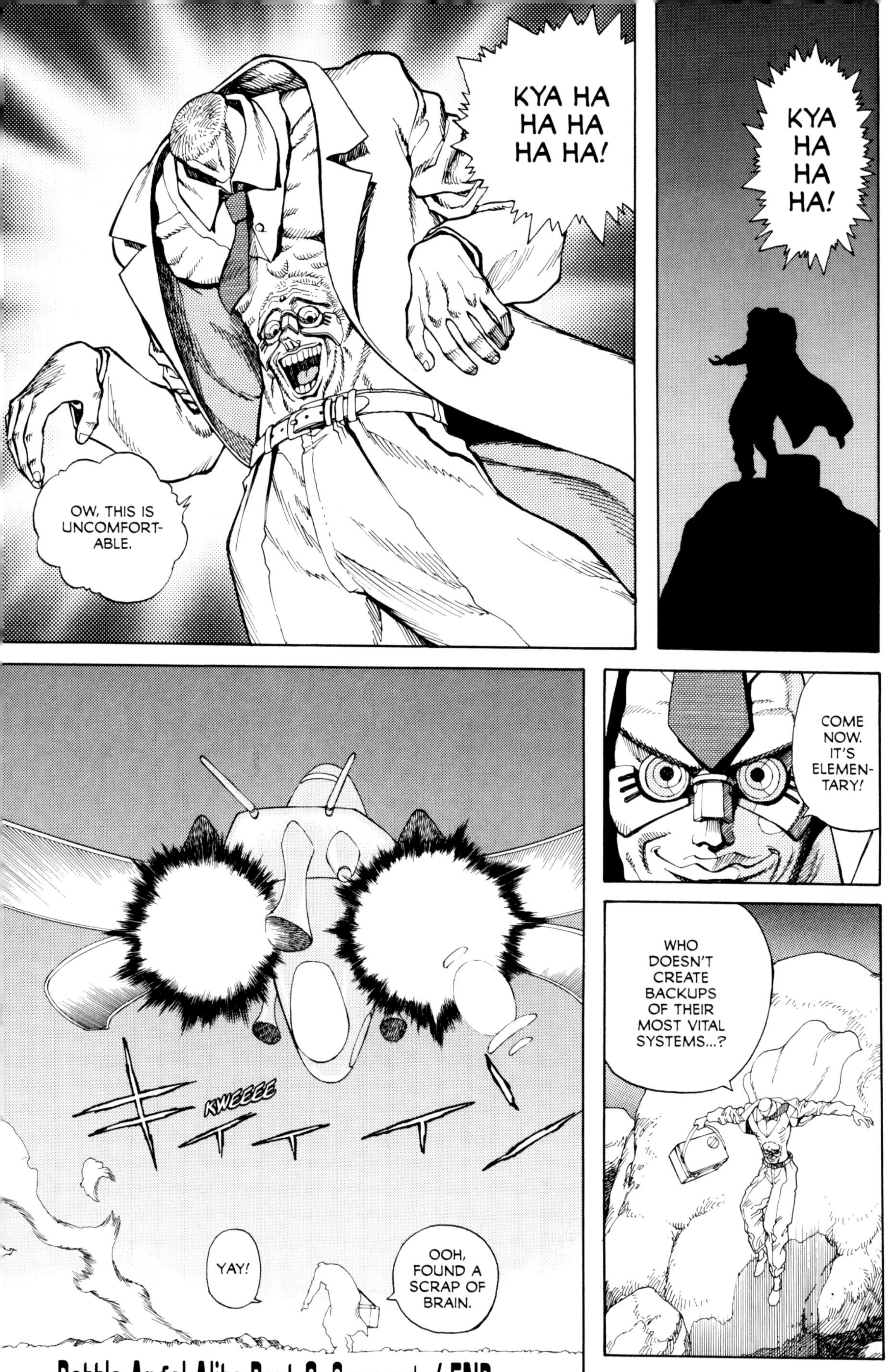
KYA HA HA HA HA!
KYA HA HA HA HA HA!
OW, THIS IS UNCOMFORTABLE.
COME NOW. IT'S ELEMENTARY!
WHO DOESN'T CREATE BACKUPS OF THEIR MOST VITAL SYSTEMS...?
KWEEEE
OOH, FOUND A SCRAP OF BRAIN.
YAY!

Battle Angel Alita Part 9: Conquest / END

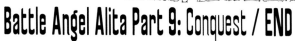

Currently, the previous chapter is the canonical end of *Battle Angel Alita*. The story of Alita eventually continued in *Battle Angel Alita: Last Order*.

The following pages are another vision of *Battle Angel Alita*, published after this ending but before *Last Order*.

Due to many requests from fans of the series for the original material, it has been included in this edition. It is not *Alita* canon; think of it as a side story, if you wish. You may find the more poetic touches of this material entertaining in a different way than the expanded view of the world presented in *Last Order*. Please enjoy.

Conquest of Zalem I

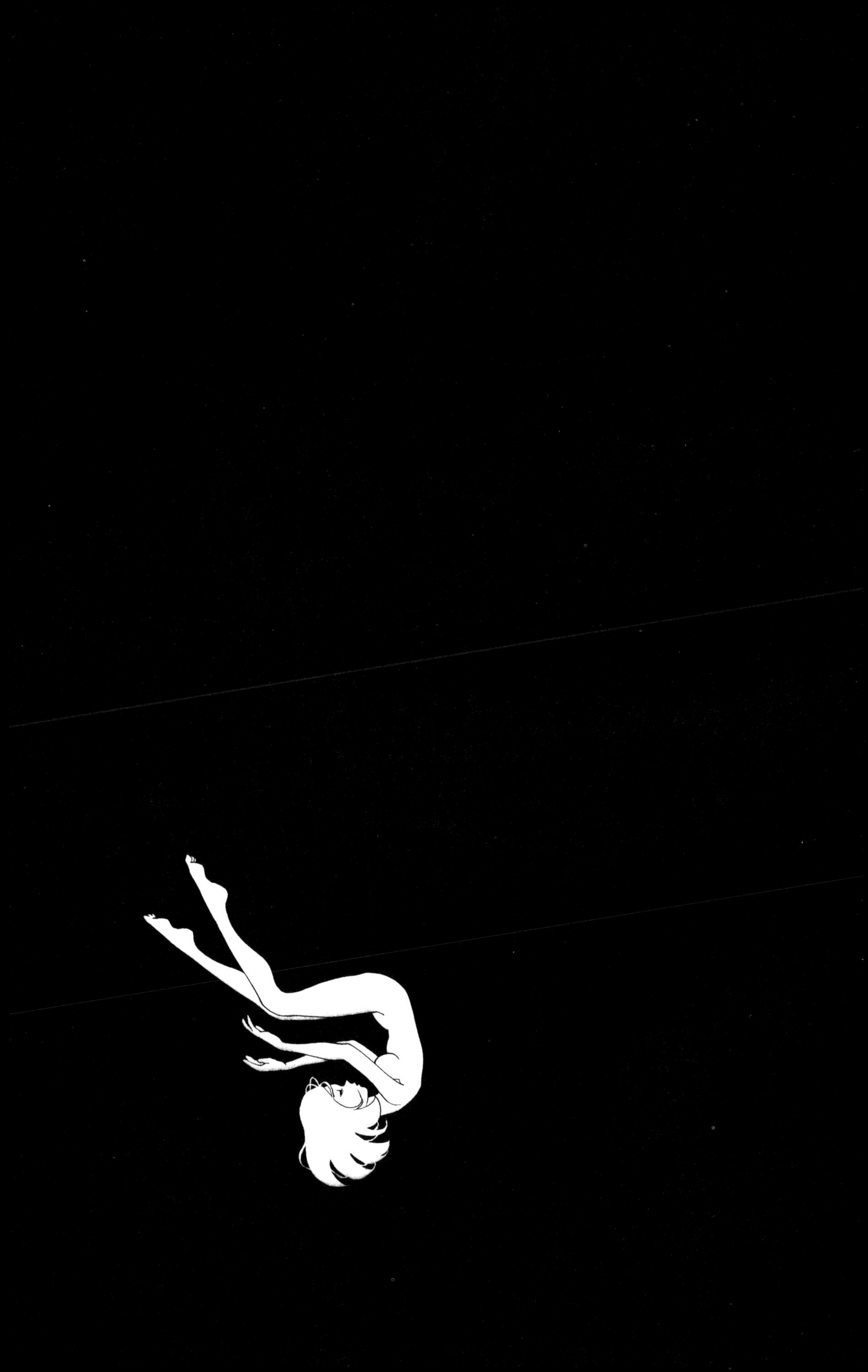

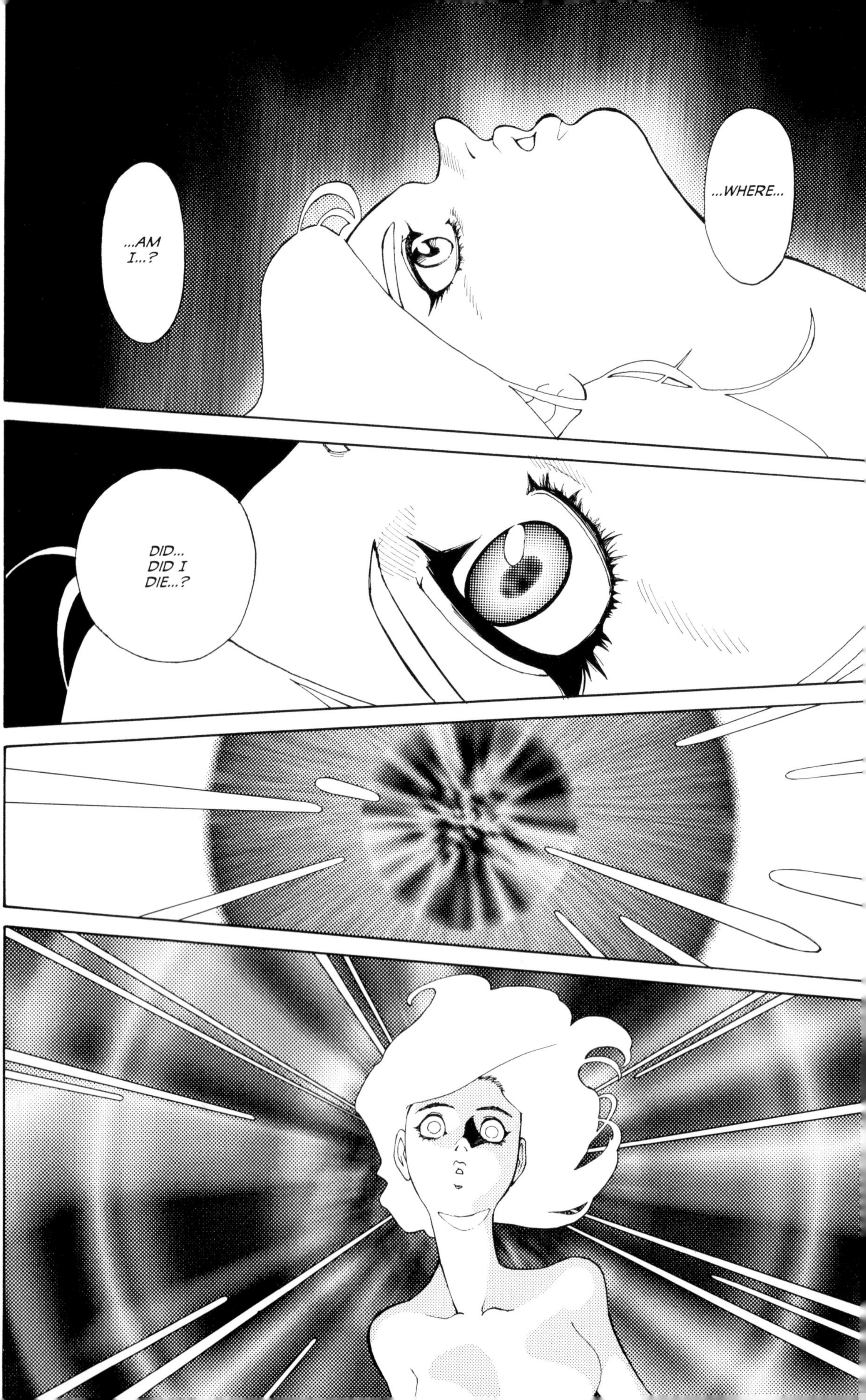
...WHERE...
...AM I...?
DID... DID I DIE...?

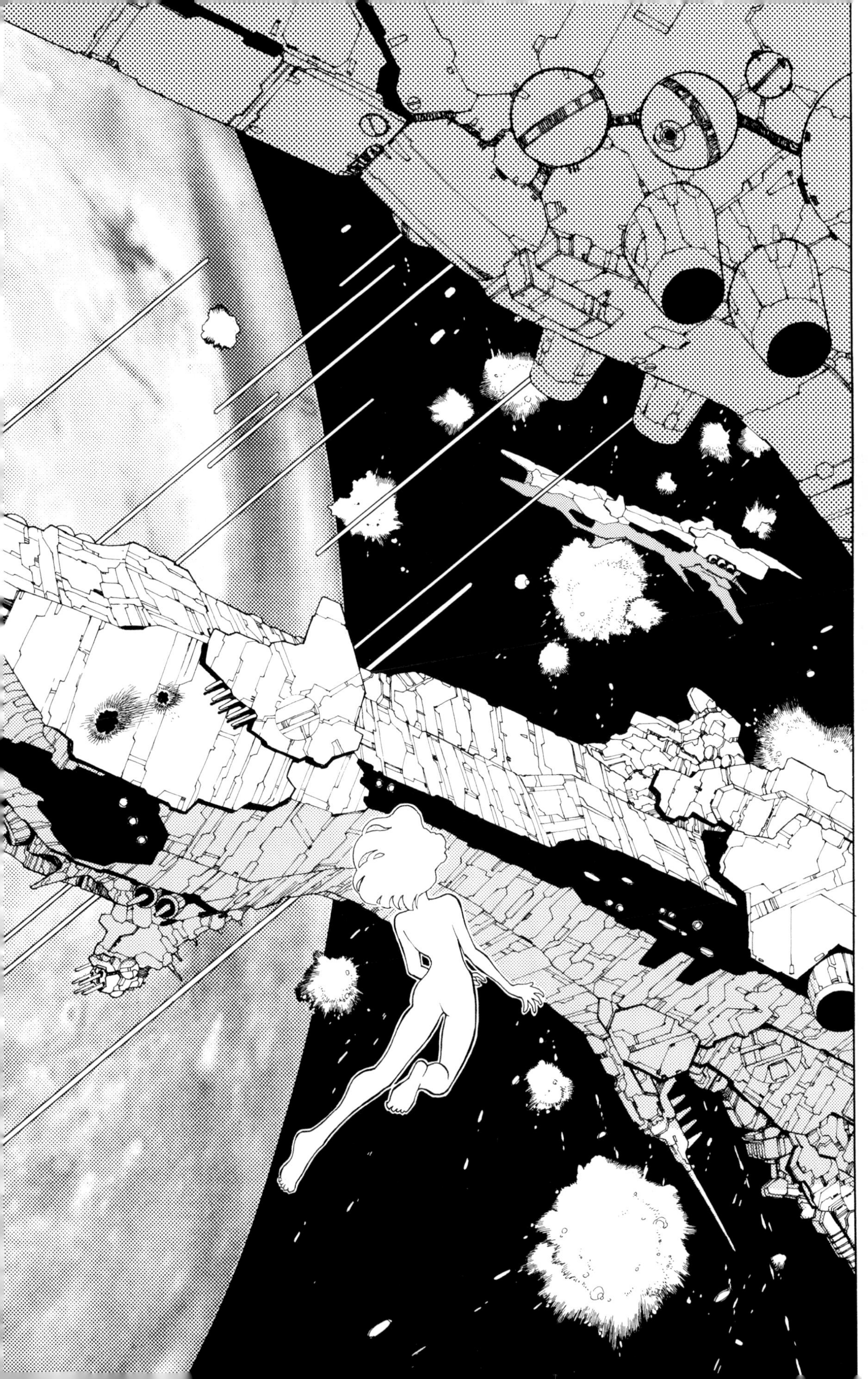

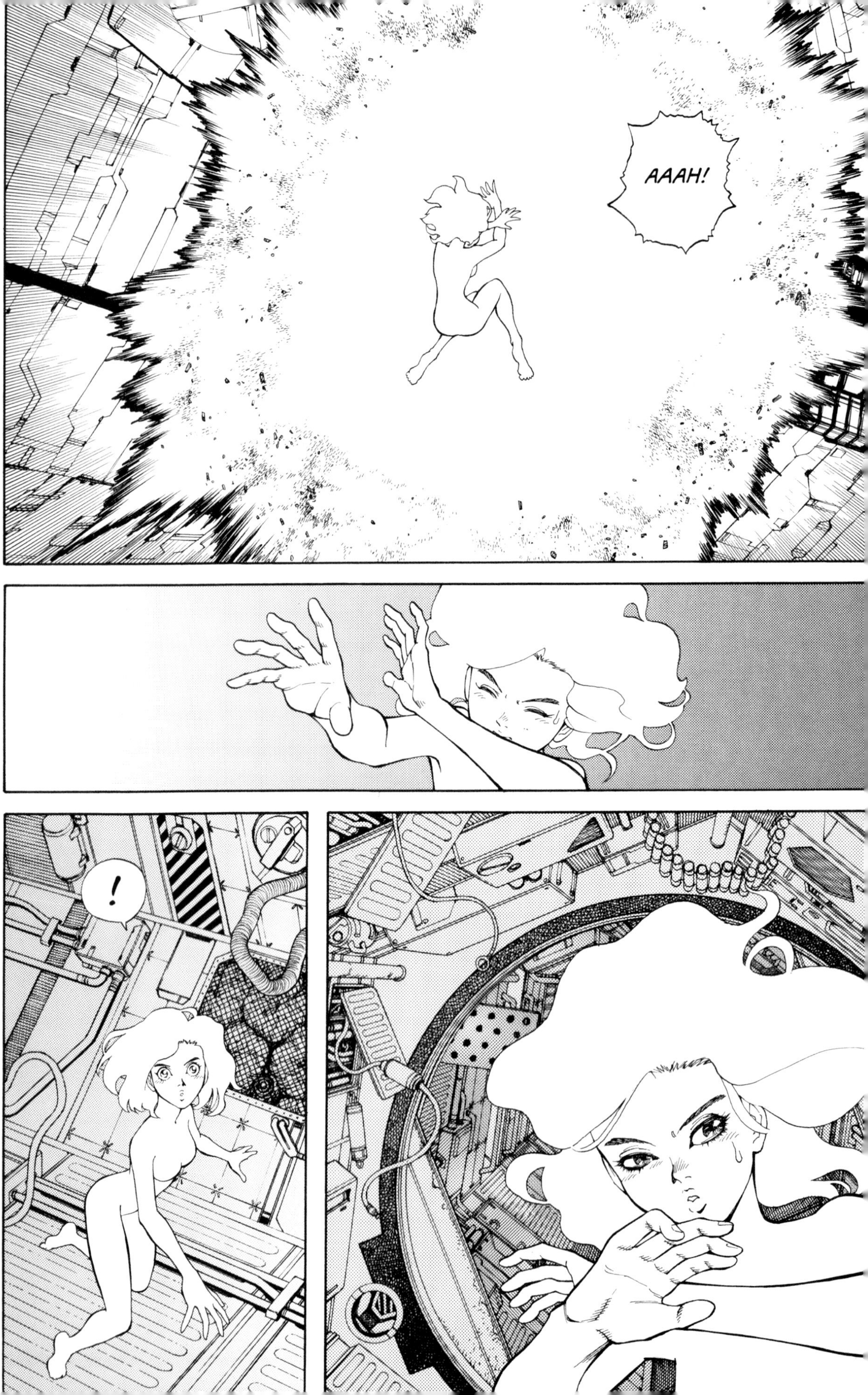
AAAH!
!

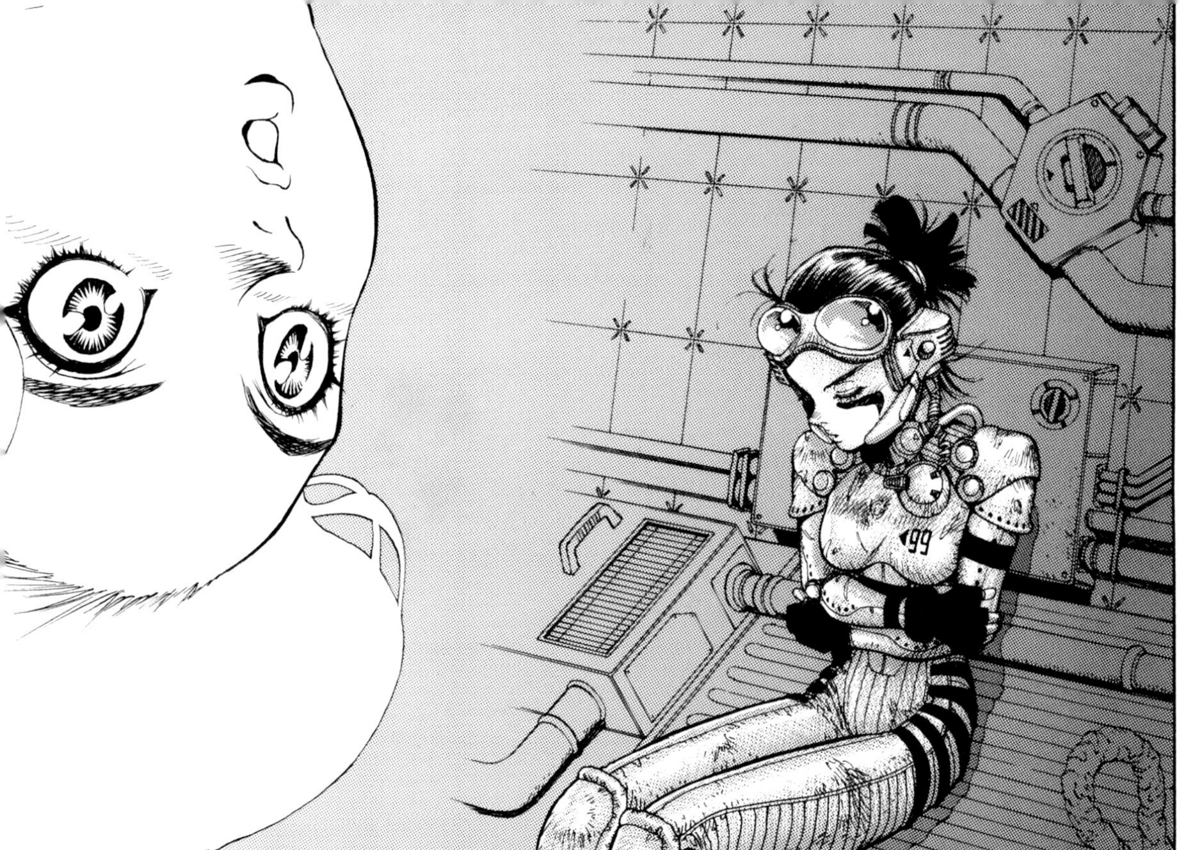

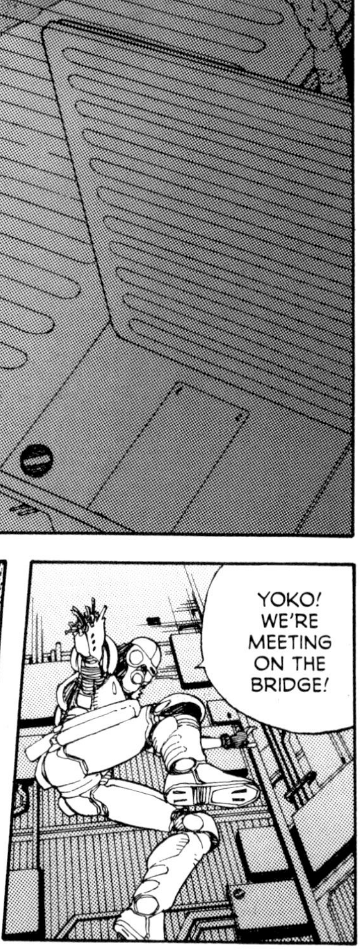
YOKO! WE'RE MEETING ON THE BRIDGE!

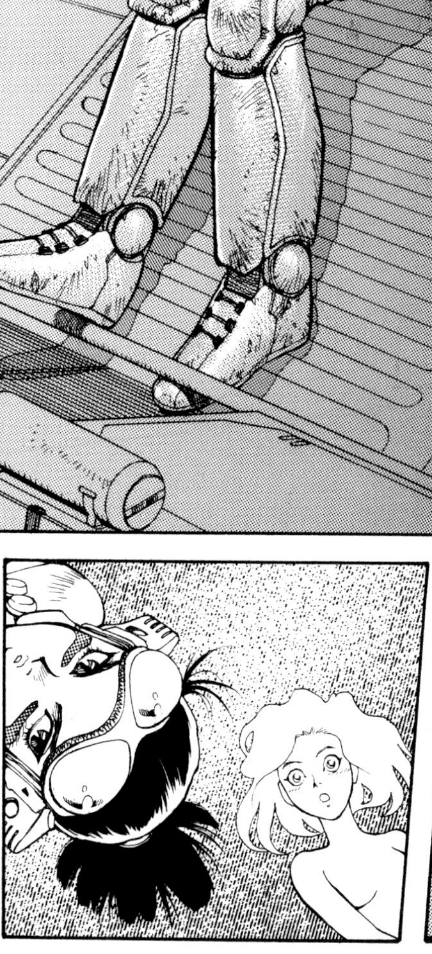

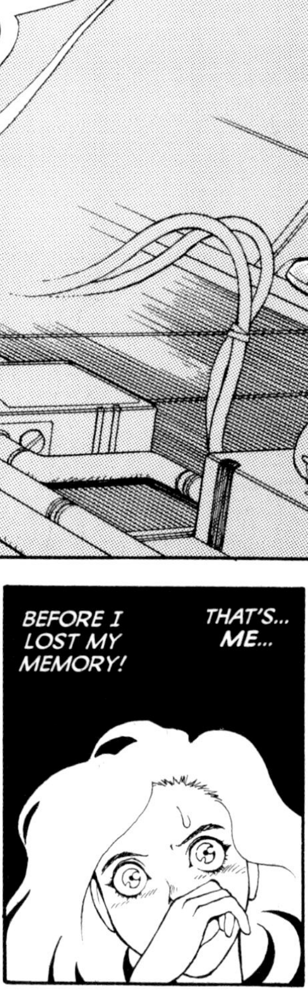
THAT'S... ME...
BEFORE I LOST MY MEMORY!

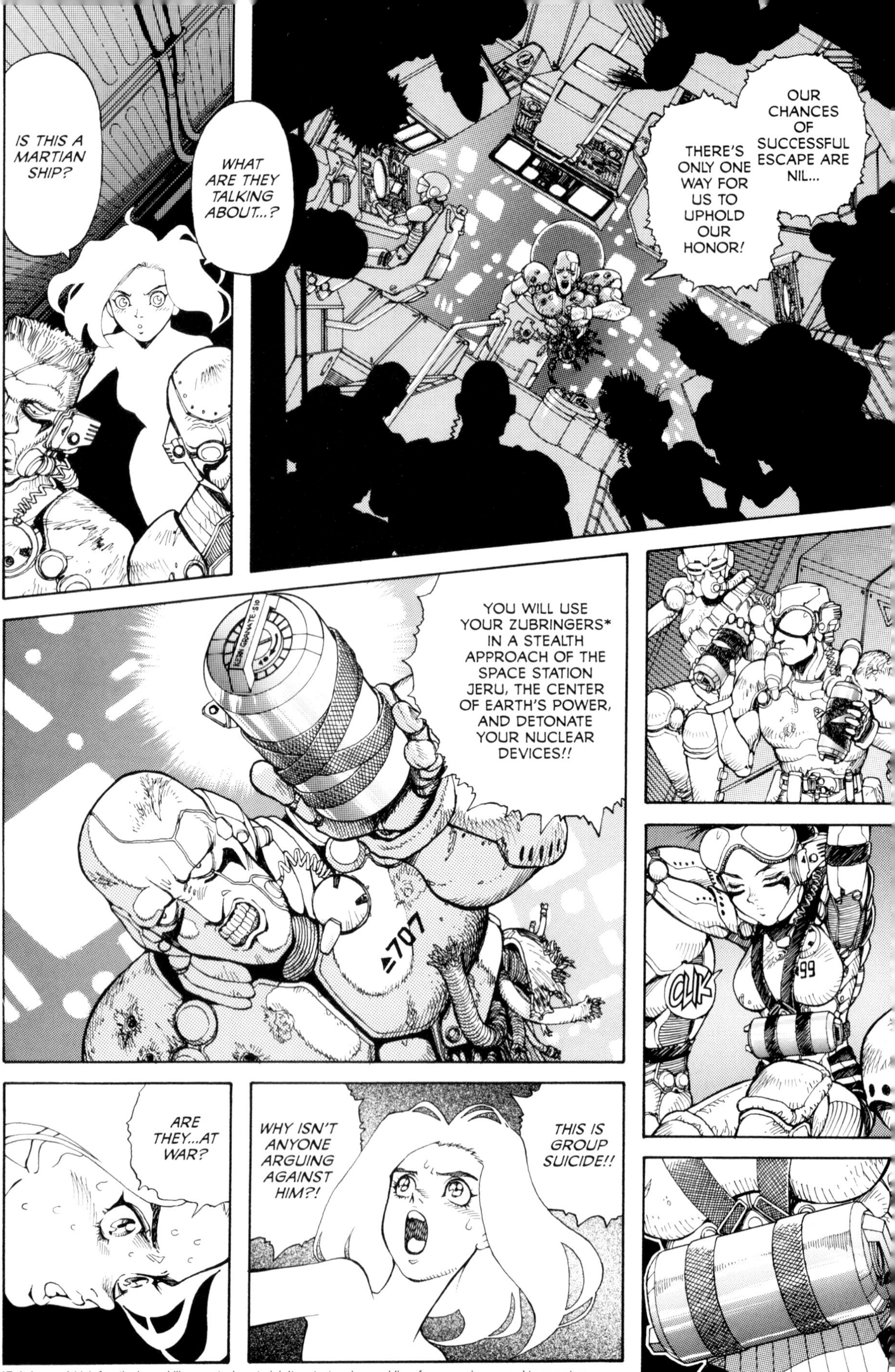
OUR CHANCES OF SUCCESSFUL ESCAPE ARE NIL...
THERE'S ONLY ONE WAY FOR US TO UPHOLD OUR HONOR!
WHAT ARE THEY TALKING ABOUT...?
IS THIS A MARTIAN SHIP?
CLIK
YOU WILL USE YOUR ZUBRINGERS* IN A STEALTH APPROACH OF THE SPACE STATION JERU, THE CENTER OF EARTH'S POWER, AND DETONATE YOUR NUCLEAR DEVICES!!
707
THIS IS GROUP SUICIDE!!
WHY ISN'T ANYONE ARGUING AGAINST HIM?!
ARE THEY...AT WAR?

***Zubringer:** A high-functioning gel-like nanotech material. It protects cyborg soldiers from cosmic rays and temperature fluctuations, and synthesizes oxygen to breathe. The surface color, texture, and hardness can be controlled electronically, making it useful as a kind of minimalistic stealth space suit.

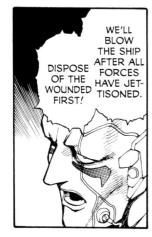

JERU IS THE TERMINAL AT THE END OF THE ORBITAL TOWER, AND THAT TOWER IS SUPPORTED BY THE ORBITAL RING–IT'S ALL MAINTAINED IN A DELICATE BALANCE!
ALL YOU NEED TO DO IS DETONATE AN EXPLOSIVE ON IT! I DON'T CARE WHERE!
THAT'S ALL IT WILL TAKE TO MAKE THEM SPEND THEIR DYING MOMENTS REGRETTING THEIR ARROGANCE!!
WE'LL BLOW THE SHIP AFTER ALL FORCES HAVE JETTISONED.
DISPOSE OF THE WOUNDED FIRST!
BUT, LEHRER! THEY SAY THAT WHEN A ZUBRINGER CONTACTS ORGANIC MATTER, IT PERMEATES AND PLASTICIZES THEM IN A KIND OF NEAR-DEATH STATE...
WHAT'S YOUR POINT?
WHY CAN'T WE PLASTICIZE THE BRAINS OF THE WOUNDED TO KEEP THEM ALIVE?
IT SEEMS TOO CRUEL TO KILL THEM JUST BECAUSE THEY ARE UNABLE TO FIGHT...
NO METHOD TO UNFREEZE THE SEALED ORGANIC MATERIAL HAS YET BEEN DISCOVERED.
AND EVEN IF WE KNEW THE WAY...WHAT IF THE ENEMY RECOVERED THE BRAINS?
MAY MARS BESTOW HIS FAVOR UPON US!!

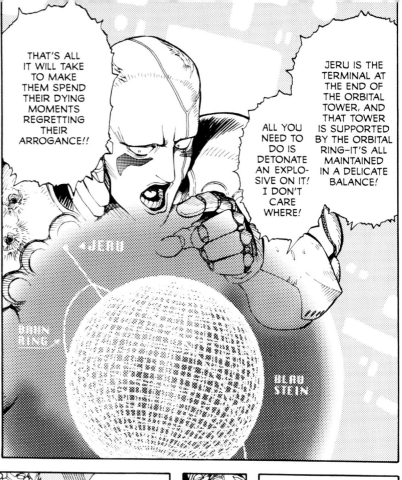

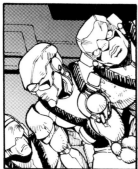

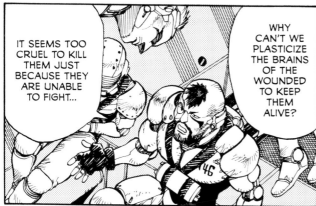

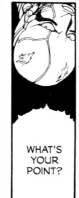

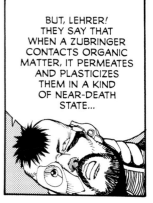

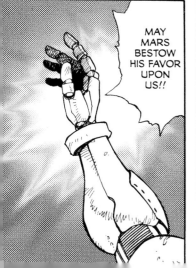

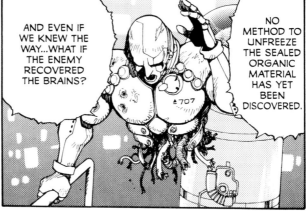

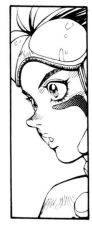

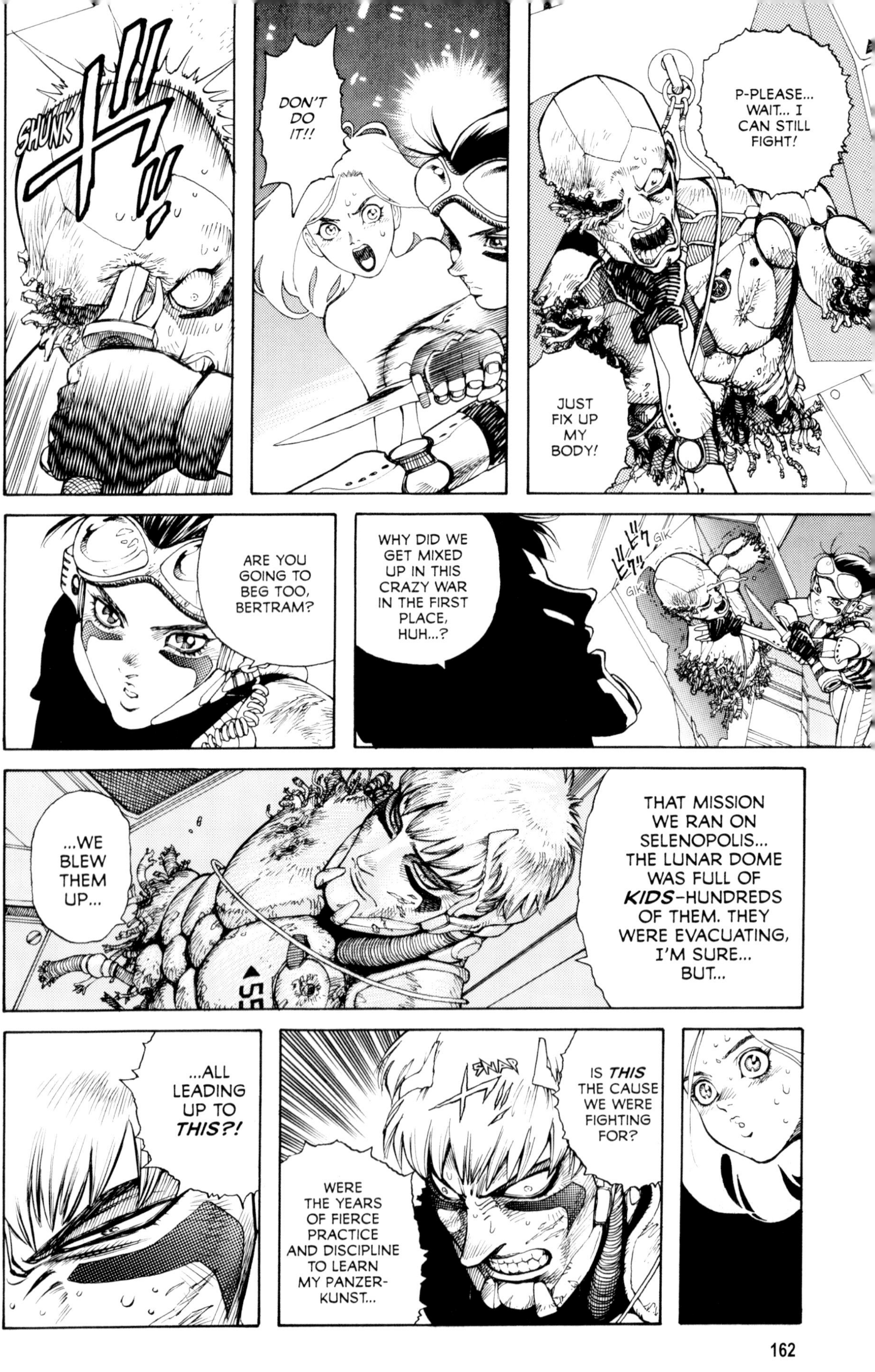
P-PLEASE... WAIT... I CAN STILL FIGHT!
JUST FIX UP MY BODY!
DON'T DO IT!!
SHUNK
GIK
GIK
WHY DID WE GET MIXED UP IN THIS CRAZY WAR IN THE FIRST PLACE, HUH...?
ARE YOU GOING TO BEG TOO, BERTRAM?
THAT MISSION WE RAN ON SELENOPOLIS... THE LUNAR DOME WAS FULL OF KIDS–HUNDREDS OF THEM. THEY WERE EVACUATING, I'M SURE... BUT...
...WE BLEW THEM UP...
IS THIS THE CAUSE WE WERE FIGHTING FOR?
WERE THE YEARS OF FIERCE PRACTICE AND DISCIPLINE TO LEARN MY PANZER-KUNST...
...ALL LEADING UP TO THIS?!

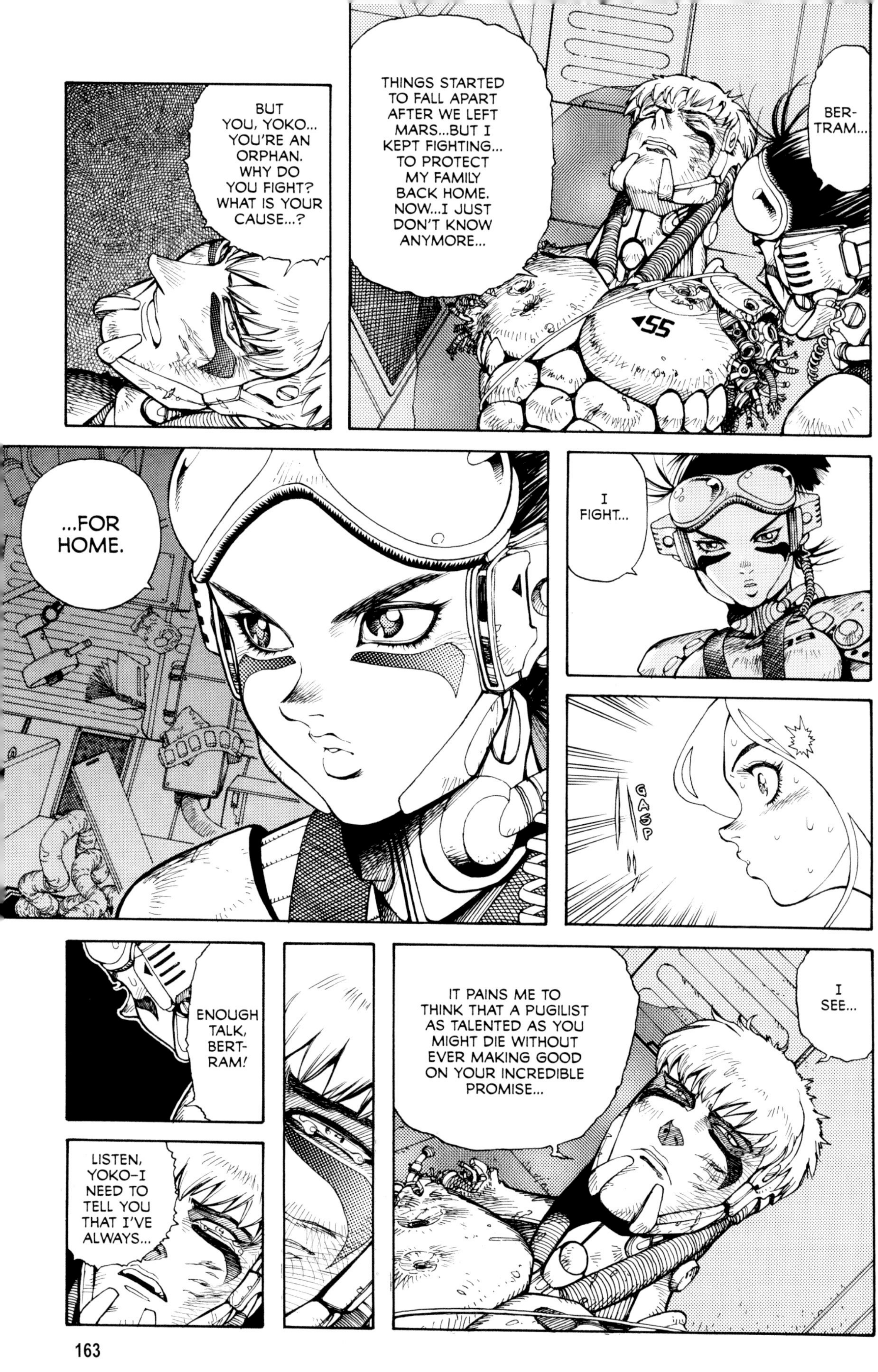
BER-TRAM...
THINGS STARTED TO FALL APART AFTER WE LEFT MARS...BUT I KEPT FIGHTING... TO PROTECT MY FAMILY BACK HOME. NOW...I JUST DON'T KNOW ANYMORE...
BUT YOU, YOKO... YOU'RE AN ORPHAN. WHY DO YOU FIGHT? WHAT IS YOUR CAUSE...?
I FIGHT...
GASP
...FOR HOME.
I SEE...
IT PAINS ME TO THINK THAT A PUGILIST AS TALENTED AS YOU MIGHT DIE WITHOUT EVER MAKING GOOD ON YOUR INCREDIBLE PROMISE...
ENOUGH TALK, BERT-RAM!
LISTEN, YOKO–I NEED TO TELL YOU THAT I'VE ALWAYS...

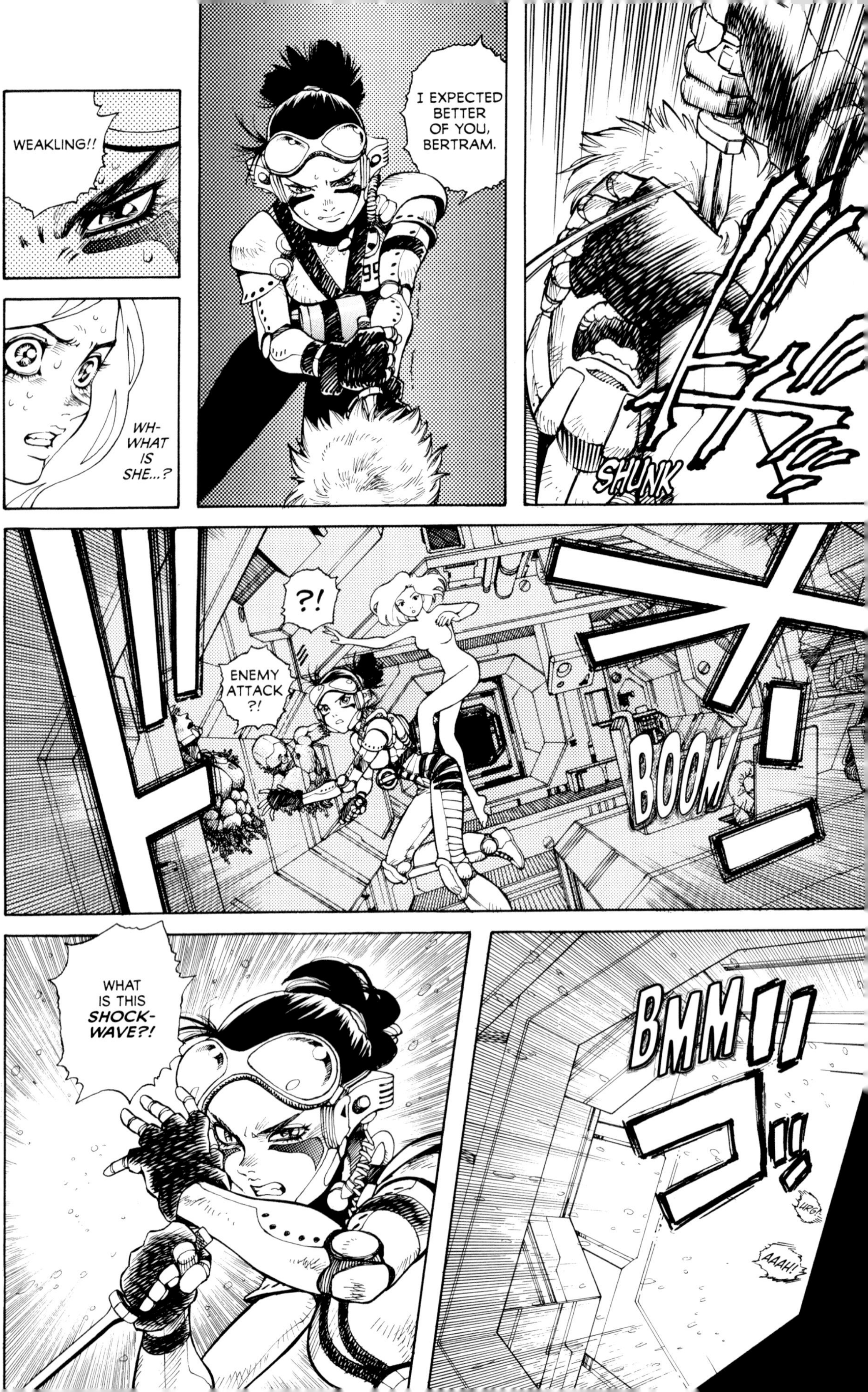
SHUNK
I EXPECTED BETTER OF YOU, BERTRAM.
WEAKLING!!
WH- WHAT IS SHE...?
?!
ENEMY ATTACK ?!
BOOM
BMM
URG!
AAAH!
WHAT IS THIS *SHOCK-WAVE?!*

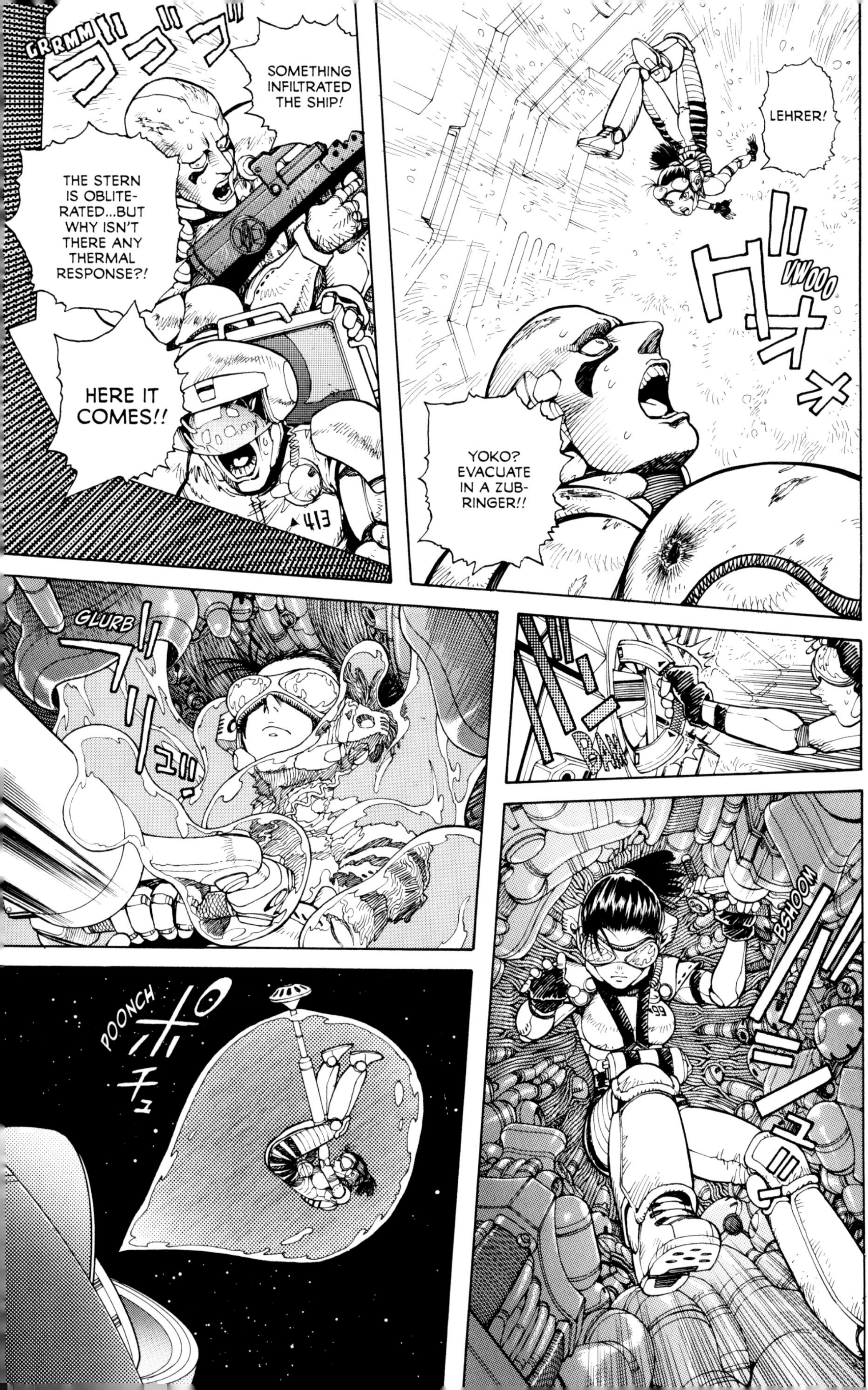
LEHRER!
VWOOO
YOKO? EVACUATE IN A ZUB-RINGER!!
GRRMM
SOMETHING INFILTRATED THE SHIP!
THE STERN IS OBLITE-RATED...BUT WHY ISN'T THERE ANY THERMAL RESPONSE?!
HERE IT COMES!!
BAM
GLURB
BSHOOM
POONCH

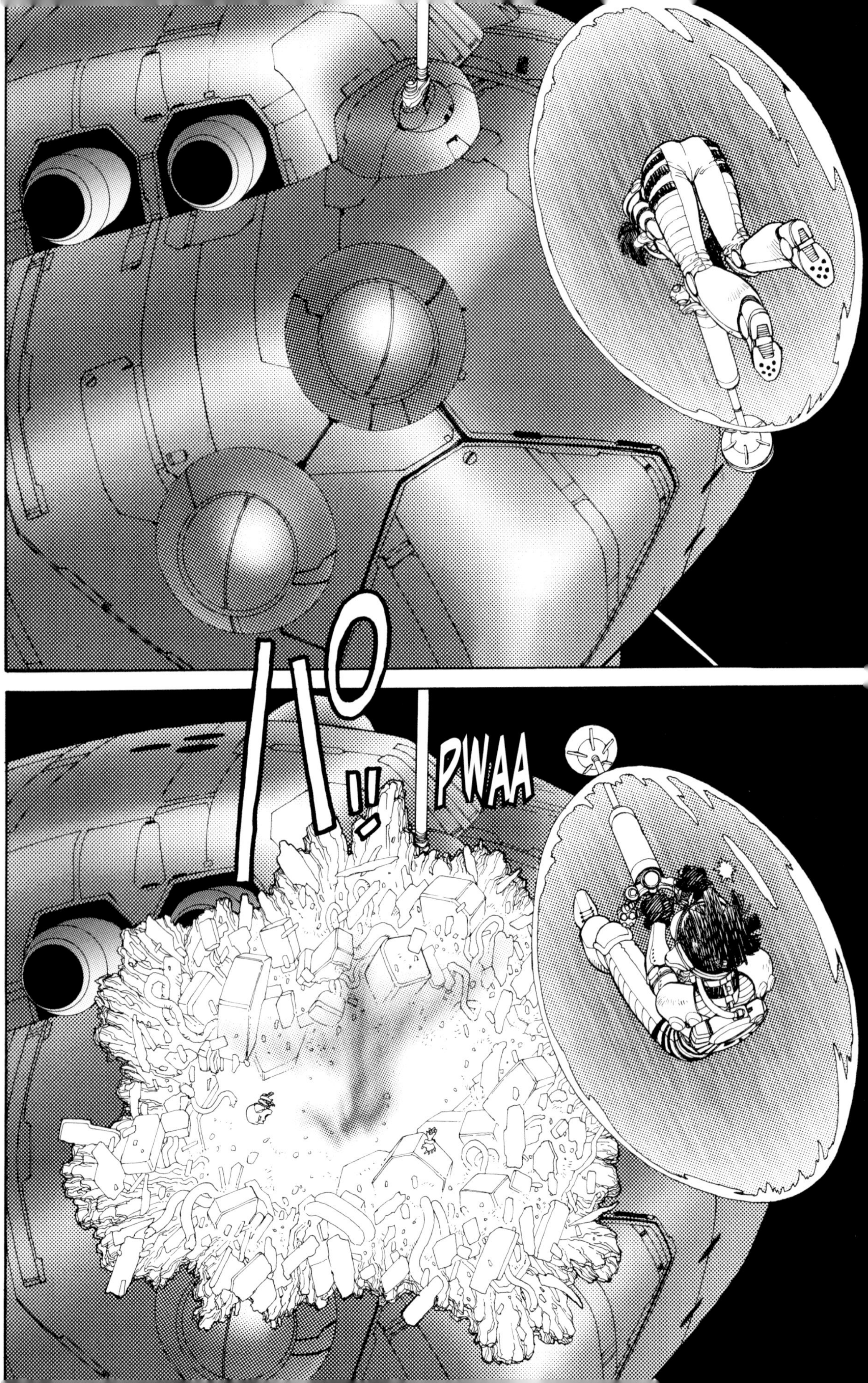
パ!!
PWAA

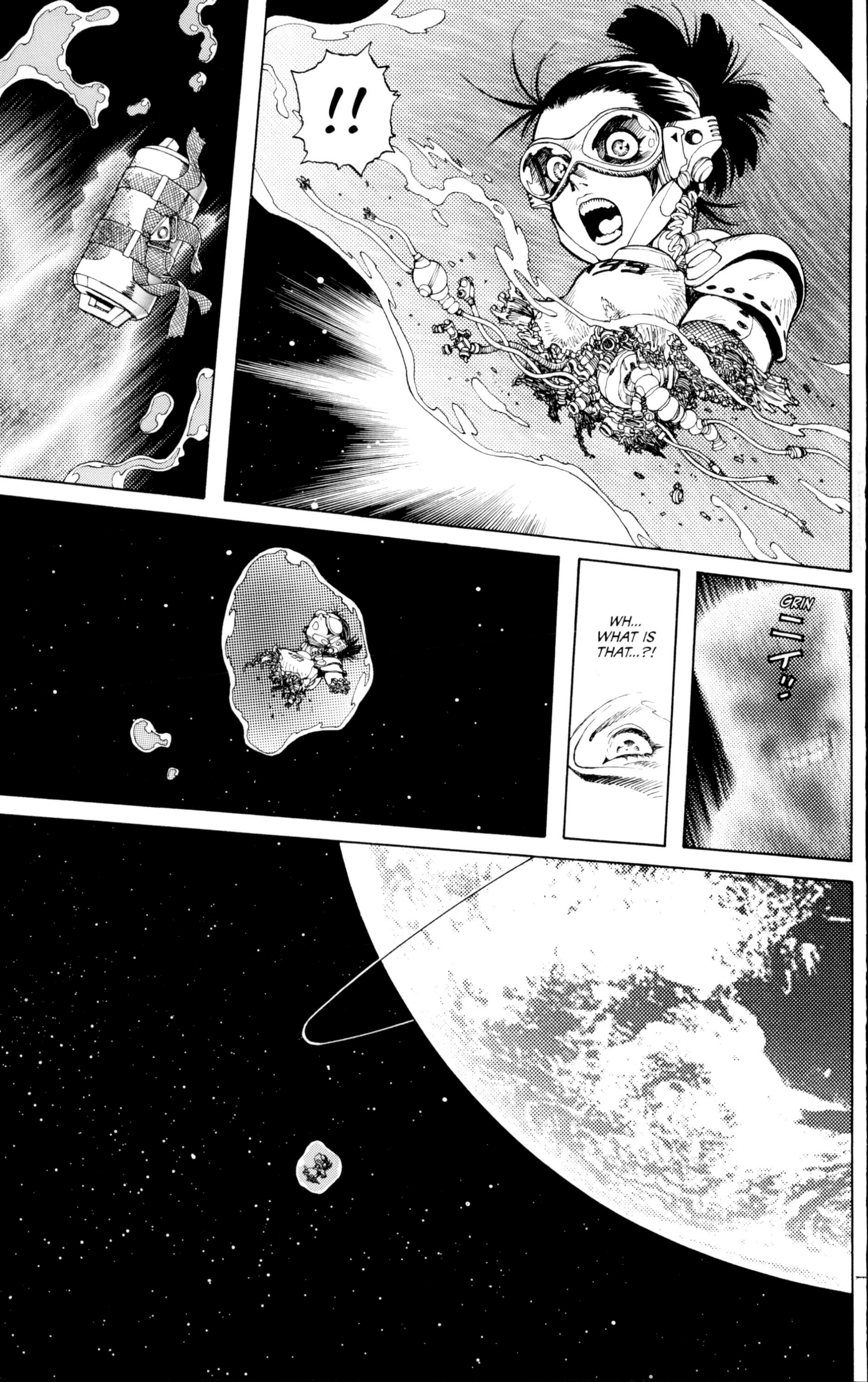
!!
GRIN
WH... WHAT IS THAT...?!

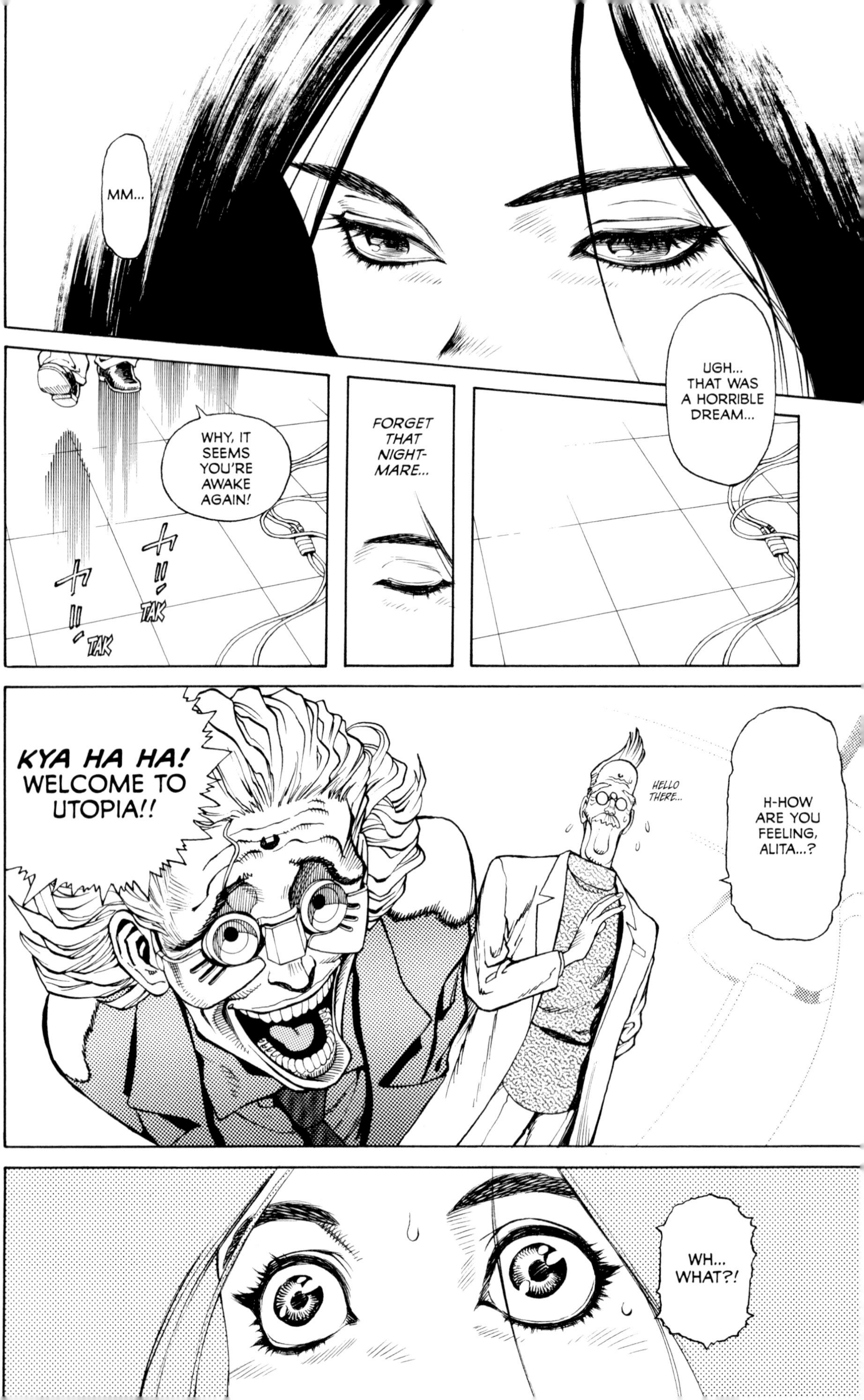
MM...
UGH... THAT WAS A HORRIBLE DREAM...
FORGET THAT NIGHT-MARE...
WHY, IT SEEMS YOU'RE AWAKE AGAIN!
TAK
TAK
H-HOW ARE YOU FEELING, ALITA...?
HELLO THERE...
KYA HA HA! WELCOME TO UTOPIA!!
WH... WHAT?!

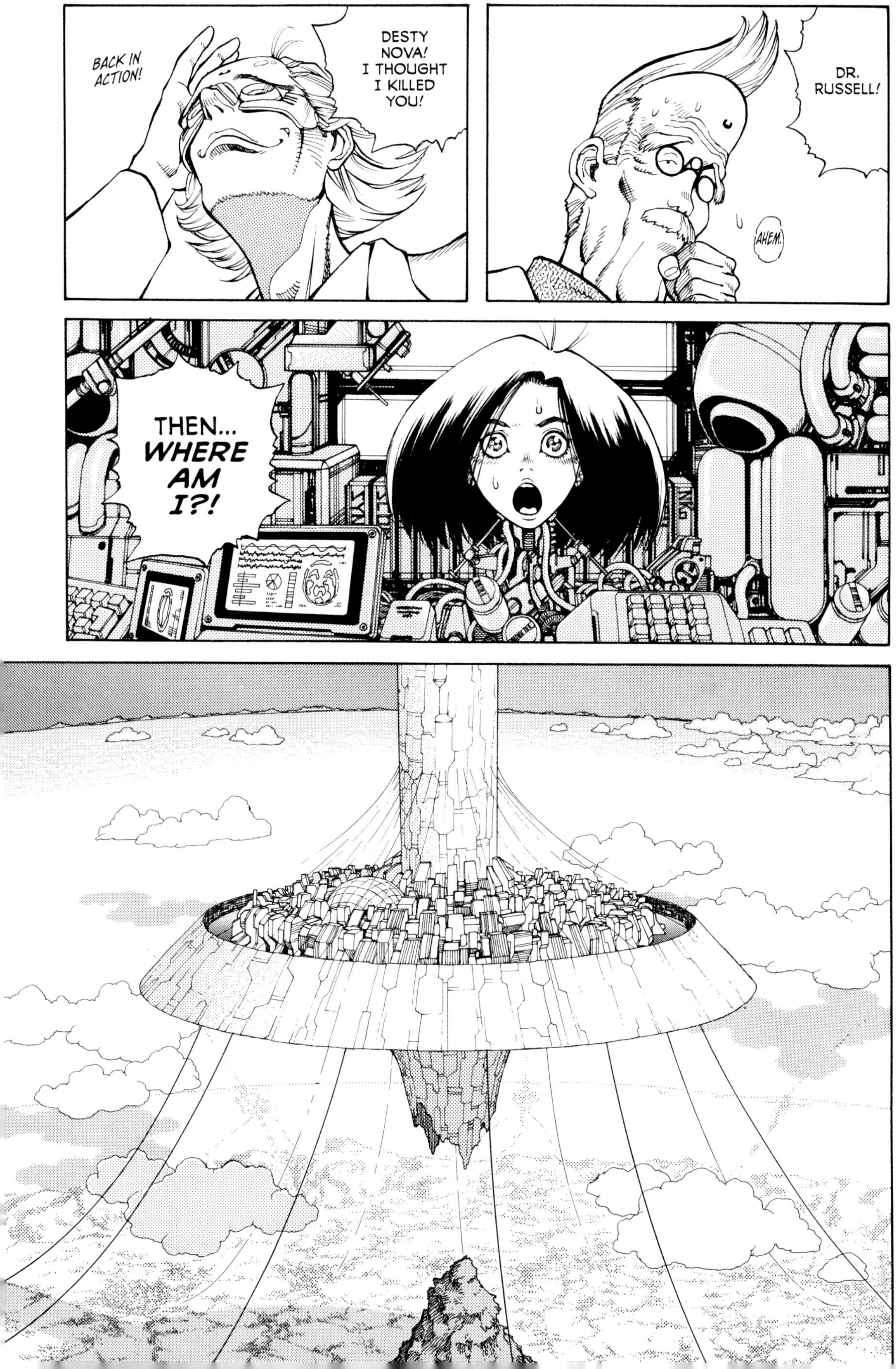
DR. RUSSELL!
AHEM.
DESTY NOVA! I THOUGHT I KILLED YOU!
BACK IN ACTION!
THEN... WHERE AM I?!

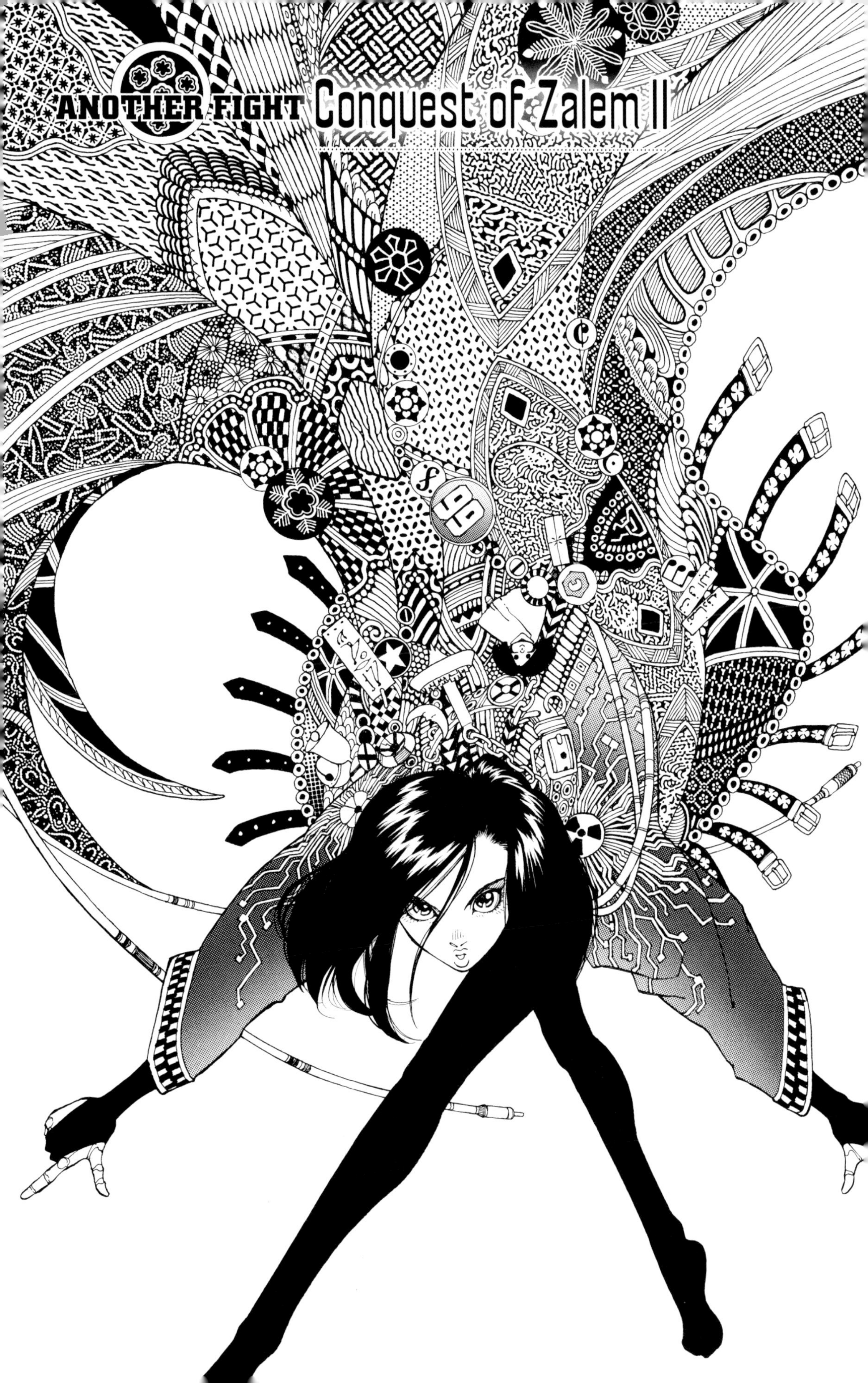
ANOTHER FIGHT Conquest of Zalem II

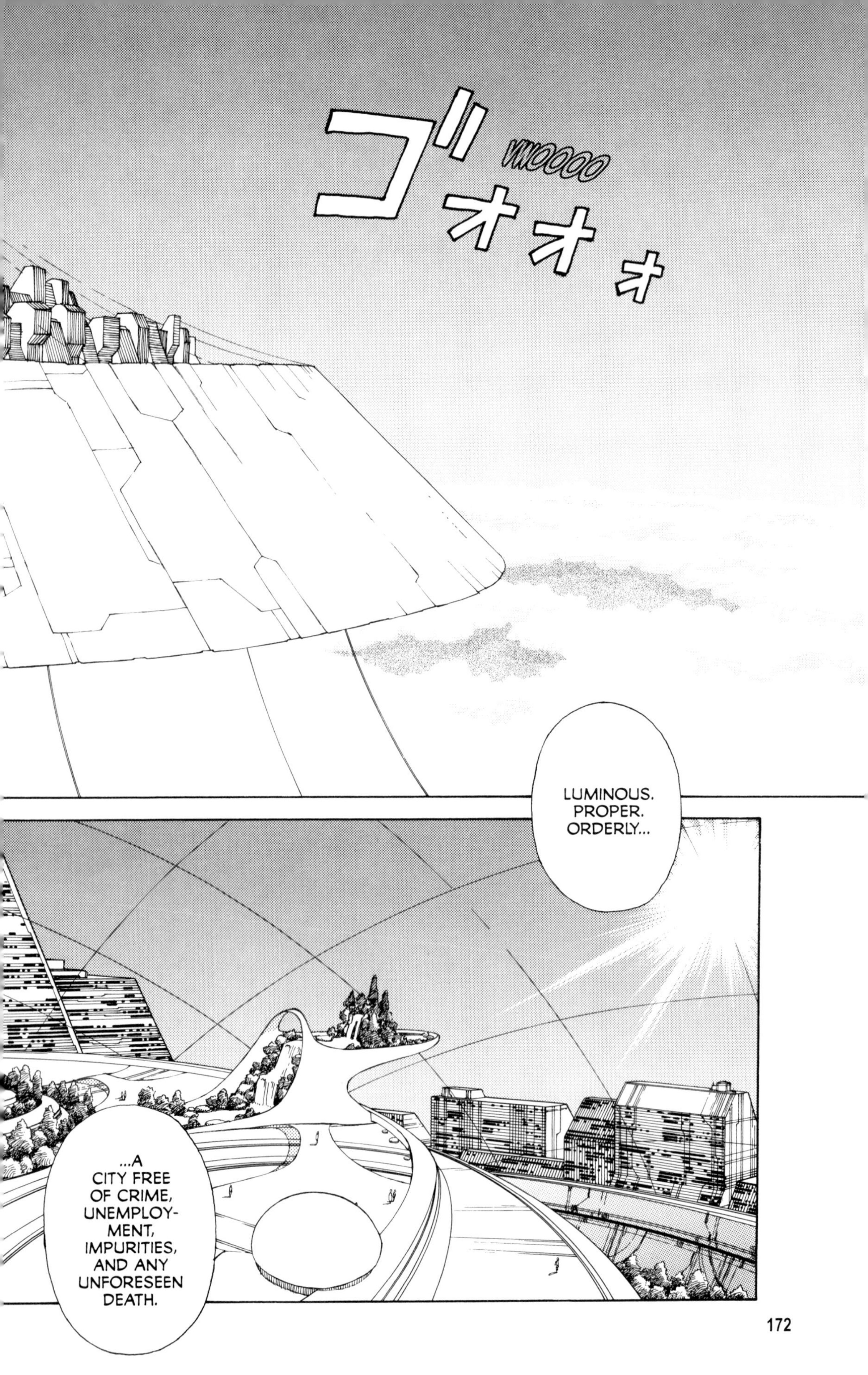
ゴオオォ
VWOOOO
LUMINOUS. PROPER. ORDERLY...
...A CITY FREE OF CRIME, UNEMPLOYMENT, IMPURITIES, AND ANY UNFORESEEN DEATH.

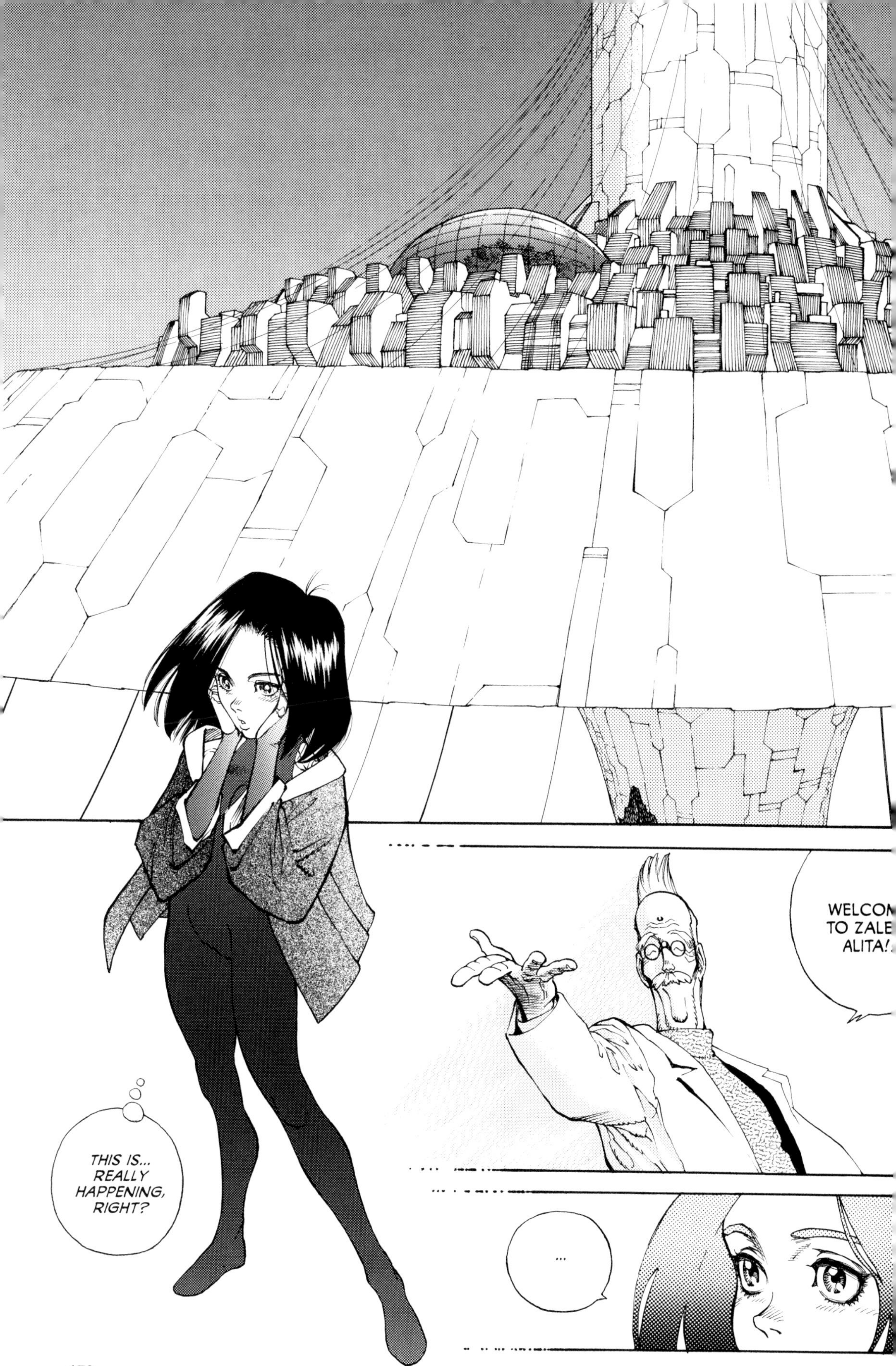
WELCOM TO ZALE ALITA!
...
THIS IS... REALLY HAPPENING, RIGHT?

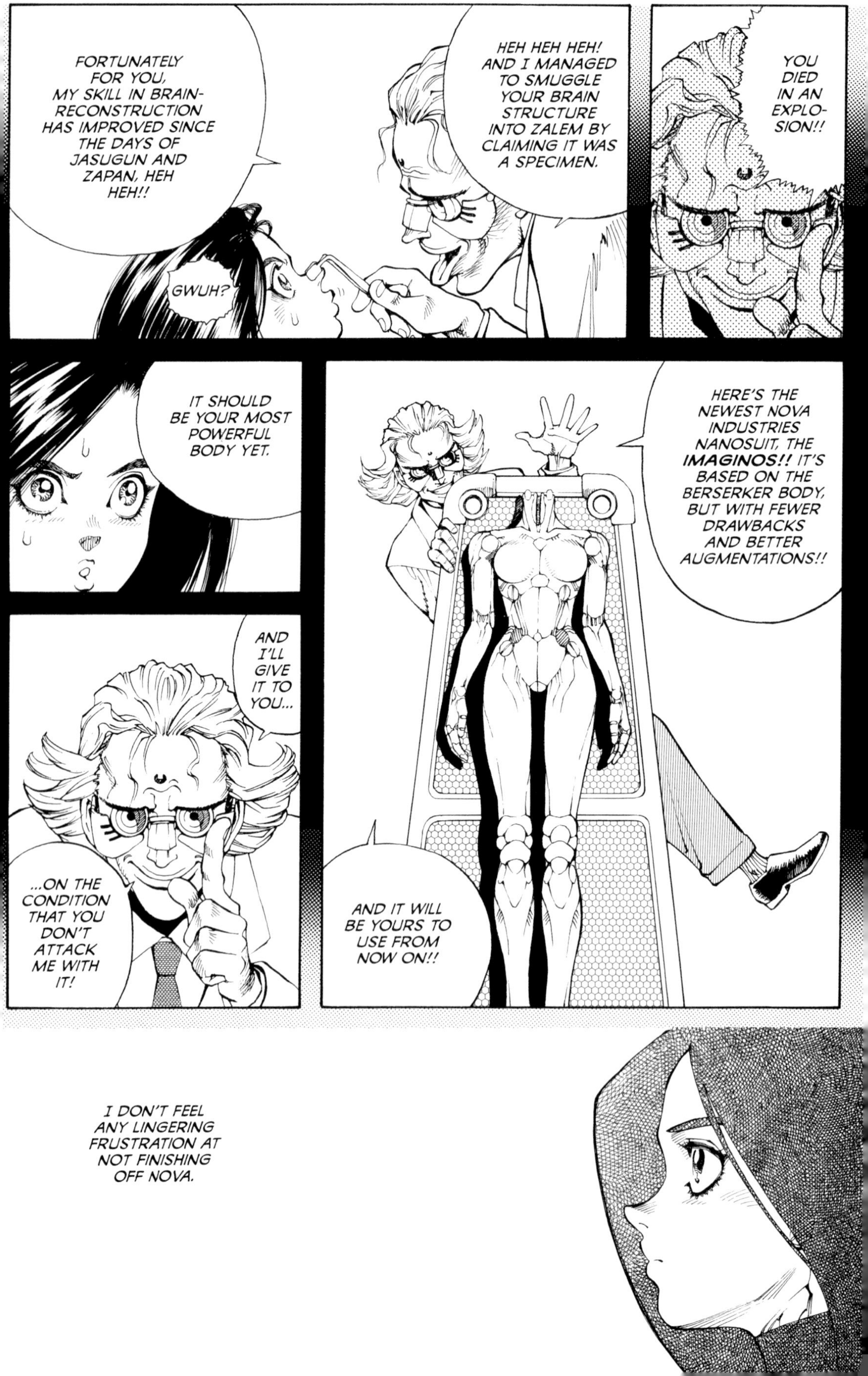
YOU DIED IN AN EXPLOSION!!
HEH HEH HEH! AND I MANAGED TO SMUGGLE YOUR BRAIN STRUCTURE INTO ZALEM BY CLAIMING IT WAS A SPECIMEN.
FORTUNATELY FOR YOU, MY SKILL IN BRAIN-RECONSTRUCTION HAS IMPROVED SINCE THE DAYS OF JASUGUN AND ZAPAN, HEH HEH!!
GWUH?
HERE'S THE NEWEST NOVA INDUSTRIES NANOSUIT, THE **IMAGINOS!!** IT'S BASED ON THE BERSERKER BODY, BUT WITH FEWER DRAWBACKS AND BETTER AUGMENTATIONS!!
AND IT WILL BE YOURS TO USE FROM NOW ON!!
IT SHOULD BE YOUR MOST POWERFUL BODY YET.
AND I'LL GIVE IT TO YOU...
...ON THE CONDITION THAT YOU DON'T ATTACK ME WITH IT!
I DON'T FEEL ANY LINGERING FRUSTRATION AT NOT FINISHING OFF NOVA.

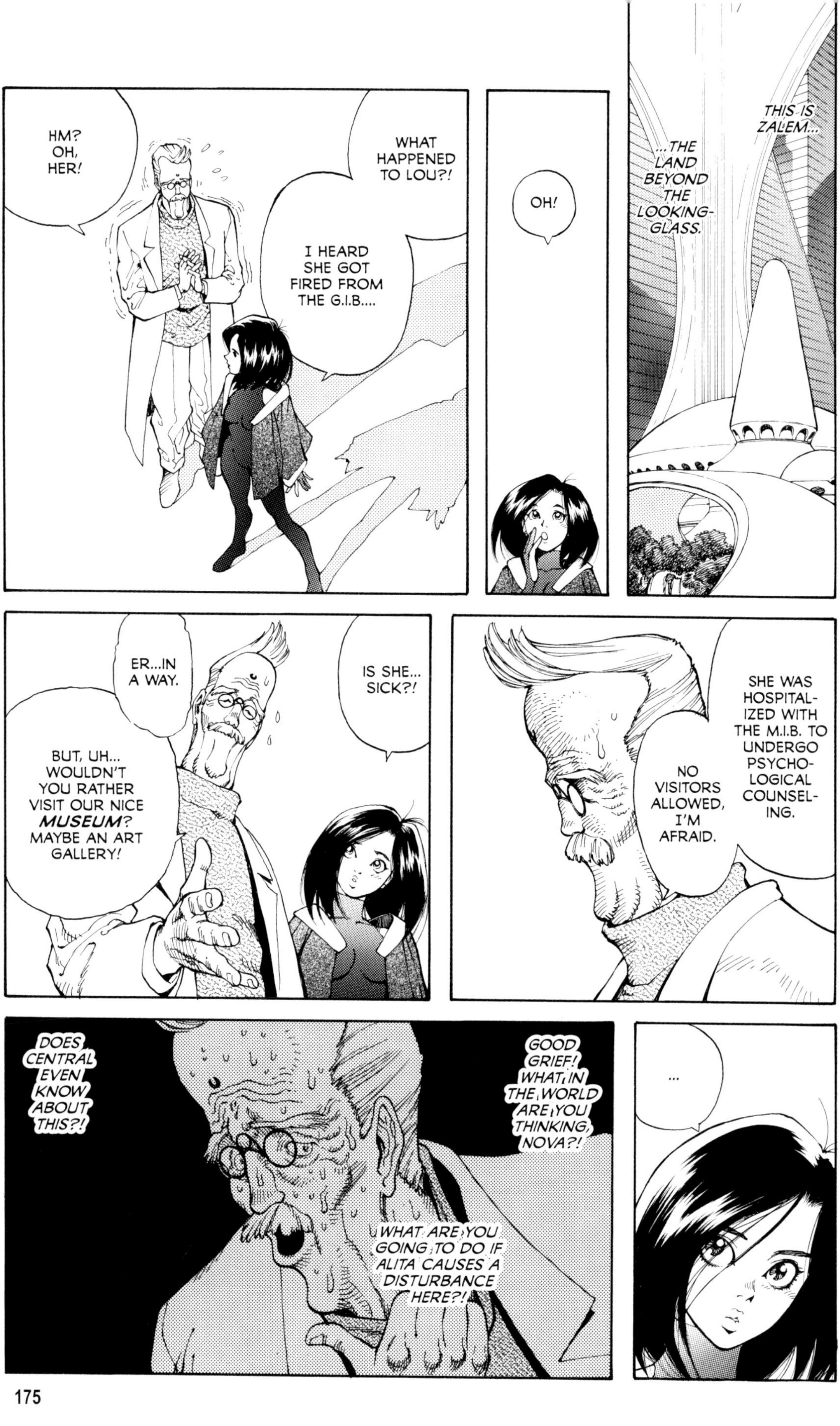
THIS IS ZALEM...
...THE LAND BEYOND THE LOOKING-GLASS.
OH!
WHAT HAPPENED TO LOU?!
I HEARD SHE GOT FIRED FROM THE G.I.B....
HM? OH, HER!
SHE WAS HOSPITALIZED WITH THE M.I.B. TO UNDERGO PSYCHOLOGICAL COUNSELING.
NO VISITORS ALLOWED, I'M AFRAID.
IS SHE... SICK?!
ER...IN A WAY.
BUT, UH... WOULDN'T YOU RATHER VISIT OUR NICE ***MUSEUM***? MAYBE AN ART GALLERY!
...
GOOD GRIEF! WHAT IN THE WORLD ARE YOU THINKING, NOVA?!
DOES CENTRAL EVEN KNOW ABOUT THIS?!
WHAT ARE YOU GOING TO DO IF ALITA CAUSES A DISTURBANCE HERE?!

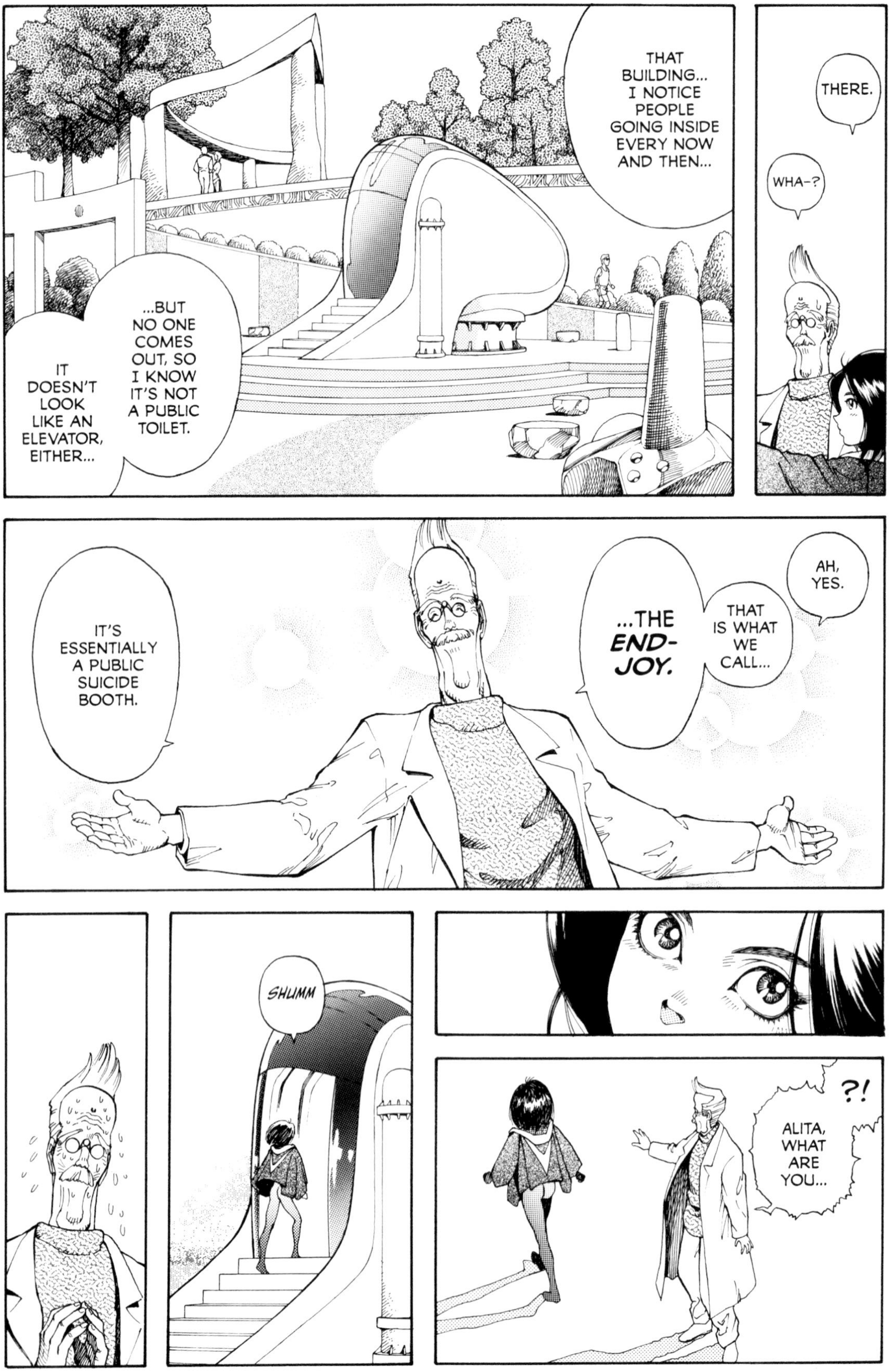
THERE.
WHA-?
THAT BUILDING... I NOTICE PEOPLE GOING INSIDE EVERY NOW AND THEN...
...BUT NO ONE COMES OUT, SO I KNOW IT'S NOT A PUBLIC TOILET.
IT DOESN'T LOOK LIKE AN ELEVATOR, EITHER...
AH, YES.
THAT IS WHAT WE CALL...
...THE *END-JOY.*
IT'S ESSENTIALLY A PUBLIC SUICIDE BOOTH.
?!
ALITA, WHAT ARE YOU...
SHUMM

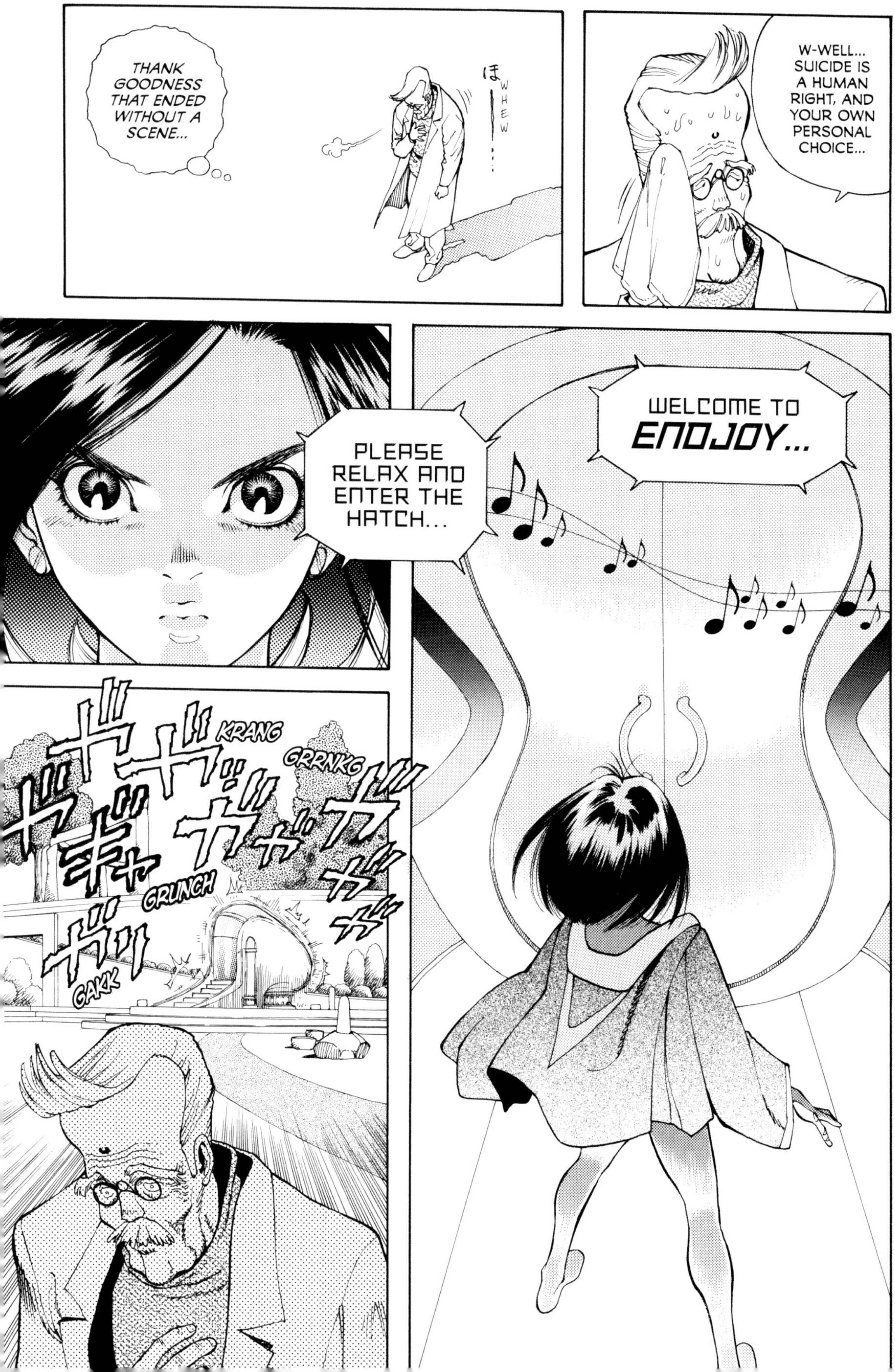
W-WELL... SUICIDE IS A HUMAN RIGHT, AND YOUR OWN PERSONAL CHOICE...
THANK GOODNESS THAT ENDED WITHOUT A SCENE...
ほ
WHEW
WELCOME TO ENDJOY...
PLEASE RELAX AND ENTER THE HATCH...
KRANG
GRRNKG
GRUNCH
GAKK

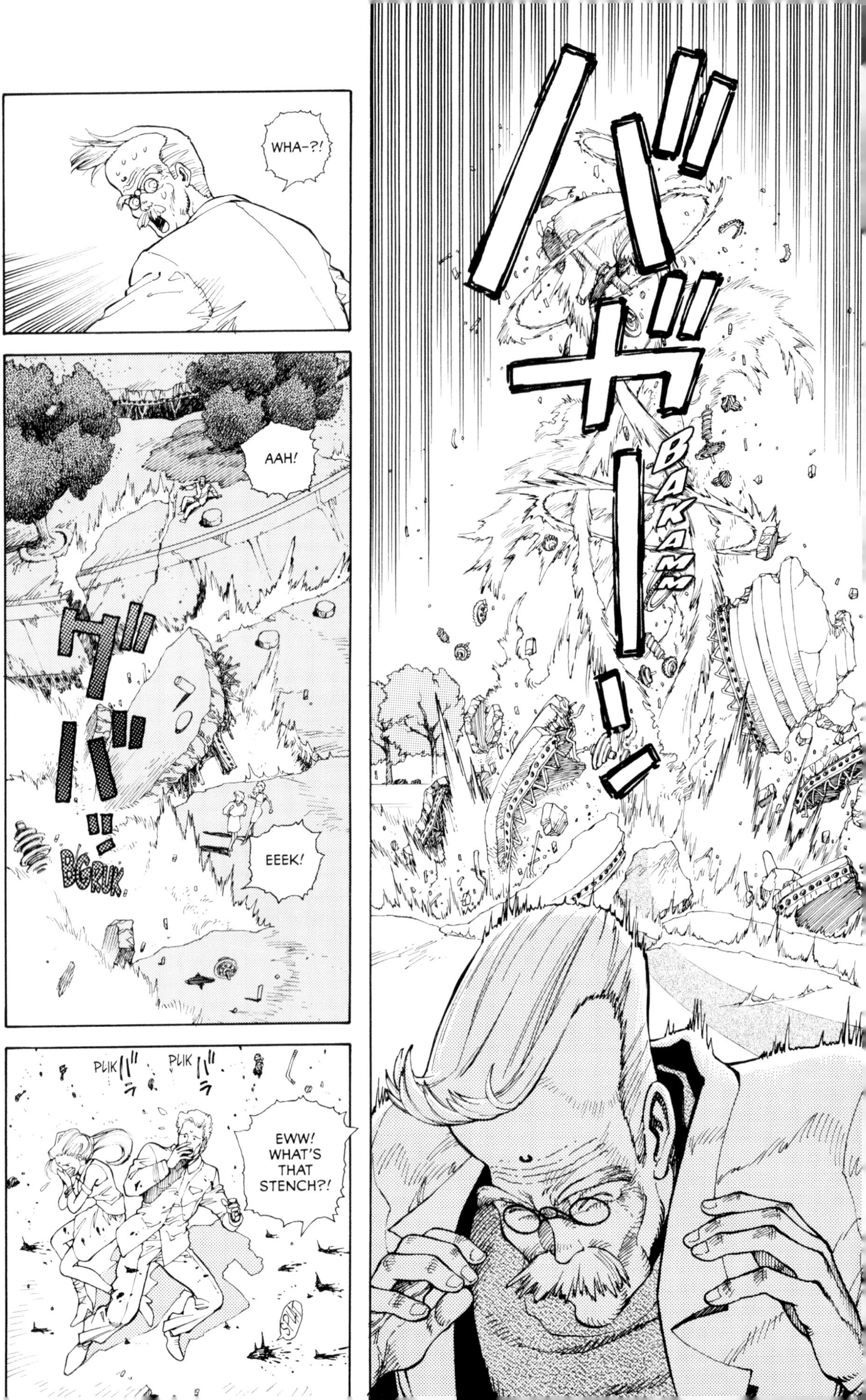

BAKAMM
WHA-?!
AAH!
BGRUK
EEEK!
PLIK
PLIK
EWW! WHAT'S THAT STENCH?!

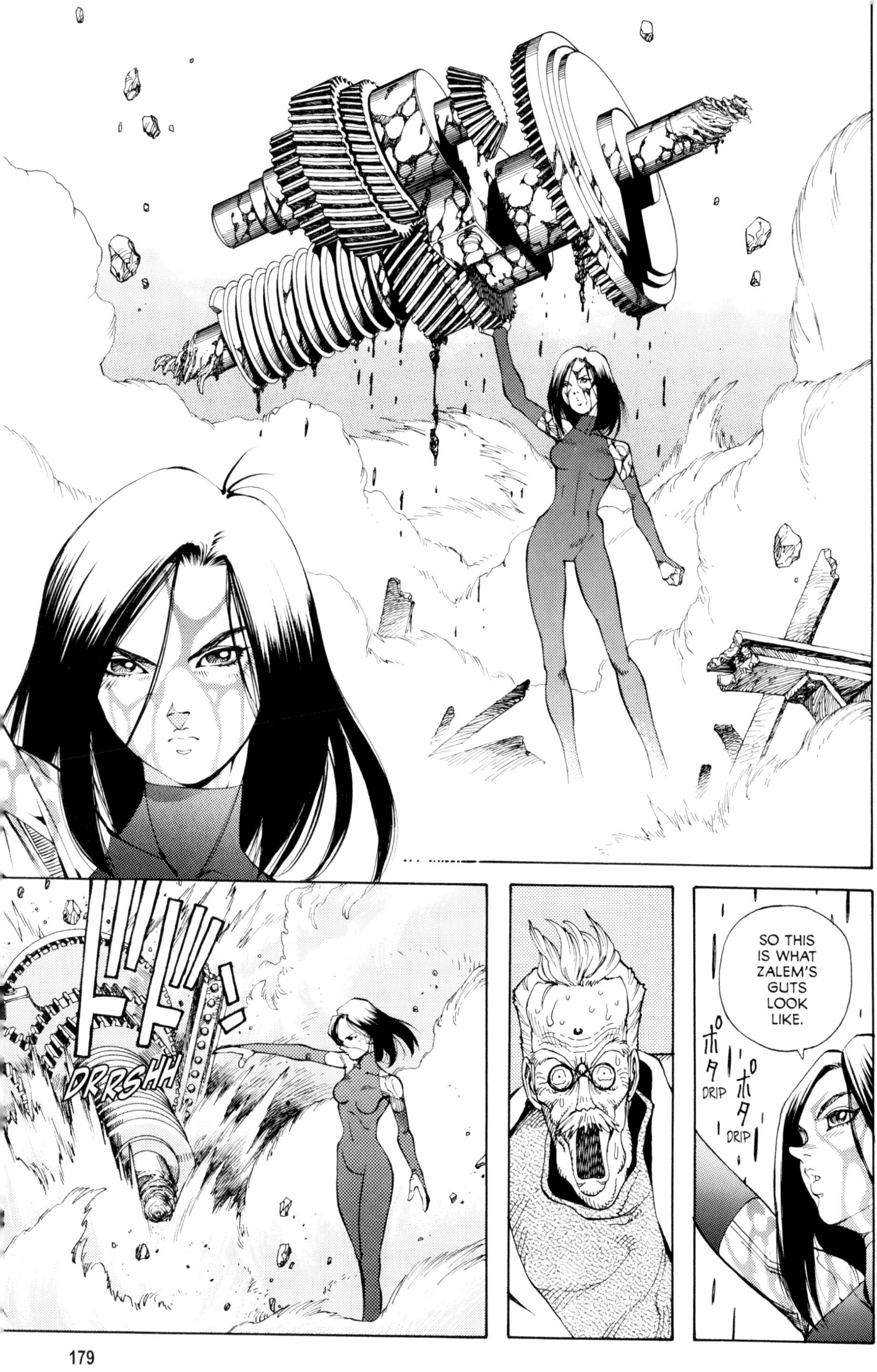
SO THIS IS WHAT ZALEM'S GUTS LOOK LIKE.
ポタ
DRIP
ポタ
DRIP
DRRSHH

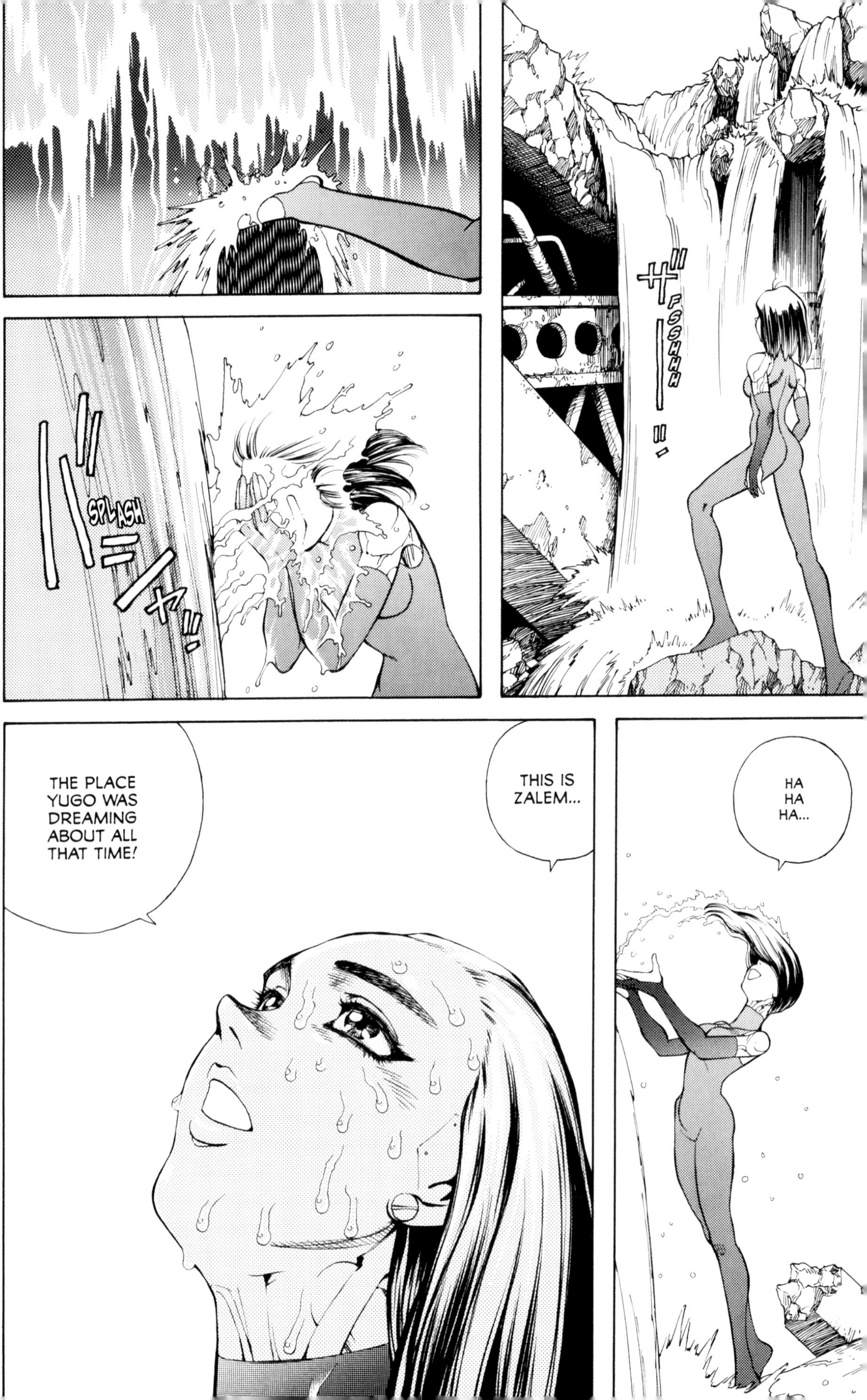

FSSHHH
SPLASH
HA HA HA...
THIS IS ZALEM...
THE PLACE YUGO WAS DREAMING ABOUT ALL THAT TIME!

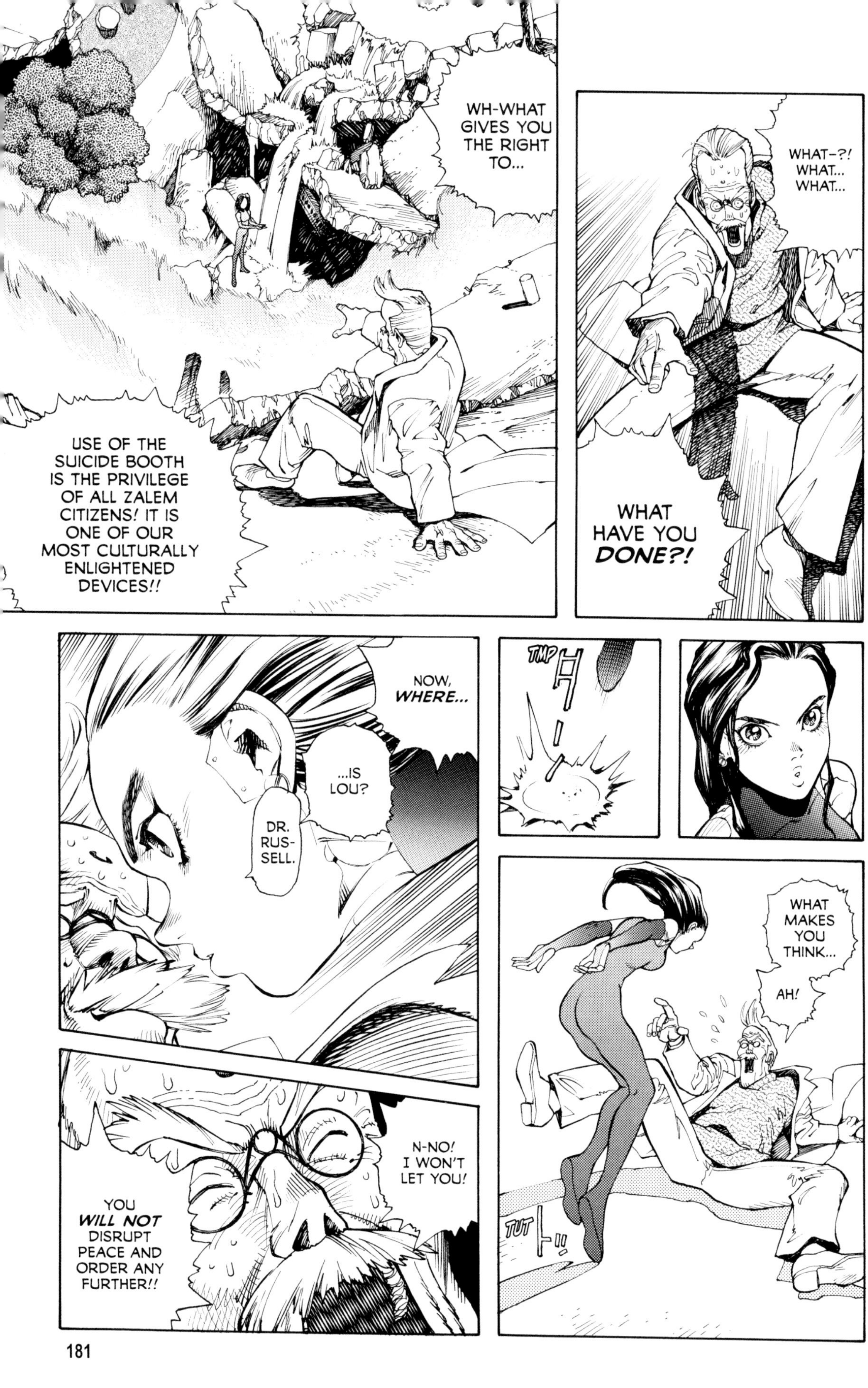
WHAT-?! WHAT... WHAT...
WHAT HAVE YOU *DONE?!*
WH-WHAT GIVES YOU THE RIGHT TO...
USE OF THE SUICIDE BOOTH IS THE PRIVILEGE OF ALL ZALEM CITIZENS! IT IS ONE OF OUR MOST CULTURALLY ENLIGHTENED DEVICES!!
TMP
NOW, *WHERE...*
...IS LOU?
DR. RUS-SELL.
WHAT MAKES YOU THINK...
AH!
TUT
N-NO! I WON'T LET YOU!
YOU *WILL NOT* DISRUPT PEACE AND ORDER ANY FURTHER!!

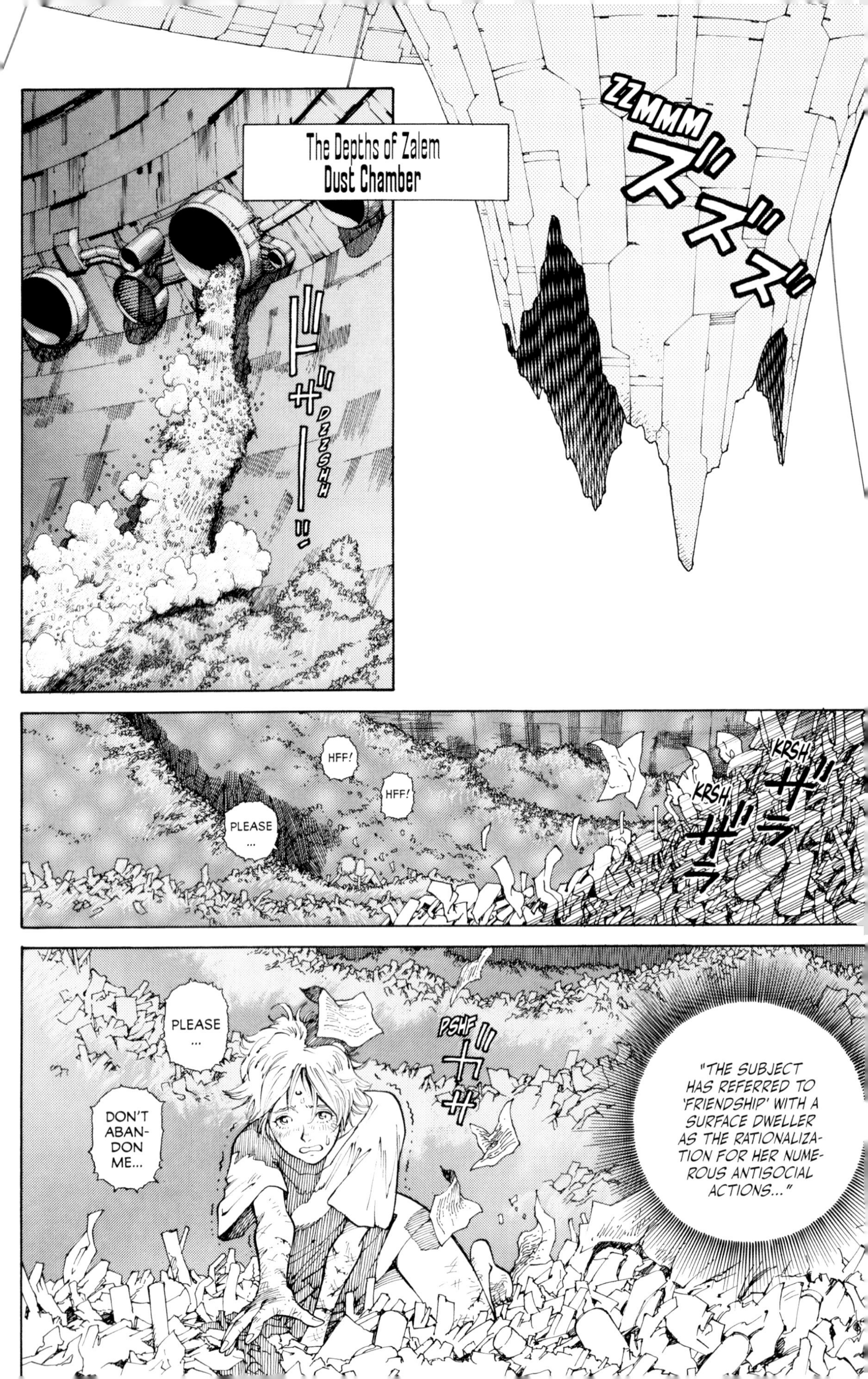
ZZMMM
ズズズズ
The Depths of Zalem
Dust Chamber
DZZSHH
ドザー!!
KRSH
ザラ
KRSH
ザラ
HFF!
HFF!
PLEASE ...
"THE SUBJECT HAS REFERRED TO 'FRIENDSHIP' WITH A SURFACE DWELLER AS THE RATIONALIZATION FOR HER NUMEROUS ANTISOCIAL ACTIONS..."
PSHF
ガサ
PLEASE ...
DON'T ABANDON ME...

GAGONG

EEK!

A... ALITA...

"WE FIND REFORM OF THE SUBJECT'S WAYS WITHOUT DESTROYING HER MIND EXCEEDINGLY UNLIKELY..."

!!

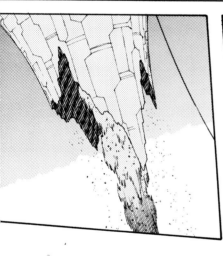

"WE DEEM HER UNFIT FOR CITIZENSHIP, AND THUS SLATED FOR DISPOSAL!!"

DWOOOSH

YAAAH!

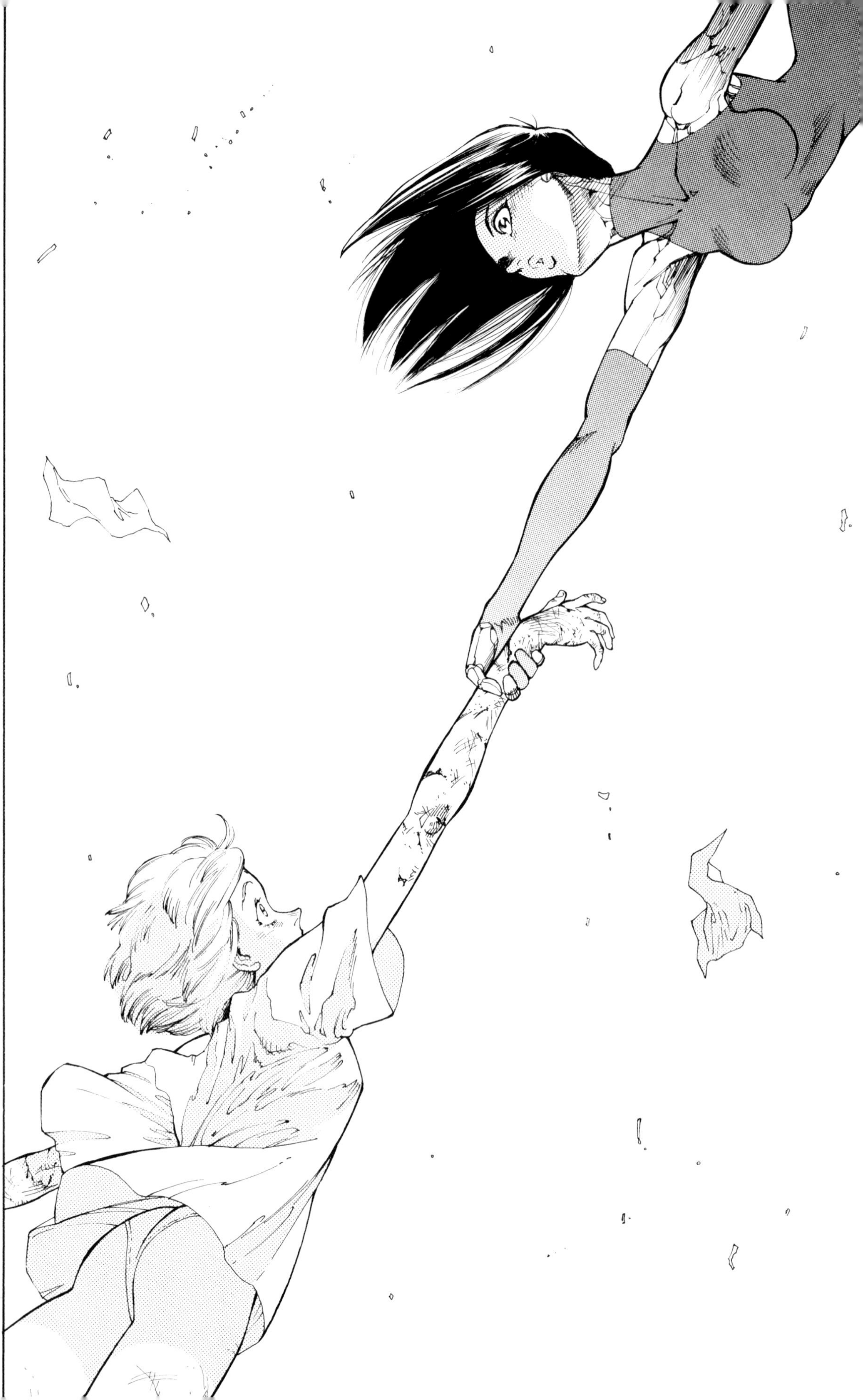

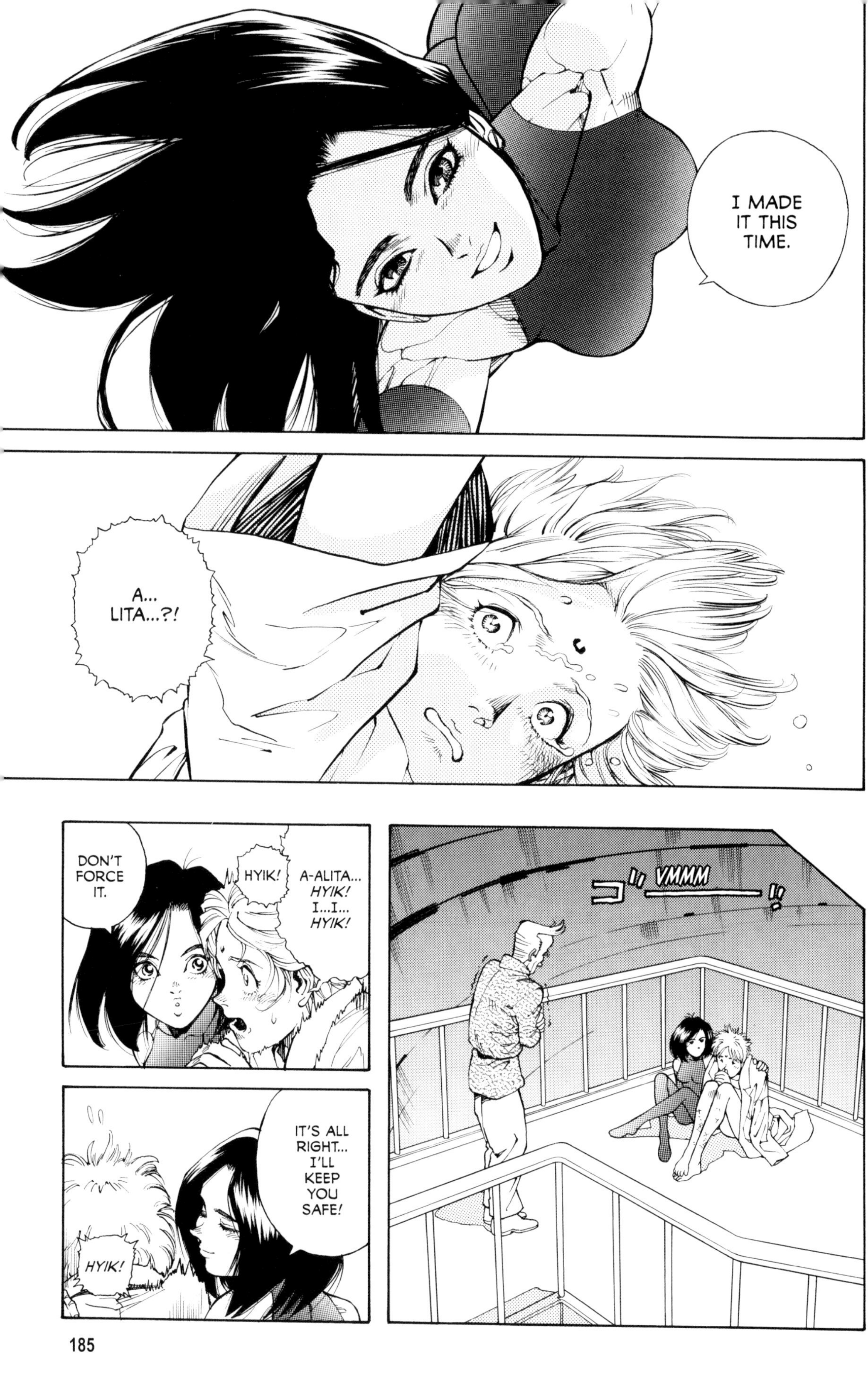
I MADE IT THIS TIME.
A... LITA...?!
VMMM
A-ALITA... HYIK! I...I... HYIK!
HYIK!
DON'T FORCE IT.
IT'S ALL RIGHT... I'LL KEEP YOU SAFE!
HYIK!

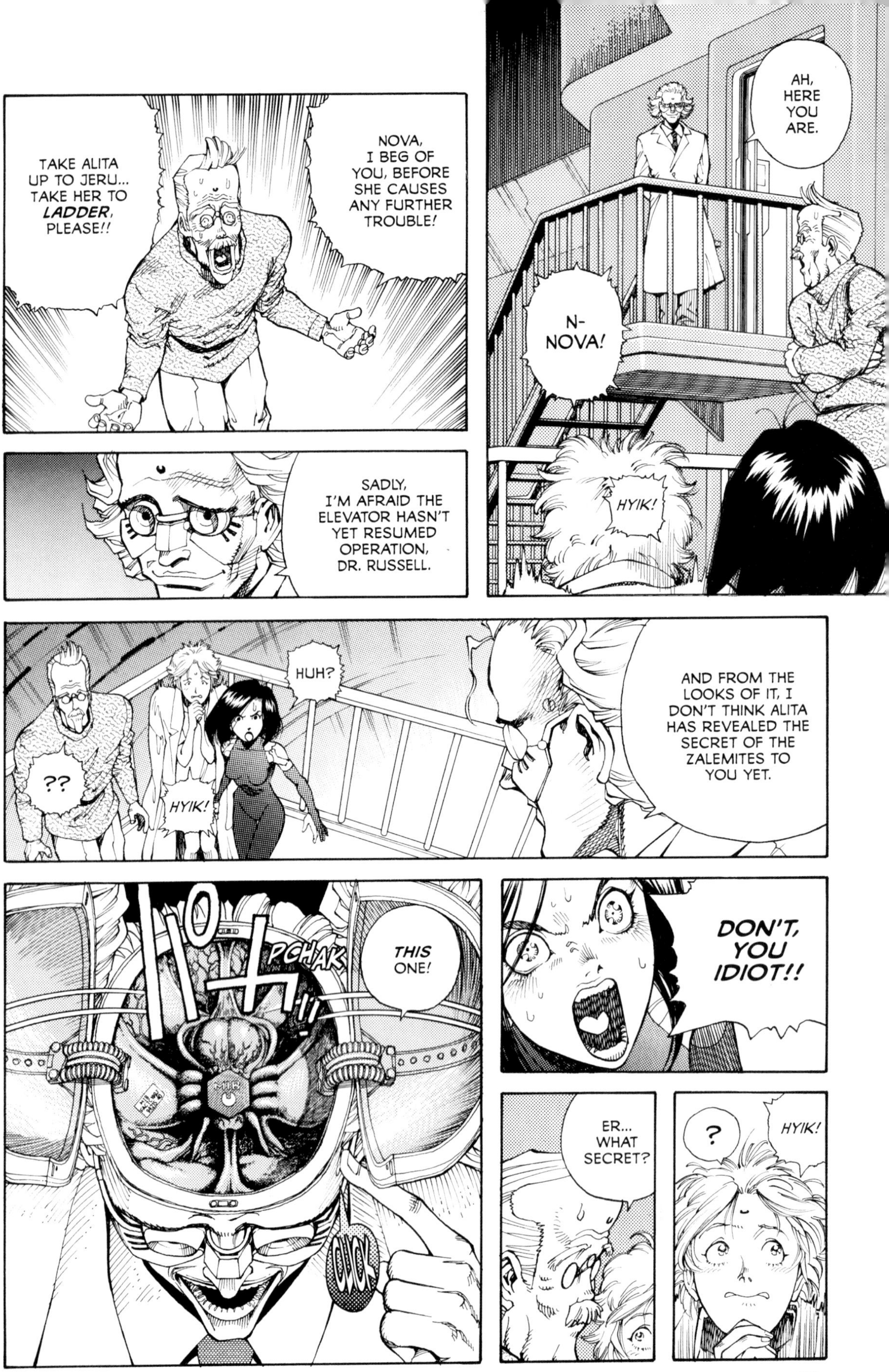
AH, HERE YOU ARE.
N-NOVA!
HYIK!
NOVA, I BEG OF YOU, BEFORE SHE CAUSES ANY FURTHER TROUBLE!
TAKE ALITA UP TO JERU... TAKE HER TO *LADDER*, PLEASE!!
SADLY, I'M AFRAID THE ELEVATOR HASN'T YET RESUMED OPERATION, DR. RUSSELL.
AND FROM THE LOOKS OF IT, I DON'T THINK ALITA HAS REVEALED THE SECRET OF THE ZALEMITES TO YOU YET.
HUH?
HYIK!
??
DON'T, YOU IDIOT!!
HYIK!
?
ER... WHAT SECRET?
THIS ONE!
PCHAK
CLICK

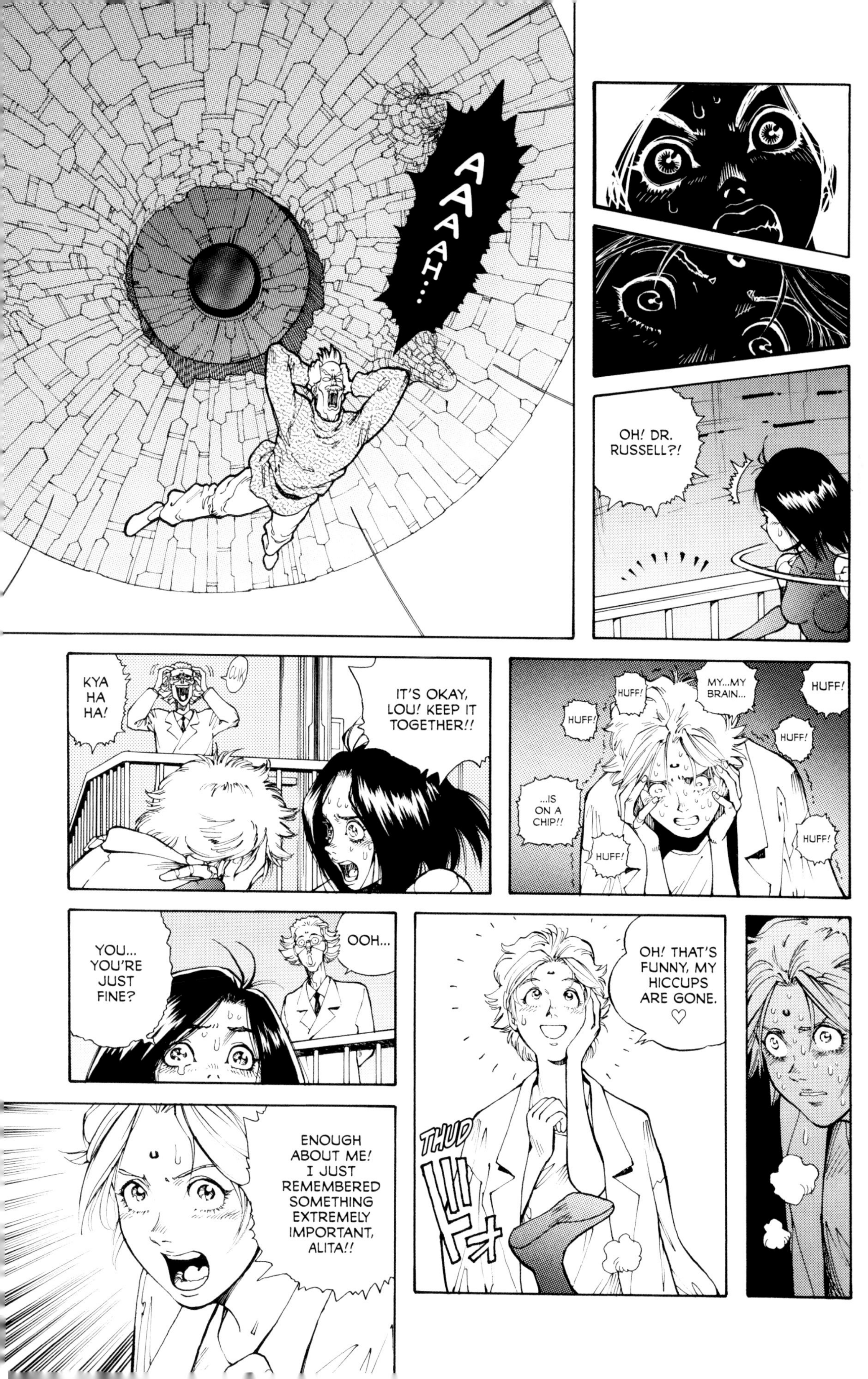
OH! DR. RUSSELL?!
AAAAH...
HUFF!
MY...MY BRAIN...
HUFF!
HUFF!
HUFF!
...IS ON A CHIP!!
HUFF!
HUFF!
IT'S OKAY, LOU! KEEP IT TOGETHER!!
KYA HA HA!
OH! THAT'S FUNNY, MY HICCUPS ARE GONE. ♡
THUD
OOH...
YOU... YOU'RE JUST FINE?
ENOUGH ABOUT ME! I JUST REMEMBERED SOMETHING EXTREMELY IMPORTANT, ALITA!!

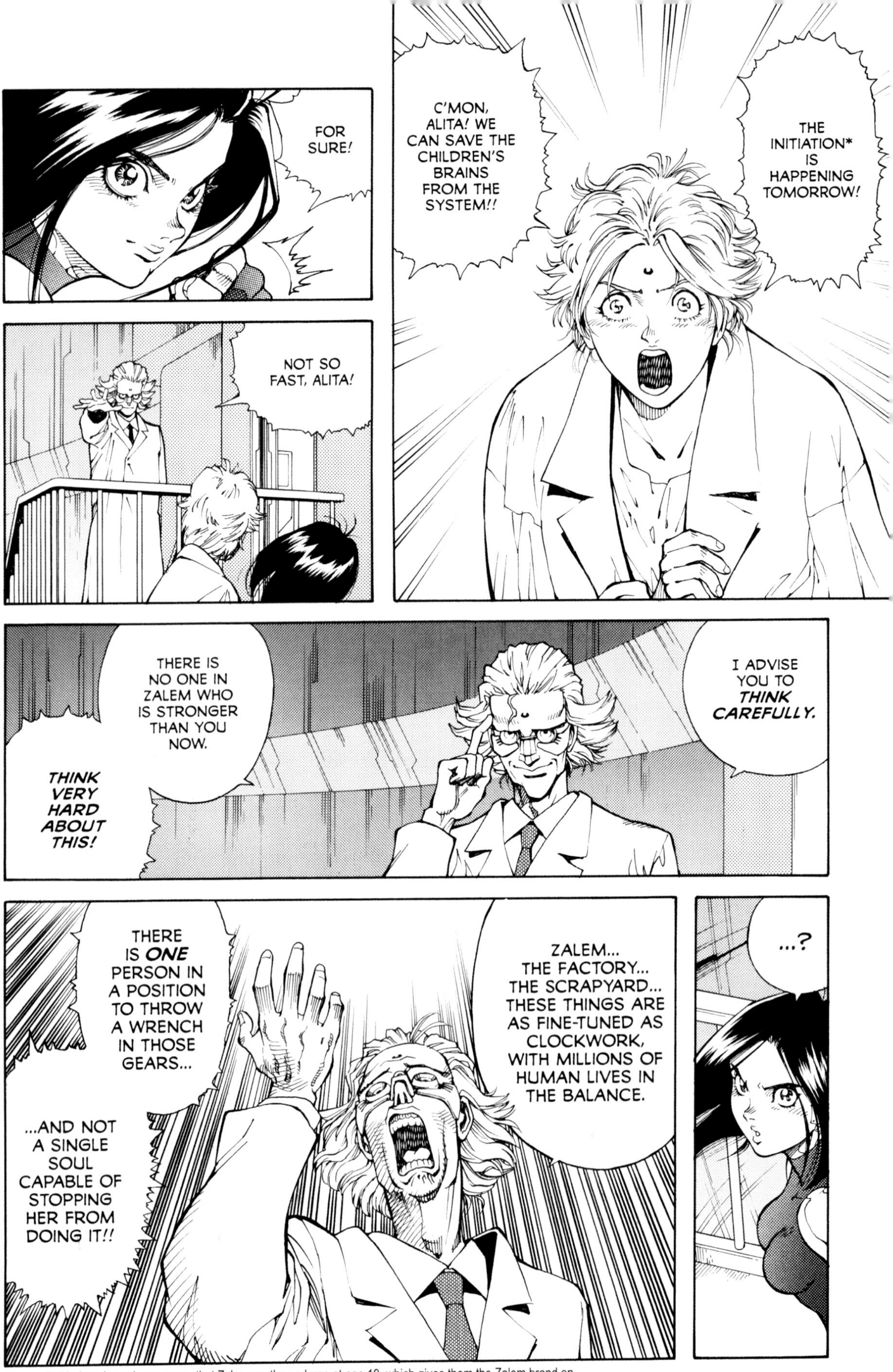
THE INITIATION* IS HAPPENING TOMORROW!
C'MON, ALITA! WE CAN SAVE THE CHILDREN'S BRAINS FROM THE SYSTEM!!
FOR SURE!
NOT SO FAST, ALITA!
I ADVISE YOU TO THINK CAREFULLY.
THERE IS NO ONE IN ZALEM WHO IS STRONGER THAN YOU NOW.
THINK VERY HARD ABOUT THIS!
...?
ZALEM... THE FACTORY... THE SCRAPYARD... THESE THINGS ARE AS FINE-TUNED AS CLOCKWORK, WITH MILLIONS OF HUMAN LIVES IN THE BALANCE.
THERE IS ONE PERSON IN A POSITION TO THROW A WRENCH IN THOSE GEARS...
...AND NOT A SINGLE SOUL CAPABLE OF STOPPING HER FROM DOING IT!!

***Initiation:** A yearly ceremony that Zalem youths undergo at age 19, which gives them the Zalem brand on the forehead and full citizenship. This is when their brains are secretly replaced by the biochip.

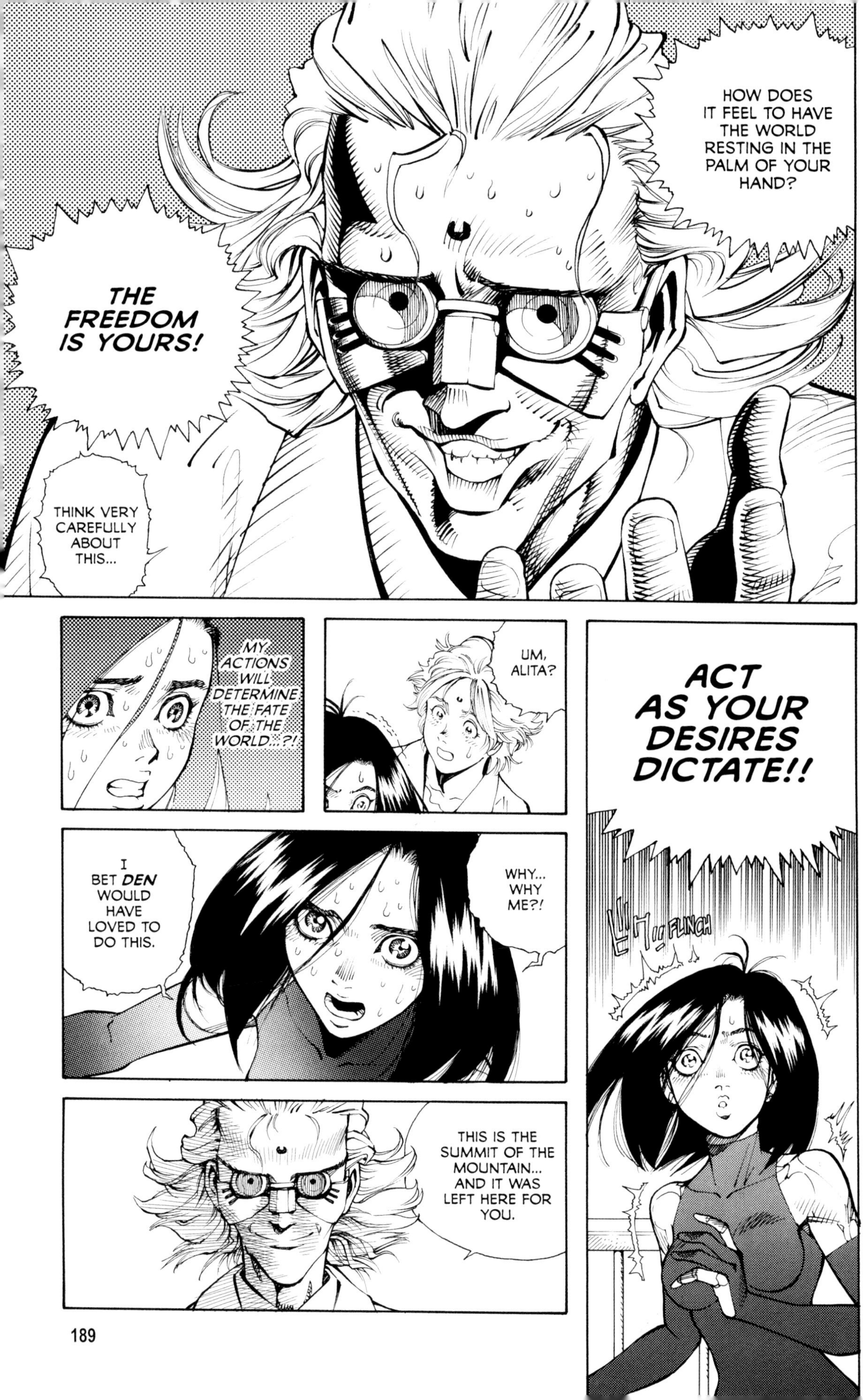
HOW DOES IT FEEL TO HAVE THE WORLD RESTING IN THE PALM OF YOUR HAND?
THE FREEDOM IS YOURS!
THINK VERY CAREFULLY ABOUT THIS...
ACT AS YOUR DESIRES DICTATE!!
FLINCH
UM, ALITA?
MY ACTIONS WILL DETERMINE THE FATE OF THE WORLD...?!
WHY... WHY ME?!
I BET *DEN* WOULD HAVE LOVED TO DO THIS.
THIS IS THE SUMMIT OF THE MOUNTAIN... AND IT WAS LEFT HERE FOR YOU.

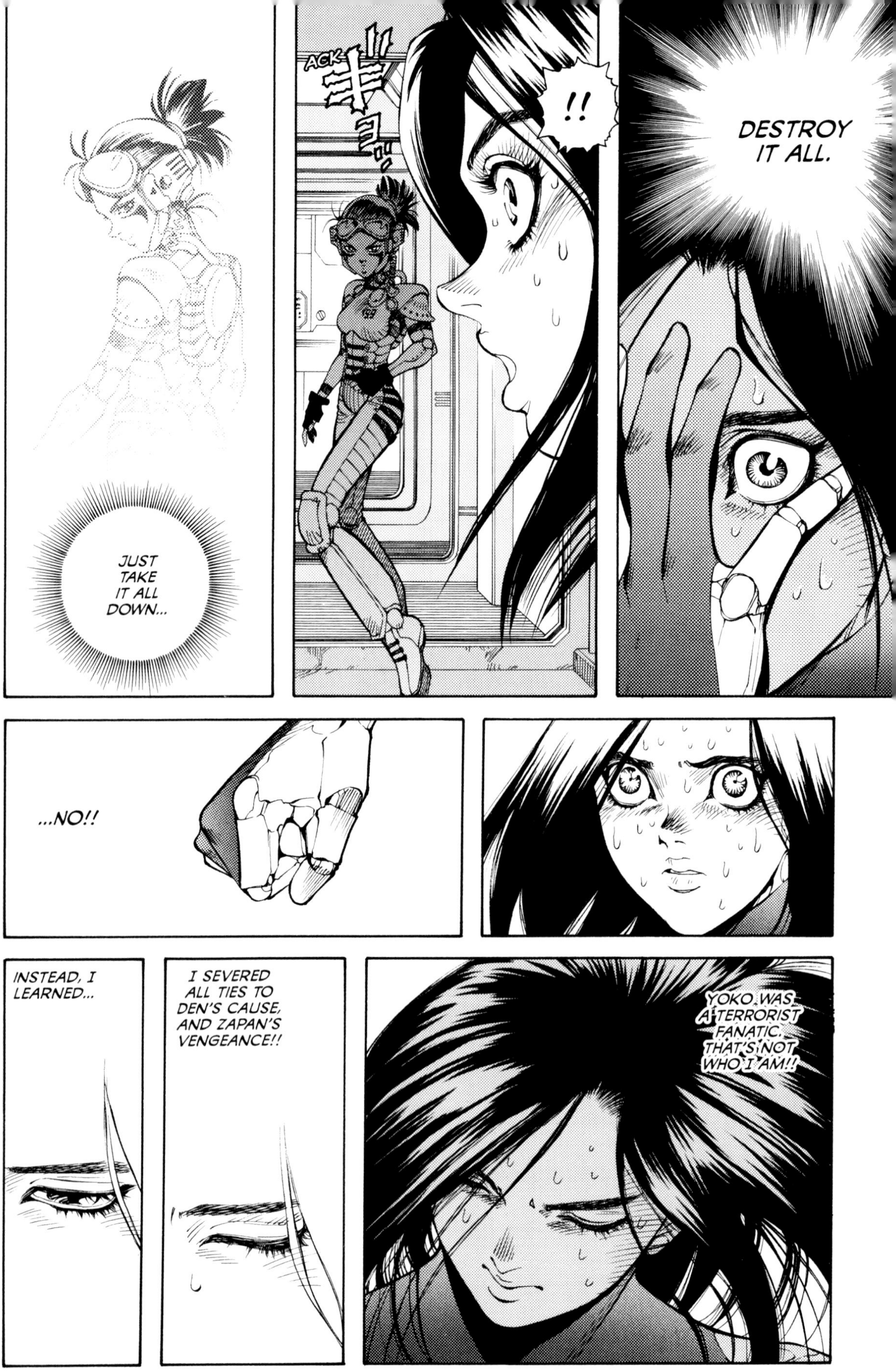
DESTROY IT ALL.
!!
ACK
JUST TAKE IT ALL DOWN...
...NO!!
YOKO WAS A TERRORIST FANATIC. THAT'S NOT WHO I AM!!
I SEVERED ALL TIES TO DEN'S CAUSE, AND ZAPAN'S VENGEANCE!!
INSTEAD, I LEARNED...

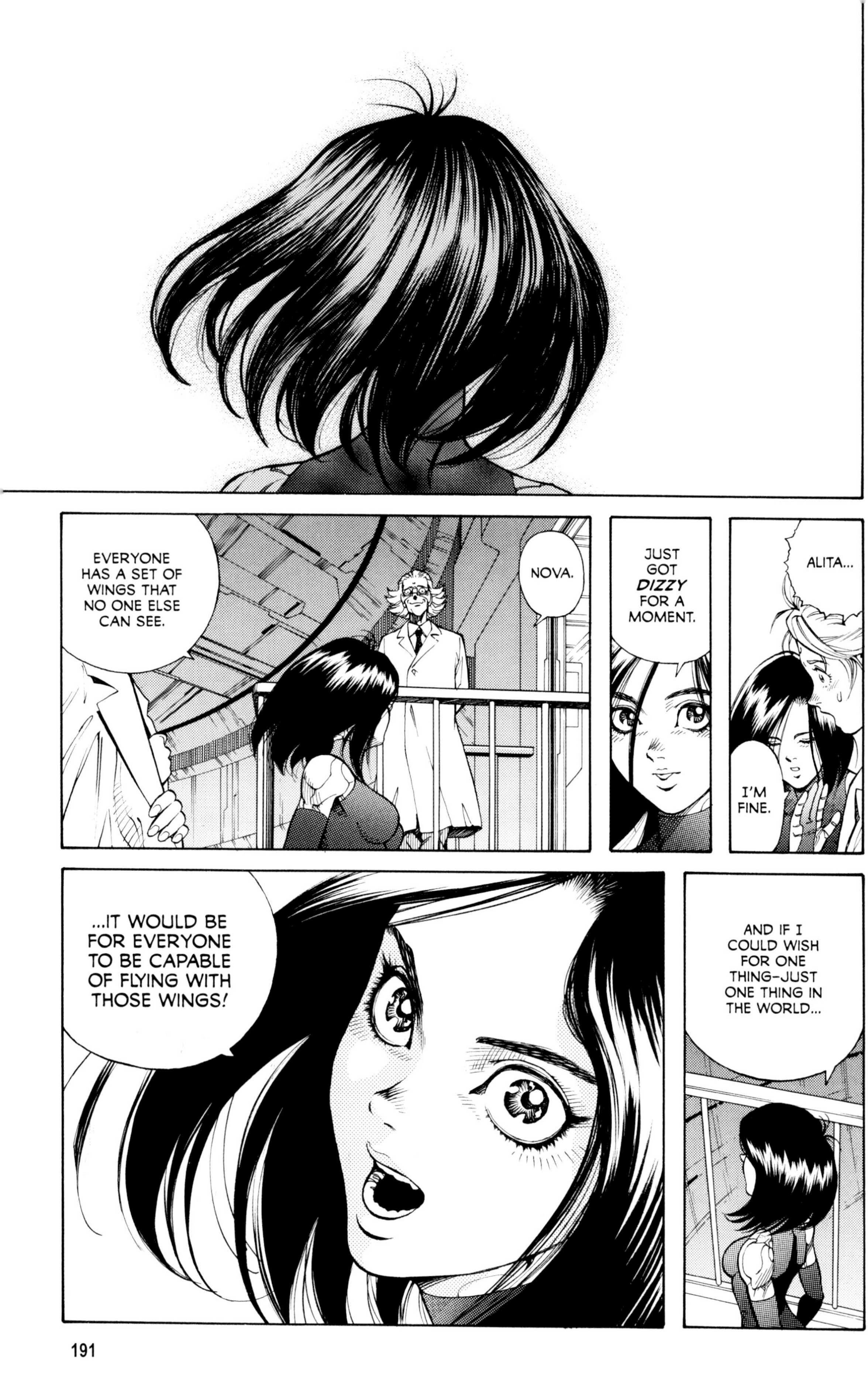
ALITA...
I'M FINE.
JUST GOT *DIZZY* FOR A MOMENT.
NOVA.
EVERYONE HAS A SET OF WINGS THAT NO ONE ELSE CAN SEE.
AND IF I COULD WISH FOR ONE THING–JUST ONE THING IN THE WORLD...
...IT WOULD BE FOR EVERYONE TO BE CAPABLE OF FLYING WITH THOSE WINGS!

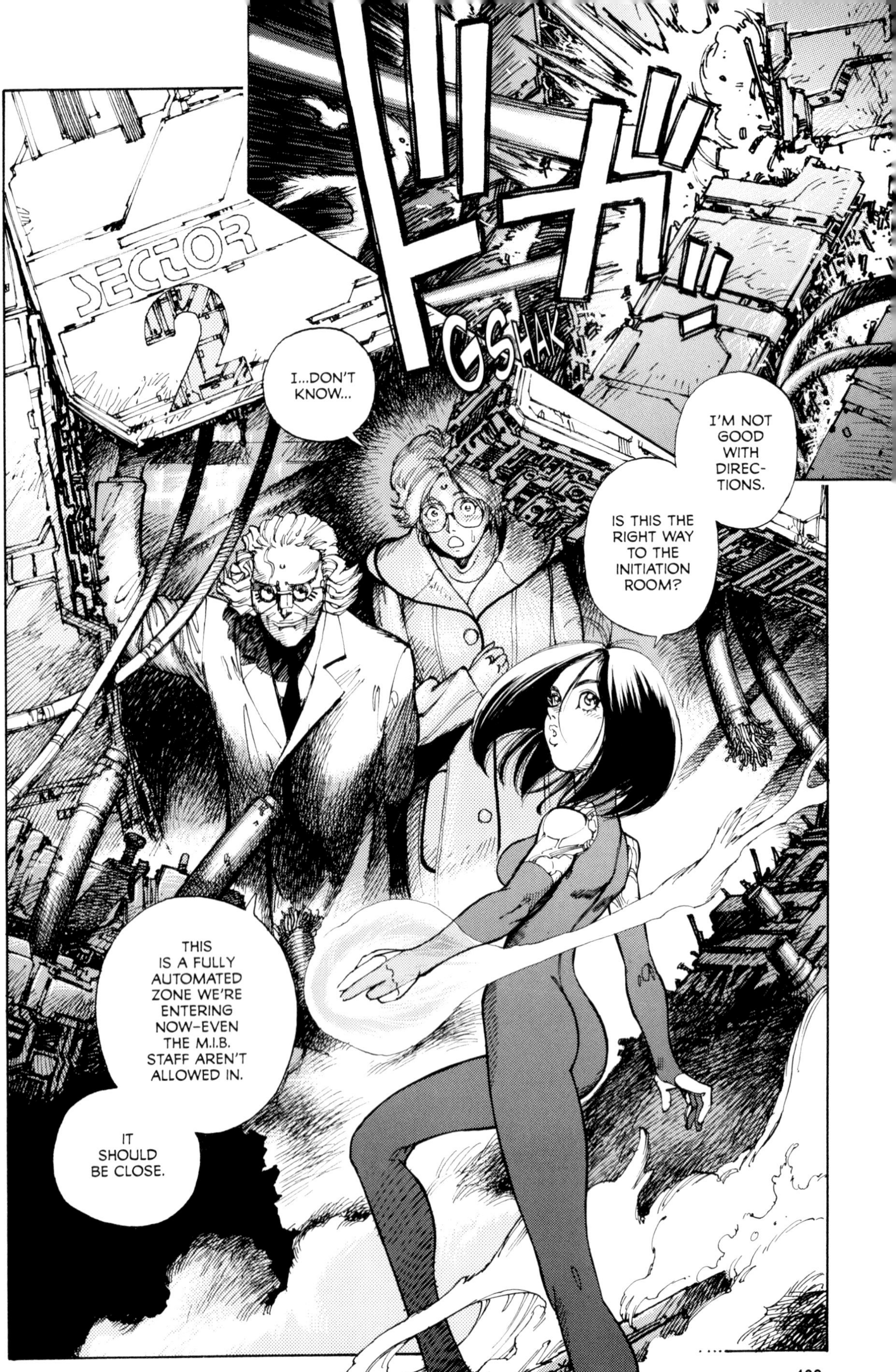
GSHAK
I'M NOT GOOD WITH DIRECTIONS.
IS THIS THE RIGHT WAY TO THE INITIATION ROOM?
SECTOR 2
I...DON'T KNOW...
THIS IS A FULLY AUTOMATED ZONE WE'RE ENTERING NOW–EVEN THE M.I.B. STAFF AREN'T ALLOWED IN.
IT SHOULD BE CLOSE.

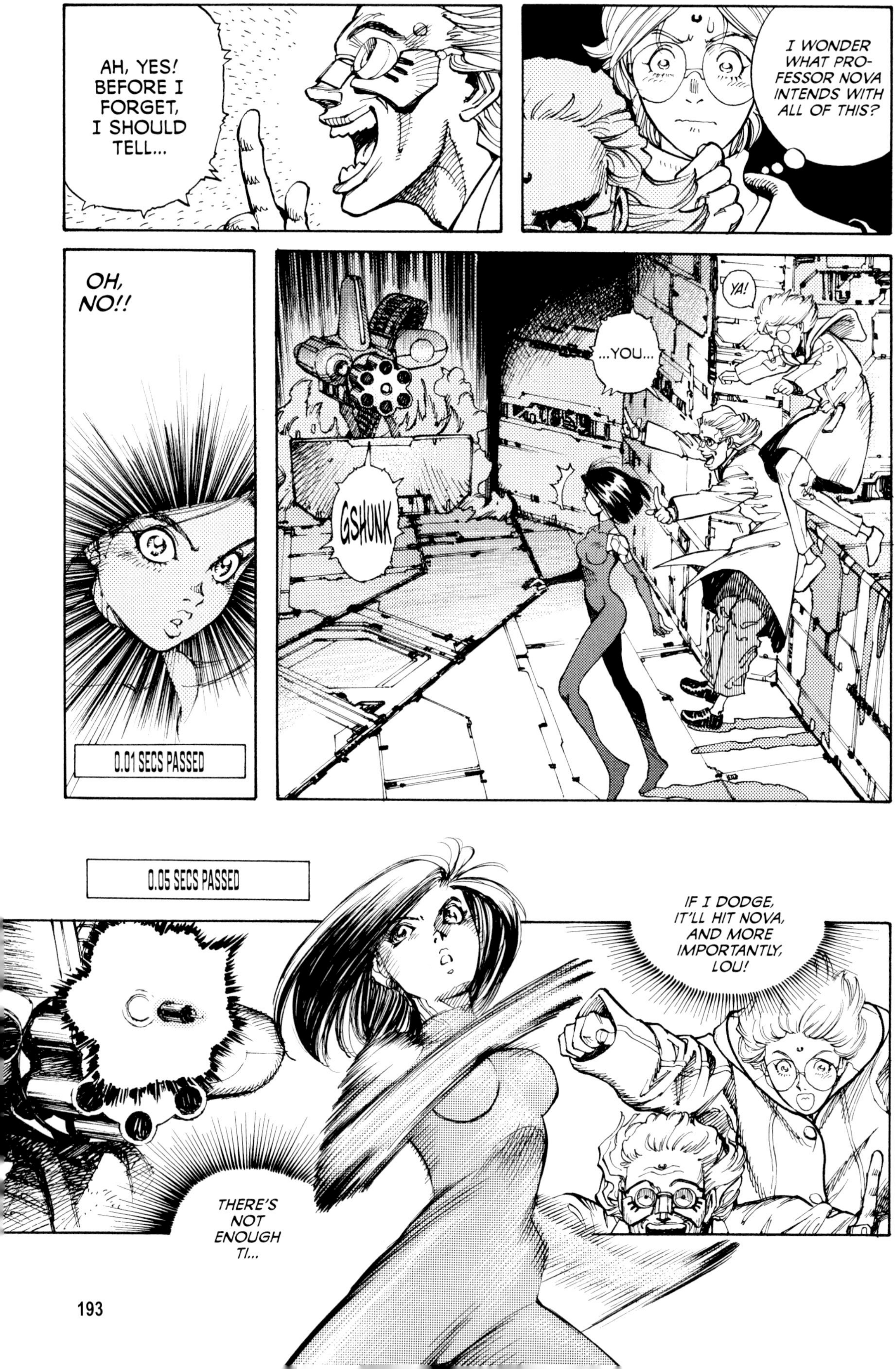
I WONDER WHAT PROFESSOR NOVA INTENDS WITH ALL OF THIS?
AH, YES! BEFORE I FORGET, I SHOULD TELL...
YA!
...YOU...
GSHUNK
OH, NO!!
0.01 SECS PASSED
0.05 SECS PASSED
IF I DODGE, IT'LL HIT NOVA, AND MORE IMPORTANTLY, LOU!
THERE'S NOT ENOUGH TI...

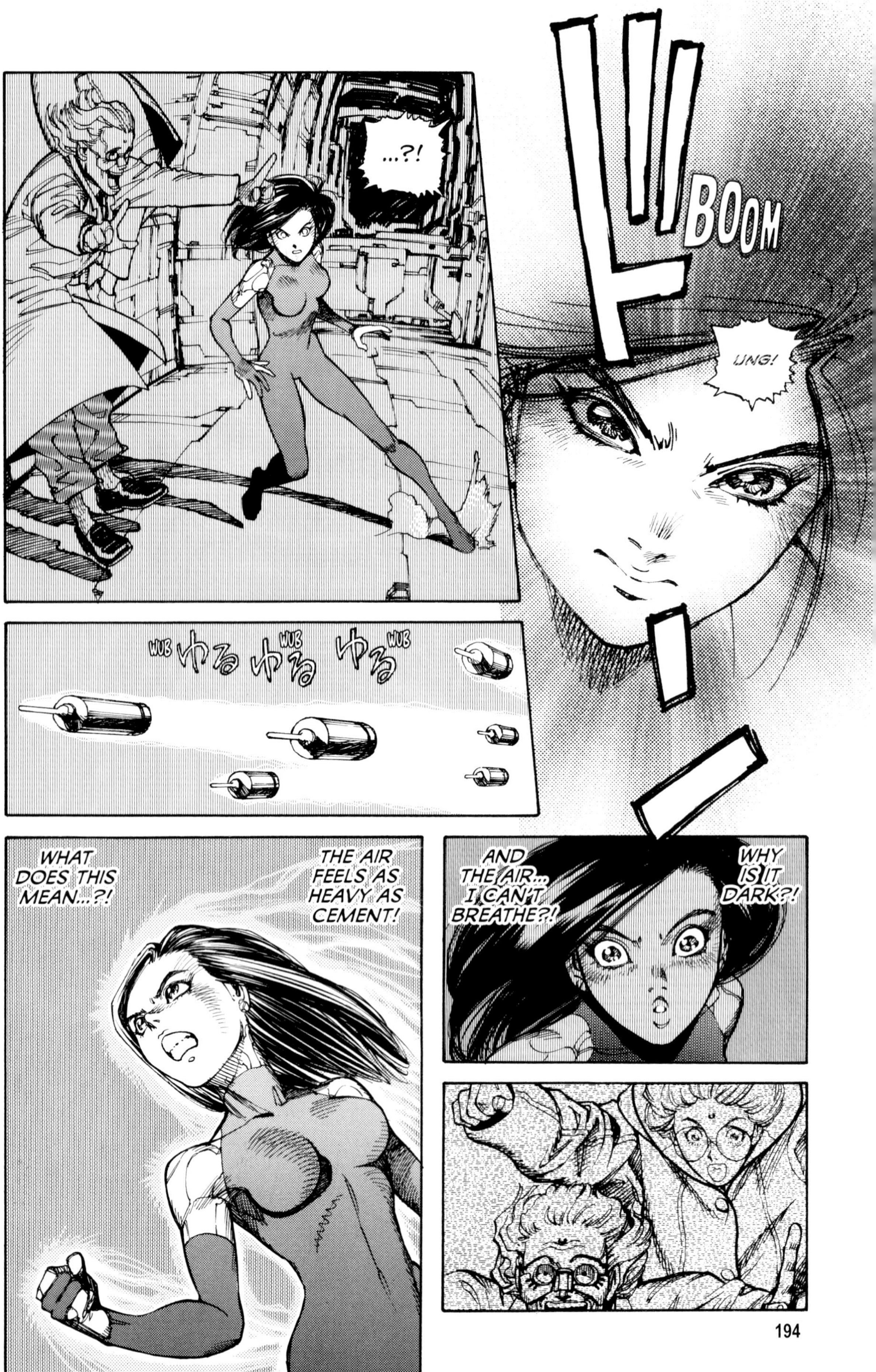
BOOM
UNG!
...?!
WUB ゆる
WUB ゆる
WUB ゆる
WHY IS IT DARK?!
AND THE AIR... I CAN'T BREATHE?!
THE AIR FEELS AS HEAVY AS CEMENT!
WHAT DOES THIS MEAN...?!

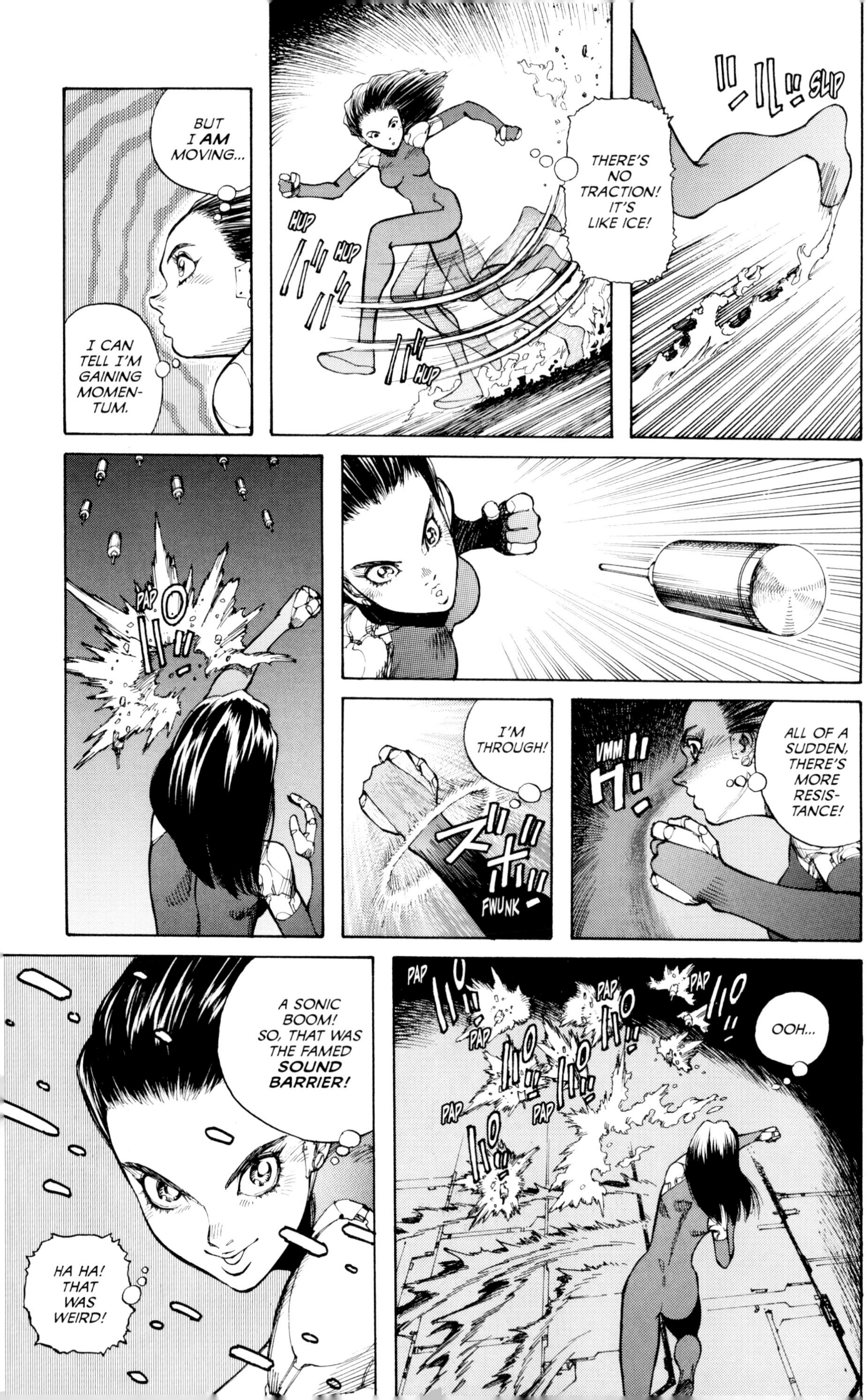
SLIP
THERE'S NO TRACTION! IT'S LIKE ICE!
HUP
HUP
HUP
BUT I **AM** MOVING...
I CAN TELL I'M GAINING MOMEN-TUM.
VMM
ALL OF A SUDDEN, THERE'S MORE RESIS-TANCE!
I'M THROUGH!
FWUNK
PAP
PAP
PAP
PAP
PAP
PAP
PAP
OOH...
A SONIC BOOM! SO, THAT WAS THE FAMED **SOUND BARRIER!**
HA HA! THAT WAS WEIRD!

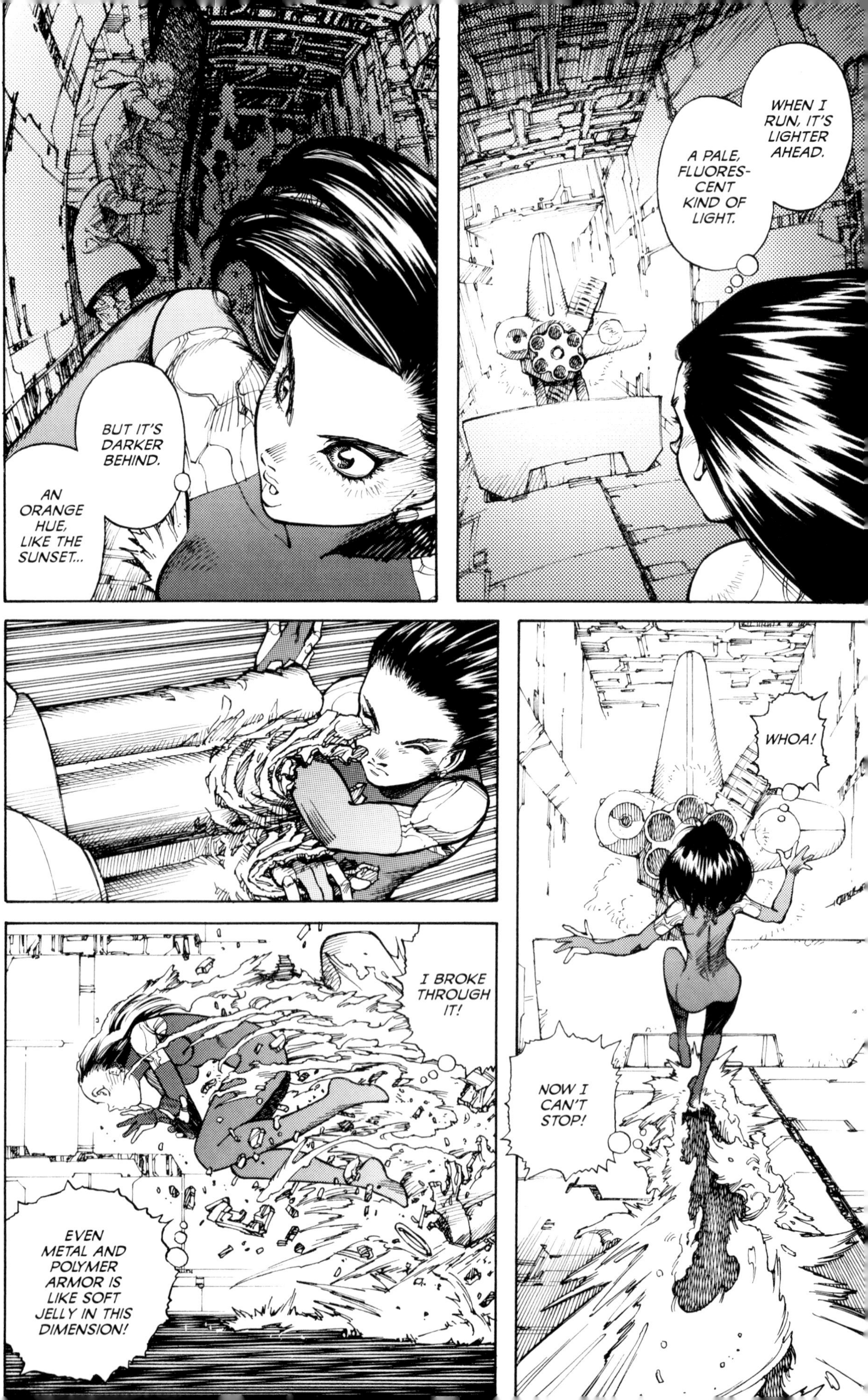
WHEN I RUN, IT'S LIGHTER AHEAD.
A PALE, FLUORES-CENT KIND OF LIGHT.
BUT IT'S DARKER BEHIND.
AN ORANGE HUE, LIKE THE SUNSET...
WHOA!
NOW I CAN'T STOP!
I BROKE THROUGH IT!
EVEN METAL AND POLYMER ARMOR IS LIKE SOFT JELLY IN THIS DIMENSION!

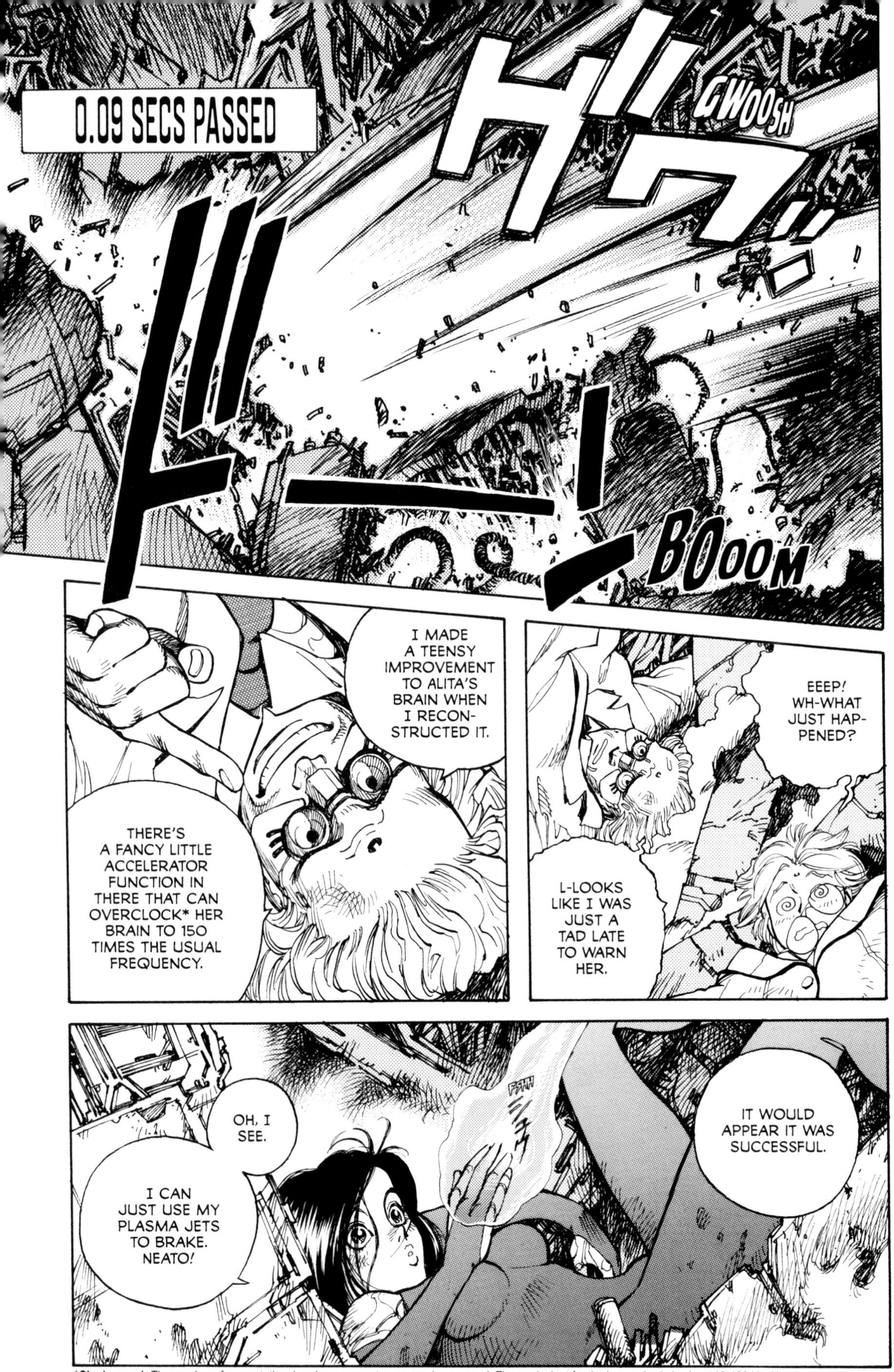
0.09 SECS PASSED
GWOOSH
BOOOM
EEEP! WH-WHAT JUST HAPPENED?
L-LOOKS LIKE I WAS JUST A TAD LATE TO WARN HER.
I MADE A TEENSY IMPROVEMENT TO ALITA'S BRAIN WHEN I RECONSTRUCTED IT.
THERE'S A FANCY LITTLE ACCELERATOR FUNCTION IN THERE THAT CAN OVERCLOCK* HER BRAIN TO 150 TIMES THE USUAL FREQUENCY.
IT WOULD APPEAR IT WAS SUCCESSFUL.
FSHH
OH, I SEE.
I CAN JUST USE MY PLASMA JETS TO BRAKE. NEATO!

***Clock speed:** The number of computational cycles a computer can run in a second. The equivalent for the human brain is about 10-100 Hz. However, information processing works entirely differently on a brain and a computer, and clock speed should not be used to compare ability.

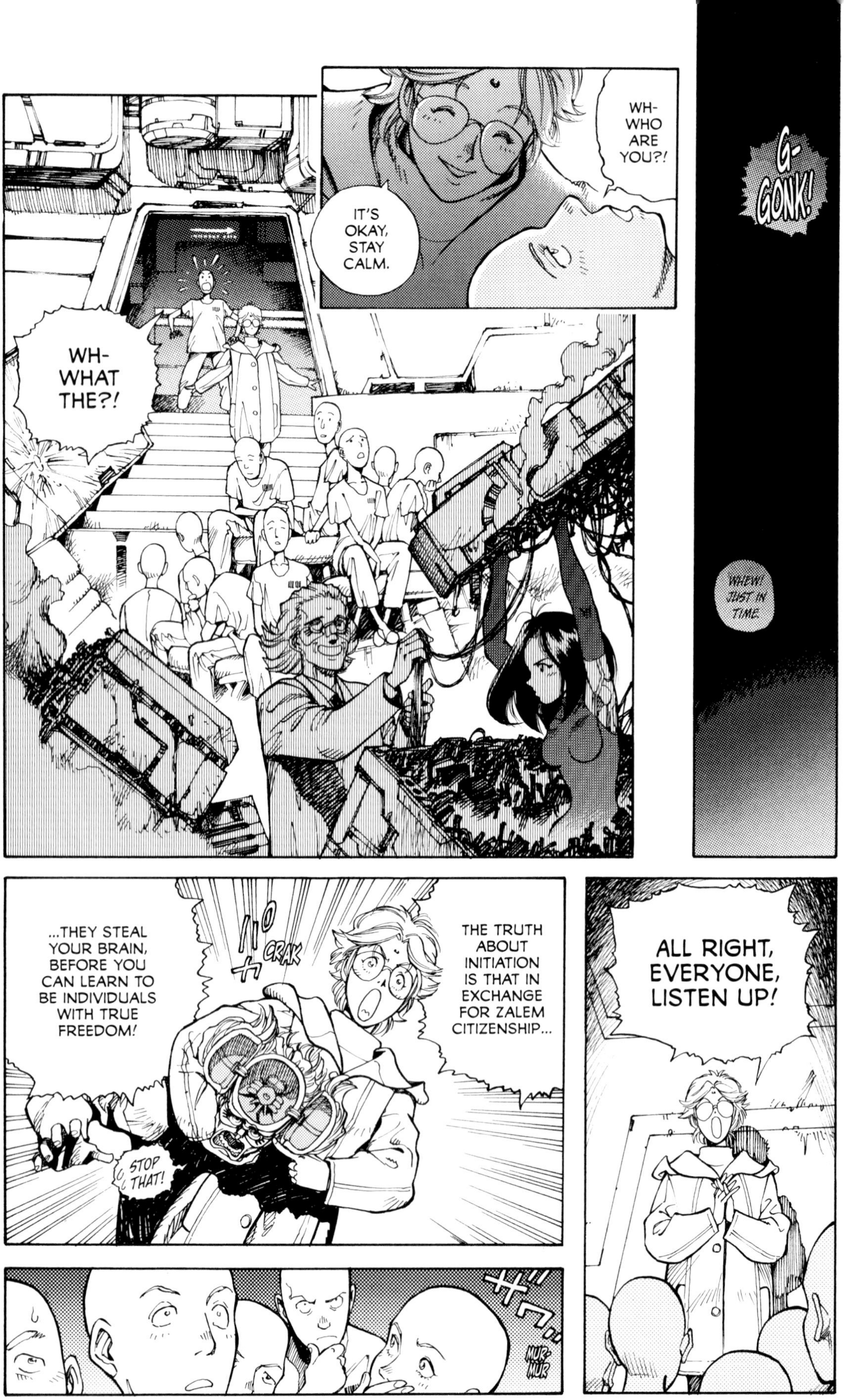
G-GONK!
WHEW! JUST IN TIME.
WH-WHO ARE YOU?!
IT'S OKAY, STAY CALM.
WH-WHAT THE?!
ALL RIGHT, EVERYONE, LISTEN UP!
THE TRUTH ABOUT INITIATION IS THAT IN EXCHANGE FOR ZALEM CITIZENSHIP...
...THEY STEAL YOUR BRAIN, BEFORE YOU CAN LEARN TO BE INDIVIDUALS WITH TRUE FREEDOM!
CRAK
STOP THAT!
MUR-MUR

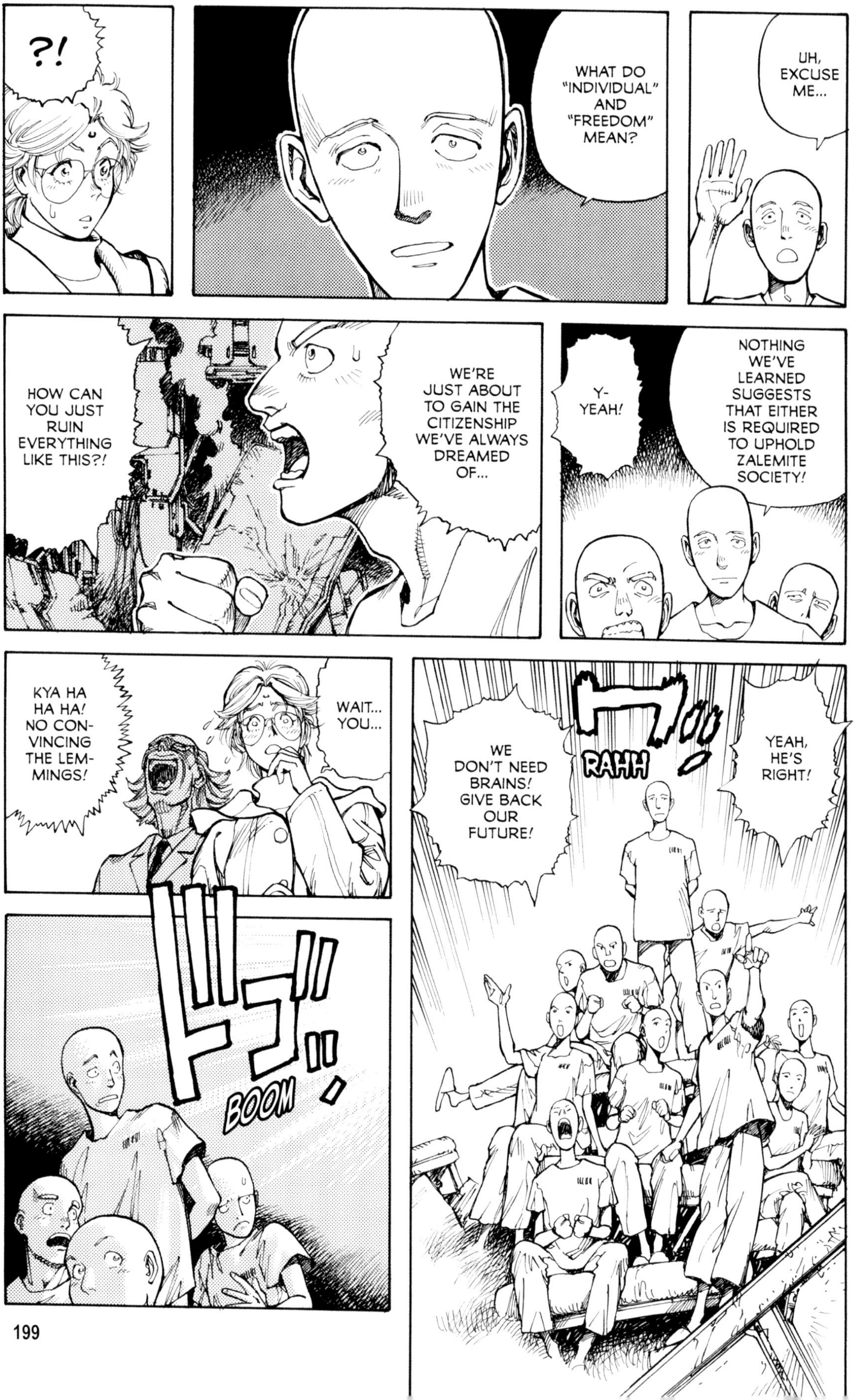

UH, EXCUSE ME...
WHAT DO "INDIVIDUAL" AND "FREEDOM" MEAN?
?!
NOTHING WE'VE LEARNED SUGGESTS THAT EITHER IS REQUIRED TO UPHOLD ZALEMITE SOCIETY!
Y-YEAH!
WE'RE JUST ABOUT TO GAIN THE CITIZENSHIP WE'VE ALWAYS DREAMED OF...
HOW CAN YOU JUST RUIN EVERYTHING LIKE THIS?!
YEAH, HE'S RIGHT!
RAHH
WE DON'T NEED BRAINS! GIVE BACK OUR FUTURE!
WAIT... YOU...
KYA HA HA HA! NO CONVINCING THE LEMMINGS!
BOOM

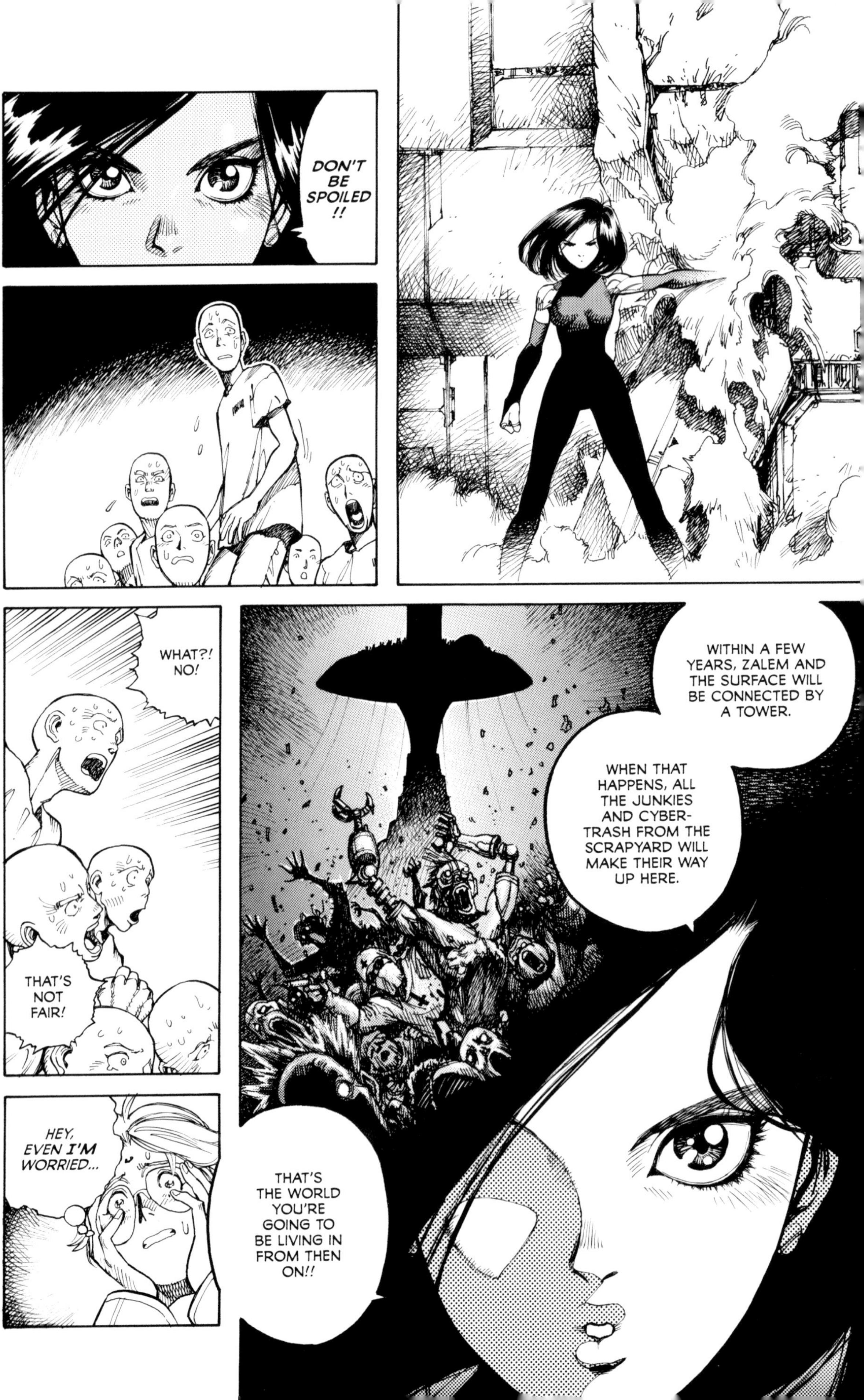
DON'T BE SPOILED!!
WITHIN A FEW YEARS, ZALEM AND THE SURFACE WILL BE CONNECTED BY A TOWER.
WHEN THAT HAPPENS, ALL THE JUNKIES AND CYBER-TRASH FROM THE SCRAPYARD WILL MAKE THEIR WAY UP HERE.
THAT'S THE WORLD YOU'RE GOING TO BE LIVING IN FROM THEN ON!!
WHAT?! NO!
THAT'S NOT FAIR!
HEY, EVEN I'M WORRIED...

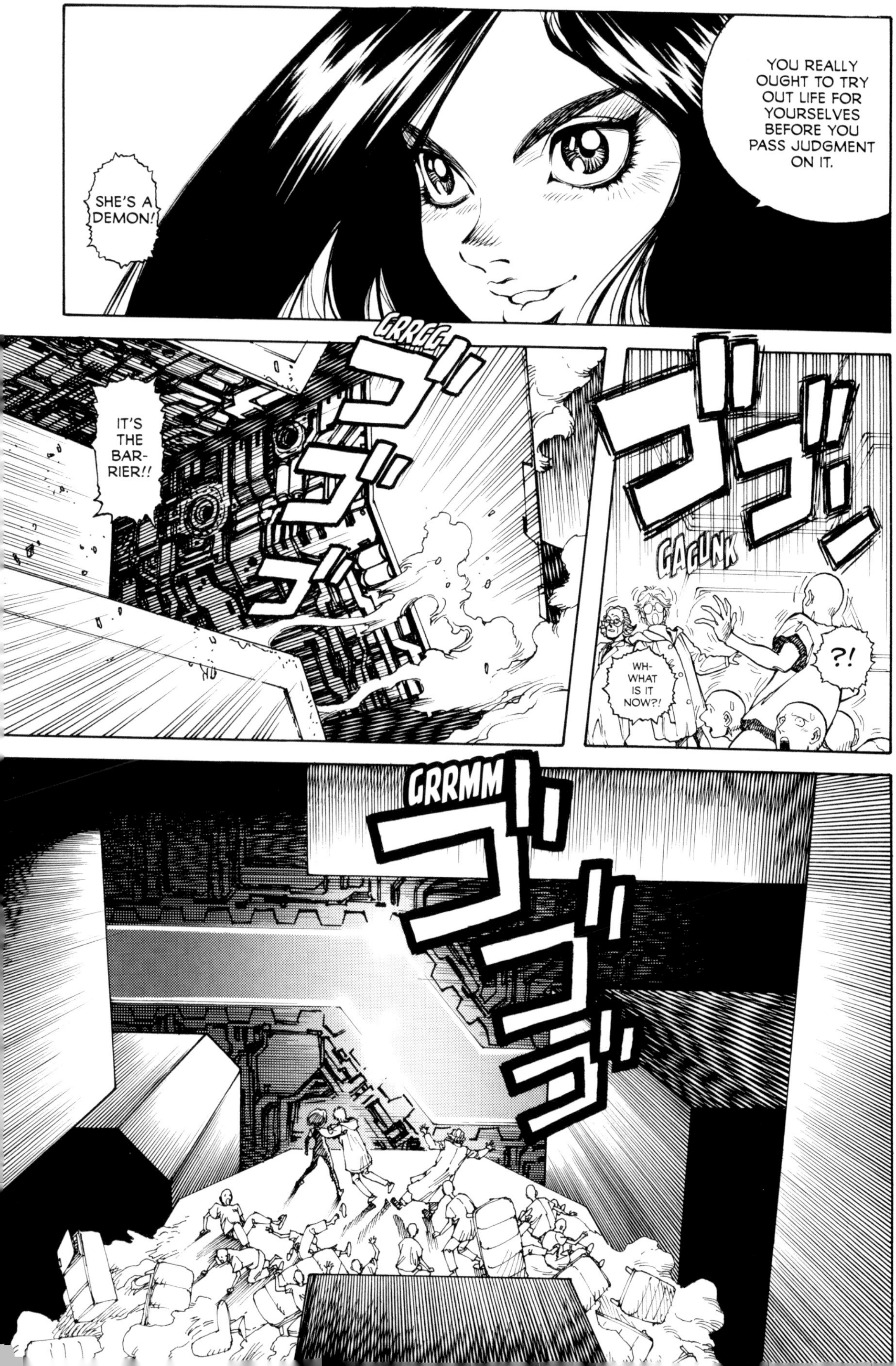
YOU REALLY OUGHT TO TRY OUT LIFE FOR YOURSELVES BEFORE YOU PASS JUDGMENT ON IT.
SHE'S A DEMON!
GAGUNK
?!
WH- WHAT IS IT NOW?!
GRRGG
IT'S THE BAR- RIER!!
GRRMM

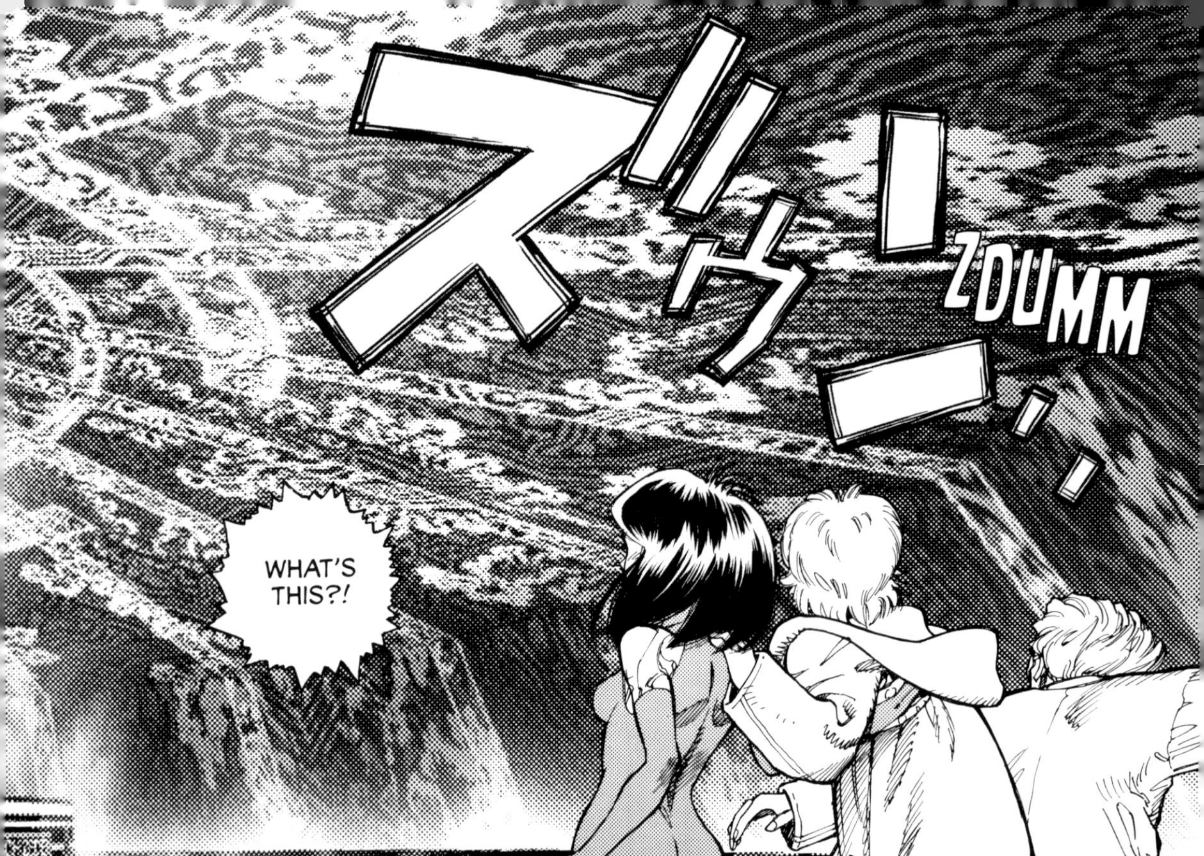
ZDUMM
WHAT'S THIS?!

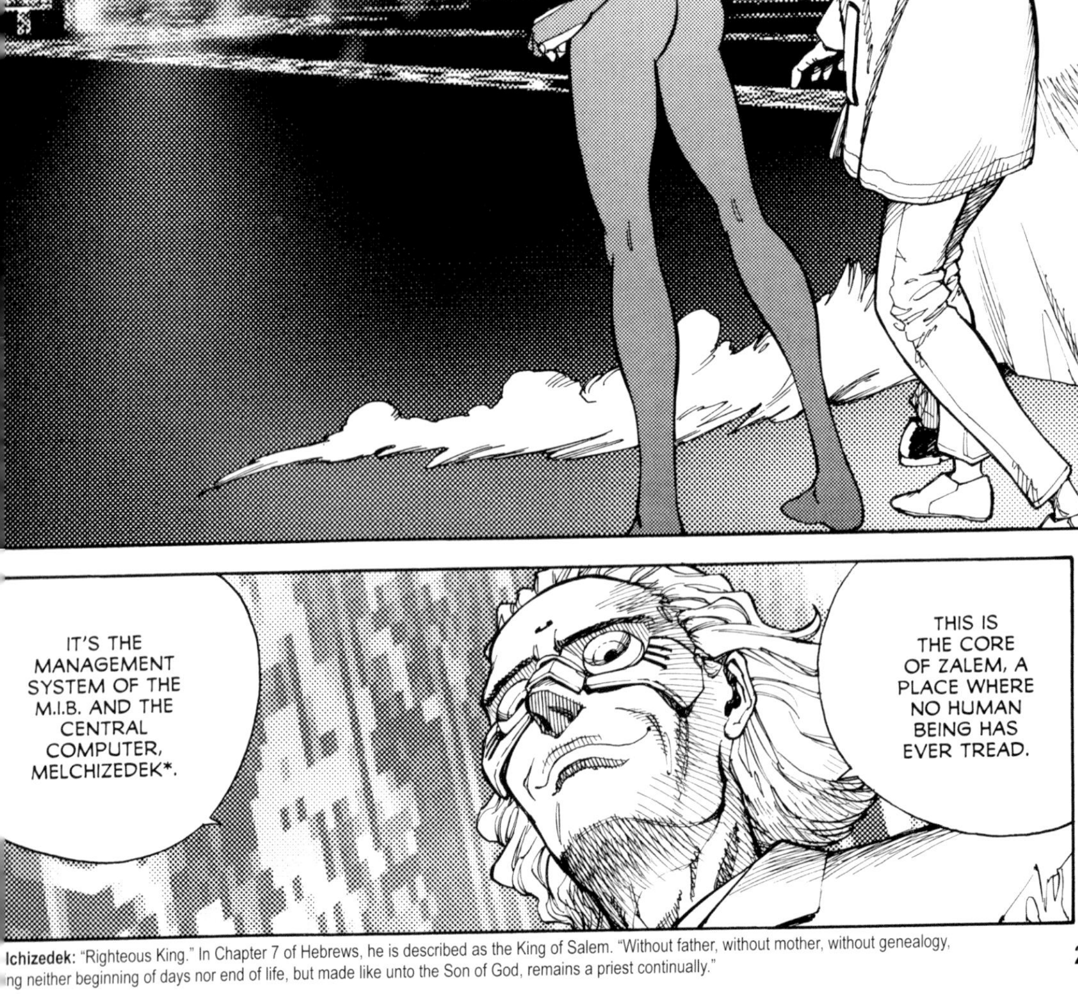
THIS IS THE CORE OF ZALEM, A PLACE WHERE NO HUMAN BEING HAS EVER TREAD.
IT'S THE MANAGEMENT SYSTEM OF THE M.I.B. AND THE CENTRAL COMPUTER, MELCHIZEDEK*.

lchizedek: "Righteous King." In Chapter 7 of Hebrews, he is described as the King of Salem. "Without father, without mother, without genealogy, ing neither beginning of days nor end of life, but made like unto the Son of God, remains a priest continually."

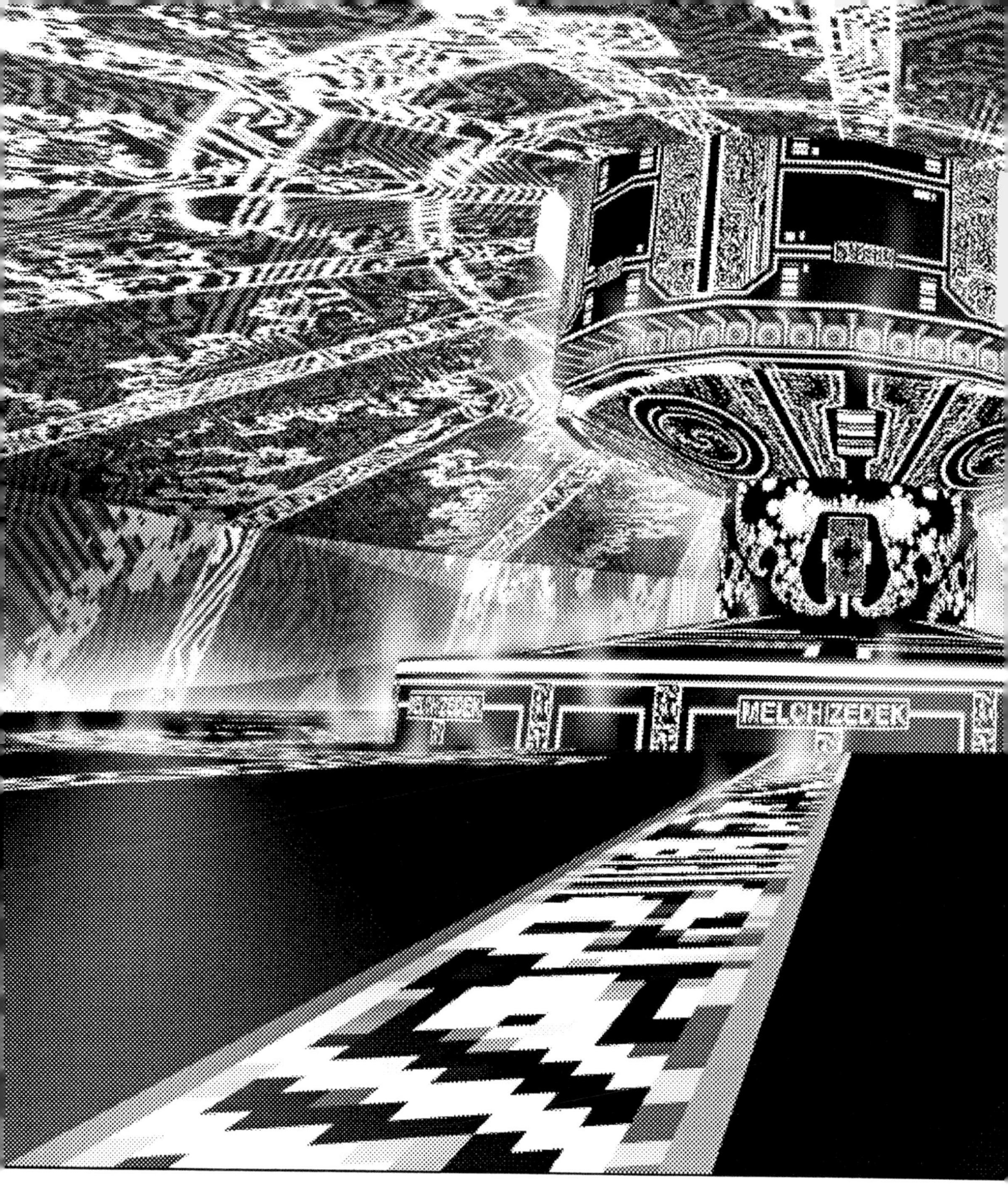
MELCHIZEDEK

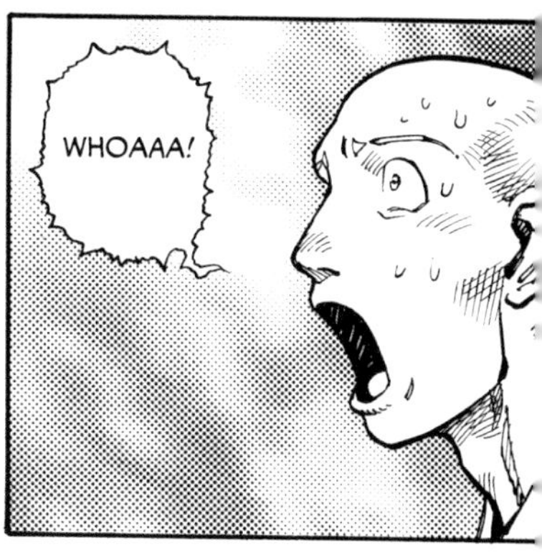
WHOAAA!

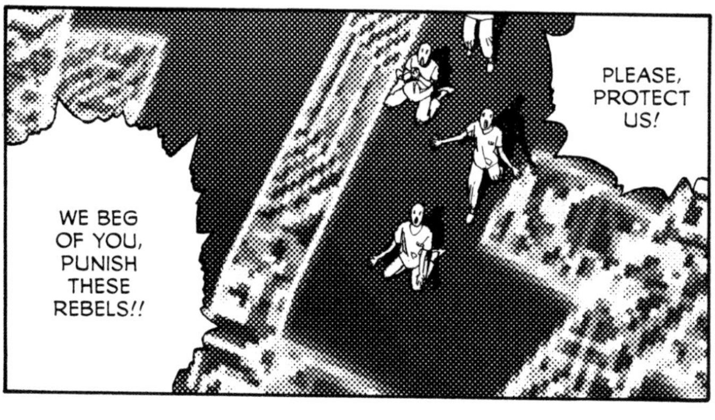
PLEASE, PROTECT US!
WE BEG OF YOU, PUNISH THESE REBELS!!

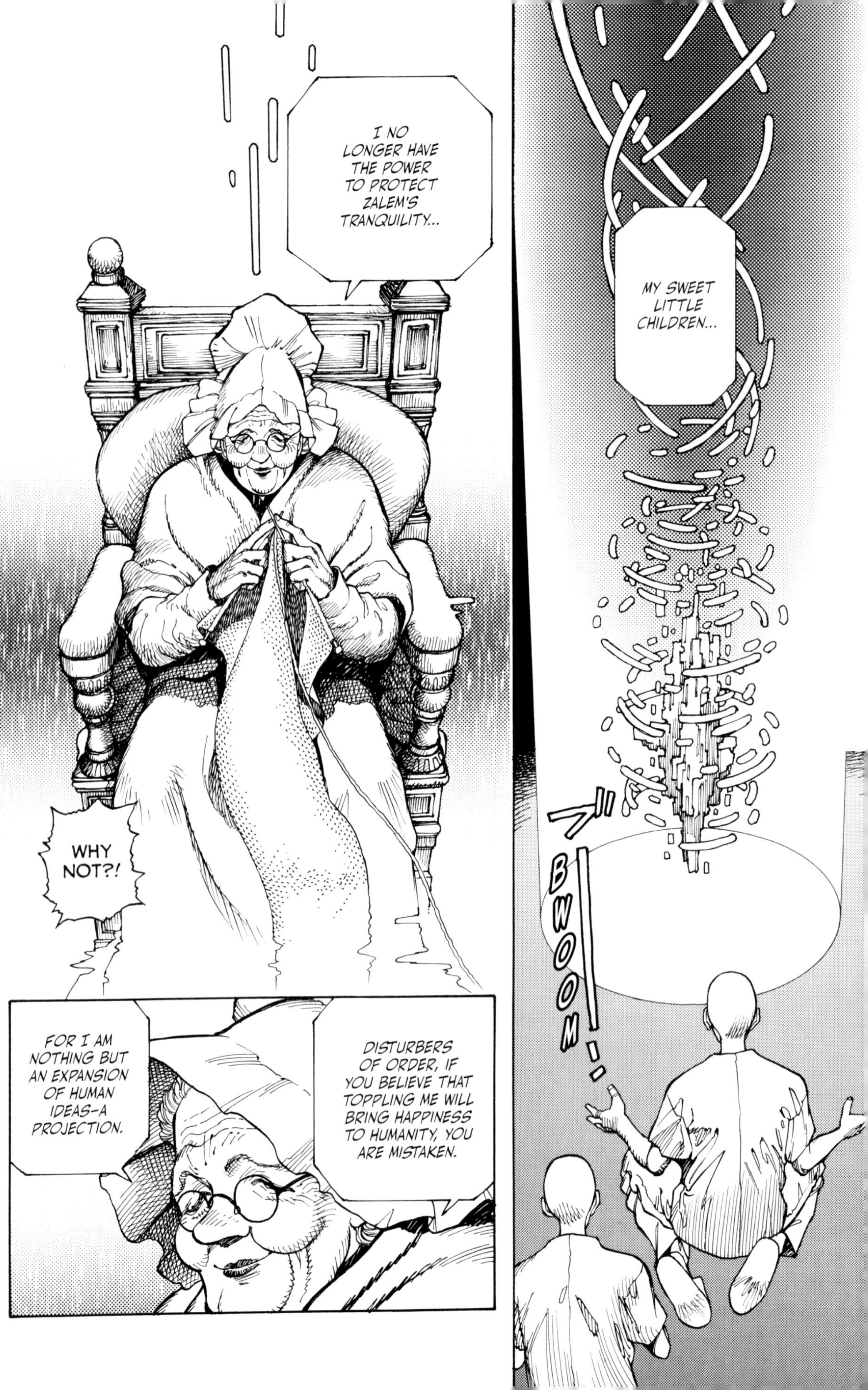
MY SWEET LITTLE CHILDREN...
BWOOM!!
I NO LONGER HAVE THE POWER TO PROTECT ZALEM'S TRANQUILITY...
WHY NOT?!
DISTURBERS OF ORDER, IF YOU BELIEVE THAT TOPPLING ME WILL BRING HAPPINESS TO HUMANITY, YOU ARE MISTAKEN.
FOR I AM NOTHING BUT AN EXPANSION OF HUMAN IDEAS-A PROJECTION.

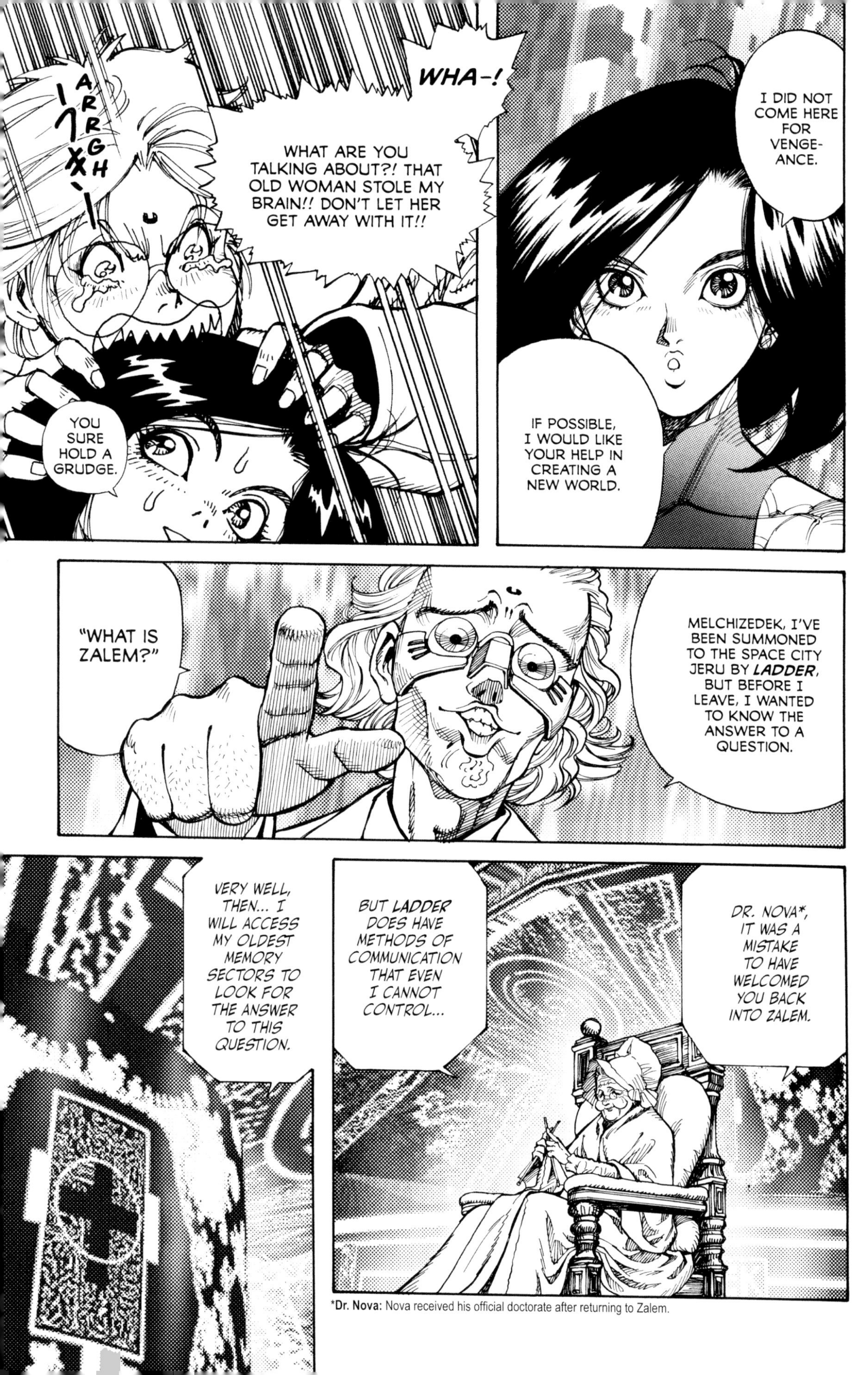
I DID NOT COME HERE FOR VENGE-ANCE.
IF POSSIBLE, I WOULD LIKE YOUR HELP IN CREATING A NEW WORLD.
WHA-!
WHAT ARE YOU TALKING ABOUT?! THAT OLD WOMAN STOLE MY BRAIN!! DON'T LET HER GET AWAY WITH IT!!
ARRGH
YOU SURE HOLD A GRUDGE.
MELCHIZEDEK, I'VE BEEN SUMMONED TO THE SPACE CITY JERU BY *LADDER*, BUT BEFORE I LEAVE, I WANTED TO KNOW THE ANSWER TO A QUESTION.
"WHAT IS ZALEM?"
DR. NOVA*, IT WAS A MISTAKE TO HAVE WELCOMED YOU BACK INTO ZALEM.
BUT *LADDER* DOES HAVE METHODS OF COMMUNICATION THAT EVEN I CANNOT CONTROL...
VERY WELL, THEN... I WILL ACCESS MY OLDEST MEMORY SECTORS TO LOOK FOR THE ANSWER TO THIS QUESTION.

*Dr. Nova: Nova received his official doctorate after returning to Zalem.

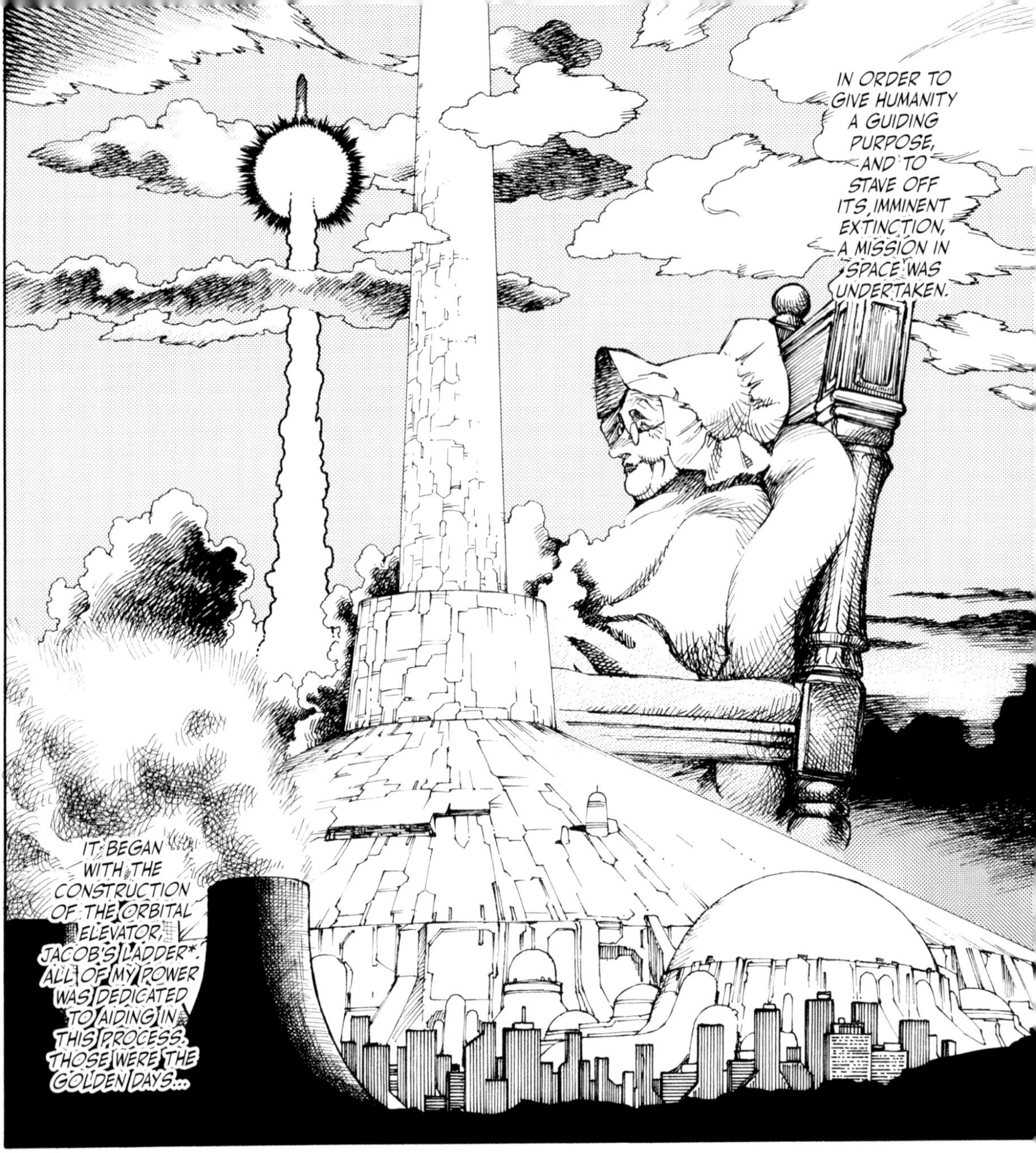
IN ORDER TO GIVE HUMANITY A GUIDING PURPOSE, AND TO STAVE OFF ITS IMMINENT EXTINCTION, A MISSION IN SPACE WAS UNDERTAKEN.
IT BEGAN WITH THE CONSTRUCTION OF THE ORBITAL ELEVATOR, JACOB'S LADDER*. ALL OF MY POWER WAS DEDICATED TO AIDING IN THIS PROCESS. THOSE WERE THE GOLDEN DAYS...

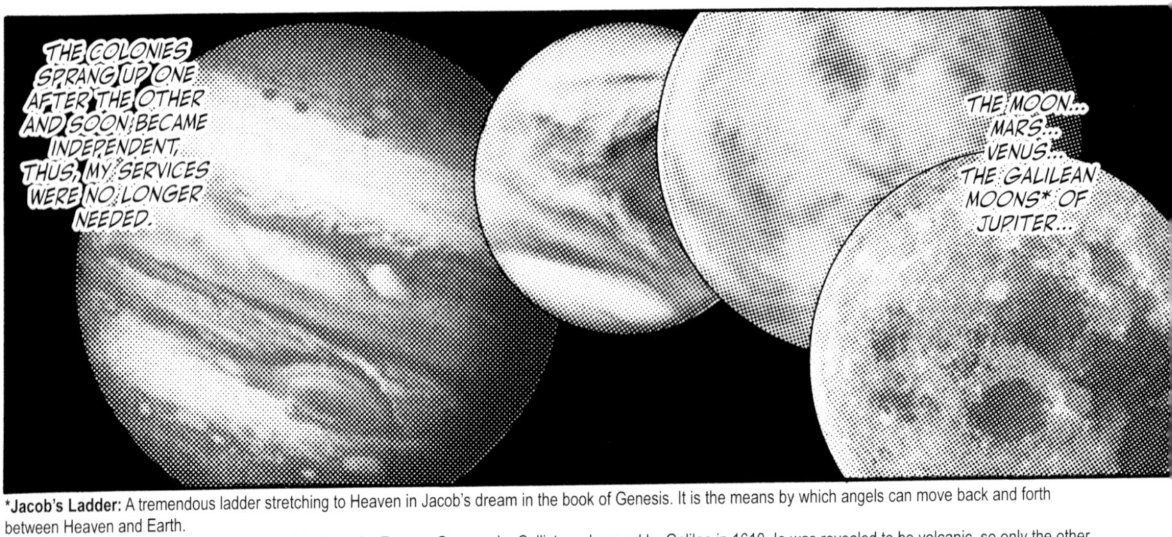
THE MOON... MARS... VENUS... THE GALILEAN MOONS* OF JUPITER...
THE COLONIES SPRANG UP ONE AFTER THE OTHER AND SOON BECAME INDEPENDENT. THUS, MY SERVICES WERE NO LONGER NEEDED.

***Jacob's Ladder:** A tremendous ladder stretching to Heaven in Jacob's dream in the book of Genesis. It is the means by which angels can move back and forth between Heaven and Earth.

***Galilean moons:** The four largest moons of Jupiter—Io, Europa, Ganymede, Callisto—observed by Galileo in 1610. Io was revealed to be volcanic, so only the other three moons were colonized.

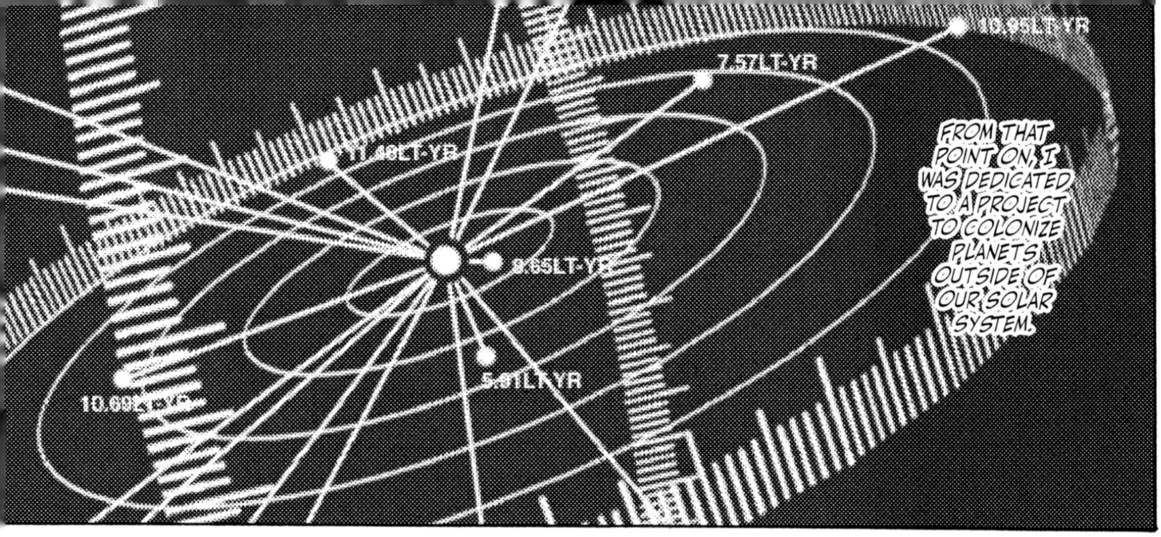
10.95LT-YR
7.57LT-YR
5.91LT-YR
FROM THAT POINT ON, I WAS DEDICATED TO A PROJECT TO COLONIZE PLANETS OUTSIDE OF OUR SOLAR SYSTEM.

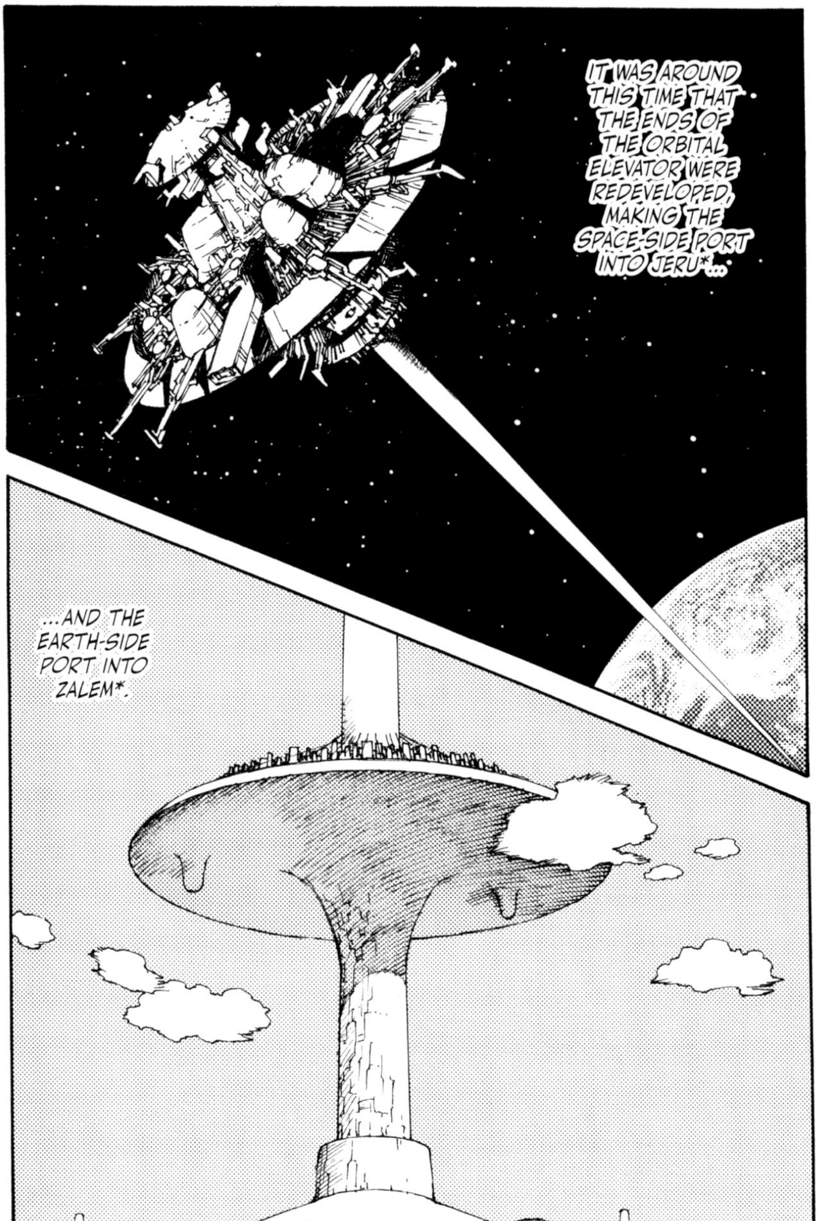
IT WAS AROUND THIS TIME THAT THE ENDS OF THE ORBITAL ELEVATOR WERE REDEVELOPED, MAKING THE SPACE-SIDE PORT INTO JERU*...
...AND THE EARTH-SIDE PORT INTO ZALEM*.

*Jeru-Zalem: Combined, they form the name "Jeru-zalem," or Jerusalem. This reference is not to the city in Israel, but the holy city that descends from Heaven in Chapter 21 of Revelations.

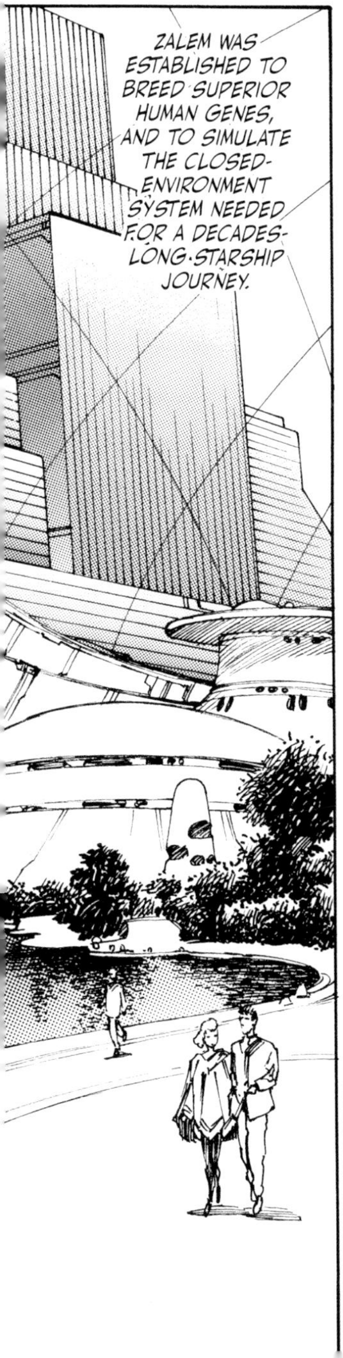
ZALEM WAS ESTABLISHED TO BREED SUPERIOR HUMAN GENES, AND TO SIMULATE THE CLOSED-ENVIRONMENT SYSTEM NEEDED FOR A DECADES-LONG STARSHIP JOURNEY.

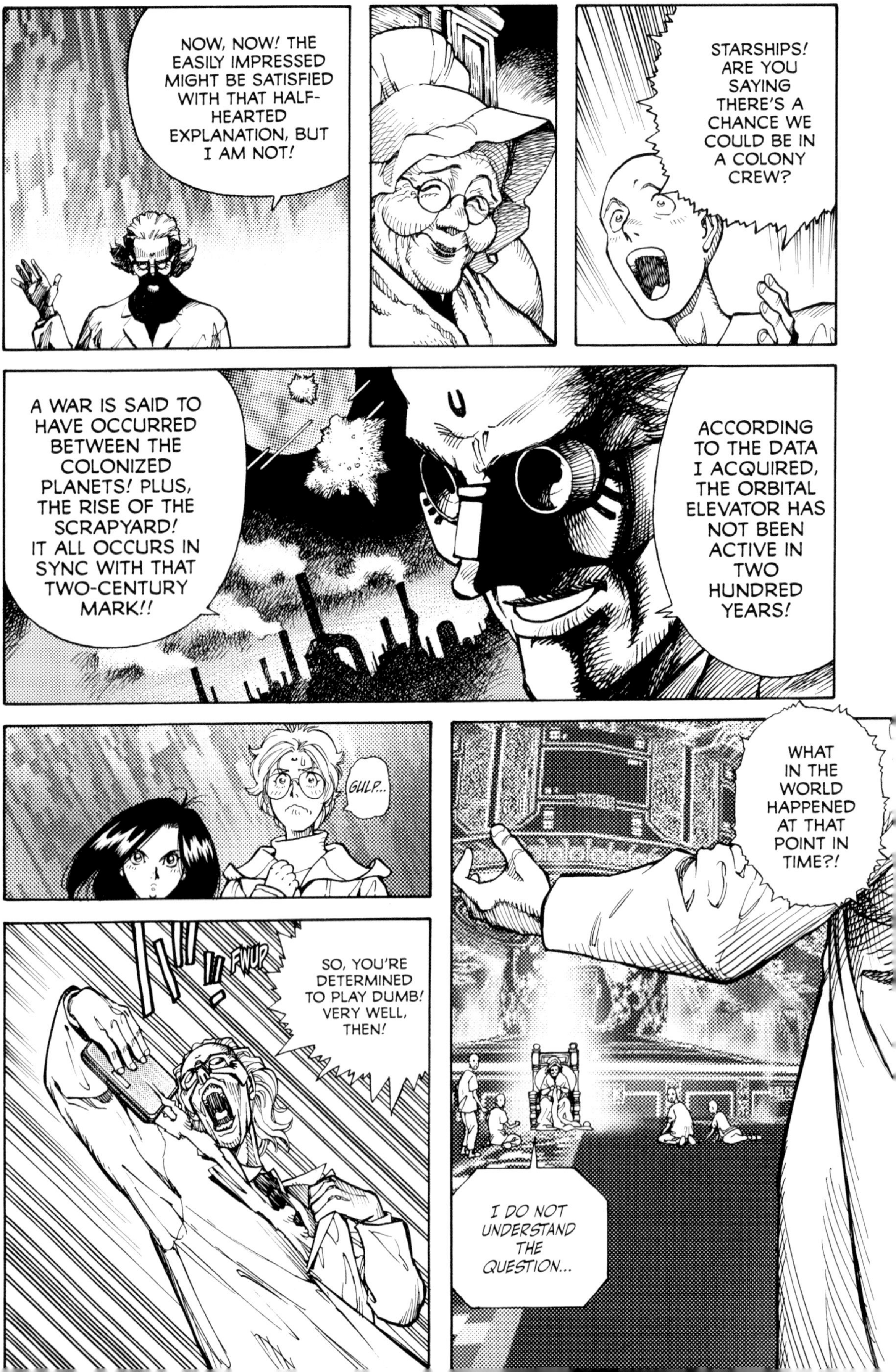
STARSHIPS! ARE YOU SAYING THERE'S A CHANCE WE COULD BE IN A COLONY CREW?
NOW, NOW! THE EASILY IMPRESSED MIGHT BE SATISFIED WITH THAT HALF-HEARTED EXPLANATION, BUT I AM NOT!
ACCORDING TO THE DATA I ACQUIRED, THE ORBITAL ELEVATOR HAS NOT BEEN ACTIVE IN TWO HUNDRED YEARS!
A WAR IS SAID TO HAVE OCCURRED BETWEEN THE COLONIZED PLANETS! PLUS, THE RISE OF THE SCRAPYARD! IT ALL OCCURS IN SYNC WITH THAT TWO-CENTURY MARK!!
WHAT IN THE WORLD HAPPENED AT THAT POINT IN TIME?!
I DO NOT UNDERSTAND THE QUESTION...
GULP...
FWUP
SO, YOU'RE DETERMINED TO PLAY DUMB! VERY WELL, THEN!

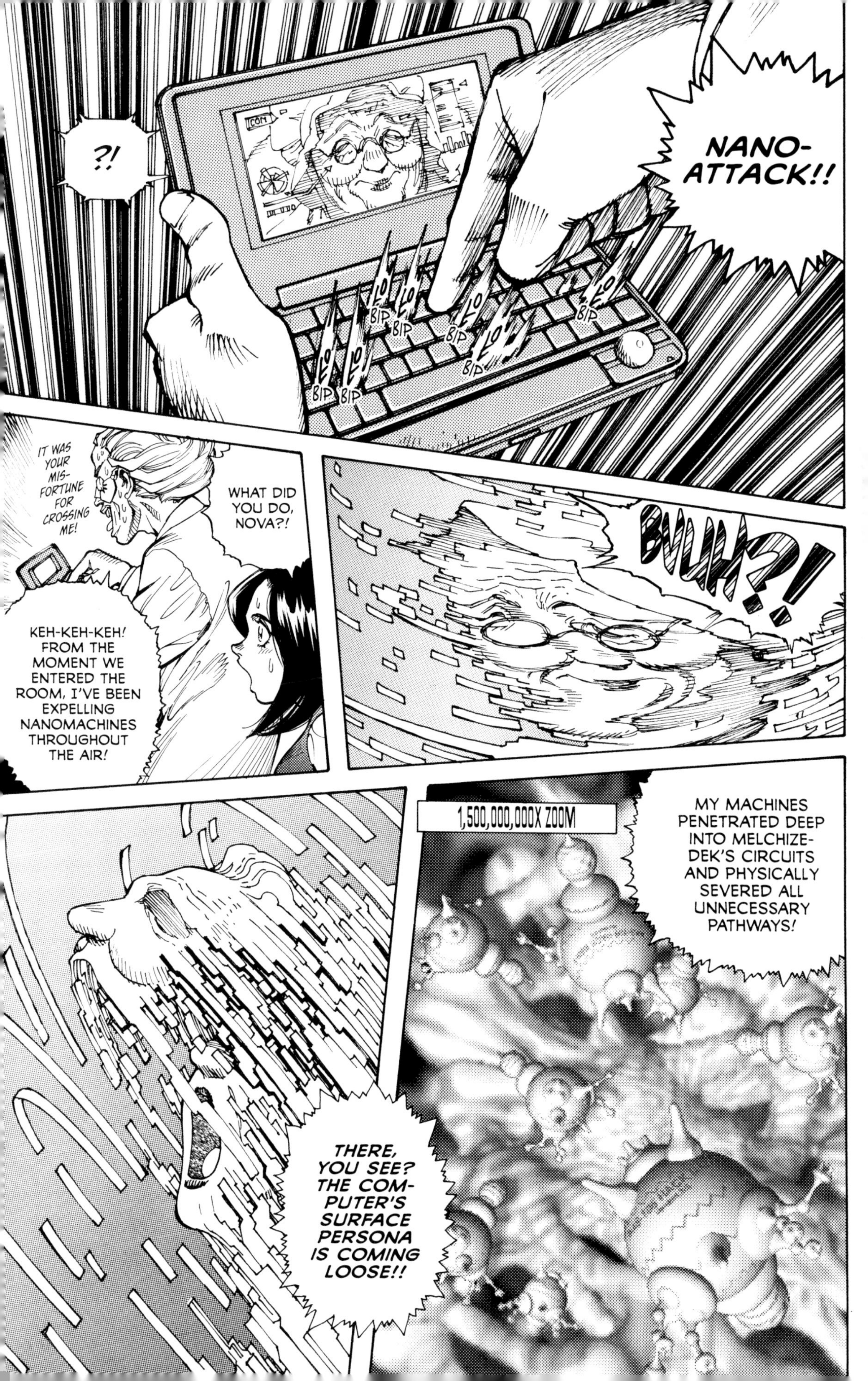
NANO-ATTACK!!
?!
BIP BIP BIP BIP BIP BIP BIP
BWUH?!!
WHAT DID YOU DO, NOVA?!
IT WAS YOUR MISFORTUNE FOR CROSSING ME!
KEH-KEH-KEH! FROM THE MOMENT WE ENTERED THE ROOM, I'VE BEEN EXPELLING NANOMACHINES THROUGHOUT THE AIR!
1,500,000,000X ZOOM
MY MACHINES PENETRATED DEEP INTO MELCHIZEDEK'S CIRCUITS AND PHYSICALLY SEVERED ALL UNNECESSARY PATHWAYS!
THERE, YOU SEE? THE COMPUTER'S SURFACE PERSONA IS COMING LOOSE!!

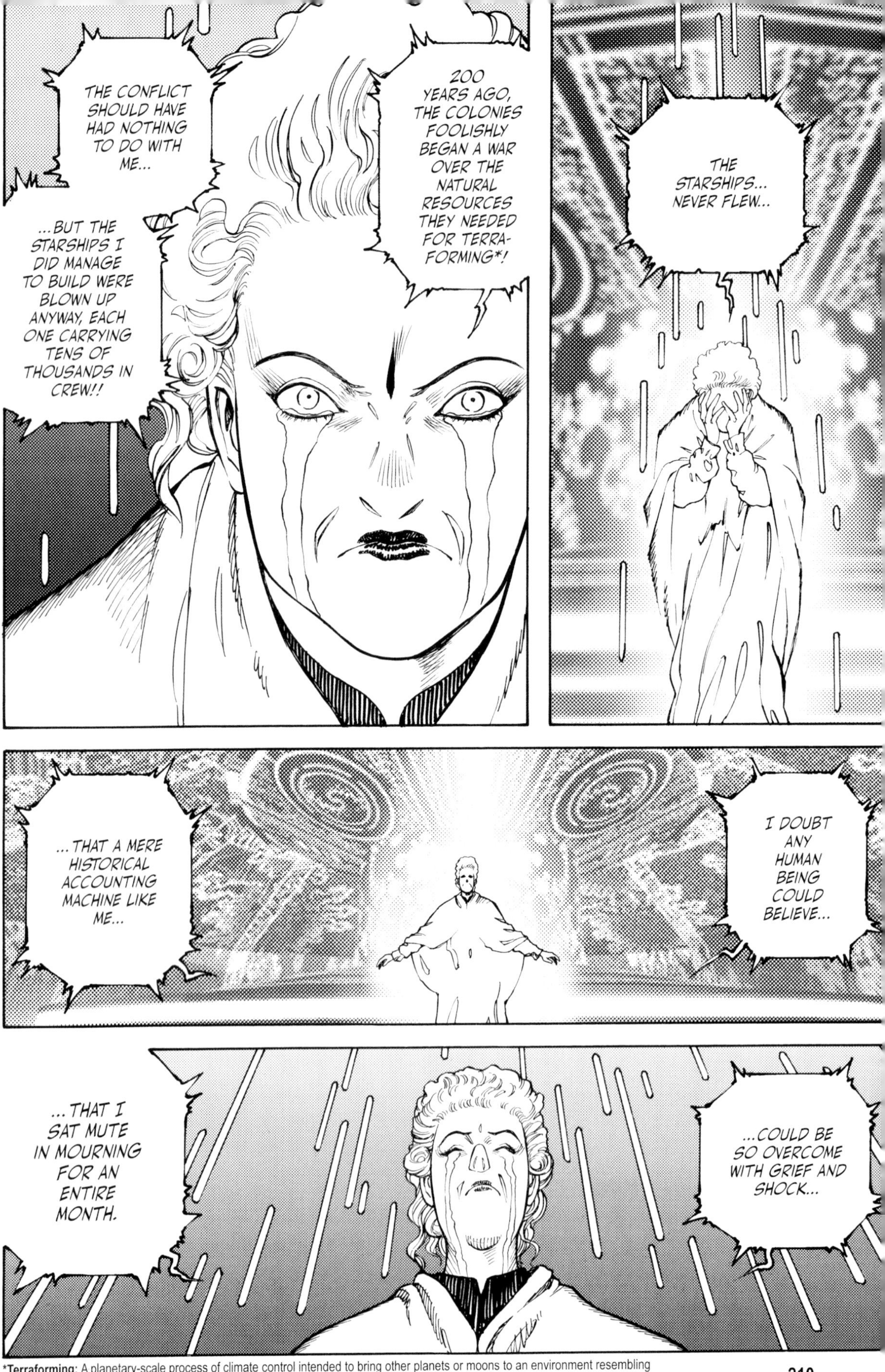
THE STARSHIPS... NEVER FLEW...
200 YEARS AGO, THE COLONIES FOOLISHLY BEGAN A WAR OVER THE NATURAL RESOURCES THEY NEEDED FOR TERRA-FORMING*!
THE CONFLICT SHOULD HAVE HAD NOTHING TO DO WITH ME...
...BUT THE STARSHIPS I DID MANAGE TO BUILD WERE BLOWN UP ANYWAY, EACH ONE CARRYING TENS OF THOUSANDS IN CREW!!
I DOUBT ANY HUMAN BEING COULD BELIEVE...
...THAT A MERE HISTORICAL ACCOUNTING MACHINE LIKE ME...
...COULD BE SO OVERCOME WITH GRIEF AND SHOCK...
...THAT I SAT MUTE IN MOURNING FOR AN ENTIRE MONTH.

***Terraforming:** A planetary-scale process of climate control intended to bring other planets or moons to an environment resembling Earth's to facilitate human habitation. The term was devised by science fiction writer Jack Williamson in the 1940s.

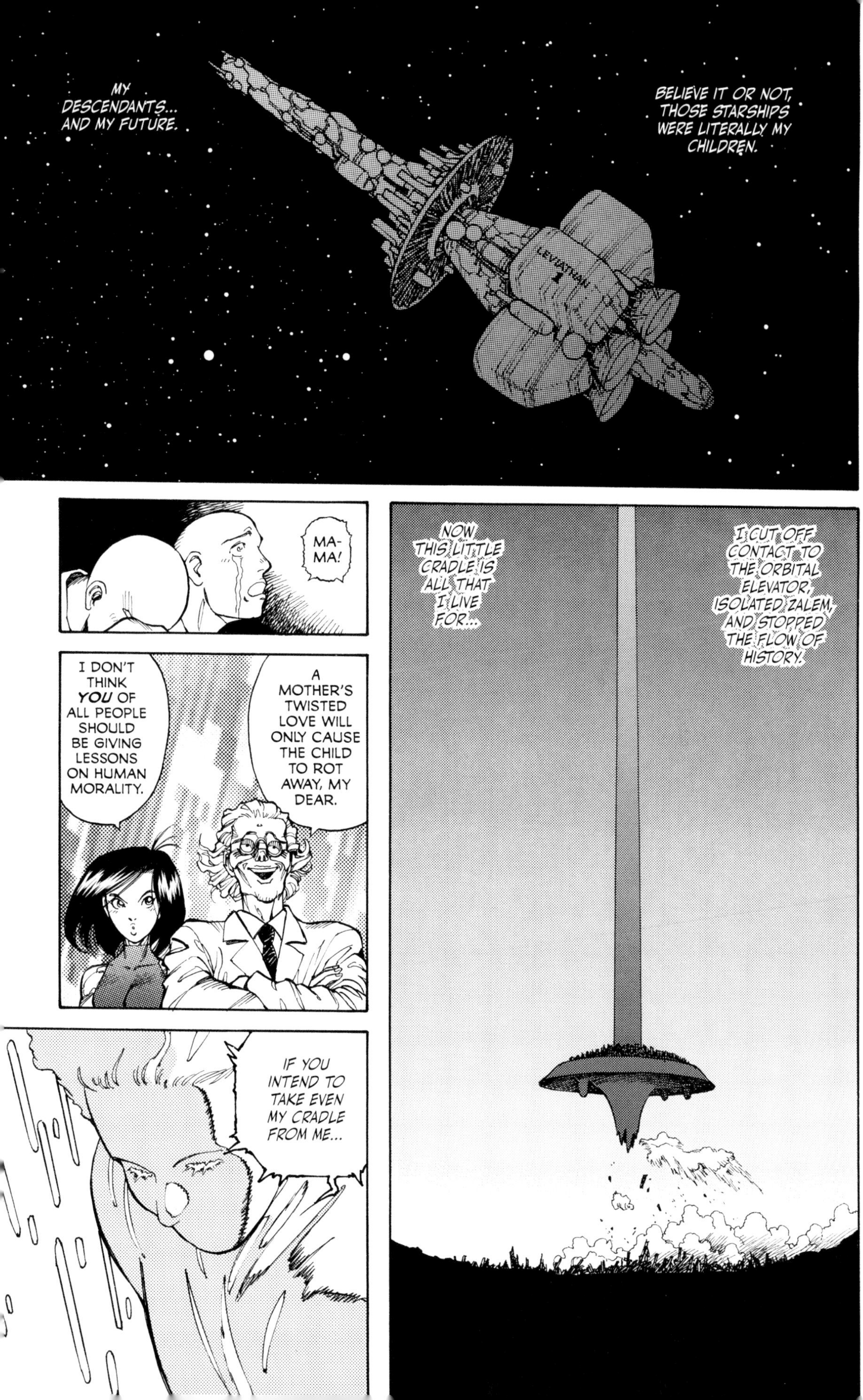
BELIEVE IT OR NOT, THOSE STARSHIPS WERE LITERALLY MY CHILDREN.
MY DESCENDANTS... AND MY FUTURE.
LEVIATHAN 1
I CUT OFF CONTACT TO THE ORBITAL ELEVATOR, ISOLATED ZALEM, AND STOPPED THE FLOW OF HISTORY.
NOW THIS LITTLE CRADLE IS ALL THAT I LIVE FOR...
MA-MA!
A MOTHER'S TWISTED LOVE WILL ONLY CAUSE THE CHILD TO ROT AWAY, MY DEAR.
I DON'T THINK ***YOU*** OF ALL PEOPLE SHOULD BE GIVING LESSONS ON HUMAN MORALITY.
IF YOU INTEND TO TAKE EVEN MY CRADLE FROM ME...

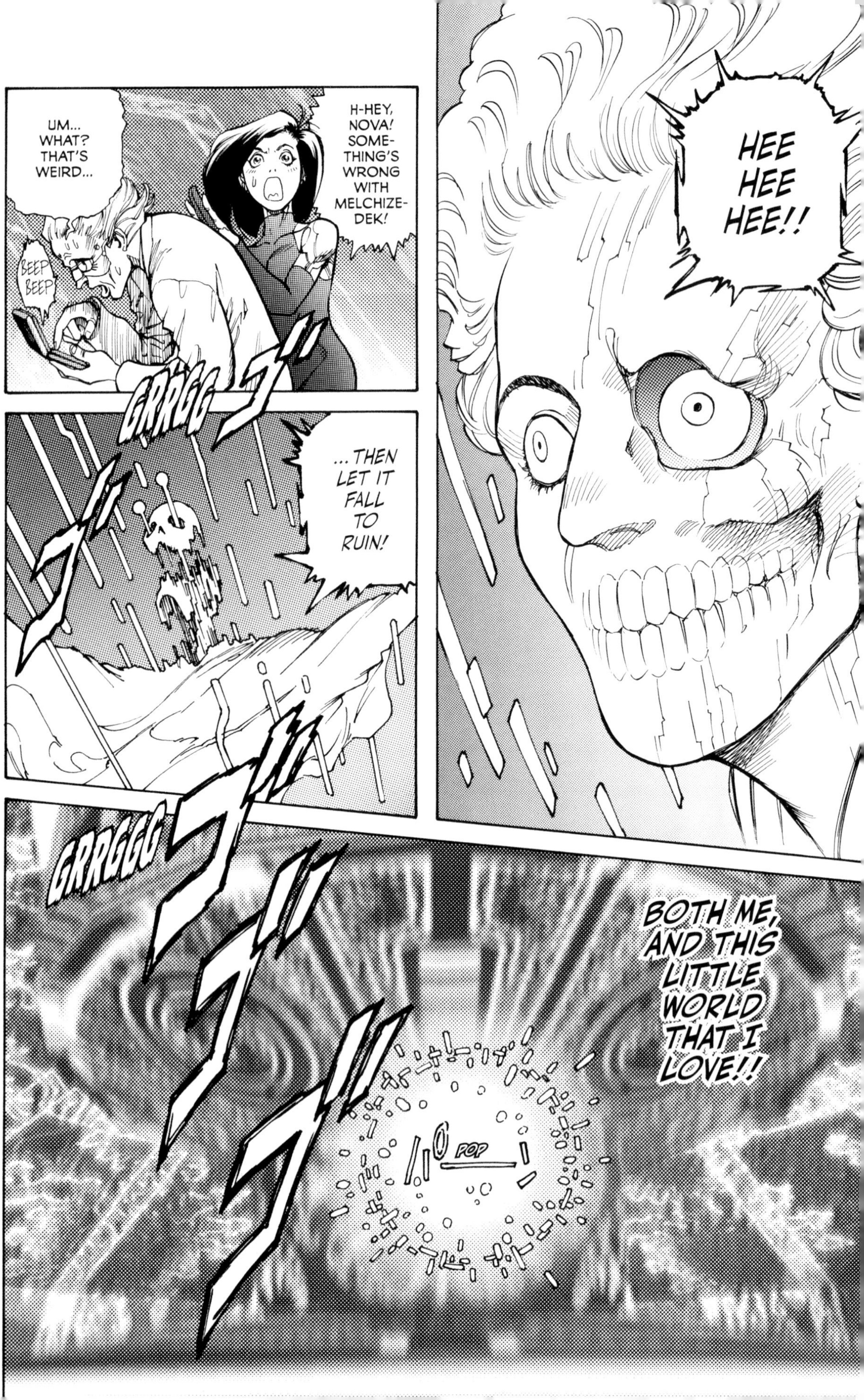
HEE HEE HEE!!
H-HEY, NOVA! SOME-THING'S WRONG WITH MELCHIZE-DEK!
UM... WHAT? THAT'S WEIRD...
BEEP BEEP
GRRGG
...THEN LET IT FALL TO RUIN!
GRRGGG
BOTH ME, AND THIS LITTLE WORLD THAT I LOVE!!
POP

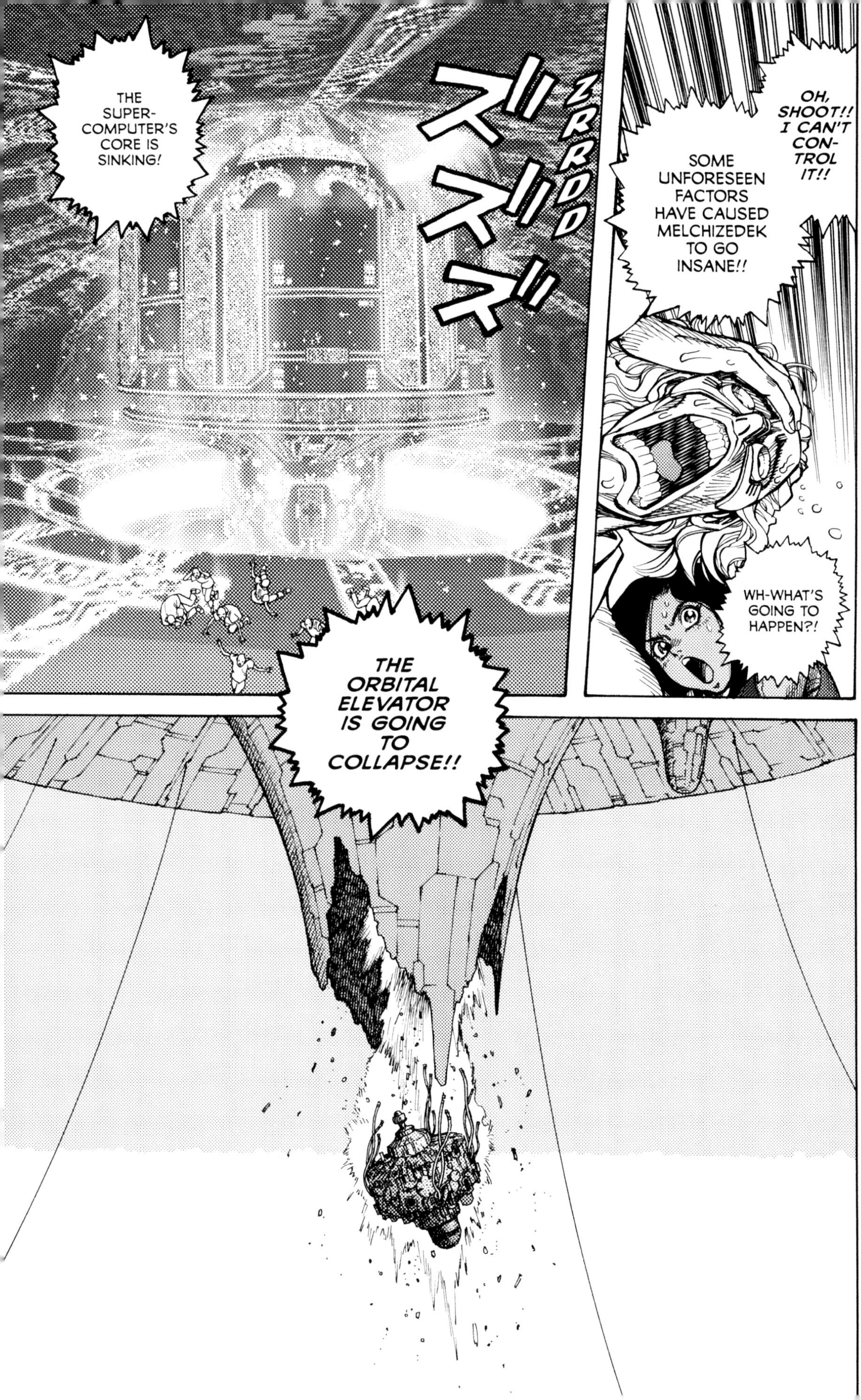
OH, SHOOT!! I CAN'T CON-TROL IT!!
SOME UNFORESEEN FACTORS HAVE CAUSED MELCHIZEDEK TO GO INSANE!!
WH-WHAT'S GOING TO HAPPEN?!
ZRRDD
THE SUPER-COMPUTER'S CORE IS SINKING!
THE ORBITAL ELEVATOR IS GOING TO COLLAPSE!!

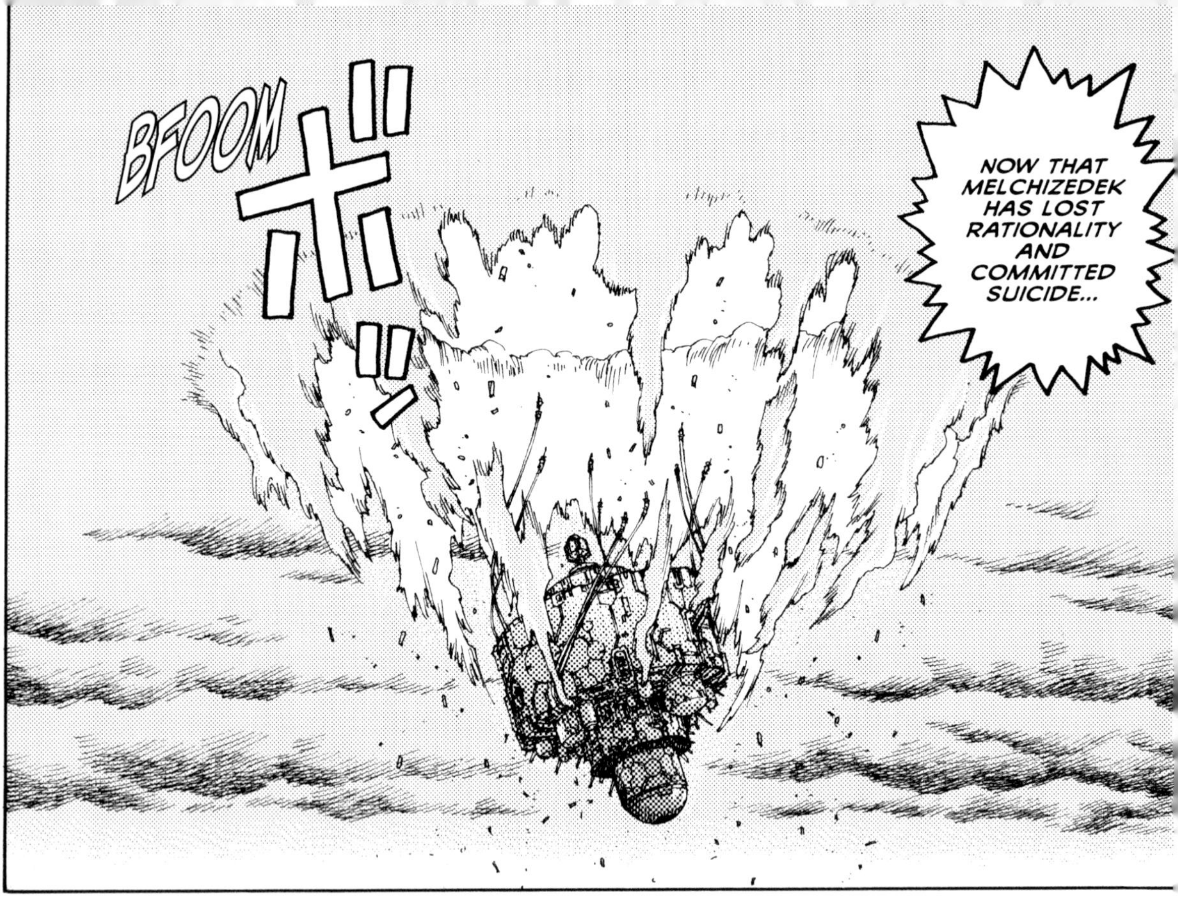
NOW THAT MELCHIZEDEK HAS LOST RATIONALITY AND COMMITTED SUICIDE...
BFOOM

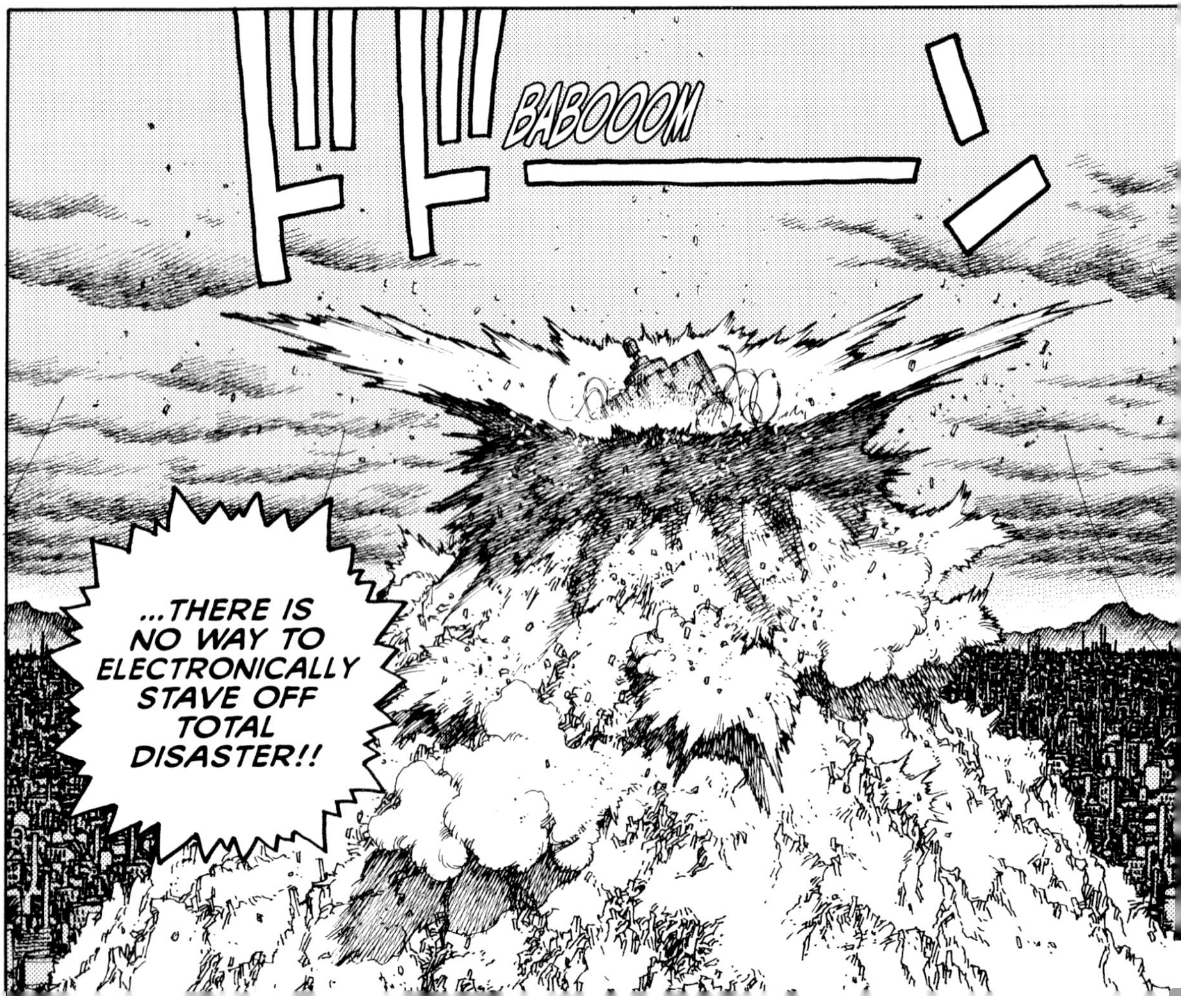
BABOOOM
...THERE IS NO WAY TO ELECTRONICALLY STAVE OFF TOTAL DISASTER!!

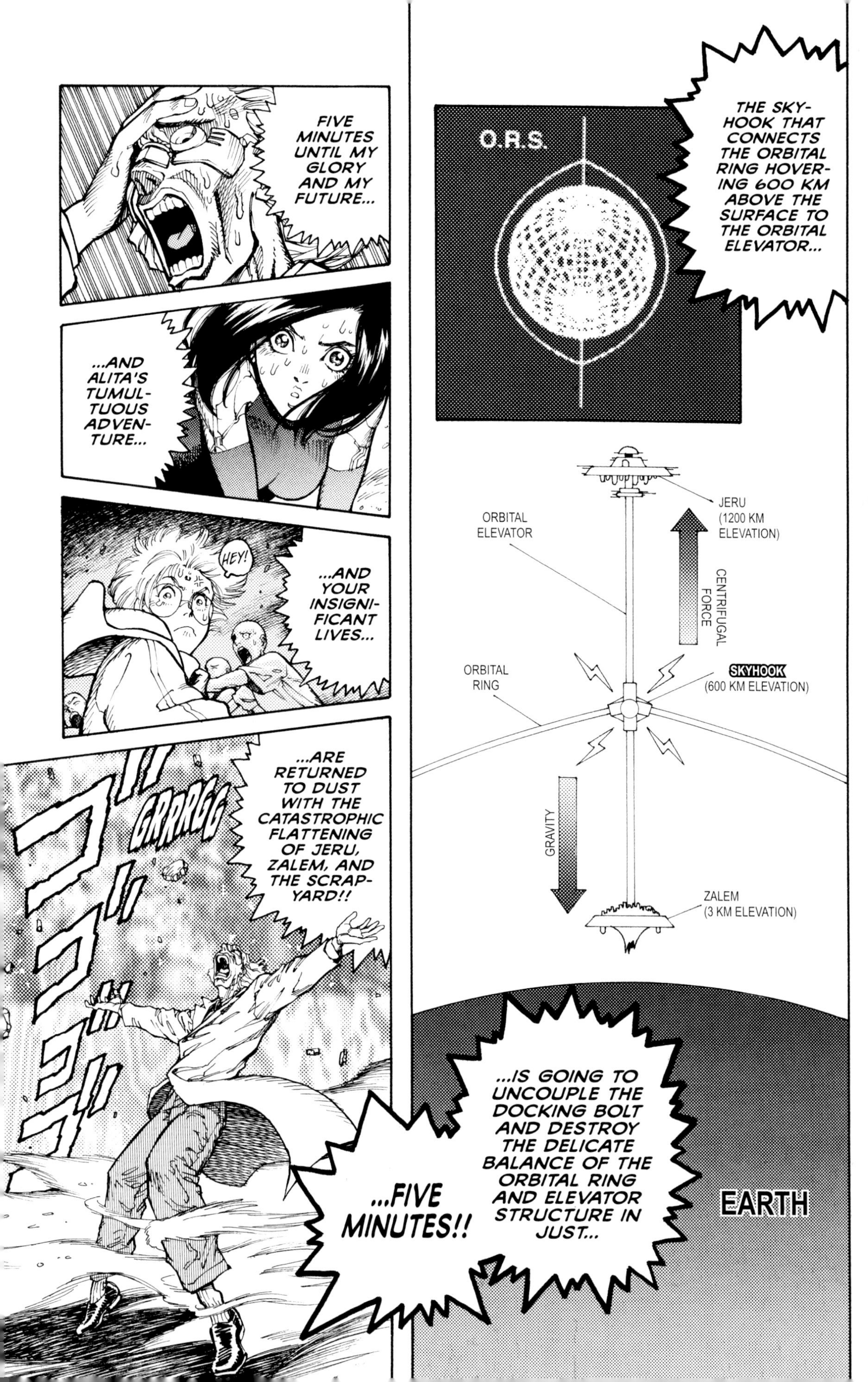
THE SKY-HOOK THAT CONNECTS THE ORBITAL RING HOVERING 600 KM ABOVE THE SURFACE TO THE ORBITAL ELEVATOR...
O.R.S.
JERU (1200 KM ELEVATION)
ORBITAL ELEVATOR
CENTRIFUGAL FORCE
ORBITAL RING
SKYHOOK (600 KM ELEVATION)
GRAVITY
ZALEM (3 KM ELEVATION)
...IS GOING TO UNCOUPLE THE DOCKING BOLT AND DESTROY THE DELICATE BALANCE OF THE ORBITAL RING AND ELEVATOR STRUCTURE IN JUST...
EARTH
...FIVE MINUTES!!
FIVE MINUTES UNTIL MY GLORY AND MY FUTURE...
...AND ALITA'S TUMULTUOUS ADVENTURE...
HEY!
...AND YOUR INSIGNIFICANT LIVES...
...ARE RETURNED TO DUST WITH THE CATASTROPHIC FLATTENING OF JERU, ZALEM, AND THE SCRAPYARD!!
GRRRGG

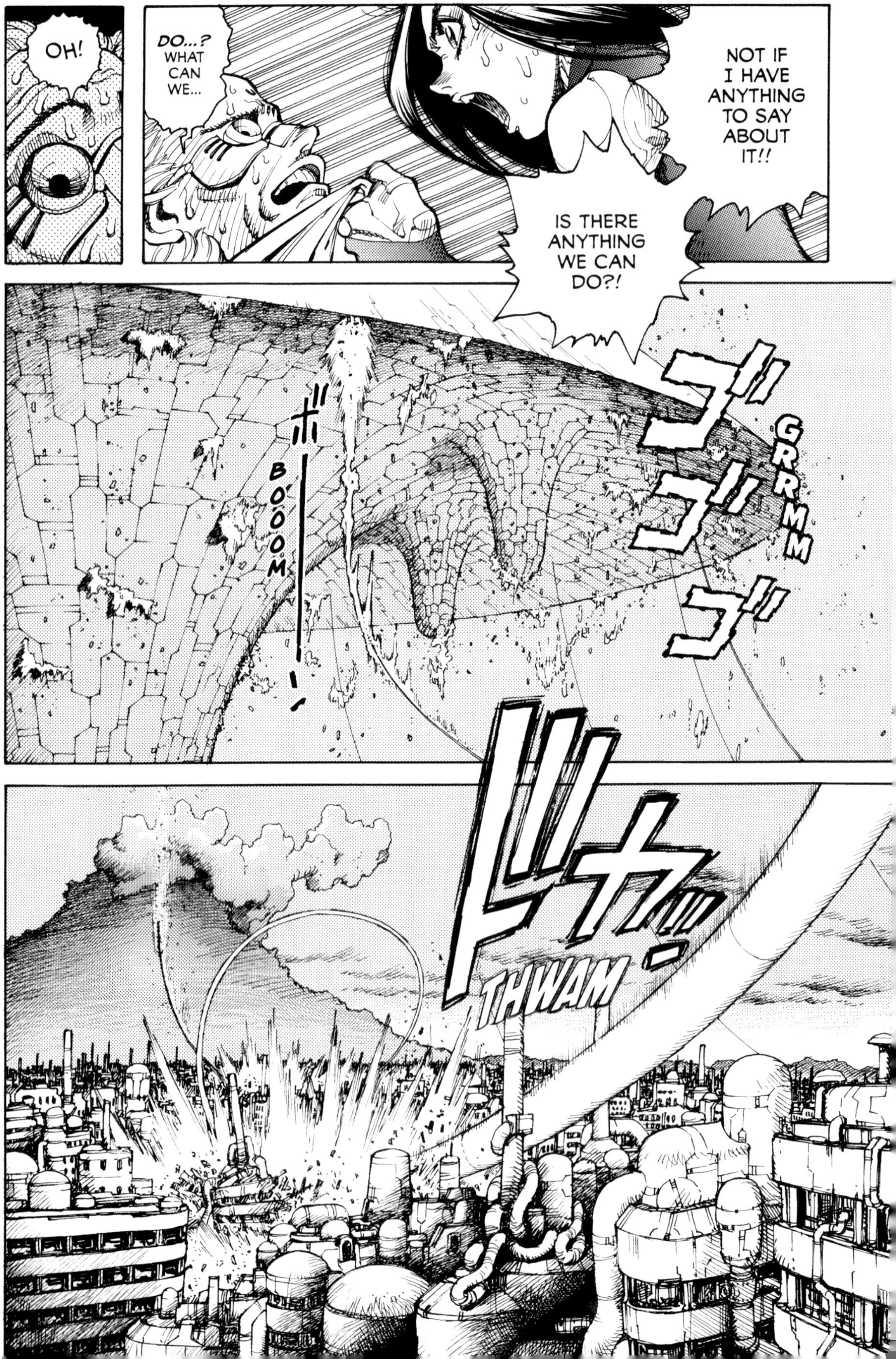
NOT IF I HAVE ANYTHING TO SAY ABOUT IT!!
DO...? WHAT CAN WE...
IS THERE ANYTHING WE CAN DO?!
OH!
GRRMM
BOOOOM
THWAM

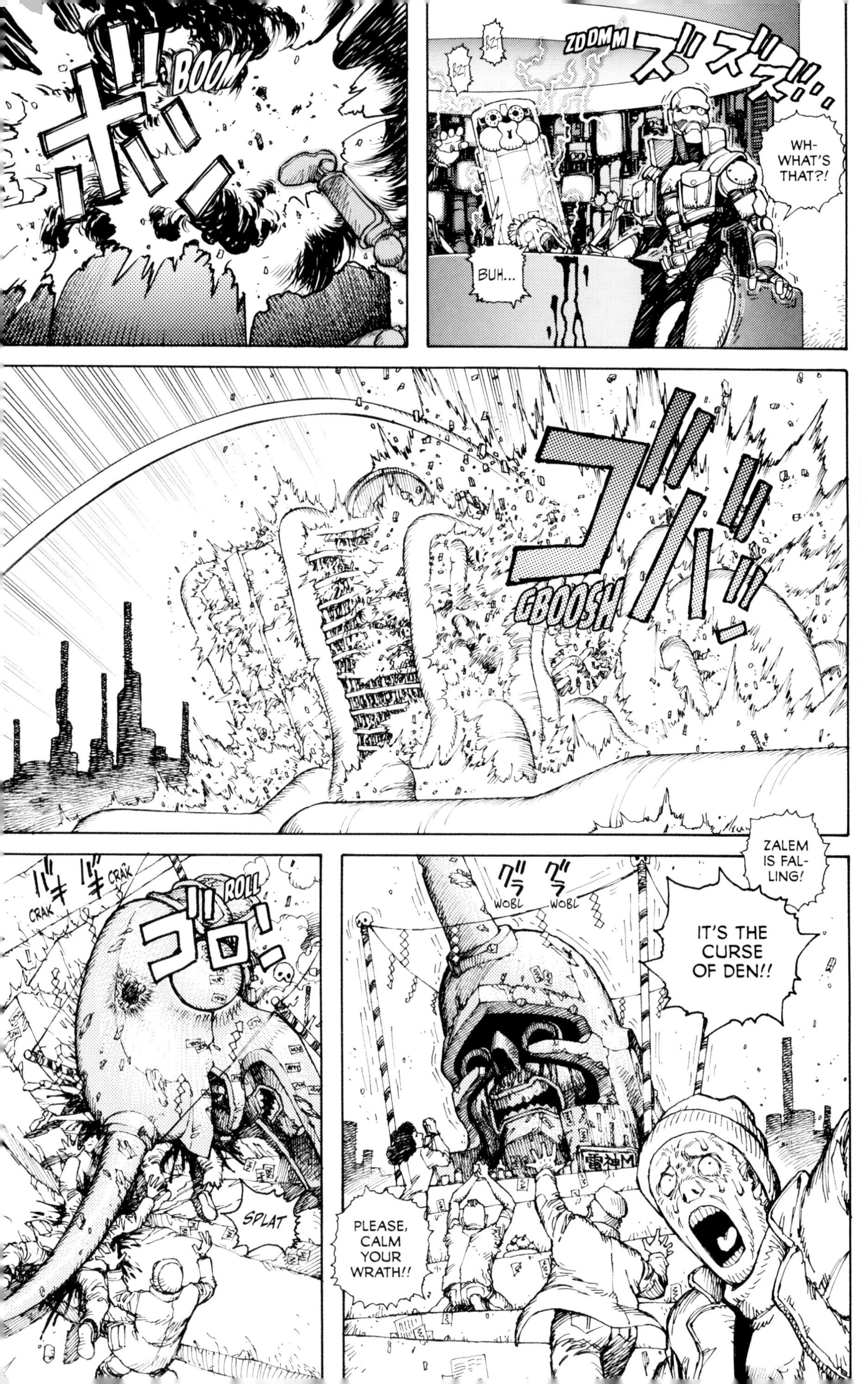

BZT
BZT
ZDOMM
ズズズ
WH-WHAT'S THAT?!
BUH...
BOOM
ボッ
ゴバッ
GBOOSH
ZALEM IS FAL-LING!
IT'S THE CURSE OF DEN!!
グラ グラ
WOBL WOBL
雷神M
PLEASE, CALM YOUR WRATH!!
バキ バキ
CRAK CRAK
ゴロッ
ROLL
SPLAT

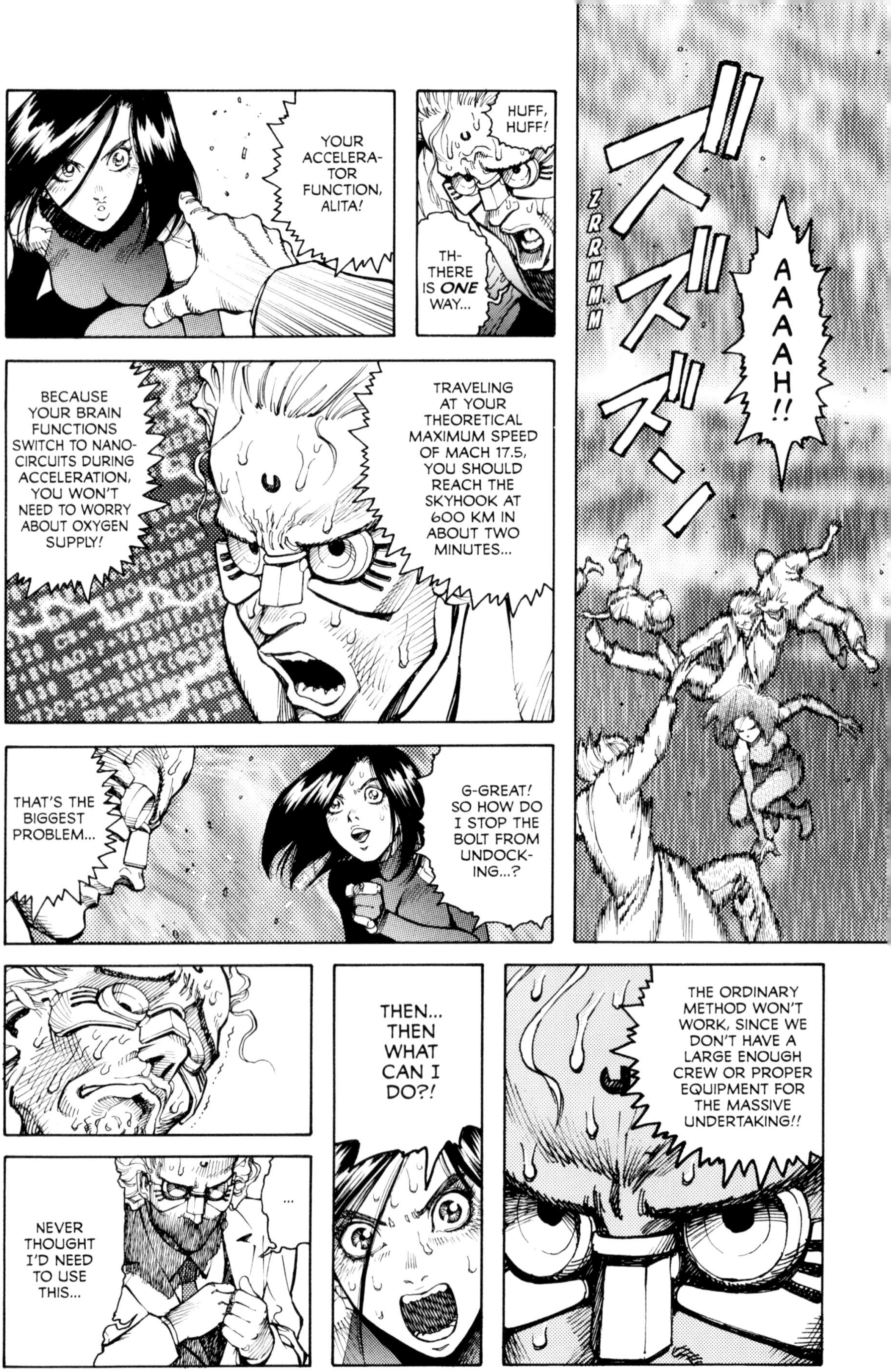
ZRRMMMM
AAAAAH!!
HUFF, HUFF!
TH-THERE IS *ONE* WAY...
YOUR ACCELERATOR FUNCTION, ALITA!
TRAVELING AT YOUR THEORETICAL MAXIMUM SPEED OF MACH 17.5, YOU SHOULD REACH THE SKYHOOK AT 600 KM IN ABOUT TWO MINUTES...
BECAUSE YOUR BRAIN FUNCTIONS SWITCH TO NANO-CIRCUITS DURING ACCELERATION, YOU WON'T NEED TO WORRY ABOUT OXYGEN SUPPLY!
G-GREAT! SO HOW DO I STOP THE BOLT FROM UNDOCKING...?
THAT'S THE BIGGEST PROBLEM...
THE ORDINARY METHOD WON'T WORK, SINCE WE DON'T HAVE A LARGE ENOUGH CREW OR PROPER EQUIPMENT FOR THE MASSIVE UNDERTAKING!!
THEN... THEN WHAT CAN I DO?!
...
NEVER THOUGHT I'D NEED TO USE THIS...

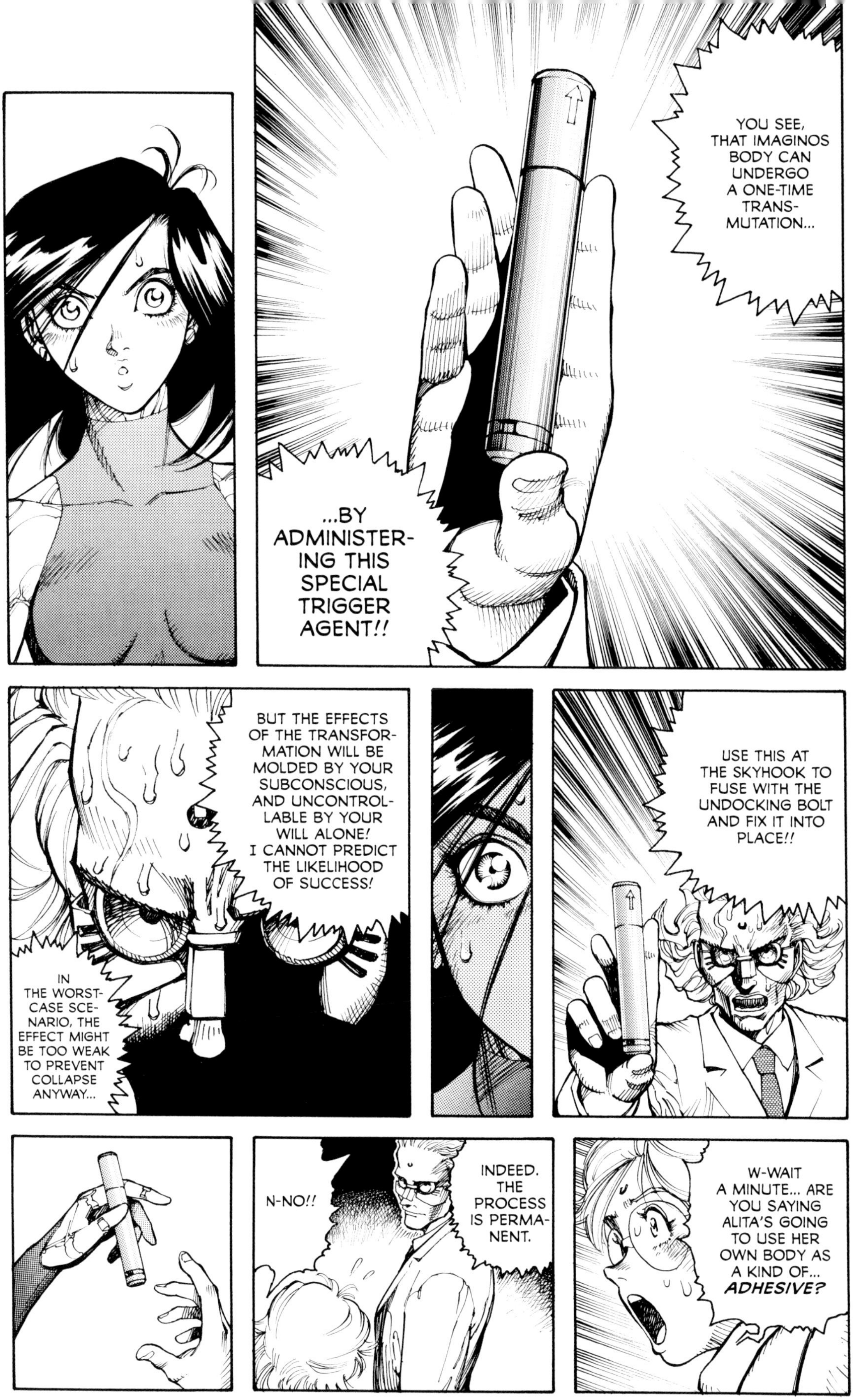
YOU SEE, THAT IMAGINOS BODY CAN UNDERGO A ONE-TIME TRANS-MUTATION...
...BY ADMINISTER-ING THIS SPECIAL TRIGGER AGENT!!
USE THIS AT THE SKYHOOK TO FUSE WITH THE UNDOCKING BOLT AND FIX IT INTO PLACE!!
BUT THE EFFECTS OF THE TRANSFOR-MATION WILL BE MOLDED BY YOUR SUBCONSCIOUS, AND UNCONTROL-LABLE BY YOUR WILL ALONE! I CANNOT PREDICT THE LIKELIHOOD OF SUCCESS!
IN THE WORST-CASE SCE-NARIO, THE EFFECT MIGHT BE TOO WEAK TO PREVENT COLLAPSE ANYWAY...
W-WAIT A MINUTE... ARE YOU SAYING ALITA'S GOING TO USE HER OWN BODY AS A KIND OF... *ADHESIVE?*
INDEED. THE PROCESS IS PERMA-NENT.
N-NO!!

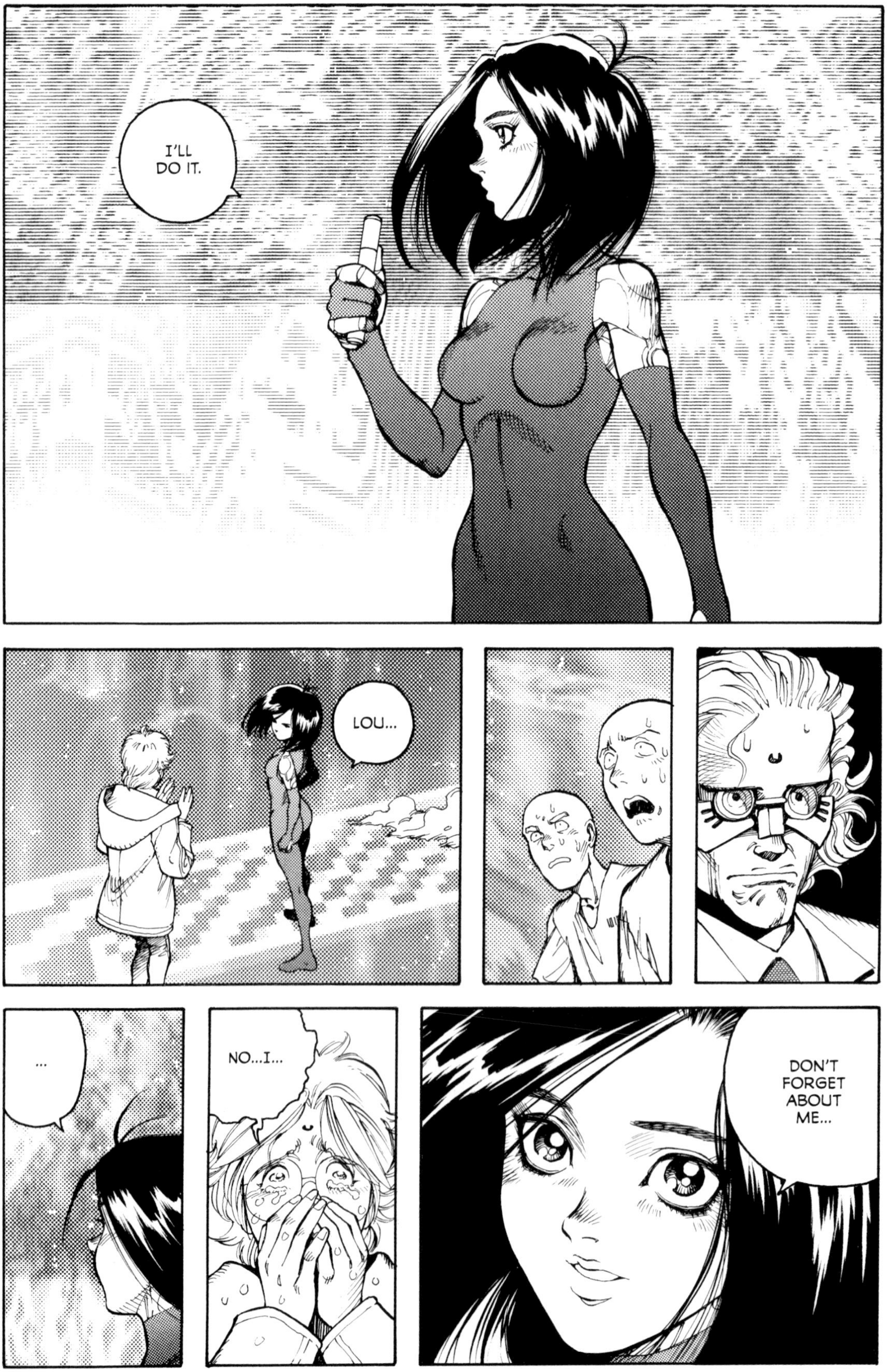
I'LL DO IT.
LOU...
DON'T FORGET ABOUT ME...
NO...I...
...

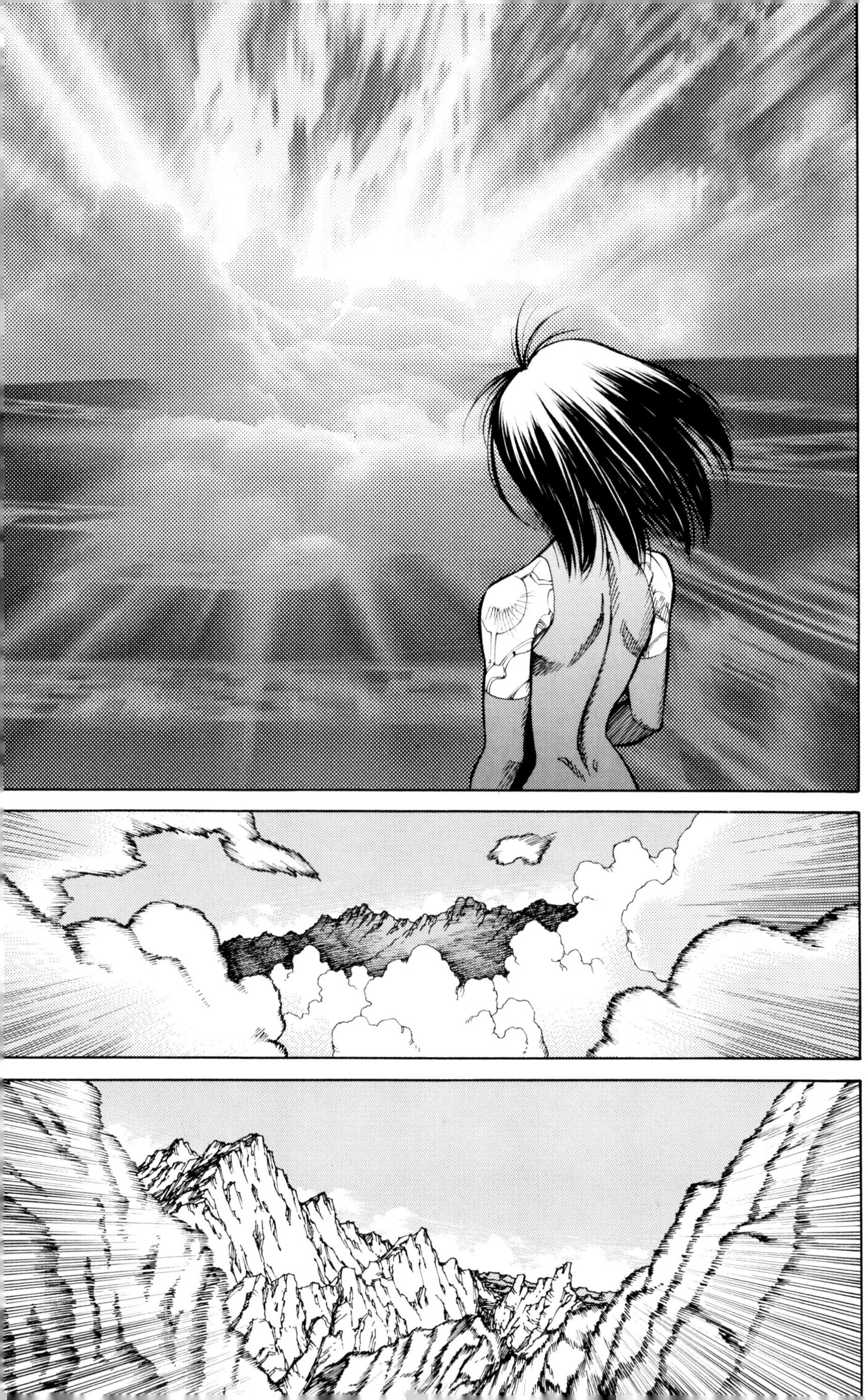

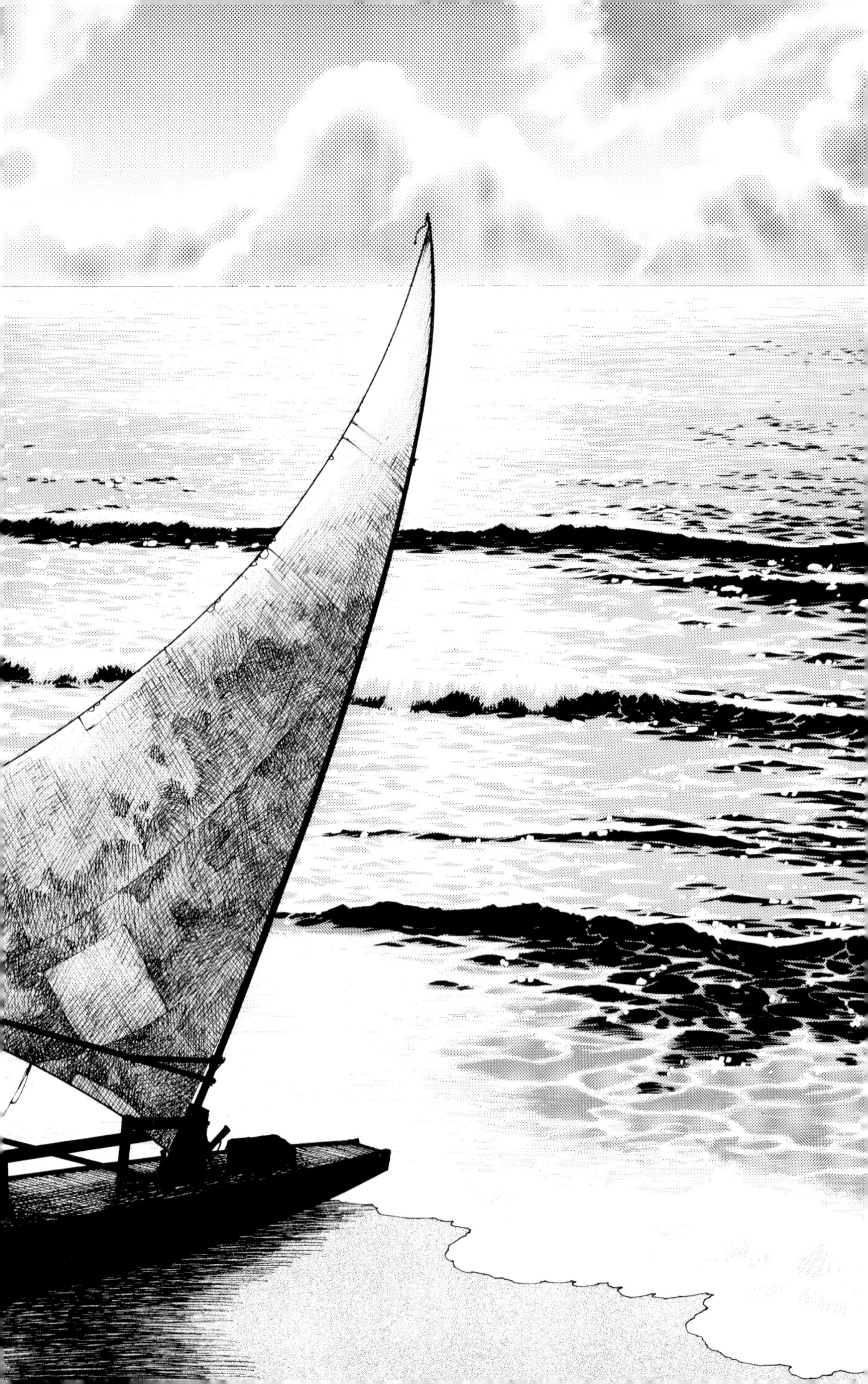

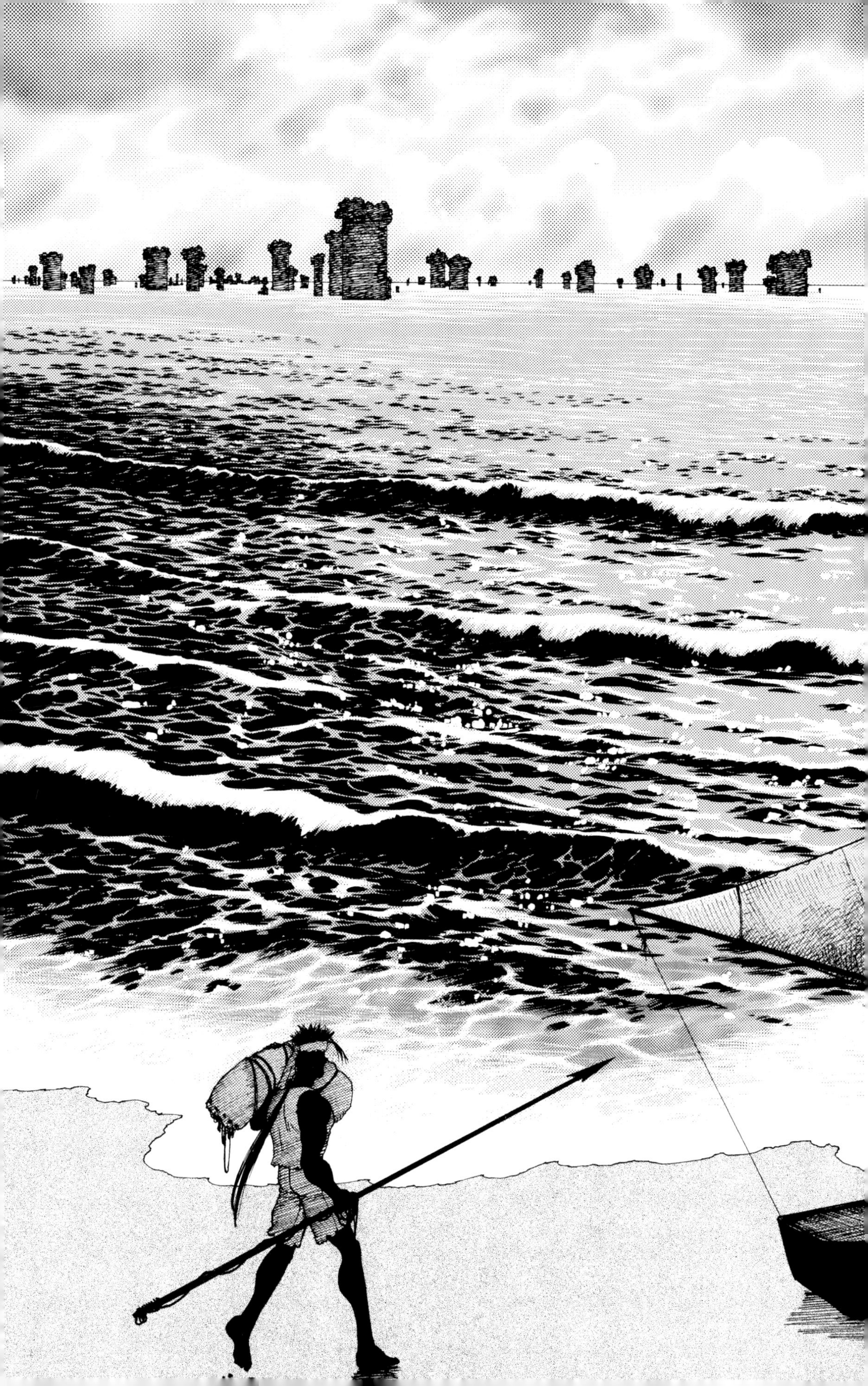

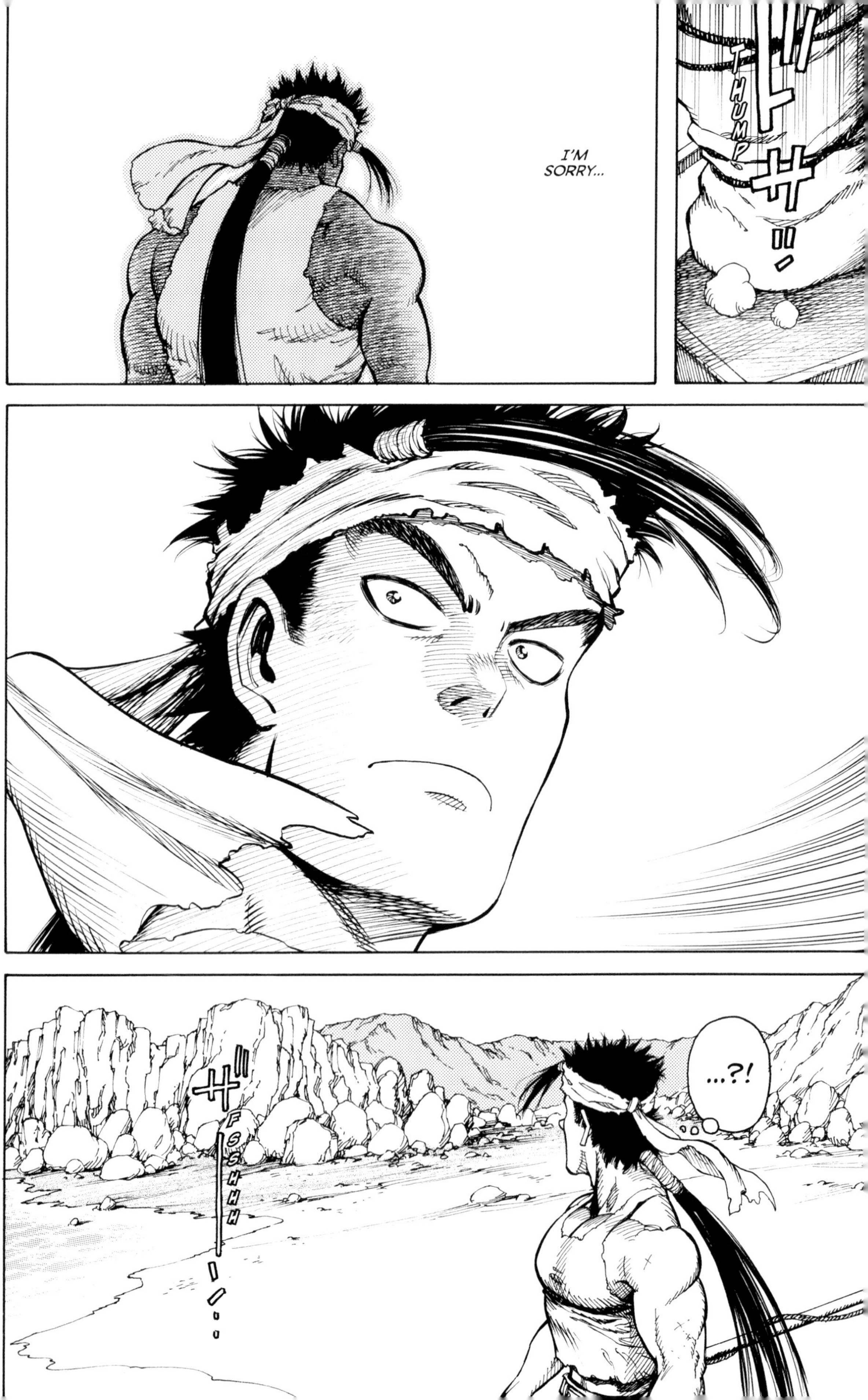
THUMP
I'M SORRY...
FSSHHH
...?!

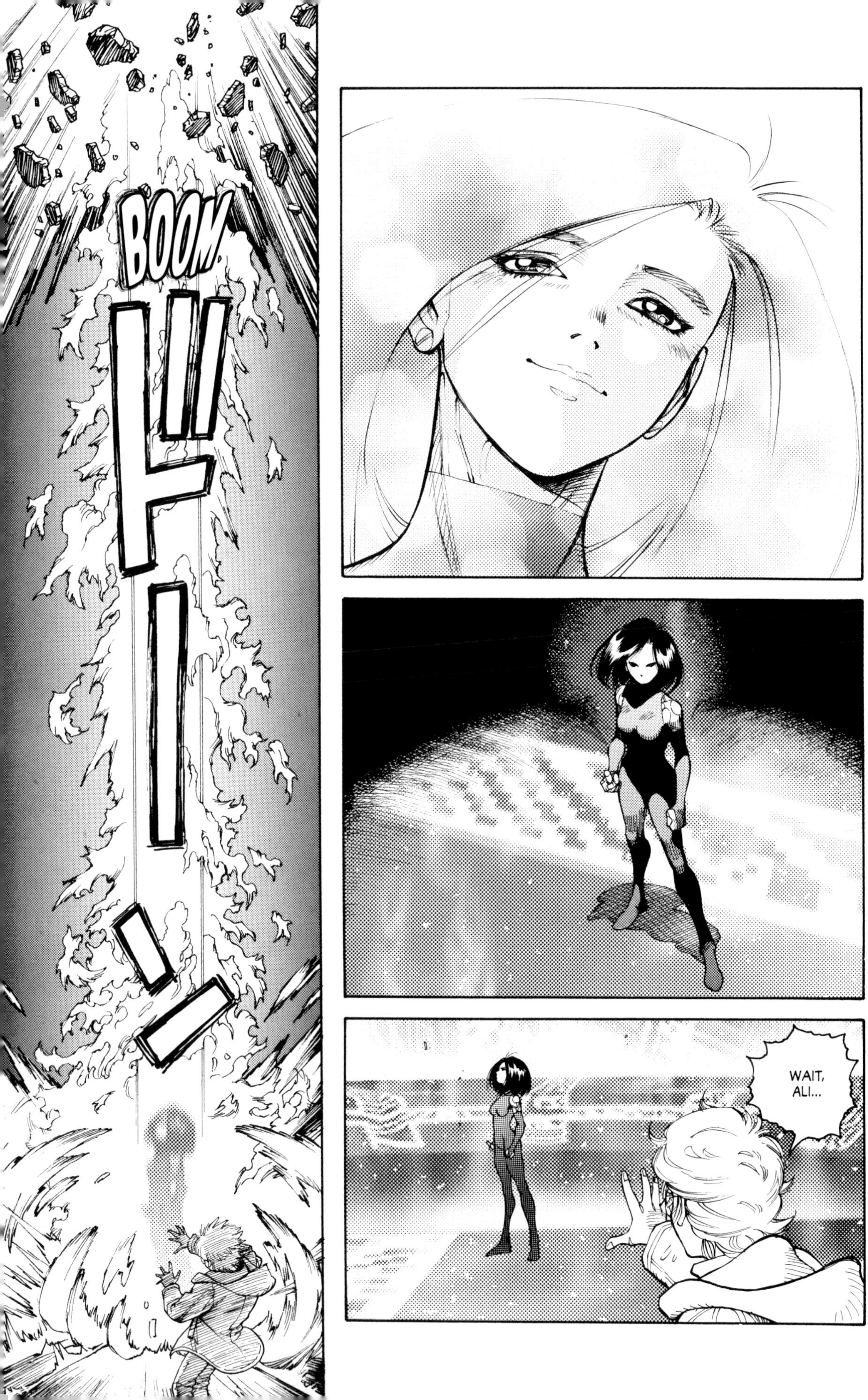
WAIT, ALI...
BOOM
ドーン

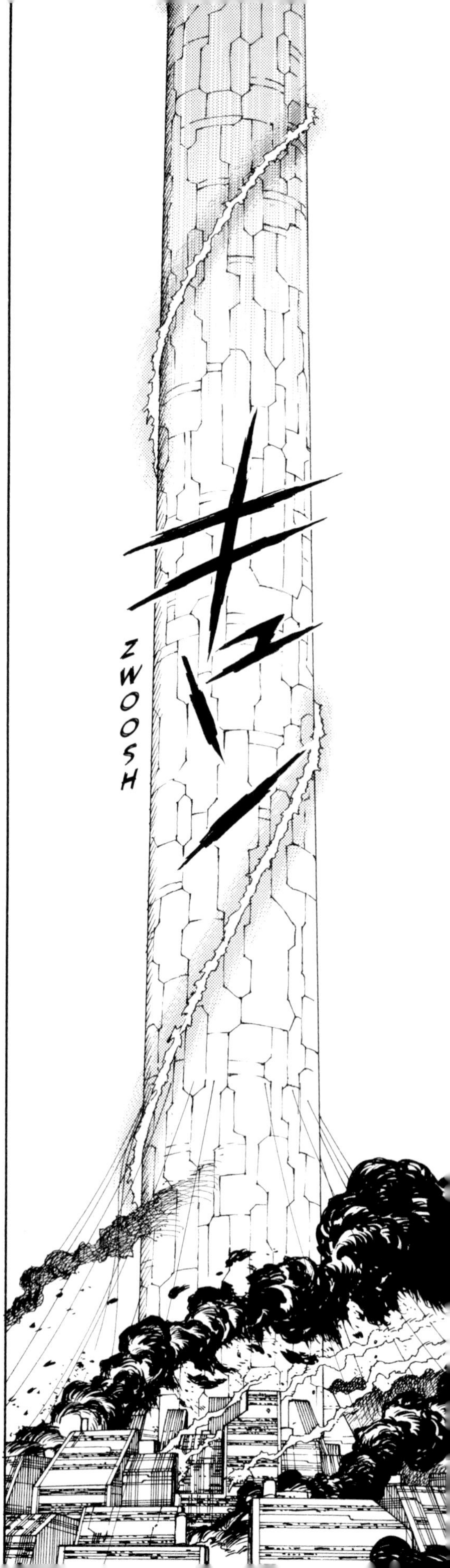
ZWOOSH
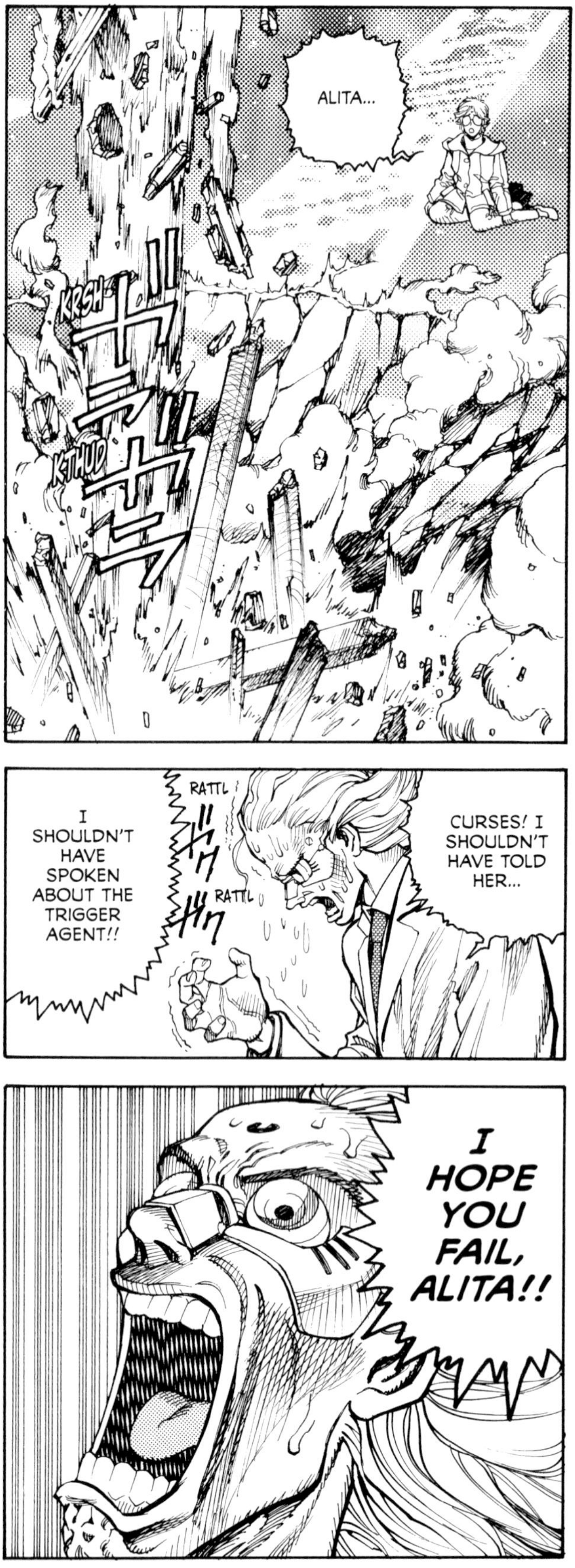
ALITA...
KRSH
KTHUD
CURSES! I SHOULDN'T HAVE TOLD HER...
RATTL
RATTL
I SHOULDN'T HAVE SPOKEN ABOUT THE TRIGGER AGENT!!
I HOPE YOU FAIL, ALITA!!

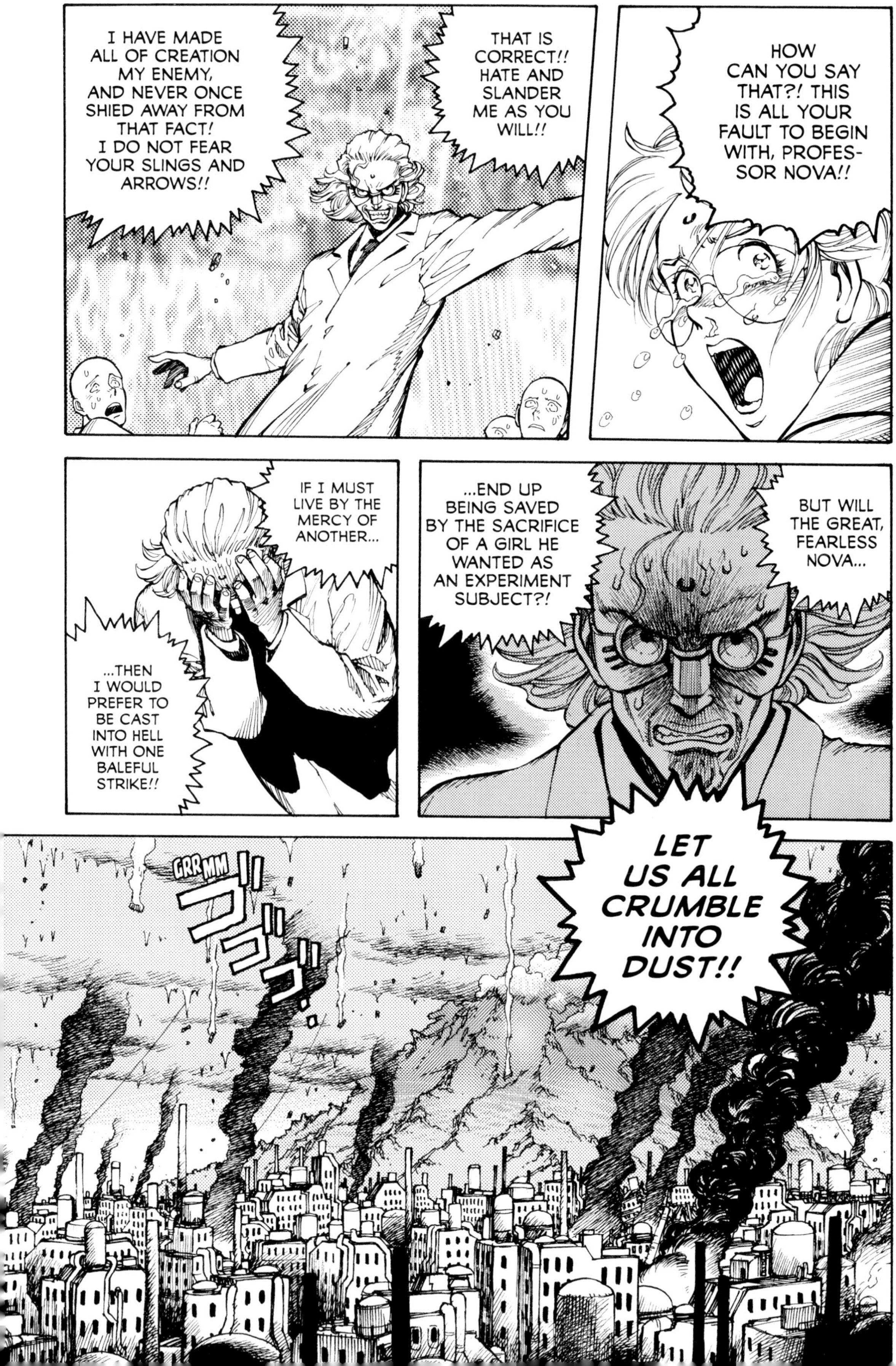
HOW CAN YOU SAY THAT?! THIS IS ALL YOUR FAULT TO BEGIN WITH, PROFESSOR NOVA!!
THAT IS CORRECT!! HATE AND SLANDER ME AS YOU WILL!!
I HAVE MADE ALL OF CREATION MY ENEMY, AND NEVER ONCE SHIED AWAY FROM THAT FACT! I DO NOT FEAR YOUR SLINGS AND ARROWS!!
BUT WILL THE GREAT, FEARLESS NOVA...
...END UP BEING SAVED BY THE SACRIFICE OF A GIRL HE WANTED AS AN EXPERIMENT SUBJECT?!
IF I MUST LIVE BY THE MERCY OF ANOTHER...
...THEN I WOULD PREFER TO BE CAST INTO HELL WITH ONE BALEFUL STRIKE!!
LET US ALL CRUMBLE INTO DUST!!
GRRMM

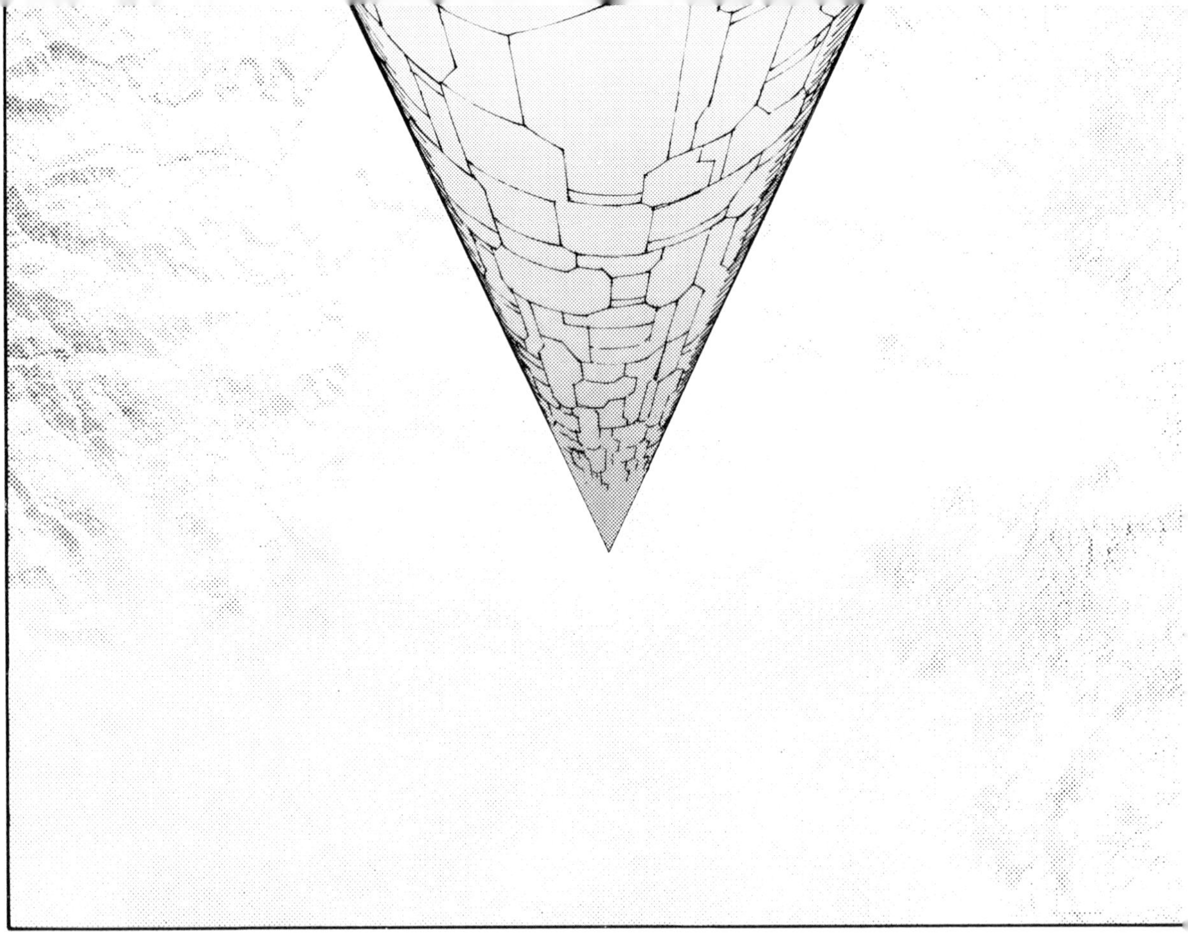
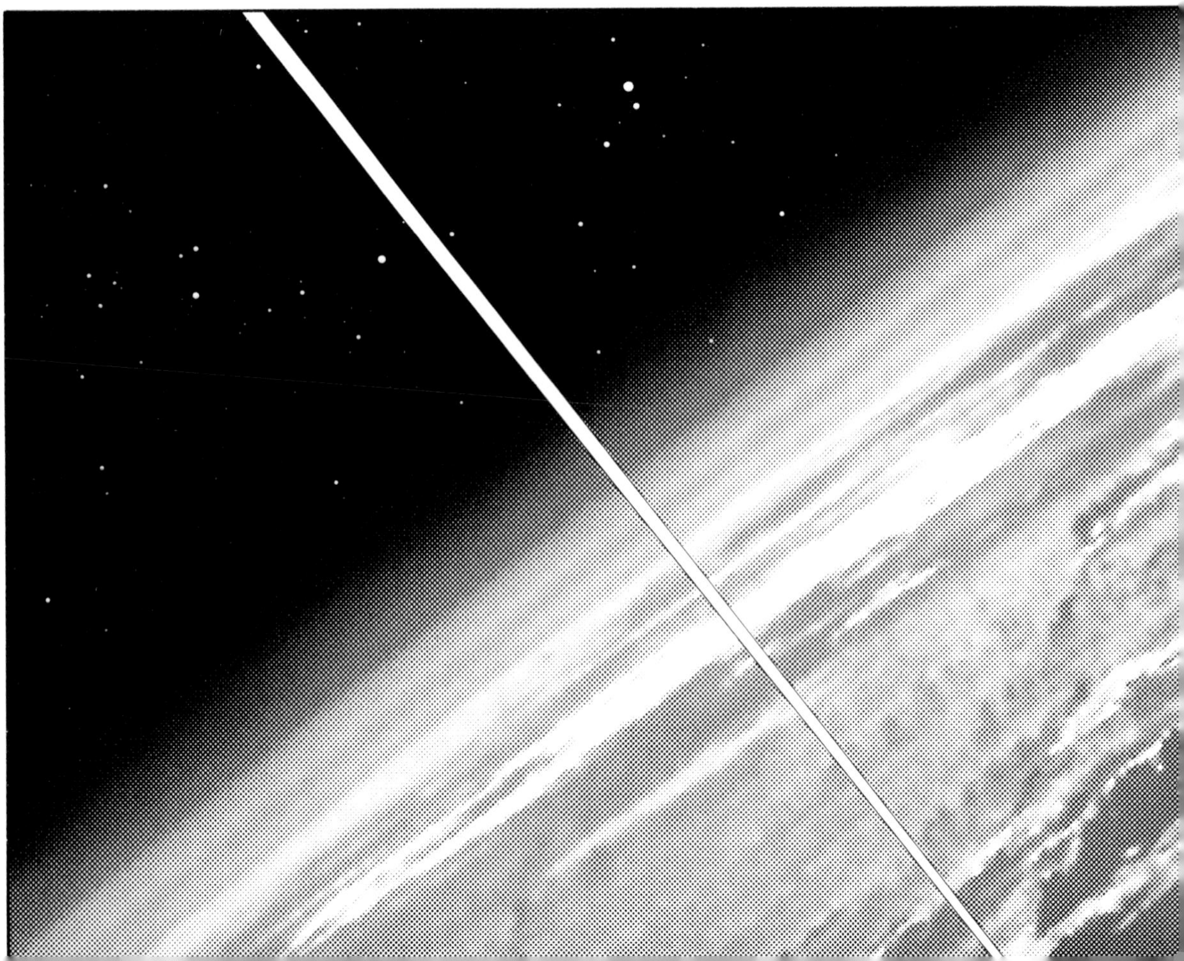

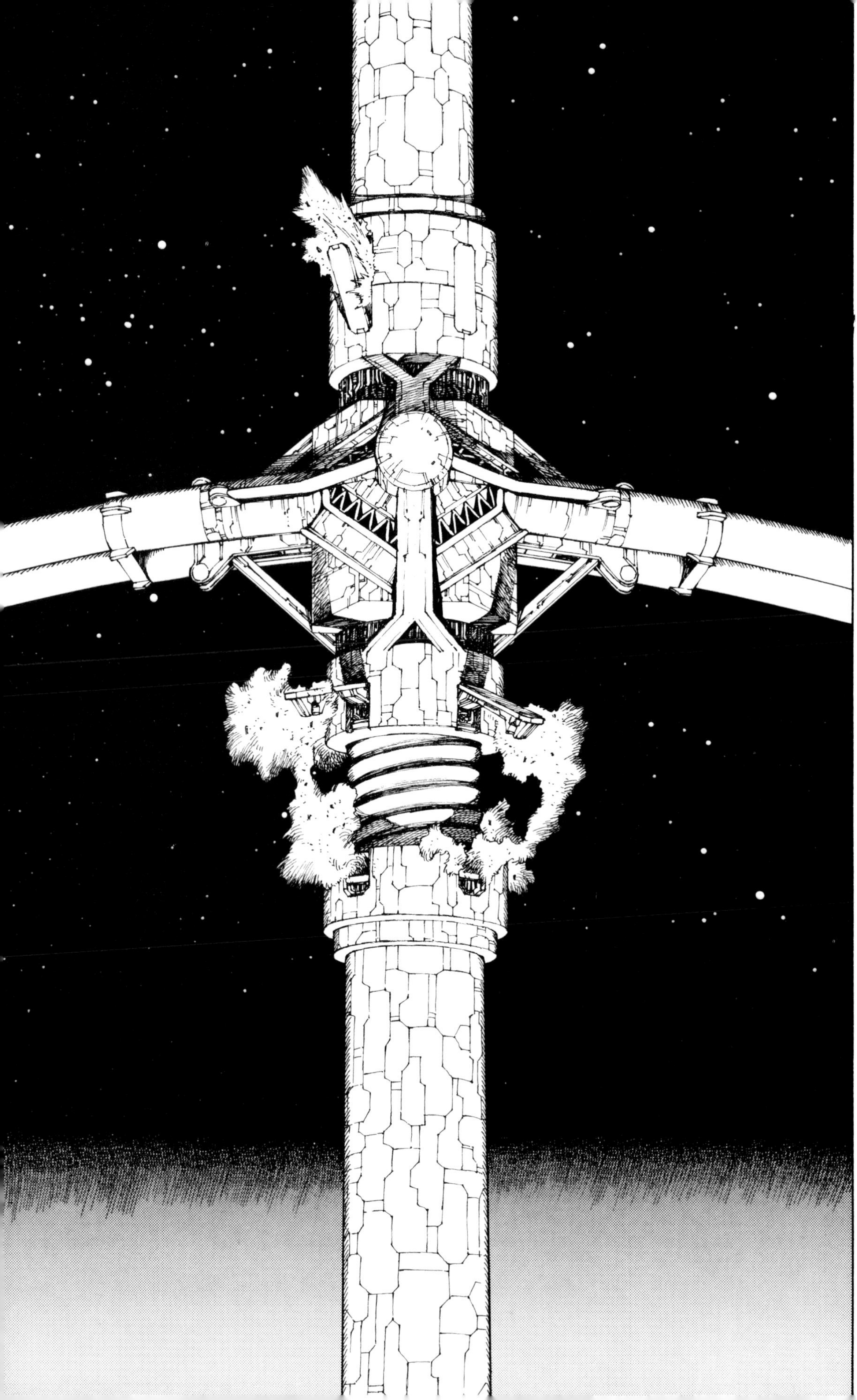

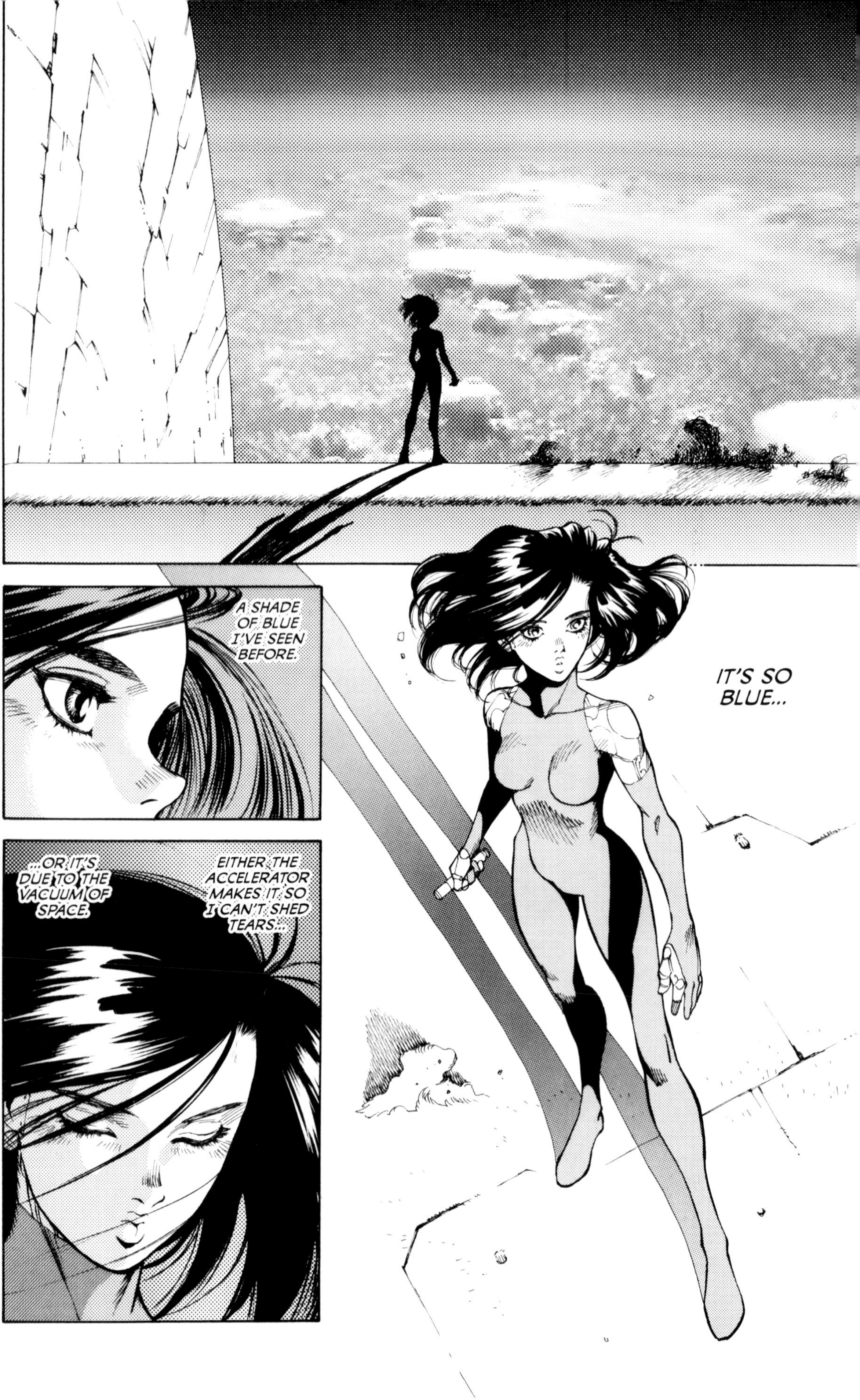
IT'S SO BLUE...
A SHADE OF BLUE I'VE SEEN BEFORE.
EITHER THE ACCELERATOR MAKES IT SO I CAN'T SHED TEARS...
...OR IT'S DUE TO THE VACUUM OF SPACE.

SO MOURNFUL.

YET, I FEEL SO LONELY.

AND EVEN THESE EMOTIONS ARE GOING TO VANISH IN A MOMENT.

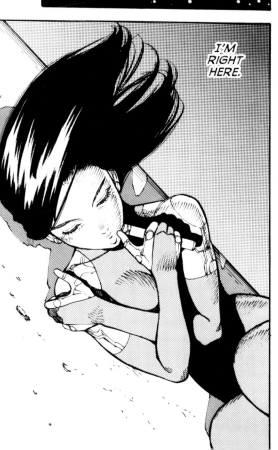

I'M RIGHT HERE.

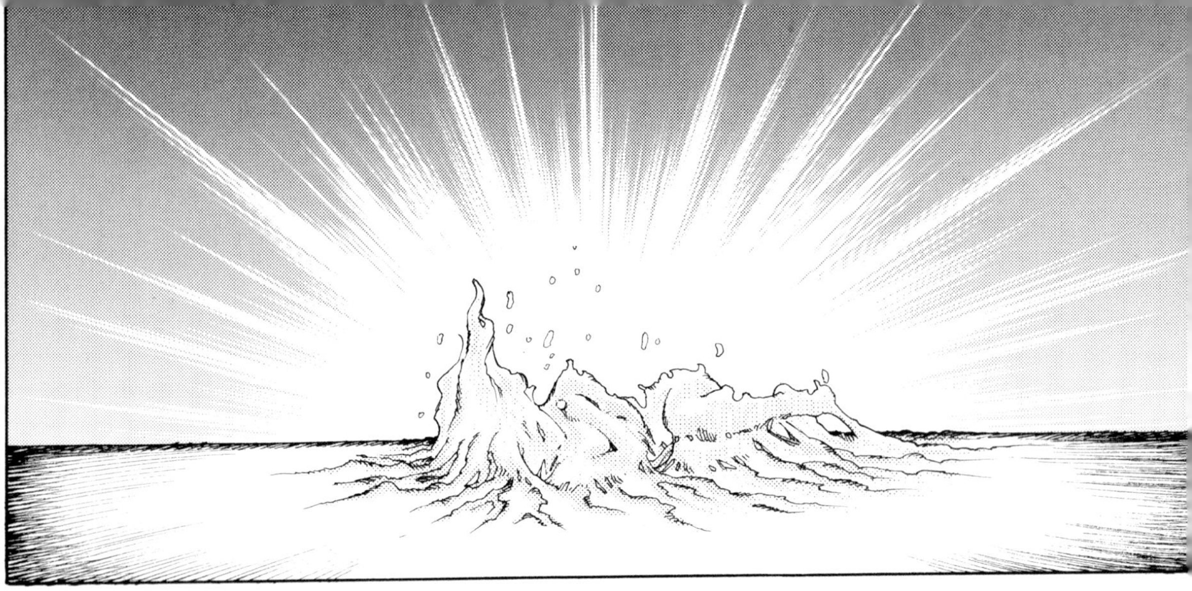
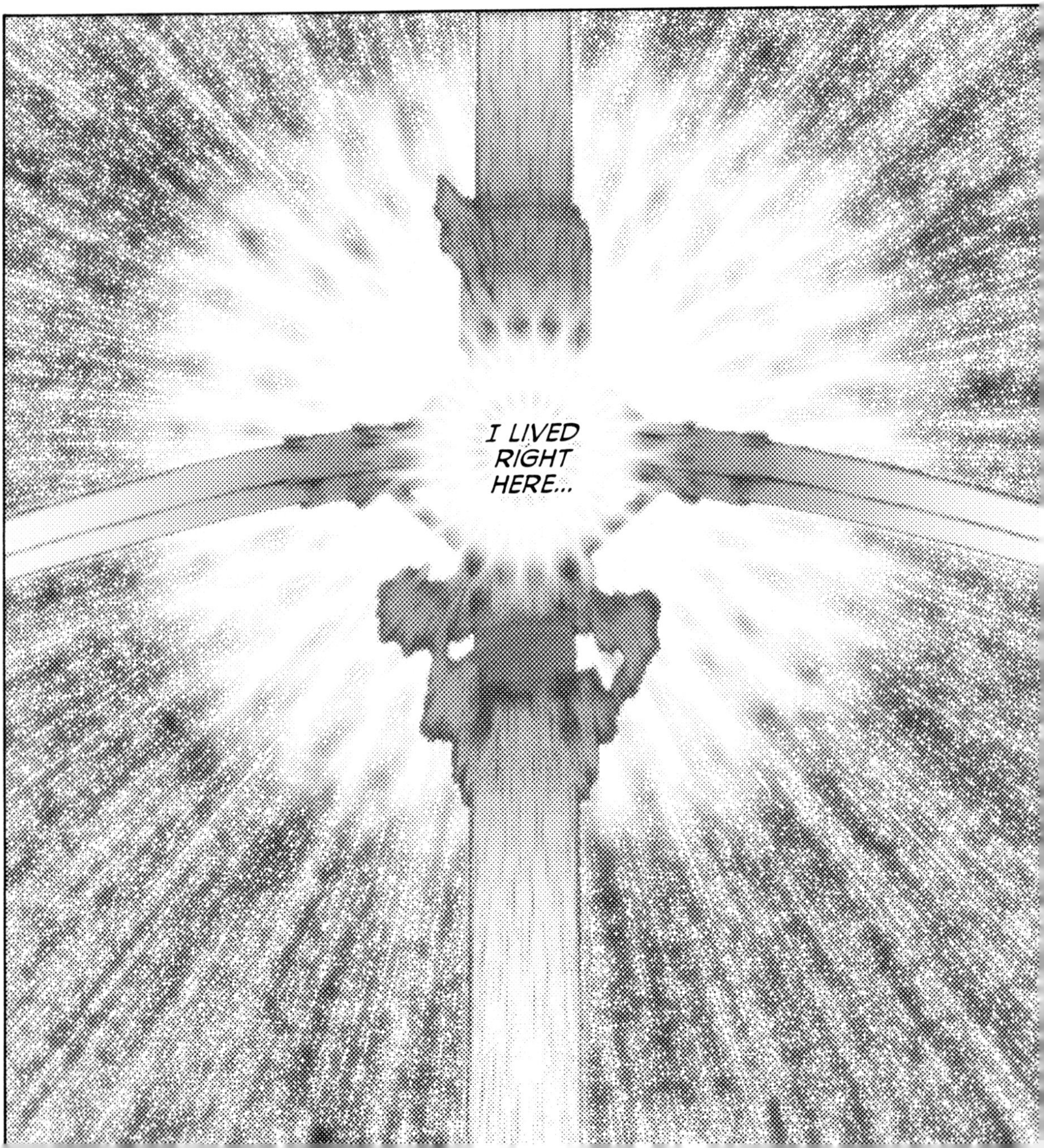
I LIVED RIGHT HERE...

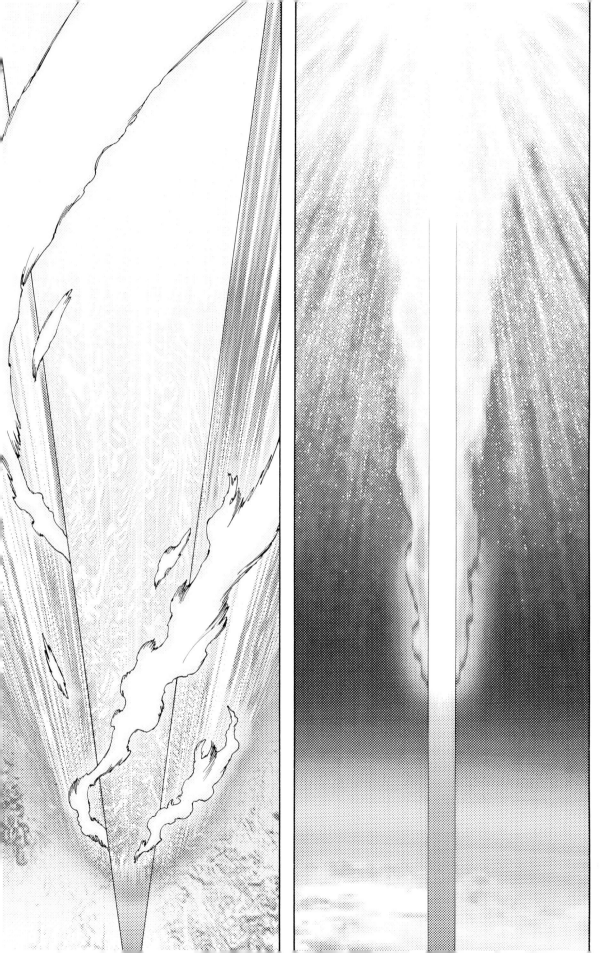

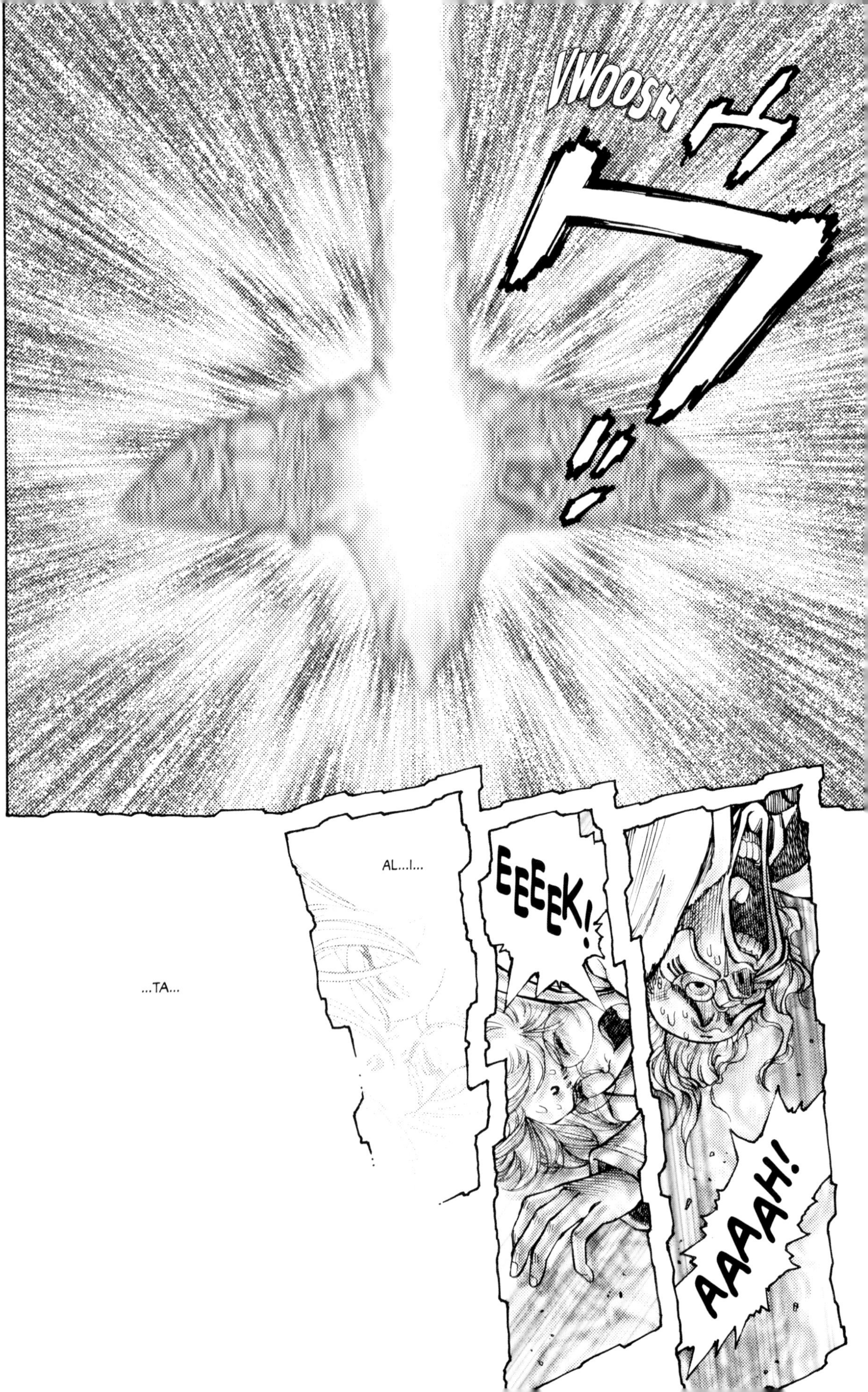
VWOOSH
AAAAH!
EEEEK!
AL...I...
...TA...

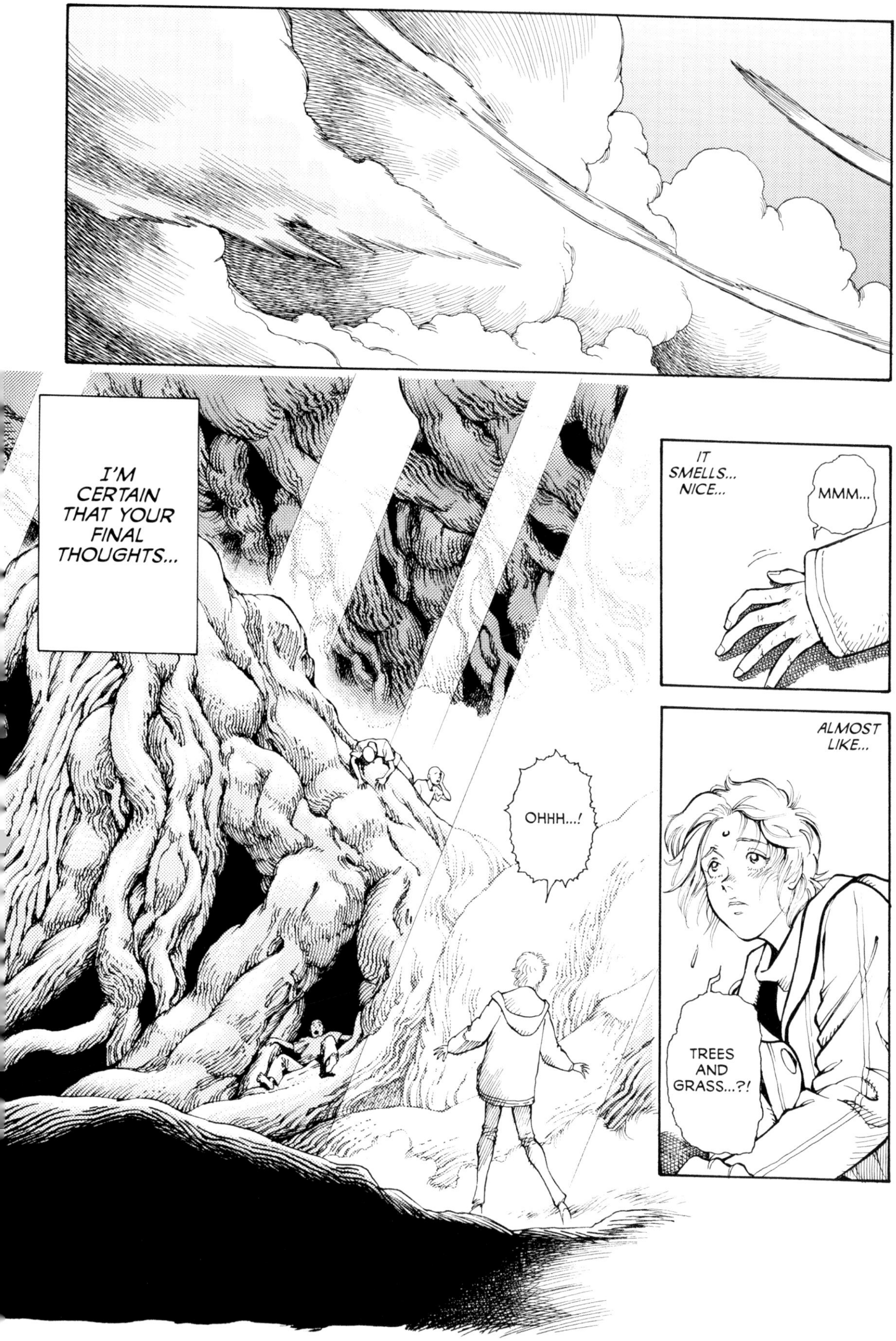
IT SMELLS... NICE...
MMM...
ALMOST LIKE...
TREES AND GRASS...?!
I'M CERTAIN THAT YOUR FINAL THOUGHTS...
OHHH...!

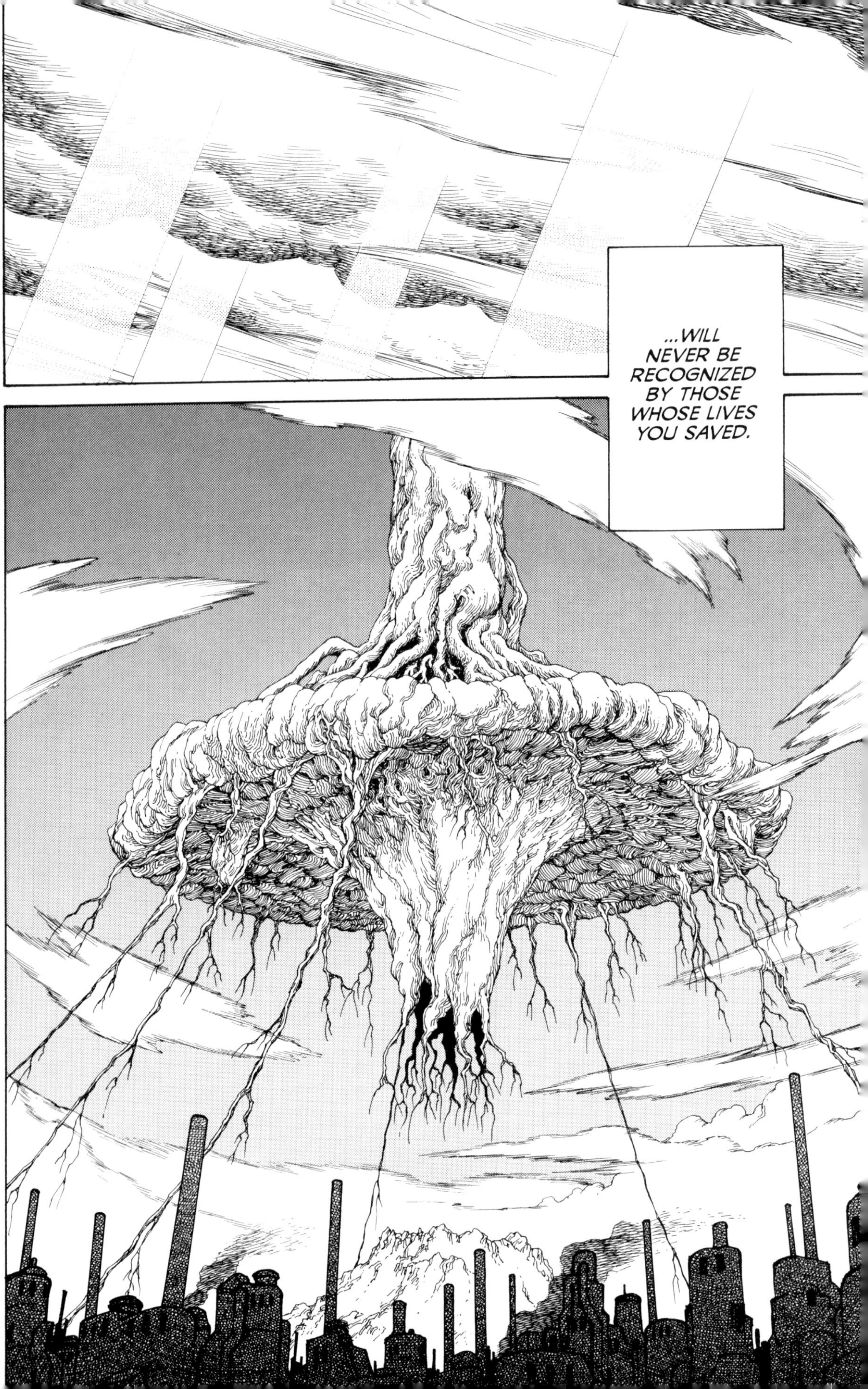
...WILL NEVER BE RECOGNIZED BY THOSE WHOSE LIVES YOU SAVED.

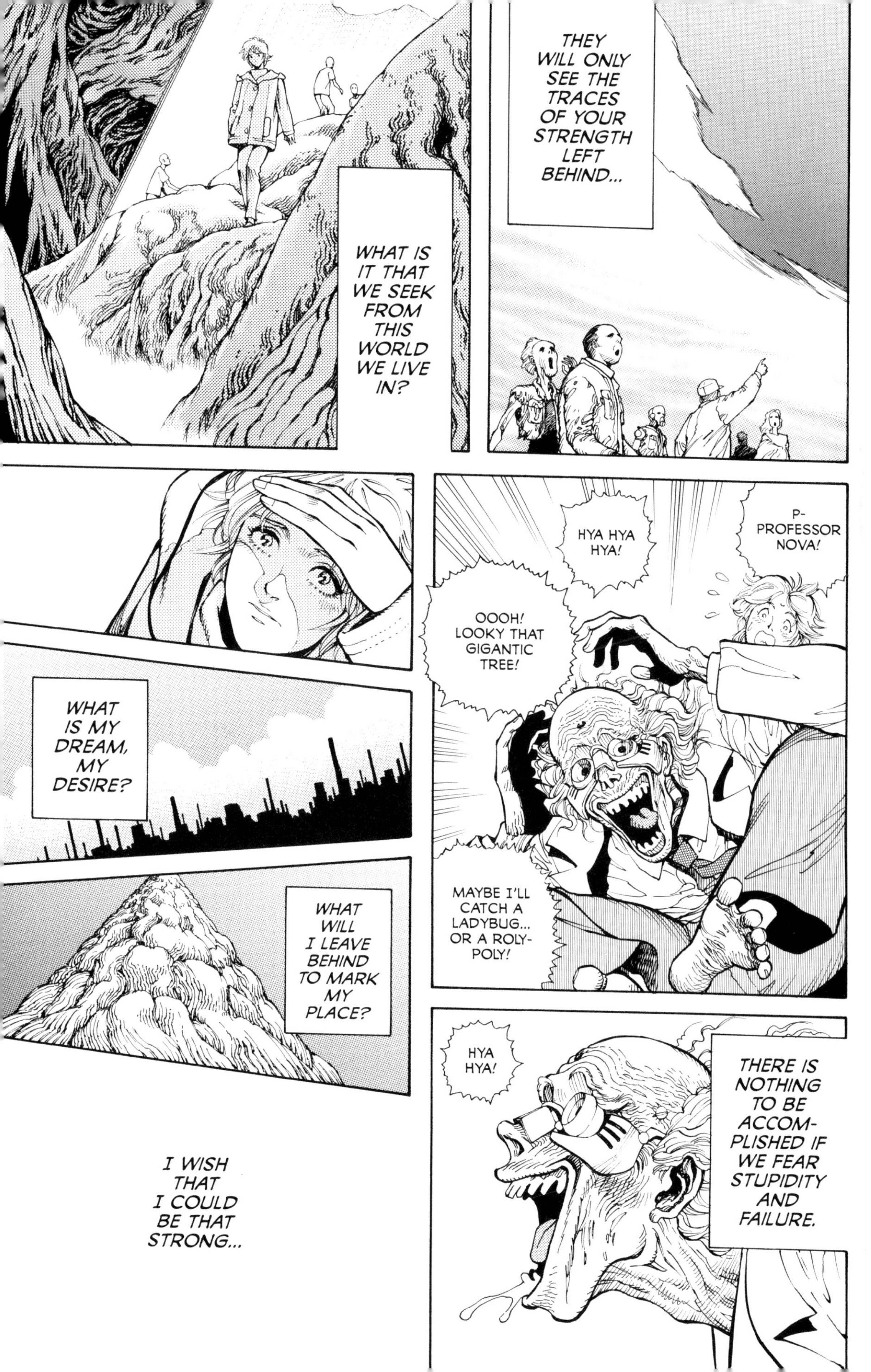
THEY WILL ONLY SEE THE TRACES OF YOUR STRENGTH LEFT BEHIND...
WHAT IS IT THAT WE SEEK FROM THIS WORLD WE LIVE IN?
P- PROFESSOR NOVA!
HYA HYA HYA!
OOOH! LOOKY THAT GIGANTIC TREE!
MAYBE I'LL CATCH A LADYBUG... OR A ROLY-POLY!
HYA HYA!
THERE IS NOTHING TO BE ACCOM-PLISHED IF WE FEAR STUPIDITY AND FAILURE.
WHAT IS MY DREAM, MY DESIRE?
WHAT WILL I LEAVE BEHIND TO MARK MY PLACE?
I WISH THAT I COULD BE THAT STRONG...

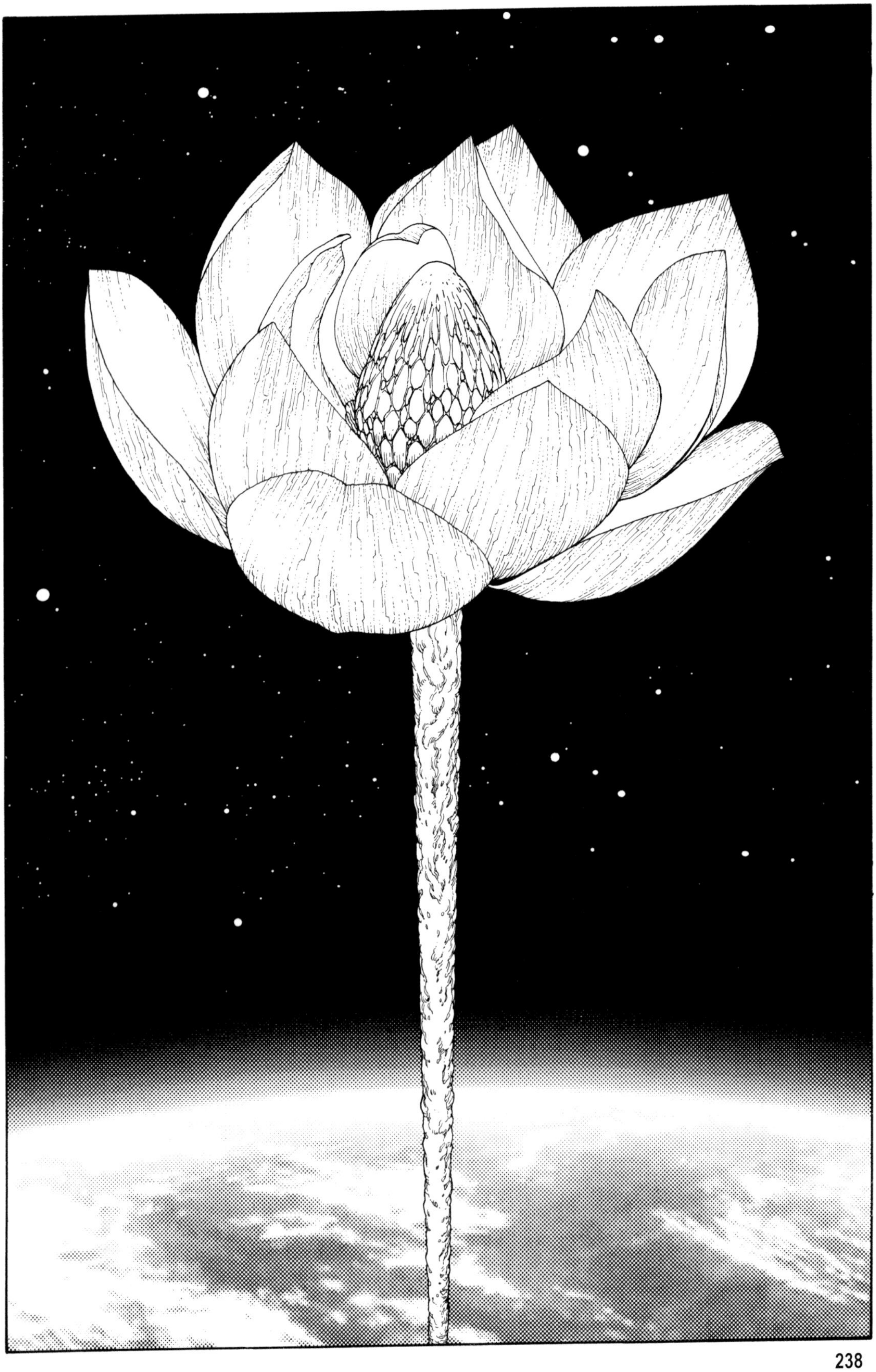

ANOTHER FIGHT Epilogue

BARJACK
WAR CHRONICLE
B.B.BUICK
AND
KOYOMI.K

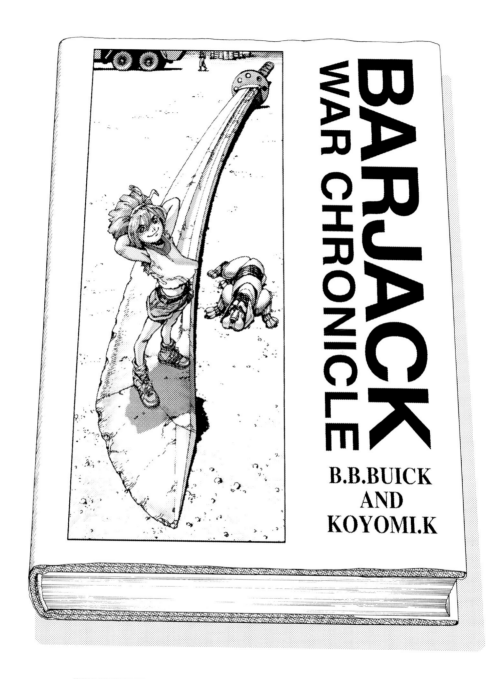

BARJACK CHRONICLE **Photos by: Buick Edited by: Koyomi**
This photography collection, published when Koyomi was fifteen years old, became an unprecedented bestseller in the Scrapyard. (The book includes a series of audio recordings, including interviews with Den and others.)

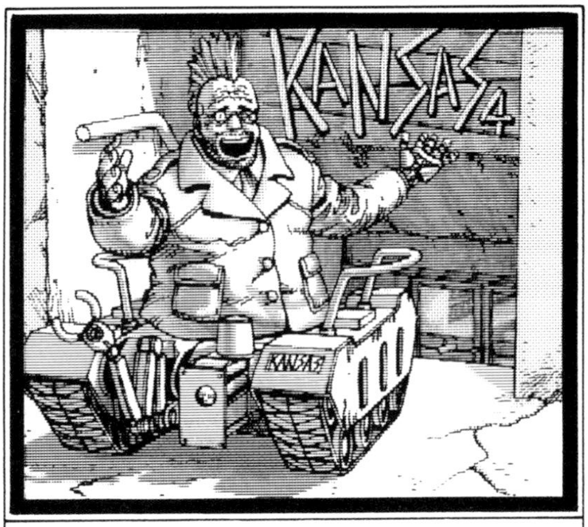
KANSAS 4
KANSAS

Thanks to the royalties from Barjack Chronicle, Koyomi's foster father was able to build his fourth attempt at the "Kansas" bar. It seems that it's actually working out this time.

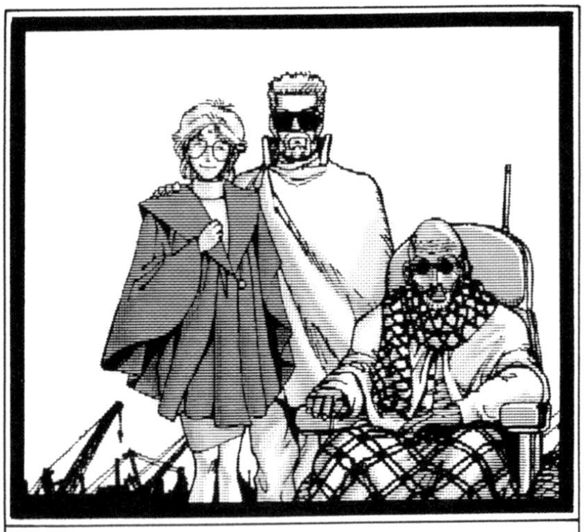

The Factory ground to a halt, and the ensuing chaos in the Scrapyard was only calmed through the efforts of two heroes: Kaos and Vector. For Lou, a years-long loving relationship between her and Kaos blossomed into matrimony.

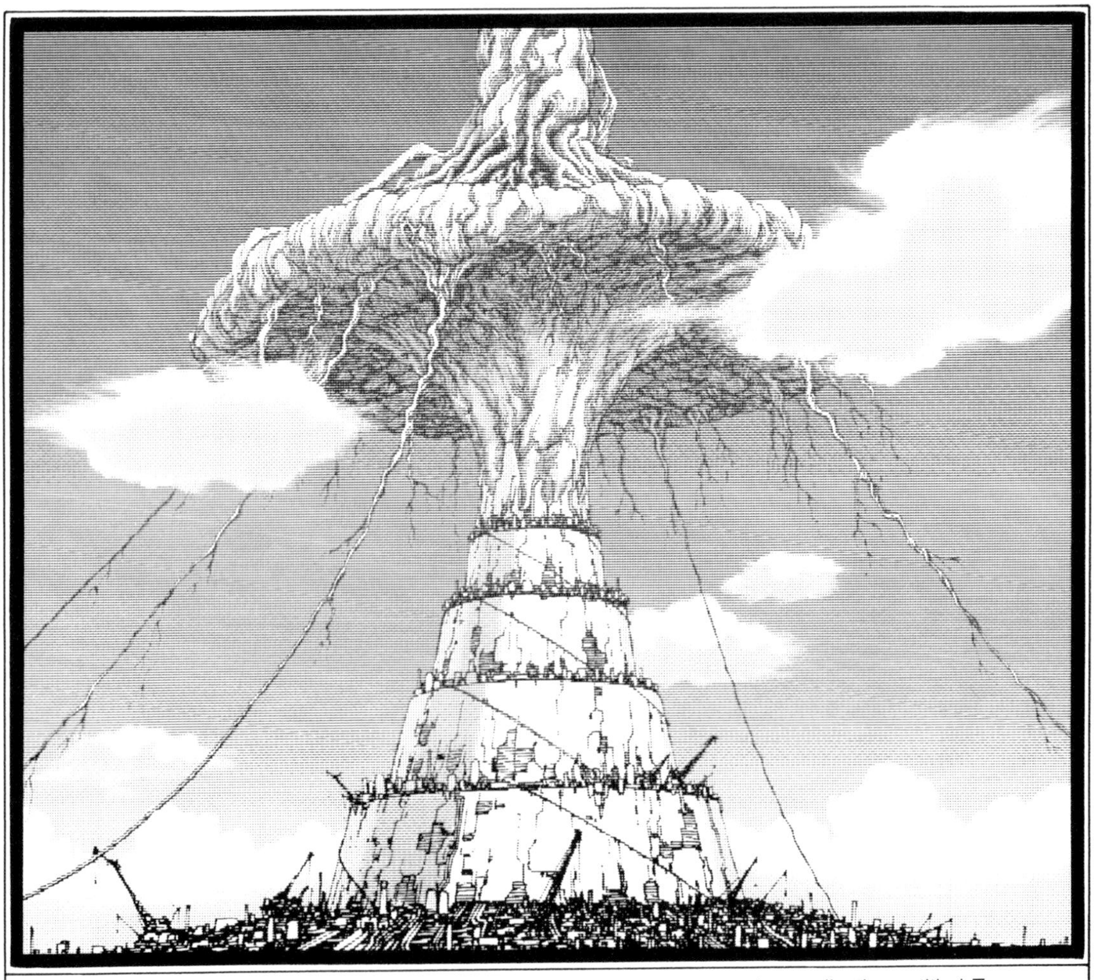

The completed Tower of Zalem. Next month, Koyomi will release her own photo collection entitled *Tower of the Sky* (preorders available), containing various anecdotes about its construction gathered over a five-year research period.

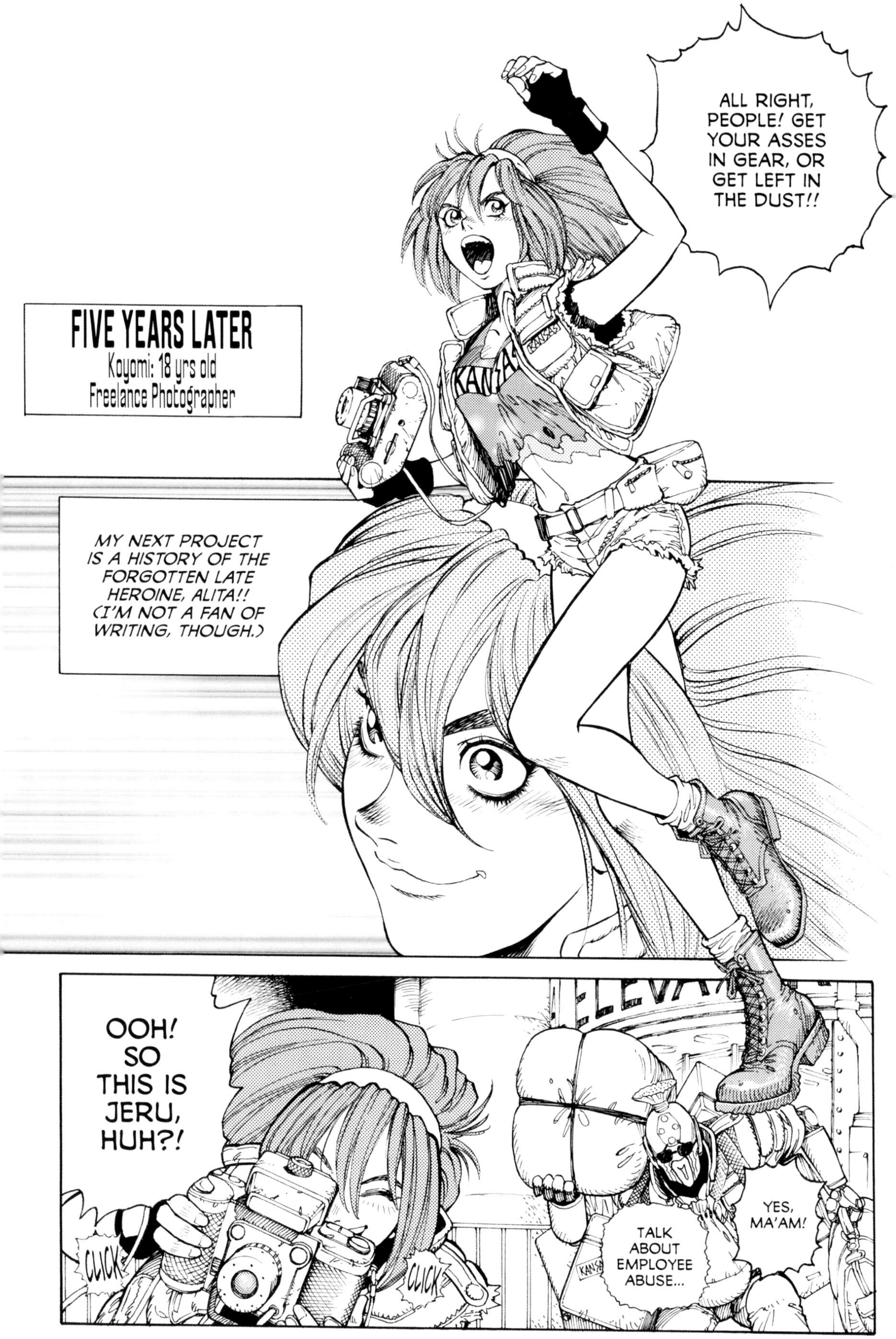
ALL RIGHT, PEOPLE! GET YOUR ASSES IN GEAR, OR GET LEFT IN THE DUST!!
FIVE YEARS LATER
Koyomi: 18 yrs old
Freelance Photographer
MY NEXT PROJECT IS A HISTORY OF THE FORGOTTEN LATE HEROINE, ALITA!! (I'M NOT A FAN OF WRITING, THOUGH.)
YES, MA'AM!
TALK ABOUT EMPLOYEE ABUSE...
CLICK
CLICK
OOH! SO THIS IS JERU, HUH?!

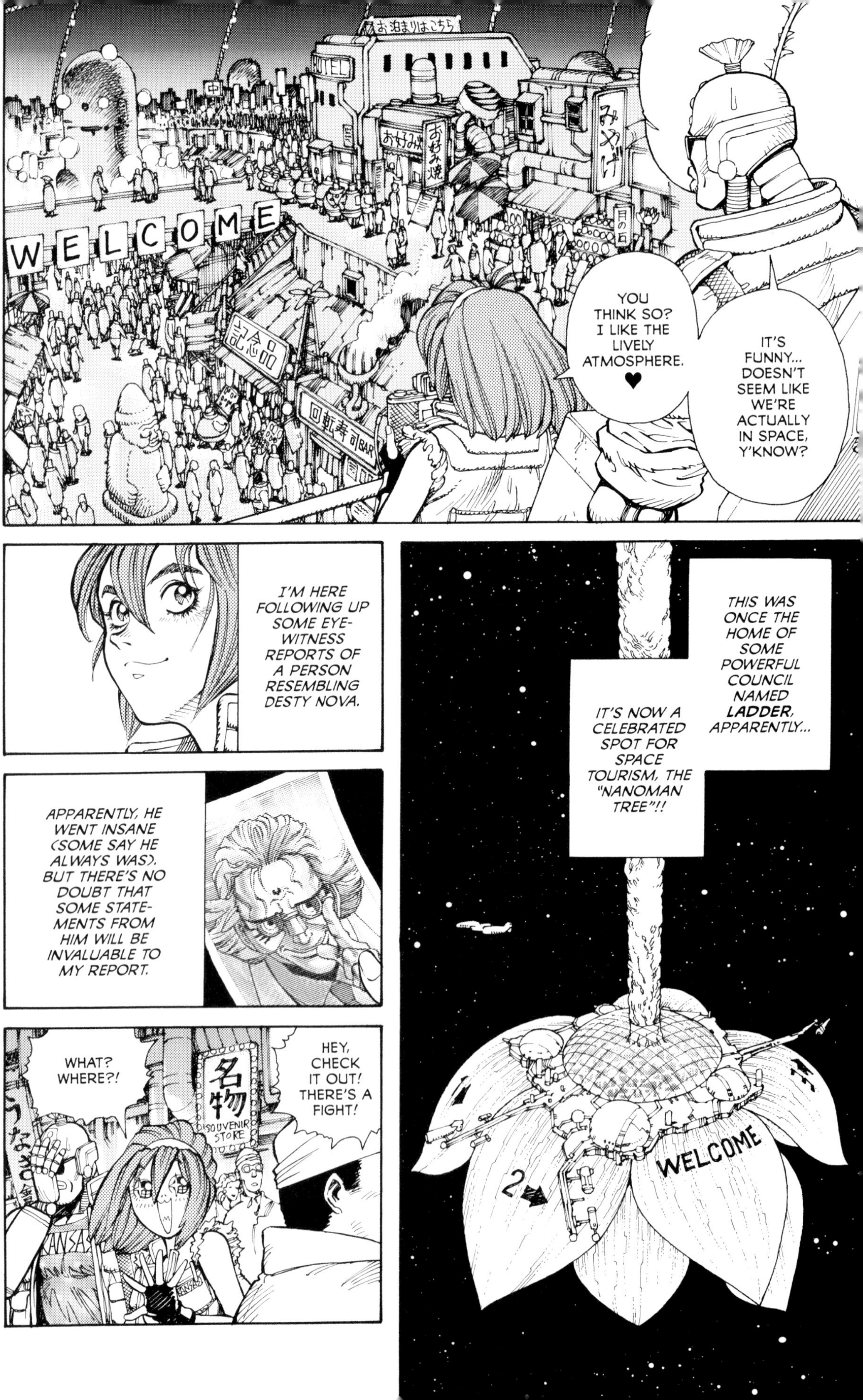
お泊まりはこちら
HOTEL
みやげ
お好み焼
WELCOME
記念品
回転寿司BAR
IT'S FUNNY... DOESN'T SEEM LIKE WE'RE ACTUALLY IN SPACE, Y'KNOW?
YOU THINK SO? I LIKE THE LIVELY ATMOSPHERE. ♥
THIS WAS ONCE THE HOME OF SOME POWERFUL COUNCIL NAMED **LADDER**, APPARENTLY...
IT'S NOW A CELEBRATED SPOT FOR SPACE TOURISM, THE "NANOMAN TREE"!!
WELCOME
I'M HERE FOLLOWING UP SOME EYE-WITNESS REPORTS OF A PERSON RESEMBLING DESTY NOVA.
APPARENTLY, HE WENT INSANE (SOME SAY HE ALWAYS WAS). BUT THERE'S NO DOUBT THAT SOME STATE-MENTS FROM HIM WILL BE INVALUABLE TO MY REPORT.
名物
SOUVENIR STORE
HEY, CHECK IT OUT! THERE'S A FIGHT!
WHAT? WHERE?!

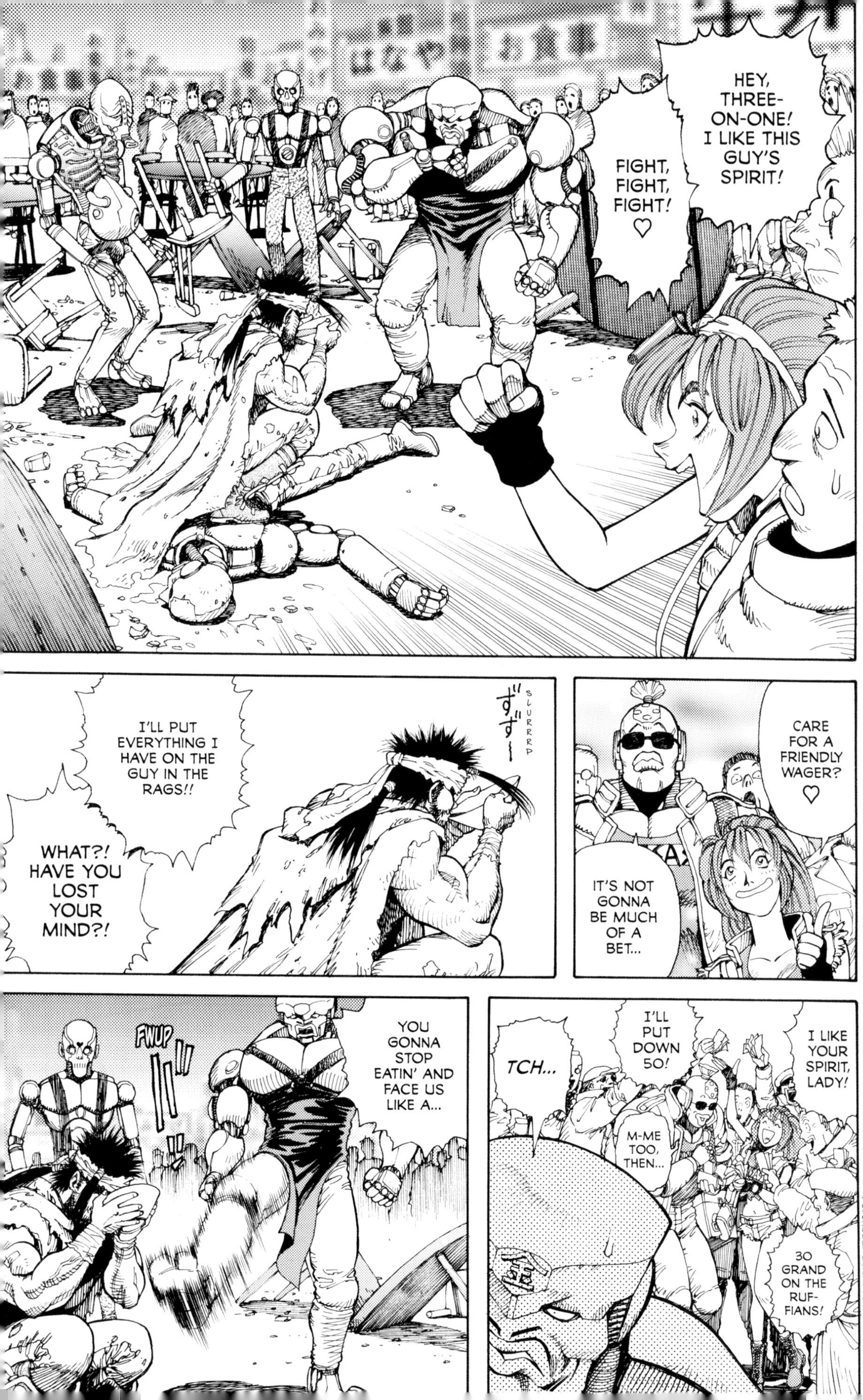
HEY, THREE-ON-ONE! I LIKE THIS GUY'S SPIRIT!
FIGHT, FIGHT, FIGHT! ♡
CARE FOR A FRIENDLY WAGER? ♡
IT'S NOT GONNA BE MUCH OF A BET...
ずず～ SLURRRP
I'LL PUT EVERYTHING I HAVE ON THE GUY IN THE RAGS!!
WHAT?! HAVE YOU LOST YOUR MIND?!
I LIKE YOUR SPIRIT, LADY!
I'LL PUT DOWN 50!
TCH...
M-ME TOO, THEN...
30 GRAND ON THE RUF-FIANS!
YOU GONNA STOP EATIN' AND FACE US LIKE A...
FWUP

Forehead: Gold/Metal

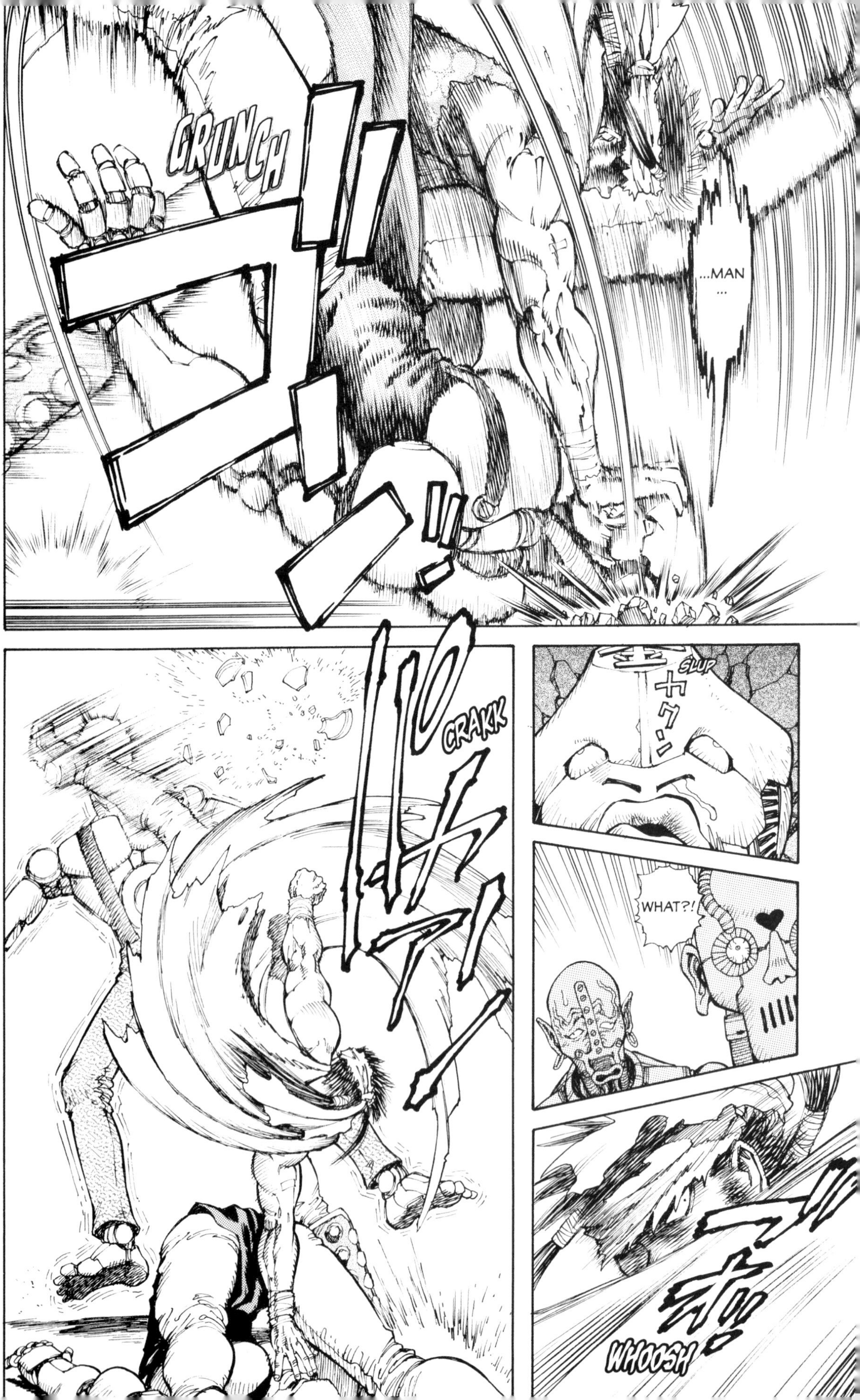

...MAN
...
GRUNCH
SLUP
WHAT?!
WHOOSH
CRAKK

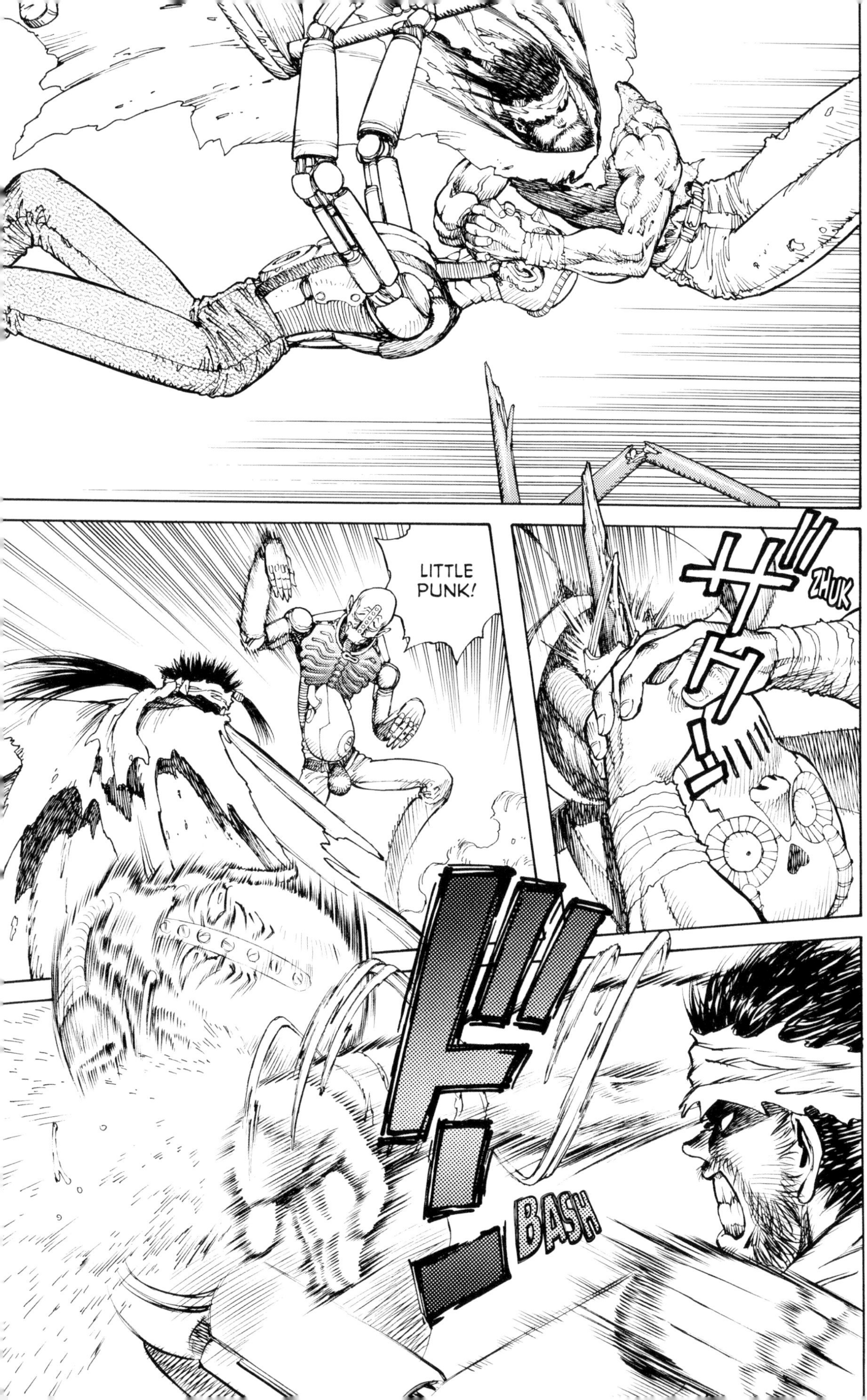
ザシュ
ZHUK
LITTLE PUNK!
ドガ
BASH

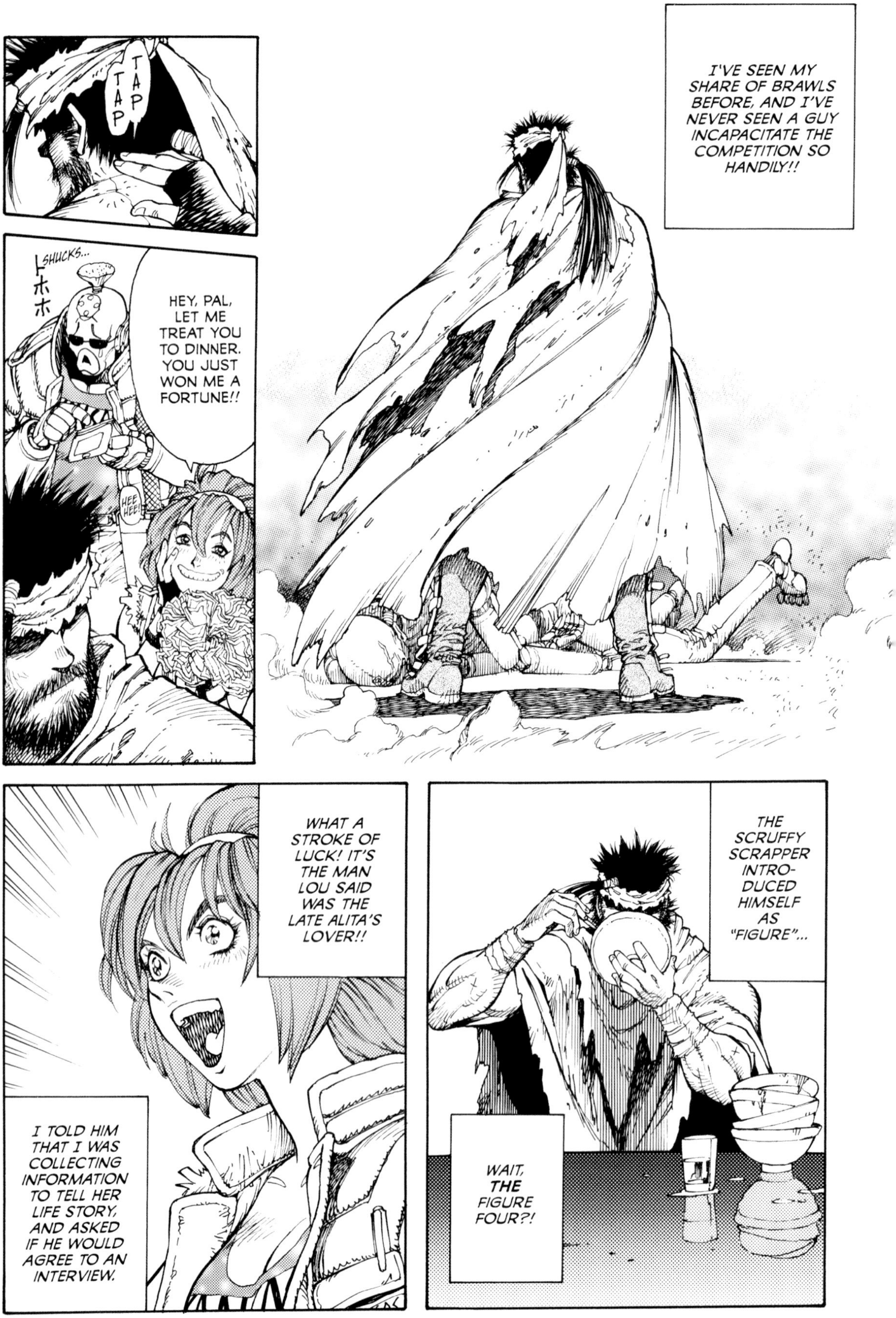
I'VE SEEN MY SHARE OF BRAWLS BEFORE, AND I'VE NEVER SEEN A GUY INCAPACITATE THE COMPETITION SO HANDILY!!
TAP TAP
トホホ SHUCKS...
HEY, PAL, LET ME TREAT YOU TO DINNER. YOU JUST WON ME A FORTUNE!!
HEE HEE!
THE SCRUFFY SCRAPPER INTRO-DUCED HIMSELF AS "FIGURE"...
WAIT, **THE** FIGURE FOUR?!
WHAT A STROKE OF LUCK! IT'S THE MAN LOU SAID WAS THE LATE ALITA'S LOVER!!
I TOLD HIM THAT I WAS COLLECTING INFORMATION TO TELL HER LIFE STORY, AND ASKED IF HE WOULD AGREE TO AN INTERVIEW.

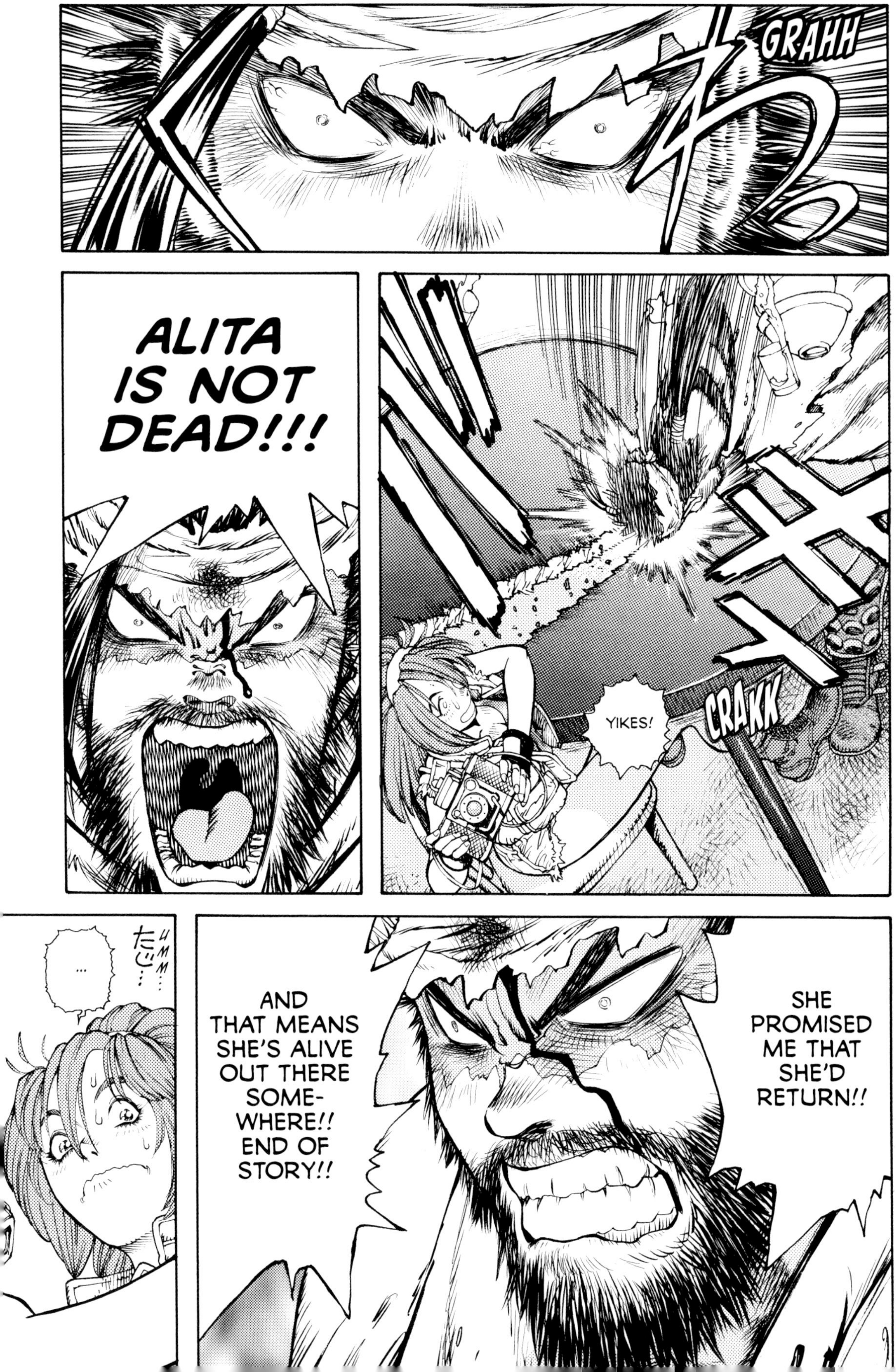
GRAHH
CRAKK
YIKES!
ALITA IS NOT DEAD!!!
SHE PROMISED ME THAT SHE'D RETURN!!
AND THAT MEANS SHE'S ALIVE OUT THERE SOME-WHERE!! END OF STORY!!
UMM...
たじ…
...

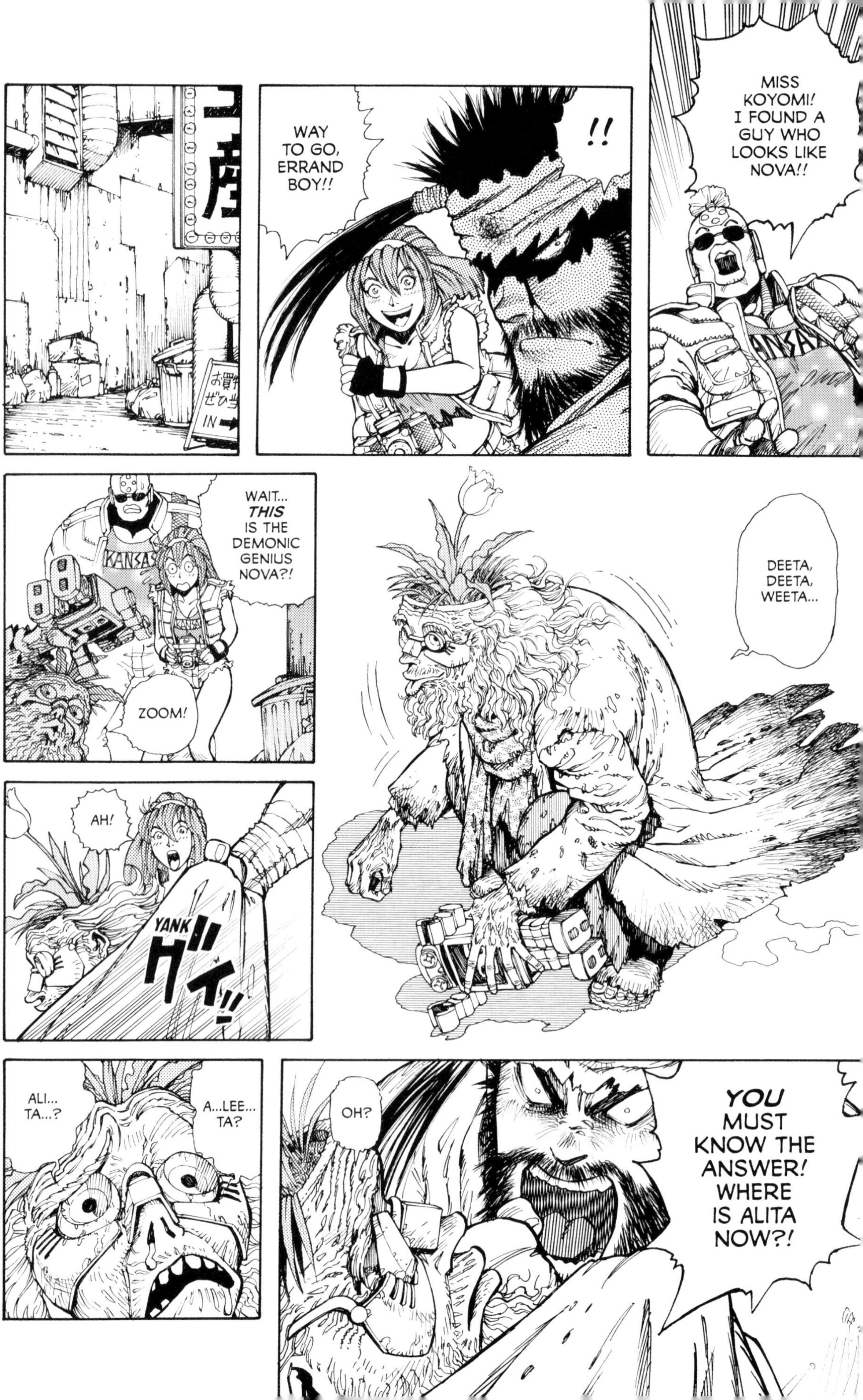
MISS KOYOMI! I FOUND A GUY WHO LOOKS LIKE NOVA!!
!!
WAY TO GO, ERRAND BOY!!
DEETA, DEETA, WEETA...
WAIT... *THIS* IS THE DEMONIC GENIUS NOVA?!
ZOOM!
AH!
YANK
グイ!!
YOU MUST KNOW THE ANSWER! WHERE IS ALITA NOW?!
OH?
A...LEE... TA?
ALI... TA...?

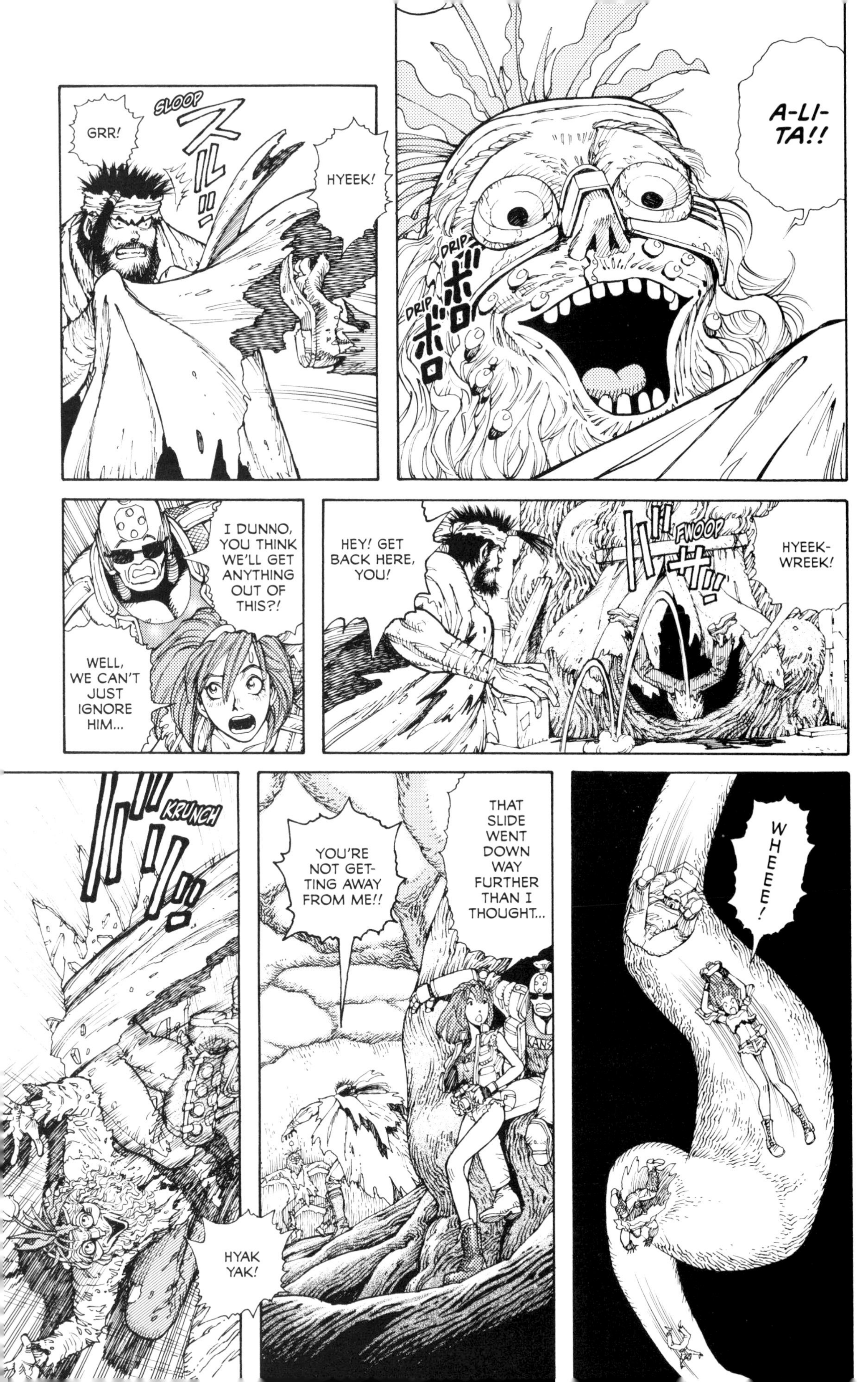

A-LI-TA!!
DRIP
DRIP
HYEEK!
SLOOP
GRR!
HYEEK-WREEK!
FWOOP
HEY! GET BACK HERE, YOU!
I DUNNO, YOU THINK WE'LL GET ANYTHING OUT OF THIS?!
WELL, WE CAN'T JUST IGNORE HIM...
WHEEEE!
THAT SLIDE WENT DOWN WAY FURTHER THAN I THOUGHT...
YOU'RE NOT GETTING AWAY FROM ME!!
KRUNCH
HYAK YAK!

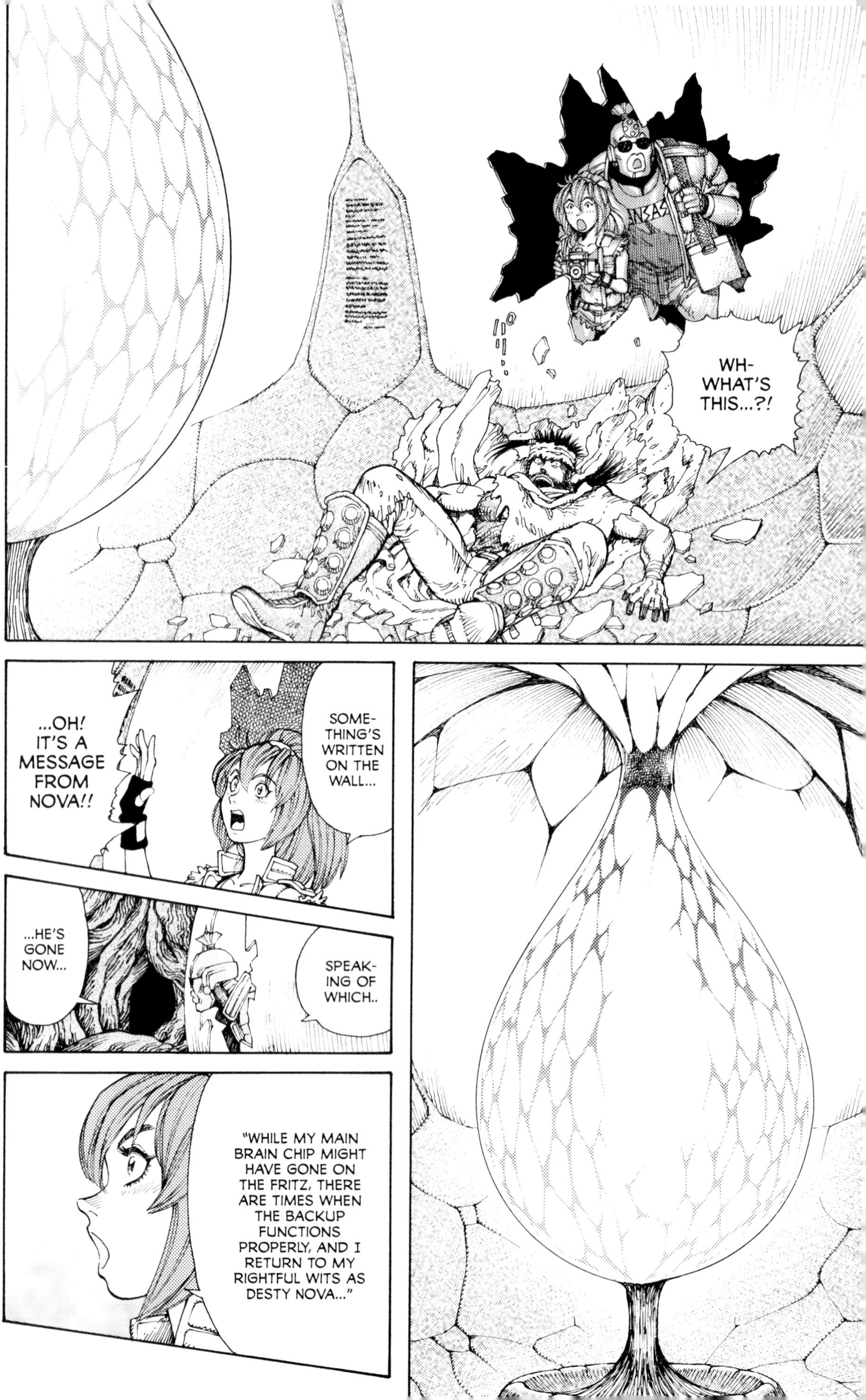
WH- WHAT'S THIS...?!
SOMETHING'S WRITTEN ON THE WALL...
...OH! IT'S A MESSAGE FROM NOVA!!
SPEAKING OF WHICH..
...HE'S GONE NOW...
"WHILE MY MAIN BRAIN CHIP MIGHT HAVE GONE ON THE FRITZ, THERE ARE TIMES WHEN THE BACKUP FUNCTIONS PROPERLY, AND I RETURN TO MY RIGHTFUL WITS AS DESTY NOVA..."

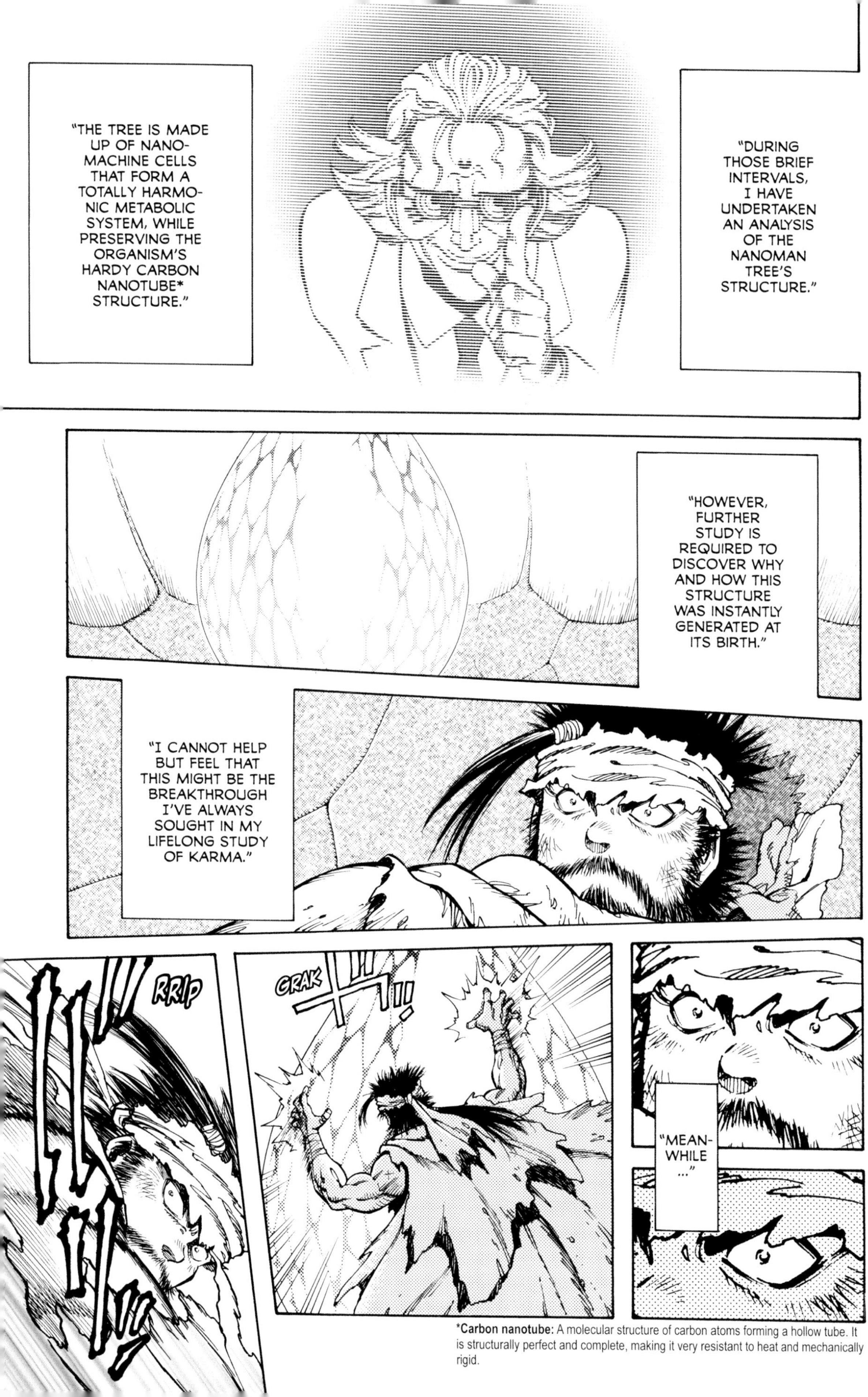
"DURING THOSE BRIEF INTERVALS, I HAVE UNDERTAKEN AN ANALYSIS OF THE NANOMAN TREE'S STRUCTURE."
"THE TREE IS MADE UP OF NANO-MACHINE CELLS THAT FORM A TOTALLY HARMONIC METABOLIC SYSTEM, WHILE PRESERVING THE ORGANISM'S HARDY CARBON NANOTUBE* STRUCTURE."
"HOWEVER, FURTHER STUDY IS REQUIRED TO DISCOVER WHY AND HOW THIS STRUCTURE WAS INSTANTLY GENERATED AT ITS BIRTH."
"I CANNOT HELP BUT FEEL THAT THIS MIGHT BE THE BREAKTHROUGH I'VE ALWAYS SOUGHT IN MY LIFELONG STUDY OF KARMA."
"MEAN-WHILE ..."
GRAK
RRIP

***Carbon nanotube:** A molecular structure of carbon atoms forming a hollow tube. It is structurally perfect and complete, making it very resistant to heat and mechanically rigid.

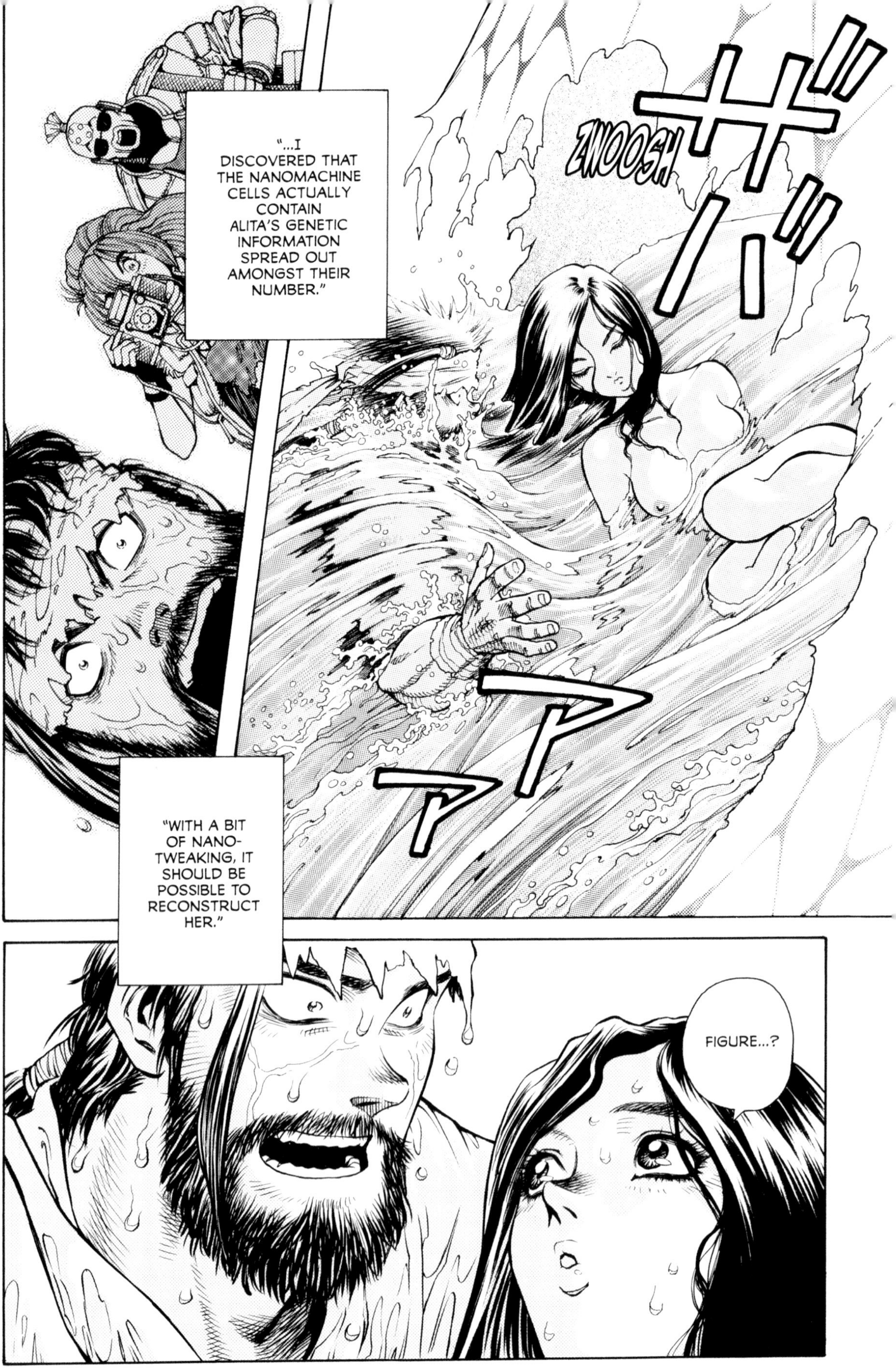
ザバ
ZWOOSH
"...I DISCOVERED THAT THE NANOMACHINE CELLS ACTUALLY CONTAIN ALITA'S GENETIC INFORMATION SPREAD OUT AMONGST THEIR NUMBER."
アア
"WITH A BIT OF NANO-TWEAKING, IT SHOULD BE POSSIBLE TO RECONSTRUCT HER."
FIGURE...?

"VERY, VERY
SLOWLY..."

Another Fight / End

Mars King, page 92

If the "Mars King" looks suspiciously like an old-fashioned toy robot, that's because it is. The design is directly based on the 1970s "Jumbo Mars King" toy robot, a battery-operated walking robot in Horikawa's "Mars King" line of toys. The original Mars King was produced in the 1960s and was part of a variety of tin-and-plastic toy robots designed by Horikawa. Many of them (including the original Mars King) were also boxed for sale in English-speaking territories, although it appears that Jumbo Mars King was not. When switched on, the Jumbo Mars King walks forward a few steps, then opens its chest cavity (as seen on page 94) and spins its torso around, emitting missile or bullet noises.

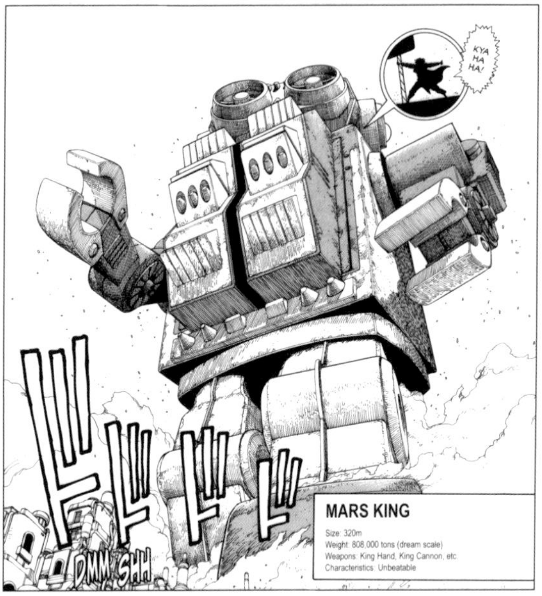
KYA HA HA!
MARS KING
Size: 320m
Weight: 808,000 tons (dream scale)
Weapons: King Hand, King Cannon, etc.
Characteristics: Unbeatable
DMM SHH

Carmina Burana, page 126-127

A collection of 12th- and 13th-century poems, mostly written in Latin. The poems grew in contemporary recognition when Carl Orff put several of them to classical music in 1936. The highly dramatic "O Fortuna" in particular is a frequently-used piece of background music in modern advertisements, movie trailers, bumpers, etc.

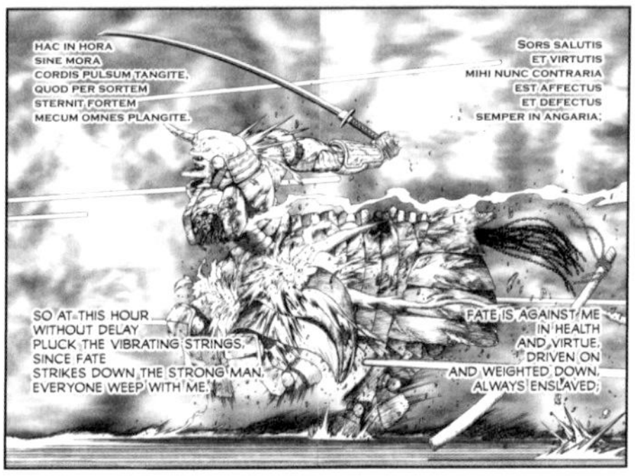
SORS SALUTIS
ET VIRTUTIS
MIHI NUNC CONTRARIA
EST AFFECTUS
ET DEFECTUS
SEMPER IN ANGARIA;
HAC IN HORA
SINE MORA
CORDIS PULSUM TANGITE,
QUOD PER SORTEM
STERNIT FORTEM
MECUM OMNES PLANGITE.
FATE IS AGAINST ME
IN HEALTH
AND VIRTUE,
DRIVEN ON
AND WEIGHTED DOWN,
ALWAYS ENSLAVED;
SO AT THIS HOUR
WITHOUT DELAY
PLUCK THE VIBRATING STRINGS,
SINCE FATE
STRIKES DOWN THE STRONG MAN,
EVERYONE WEEP WITH ME.

Lehrer, page 165

The Martian culture (beginning with the references to Panzer Kunst) of *Battle Angel Alita* seems to have developed using the German language as its foundation. The soldiers call the leader here "Lehrer," which means teacher. They refer to Earth by the word "Blau" or "Blau Stein" in the diagram pictured here, which means "blue rock," and their home of Mars is "Rot," or "red." The word "body" is also called "Körper." (As these pronunciations are accompanied by the kanji that define their intended meaning to a Japanese reader, many of them are translated into their plain English equivalent in the text for the sake of comprehension.)

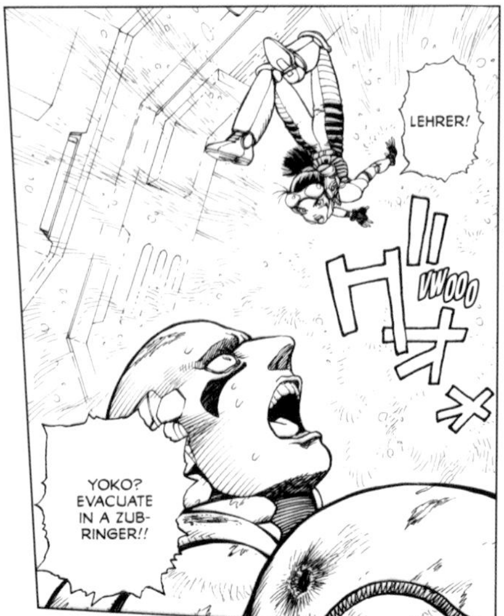
LEHRER!
VWOOO
YOKO? EVACUATE IN A ZUB-RINGER!!

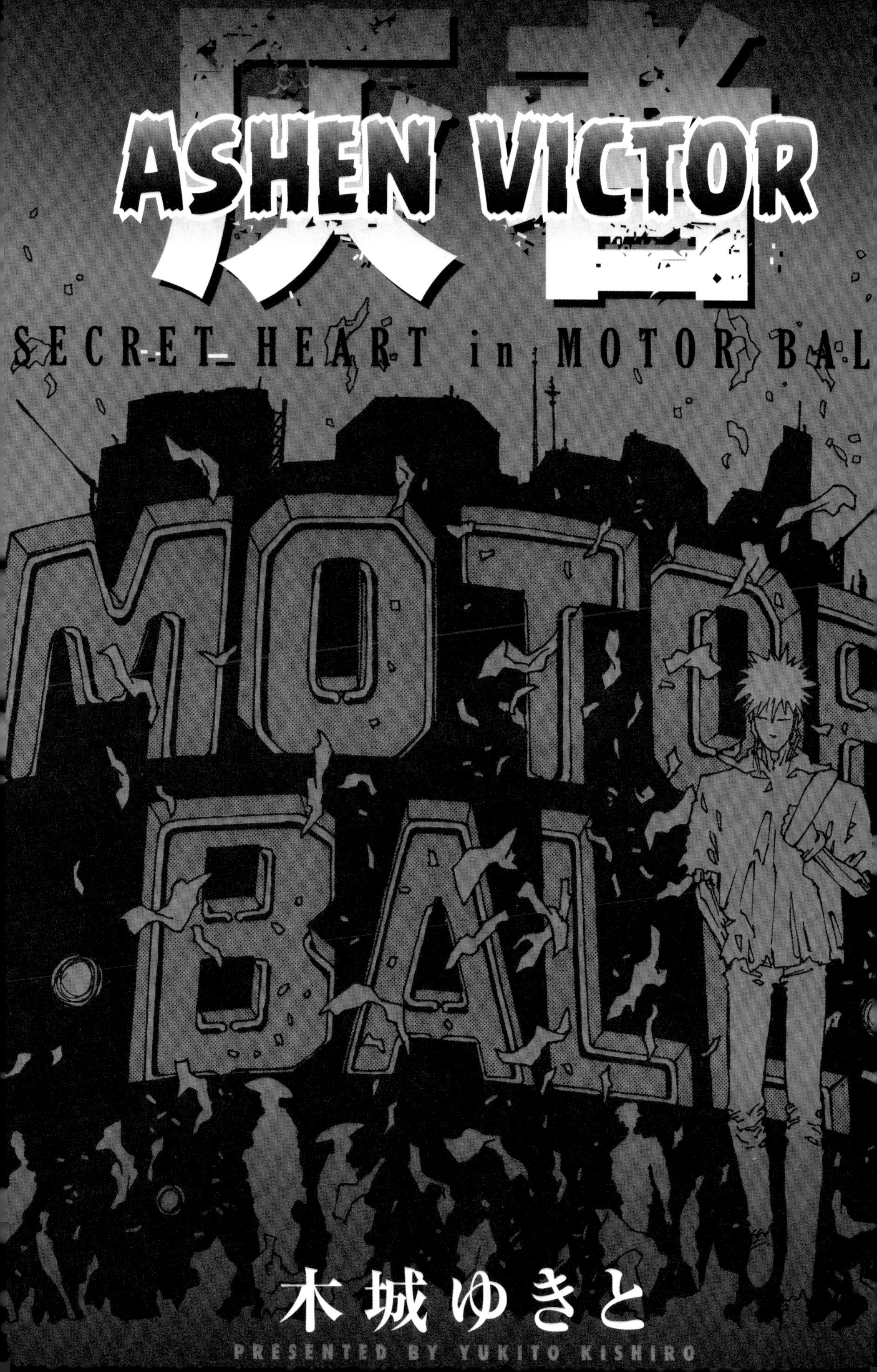
ASHEN VICTOR
SECRET HEART in MOTOR BAL
木城ゆきと
PRESENTED BY YUKITO KISHIRO

ASHEN VICTOR

SECRET–HEART in MOTOR BALL

PRESENTED BY YUKITO KISHIRO

SECRET HEART in MOTOR BALL

PRESENTED BY YUKITO KISHIRO

CONTENTS

SNEV
MOTORBALLER
NUMBER:5

DRAGUNOV
MOTORBALLER
NUMBER:4

BERETTA
PROSTITUTE

HOLMEGOLUD
ENGINEER WITH
TEAM SPANDAU

BEN
MANAGER OF
TEAM SPANDAU

MARVIN
STREET PAINTER

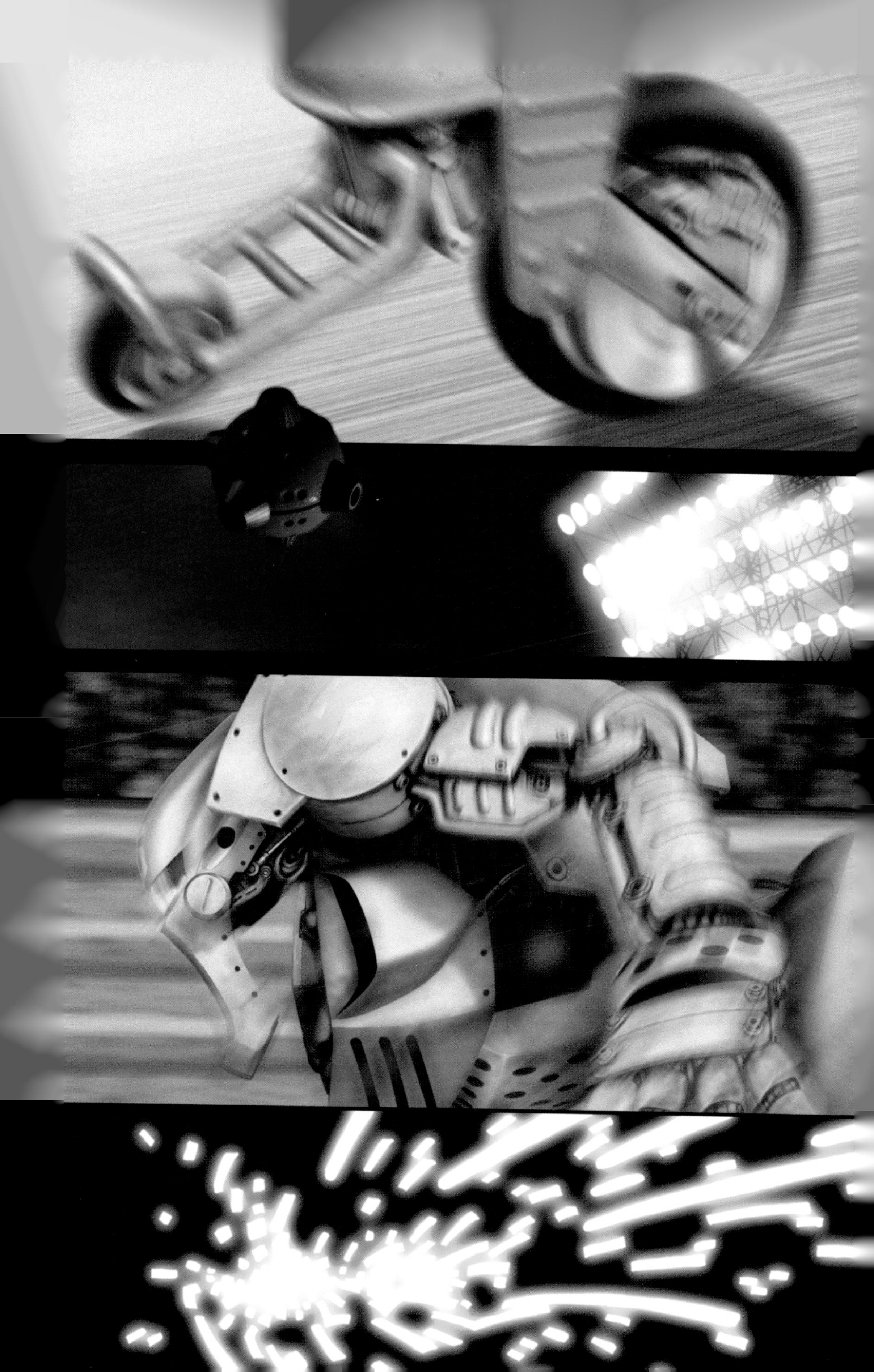

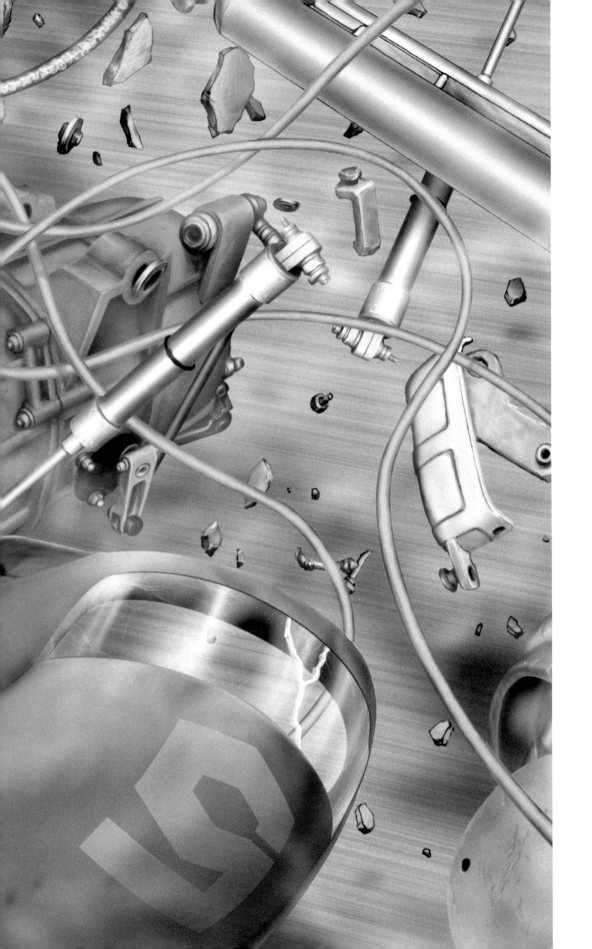

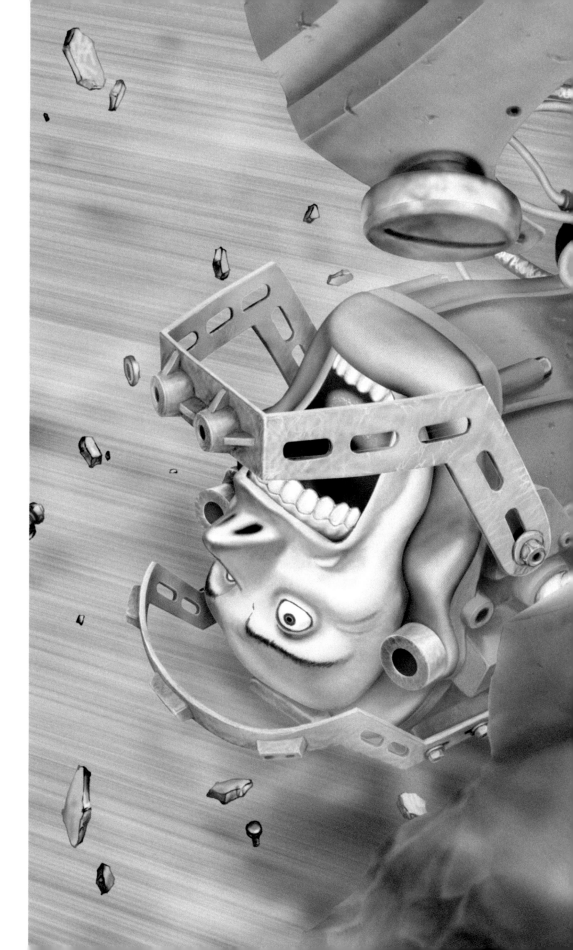

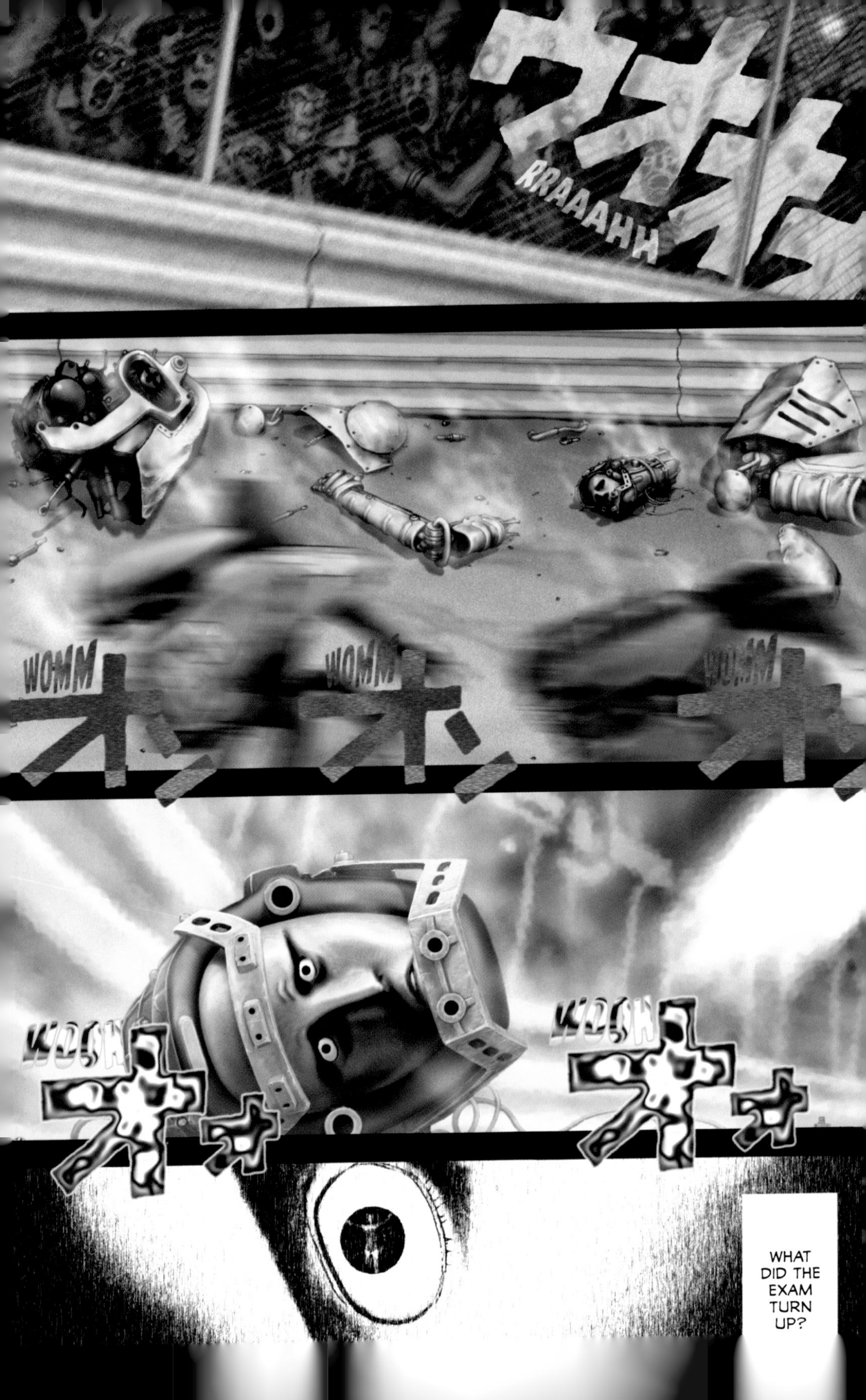
RRAAAAHH
WOMM
WOMM
WOMM
WOOSH
WOOSH
WHAT DID THE EXAM TURN UP?

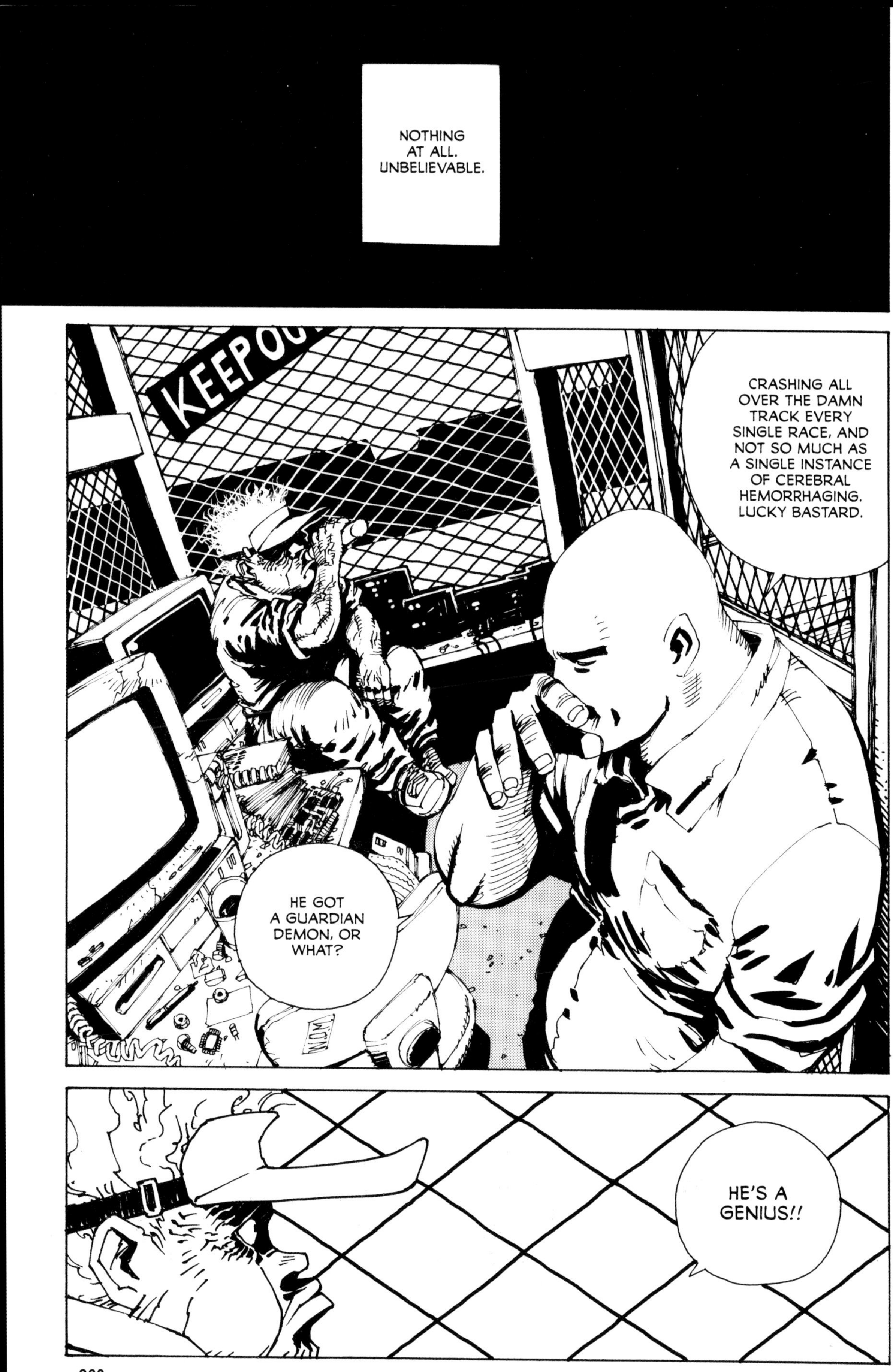
NOTHING AT ALL. UNBELIEVABLE.
CRASHING ALL OVER THE DAMN TRACK EVERY SINGLE RACE, AND NOT SO MUCH AS A SINGLE INSTANCE OF CEREBRAL HEMORRHAGING. LUCKY BASTARD.
HE GOT A GUARDIAN DEMON, OR WHAT?
HE'S A GENIUS!!

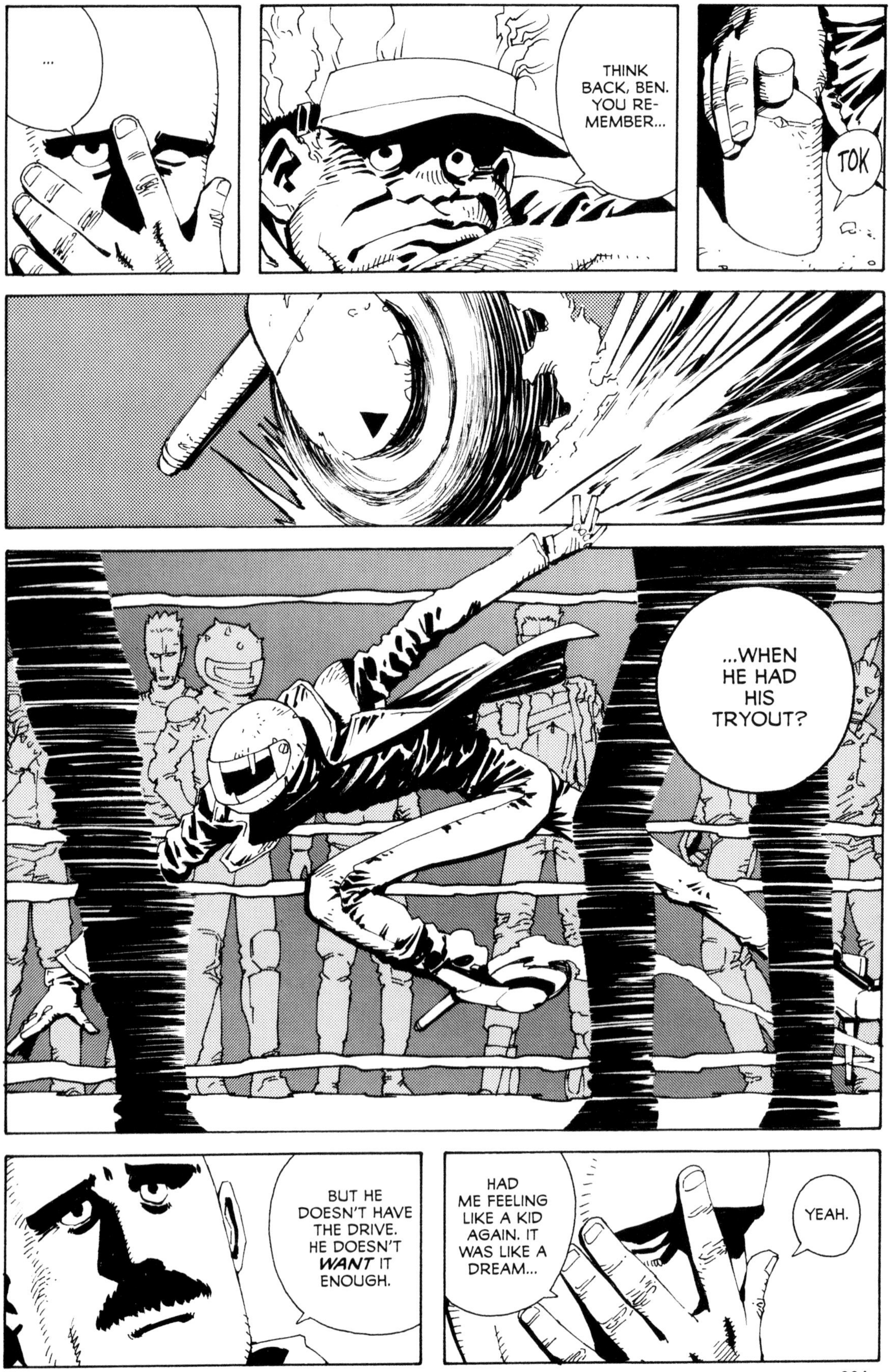
TOK
THINK BACK, BEN. YOU RE-MEMBER...
...
...WHEN HE HAD HIS TRYOUT?
YEAH.
HAD ME FEELING LIKE A KID AGAIN. IT WAS LIKE A DREAM...
BUT HE DOESN'T HAVE THE DRIVE. HE DOESN'T *WANT* IT ENOUGH.

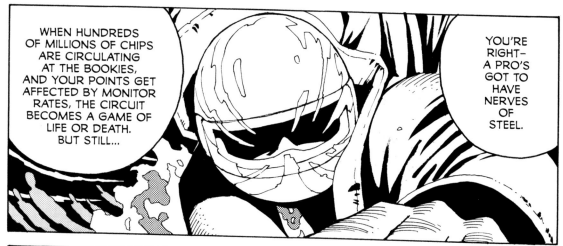

YOU'RE RIGHT– A PRO'S GOT TO HAVE NERVES OF STEEL.
WHEN HUNDREDS OF MILLIONS OF CHIPS ARE CIRCULATING AT THE BOOKIES, AND YOUR POINTS GET AFFECTED BY MONITOR RATES, THE CIRCUIT BECOMES A GAME OF LIFE OR DEATH. BUT STILL...
HE'S A GENIUS! WE OUGHTA TAKE THE LONG VIEW!
TEN OR TWENTY FALLS AIN'T NOTHIN' TO WHINE ABOUT...
AT THE VERY LEAST...
...I WOULDN'T LOOK SO INCOMPETENT IF HE FINISHED ***ONE*** RACE.
PLEASE... JUST TALK TO THE TEAM OWNER, WOULDJA?
I'M NOT A MIRACLE WORKER.
FIRE PRO
I JUST WANNA SEE A TRUE MOTORBALLER, ONE WHO DOESN'T NEED TO THROW HIS STRENGTH OR WEIGHT AROUND!!
YOU'RE TOO OLD, POPS.
MOTORBALL AIN'T A SPORT ANYMORE, IT'S A SHOW OF VIOLENCE. IT'S WHAT THE AUDIENCE WANTS.

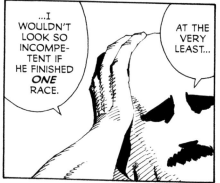

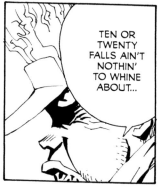

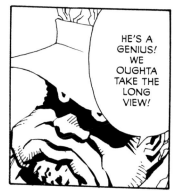

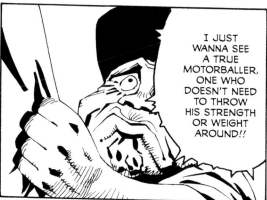

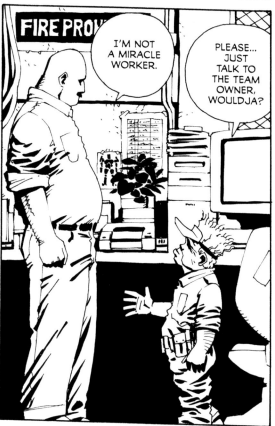

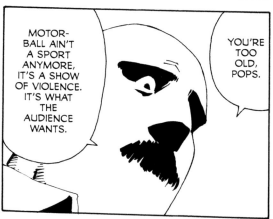

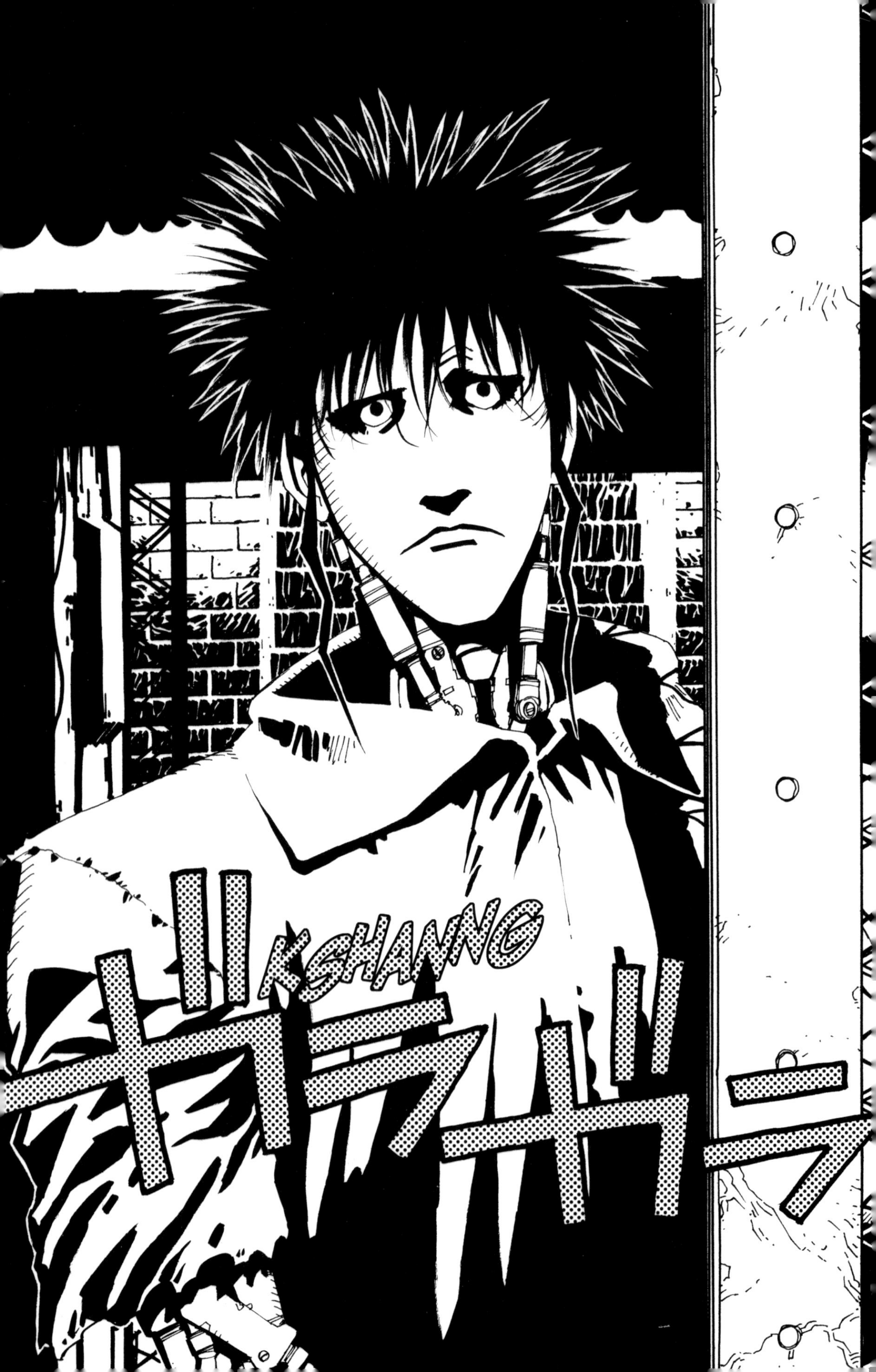
KSHANNG

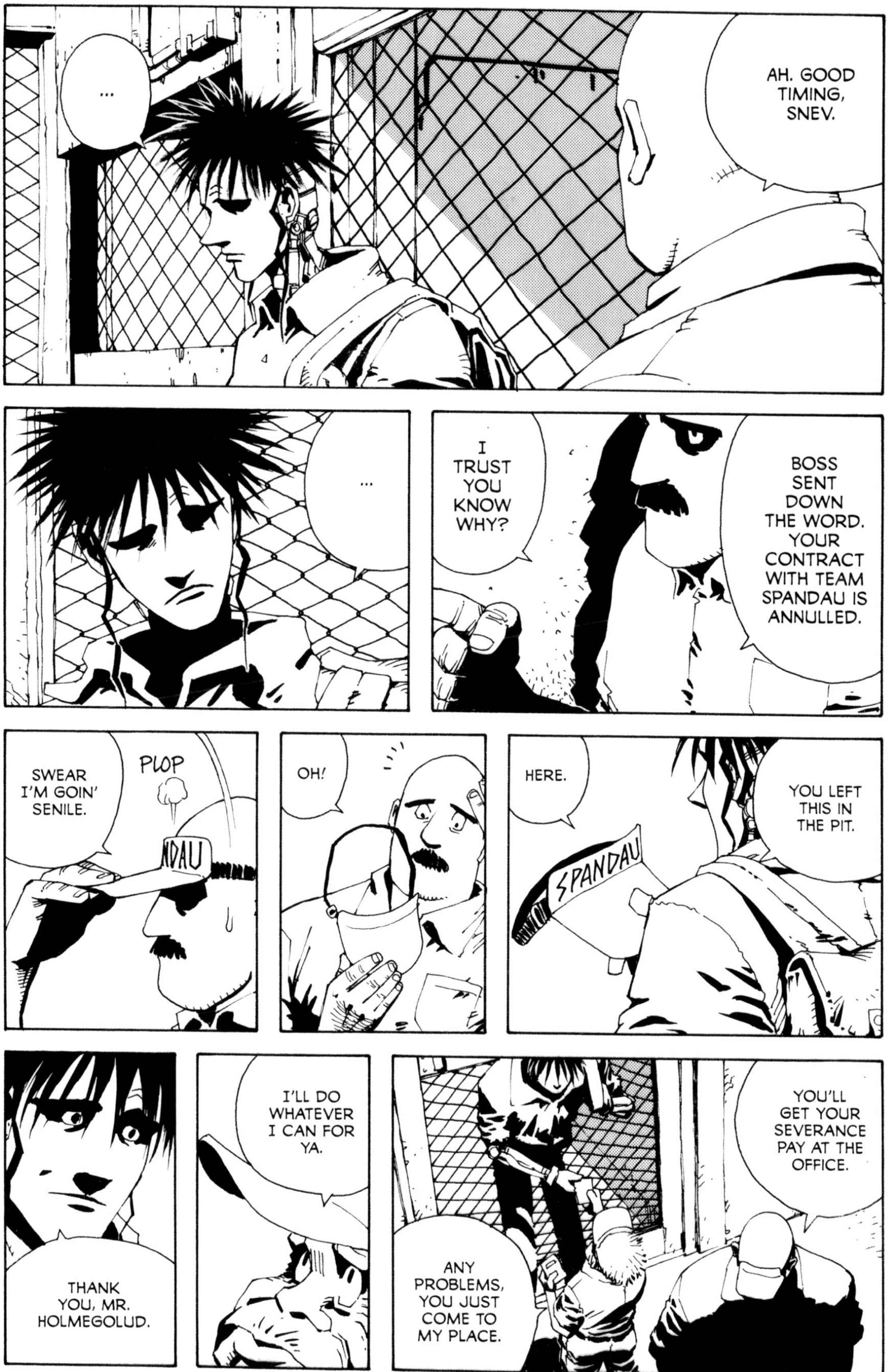
AH. GOOD TIMING, SNEV.
...
BOSS SENT DOWN THE WORD. YOUR CONTRACT WITH TEAM SPANDAU IS ANNULLED.
I TRUST YOU KNOW WHY?
...
YOU LEFT THIS IN THE PIT.
HERE.
SPANDAU
OH!
SWEAR I'M GOIN' SENILE.
PLOP
NDAU
YOU'LL GET YOUR SEVERANCE PAY AT THE OFFICE.
ANY PROBLEMS, YOU JUST COME TO MY PLACE.
I'LL DO WHATEVER I CAN FOR YA.
THANK YOU, MR. HOLMEGOLUD.

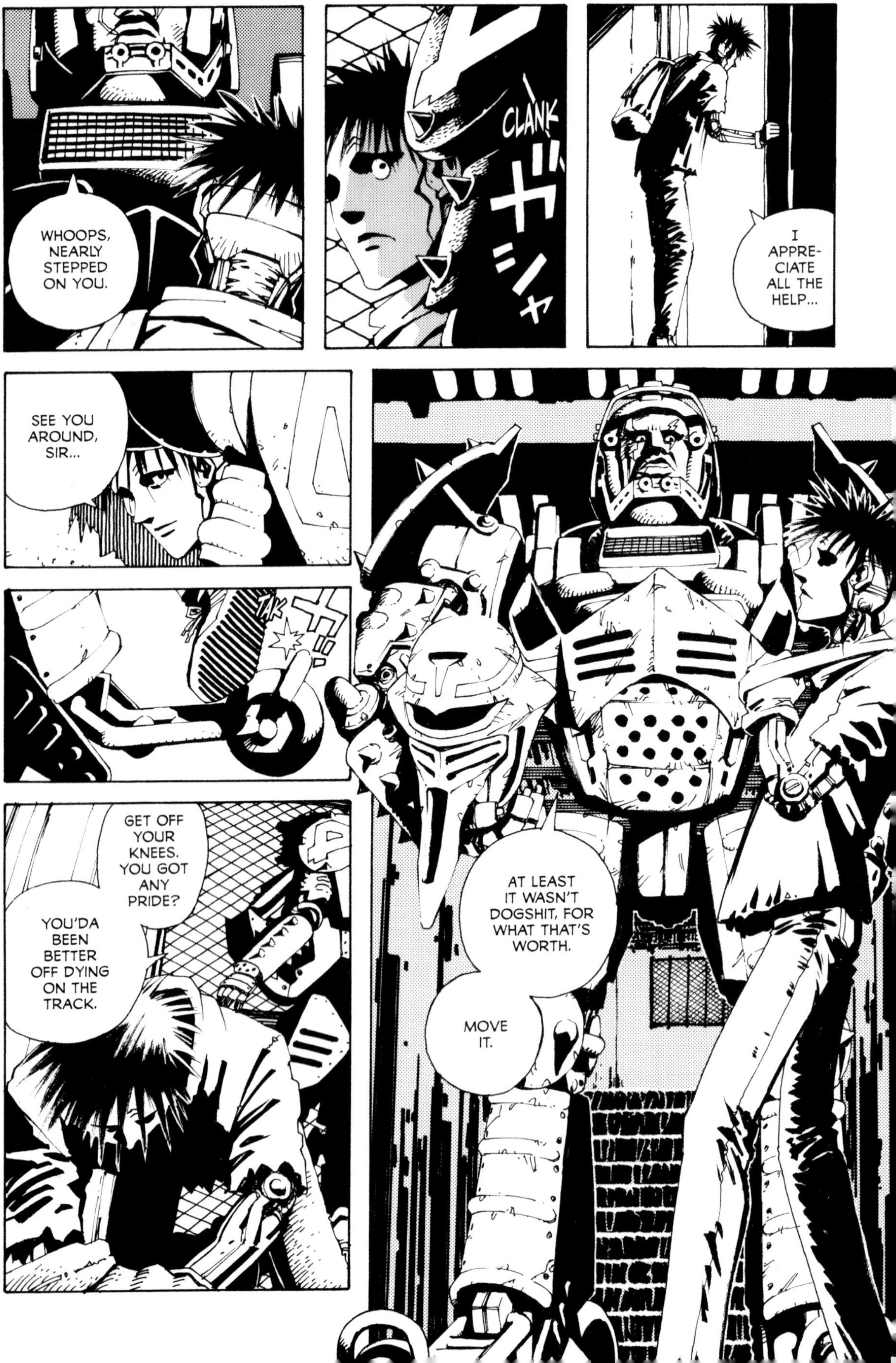
I APPRECIATE ALL THE HELP...
CLANK
ガシャ
WHOOPS, NEARLY STEPPED ON YOU.
AT LEAST IT WASN'T DOGSHIT, FOR WHAT THAT'S WORTH.
MOVE IT.
SEE YOU AROUND, SIR...
TAK
GET OFF YOUR KNEES. YOU GOT ANY PRIDE?
YOU'DA BEEN BETTER OFF DYING ON THE TRACK.

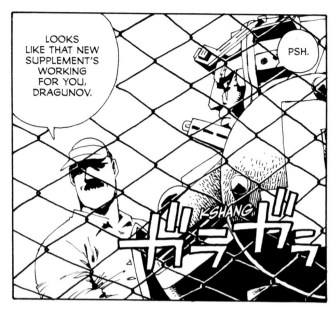

...
LOOKS LIKE THAT NEW SUPPLEMENT'S WORKING FOR YOU, DRAGUNOV.
PSH.
KSHANG
ガラガラ
YOU BET. NEXT RACE IS *MINE.*
WHAT SUPPLE-MENT?
SPANDAU
NEW PRODUCT FROM MEGIL INC. CALLED "ACCEL."
SO NEW, IT'S NOT EVEN ON THE MARKET YET.
FEELS LIKE SOMEONE JAMMED NITRO RIGHT INTO MY BRAIN.
YOUR VISION EXPANDS, AND IT FEELS LIKE YOUR BODY'S TEN TIMES BIGGER THAN IT IS.
GOTTA GET THE HANG OF IT TO USE IN A RACE, THOUGH.
CAN'T WAIT TO SEE YOU IN ACTION!
GOOD GRIEF. STOOPIN' TO *DRUGS*...

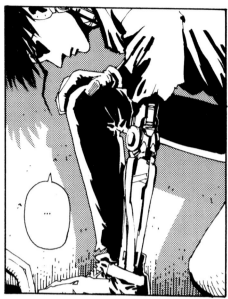

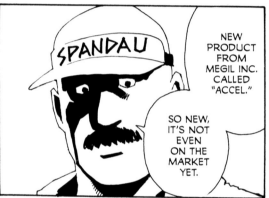

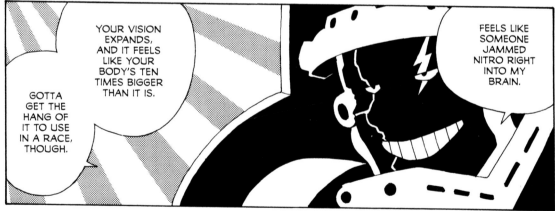

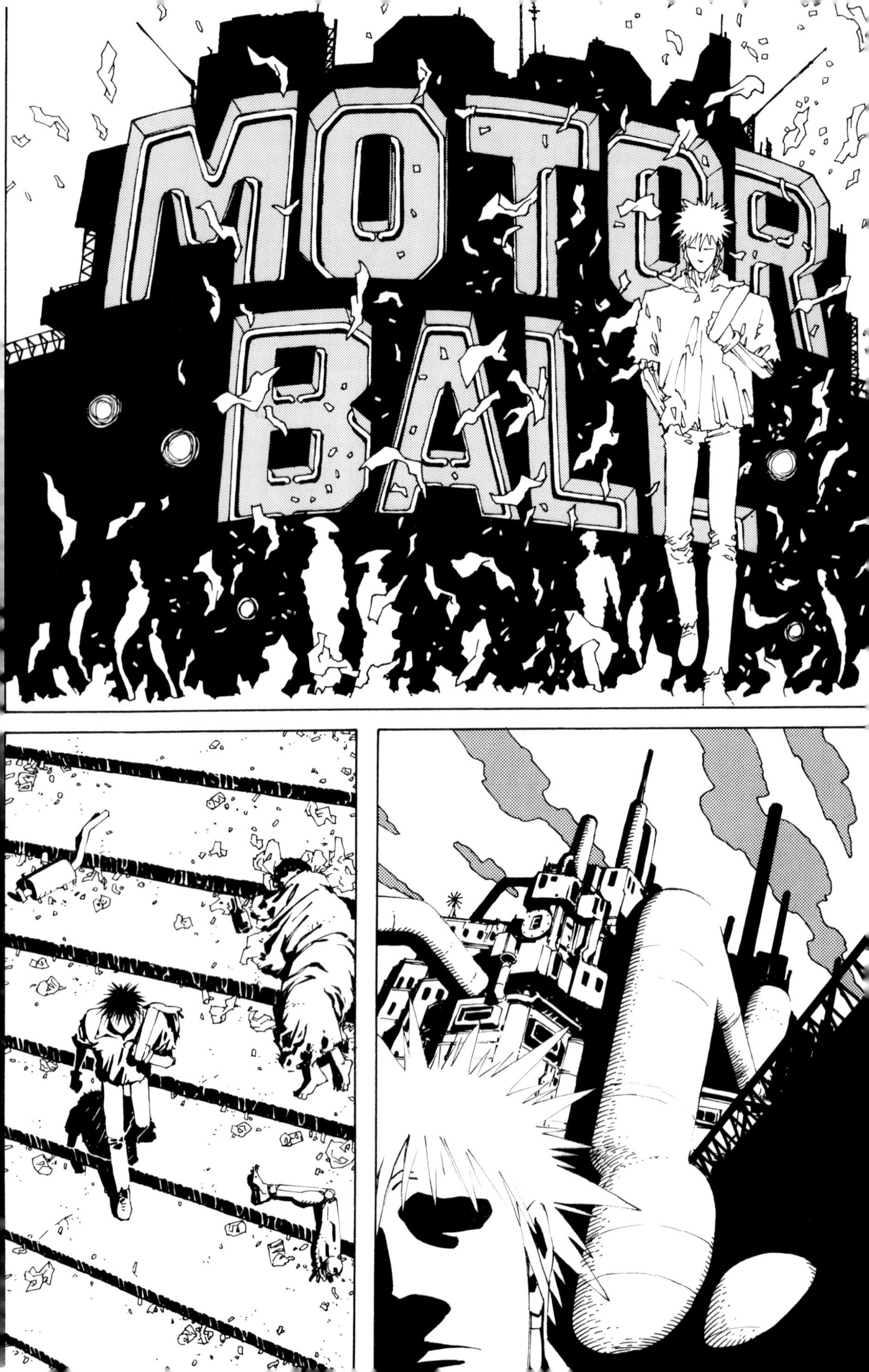
MOTOR
BAL

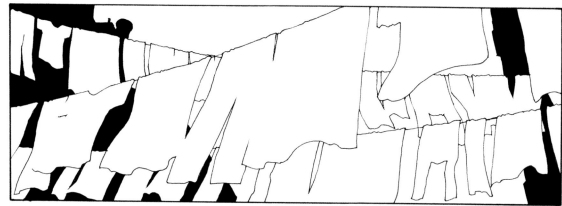

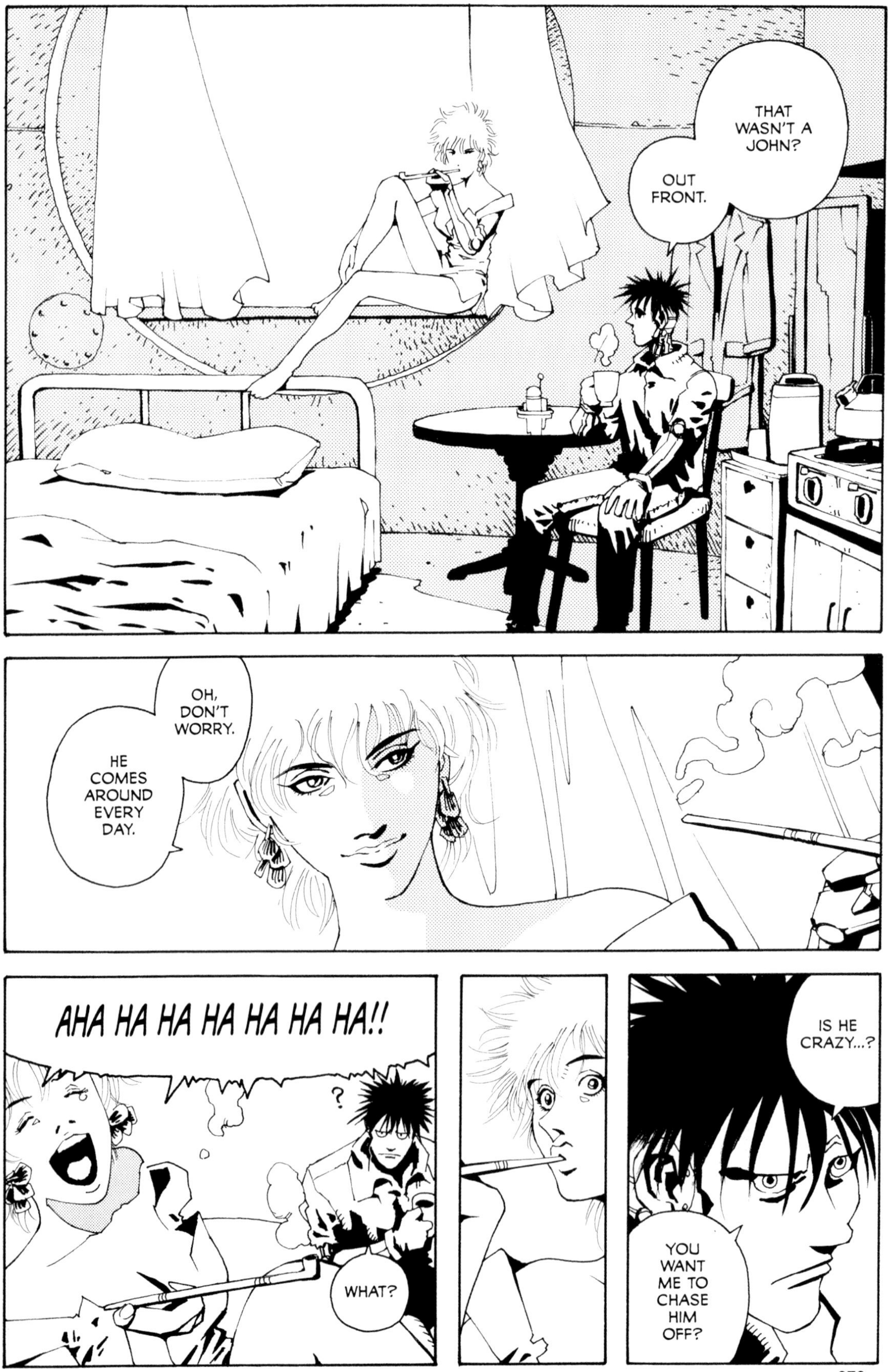
THAT WASN'T A JOHN?
OUT FRONT.
OH, DON'T WORRY.
HE COMES AROUND EVERY DAY.
IS HE CRAZY...?
YOU WANT ME TO CHASE HIM OFF?
AHA HA HA HA HA HA HA!!
?
WHAT?

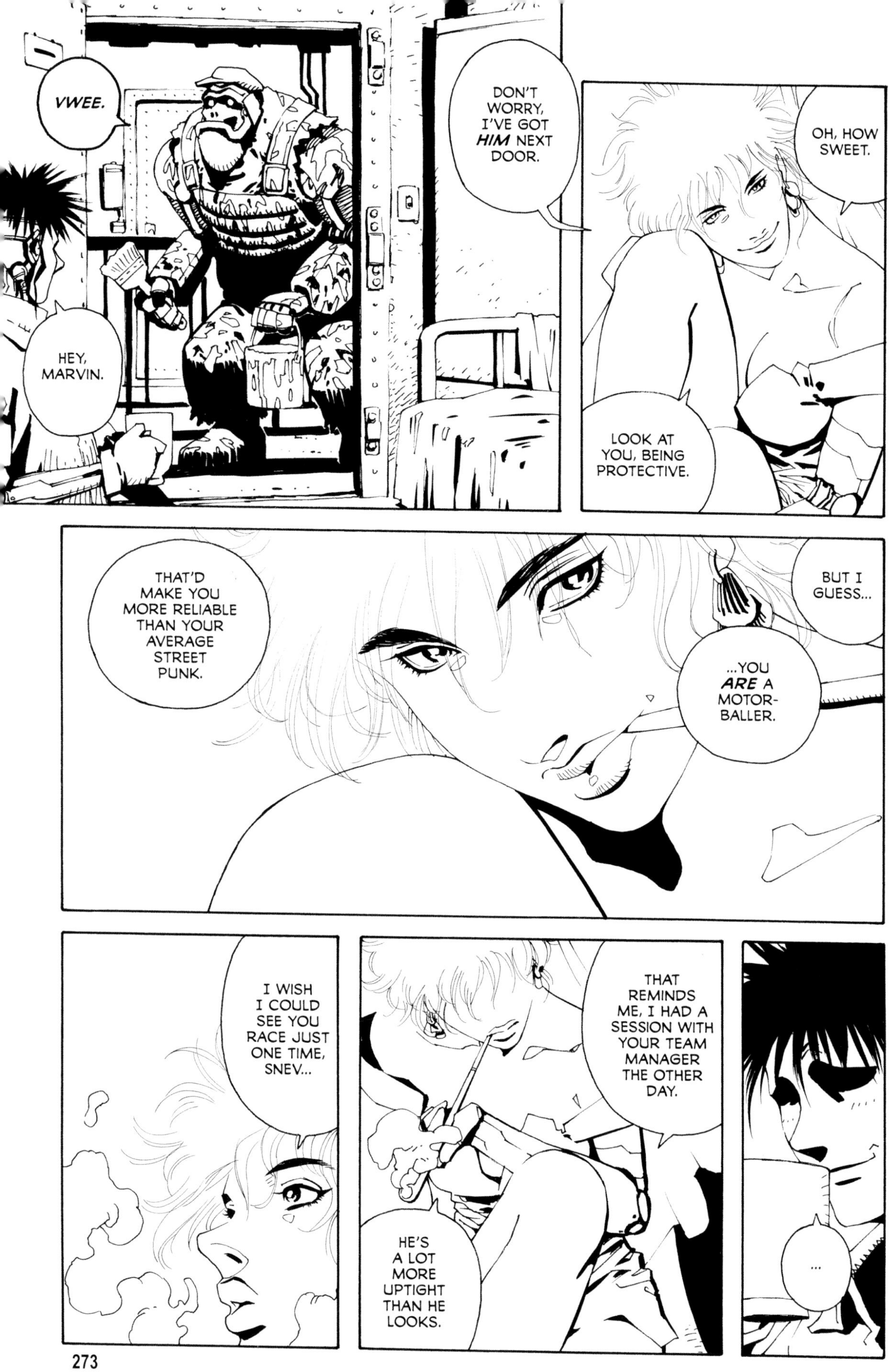
OH, HOW SWEET.
LOOK AT YOU, BEING PROTECTIVE.
DON'T WORRY, I'VE GOT *HIM* NEXT DOOR.
VWEE.
HEY, MARVIN.
BUT I GUESS...
...YOU *ARE* A MOTOR-BALLER.
THAT'D MAKE YOU MORE RELIABLE THAN YOUR AVERAGE STREET PUNK.
...
THAT REMINDS ME, I HAD A SESSION WITH YOUR TEAM MANAGER THE OTHER DAY.
HE'S A LOT MORE UPTIGHT THAN HE LOOKS.
I WISH I COULD SEE YOU RACE JUST ONE TIME, SNEV...

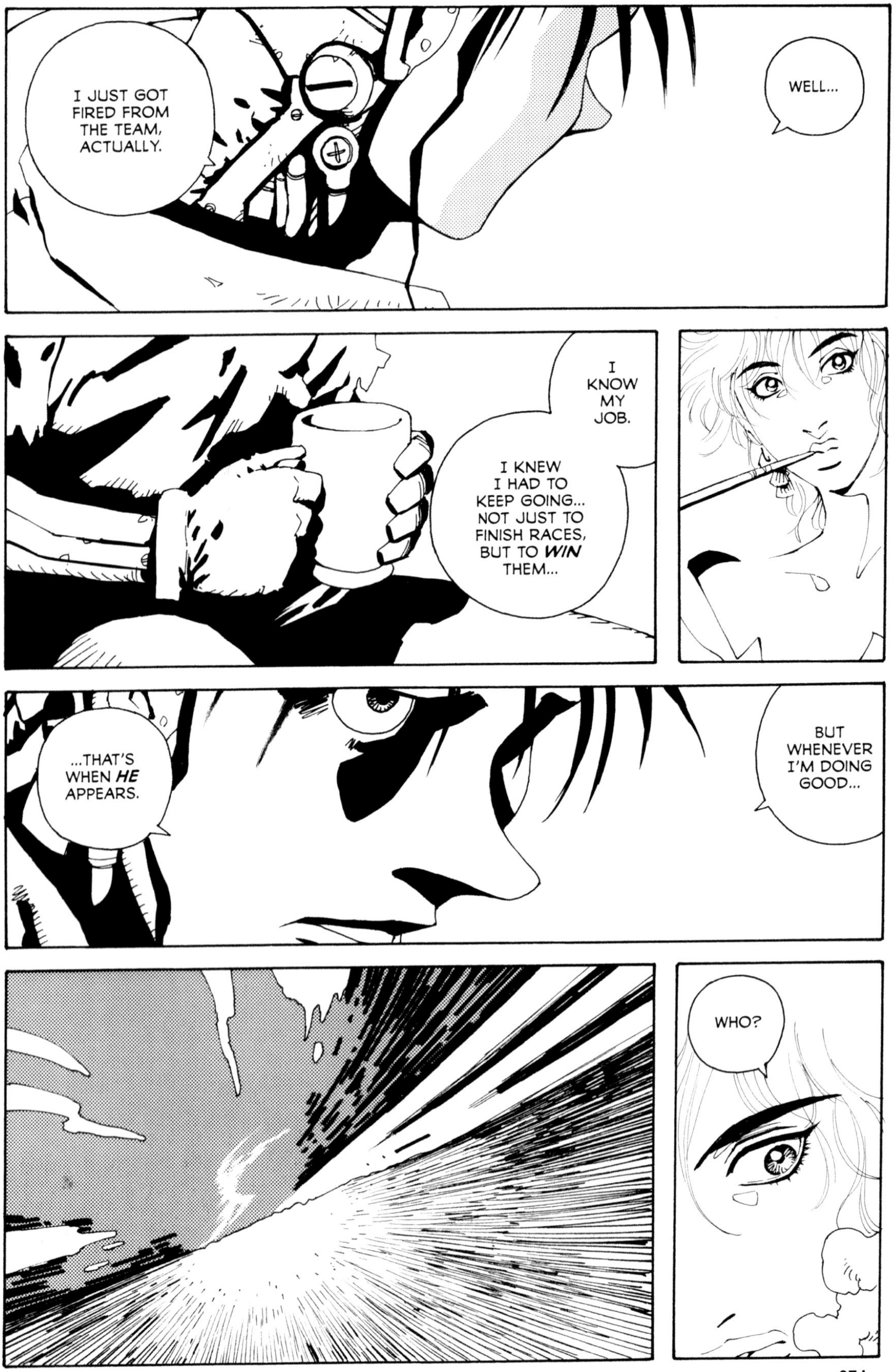
WELL...
I JUST GOT FIRED FROM THE TEAM, ACTUALLY.
I KNOW MY JOB.
I KNEW I HAD TO KEEP GOING... NOT JUST TO FINISH RACES, BUT TO **WIN** THEM...
BUT WHENEVER I'M DOING GOOD...
...THAT'S WHEN **HE** APPEARS.
WHO?

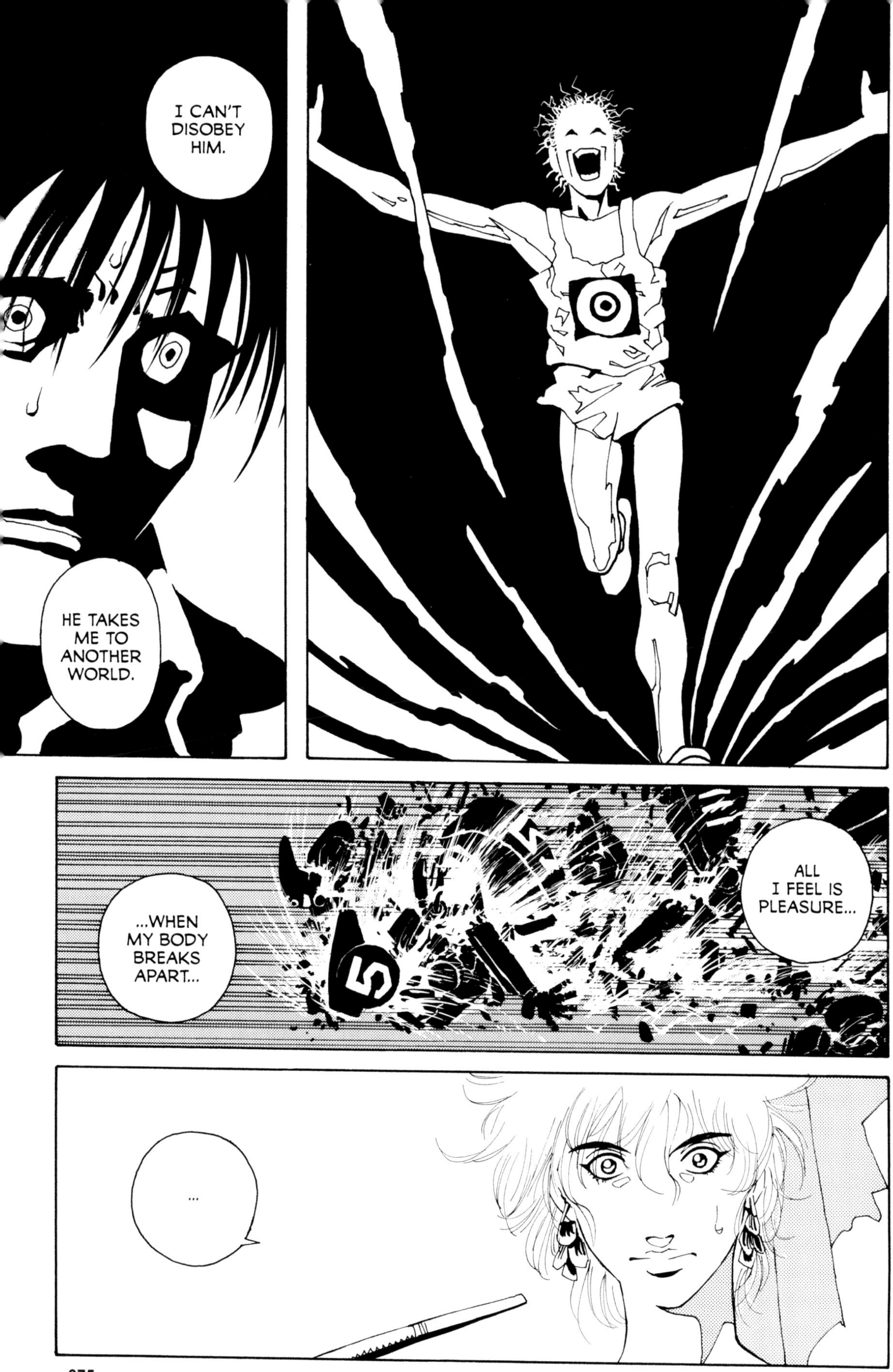
I CAN'T DISOBEY HIM.
HE TAKES ME TO ANOTHER WORLD.
ALL I FEEL IS PLEASURE...
...WHEN MY BODY BREAKS APART...
...

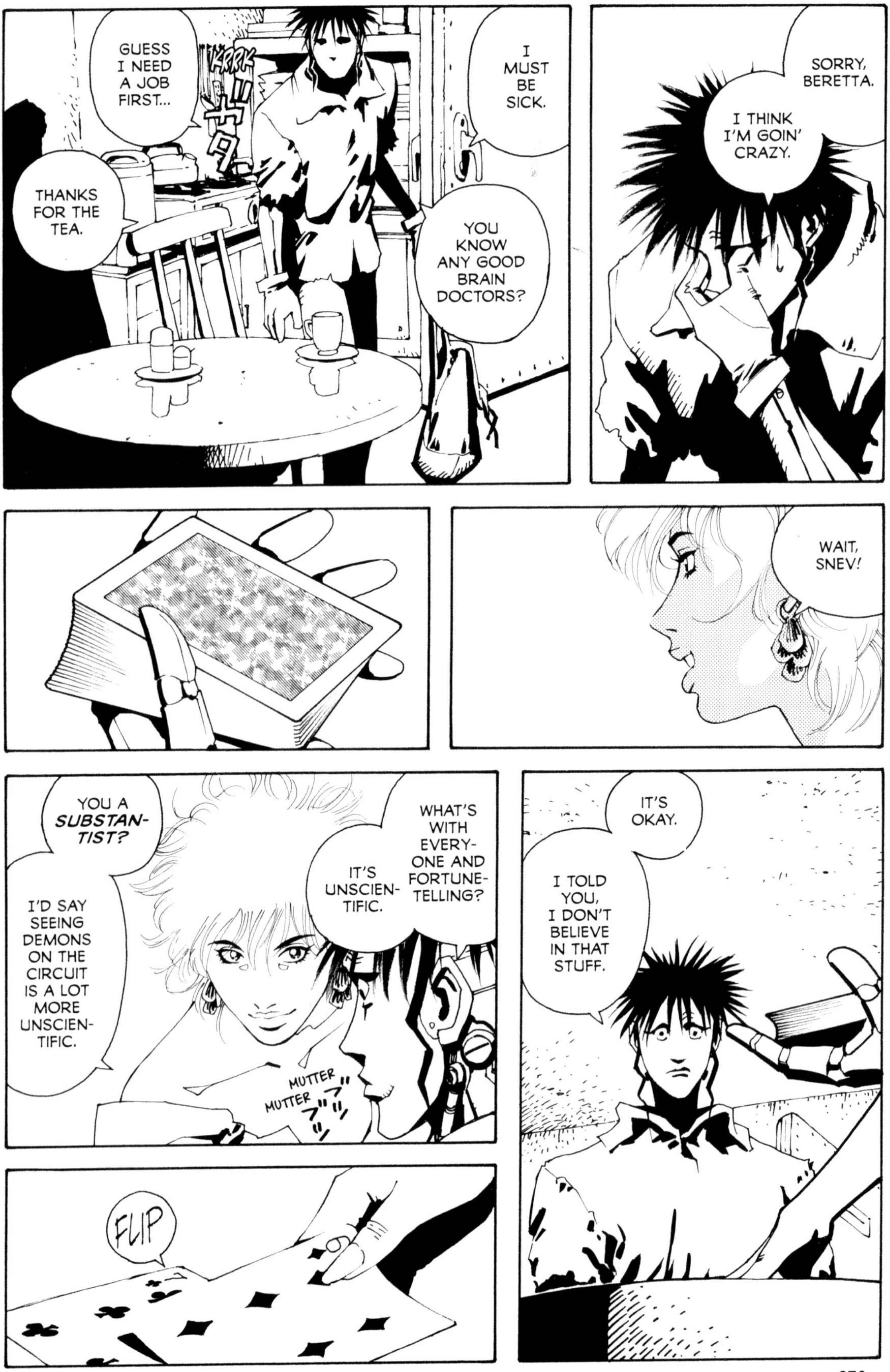
SORRY, BERETTA.
I THINK I'M GOIN' CRAZY.
I MUST BE SICK.
YOU KNOW ANY GOOD BRAIN DOCTORS?
KRRK
GUESS I NEED A JOB FIRST...
THANKS FOR THE TEA.
WAIT, SNEV!
IT'S OKAY.
I TOLD YOU, I DON'T BELIEVE IN THAT STUFF.
WHAT'S WITH EVERYONE AND FORTUNE-TELLING?
IT'S UNSCIENTIFIC.
YOU A *SUBSTANTIST?*
I'D SAY SEEING DEMONS ON THE CIRCUIT IS A LOT MORE UNSCIENTIFIC.
MUTTER MUTTER
FLIP

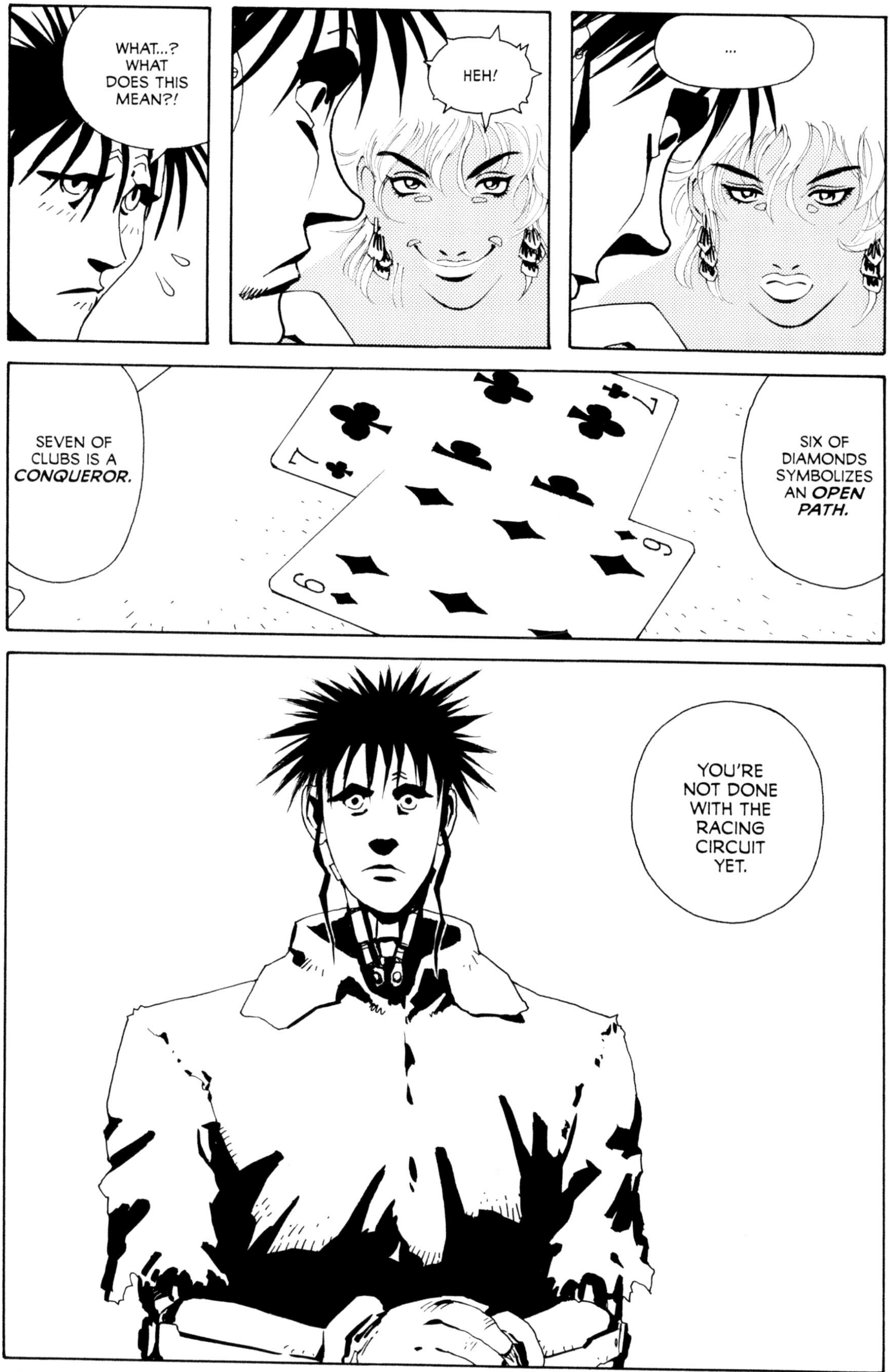
...
HEH!
WHAT...? WHAT DOES THIS MEAN?!
SIX OF DIAMONDS SYMBOLIZES AN ***OPEN PATH.***
SEVEN OF CLUBS IS A ***CONQUEROR.***
YOU'RE NOT DONE WITH THE RACING CIRCUIT YET.

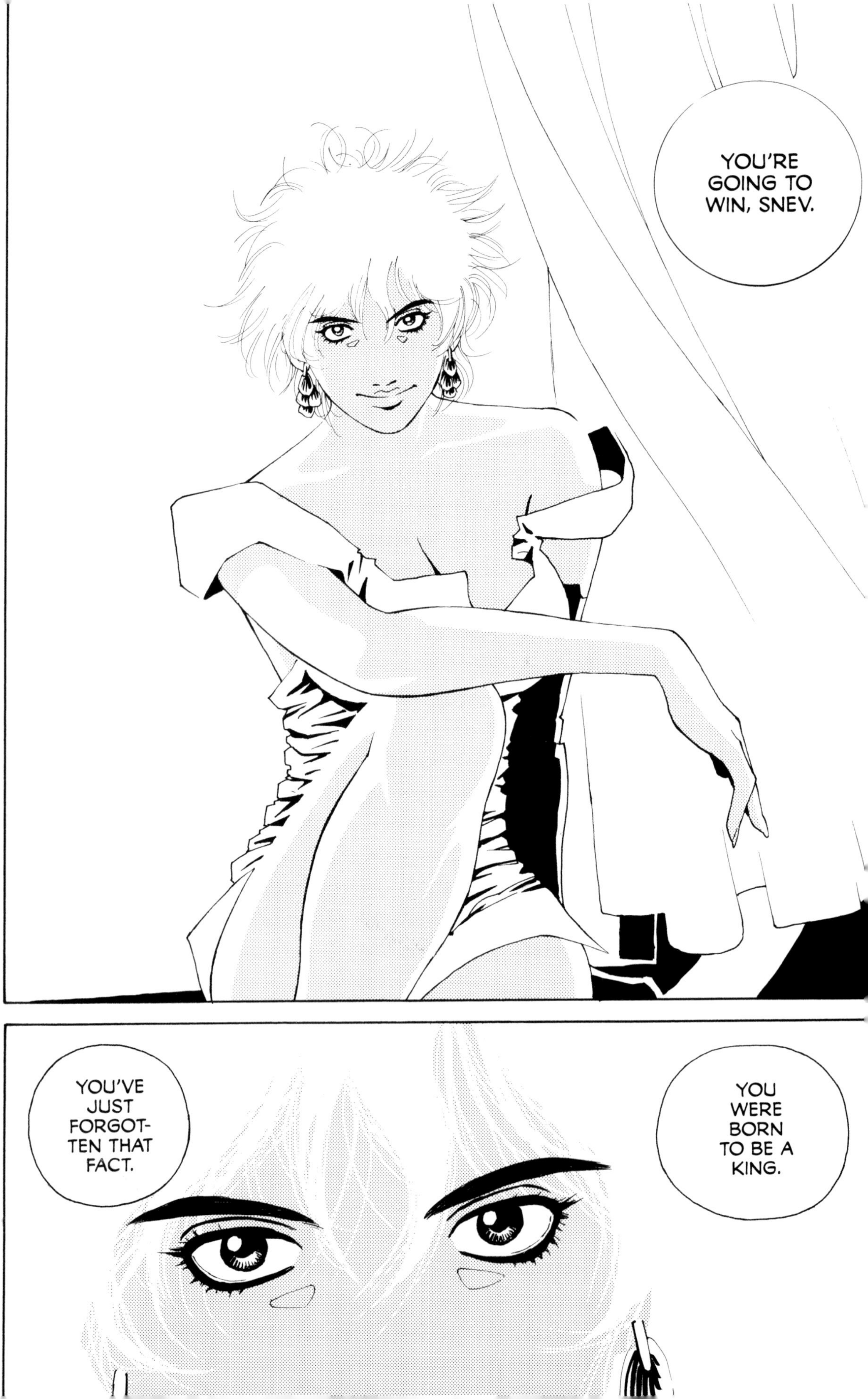
YOU'RE GOING TO WIN, SNEV.
YOU WERE BORN TO BE A KING.
YOU'VE JUST FORGOT-TEN THAT FACT.

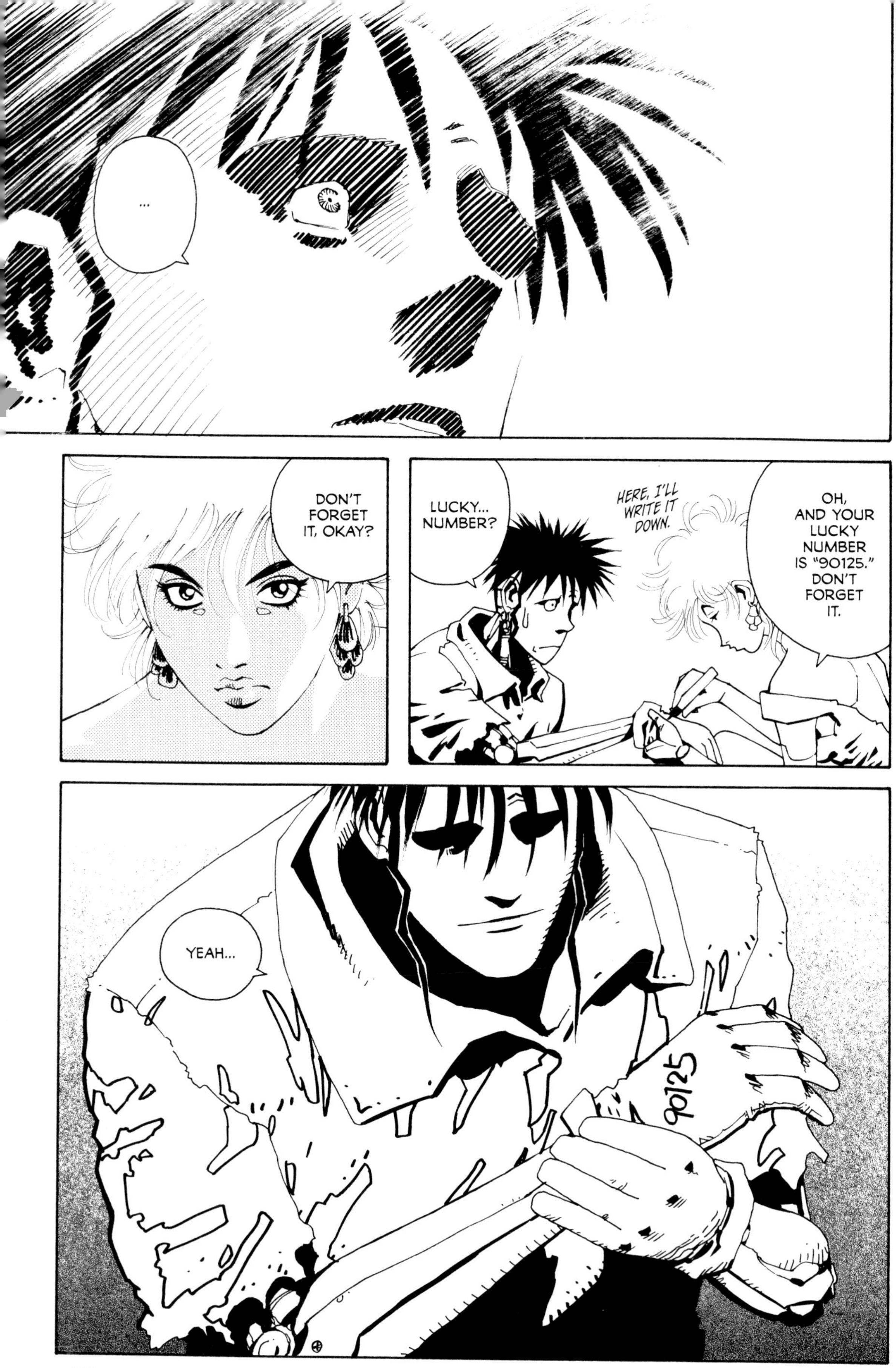
...
OH, AND YOUR LUCKY NUMBER IS "90125." DON'T FORGET IT.
HERE, I'LL WRITE IT DOWN.
LUCKY... NUMBER?
DON'T FORGET IT, OKAY?
YEAH...
90125

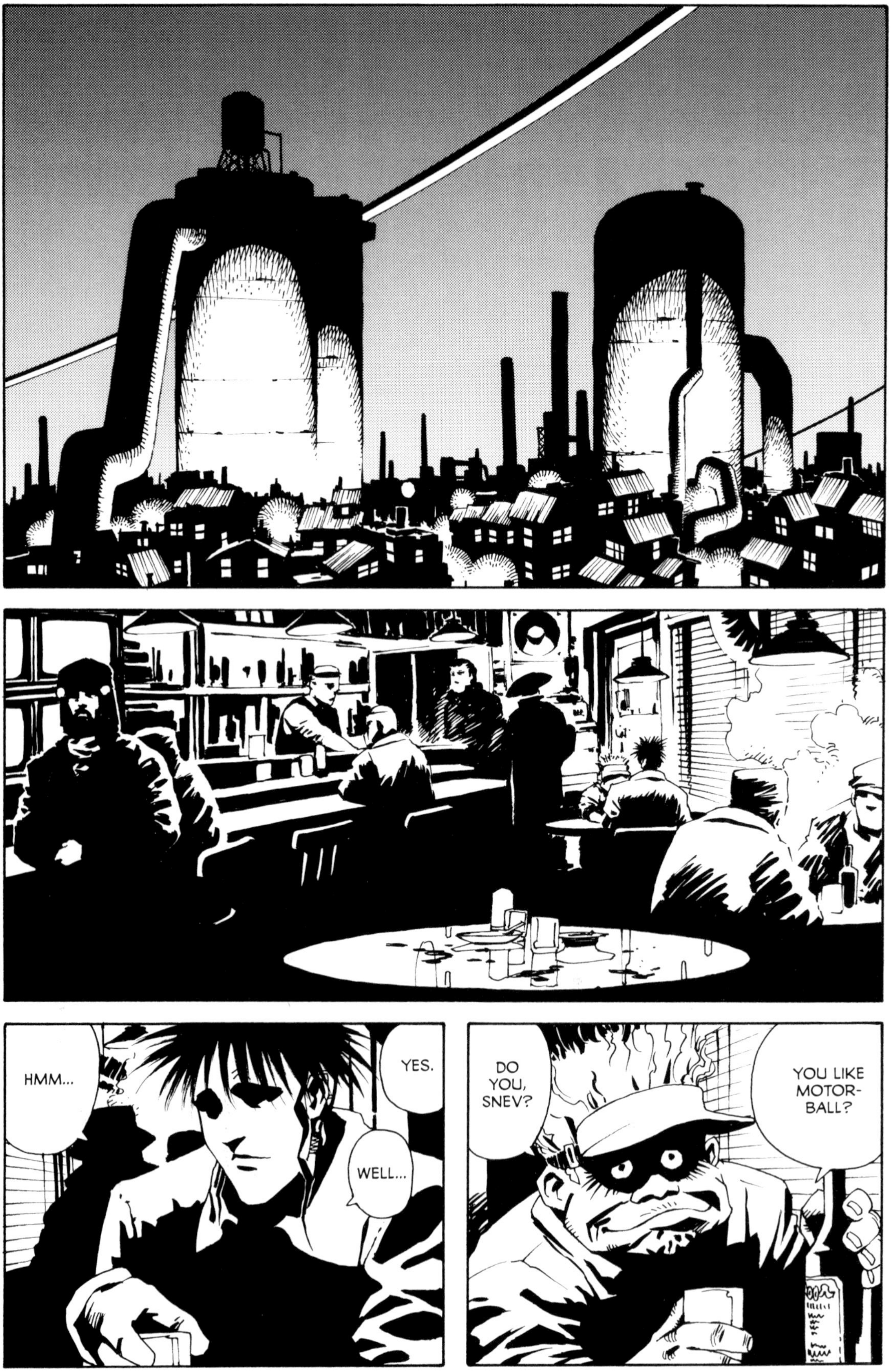
YOU LIKE MOTOR-BALL?
DO YOU, SNEV?
YES.
WELL...
HMM...

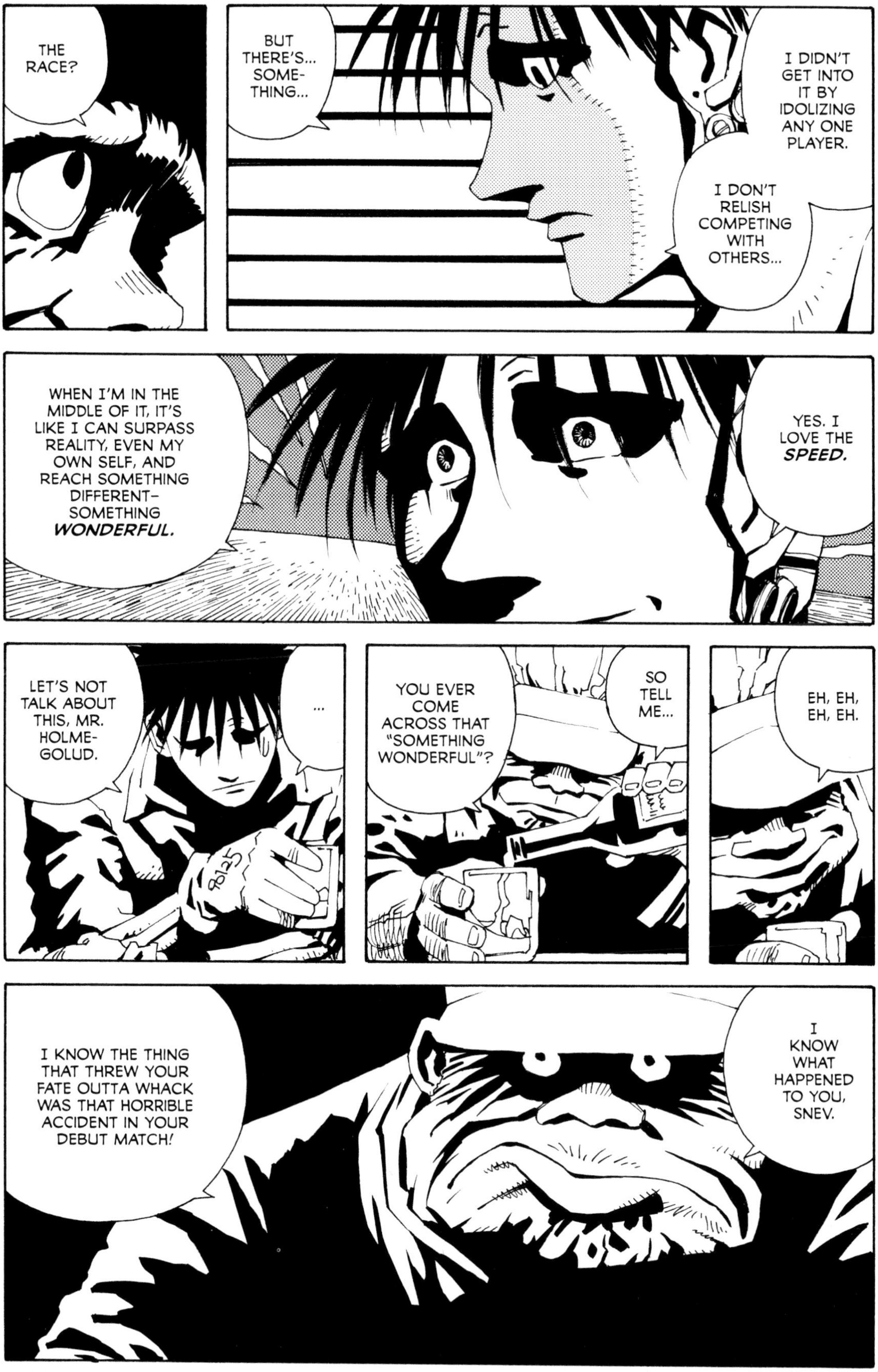
I DIDN'T GET INTO IT BY IDOLIZING ANY ONE PLAYER.
I DON'T RELISH COMPETING WITH OTHERS...
BUT THERE'S... SOME-THING...
THE RACE?
YES. I LOVE THE *SPEED.*
WHEN I'M IN THE MIDDLE OF IT, IT'S LIKE I CAN SURPASS REALITY, EVEN MY OWN SELF, AND REACH SOMETHING DIFFERENT–SOMETHING *WONDERFUL.*
EH, EH, EH, EH.
SO TELL ME...
YOU EVER COME ACROSS THAT "SOMETHING WONDERFUL"?
...
LET'S NOT TALK ABOUT THIS, MR. HOLME-GOLUD.
I KNOW WHAT HAPPENED TO YOU, SNEV.
I KNOW THE THING THAT THREW YOUR FATE OUTTA WHACK WAS THAT HORRIBLE ACCIDENT IN YOUR DEBUT MATCH!

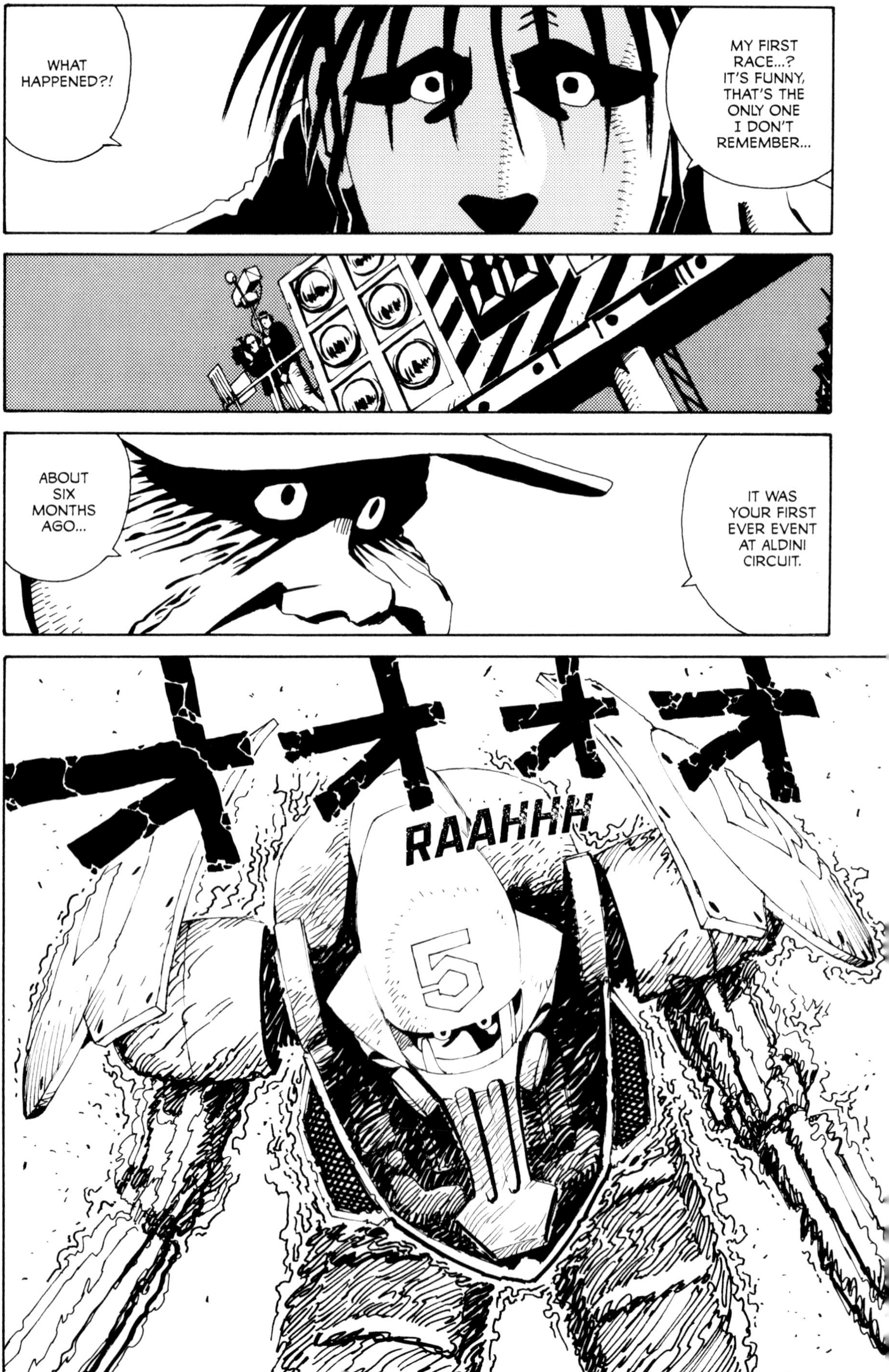
MY FIRST RACE...? IT'S FUNNY, THAT'S THE ONLY ONE I DON'T REMEMBER...
WHAT HAPPENED?!
IT WAS YOUR FIRST EVER EVENT AT ALDINI CIRCUIT.
ABOUT SIX MONTHS AGO...
オオオオ
RAAHHH

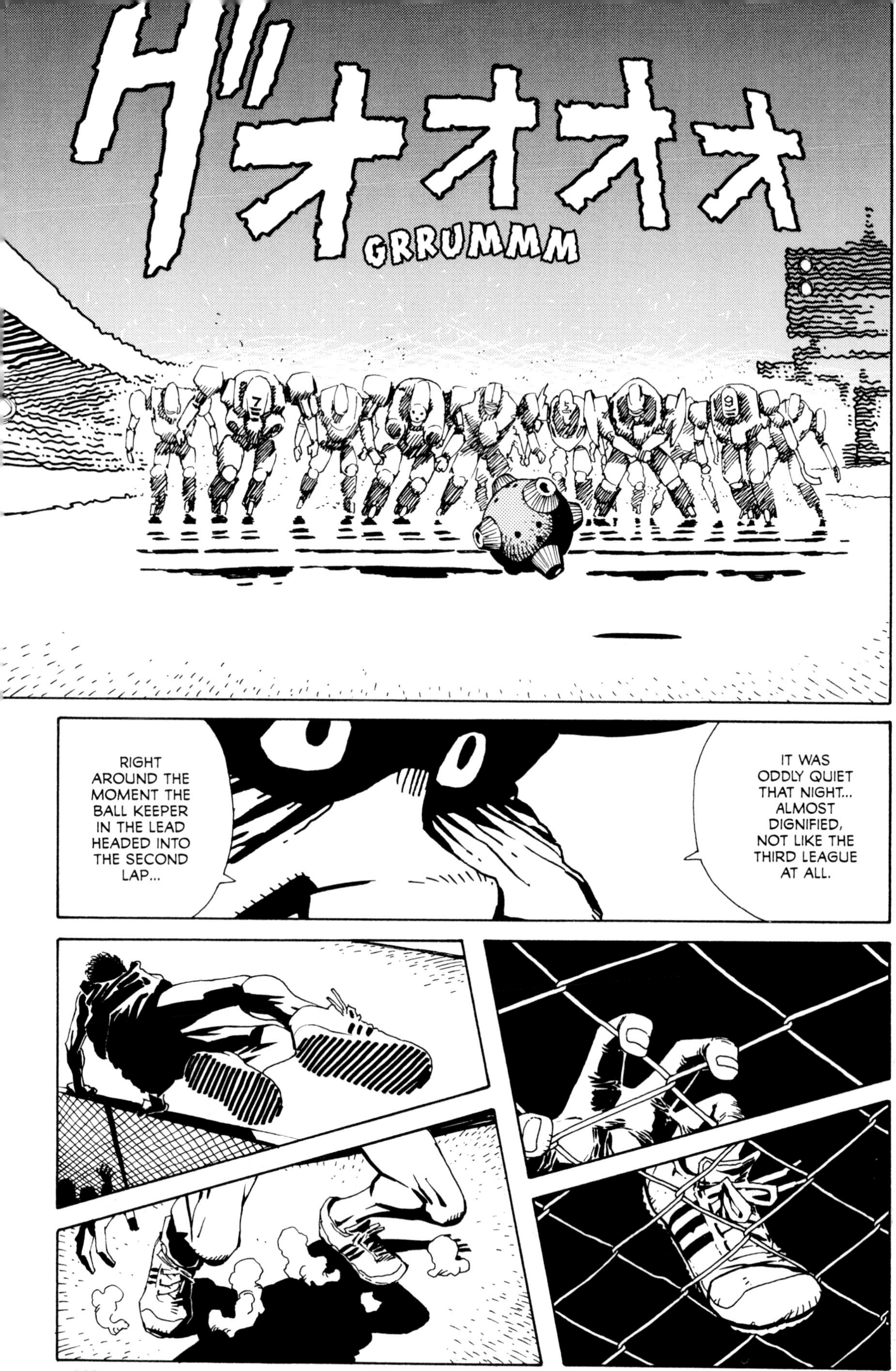
GRRUMMM
IT WAS ODDLY QUIET THAT NIGHT... ALMOST DIGNIFIED, NOT LIKE THE THIRD LEAGUE AT ALL.
RIGHT AROUND THE MOMENT THE BALL KEEPER IN THE LEAD HEADED INTO THE SECOND LAP...

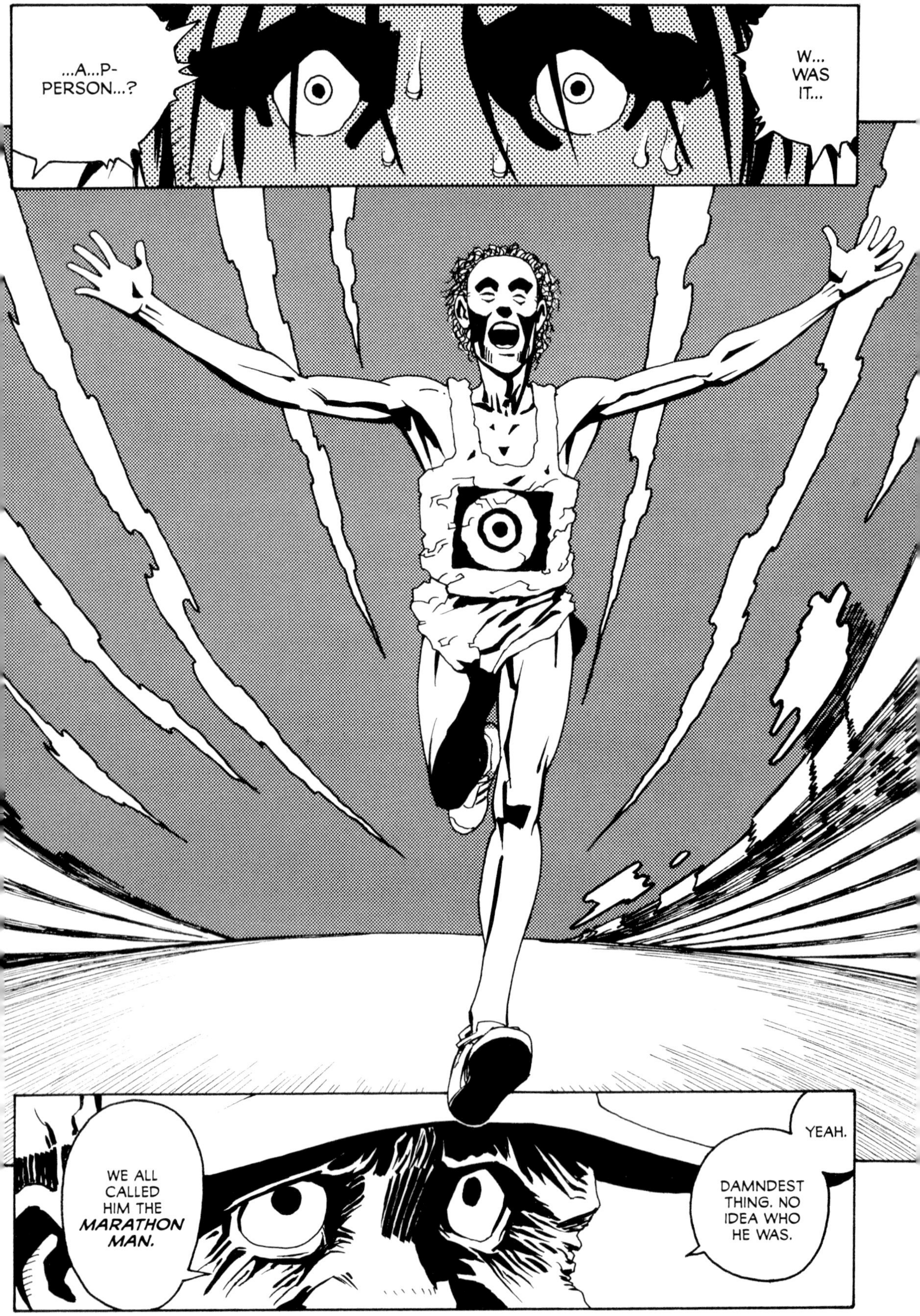
W... WAS IT...
...A...P- PERSON...?
YEAH.
DAMNDEST THING. NO IDEA WHO HE WAS.
WE ALL CALLED HIM THE *MARATHON MAN.*

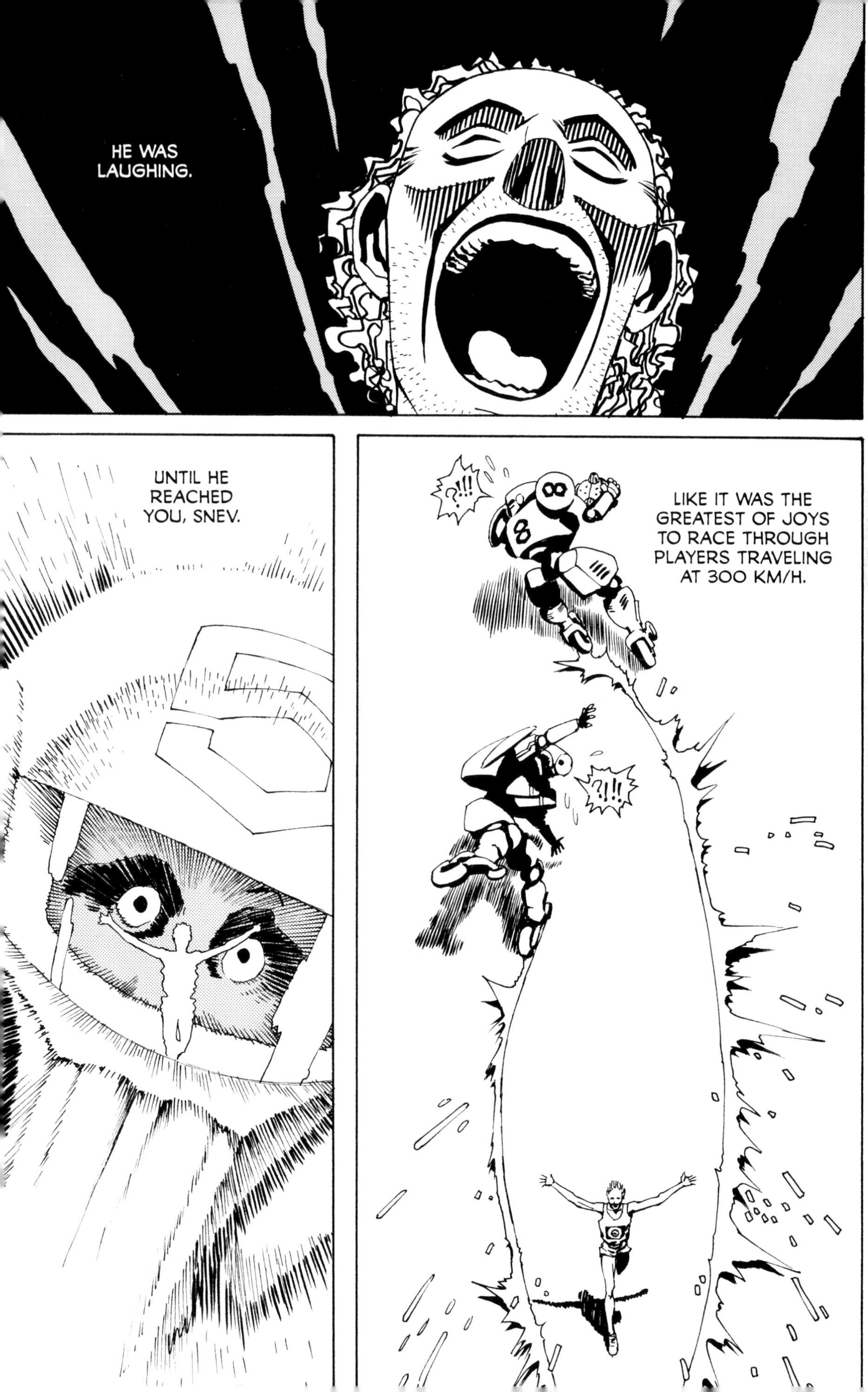
HE WAS LAUGHING.
LIKE IT WAS THE GREATEST OF JOYS TO RACE THROUGH PLAYERS TRAVELING AT 300 KM/H.
?!!!
?!!!
UNTIL HE REACHED YOU, SNEV.

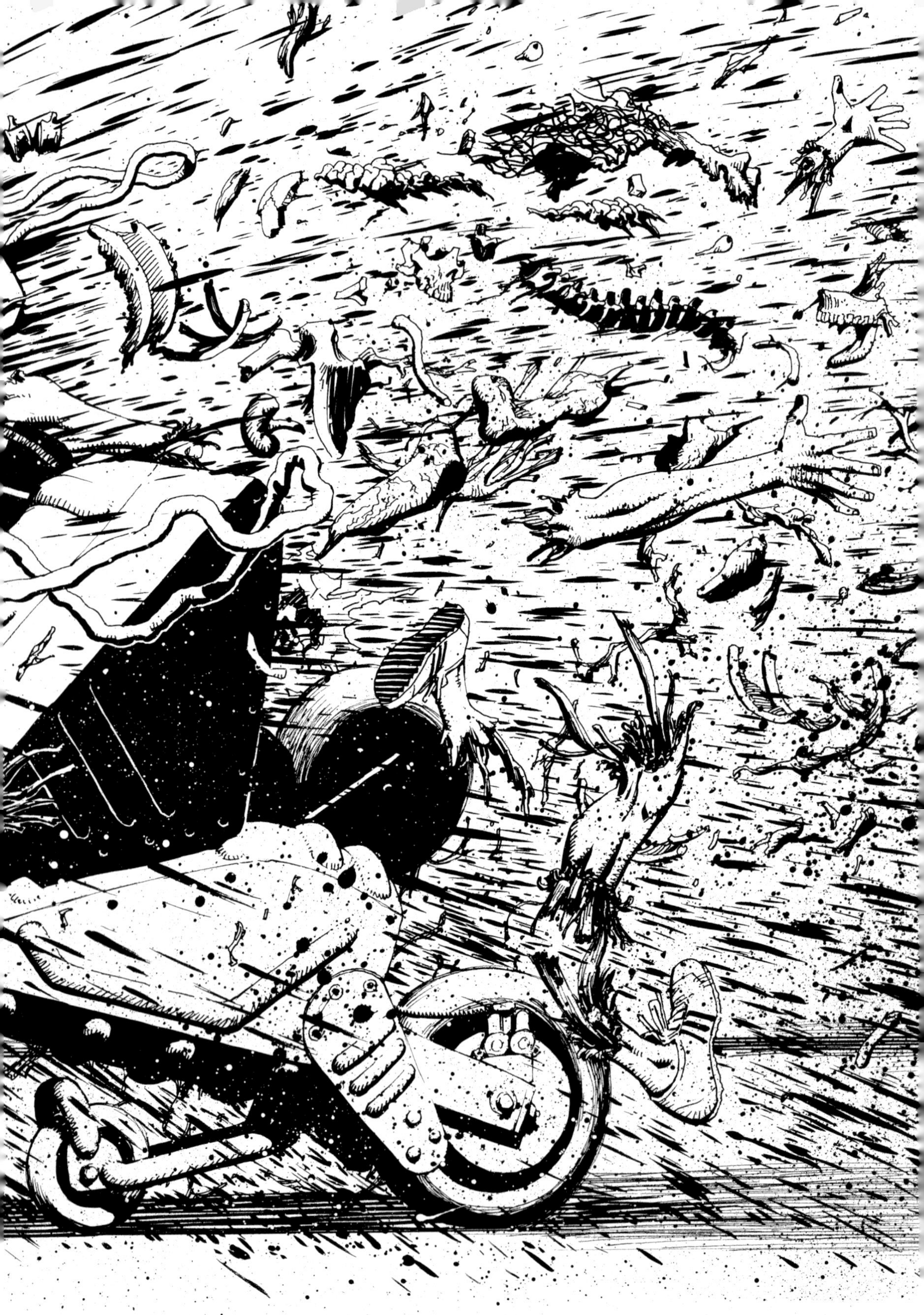

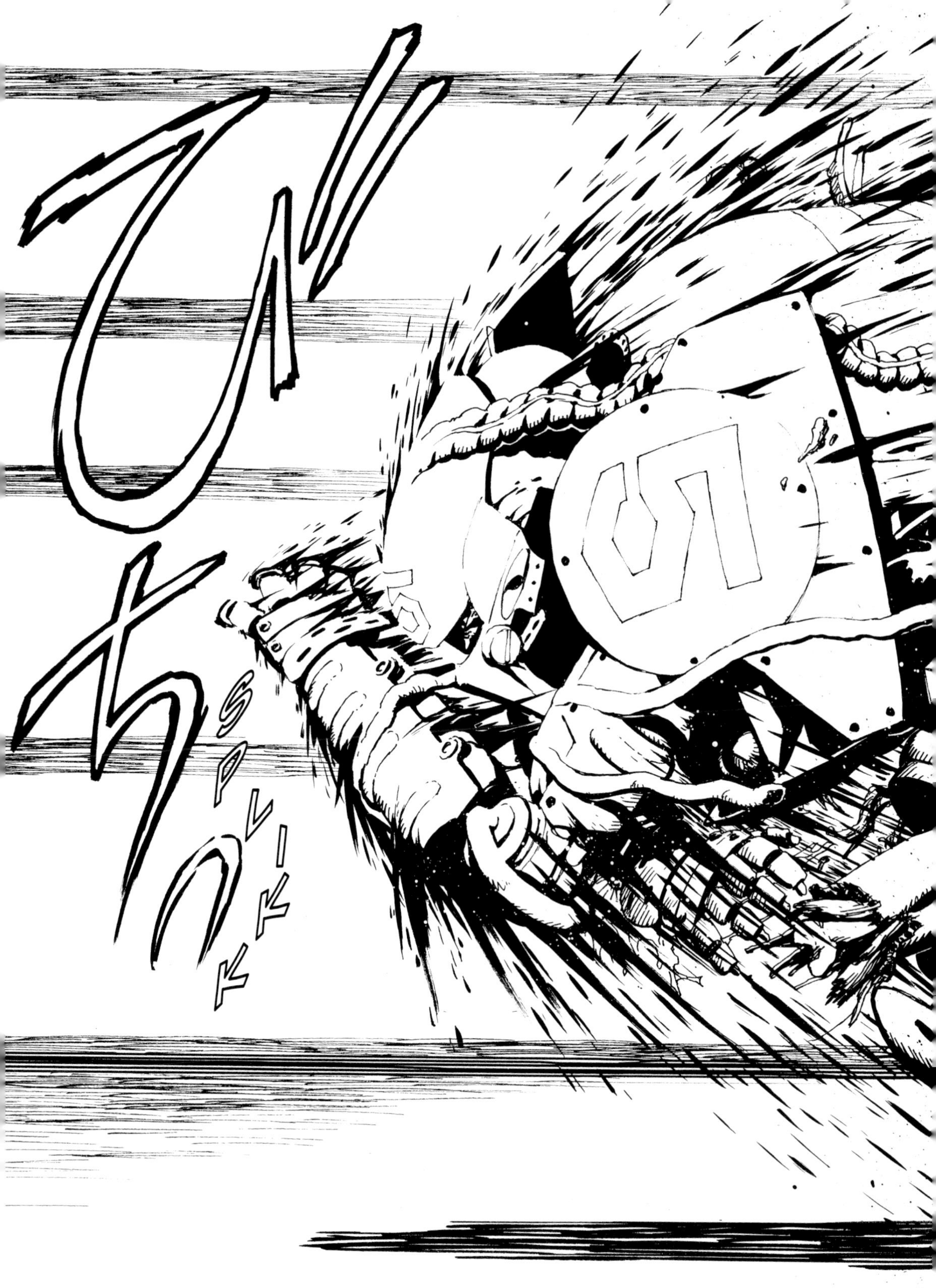
SPLIKK

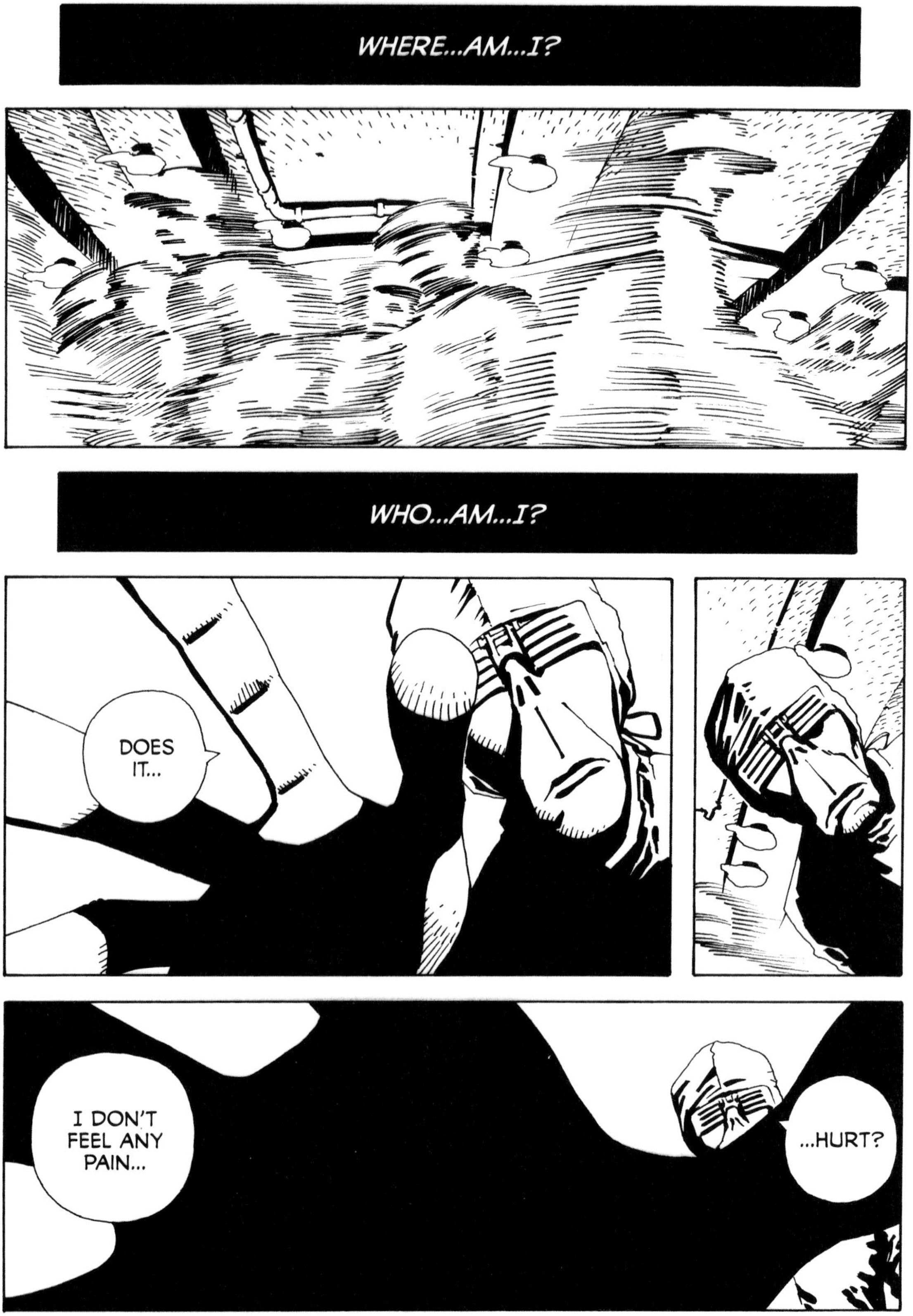
WHERE...AM...I?
WHO...AM...I?
DOES IT...
...HURT?
I DON'T FEEL ANY PAIN...

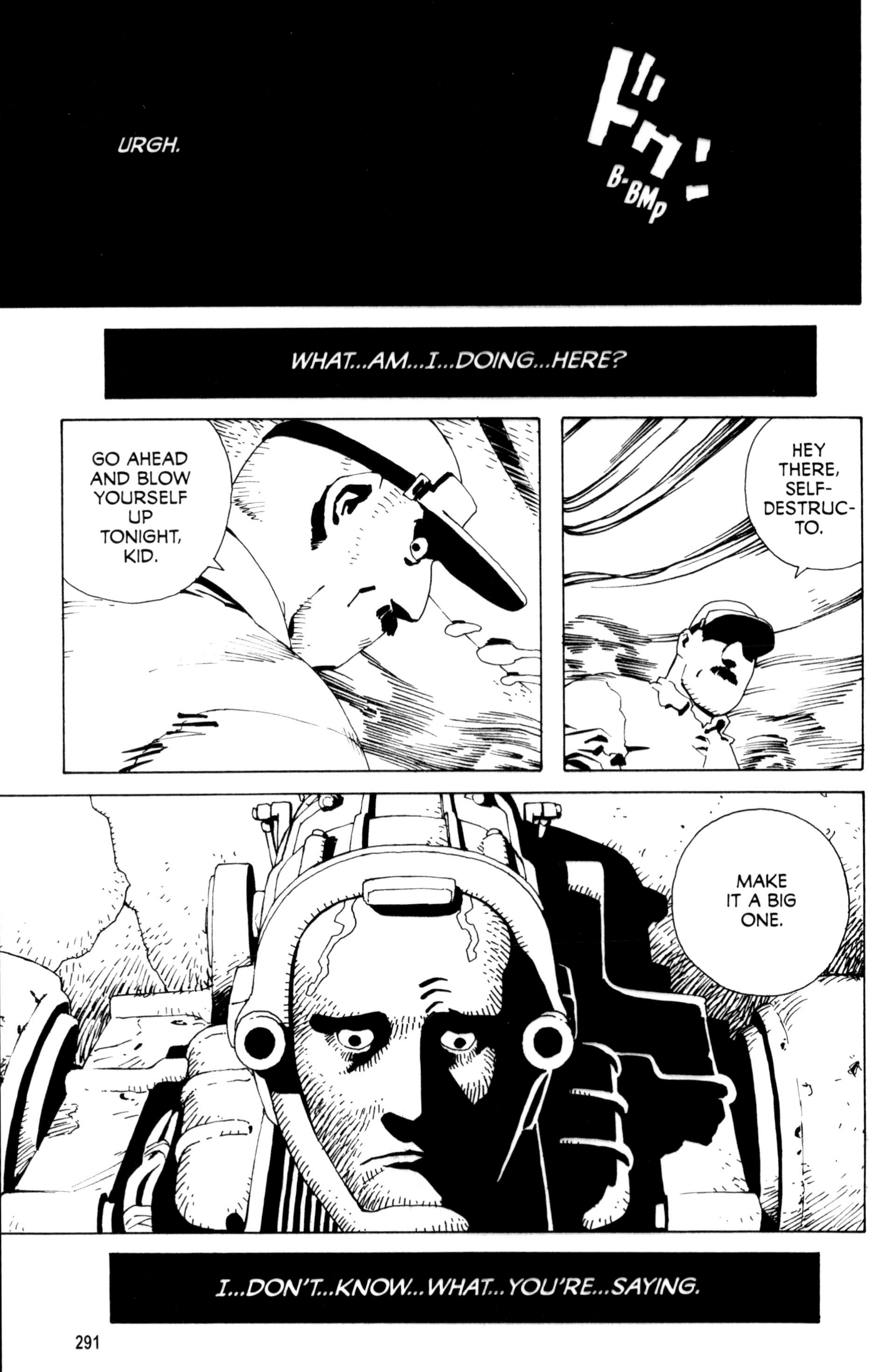
ドクン!
B-BMp
URGH.
WHAT...AM...I...DOING...HERE?
HEY THERE, SELF-DESTRUC-TO.
GO AHEAD AND BLOW YOURSELF UP TONIGHT, KID.
MAKE IT A BIG ONE.
I...DON'T...KNOW...WHAT...YOU'RE...SAYING.

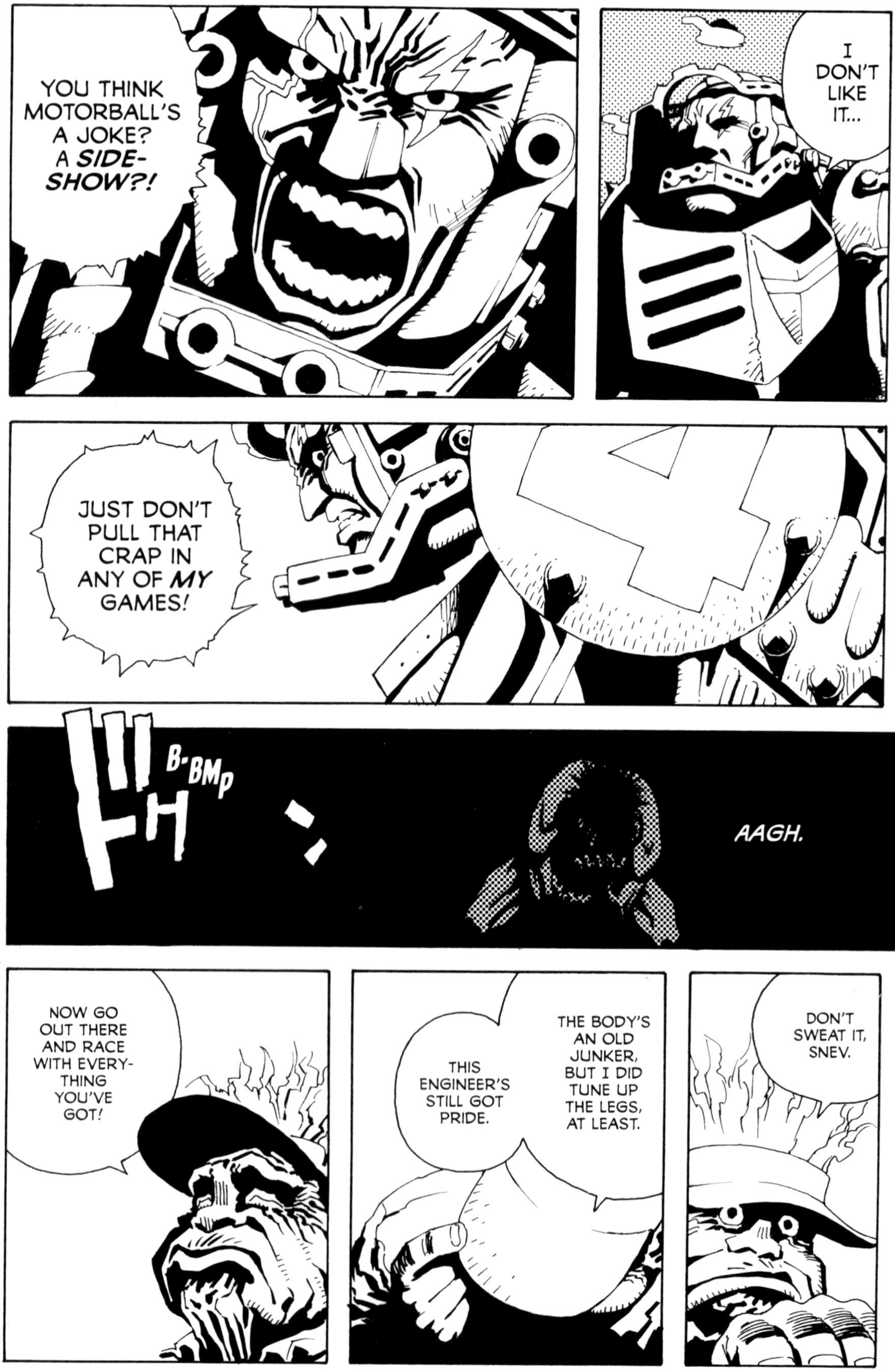
I DON'T LIKE IT...
YOU THINK MOTORBALL'S A JOKE? A *SIDE-SHOW?!*
JUST DON'T PULL THAT CRAP IN ANY OF *MY* GAMES!
AAGH.
B-BMP
DON'T SWEAT IT, SNEV.
THE BODY'S AN OLD JUNKER, BUT I DID TUNE UP THE LEGS, AT LEAST.
THIS ENGINEER'S STILL GOT PRIDE.
NOW GO OUT THERE AND RACE WITH EVERY-THING YOU'VE GOT!

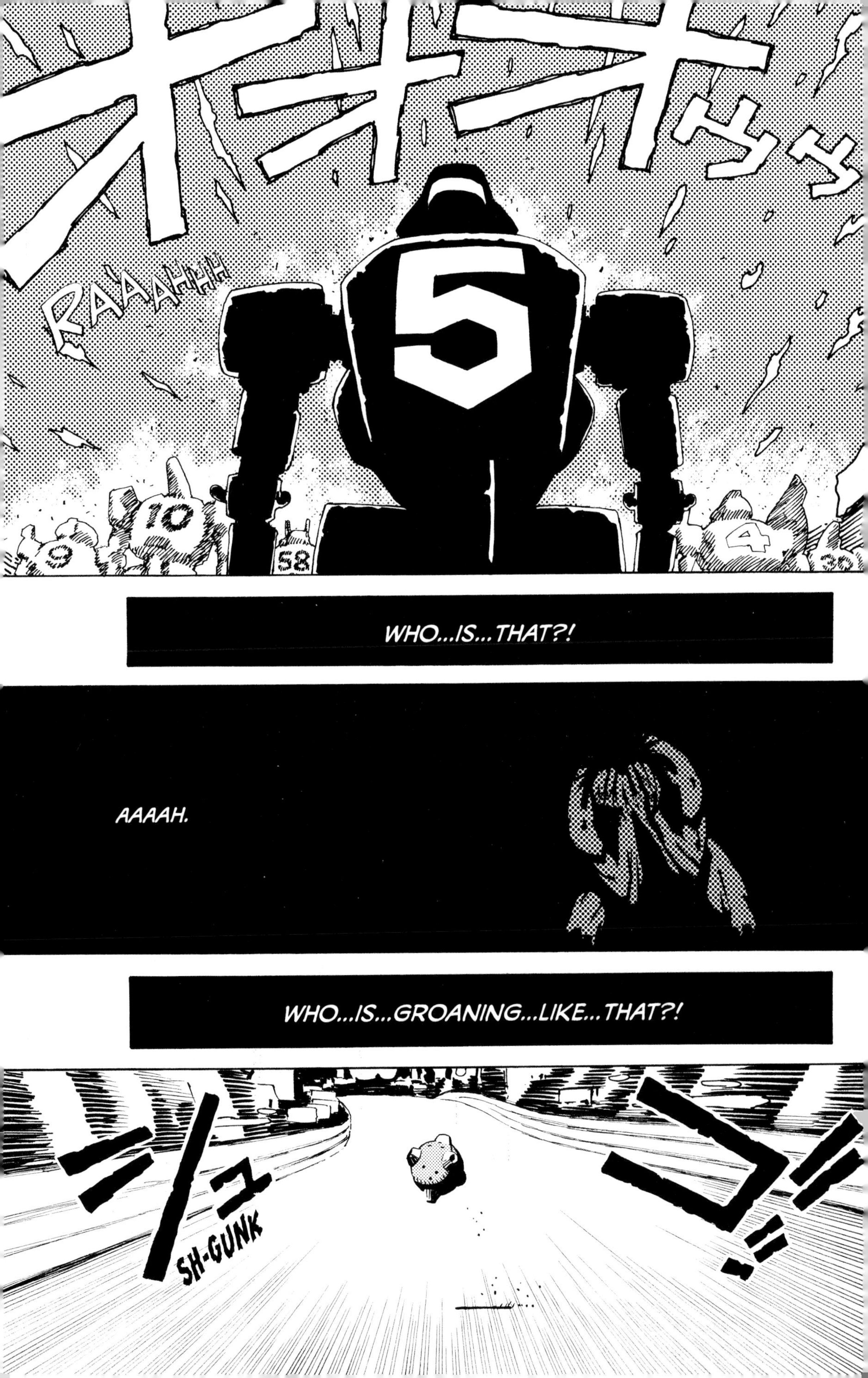
RAAAHHH
WHO...IS...THAT?!
AAAAH.
WHO...IS...GROANING...LIKE...THAT?!
SH-GUNK

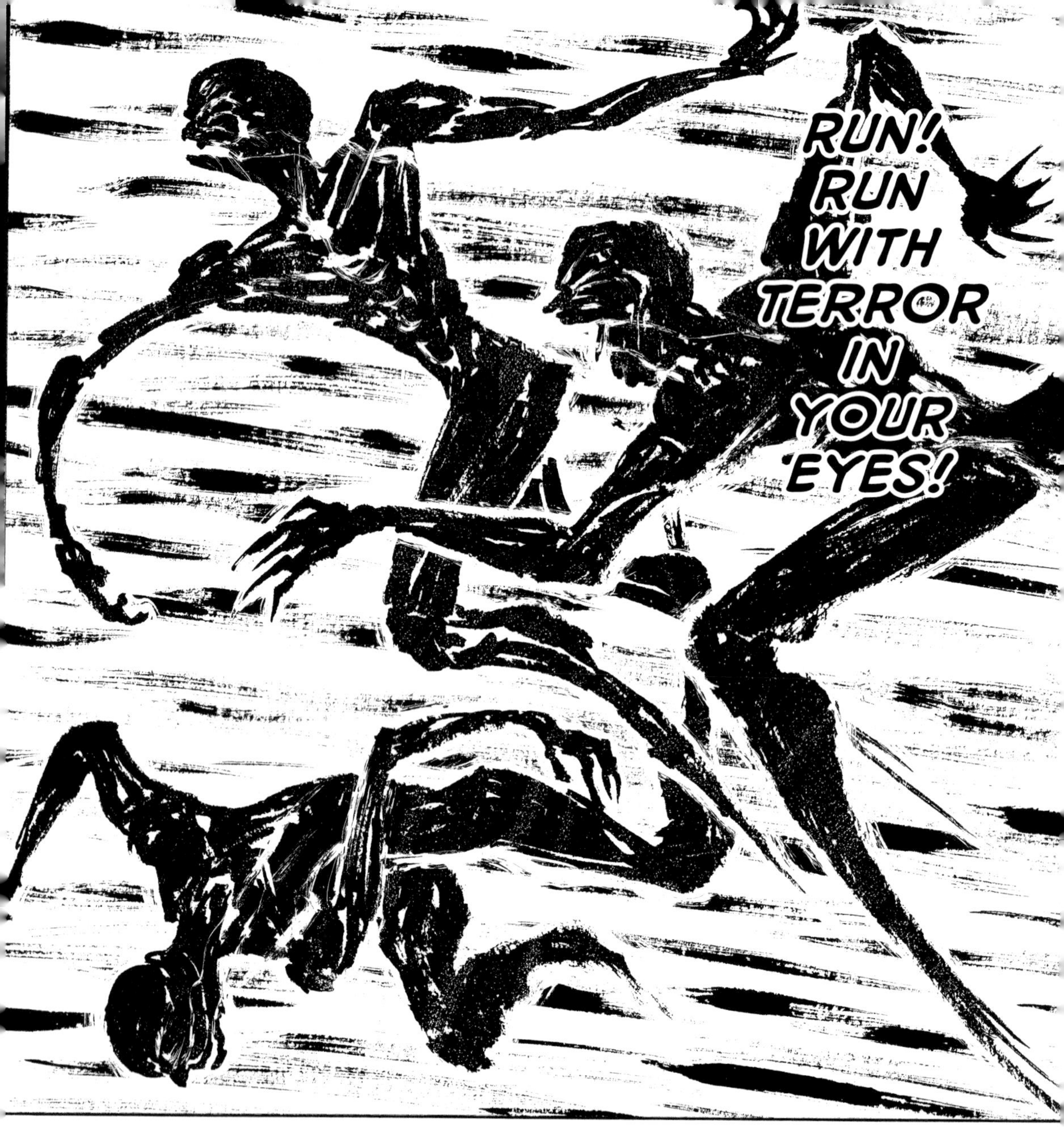
RUN! RUN WITH TERROR IN YOUR EYES!

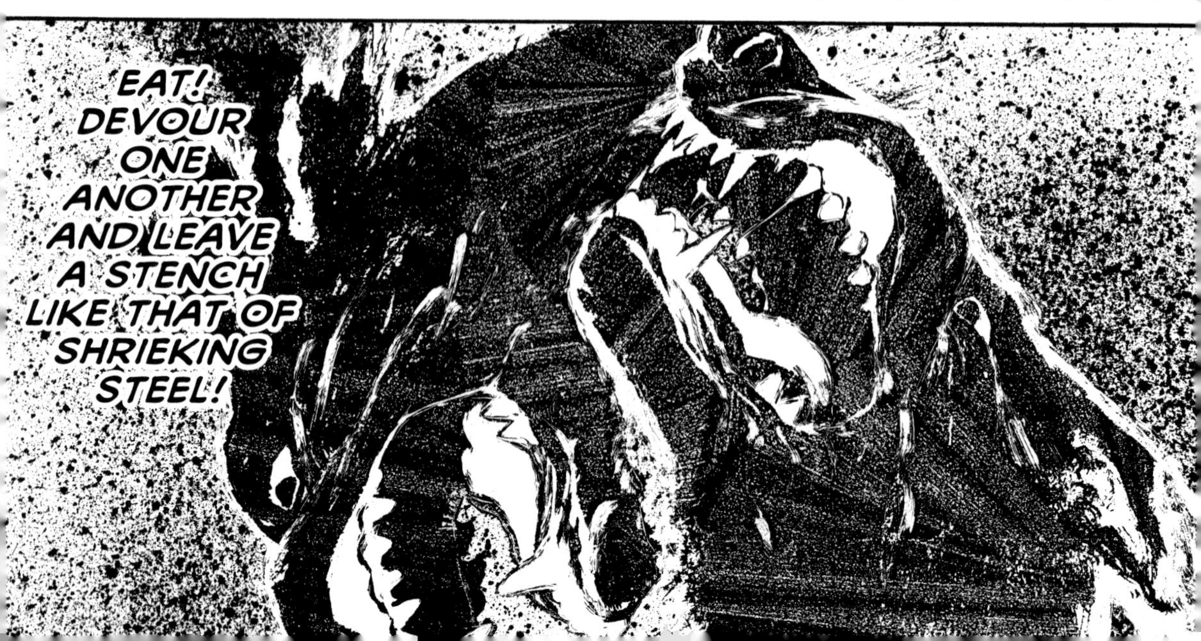
EAT! DEVOUR ONE ANOTHER AND LEAVE A STENCH LIKE THAT OF SHRIEKING STEEL!

100,000 LITERS OF PRIMAL RAGE, FILLING THE ARENA.

OOOHH

DOPA-MINE.

KE-KEH!

INDULGE YOUR APPETITE.

GEK!

KEH!

I...REMEMBER...

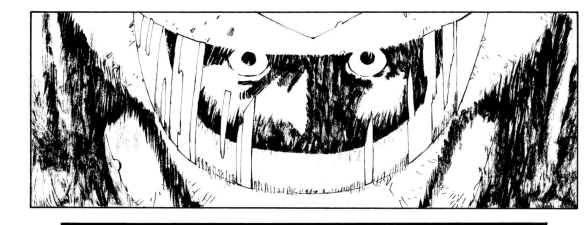

I...REMEMBER...NOW...

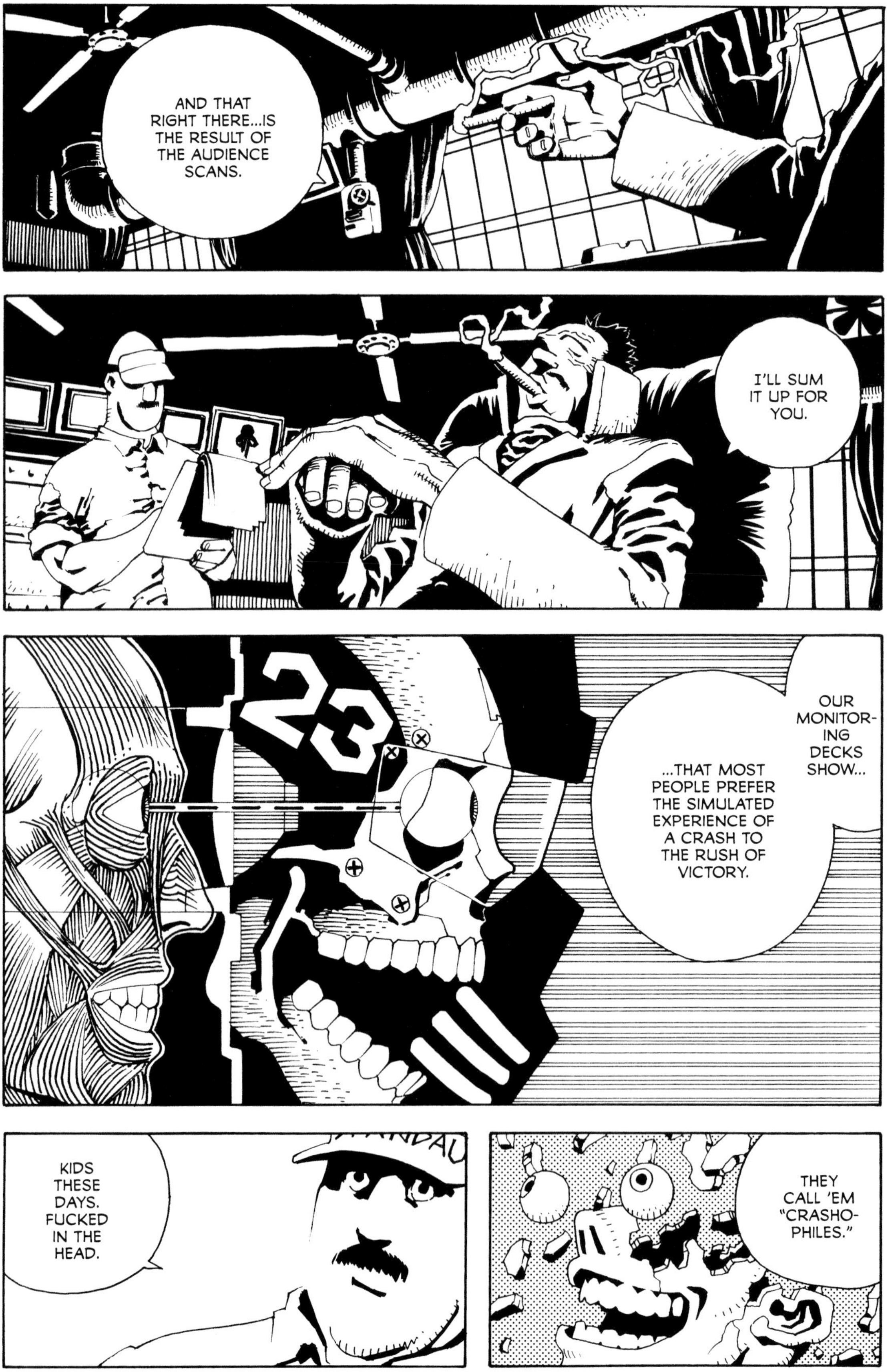
AND THAT RIGHT THERE...IS THE RESULT OF THE AUDIENCE SCANS.
I'LL SUM IT UP FOR YOU.
OUR MONITOR-ING DECKS SHOW...
...THAT MOST PEOPLE PREFER THE SIMULATED EXPERIENCE OF A CRASH TO THE RUSH OF VICTORY.
23
THEY CALL 'EM "CRASHO-PHILES."
KIDS THESE DAYS. FUCKED IN THE HEAD.

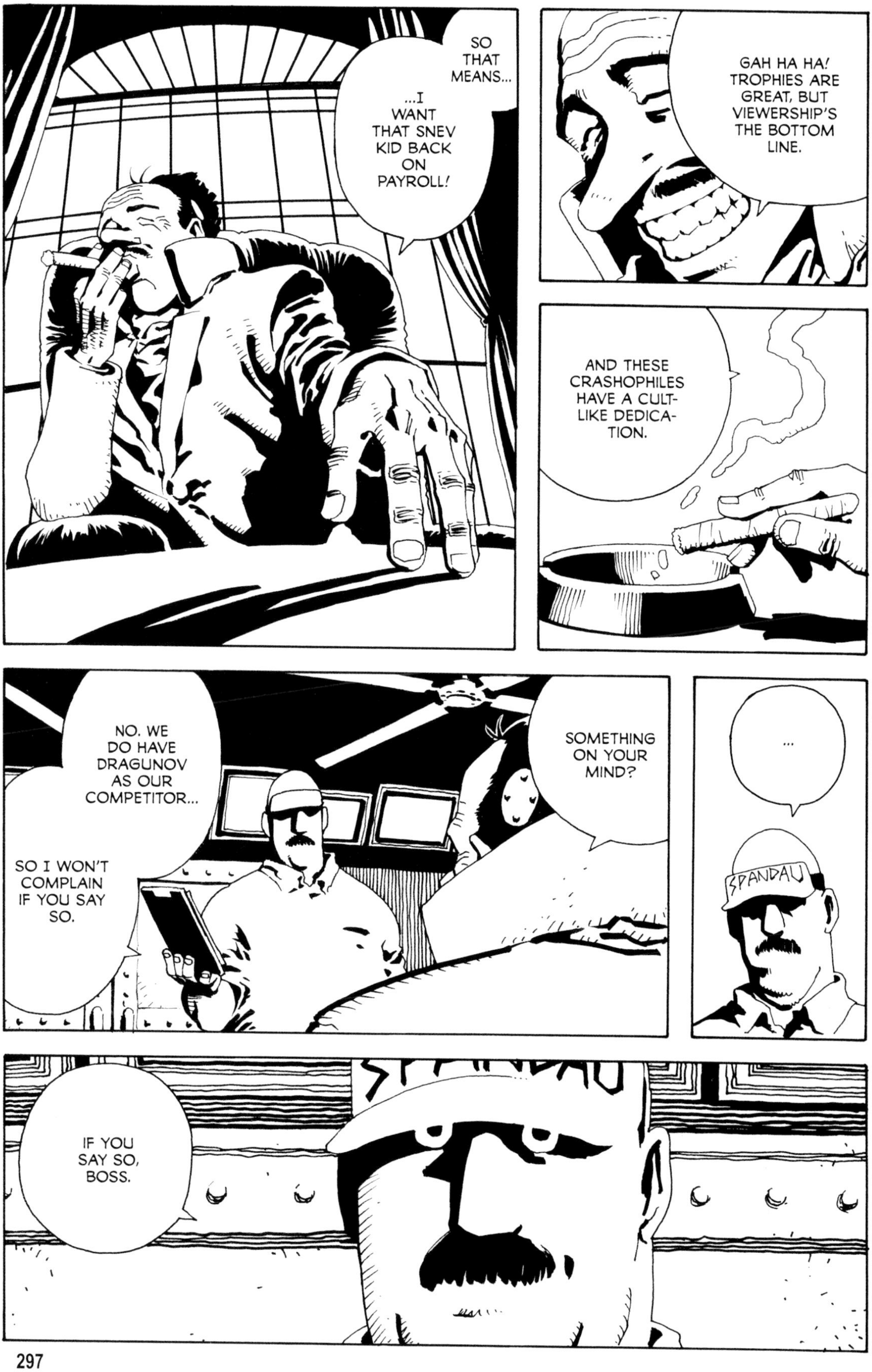
GAH HA HA! TROPHIES ARE GREAT, BUT VIEWERSHIP'S THE BOTTOM LINE.
AND THESE CRASHOPHILES HAVE A CULT-LIKE DEDICATION.
SO THAT MEANS...
...I WANT THAT SNEV KID BACK ON PAYROLL!
...
SPANDAU
SOMETHING ON YOUR MIND?
NO. WE DO HAVE DRAGUNOV AS OUR COMPETITOR...
SO I WON'T COMPLAIN IF YOU SAY SO.
IF YOU SAY SO, BOSS.

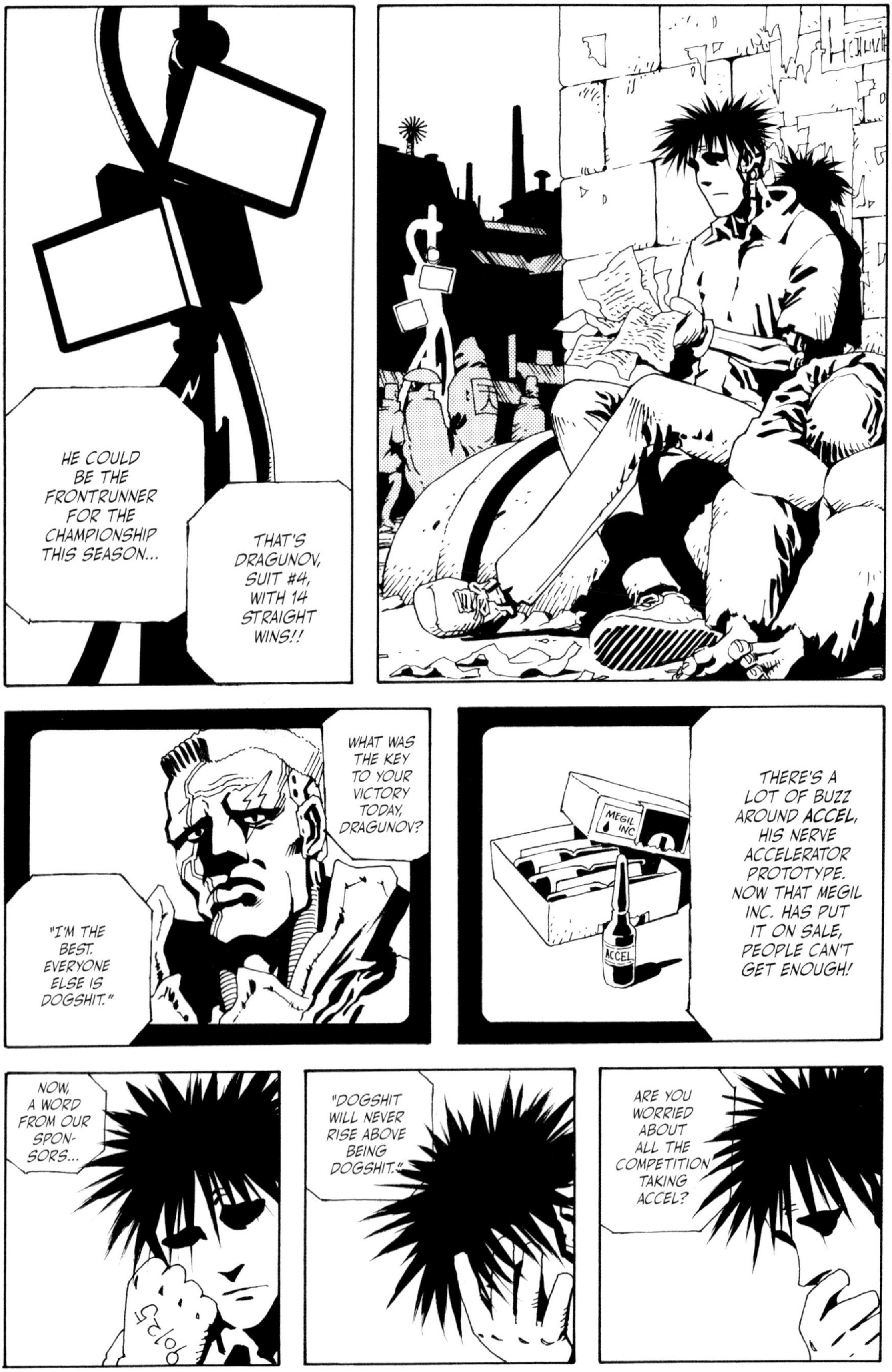
THAT'S DRAGUNOV, SUIT #4, WITH 14 STRAIGHT WINS!!
HE COULD BE THE FRONTRUNNER FOR THE CHAMPIONSHIP THIS SEASON...
THERE'S A LOT OF BUZZ AROUND ACCEL, HIS NERVE ACCELERATOR PROTOTYPE. NOW THAT MEGIL INC. HAS PUT IT ON SALE, PEOPLE CAN'T GET ENOUGH!
MEGIL INC
ACCEL
WHAT WAS THE KEY TO YOUR VICTORY TODAY, DRAGUNOV?
"I'M THE BEST. EVERYONE ELSE IS DOGSHIT."
ARE YOU WORRIED ABOUT ALL THE COMPETITION TAKING ACCEL?
"DOGSHIT WILL NEVER RISE ABOVE BEING DOGSHIT."
NOW, A WORD FROM OUR SPON-SORS...

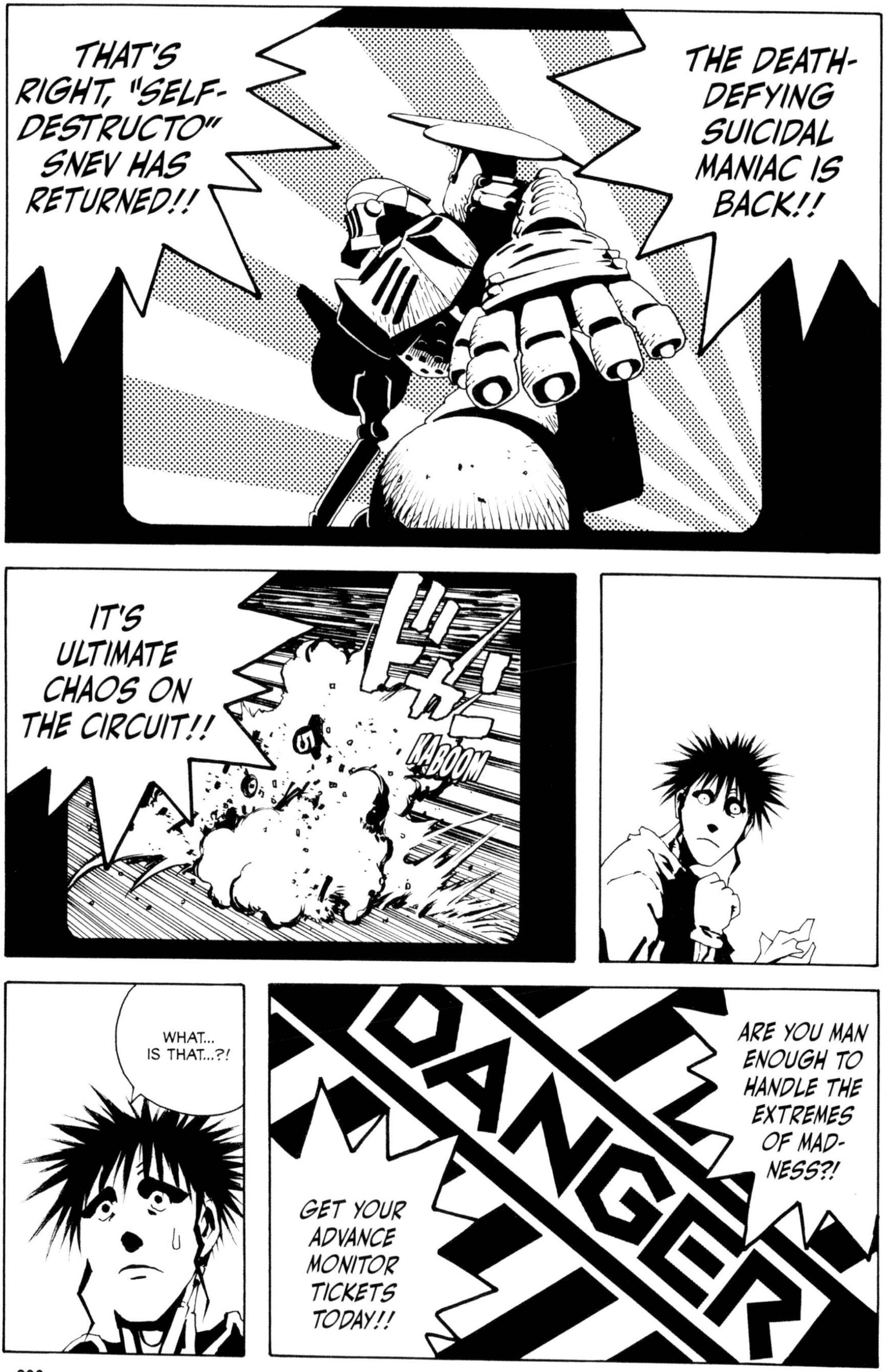
THE DEATH-DEFYING SUICIDAL MANIAC IS BACK!!
THAT'S RIGHT, "SELF-DESTRUCTO" SNEV HAS RETURNED!!
IT'S ULTIMATE CHAOS ON THE CIRCUIT!!
KABOOM
DANGER
ARE YOU MAN ENOUGH TO HANDLE THE EXTREMES OF MAD-NESS?!
GET YOUR ADVANCE MONITOR TICKETS TODAY!!
WHAT... IS THAT...?!

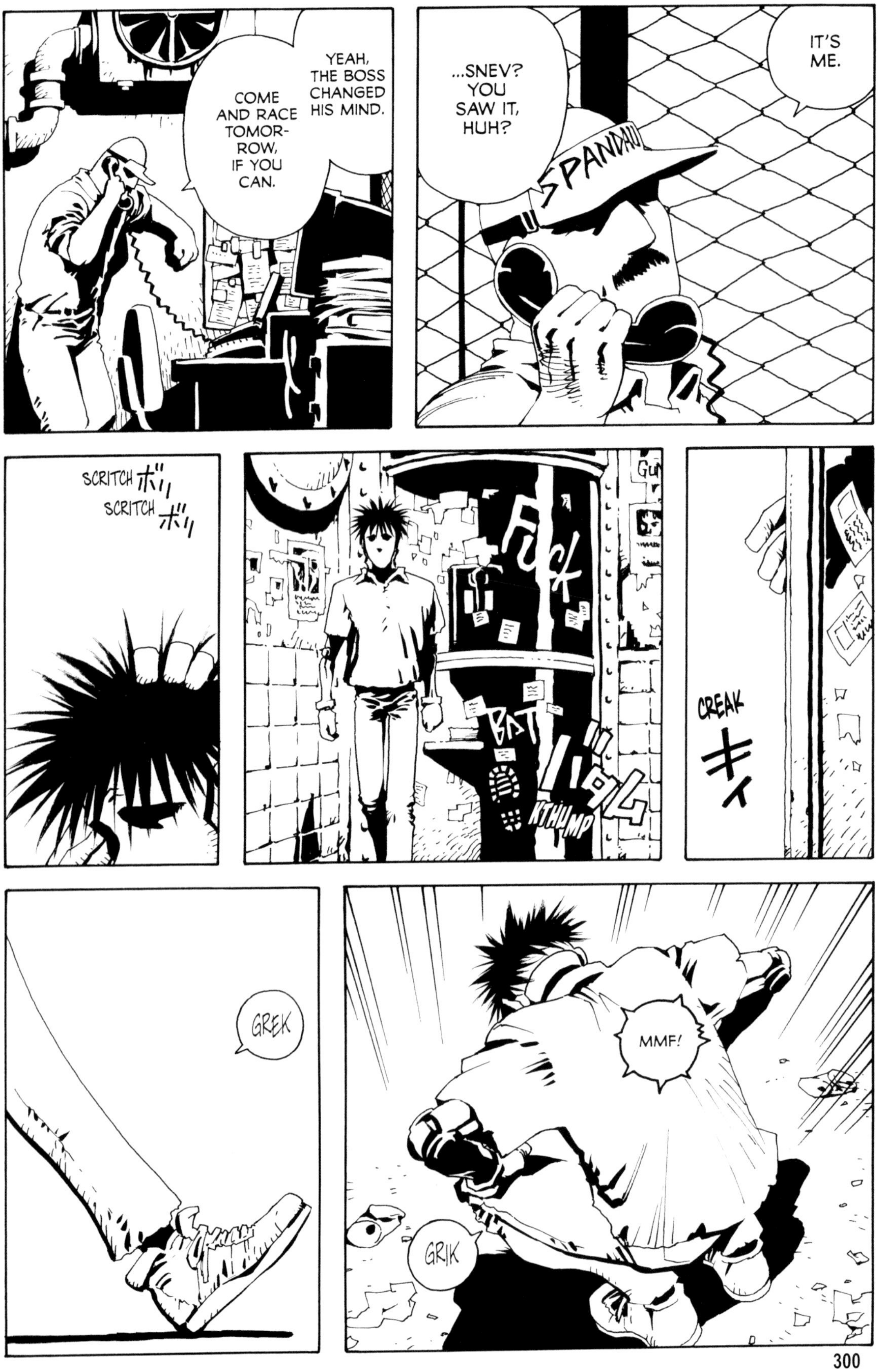
IT'S ME.
...SNEV? YOU SAW IT, HUH?
SPANDAU
YEAH, THE BOSS CHANGED HIS MIND.
COME AND RACE TOMOR-ROW, IF YOU CAN.
CREAK キィ
BAT バタム KTHUMP
SCRITCH ボリ
SCRITCH ボリ
MMF!
GRIK
GREK

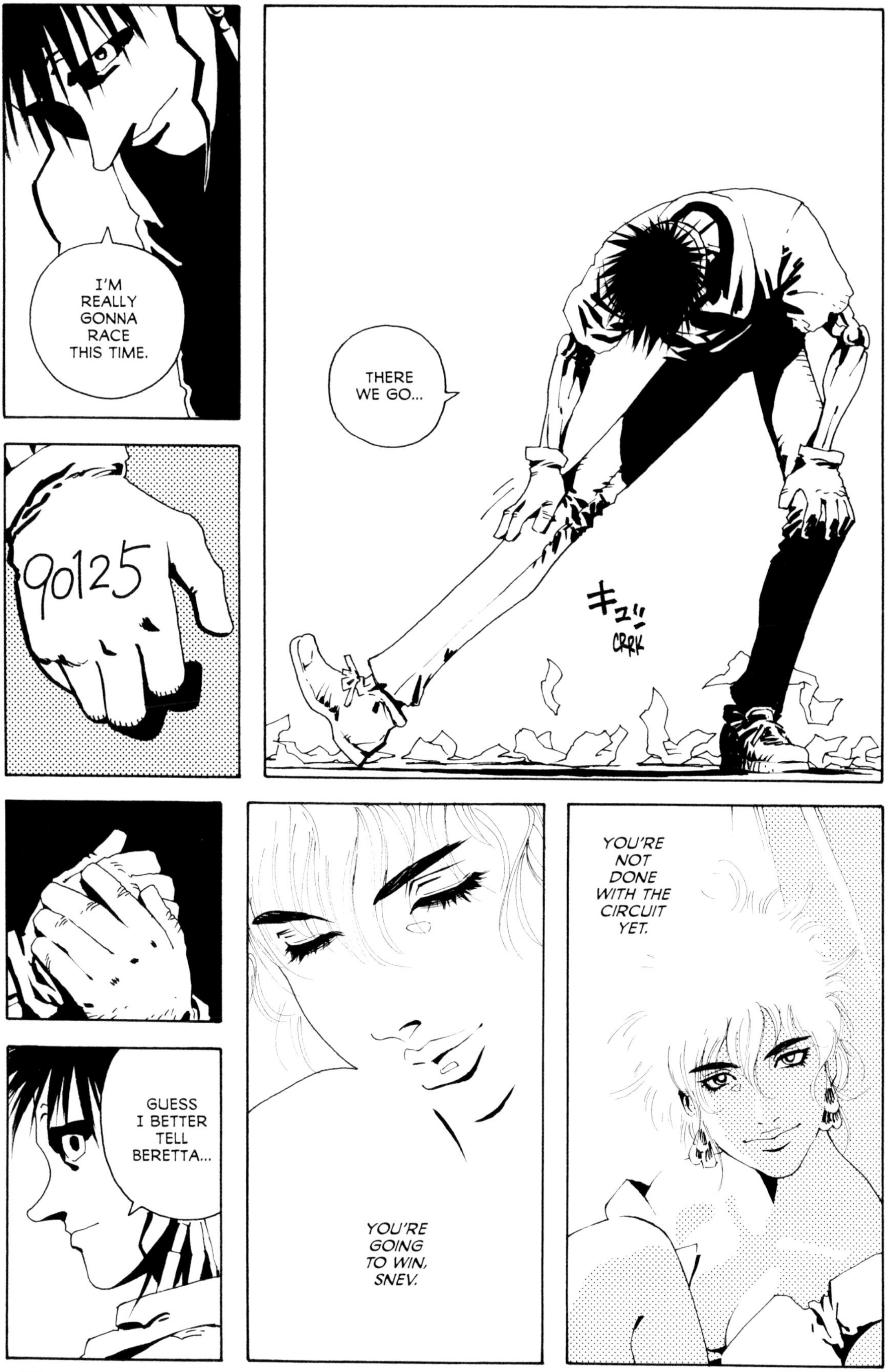
THERE WE GO...
キュッ
CRRK
I'M REALLY GONNA RACE THIS TIME.
90125
YOU'RE NOT DONE WITH THE CIRCUIT YET.
YOU'RE GOING TO WIN, SNEV.
GUESS I BETTER TELL BERETTA...

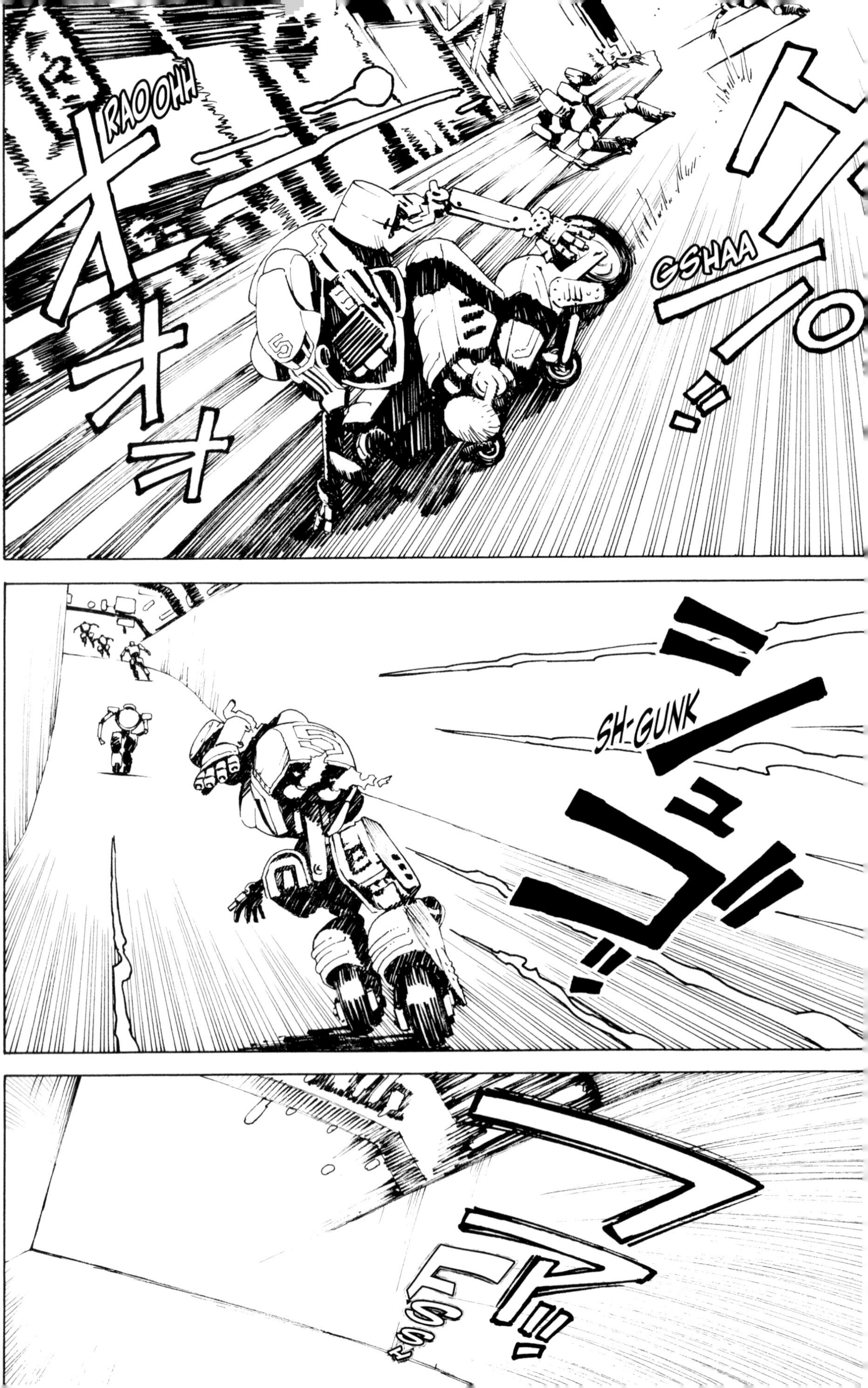
GSHAA
RAOOHH
SH-GUNK

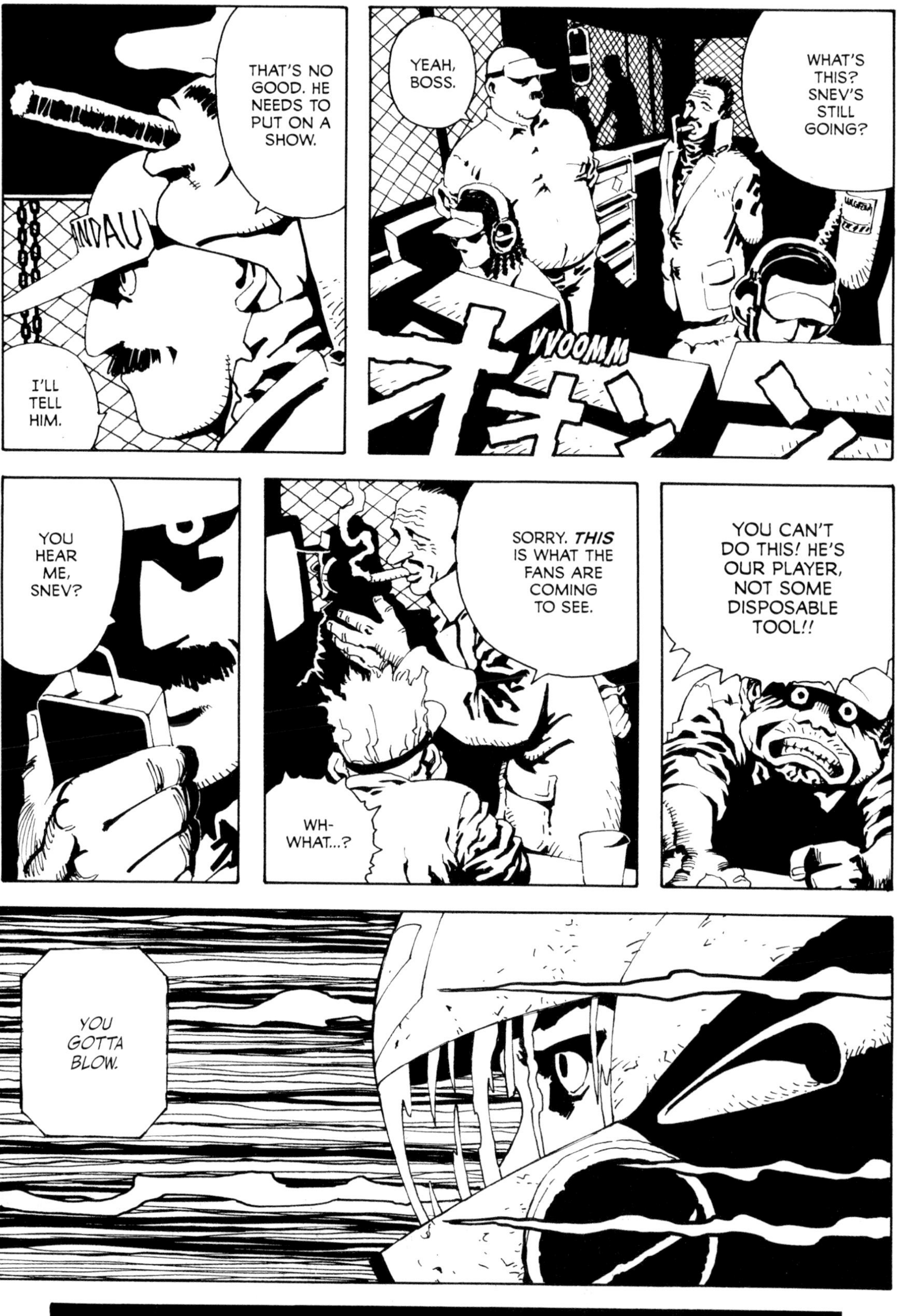
WHAT'S THIS? SNEV'S STILL GOING?
YEAH, BOSS.
VVOOMM
THAT'S NO GOOD. HE NEEDS TO PUT ON A SHOW.
I'LL TELL HIM.
YOU CAN'T DO THIS! HE'S OUR PLAYER, NOT SOME DISPOSABLE TOOL!!
SORRY. *THIS* IS WHAT THE FANS ARE COMING TO SEE.
WH- WHAT...?
YOU HEAR ME, SNEV?
YOU GOTTA BLOW.
I...REMEMBER...NOW...

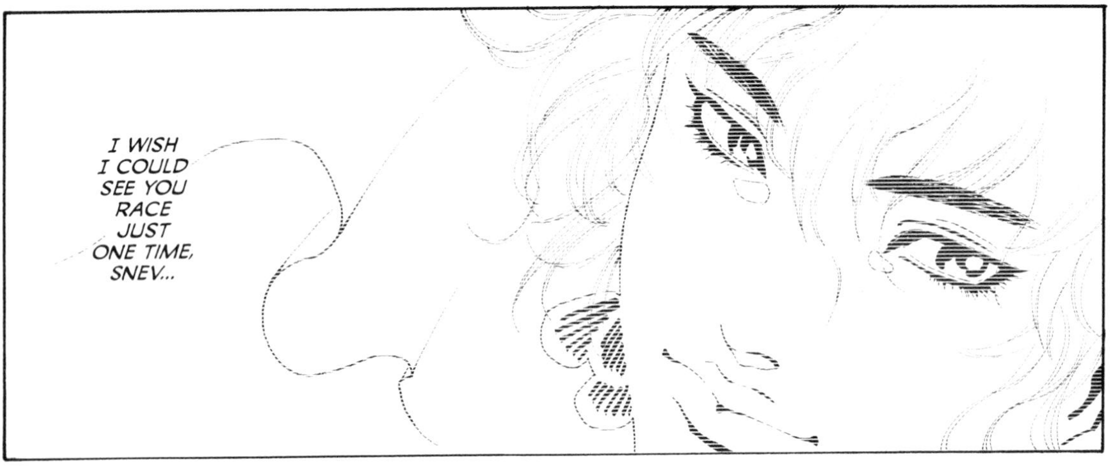
I WISH I COULD SEE YOU RACE JUST ONE TIME, SNEV...

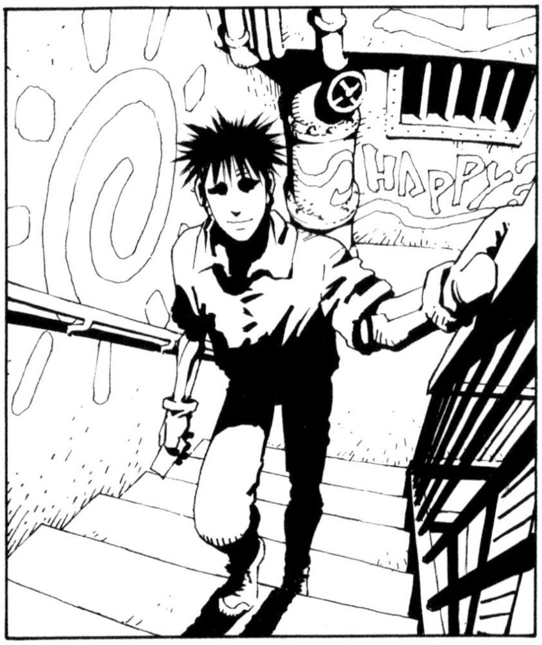

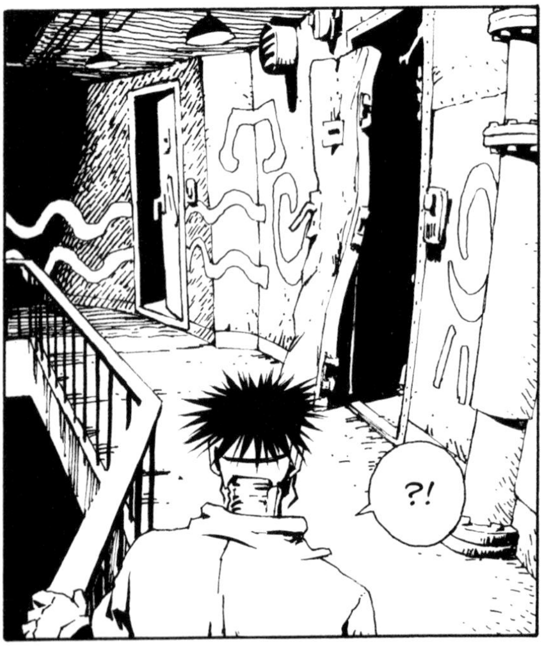
?!

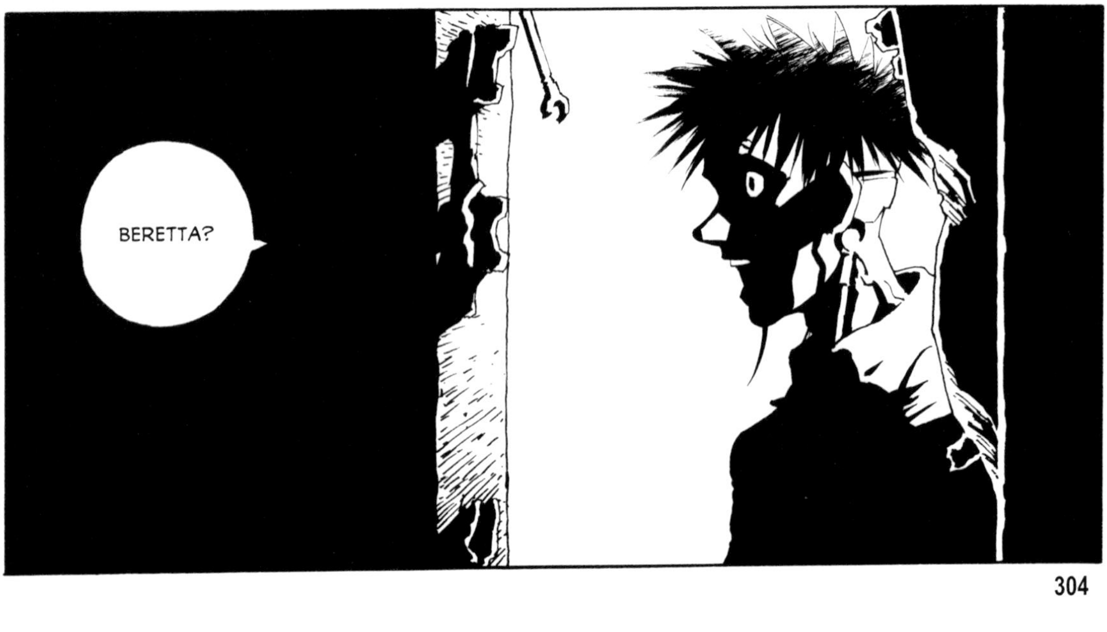
BERETTA?

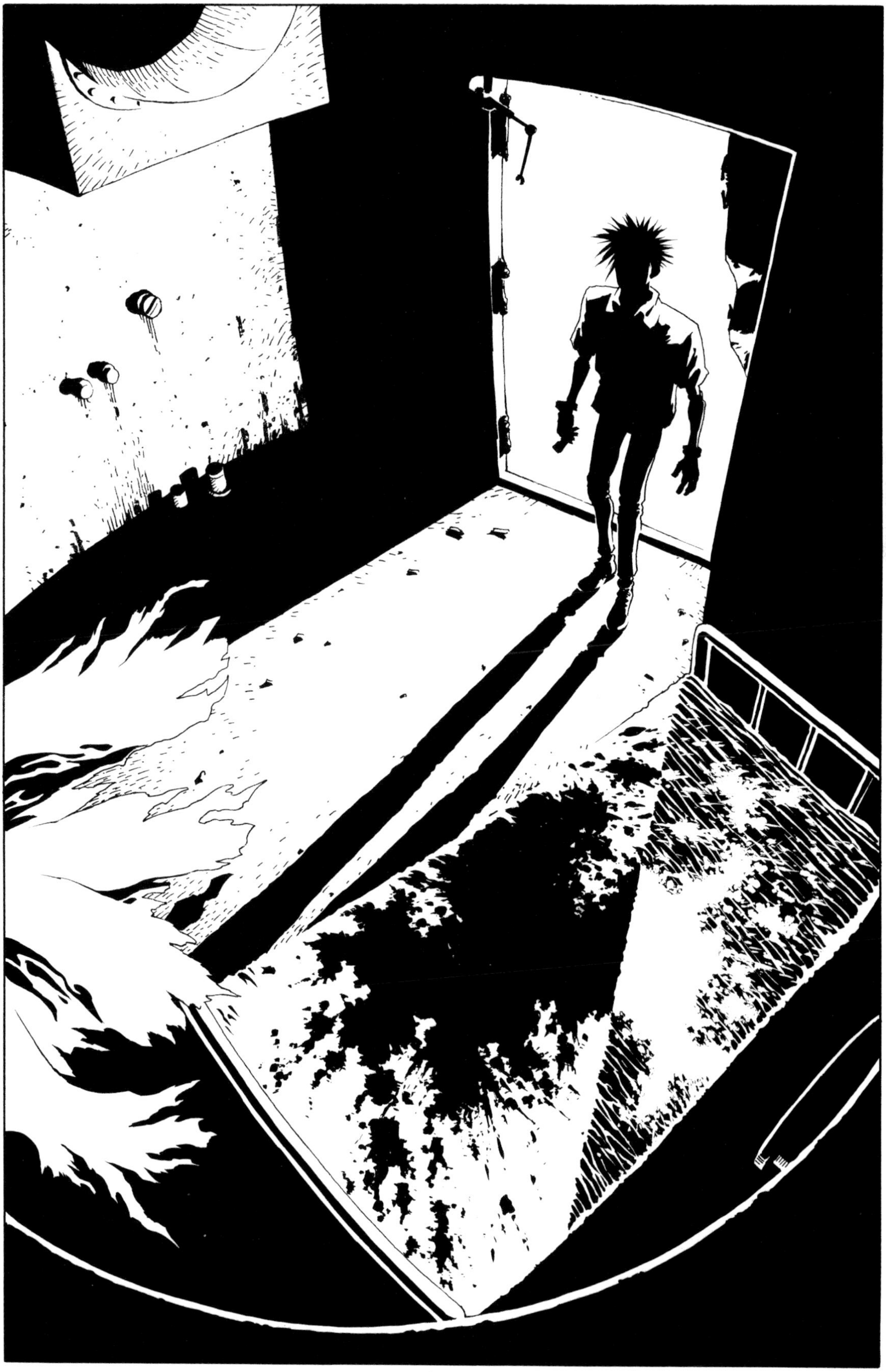

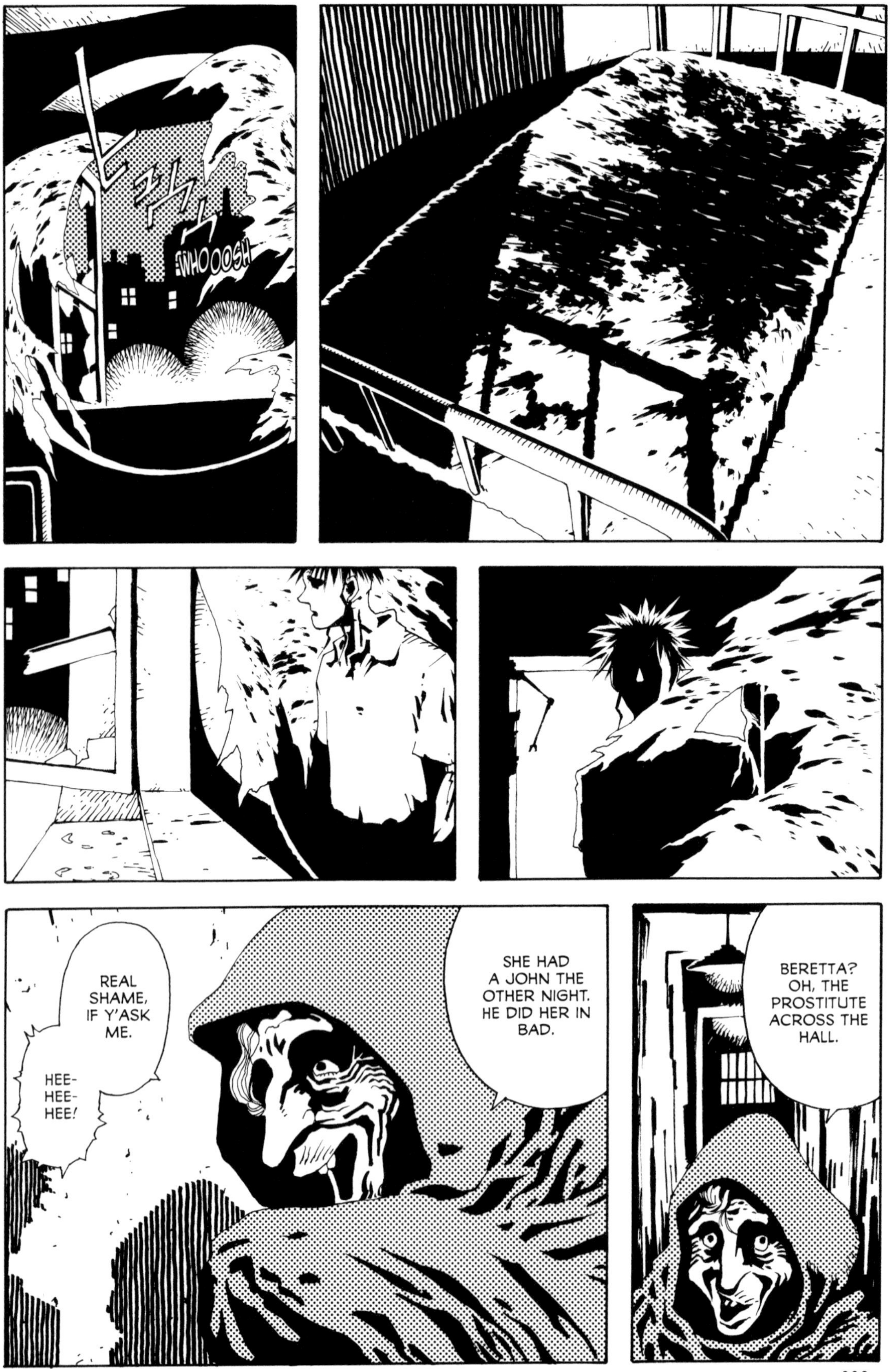
WHOOOSH
BERETTA? OH, THE PROSTITUTE ACROSS THE HALL.
SHE HAD A JOHN THE OTHER NIGHT. HE DID HER IN BAD.
REAL SHAME, IF Y'ASK ME.
HEE-HEE-HEE!

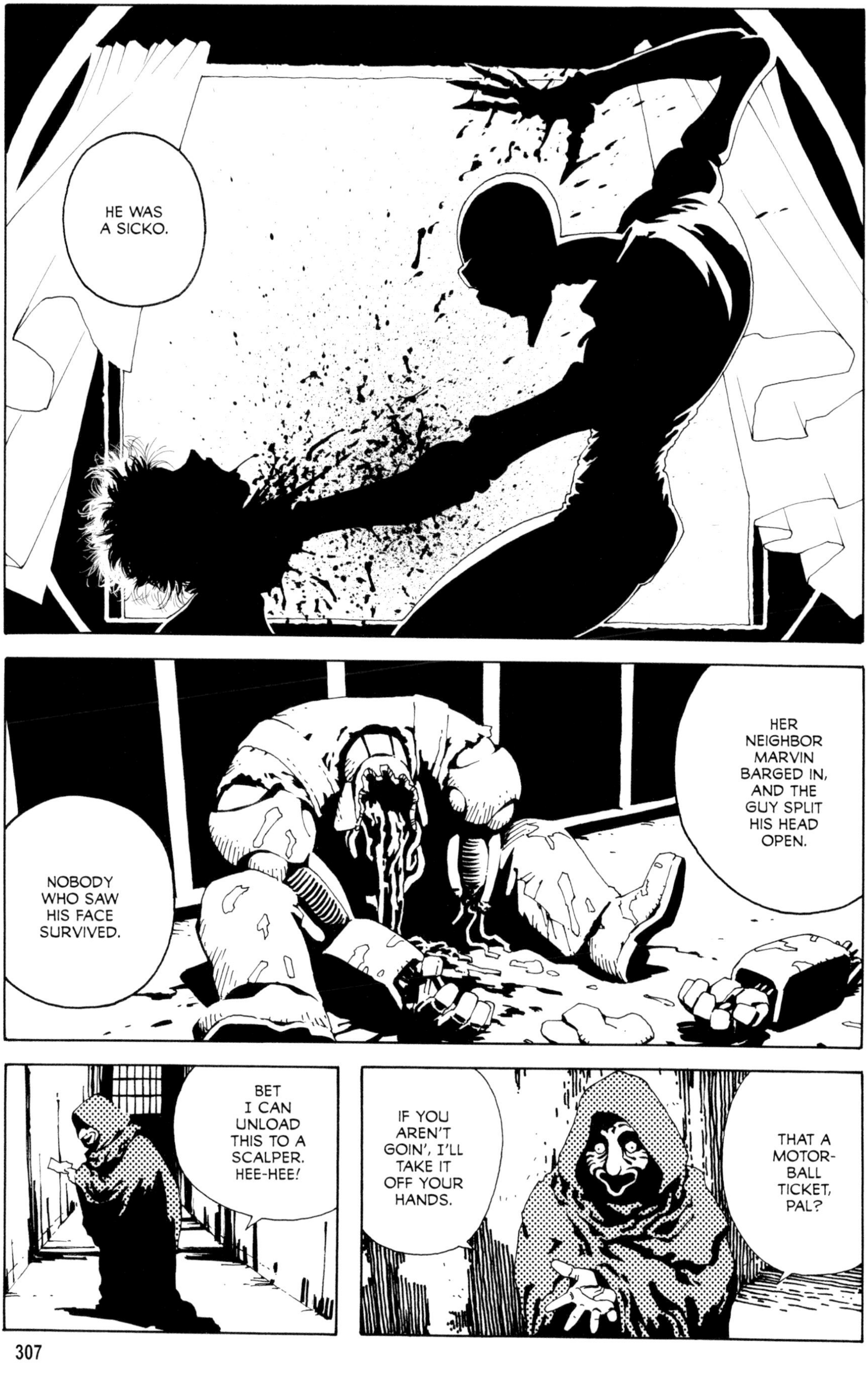
HE WAS A SICKO.
HER NEIGHBOR MARVIN BARGED IN, AND THE GUY SPLIT HIS HEAD OPEN.
NOBODY WHO SAW HIS FACE SURVIVED.
THAT A MOTOR-BALL TICKET, PAL?
IF YOU AREN'T GOIN', I'LL TAKE IT OFF YOUR HANDS.
BET I CAN UNLOAD THIS TO A SCALPER. HEE-HEE!

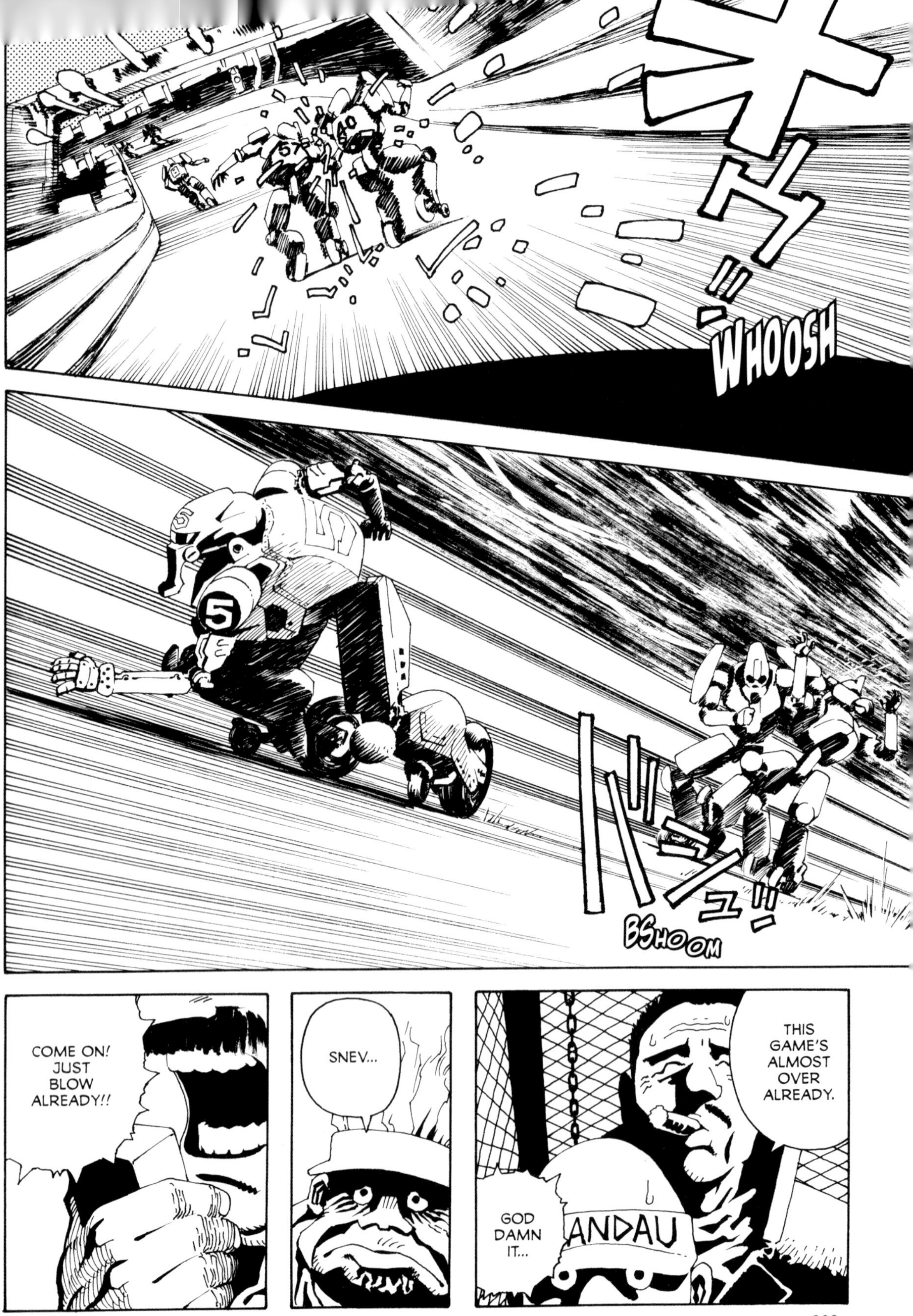
WHOOSH
BSHOOM
THIS GAME'S ALMOST OVER ALREADY.
ANDAU
GOD DAMN IT...
SNEV...
COME ON! JUST BLOW ALREADY!!

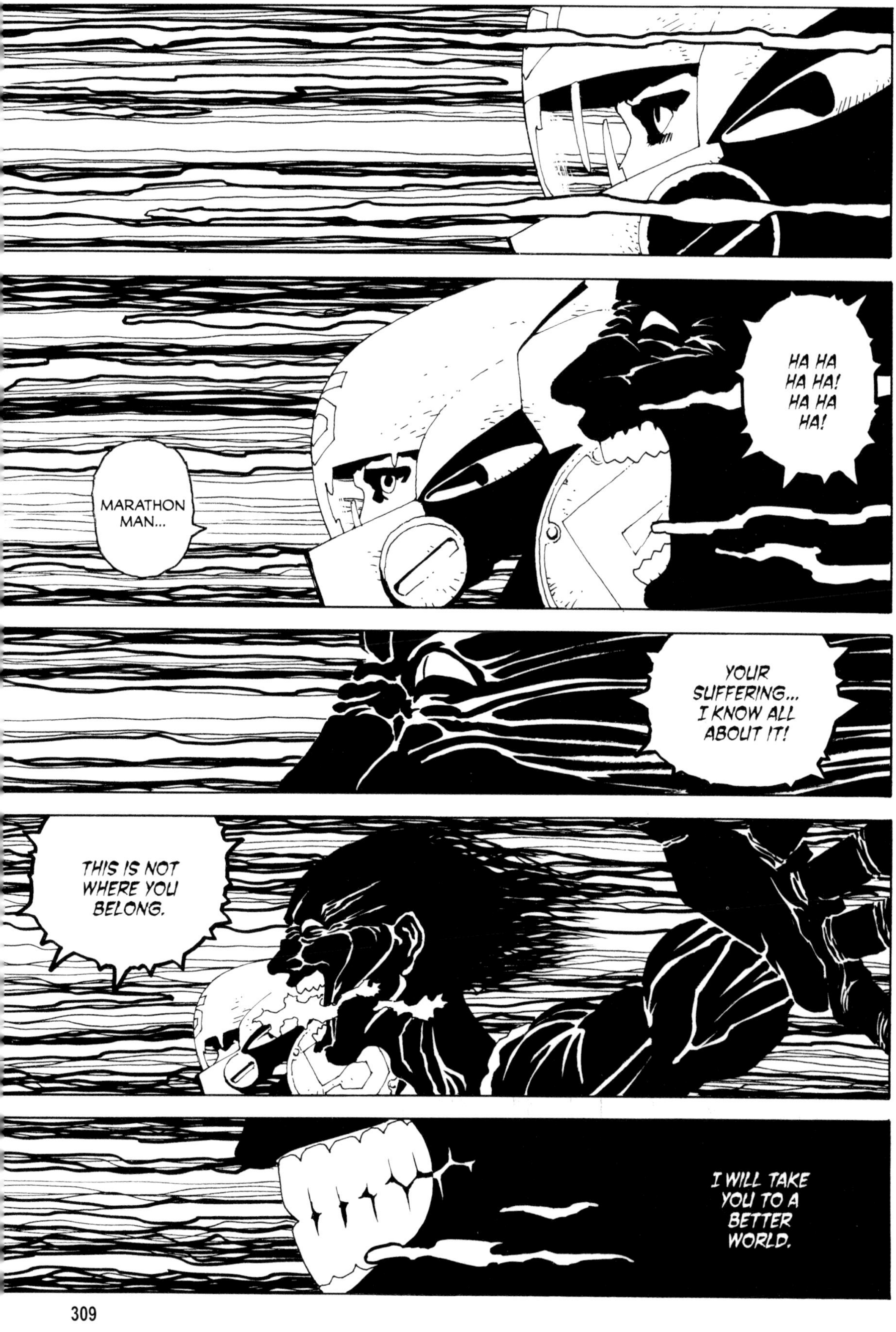
HA HA HA HA! HA HA HA!
MARATHON MAN...
YOUR SUFFERING... I KNOW ALL ABOUT IT!
THIS IS NOT WHERE YOU BELONG.
I WILL TAKE YOU TO A BETTER WORLD.

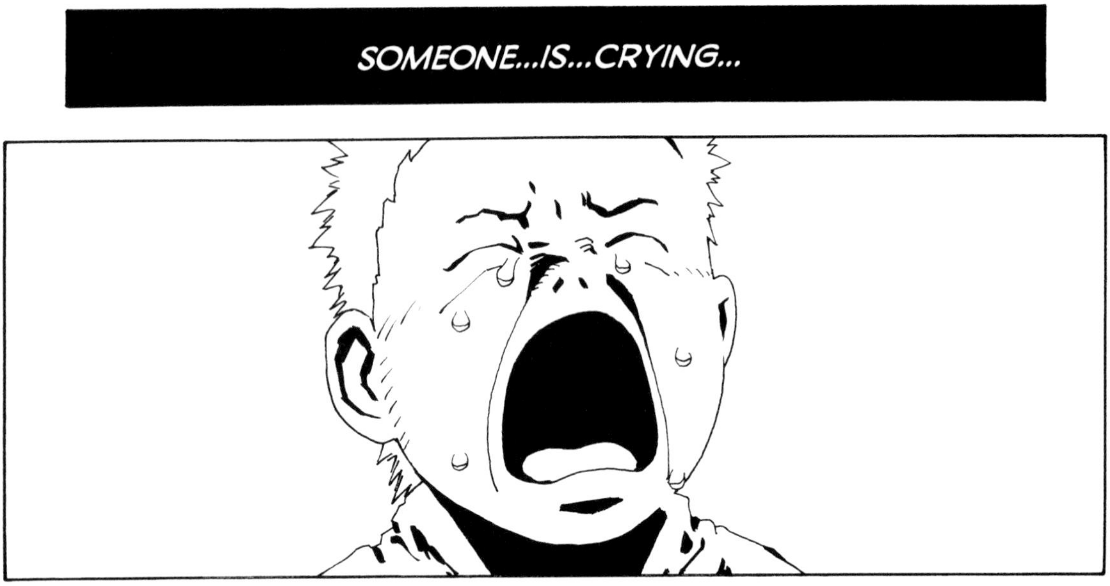
SOMEONE...IS...CRYING...

Signs: Megil Inc., Organ Resale, Flesh Augmentation

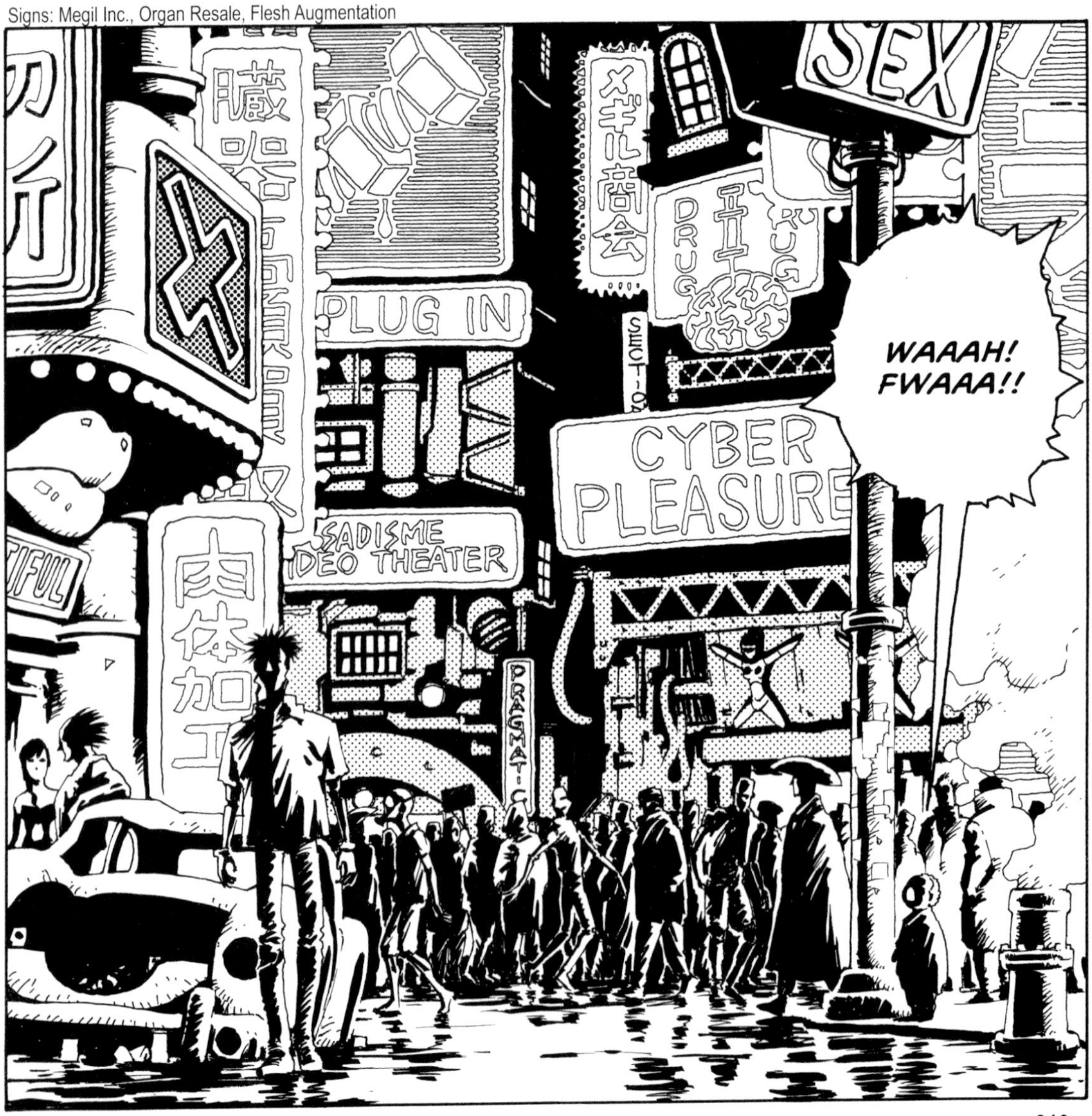
WAAAH! FWAAA!!
SEX
メギル商会
DRUG
PLUG IN
CYBER PLEASURE
SADISME
肉体加工

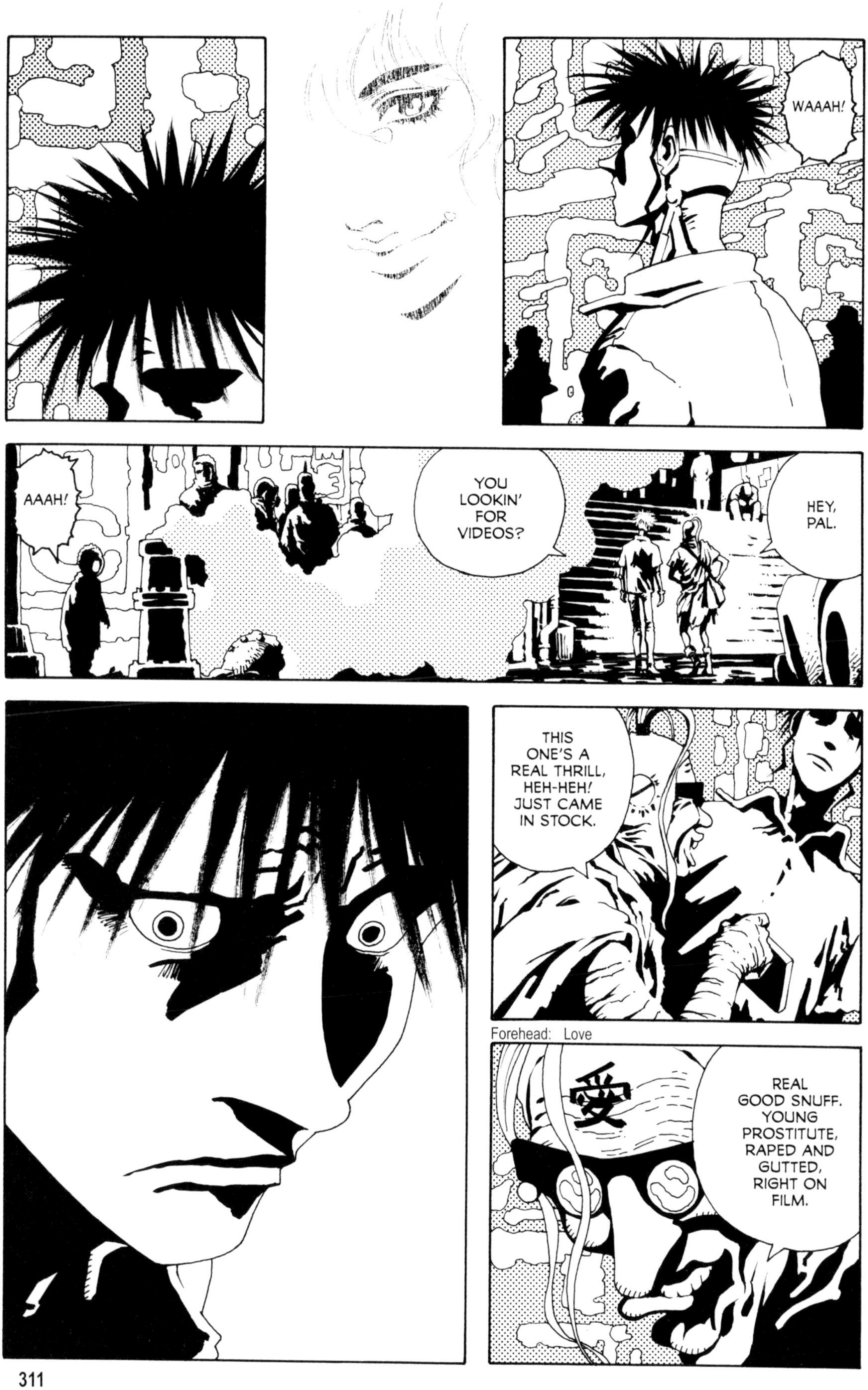
WAAAH!
HEY, PAL.
YOU LOOKIN' FOR VIDEOS?
AAAH!
THIS ONE'S A REAL THRILL, HEH-HEH! JUST CAME IN STOCK.
Forehead: Love
REAL GOOD SNUFF. YOUNG PROSTITUTE, RAPED AND GUTTED, RIGHT ON FILM.

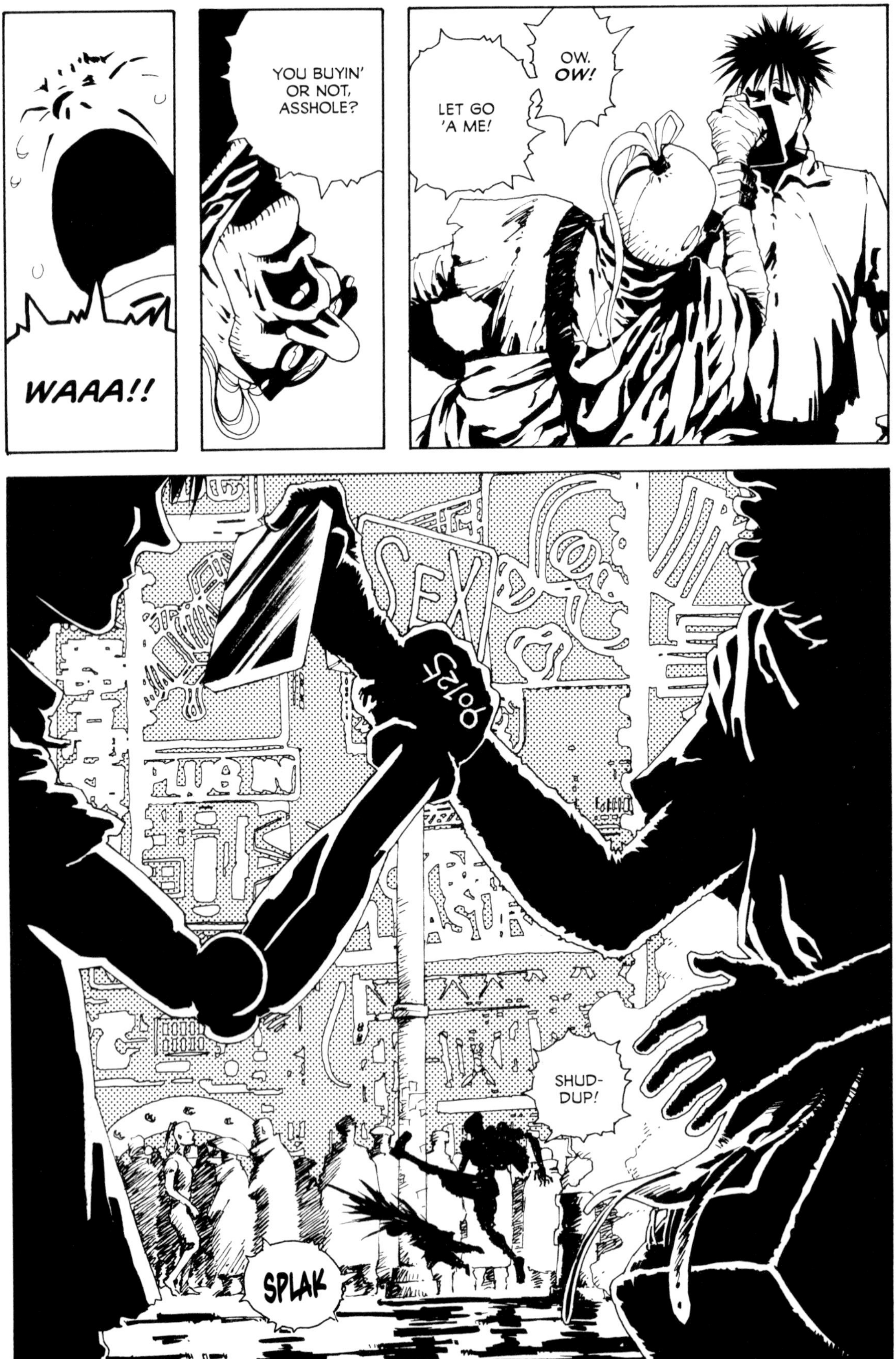
OW. OW!
LET GO 'A ME!
YOU BUYIN' OR NOT, ASSHOLE?
WAAA!!
SEX
SHUD-DUP!
SPLAK

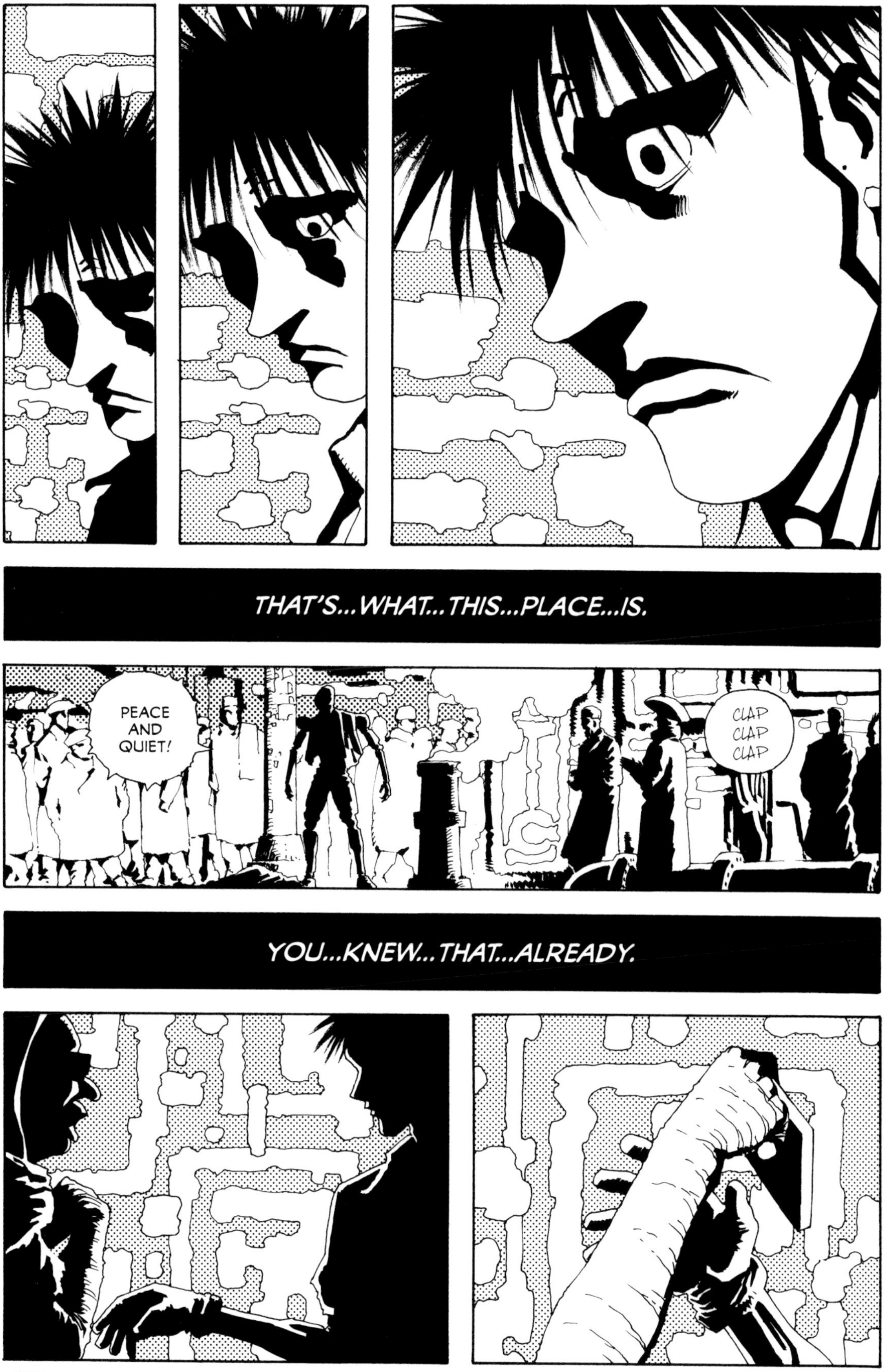
THAT'S...WHAT...THIS...PLACE...IS.
CLAP CLAP CLAP
PEACE AND QUIET!
YOU...KNEW...THAT...ALREADY.

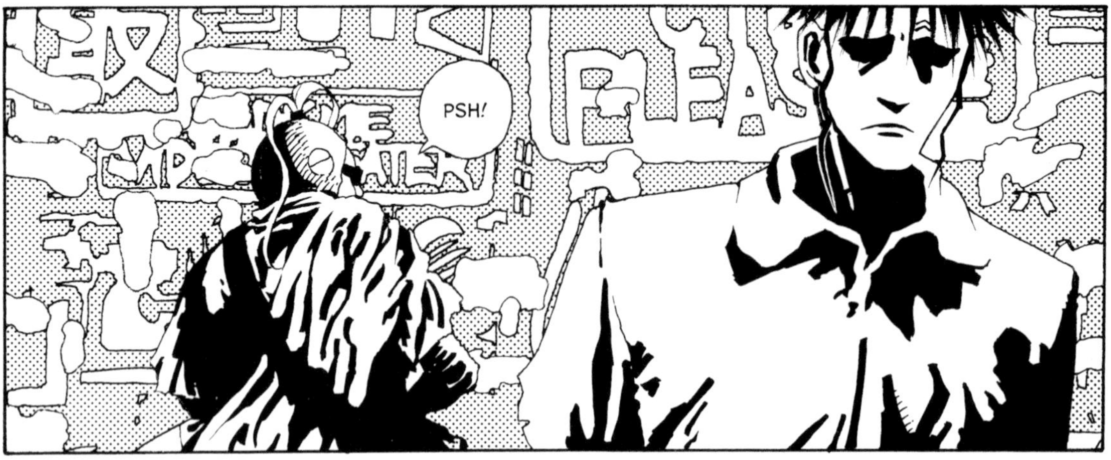
PSH!

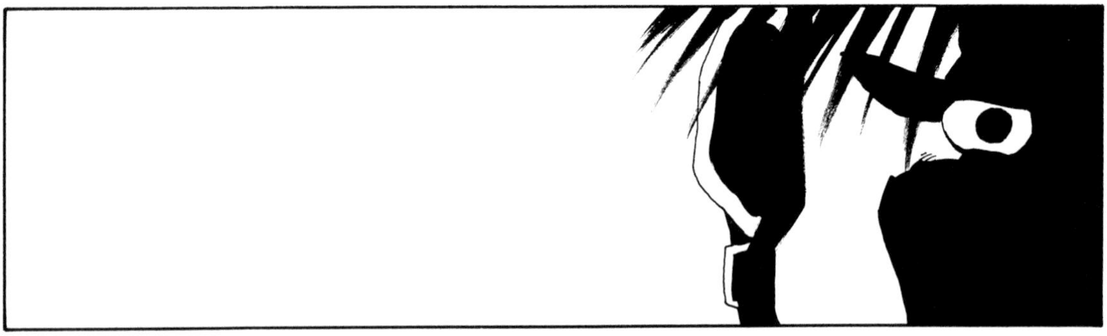

YOU...MUSTN'T...LET...THE...ANGER...SHOW.

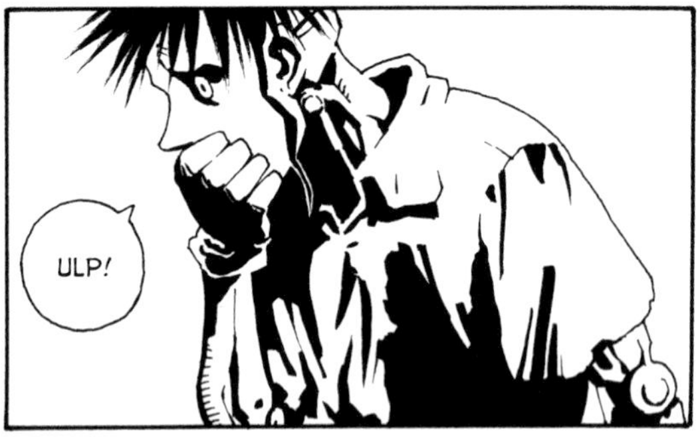
ULP!

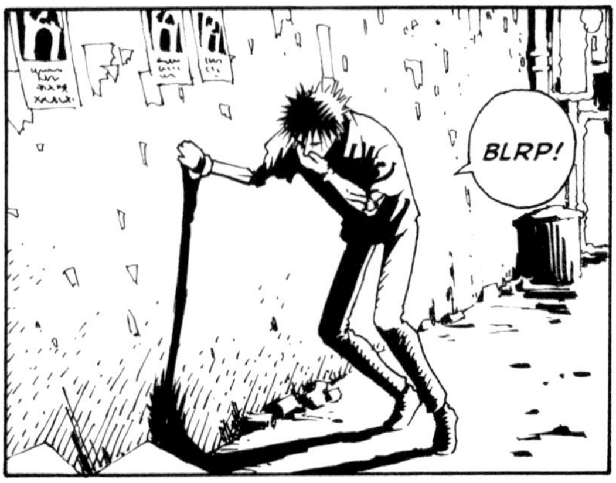
BLRP!

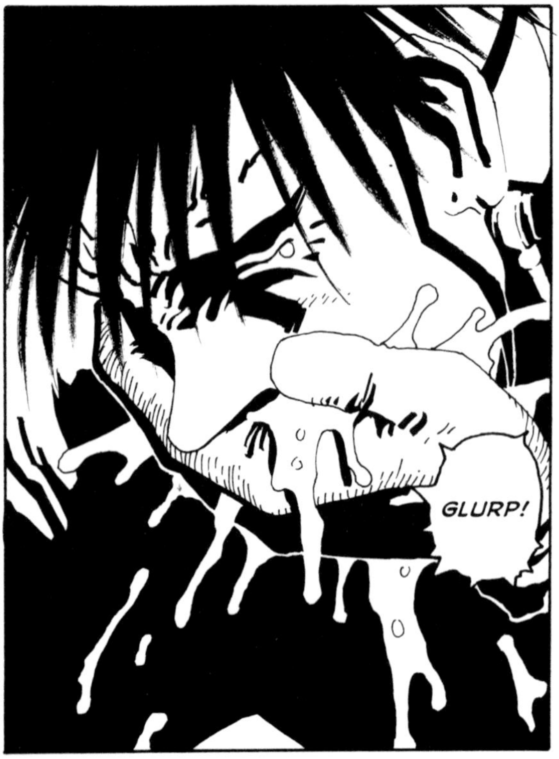
GLURP!

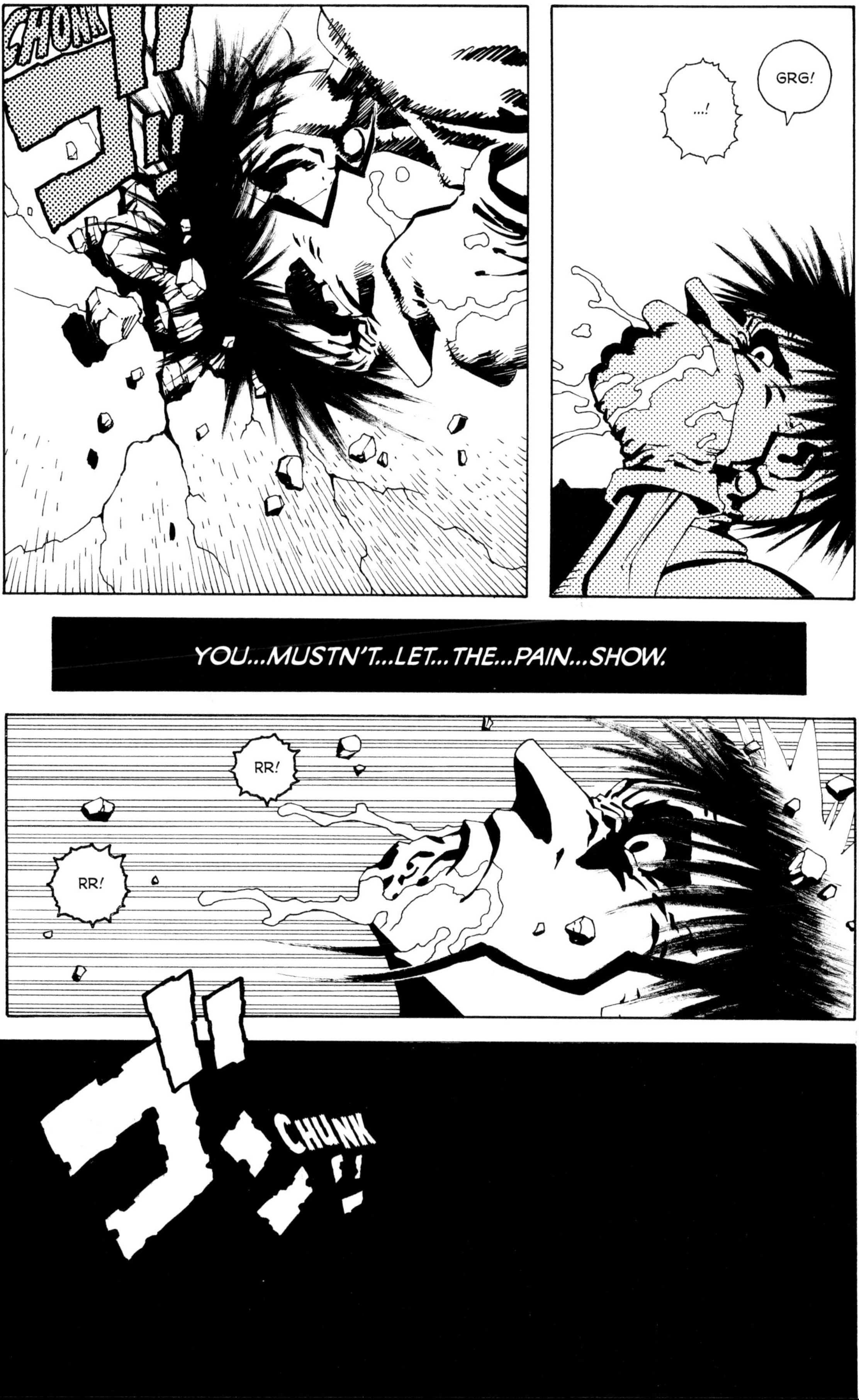
GRG!
...!
YOU...MUSTN'T...LET...THE...PAIN...SHOW.
RR!
RR!
CHUNK!!

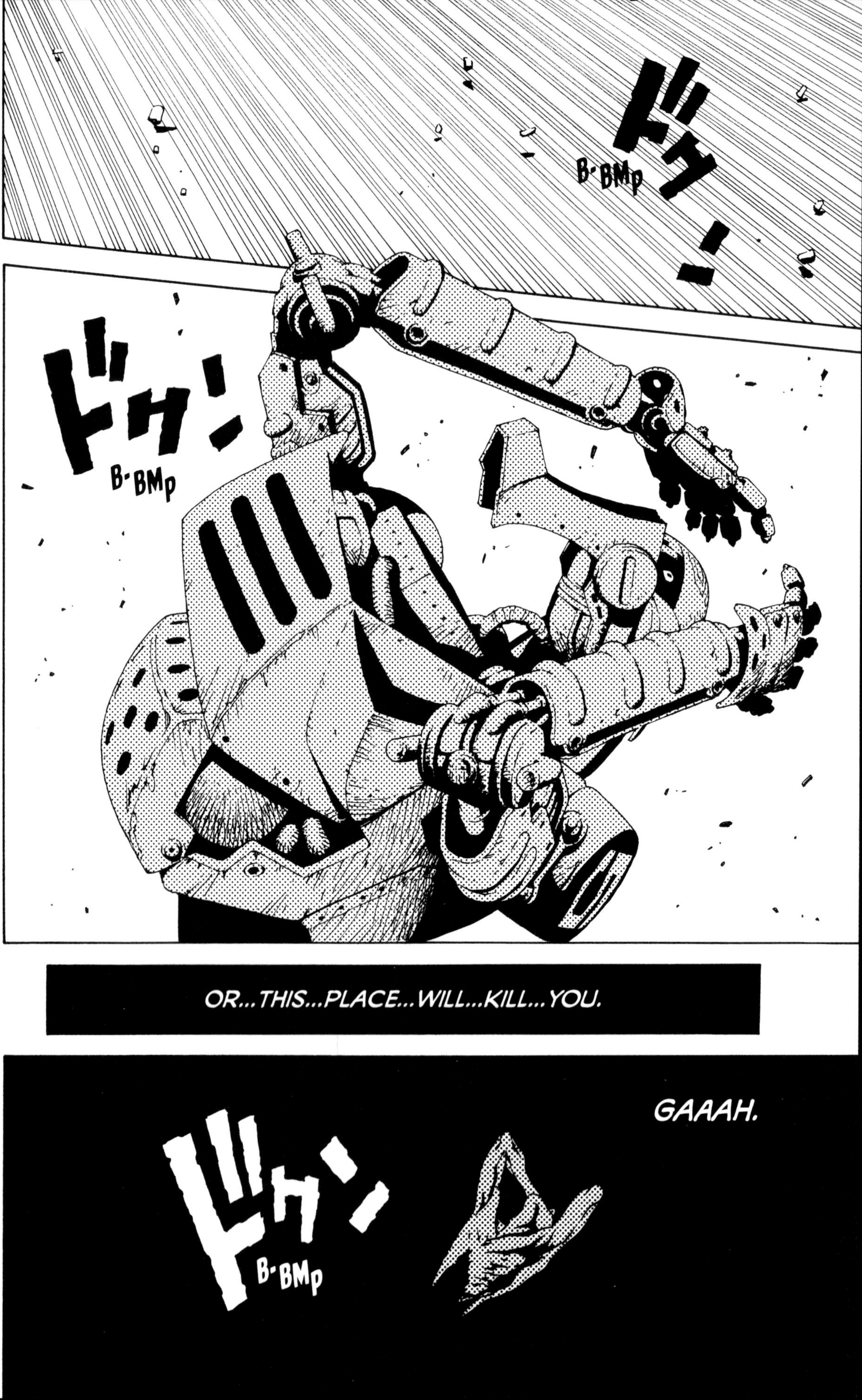
ドクン
B-BMp
ドクン
B-BMp
OR...THIS...PLACE...WILL...KILL...YOU.
GAAAH.
ドクン
B-BMp

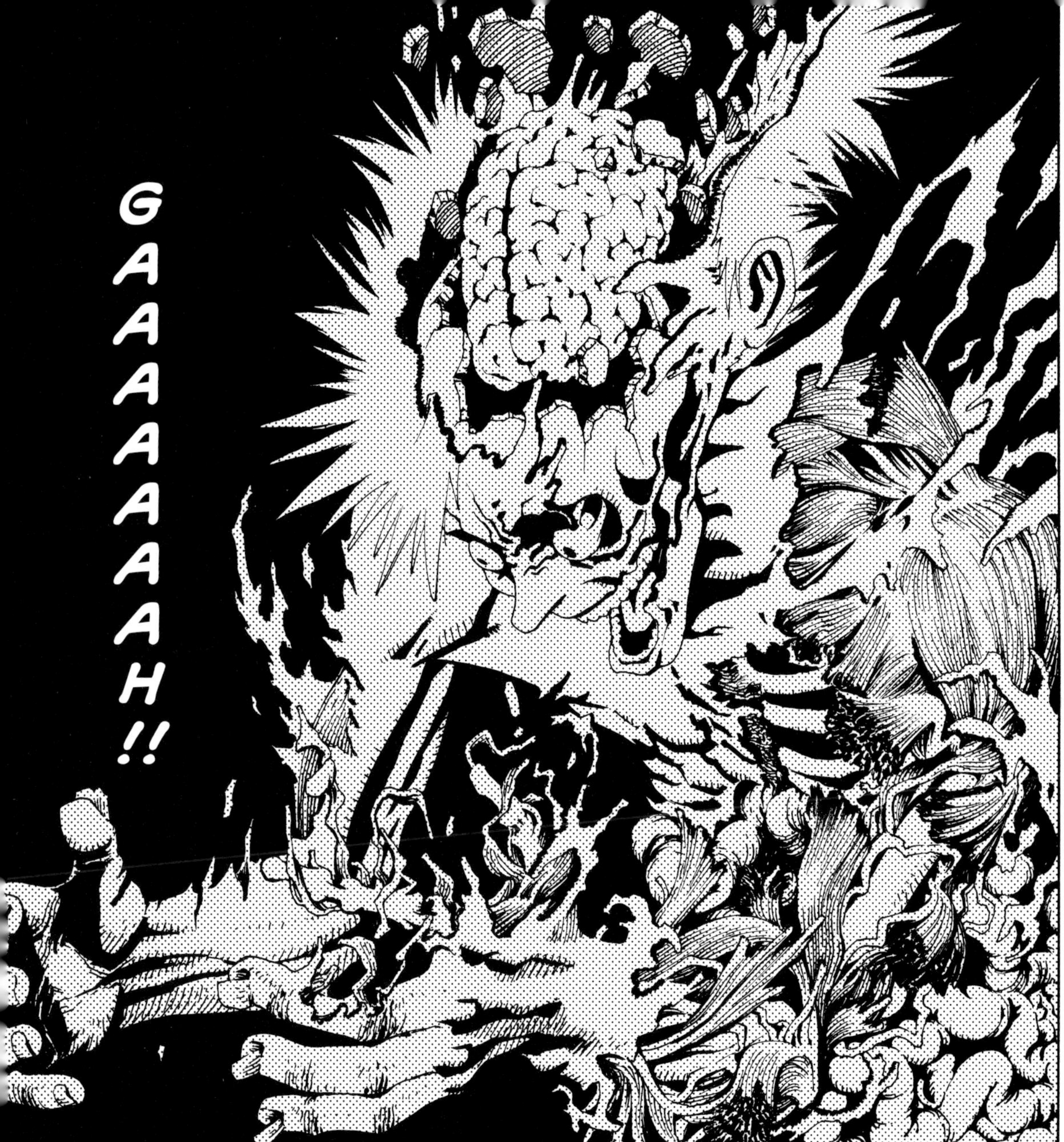
GAAAAAAAAH!!

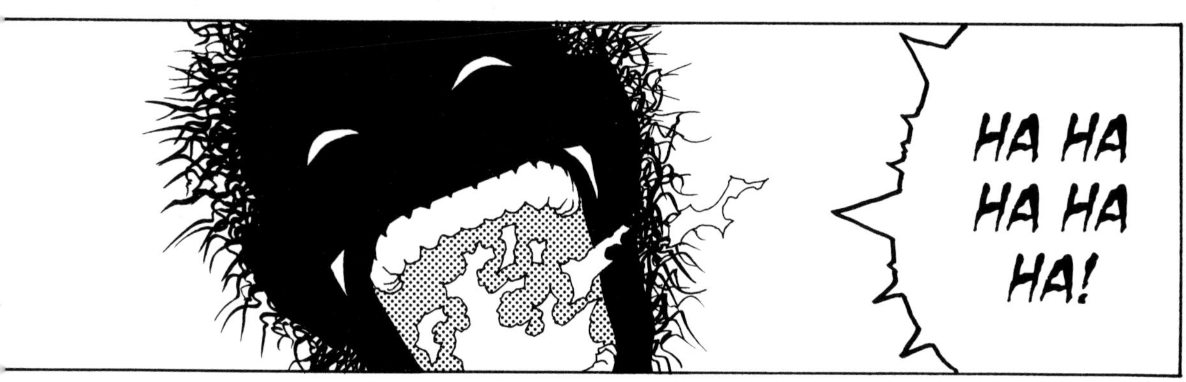
HA HA HA HA HA!

THIS...IS...ALL...I...CAN...DO.

BLOW YOUR- SELF UP

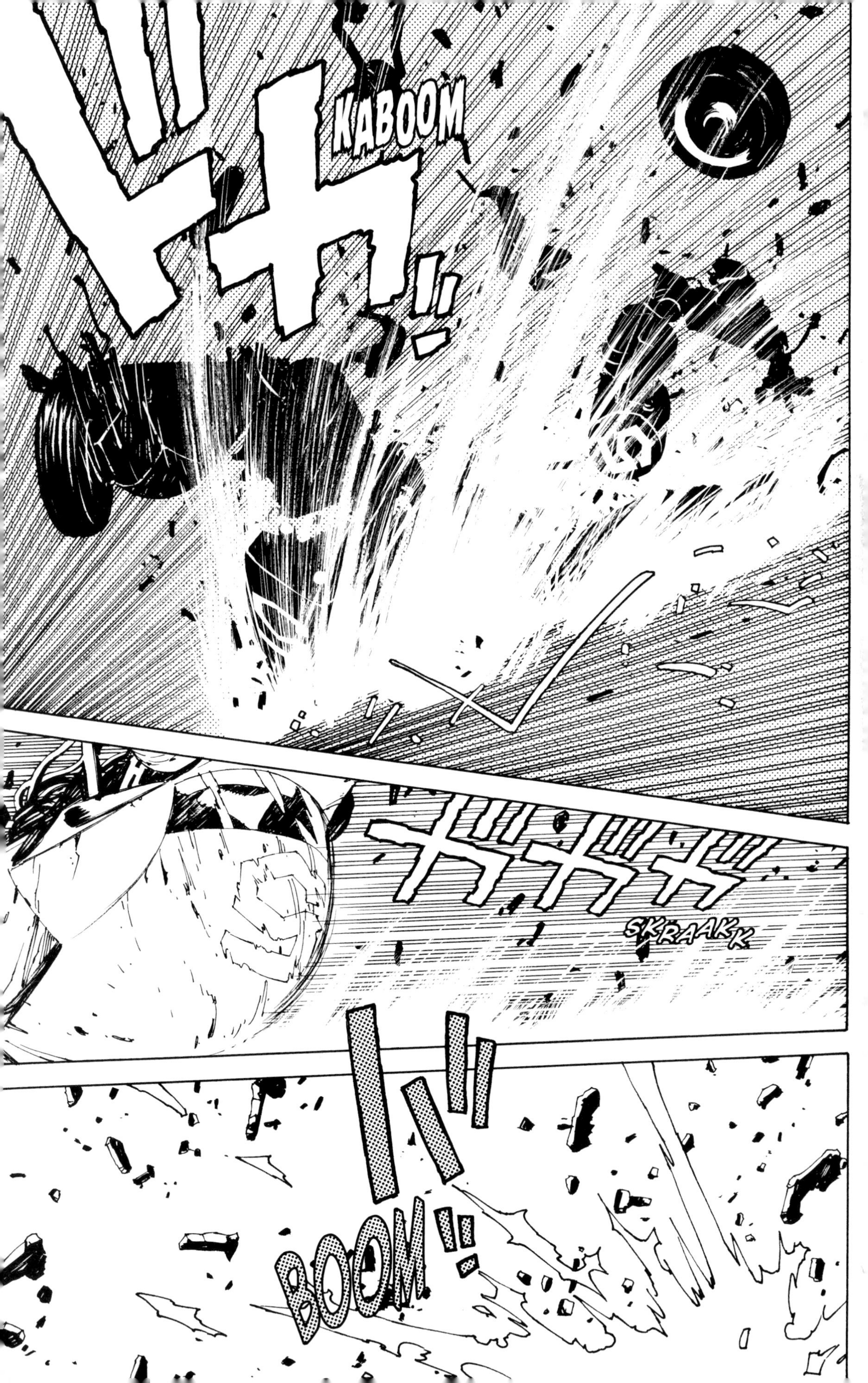
KABOOM
SKRAAKK
BOOM!!

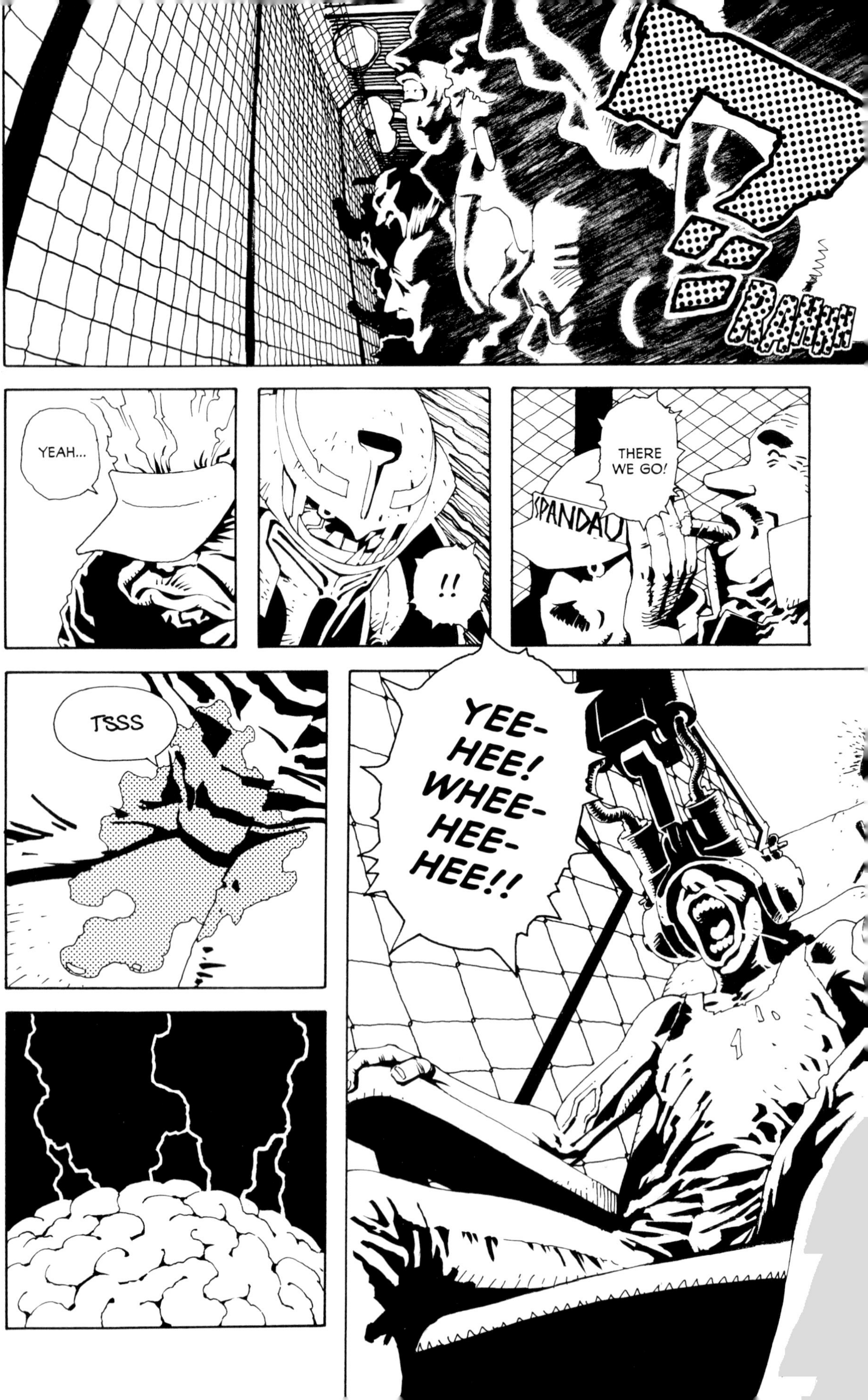
RAKKK
THERE WE GO!
SPANDAU
!!
YEAH...
YEE-HEE! WHEE-HEE-HEE!!
TSSS

LISTEN TO THE CHEERS!

THIS SINGLE MOMENT IS THE UNDENIABLE TRUTH.

IT TELLS YOU THAT YOU WERE BORN FOR JUST THIS PURPOSE...

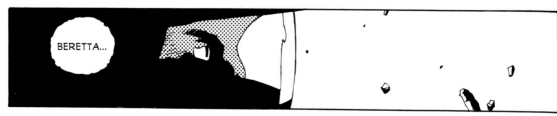

BERETTA...

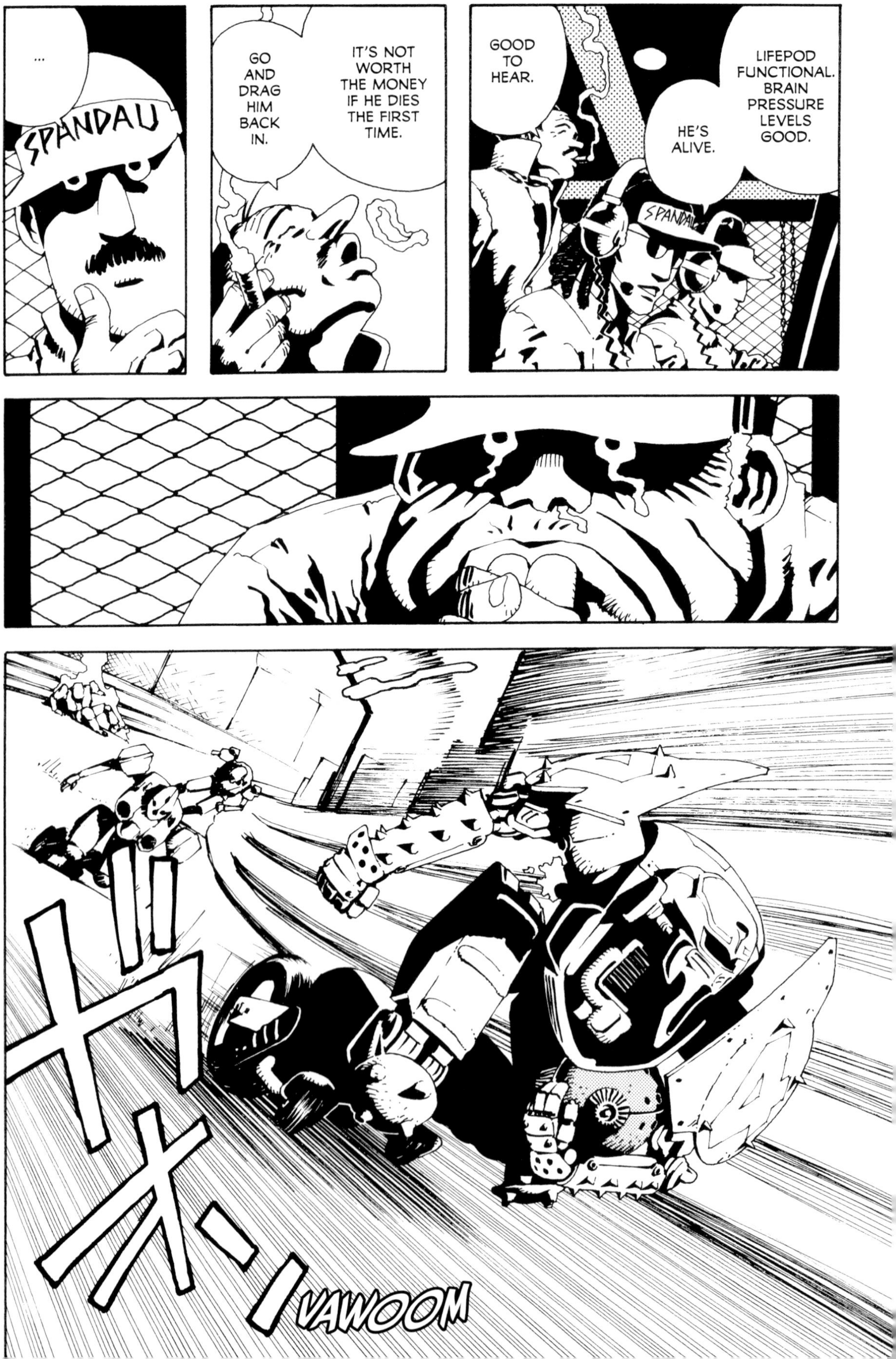
LIFEPOD FUNCTIONAL. BRAIN PRESSURE LEVELS GOOD.
HE'S ALIVE.
SPANDAU
GOOD TO HEAR.
IT'S NOT WORTH THE MONEY IF HE DIES THE FIRST TIME.
GO AND DRAG HIM BACK IN.
...
SPANDAU
VAWOOM

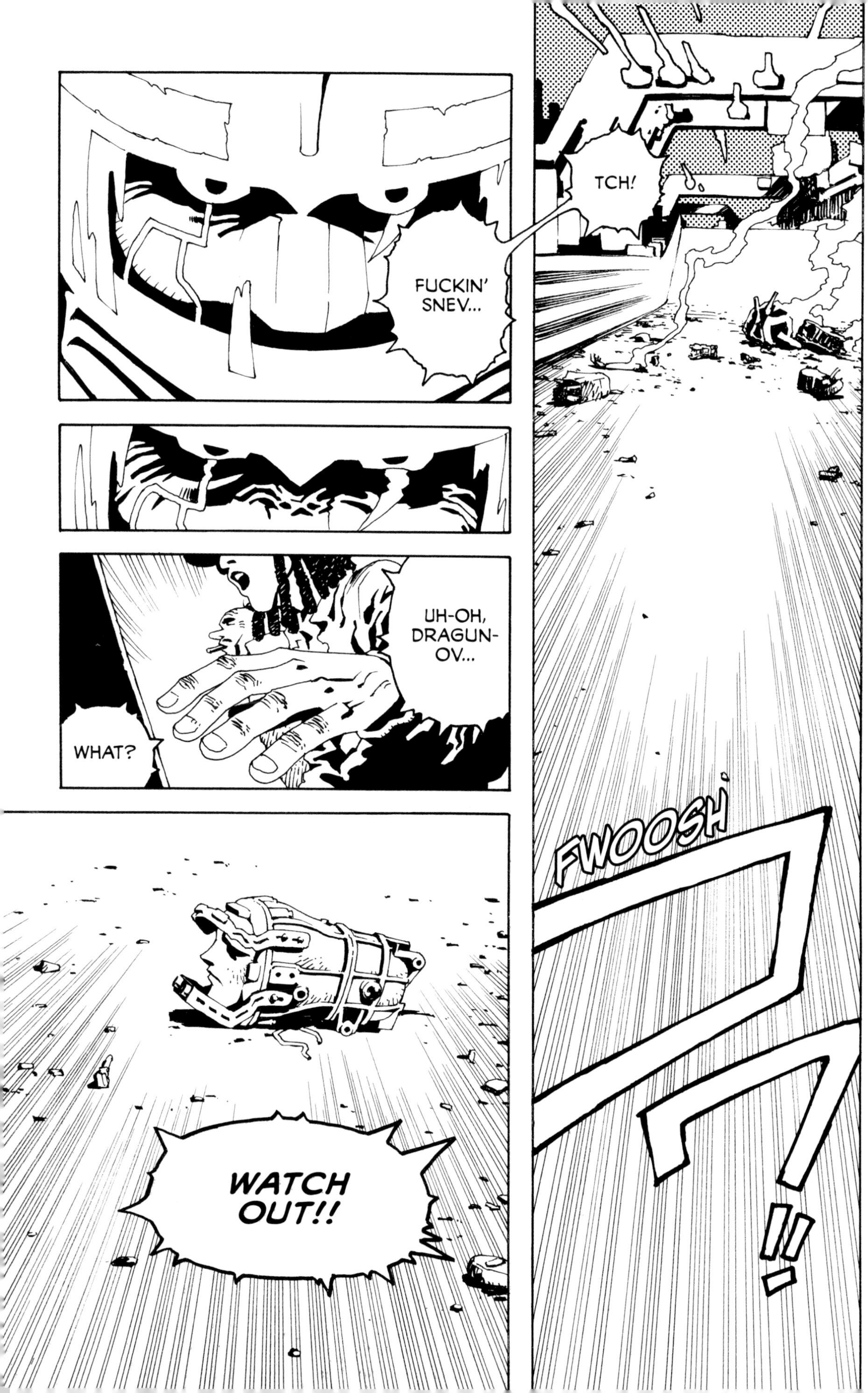
TCH!
FWOOSH
!!
FUCKIN' SNEV...
UH-OH, DRAGUN-OV...
WHAT?
WATCH OUT!!

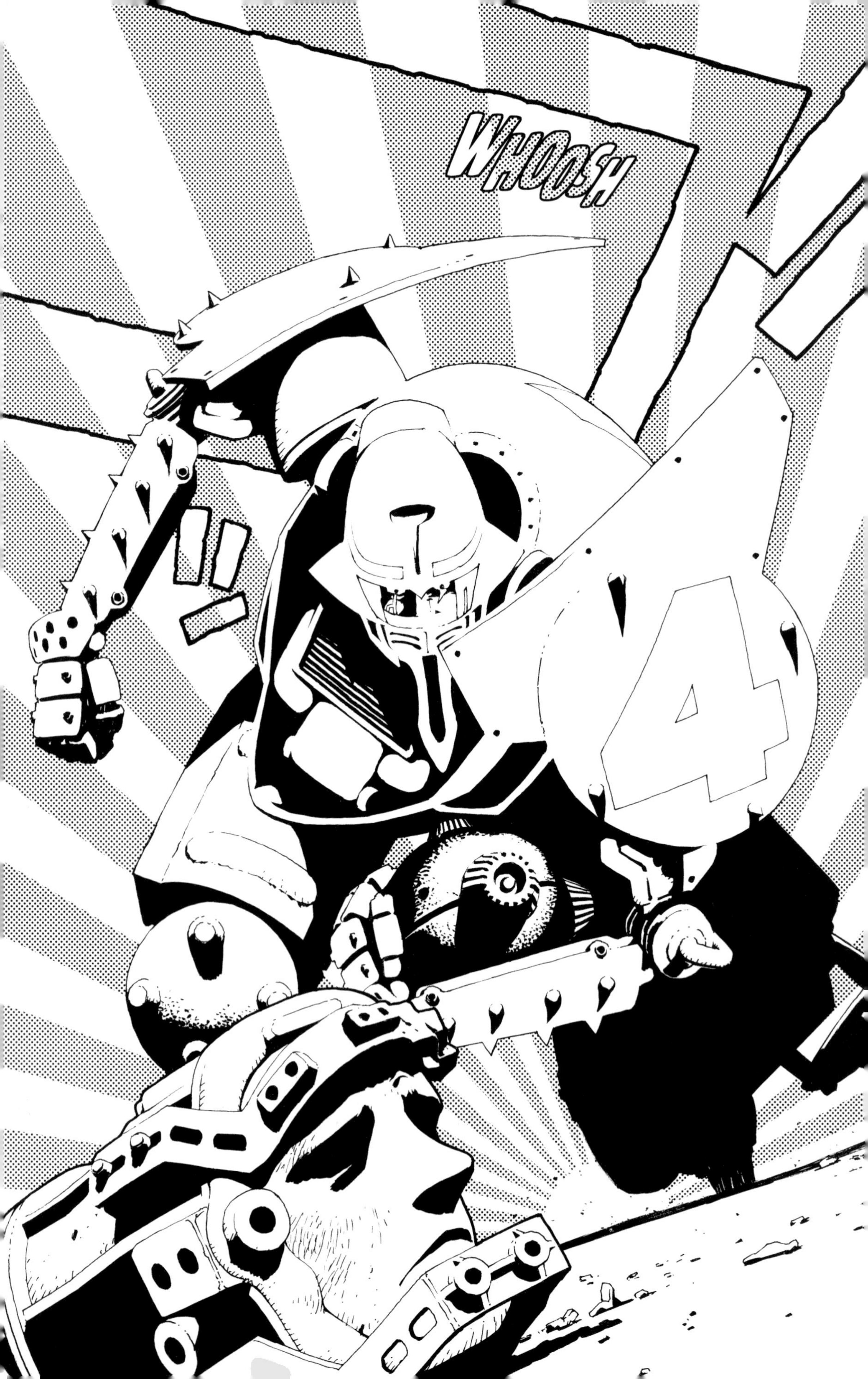
WHOOSH

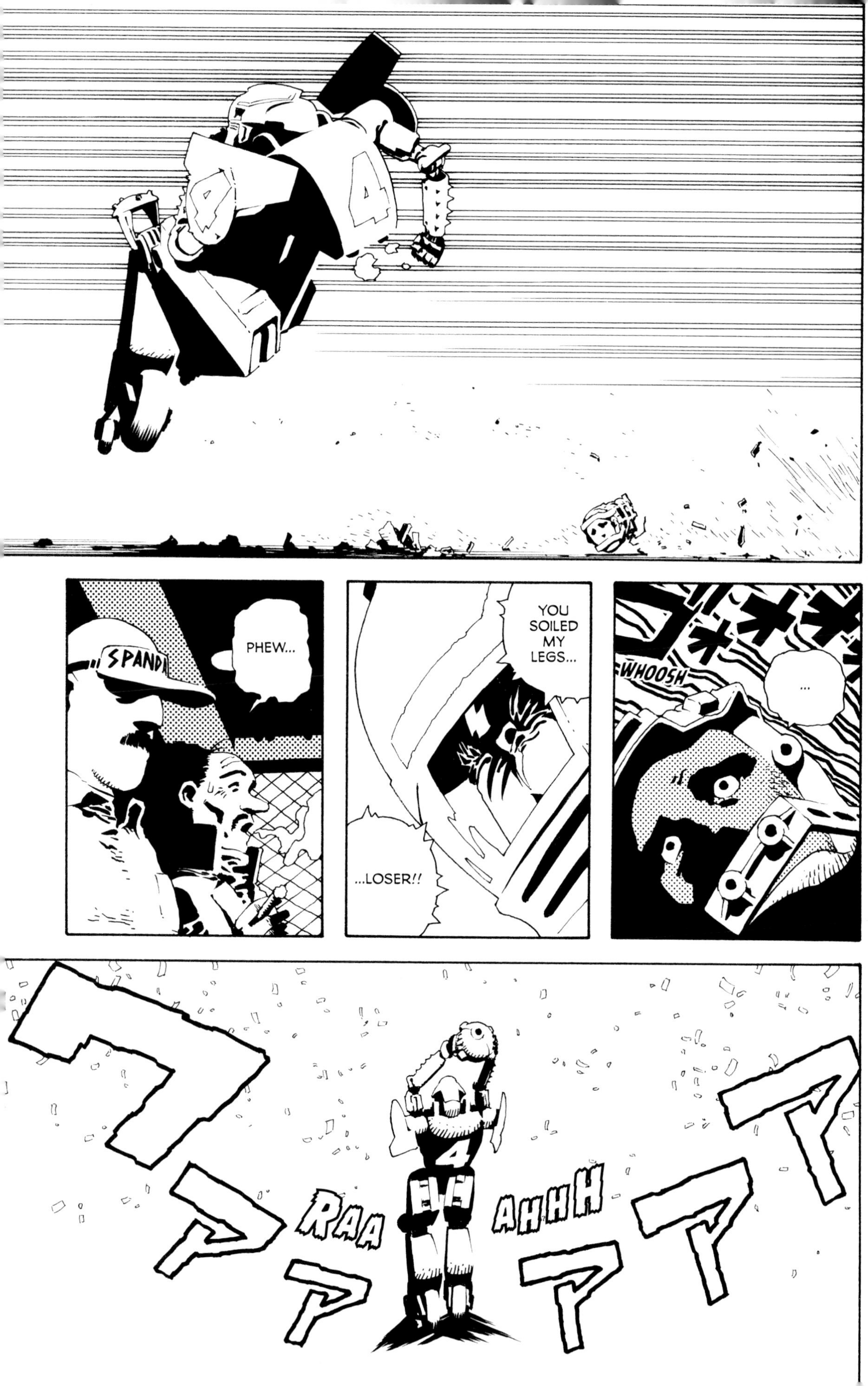
WHOOSH
...
YOU SOILED MY LEGS...
...LOSER!!
SPANDA
PHEW...
RAA AHHH

CRIKK...
ギチ‥

...

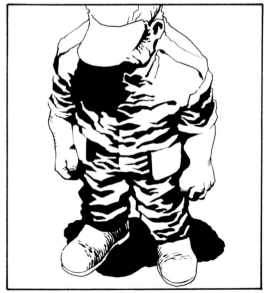

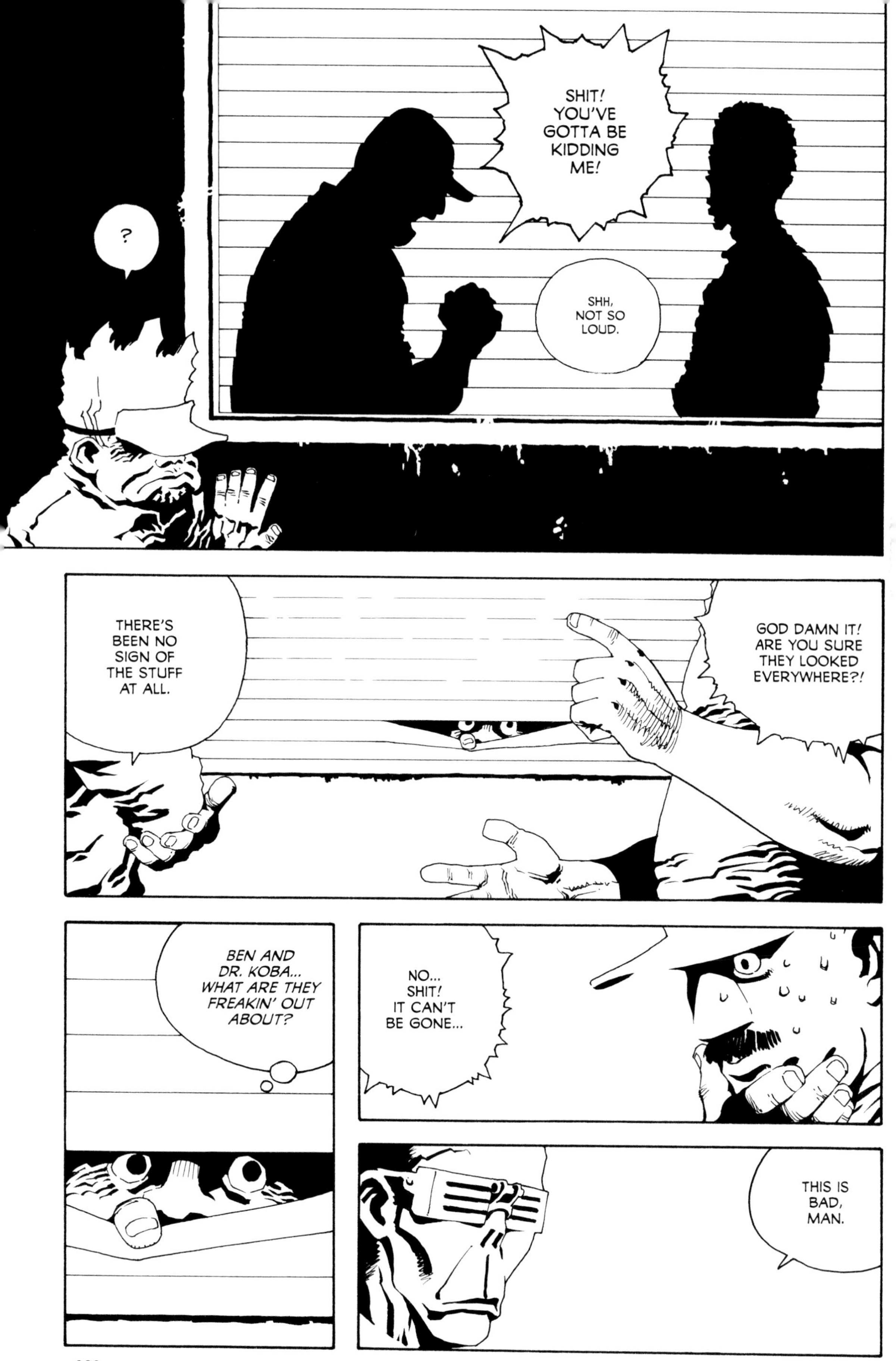
SHIT! YOU'VE GOTTA BE KIDDING ME!
SHH, NOT SO LOUD.
?
GOD DAMN IT! ARE YOU SURE THEY LOOKED EVERYWHERE?!
THERE'S BEEN NO SIGN OF THE STUFF AT ALL.
NO... SHIT! IT CAN'T BE GONE...
THIS IS BAD, MAN.
BEN AND DR. KOBA... WHAT ARE THEY FREAKIN' OUT ABOUT?

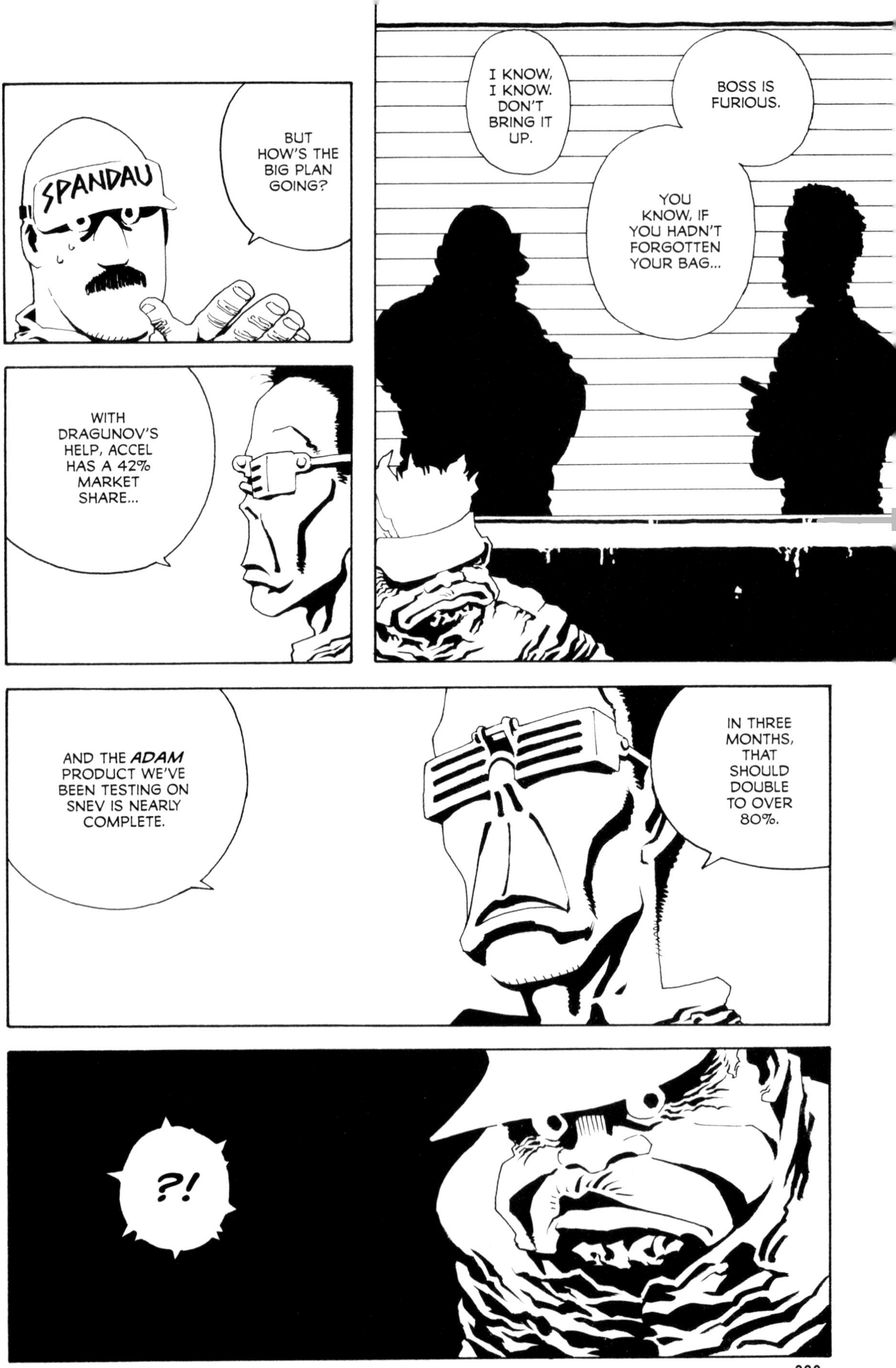
BOSS IS FURIOUS.
I KNOW, I KNOW. DON'T BRING IT UP.
YOU KNOW, IF YOU HADN'T FORGOTTEN YOUR BAG...
SPANDAU
BUT HOW'S THE BIG PLAN GOING?
WITH DRAGUNOV'S HELP, ACCEL HAS A 42% MARKET SHARE...
IN THREE MONTHS, THAT SHOULD DOUBLE TO OVER 80%.
AND THE *ADAM* PRODUCT WE'VE BEEN TESTING ON SNEV IS NEARLY COMPLETE.
?!

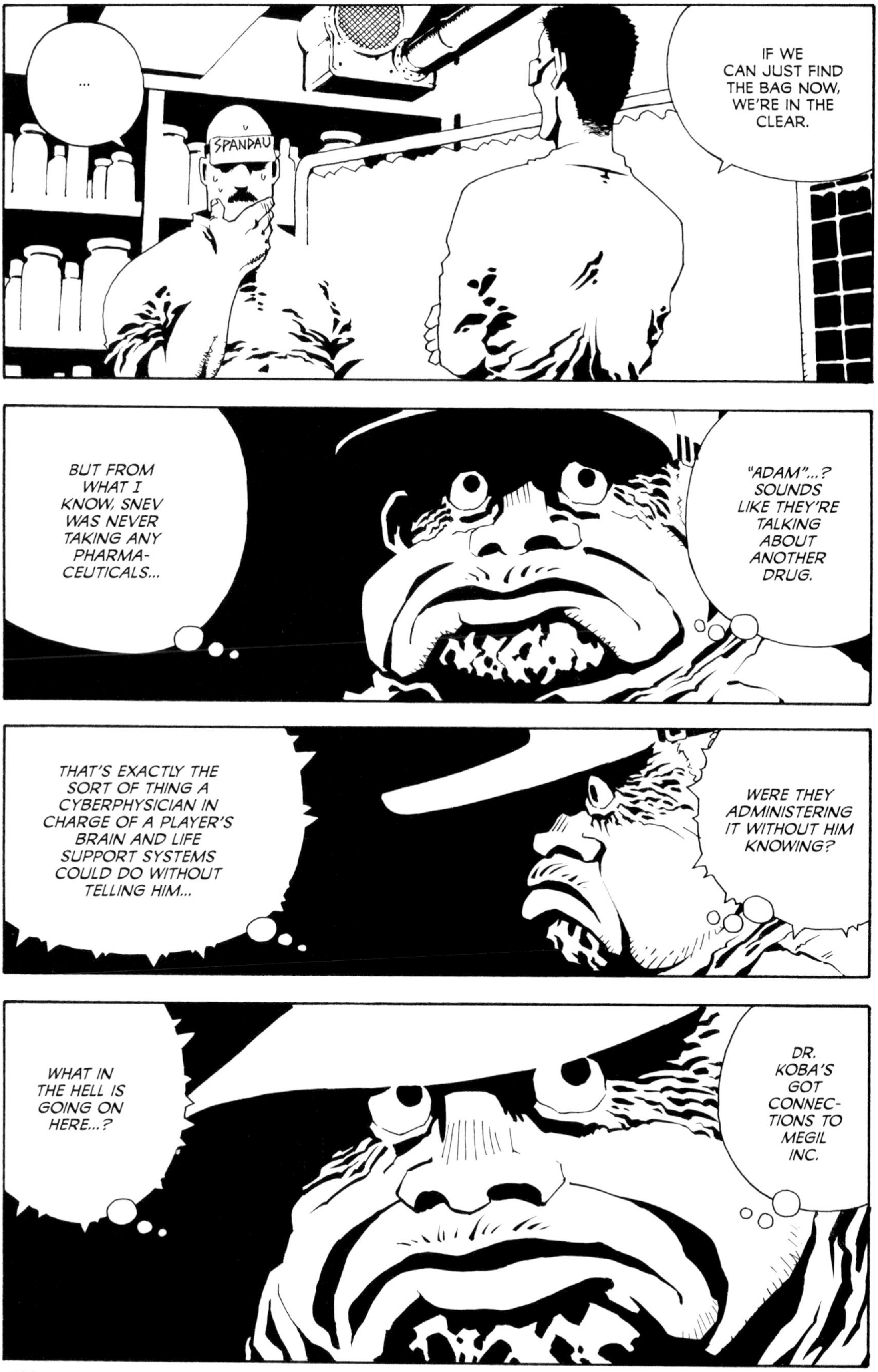
IF WE CAN JUST FIND THE BAG NOW, WE'RE IN THE CLEAR.
...
SPANDAU
"ADAM"...? SOUNDS LIKE THEY'RE TALKING ABOUT ANOTHER DRUG.
BUT FROM WHAT I KNOW, SNEV WAS NEVER TAKING ANY PHARMA-CEUTICALS...
WERE THEY ADMINISTERING IT WITHOUT HIM KNOWING?
THAT'S EXACTLY THE SORT OF THING A CYBERPHYSICIAN IN CHARGE OF A PLAYER'S BRAIN AND LIFE SUPPORT SYSTEMS COULD DO WITHOUT TELLING HIM...
DR. KOBA'S GOT CONNEC-TIONS TO MEGIL INC.
WHAT IN THE HELL IS GOING ON HERE...?

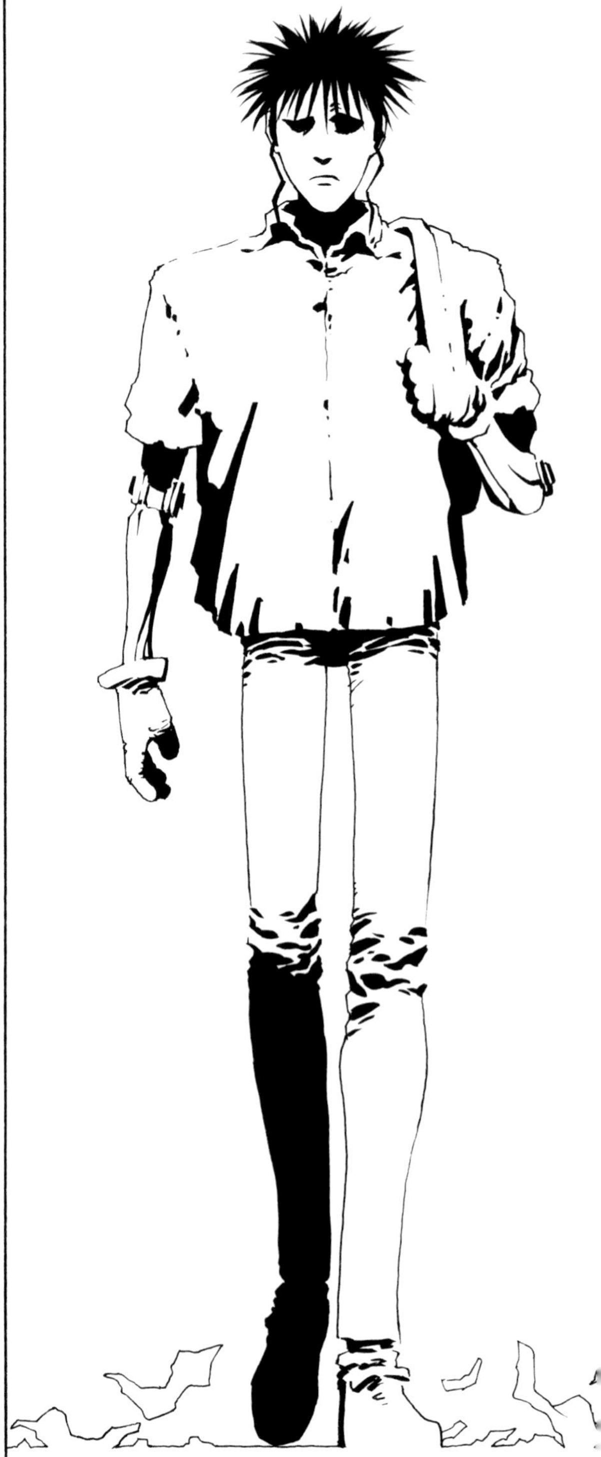

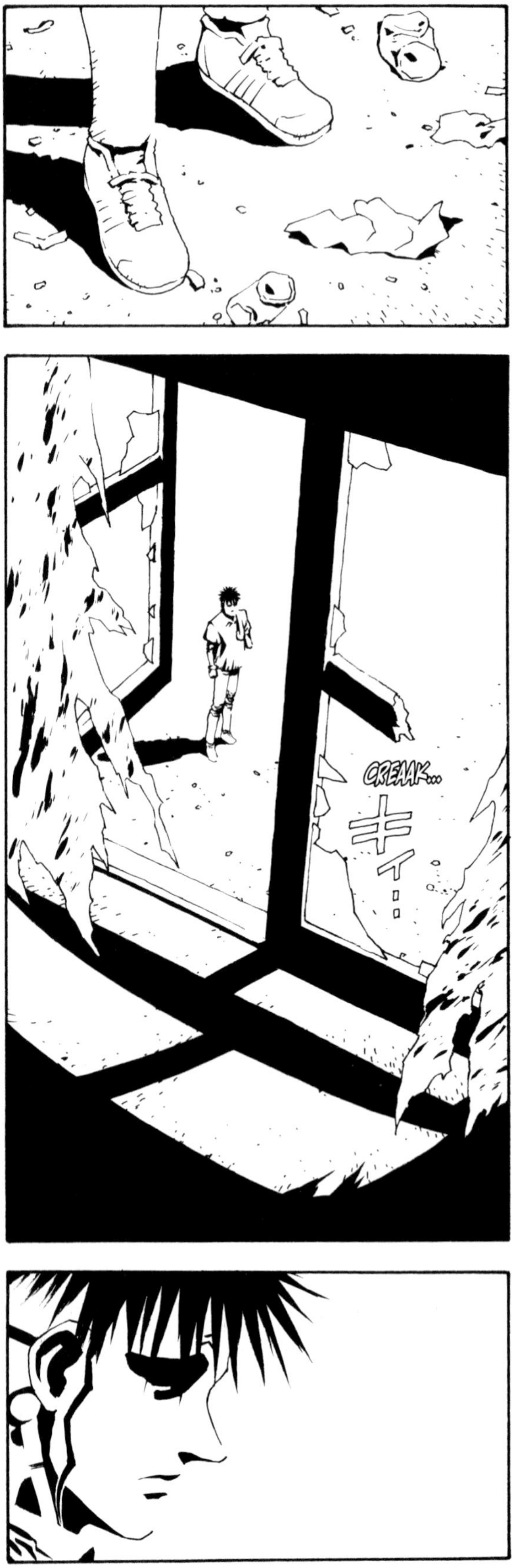
CREAAK...
キイ・・

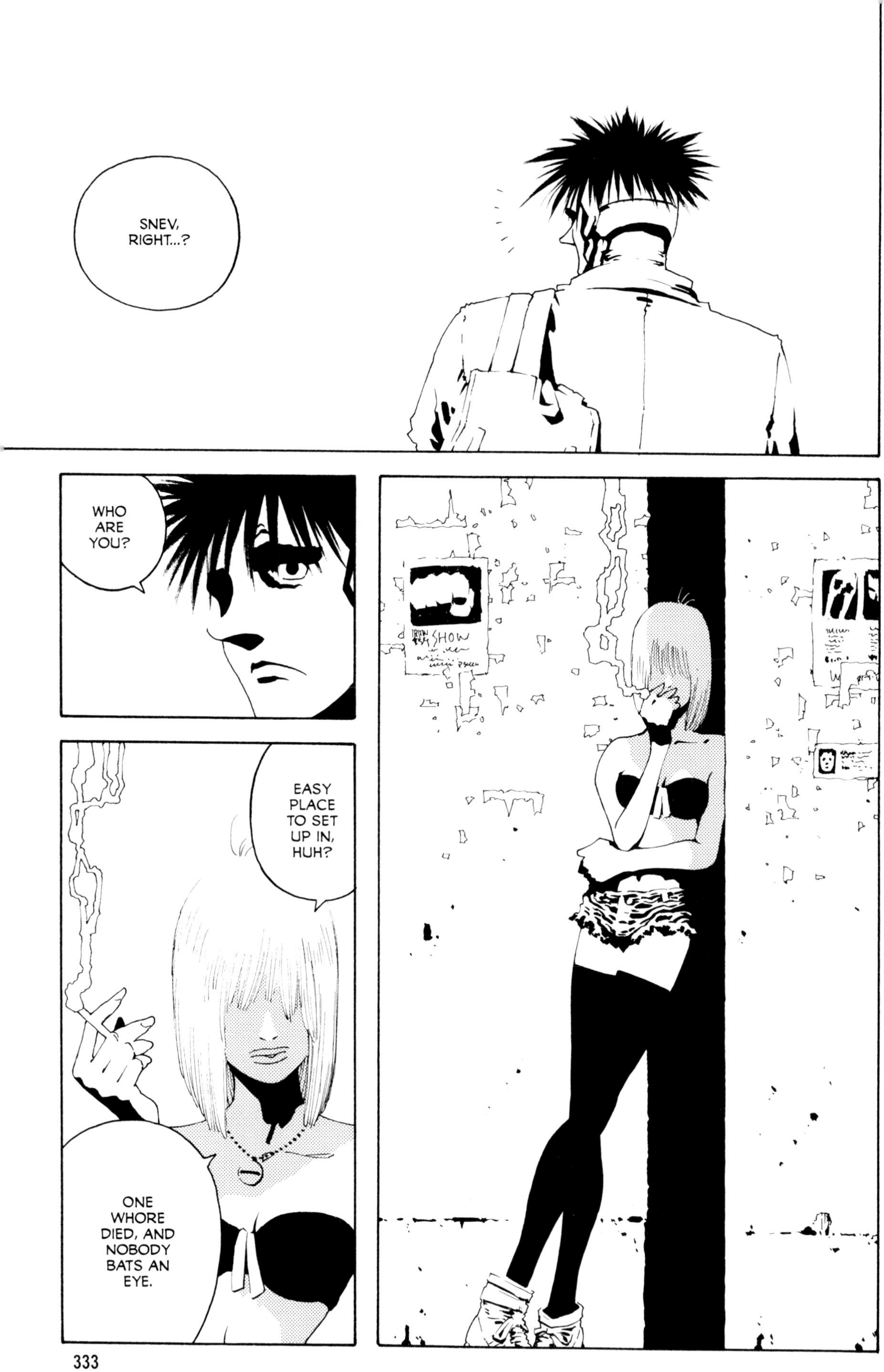
SNEV, RIGHT...?
WHO ARE YOU?
EASY PLACE TO SET UP IN, HUH?
ONE WHORE DIED, AND NOBODY BATS AN EYE.

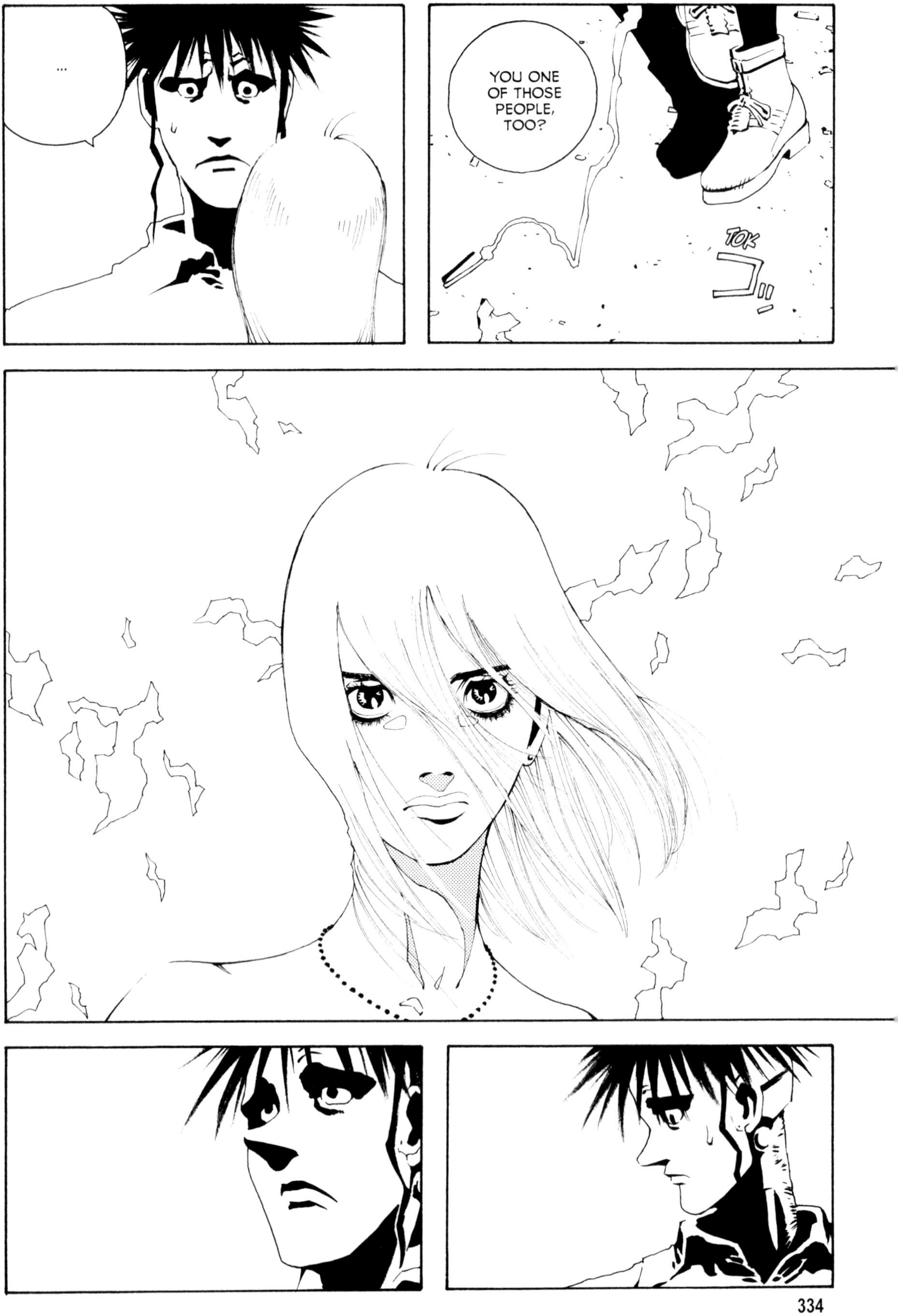
YOU ONE OF THOSE PEOPLE, TOO?
TOK
...

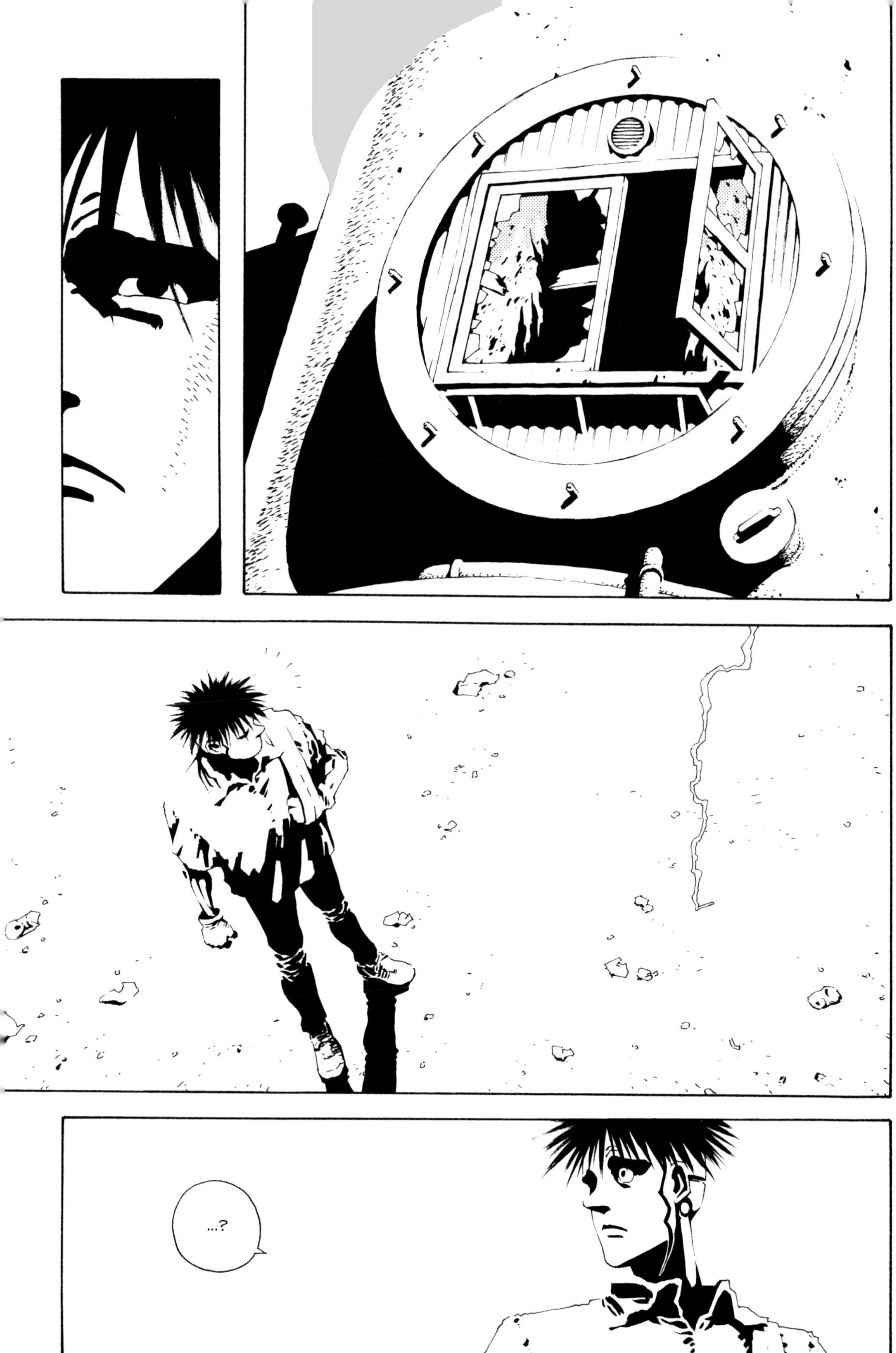
...?

07
SNEV

TAK

HUH...?

CREAK...

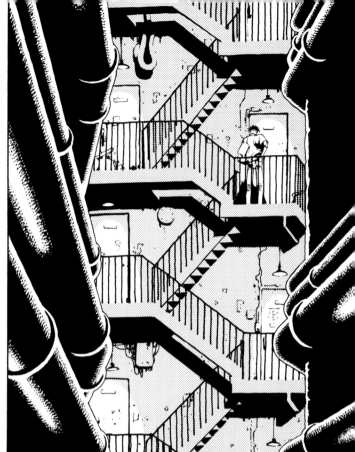

I'VE BEEN ROBBED...

THEY DIDN'T TAKE MY CHIPS...

THAT'S WEIRD.

HM?

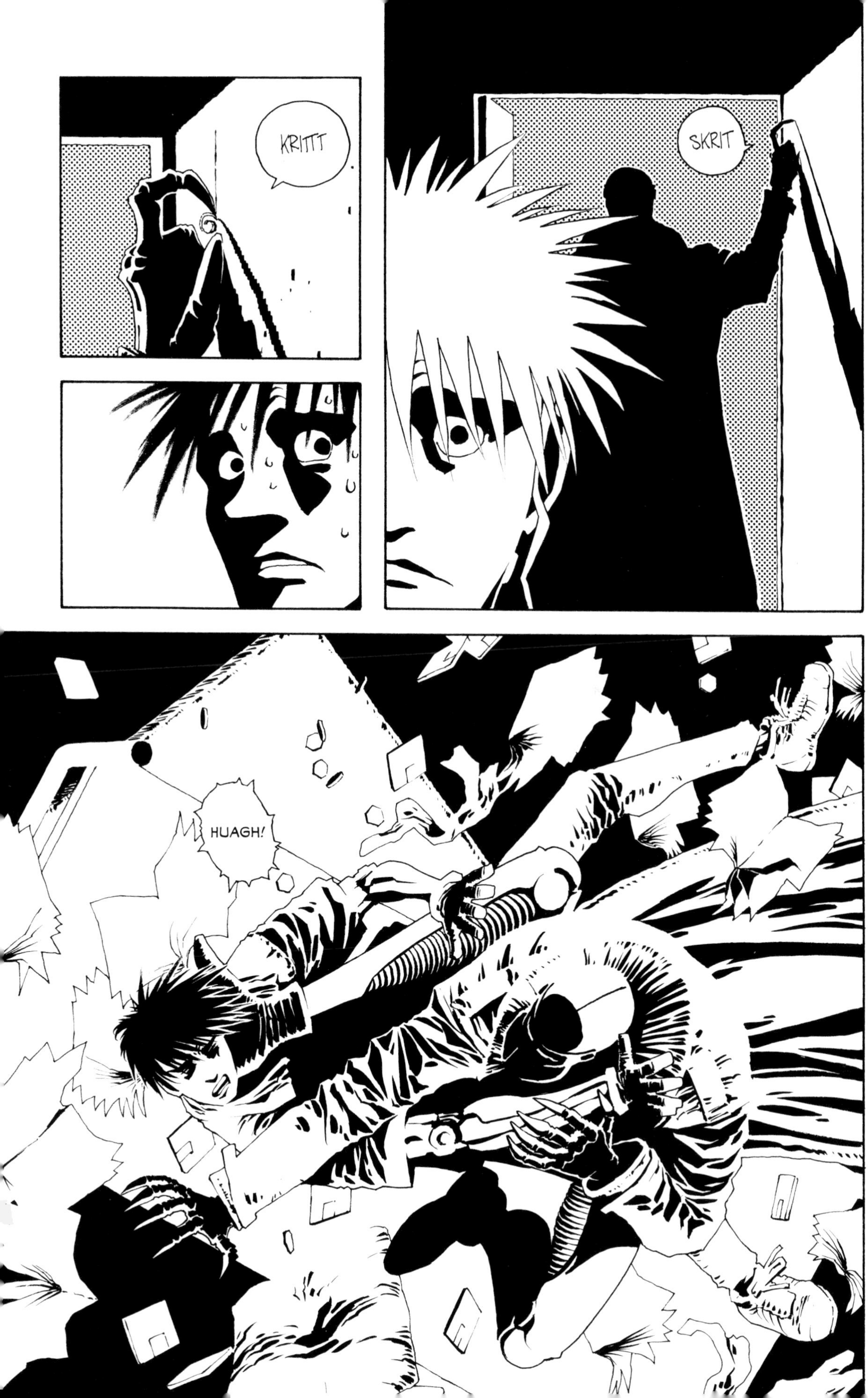
SKRIT
KRITTT
HUAGH!

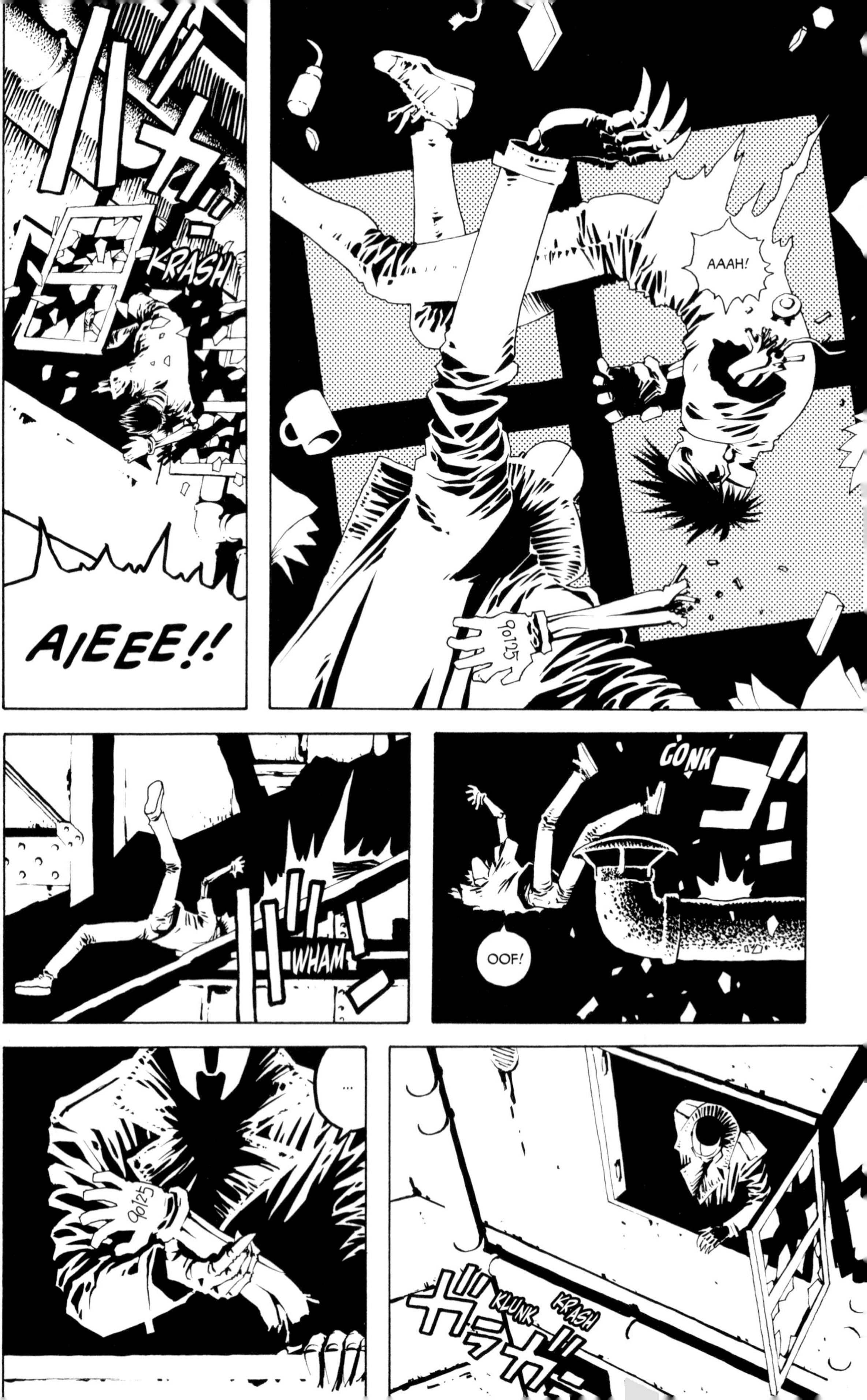
AAAH!
KRASH
AIEEE!!
GONK
OOF!
WHAM
KRASH
KLUNK
...

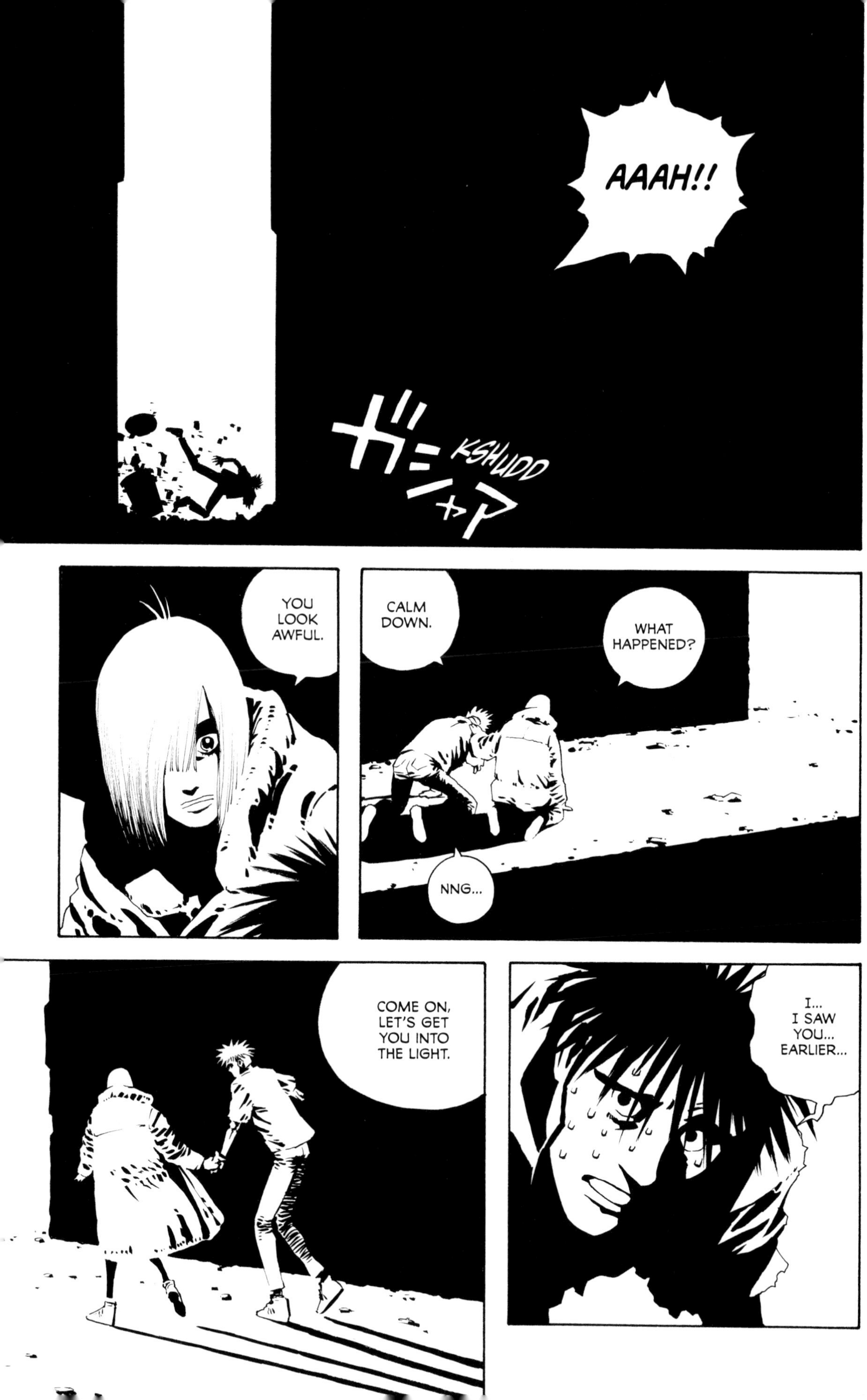
AAAH!!
ガシャア
KSHUDD
CALM DOWN.
WHAT HAPPENED?
NNG...
YOU LOOK AWFUL.
I... I SAW YOU... EARLIER...
COME ON, LET'S GET YOU INTO THE LIGHT.

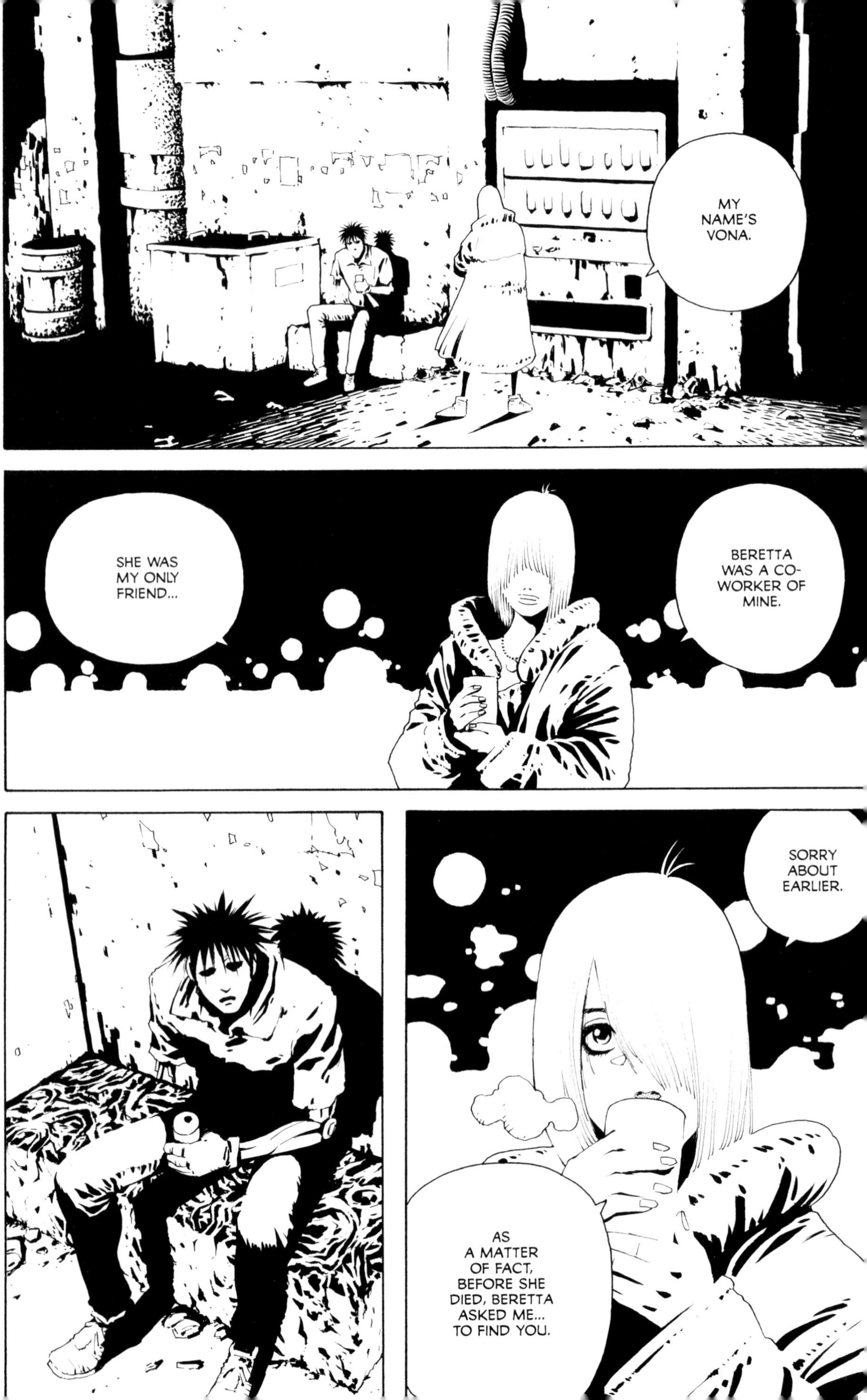
MY NAME'S VONA.
BERETTA WAS A CO-WORKER OF MINE.
SHE WAS MY ONLY FRIEND...
SORRY ABOUT EARLIER.
AS A MATTER OF FACT, BEFORE SHE DIED, BERETTA ASKED ME... TO FIND YOU.

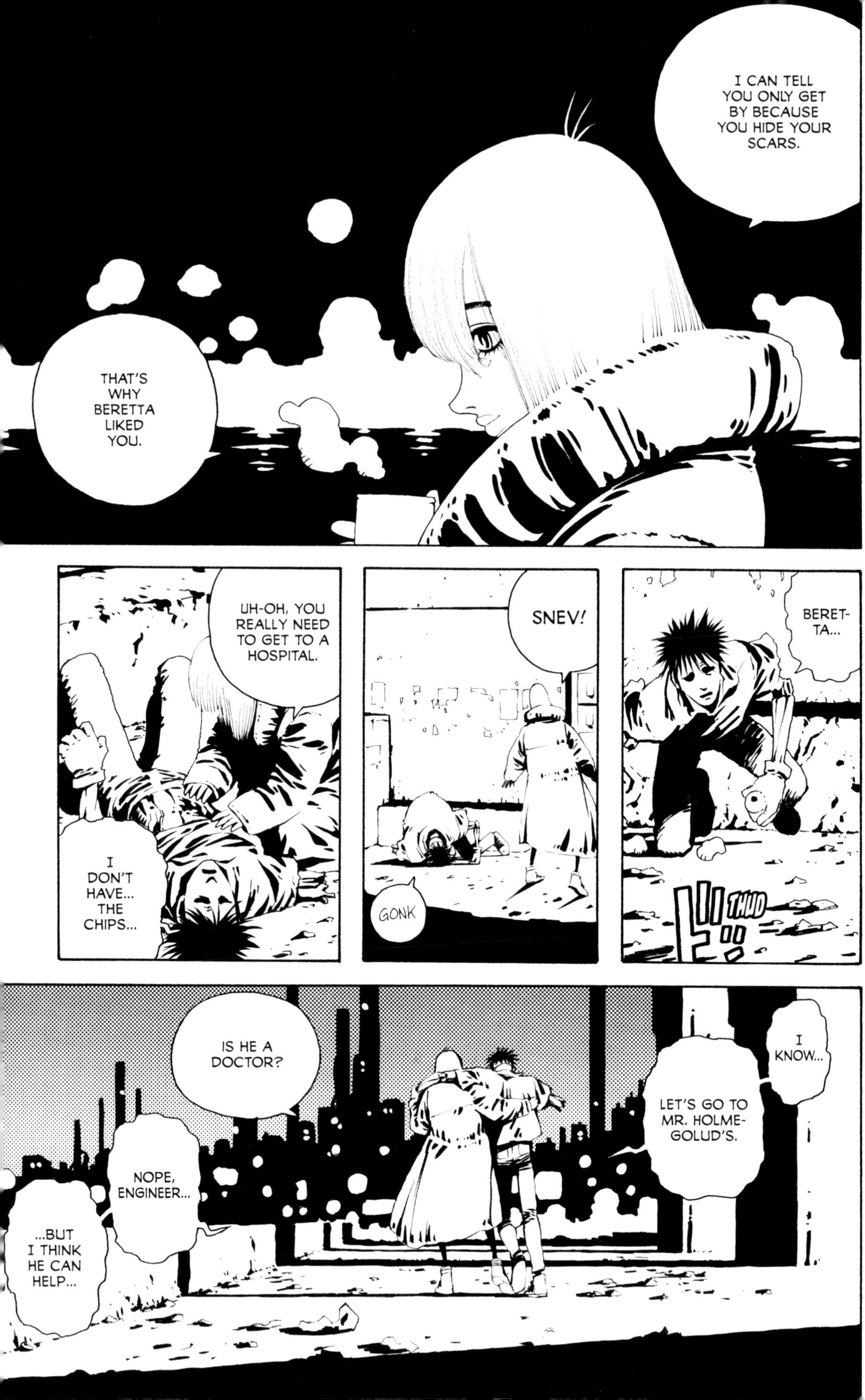
I CAN TELL YOU ONLY GET BY BECAUSE YOU HIDE YOUR SCARS.
THAT'S WHY BERETTA LIKED YOU.
BERET-TA...
THUD
SNEV!
GONK
UH-OH, YOU REALLY NEED TO GET TO A HOSPITAL.
I DON'T HAVE... THE CHIPS...
I KNOW...
LET'S GO TO MR. HOLME-GOLUD'S.
IS HE A DOCTOR?
NOPE, ENGINEER...
...BUT I THINK HE CAN HELP...

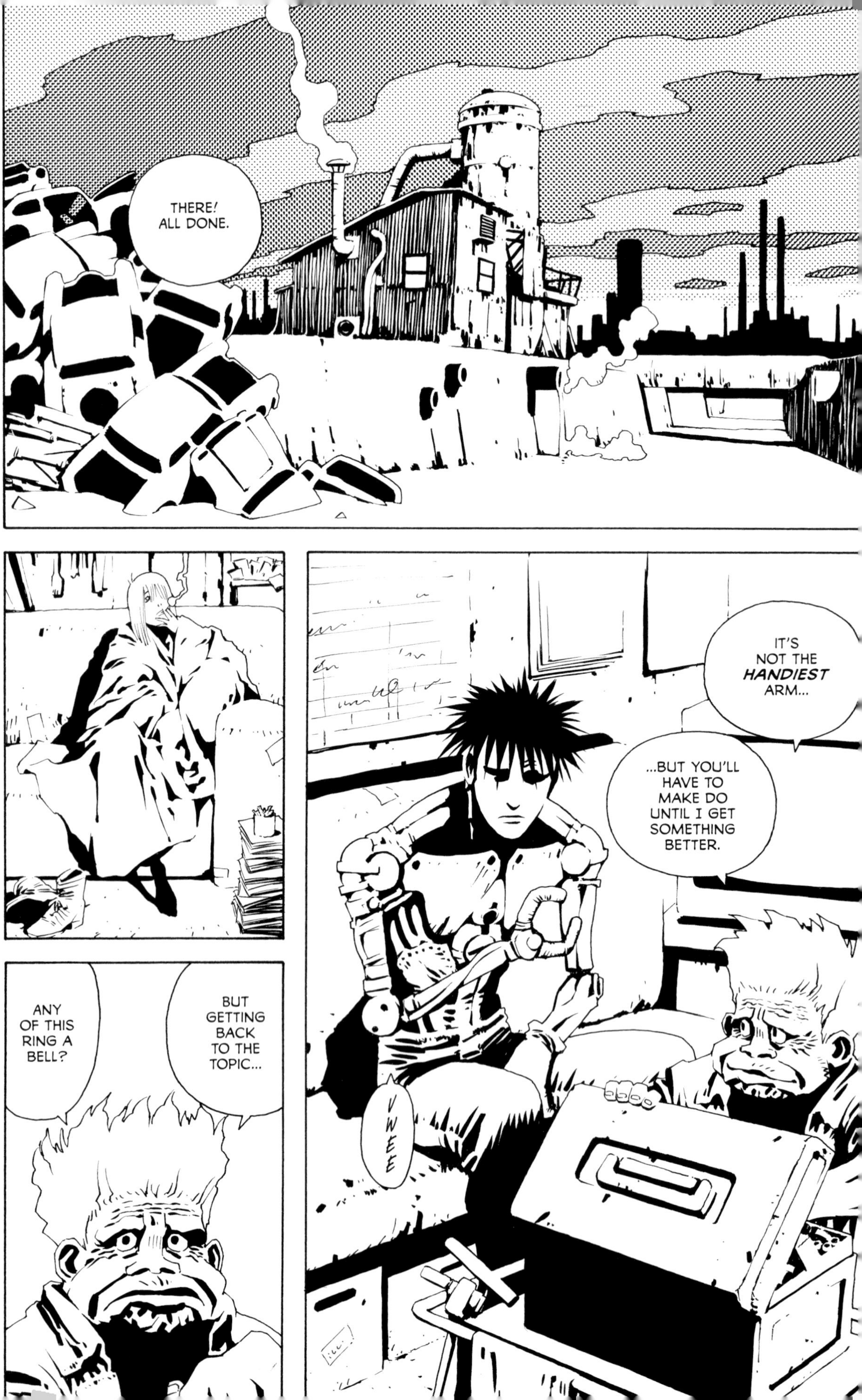
THERE! ALL DONE.
IT'S NOT THE *HANDIEST* ARM...
...BUT YOU'LL HAVE TO MAKE DO UNTIL I GET SOMETHING BETTER.
VWEE
BUT GETTING BACK TO THE TOPIC...
ANY OF THIS RING A BELL?

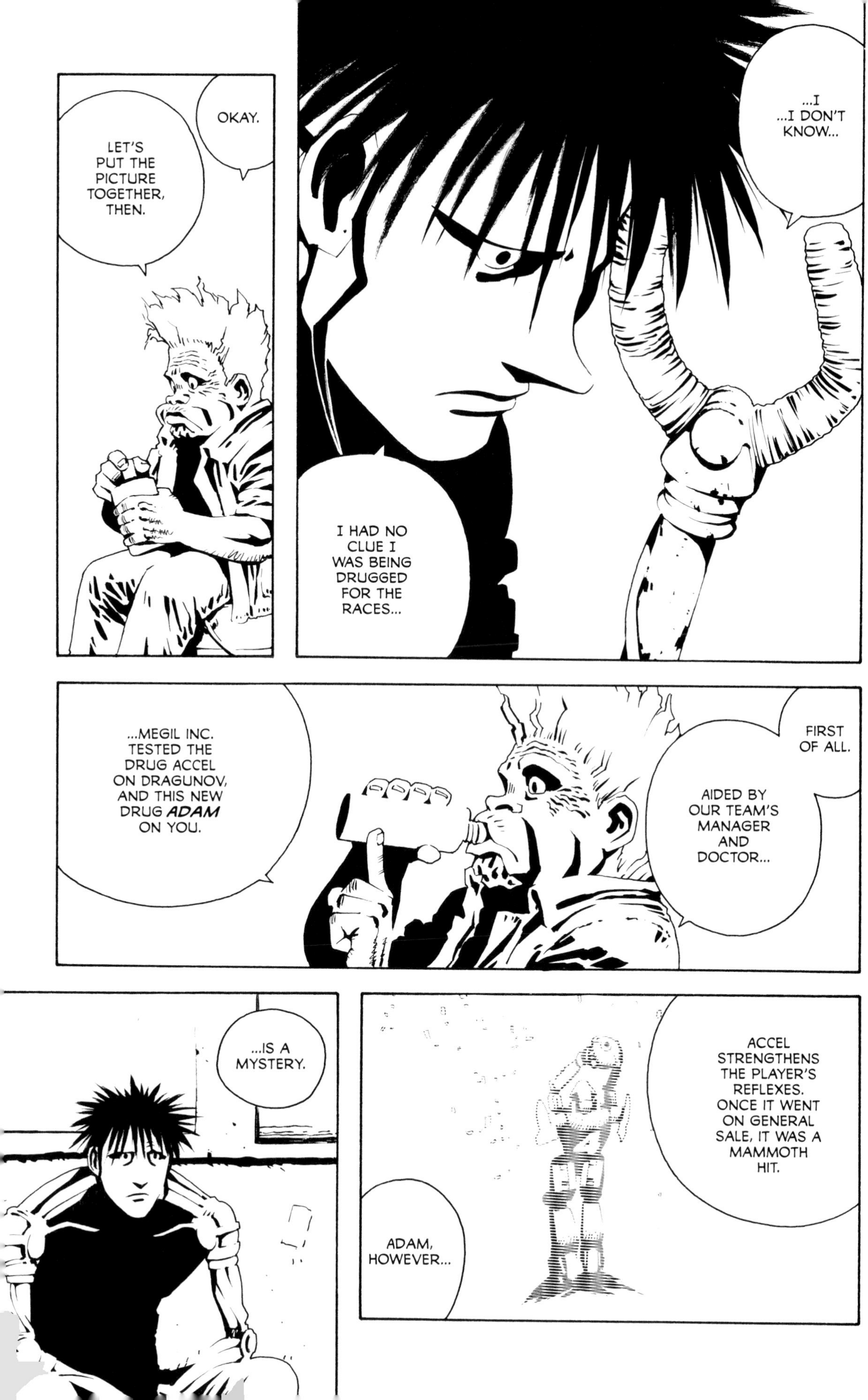
...I ...I DON'T KNOW...
I HAD NO CLUE I WAS BEING DRUGGED FOR THE RACES...
OKAY.
LET'S PUT THE PICTURE TOGETHER, THEN.
FIRST OF ALL.
AIDED BY OUR TEAM'S MANAGER AND DOCTOR...
...MEGIL INC. TESTED THE DRUG ACCEL ON DRAGUNOV, AND THIS NEW DRUG *ADAM* ON YOU.
ACCEL STRENGTHENS THE PLAYER'S REFLEXES. ONCE IT WENT ON GENERAL SALE, IT WAS A MAMMOTH HIT.
ADAM, HOWEVER...
...IS A MYSTERY.

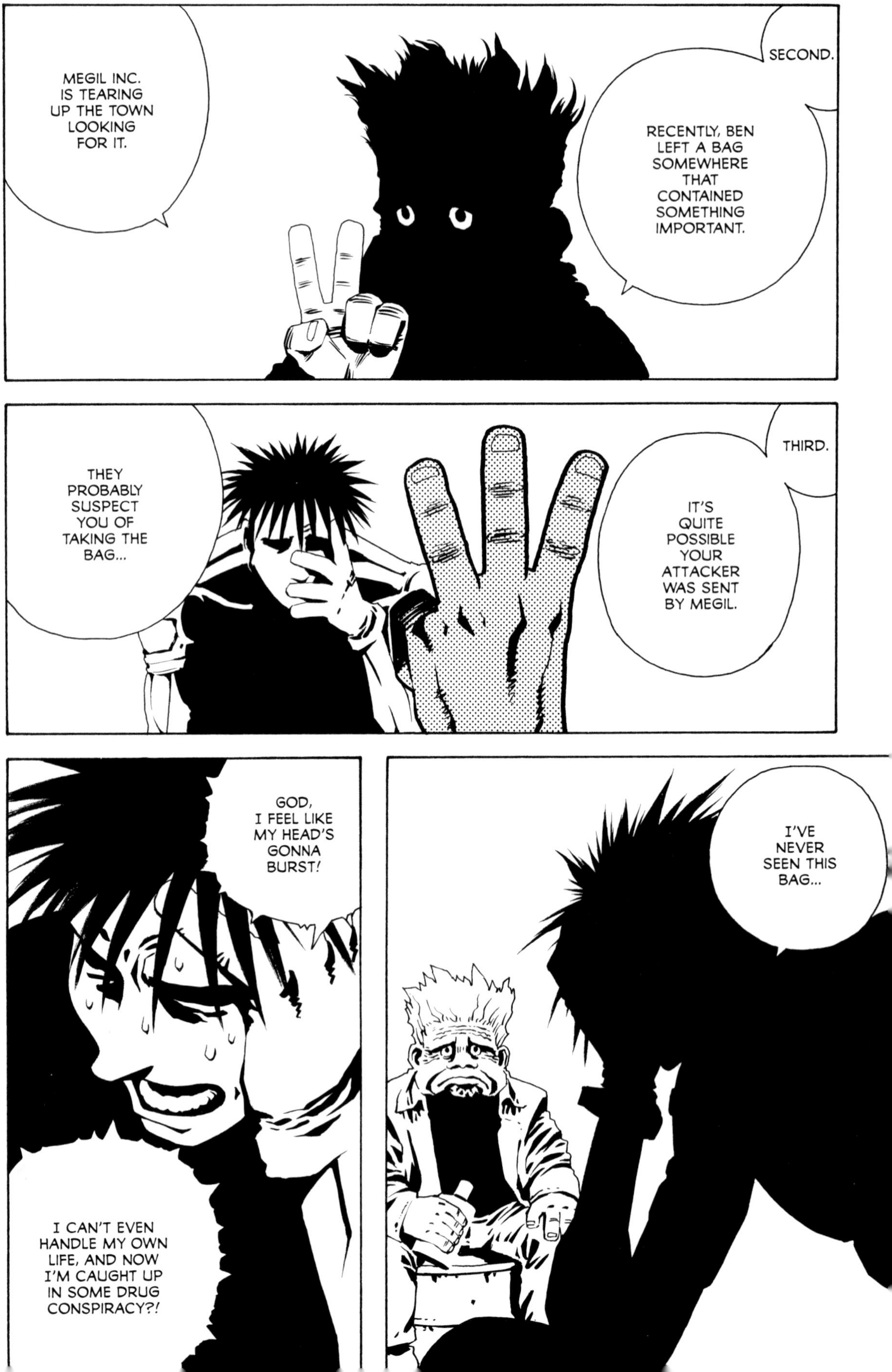
SECOND.
RECENTLY, BEN LEFT A BAG SOMEWHERE THAT CONTAINED SOMETHING IMPORTANT.
MEGIL INC. IS TEARING UP THE TOWN LOOKING FOR IT.
THIRD.
IT'S QUITE POSSIBLE YOUR ATTACKER WAS SENT BY MEGIL.
THEY PROBABLY SUSPECT YOU OF TAKING THE BAG...
I'VE NEVER SEEN THIS BAG...
GOD, I FEEL LIKE MY HEAD'S GONNA BURST!
I CAN'T EVEN HANDLE MY OWN LIFE, AND NOW I'M CAUGHT UP IN SOME DRUG CONSPIRACY?!

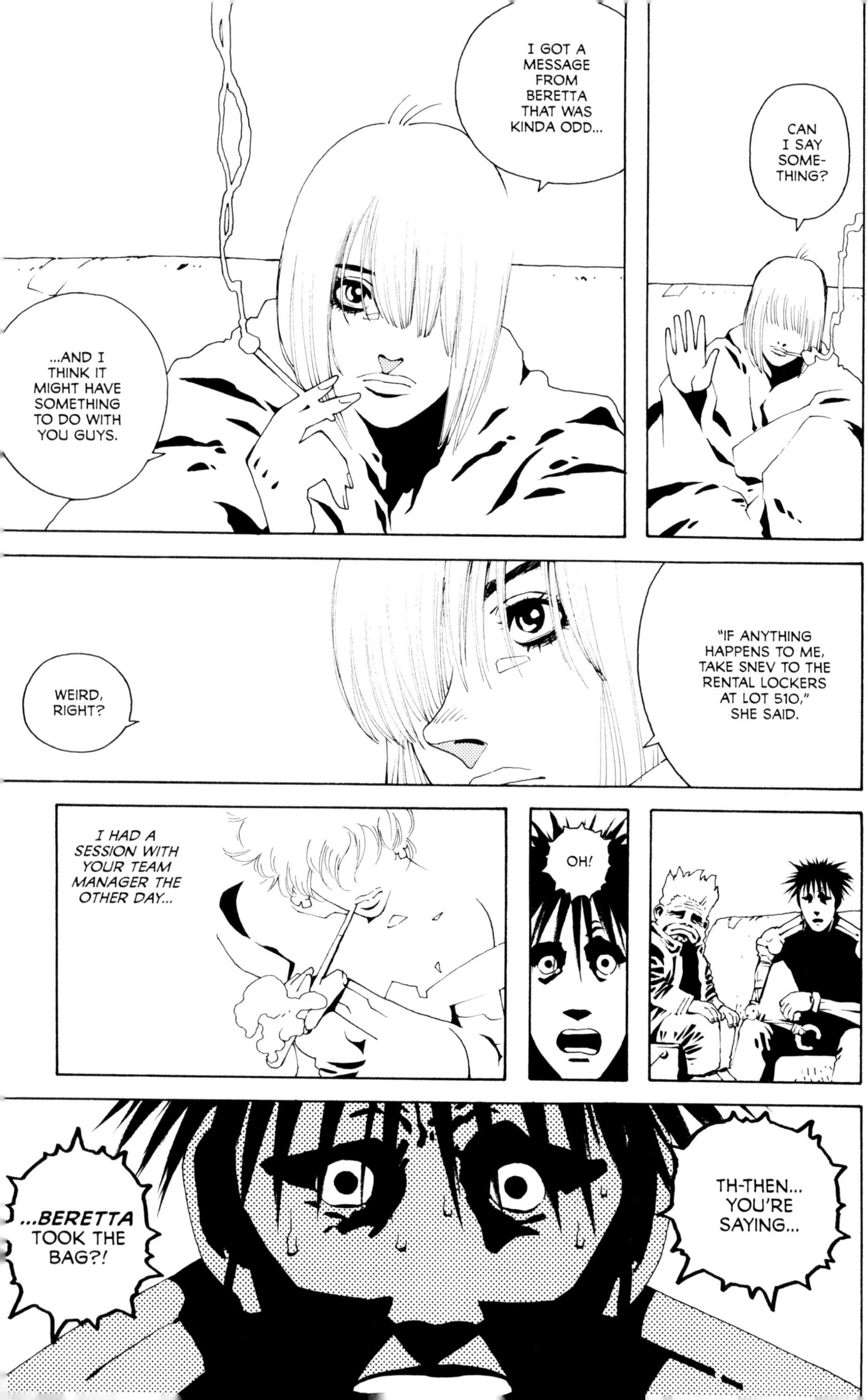
CAN I SAY SOME-THING?
I GOT A MESSAGE FROM BERETTA THAT WAS KINDA ODD...
...AND I THINK IT MIGHT HAVE SOMETHING TO DO WITH YOU GUYS.
"IF ANYTHING HAPPENS TO ME, TAKE SNEV TO THE RENTAL LOCKERS AT LOT 510," SHE SAID.
WEIRD, RIGHT?
OH!
I HAD A SESSION WITH YOUR TEAM MANAGER THE OTHER DAY...
TH-THEN... YOU'RE SAYING...
...BERETTA TOOK THE BAG?!

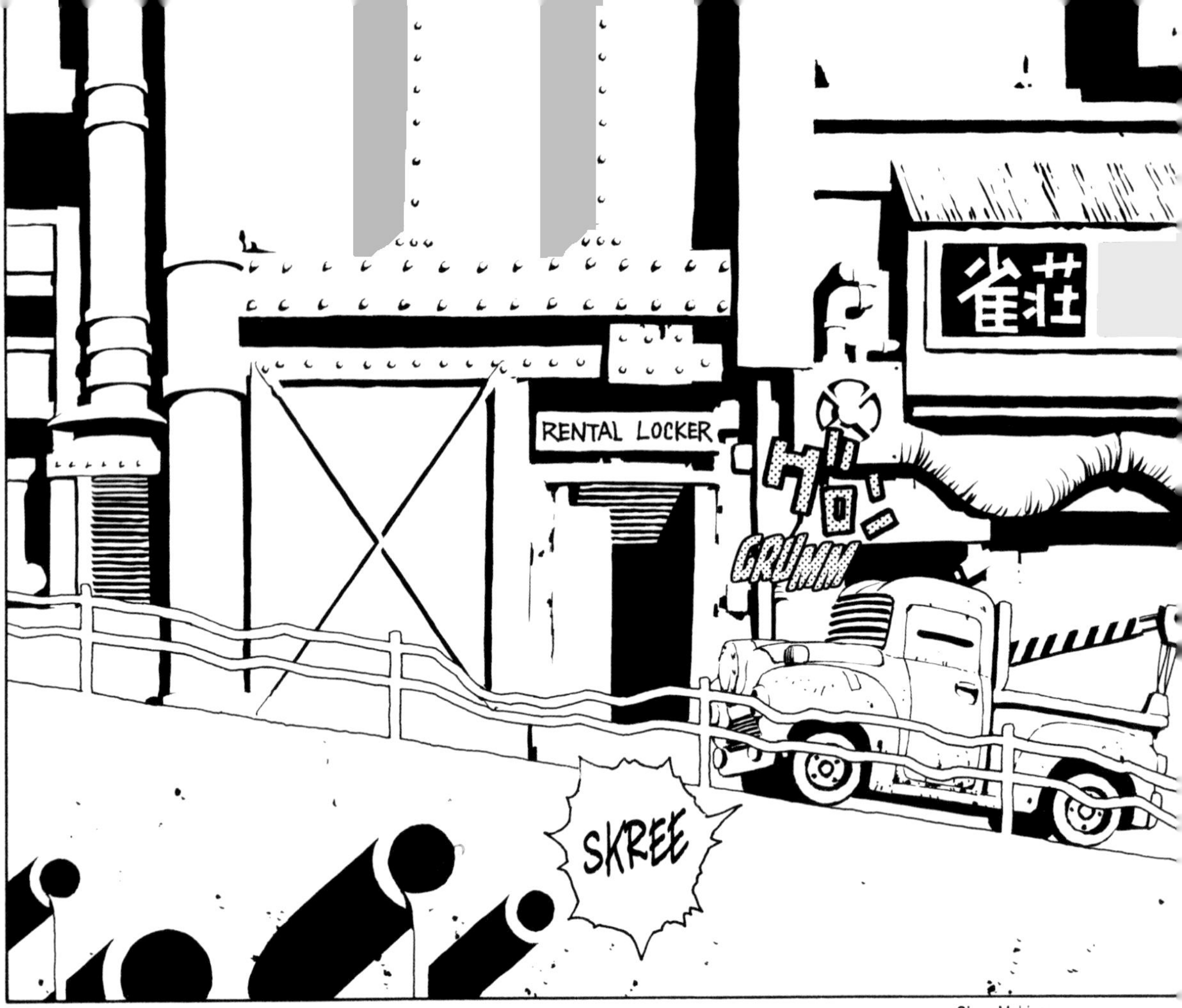
雀荘
RENTAL LOCKER
GRUMM
SKREE
Sign: Mahjong

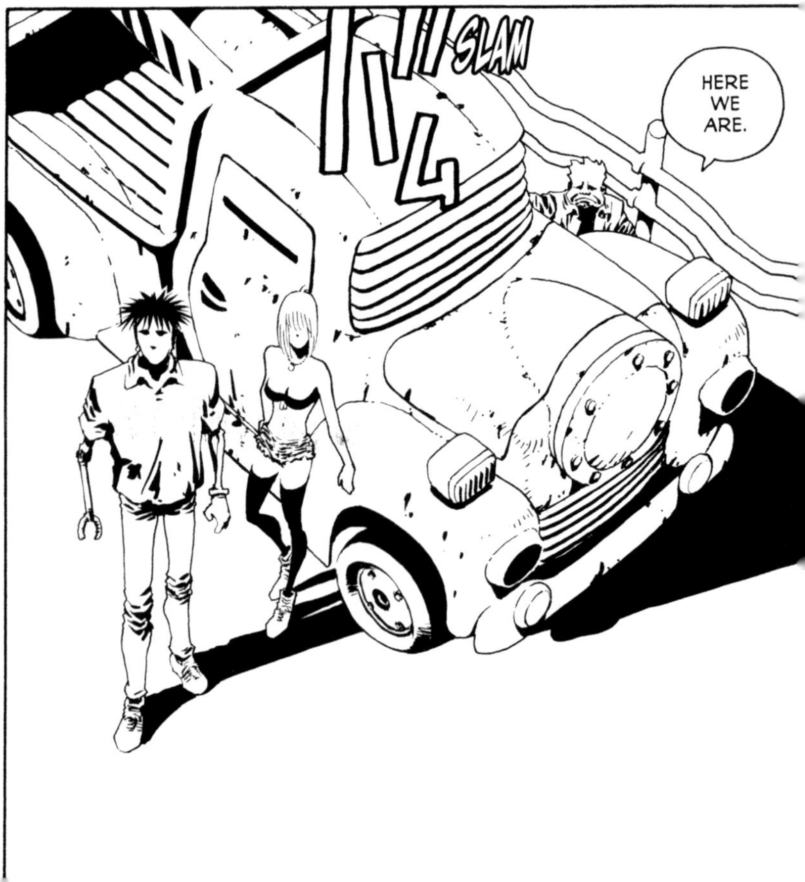
SLAM
HERE WE ARE.

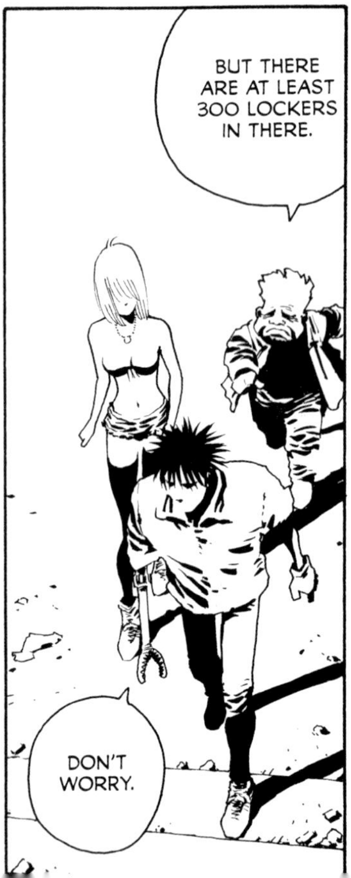
BUT THERE ARE AT LEAST 300 LOCKERS IN THERE.
DON'T WORRY.

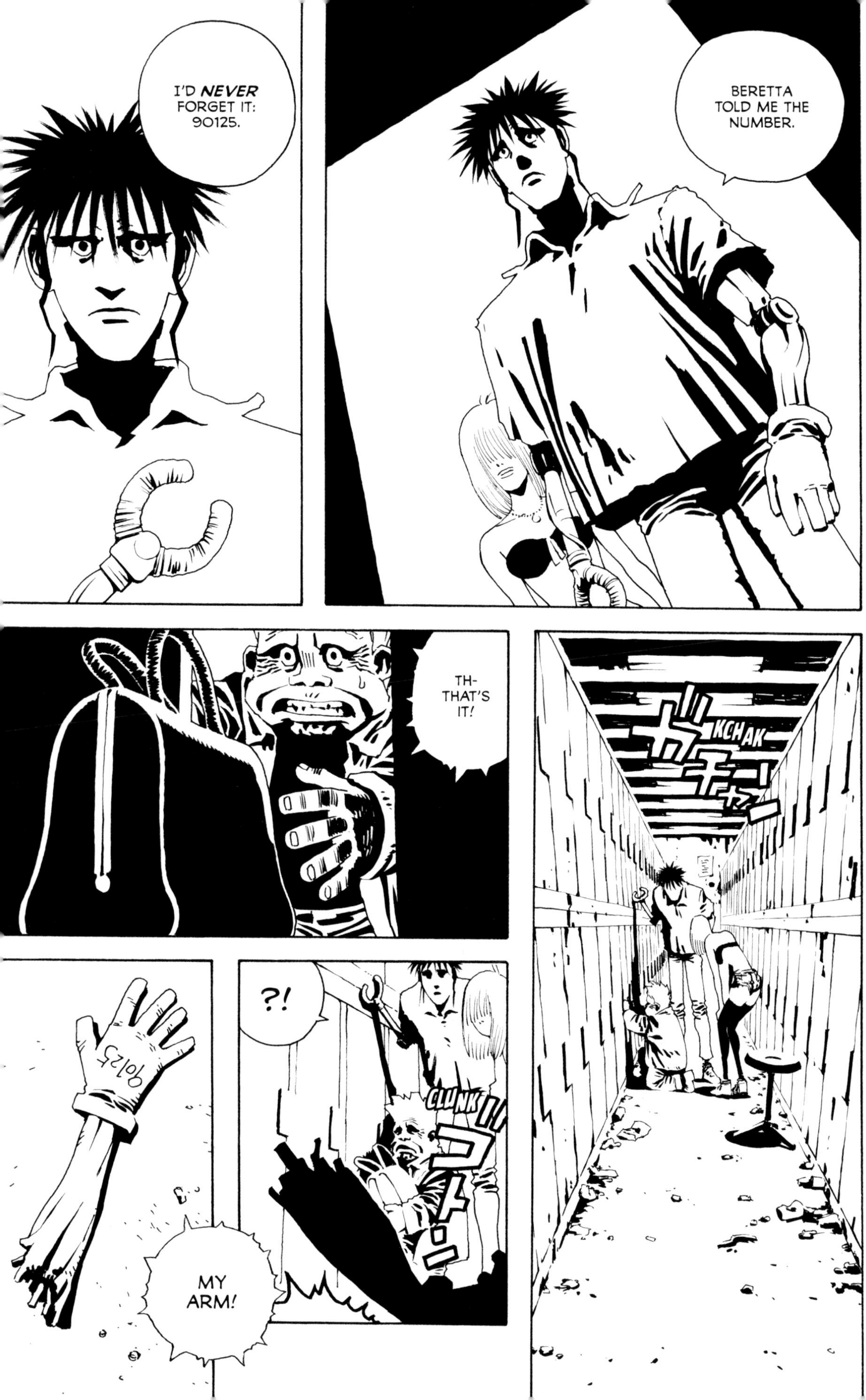
BERETTA TOLD ME THE NUMBER.
I'D **NEVER** FORGET IT: 90125.
KCHAK
TH-THAT'S IT!
?!
CLUNK
MY ARM!

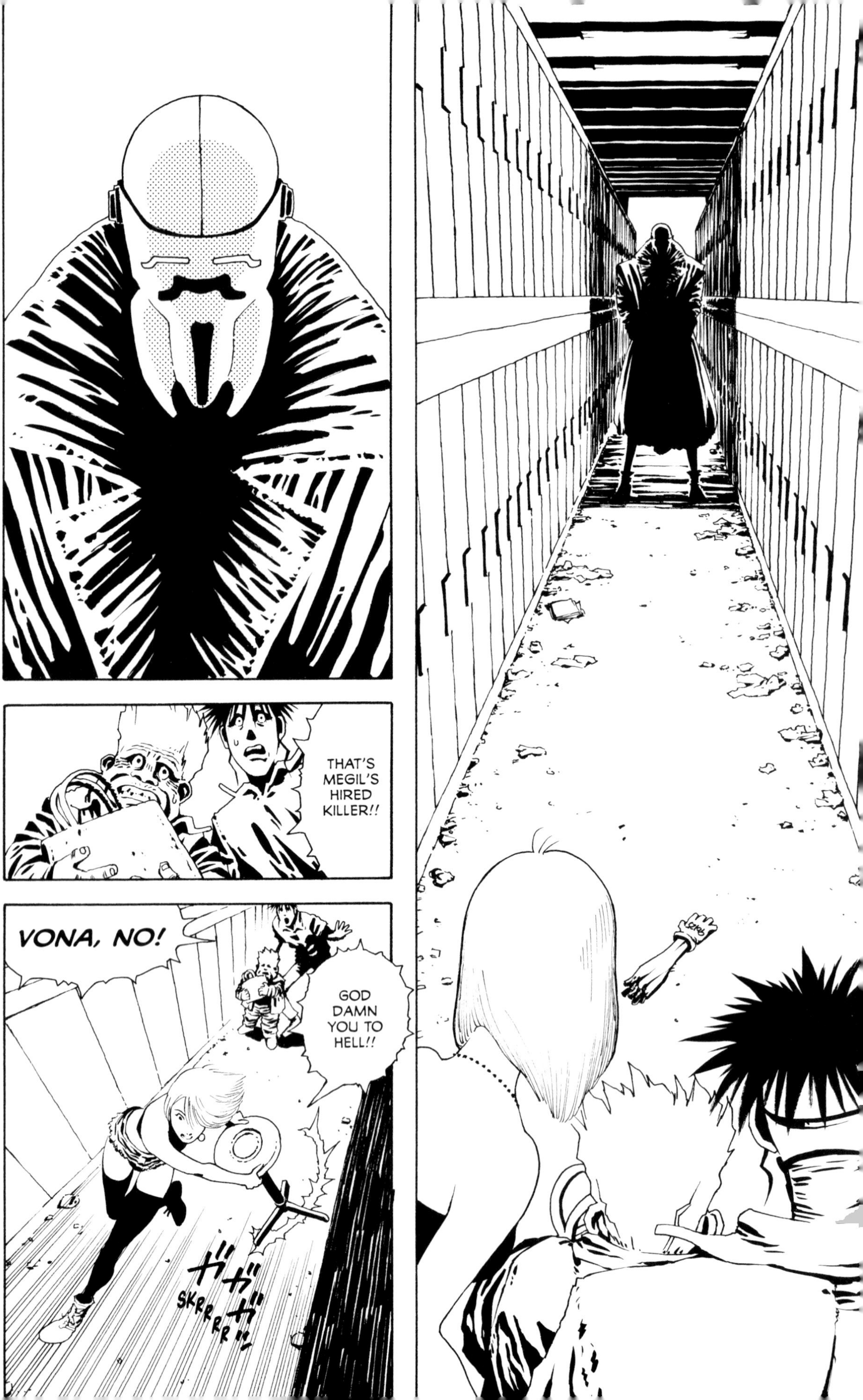
THAT'S MEGIL'S HIRED KILLER!!
VONA, NO!
GOD DAMN YOU TO HELL!!
ガガガ
SKRRRR!!

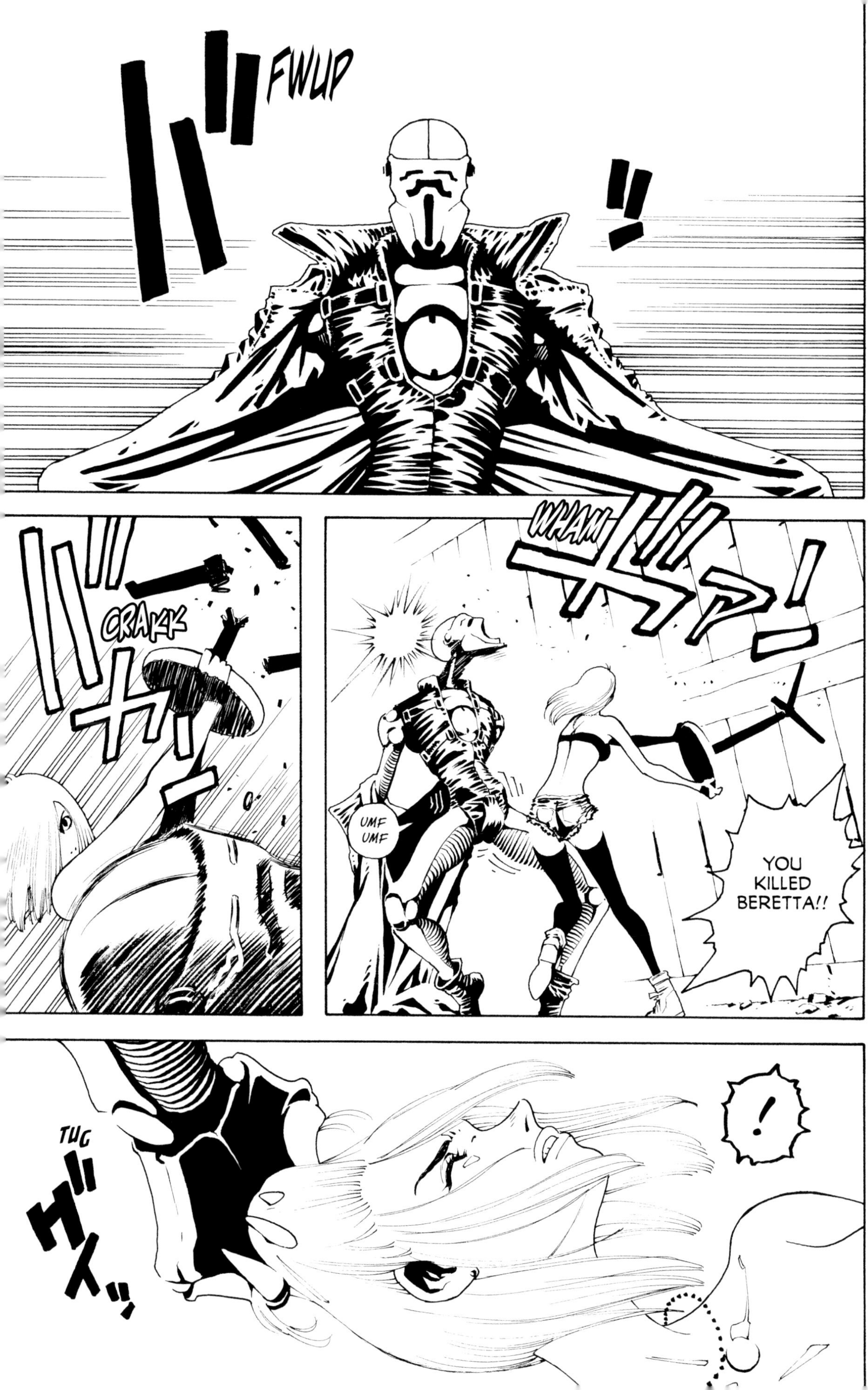
FWUP
WHAM
YOU KILLED BERETTA!!
UMF UMF
CRAKK
!
TUG

FWIK

THUD

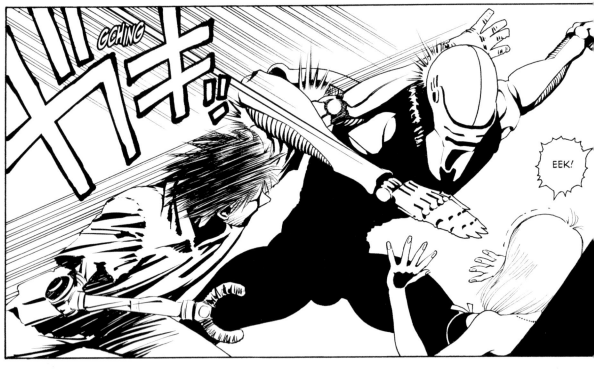

GOHING

EEK!

VONA... HURRY...

BUT SNEV!

WHAM

CRAK CRAK

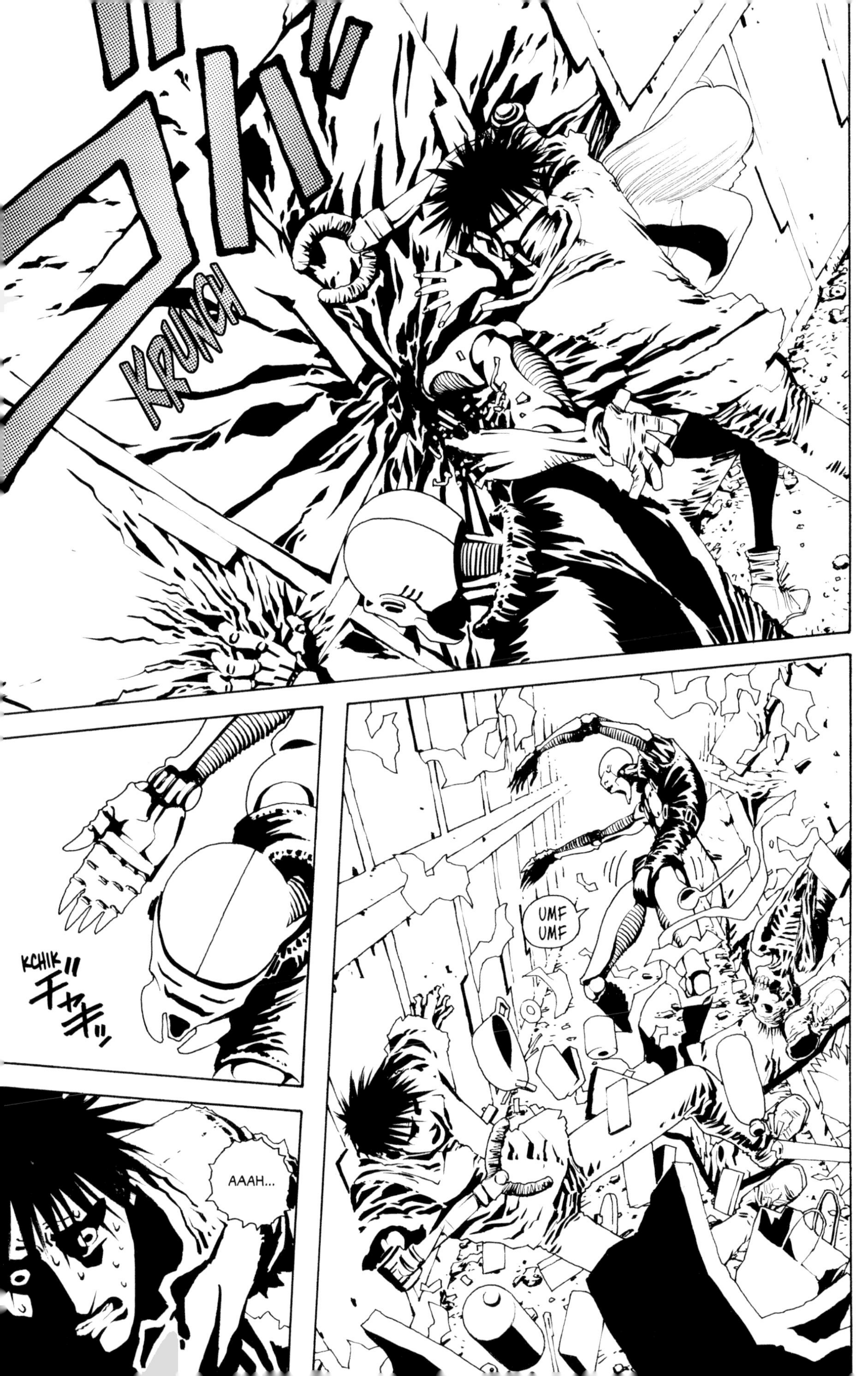
KRUNCH
UMF UMF
KCHIK
チャキッ
AAAH...

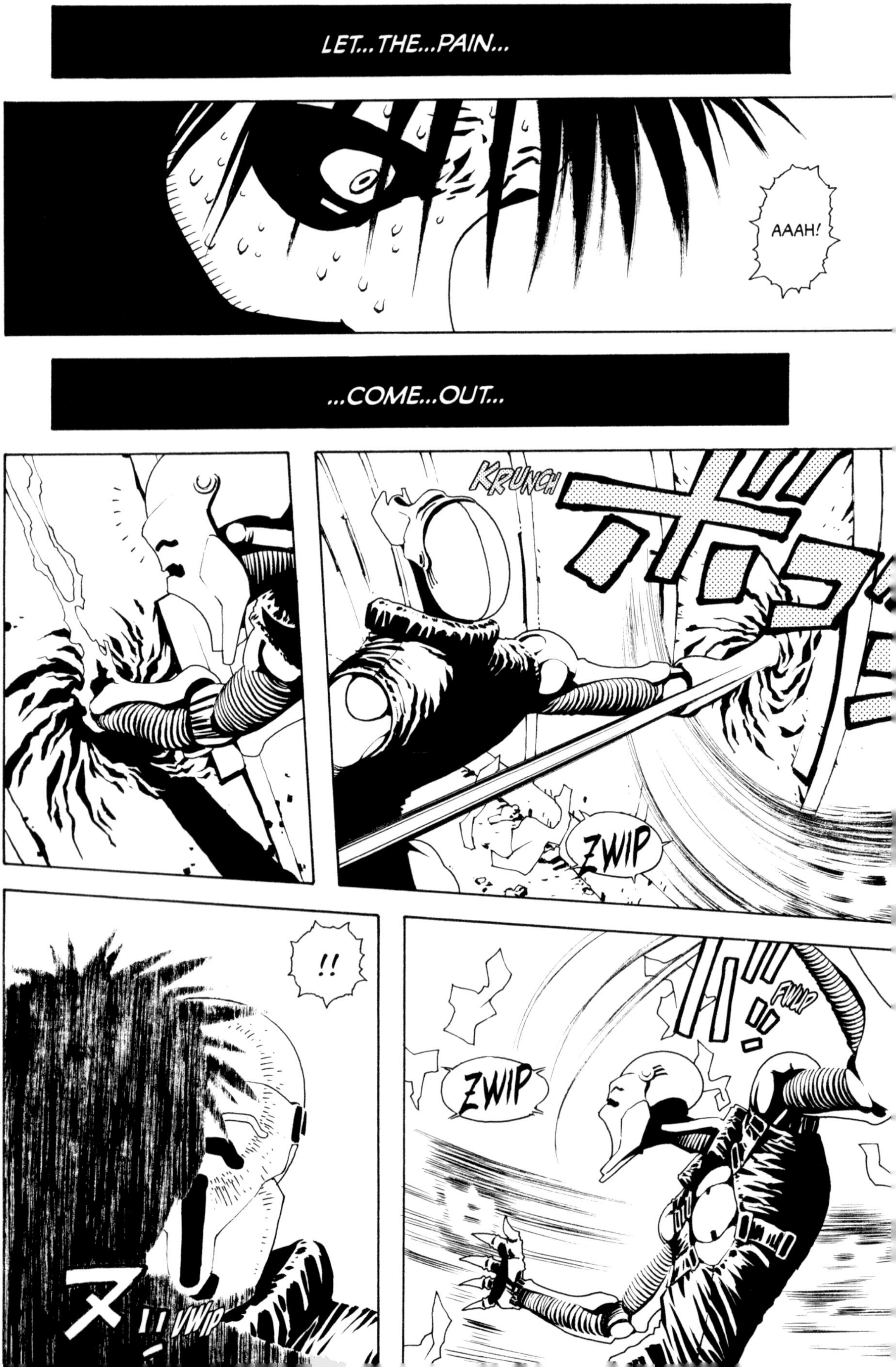
LET...THE...PAIN...
AAAH!
...COME...OUT...
KRUNCH
ZWIP
ZWIP
FWIP
!!
VWIP

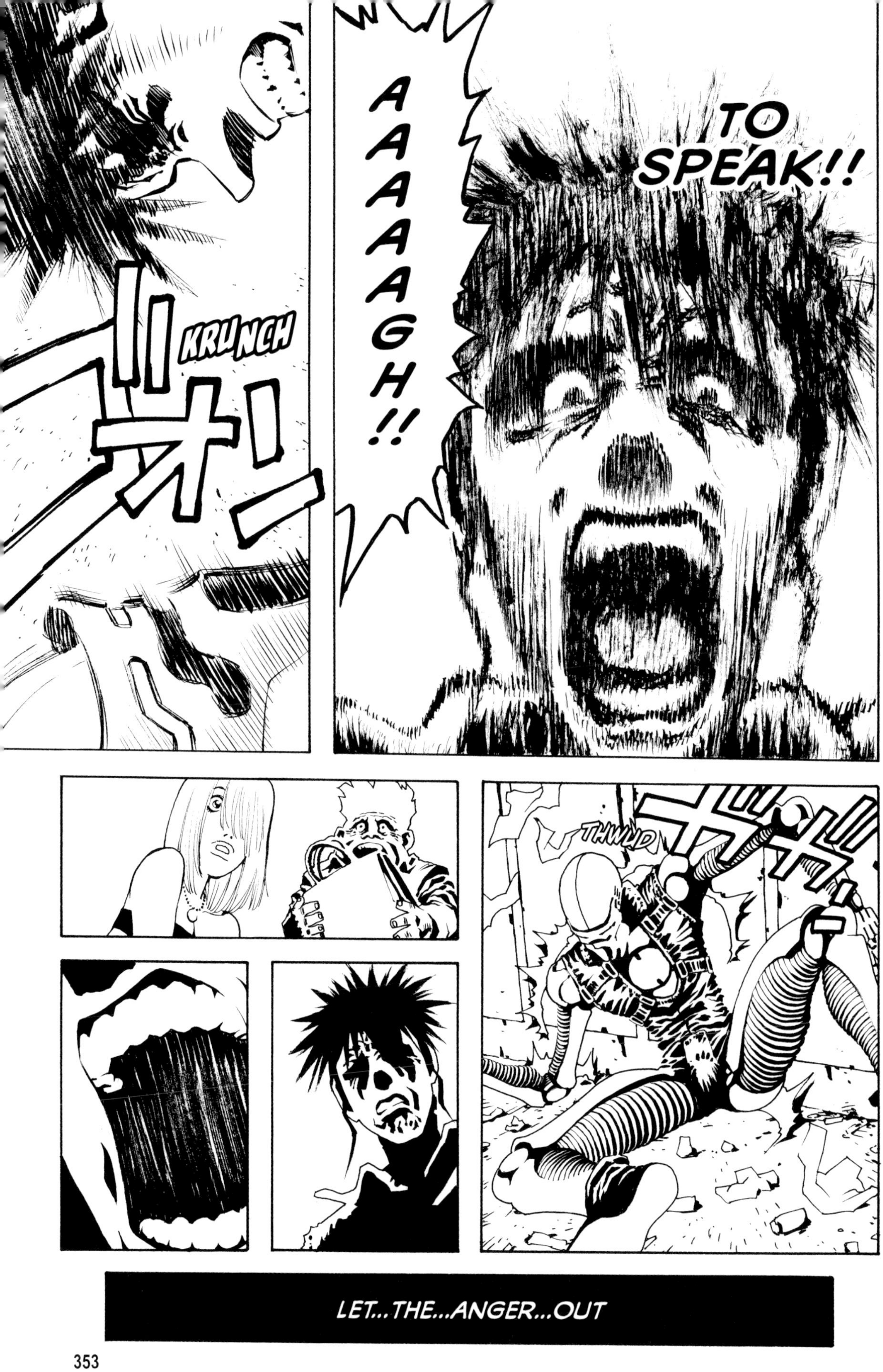
TO SPEAK!!
AAAAAGH!!
KRUNCH
THWUD
LET...THE...ANGER...OUT

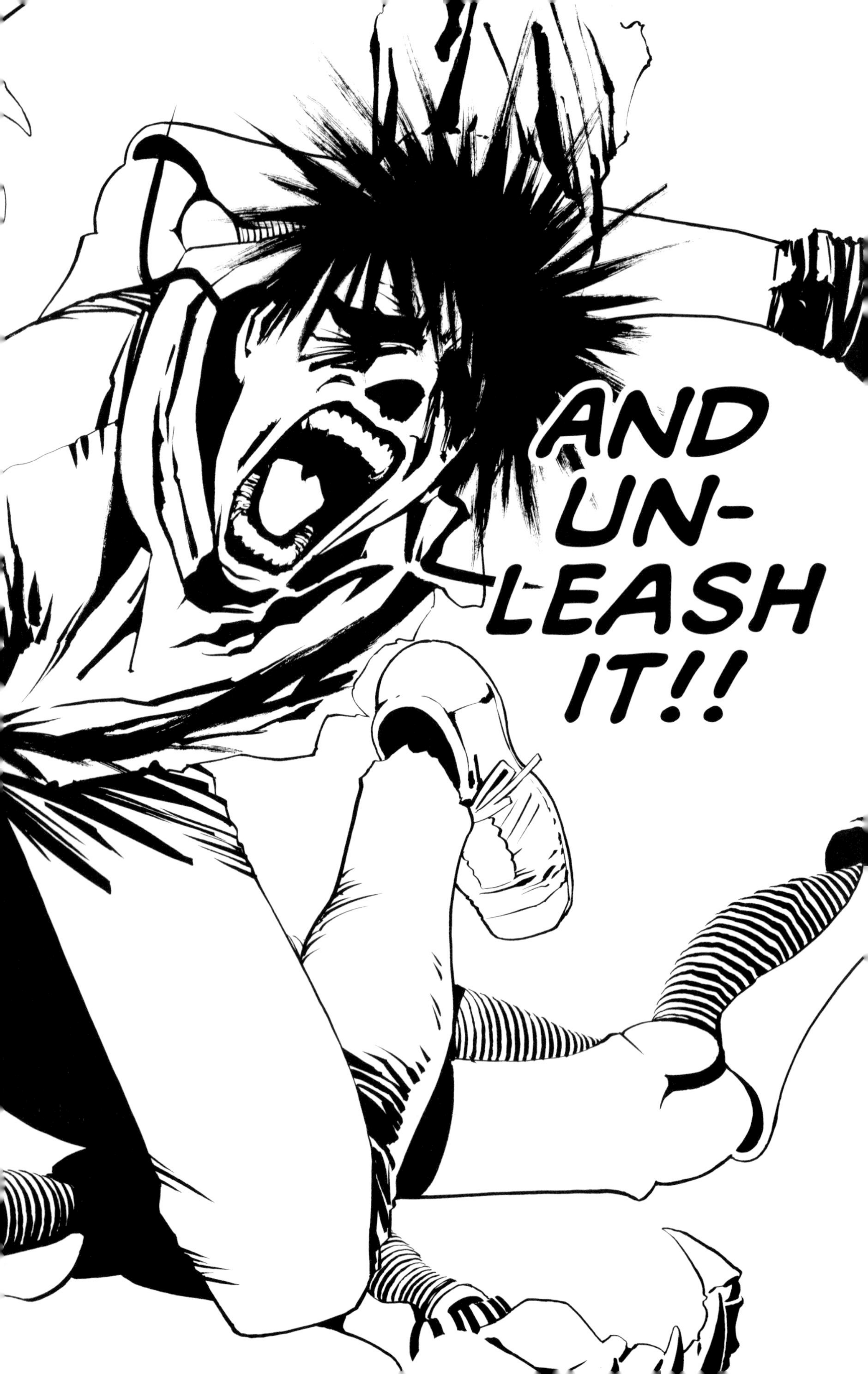
AND UN-LEASH IT!!

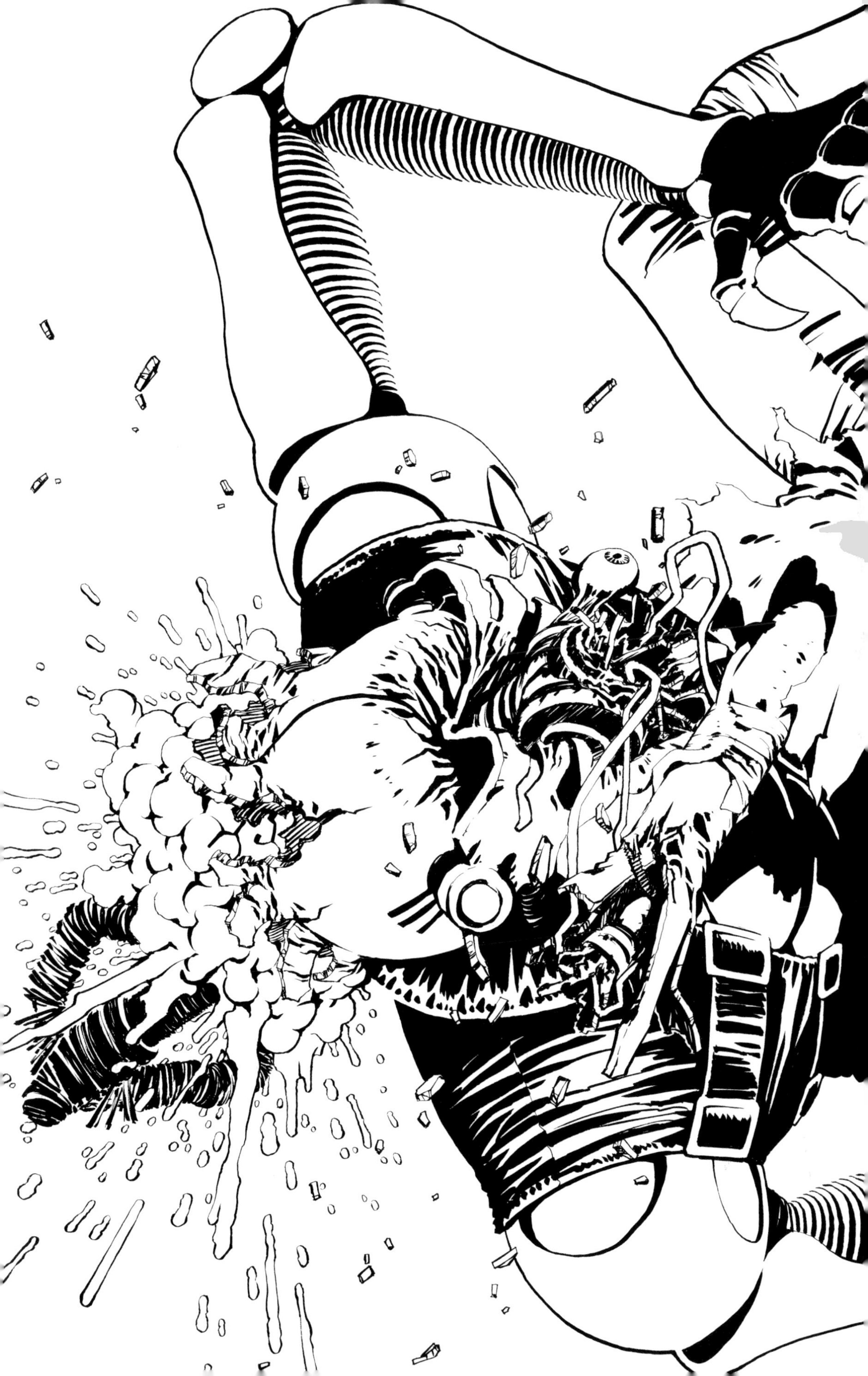

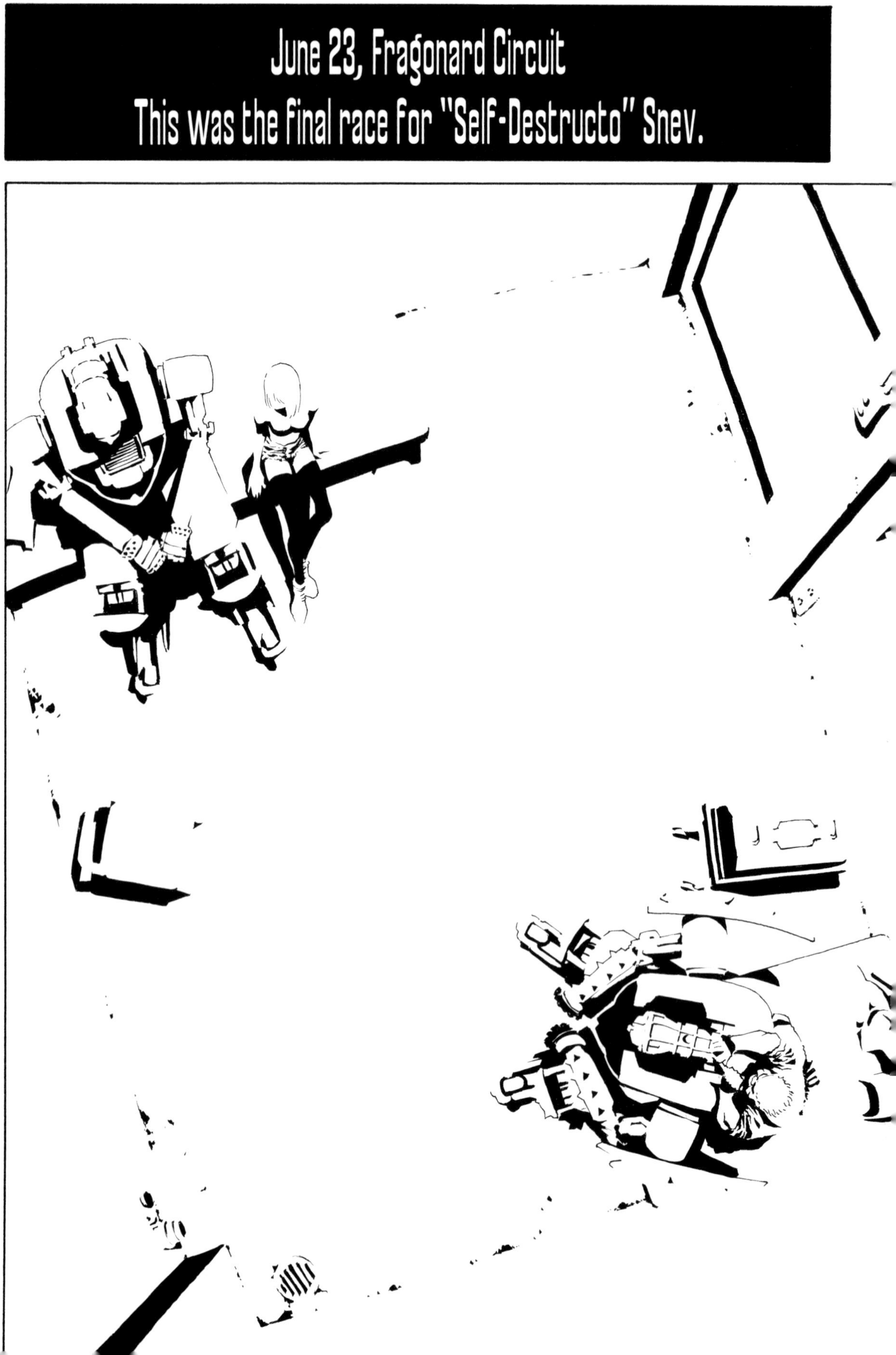
June 23, Fragonard Circuit
This was the final race for "Self-Destructo" Snev.

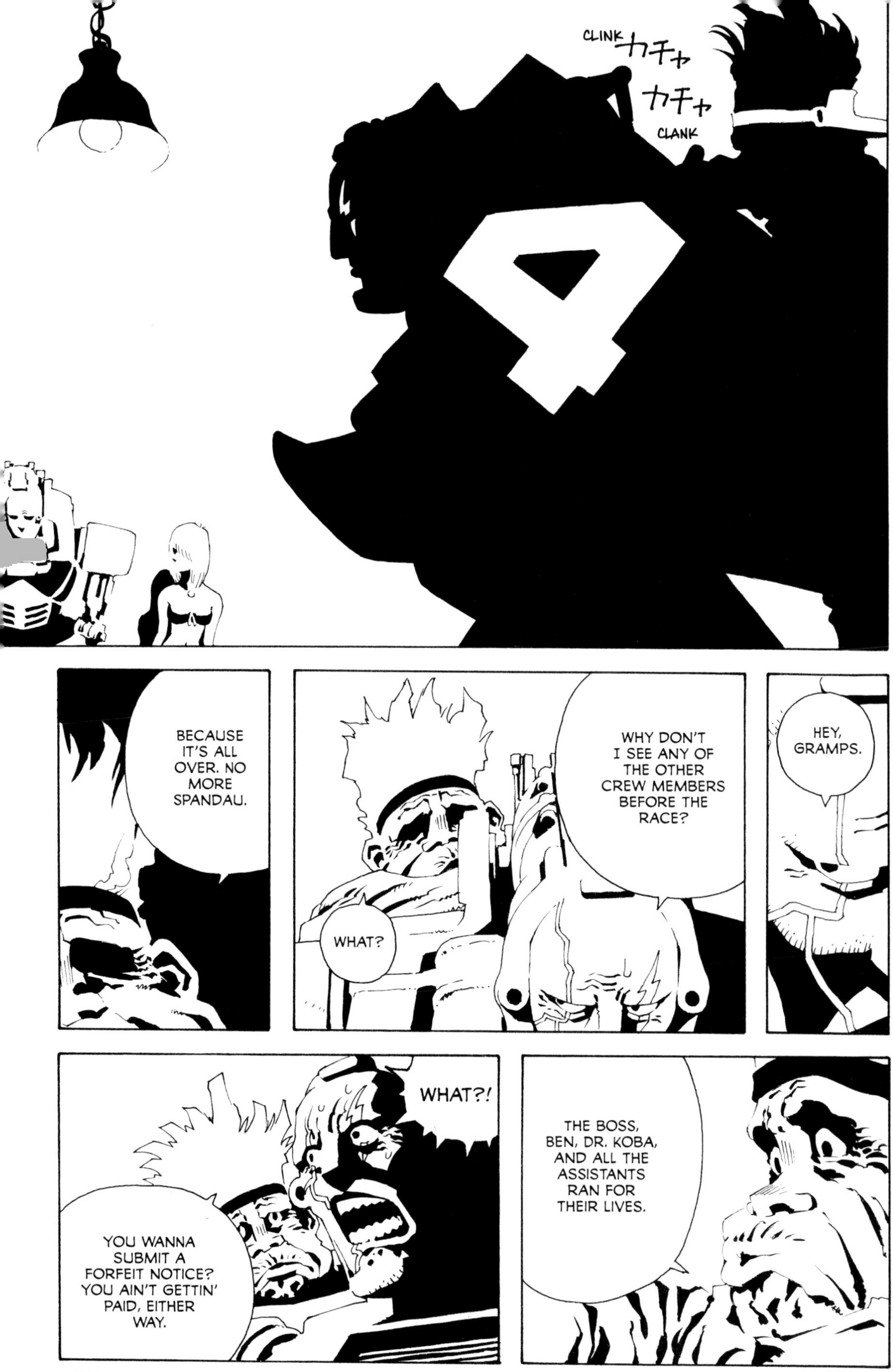
CLINK カチャ
カチャ CLANK
HEY, GRAMPS.
WHY DON'T I SEE ANY OF THE OTHER CREW MEMBERS BEFORE THE RACE?
WHAT?
BECAUSE IT'S ALL OVER. NO MORE SPANDAU.
THE BOSS, BEN, DR. KOBA, AND ALL THE ASSISTANTS RAN FOR THEIR LIVES.
WHAT?!
YOU WANNA SUBMIT A FORFEIT NOTICE? YOU AIN'T GETTIN' PAID, EITHER WAY.

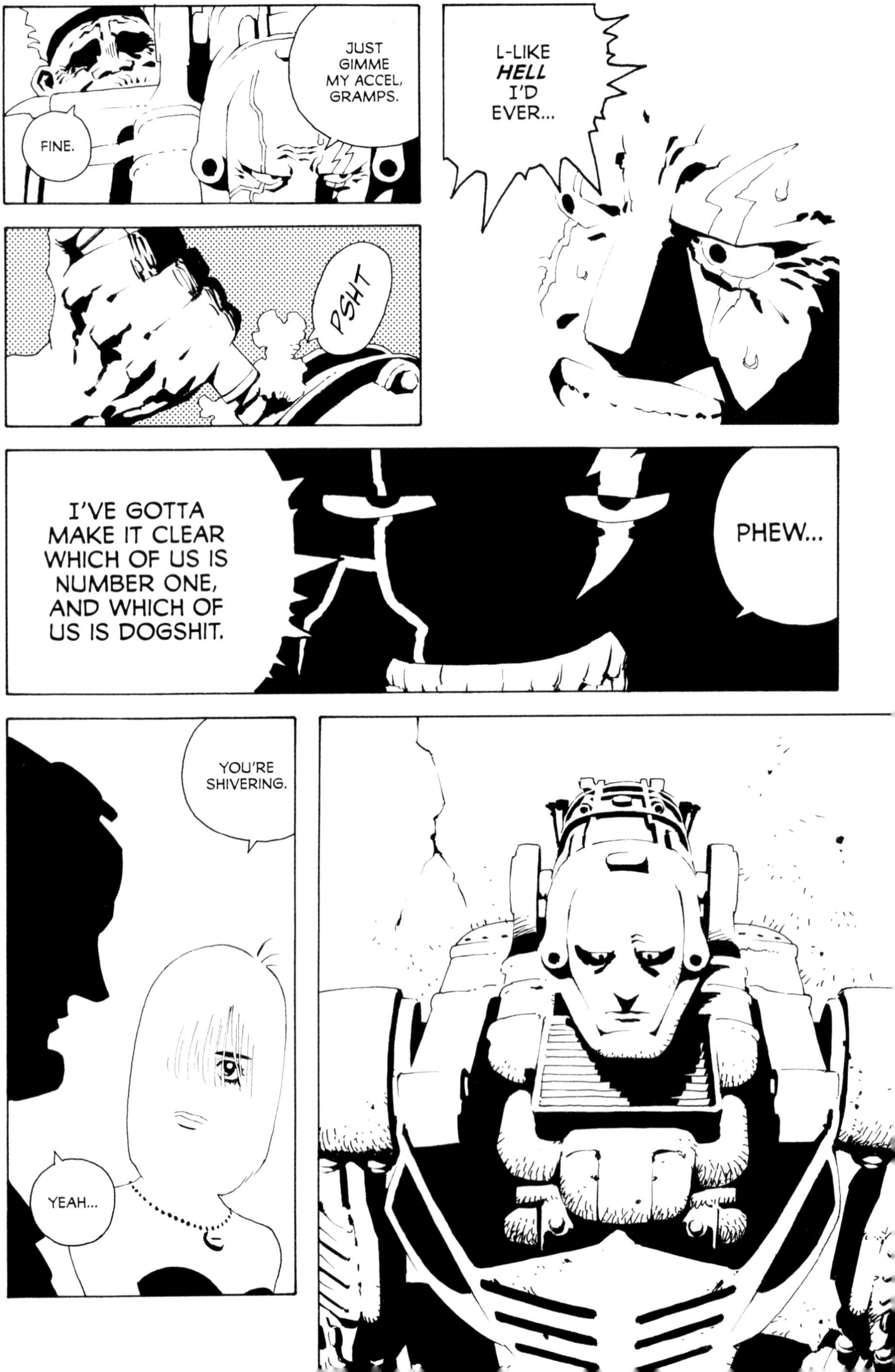
L-LIKE *HELL* I'D EVER...
JUST GIMME MY ACCEL, GRAMPS.
FINE.
PSHT
PHEW...
I'VE GOTTA MAKE IT CLEAR WHICH OF US IS NUMBER ONE, AND WHICH OF US IS DOGSHIT.
YOU'RE SHIVERING.
YEAH...

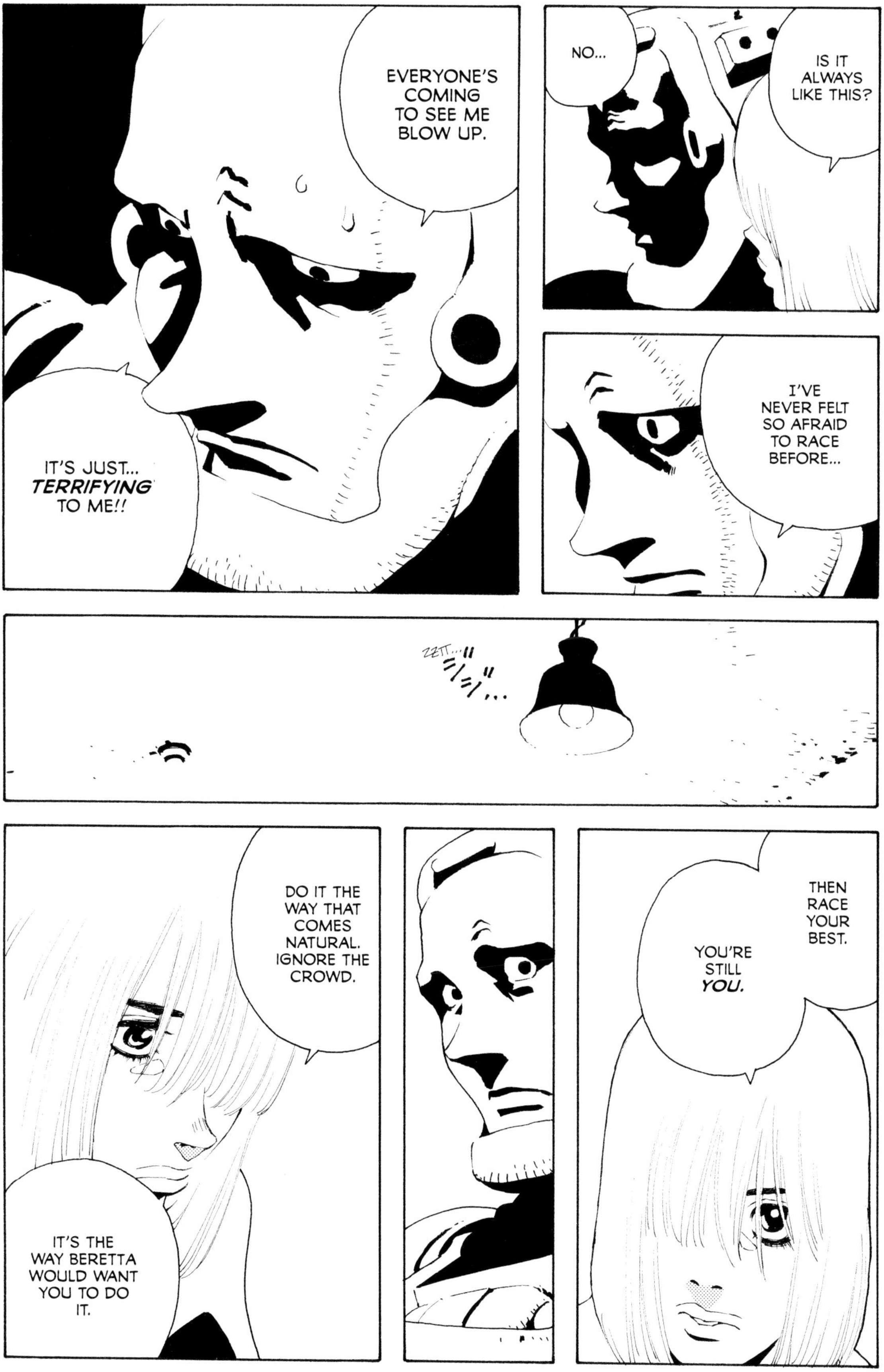
IS IT ALWAYS LIKE THIS?
NO...
I'VE NEVER FELT SO AFRAID TO RACE BEFORE...
EVERYONE'S COMING TO SEE ME BLOW UP.
IT'S JUST... *TERRIFYING* TO ME!!
ZZTT...
THEN RACE YOUR BEST.
YOU'RE STILL *YOU.*
DO IT THE WAY THAT COMES NATURAL. IGNORE THE CROWD.
IT'S THE WAY BERETTA WOULD WANT YOU TO DO IT.

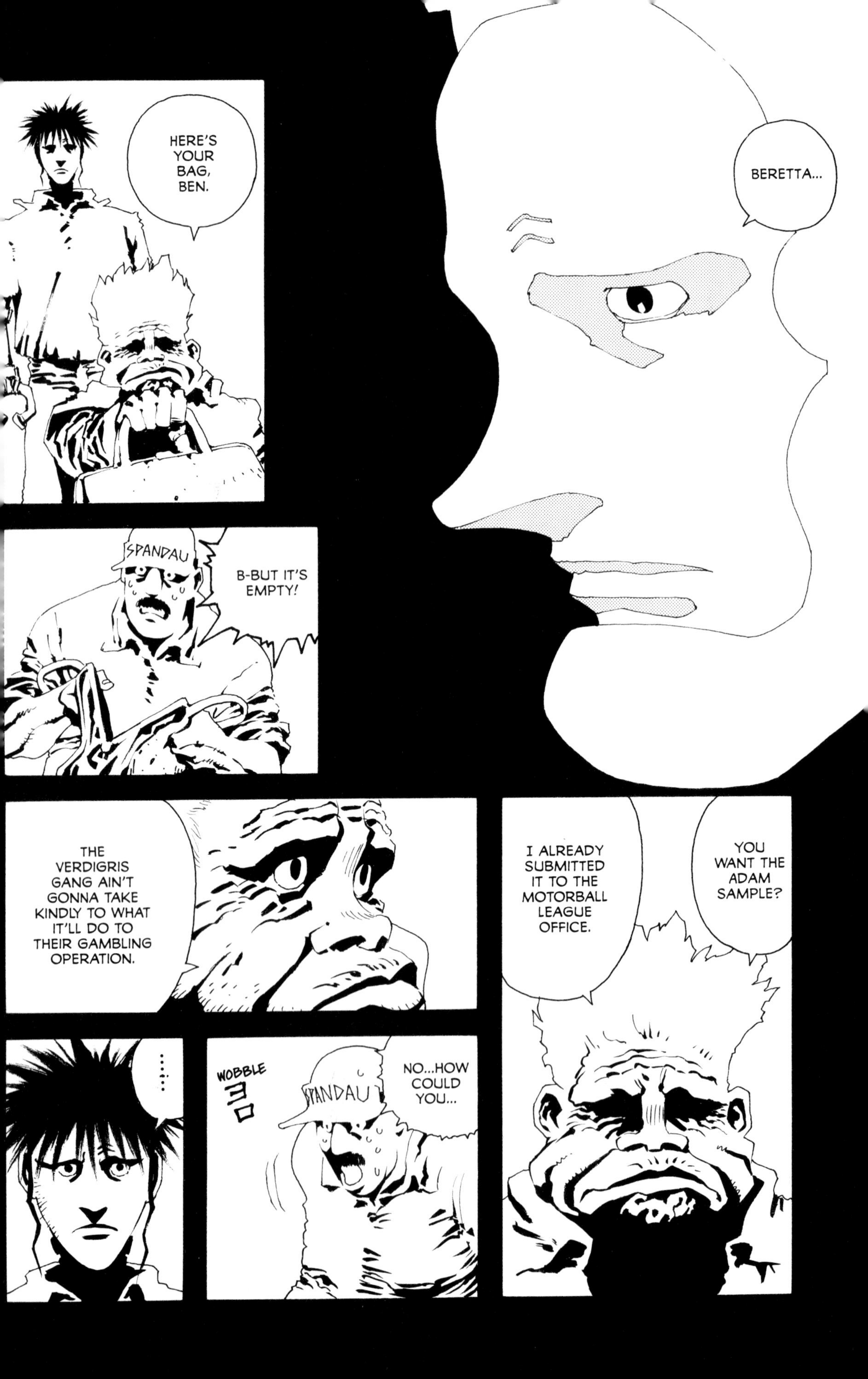
BERETTA...
HERE'S YOUR BAG, BEN.
B-BUT IT'S EMPTY!
SPANDAU
YOU WANT THE ADAM SAMPLE?
I ALREADY SUBMITTED IT TO THE MOTORBALL LEAGUE OFFICE.
THE VERDIGRIS GANG AIN'T GONNA TAKE KINDLY TO WHAT IT'LL DO TO THEIR GAMBLING OPERATION.
NO...HOW COULD YOU...
WOBBLE ヨロ
SPANDAU
.....

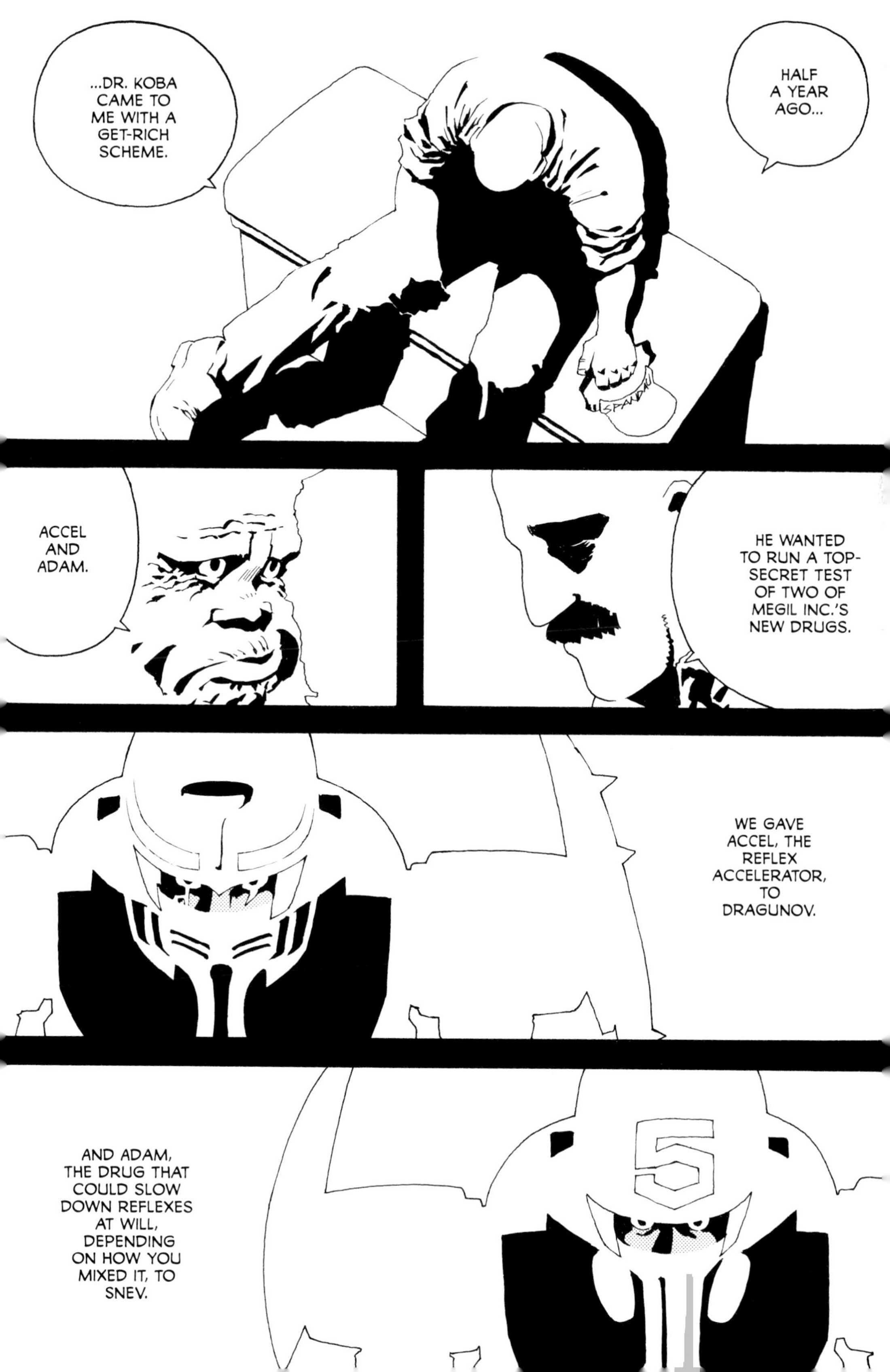
HALF A YEAR AGO...
...DR. KOBA CAME TO ME WITH A GET-RICH SCHEME.
SPANDAU
HE WANTED TO RUN A TOP-SECRET TEST OF TWO OF MEGIL INC.'S NEW DRUGS.
ACCEL AND ADAM.
WE GAVE ACCEL, THE REFLEX ACCELERATOR, TO DRAGUNOV.
AND ADAM, THE DRUG THAT COULD SLOW DOWN REFLEXES AT WILL, DEPENDING ON HOW YOU MIXED IT, TO SNEV.

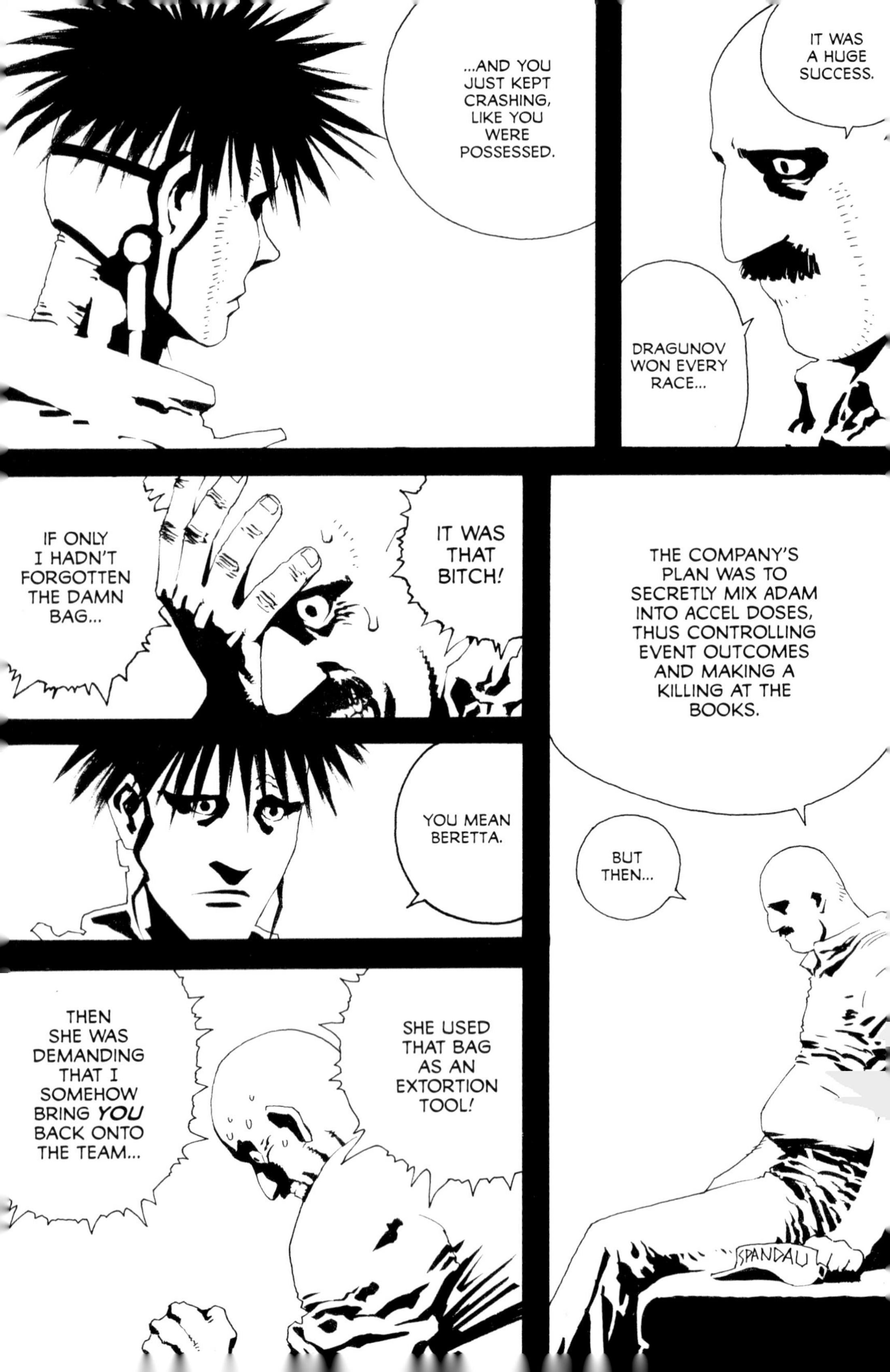
IT WAS A HUGE SUCCESS.
DRAGUNOV WON EVERY RACE...
...AND YOU JUST KEPT CRASHING, LIKE YOU WERE POSSESSED.
THE COMPANY'S PLAN WAS TO SECRETLY MIX ADAM INTO ACCEL DOSES, THUS CONTROLLING EVENT OUTCOMES AND MAKING A KILLING AT THE BOOKS.
BUT THEN...
SPANDAU
IT WAS THAT BITCH!
IF ONLY I HADN'T FORGOTTEN THE DAMN BAG...
YOU MEAN BERETTA.
SHE USED THAT BAG AS AN EXTORTION TOOL!
THEN SHE WAS DEMANDING THAT I SOMEHOW BRING *YOU* BACK ONTO THE TEAM...

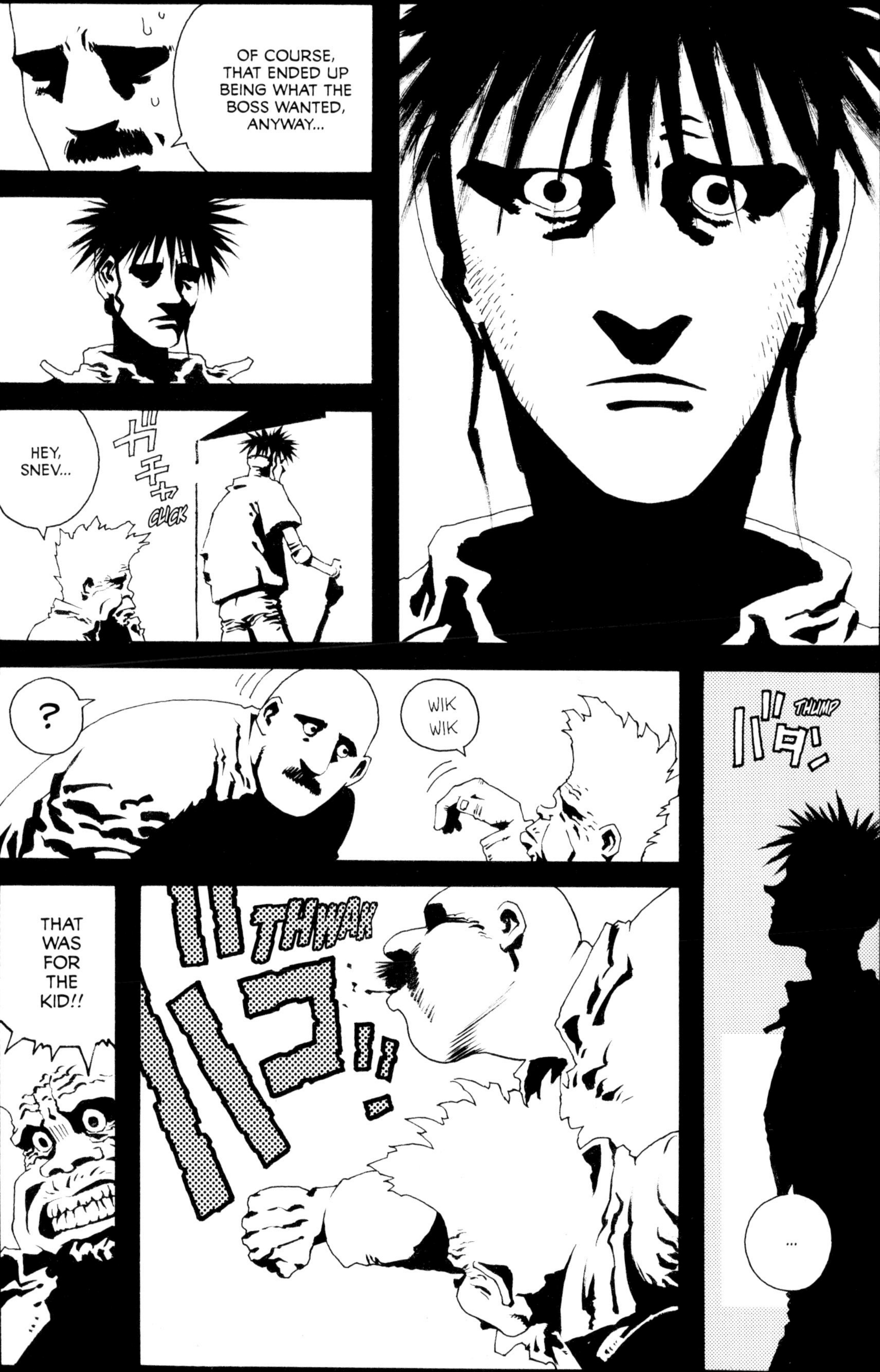
OF COURSE, THAT ENDED UP BEING WHAT THE BOSS WANTED, ANYWAY...
ガチャ
CLICK
HEY, SNEV...
バタン
THUMP
...
WIK WIK
?
バコ!!
THWAK
THAT WAS FOR THE KID!!

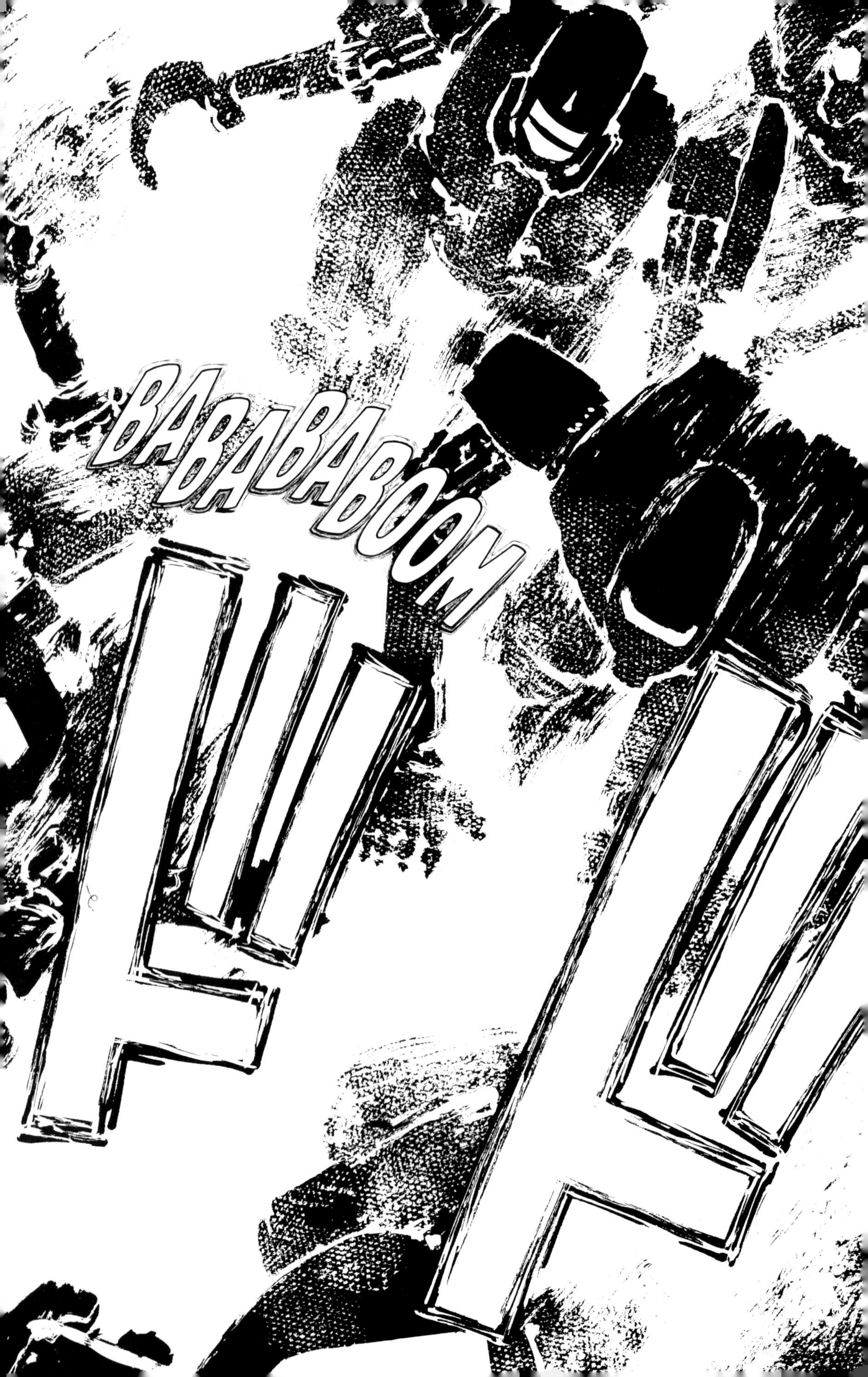
BABABABOOM

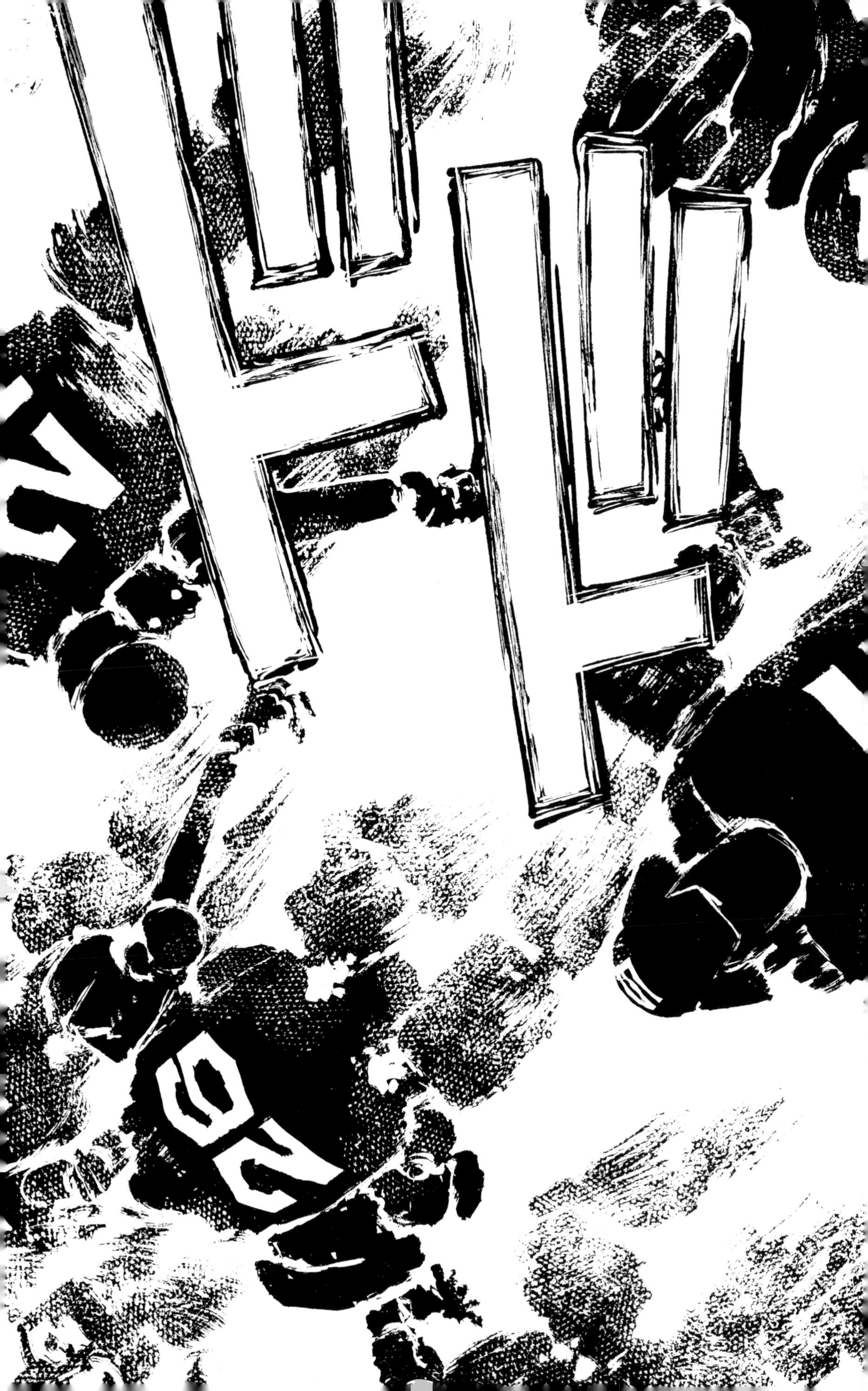

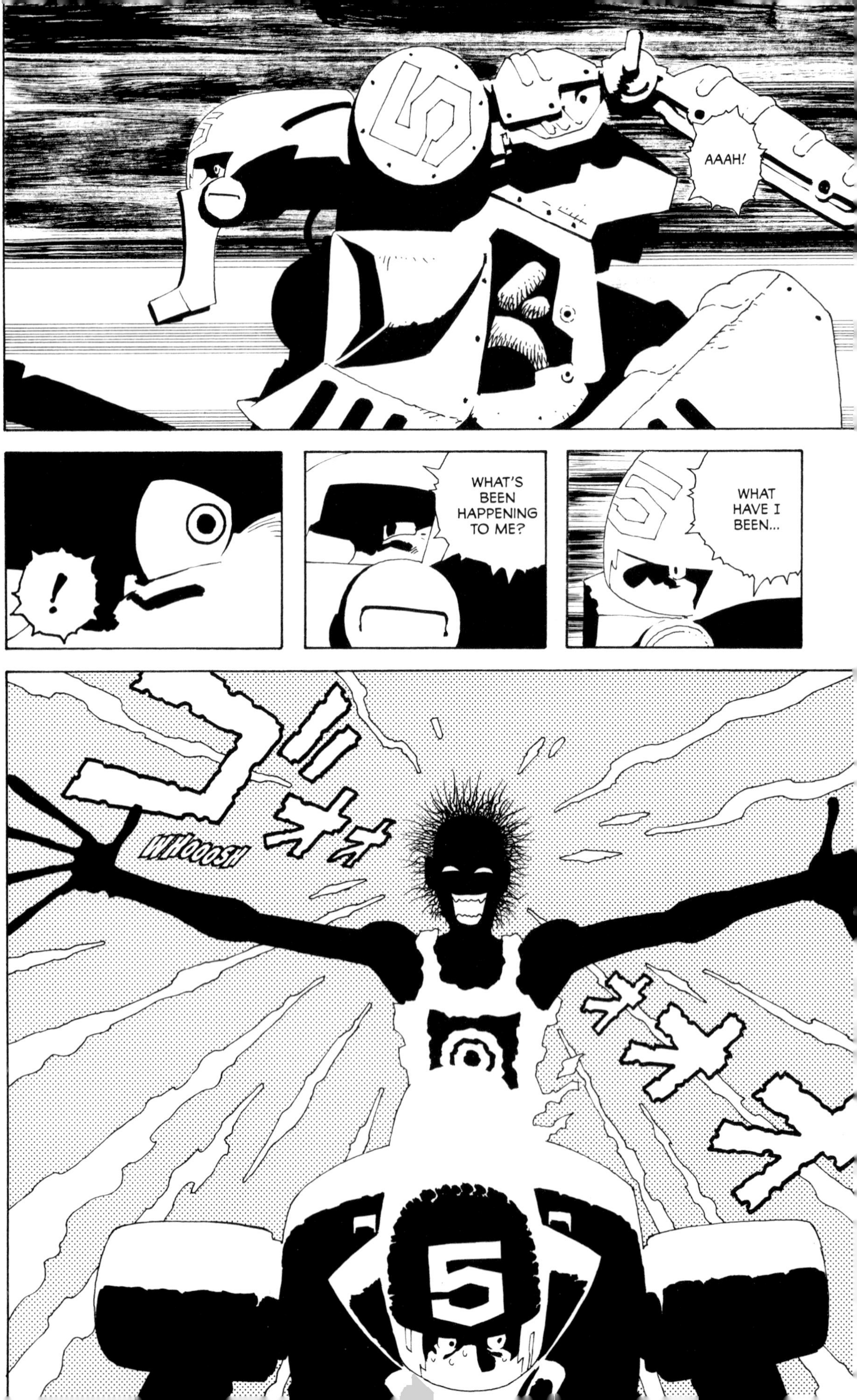
AAAH!
WHAT HAVE I BEEN...
WHAT'S BEEN HAPPENING TO ME?
!
WHOOOSH

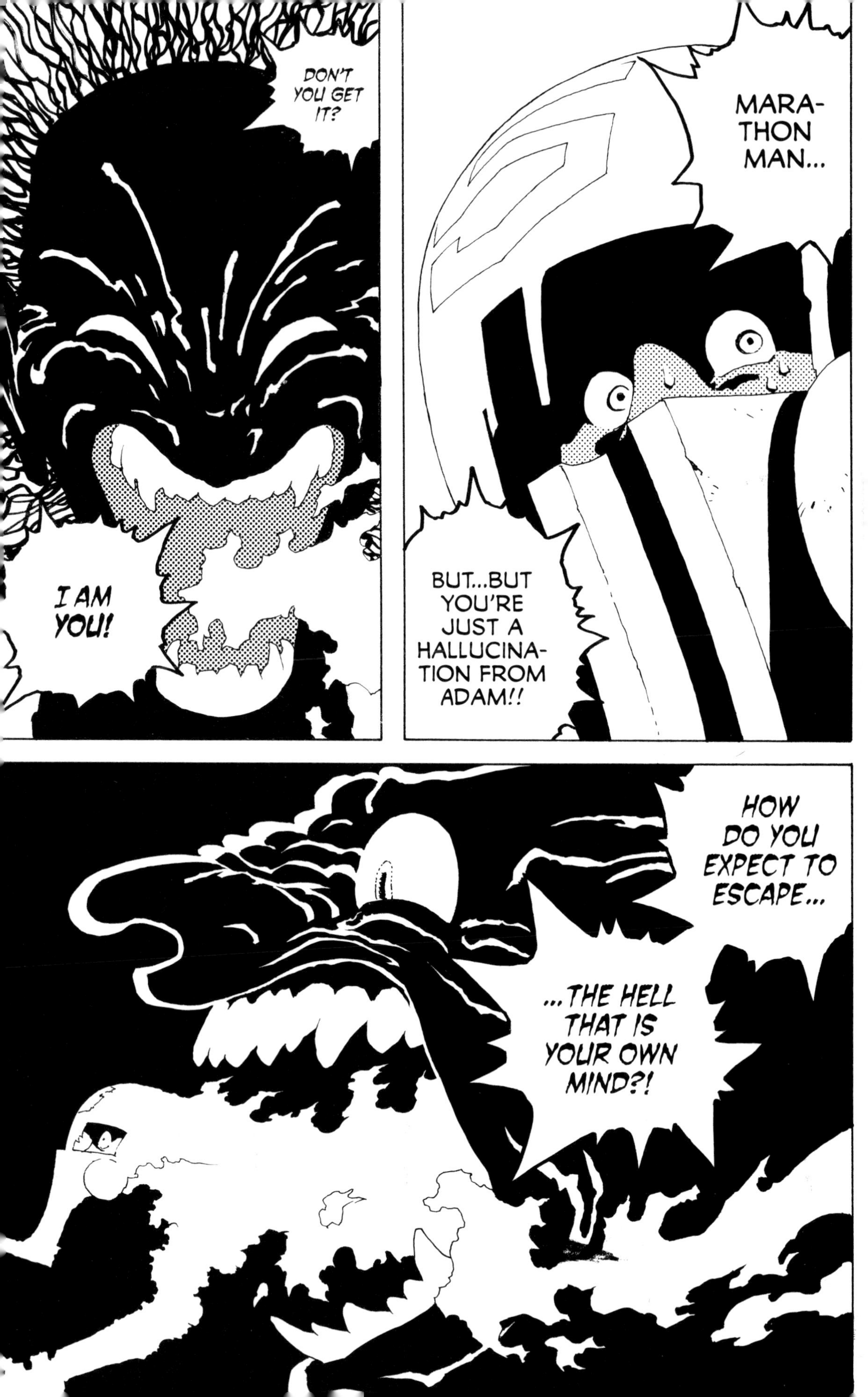
MARATHON MAN...
BUT...BUT YOU'RE JUST A HALLUCINATION FROM ADAM!!
DON'T YOU GET IT?
I AM YOU!
HOW DO YOU EXPECT TO ESCAPE...
...THE HELL THAT IS YOUR OWN MIND?!

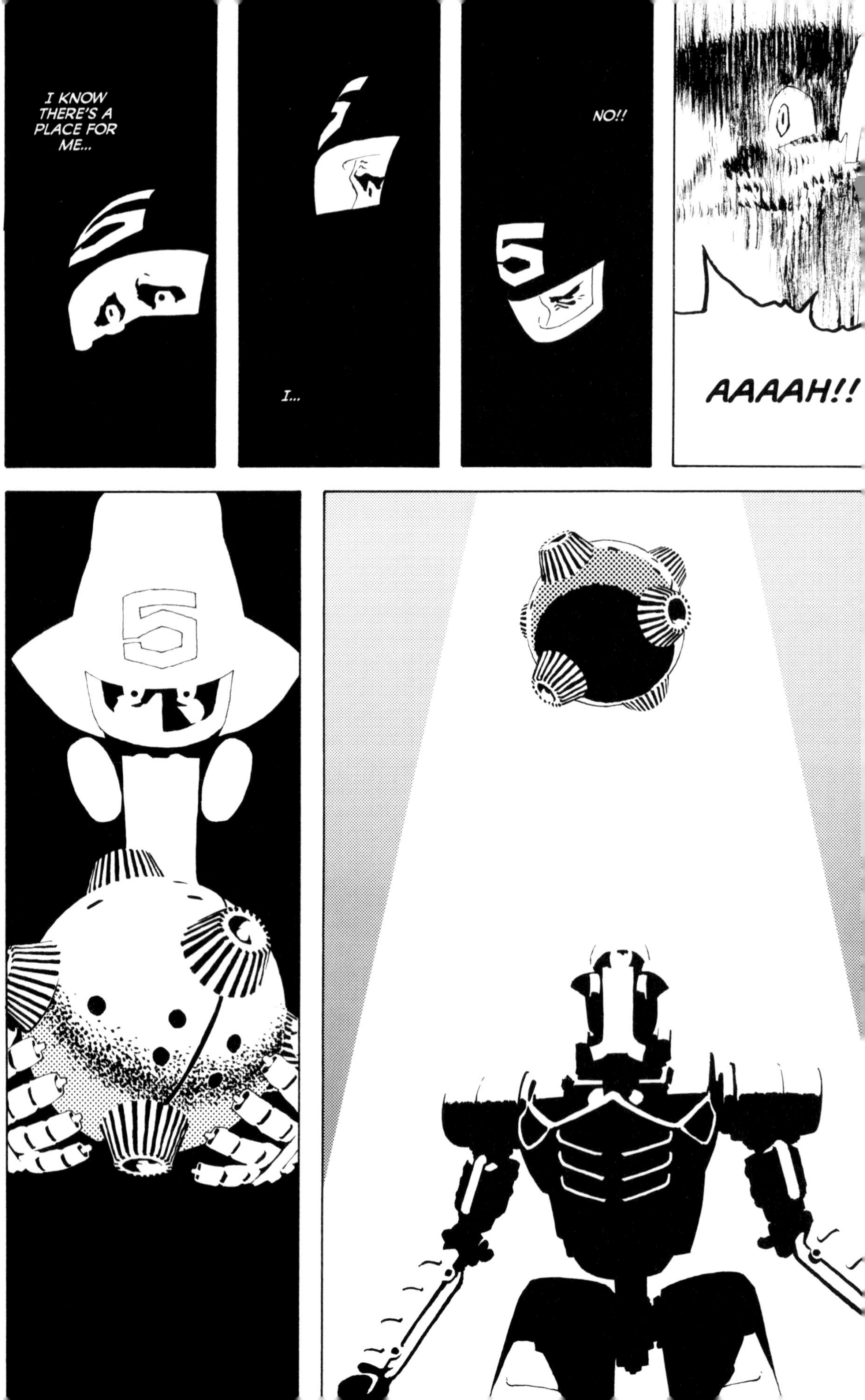
AAAAH!!
NO!!
I...
I KNOW THERE'S A PLACE FOR ME...

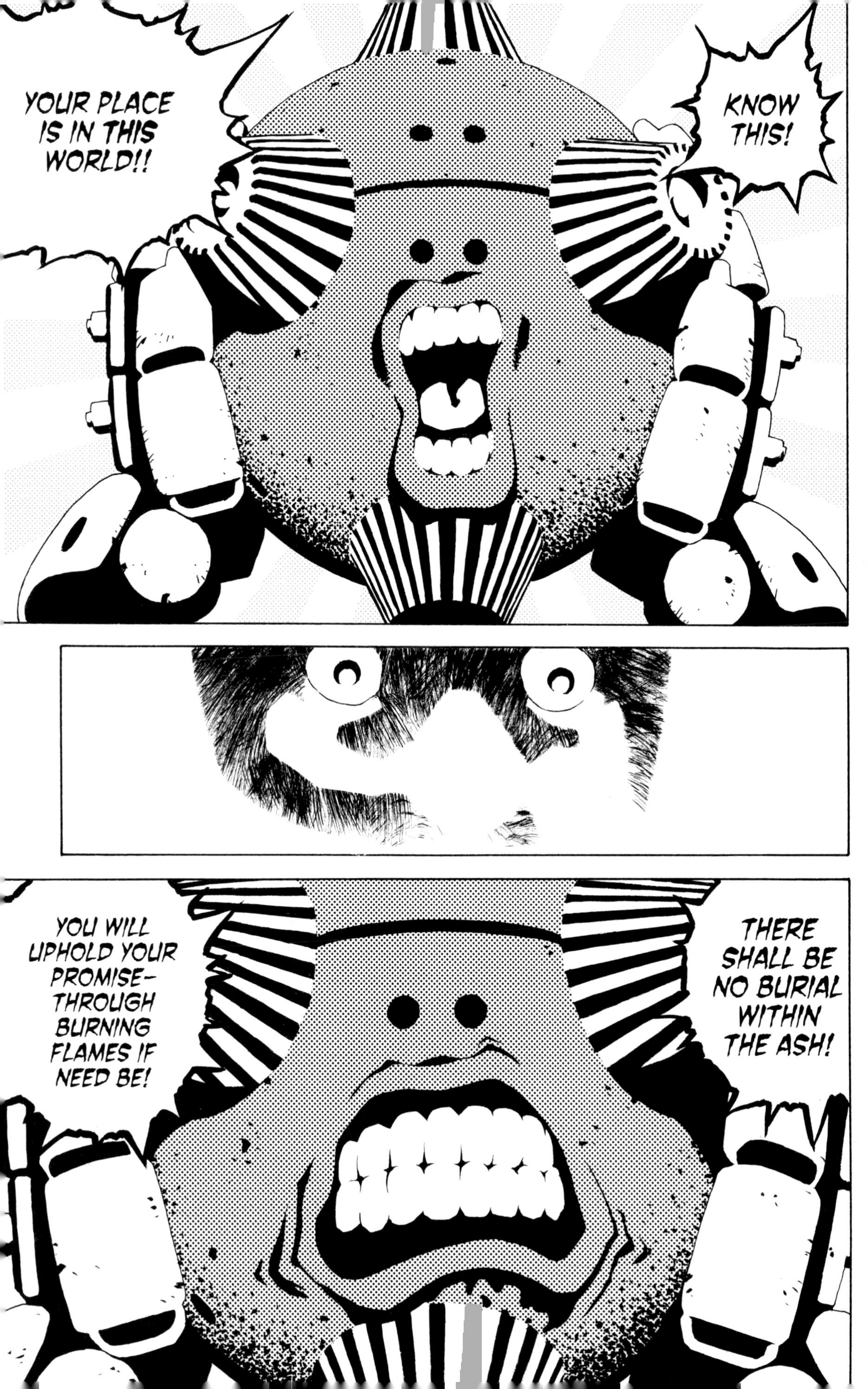
KNOW THIS!
YOUR PLACE IS IN THIS WORLD!!
THERE SHALL BE NO BURIAL WITHIN THE ASH!
YOU WILL UPHOLD YOUR PROMISE-THROUGH BURNING FLAMES IF NEED BE!

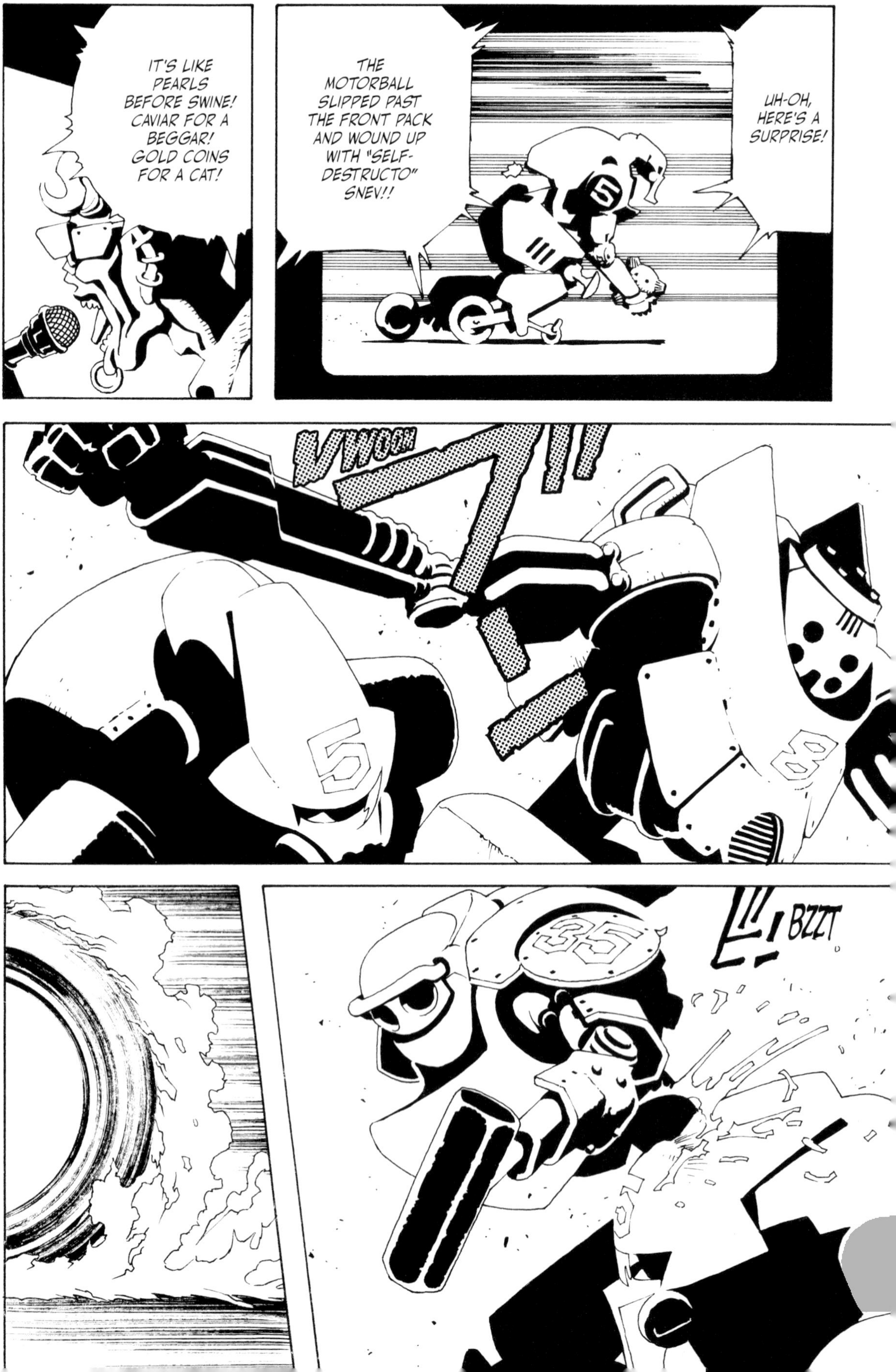
UH-OH, HERE'S A SURPRISE!
THE MOTORBALL SLIPPED PAST THE FRONT PACK AND WOUND UP WITH "SELF-DESTRUCTO" SNEV!!
IT'S LIKE PEARLS BEFORE SWINE! CAVIAR FOR A BEGGAR! GOLD COINS FOR A CAT!
VWOOM
BZZT

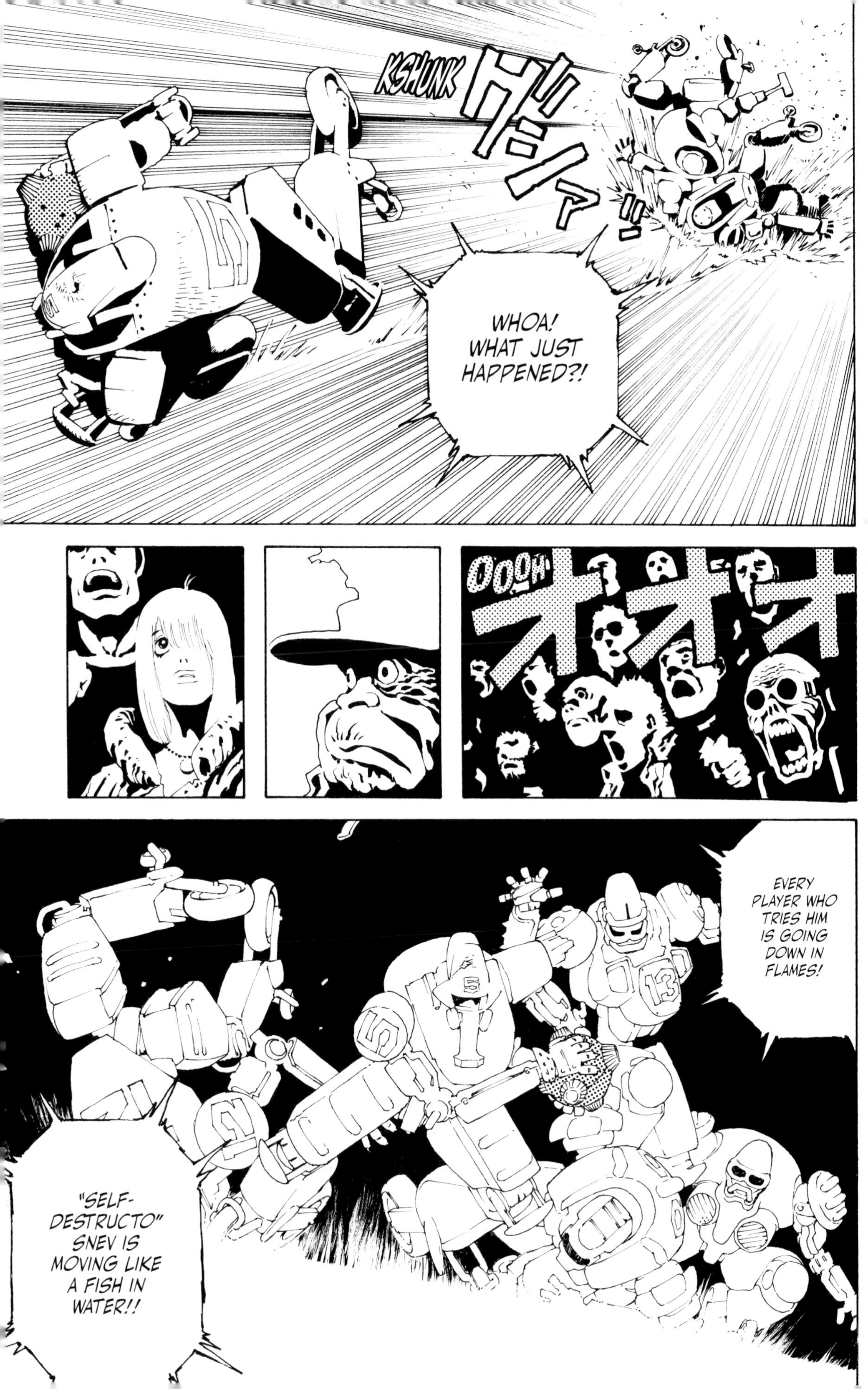
KSHUNK
WHOA! WHAT JUST HAPPENED?!
OOOH
EVERY PLAYER WHO TRIES HIM IS GOING DOWN IN FLAMES!
"SELF-DESTRUCTO" SNEV IS MOVING LIKE A FISH IN WATER!!

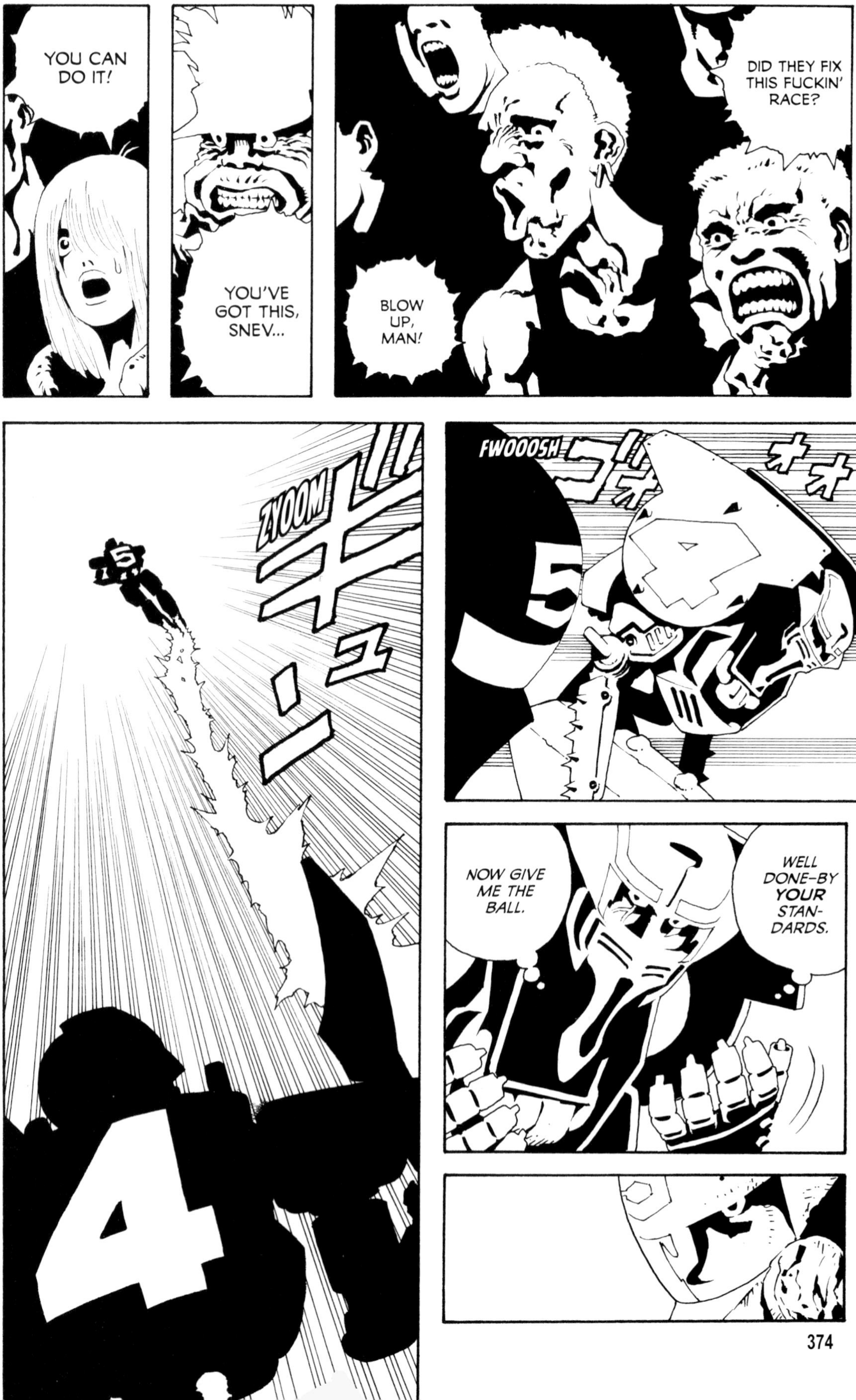
DID THEY FIX THIS FUCKIN' RACE?
BLOW UP, MAN!
YOU'VE GOT THIS, SNEV...
YOU CAN DO IT!
FWOOOSH
ゴォオオ
WELL DONE—BY **YOUR** STAN-DARDS.
NOW GIVE ME THE BALL.
ZYOOM
キュ・ー

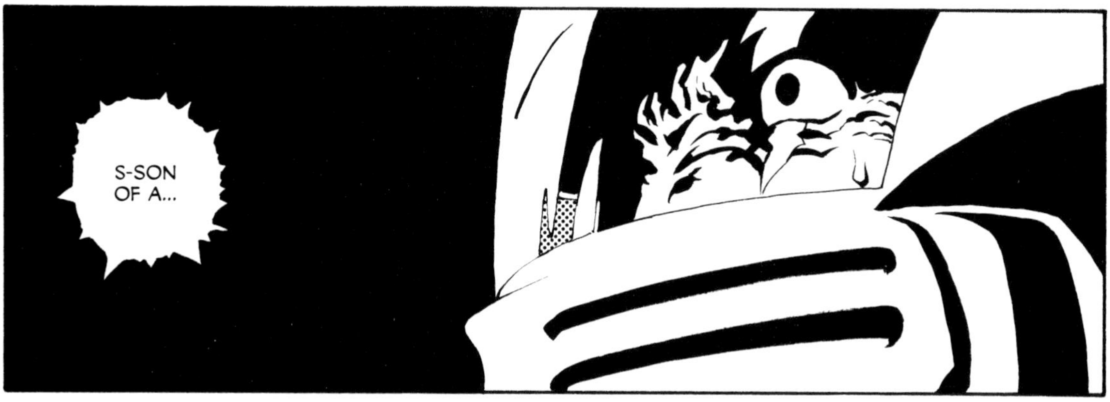
S-SON
OF A...
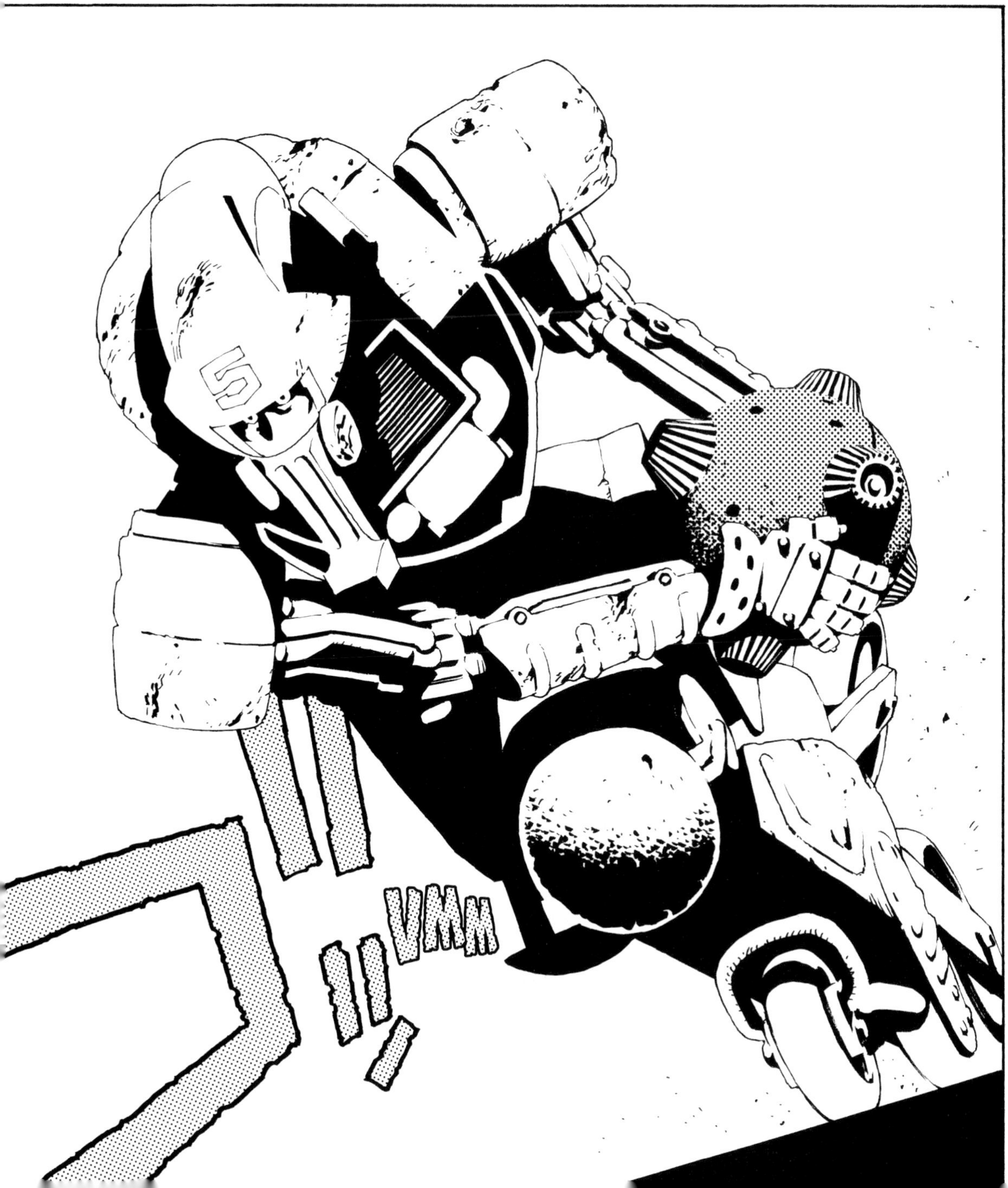
VMM

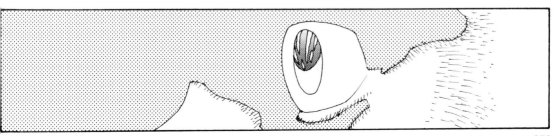

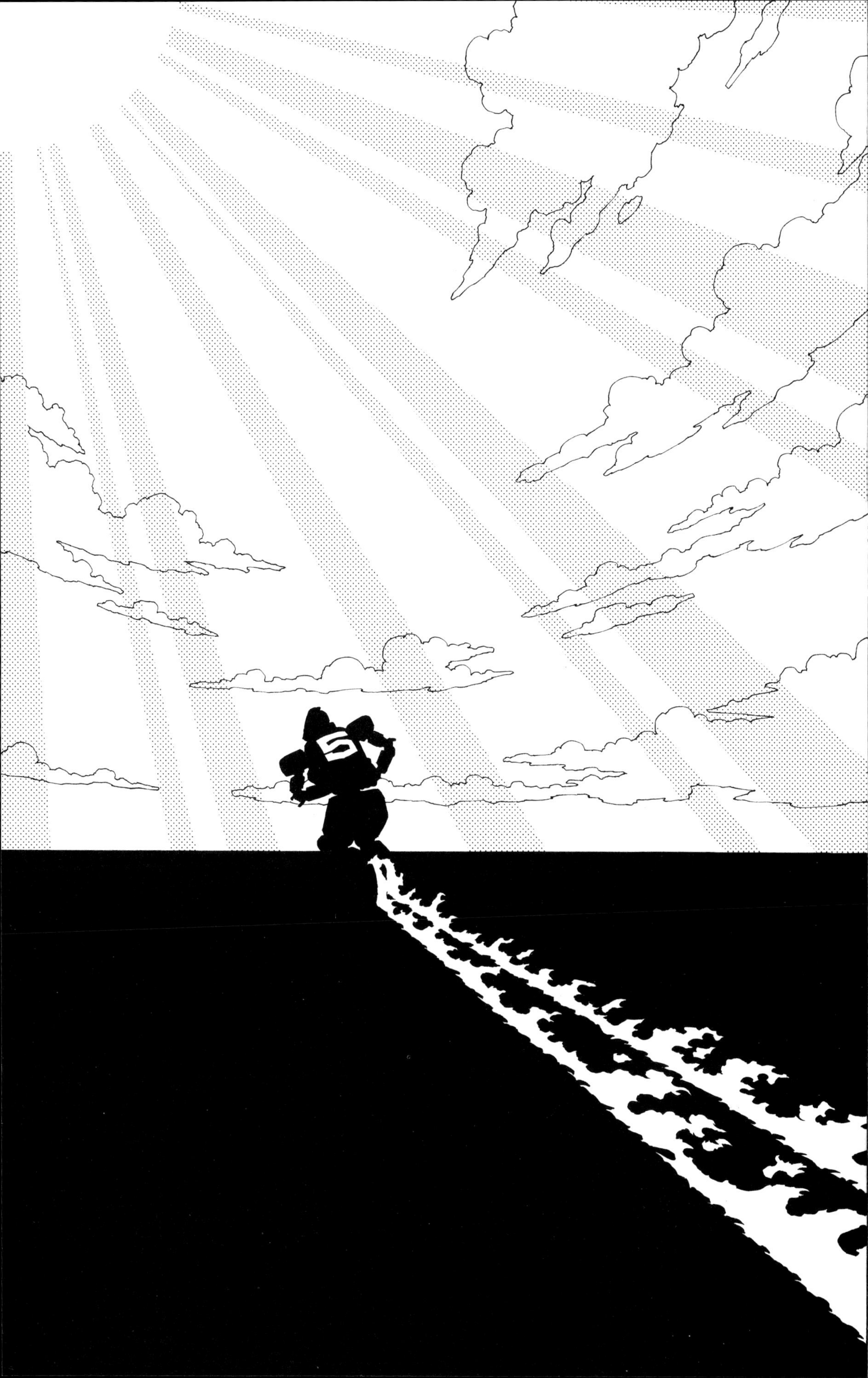
5

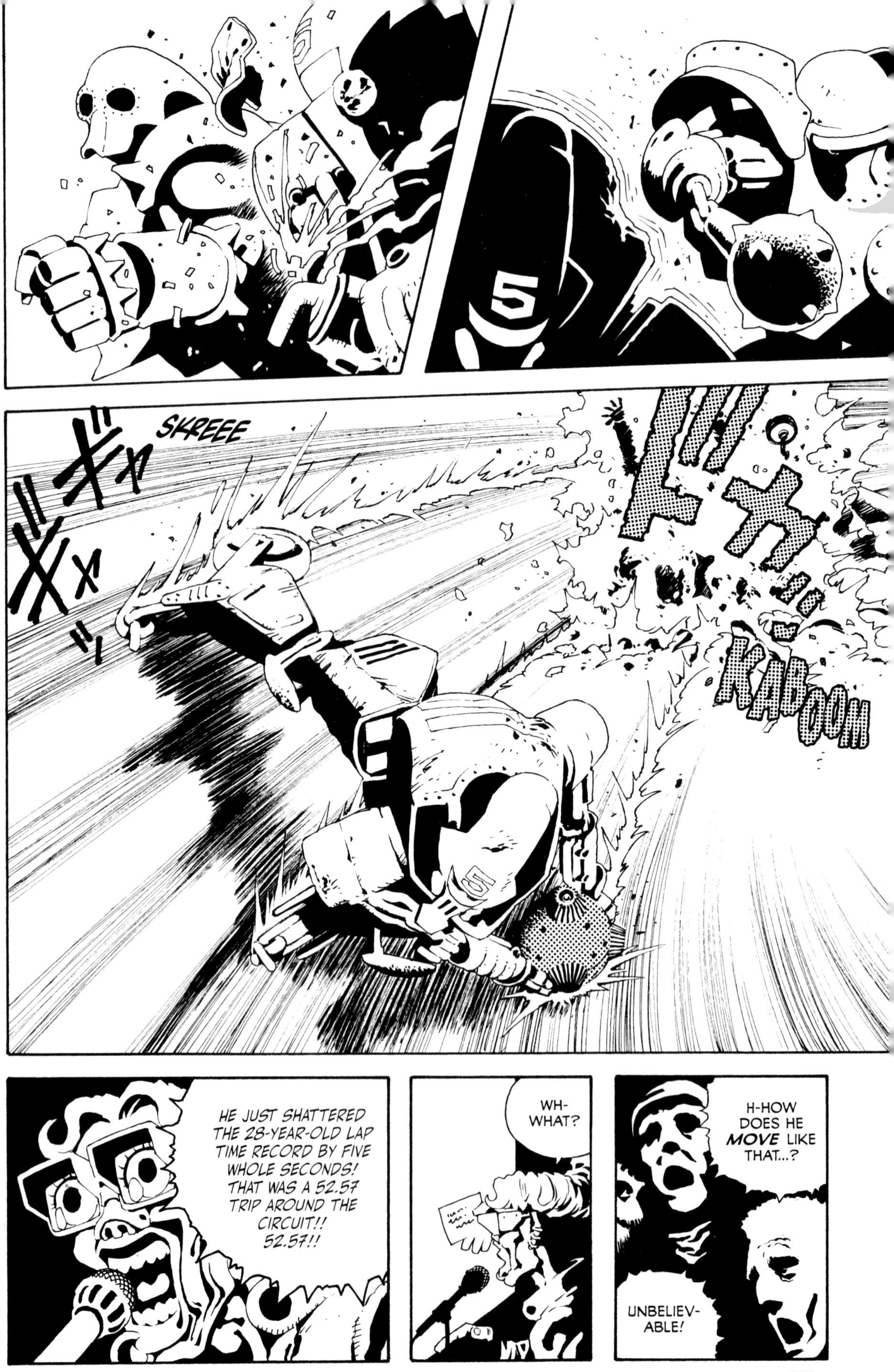
SKREEE
KABOOM
H-HOW DOES HE **MOVE** LIKE THAT...?
UNBELIEV-ABLE!
WH-WHAT?
HE JUST SHATTERED THE 28-YEAR-OLD LAP TIME RECORD BY FIVE WHOLE SECONDS! THAT WAS A 52.57 TRIP AROUND THE CIRCUIT!! 52.57!!

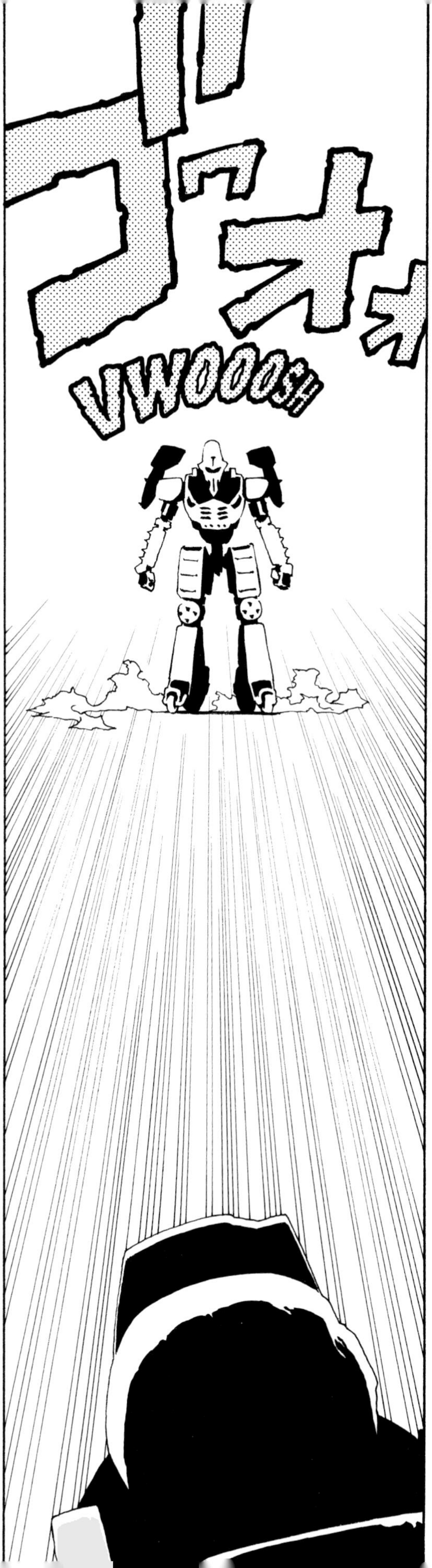
ゴァオォ
VWOOOSH

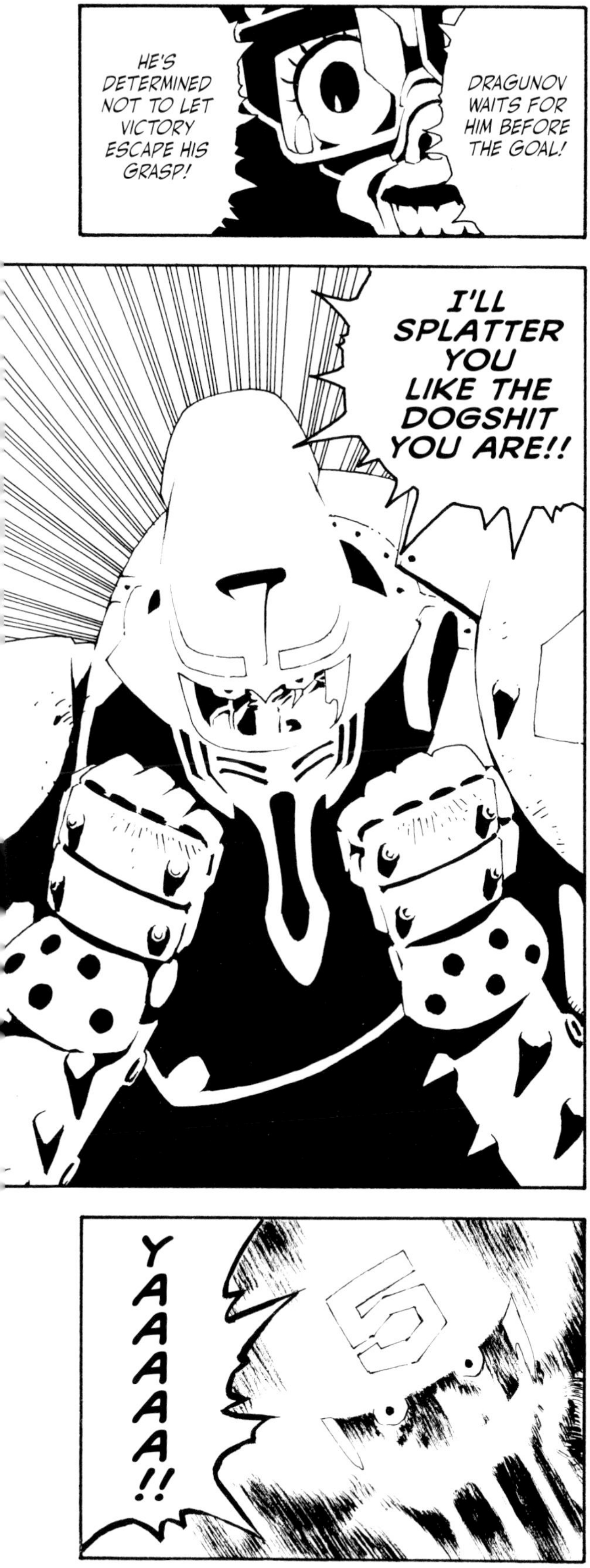
DRAGUNOV WAITS FOR HIM BEFORE THE GOAL!
HE'S DETERMINED NOT TO LET VICTORY ESCAPE HIS GRASP!
I'LL SPLATTER YOU LIKE THE DOGSHIT YOU ARE!!
YAAAAAA!!

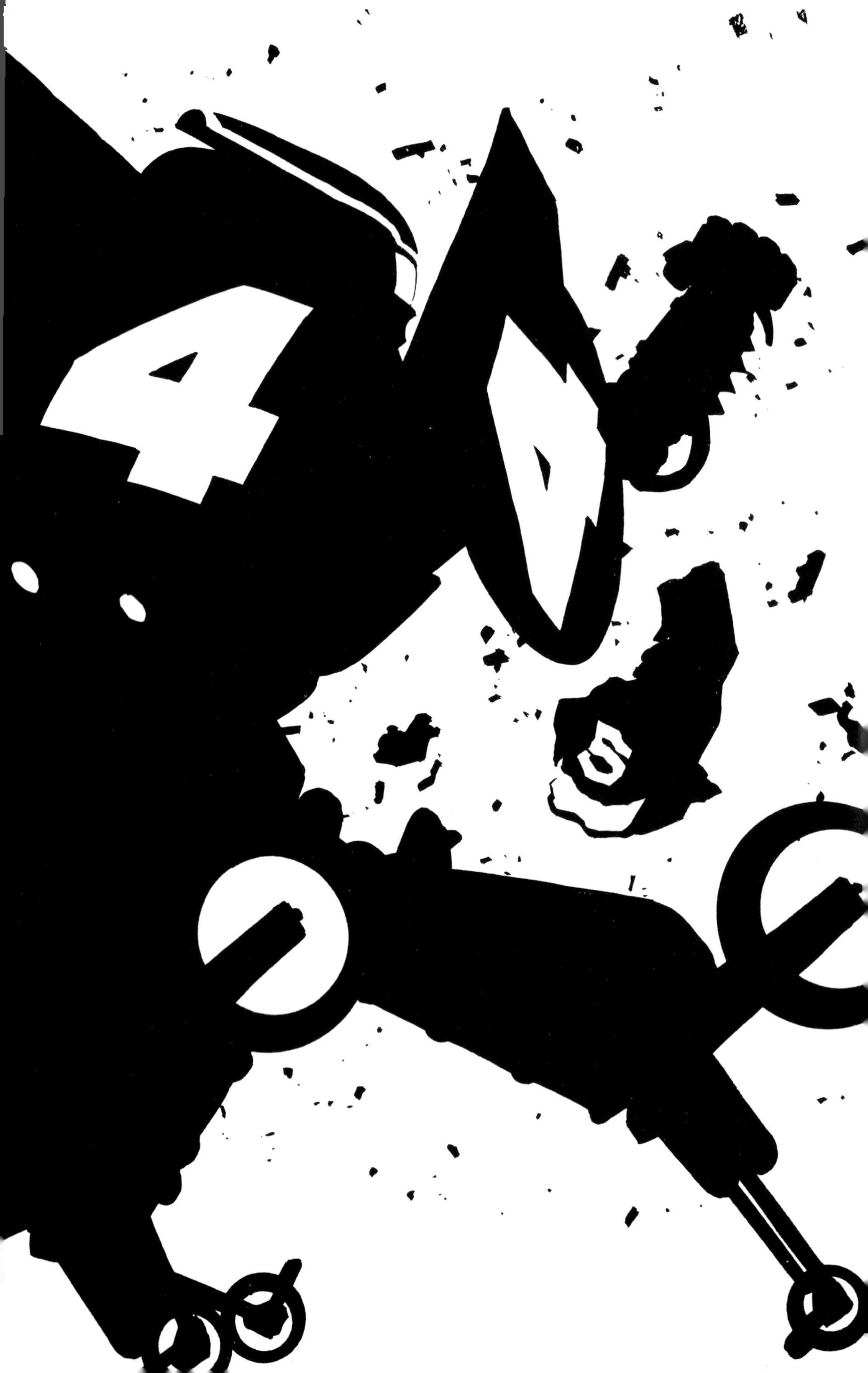

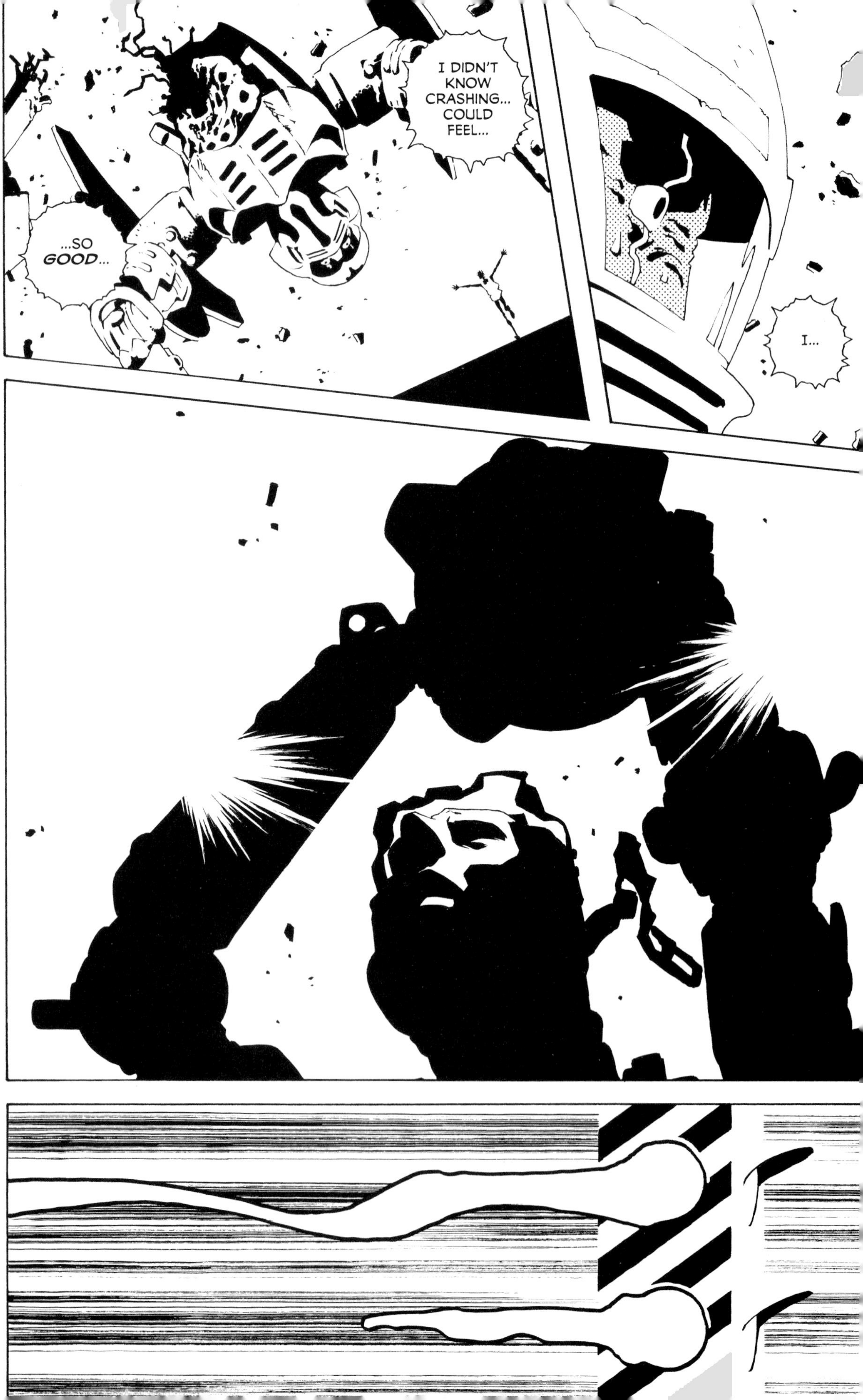
I...
I DIDN'T KNOW CRASHING... COULD FEEL...
...SO *GOOD*...

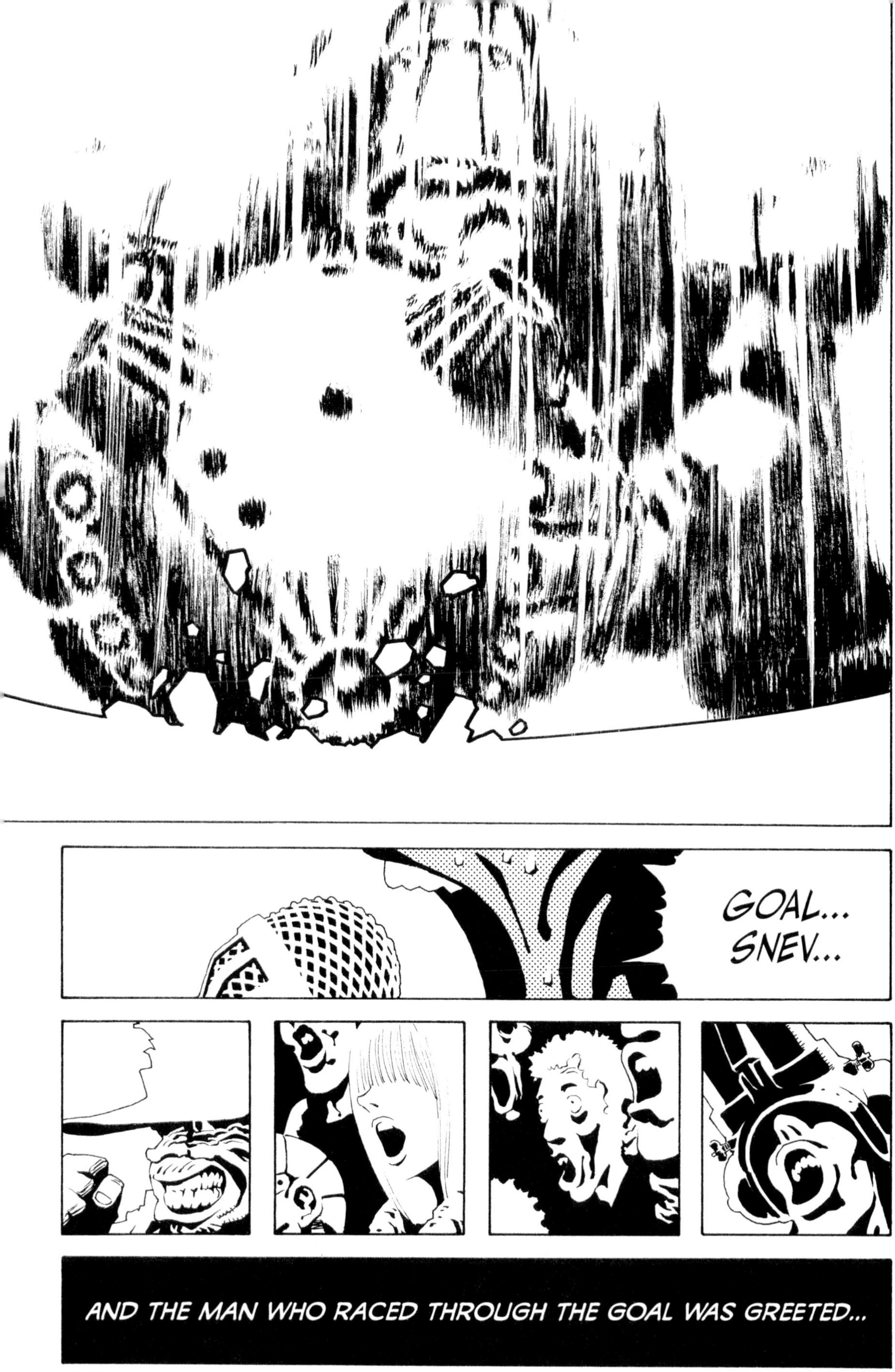
GOAL... SNEV...
AND THE MAN WHO RACED THROUGH THE GOAL WAS GREETED...

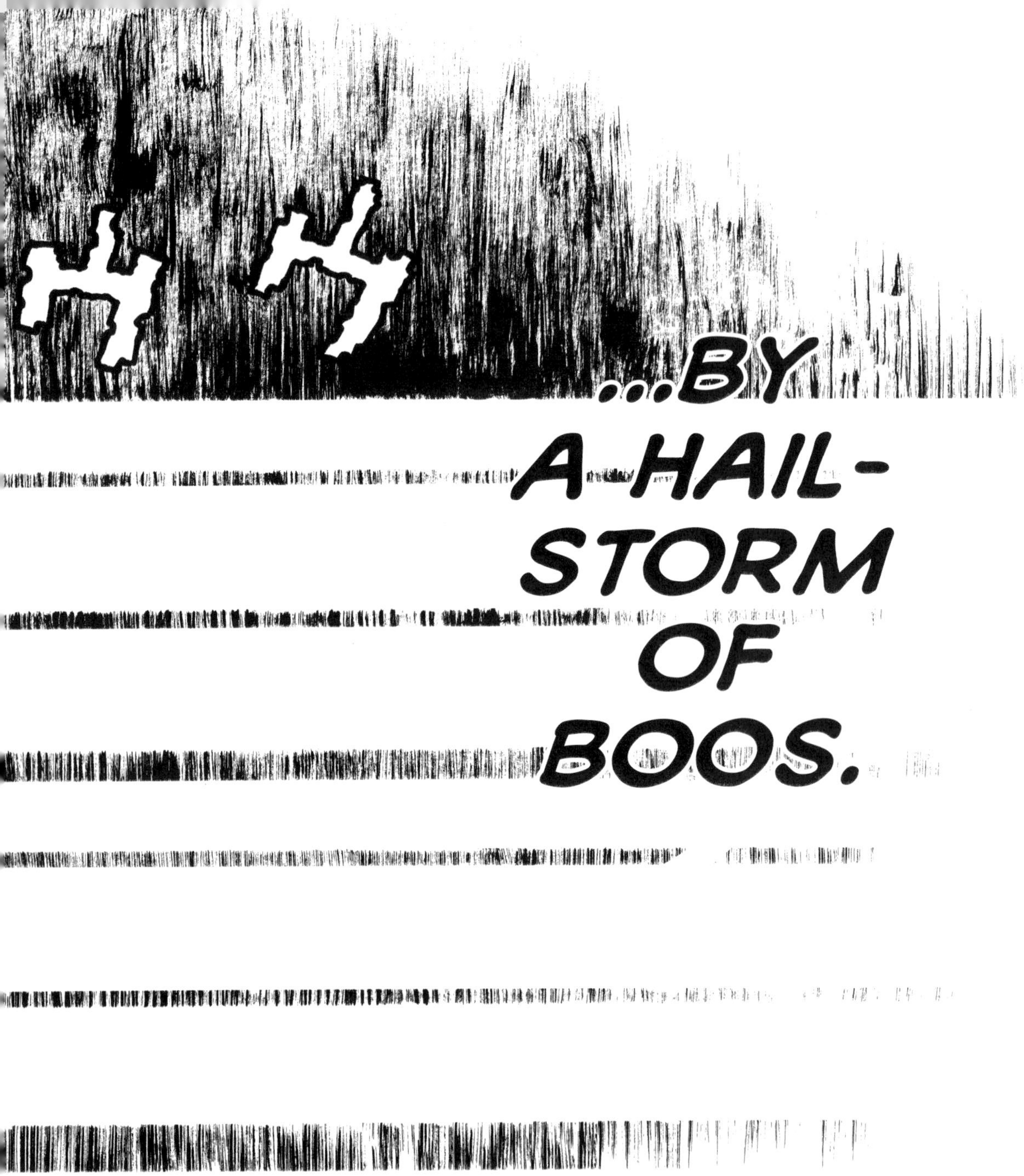
...BY A HAIL-STORM OF BOOS.

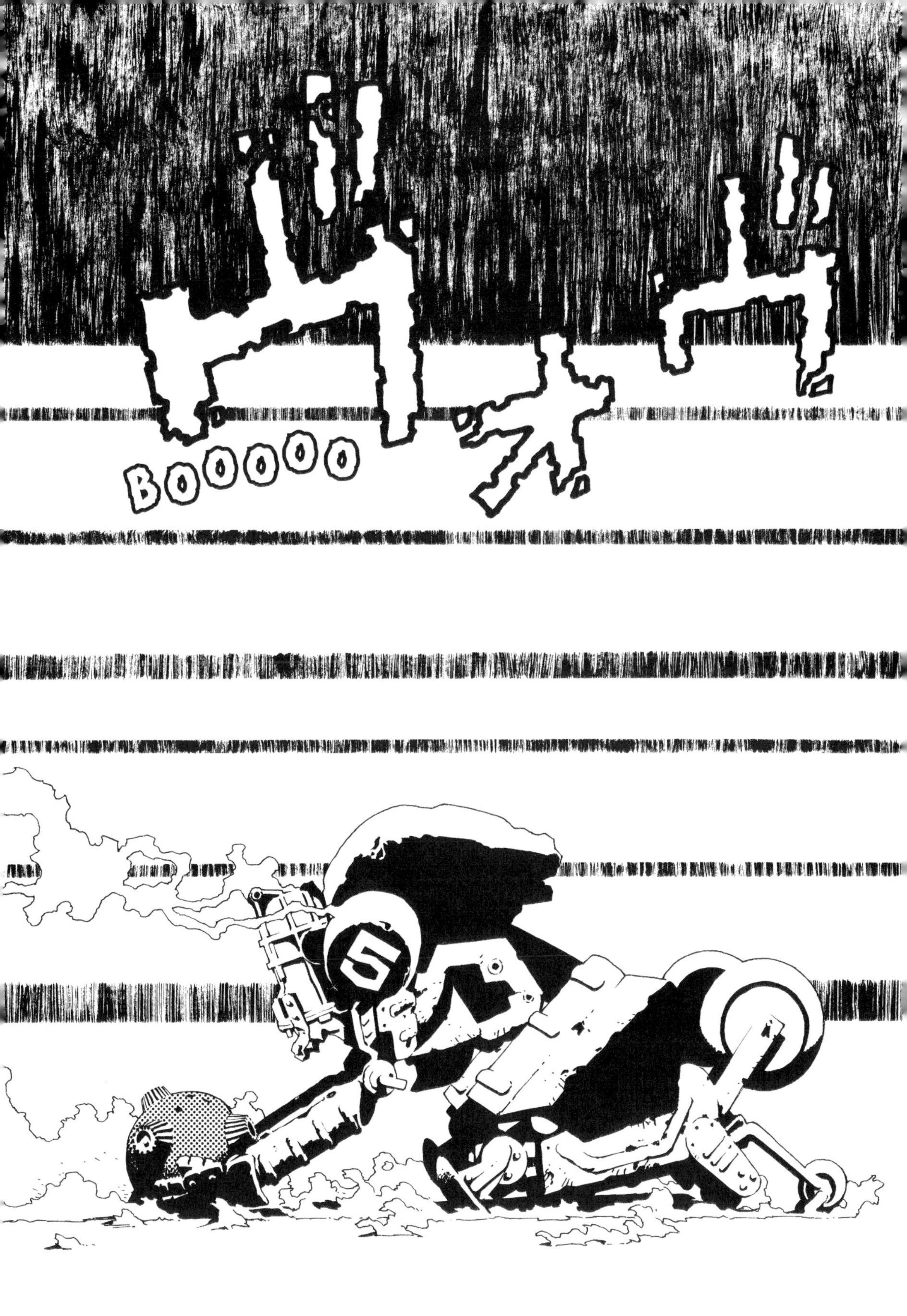
BOOOOO

THE WINNER NOBODY WANTED.

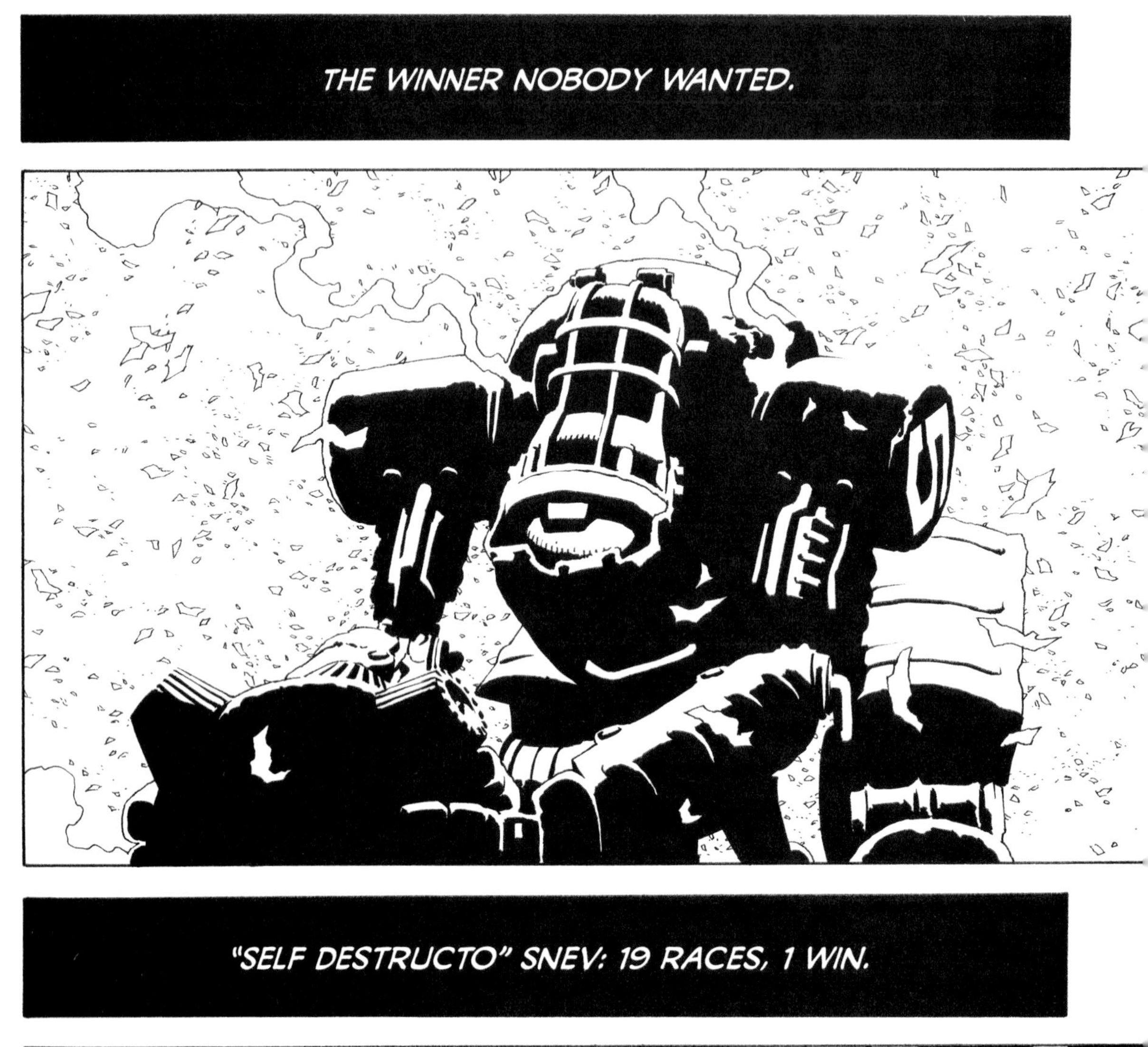

"SELF DESTRUCTO" SNEV: 19 RACES, 1 WIN.

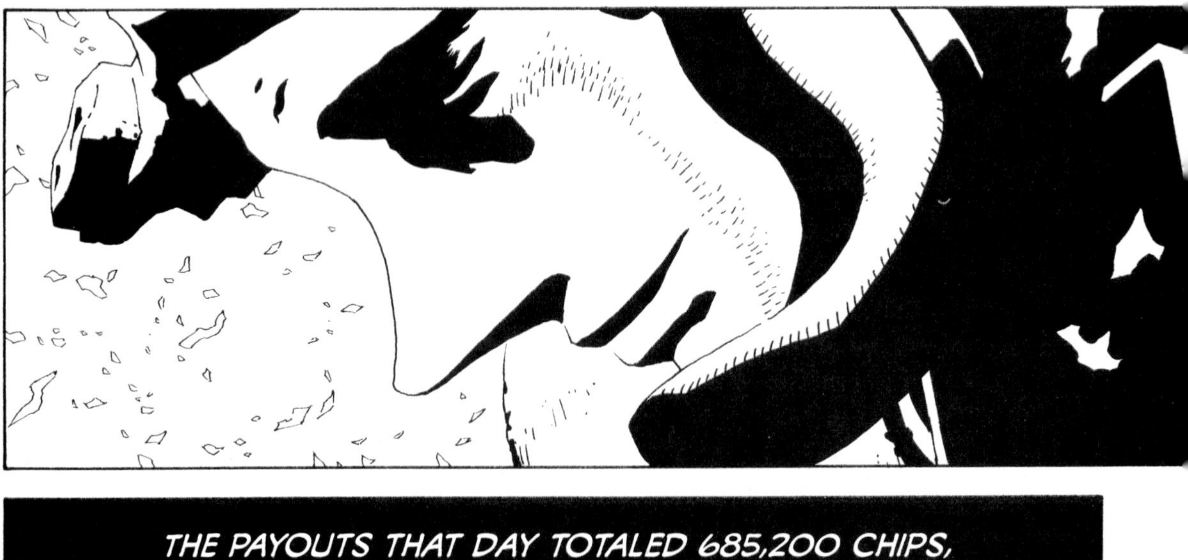

THE PAYOUTS THAT DAY TOTALED 685,200 CHIPS,
MAKING SNEV THE GREATEST LONG SHOT IN HISTORY.

THE REVELATION OF THE ADAM SCANDAL DEALT A MAJOR BLOW TO MEGIL INC., BUT IT WASN'T ENOUGH TO DRIVE IT COMPLETELY OUT OF BUSINESS. IN FACT, MEGIL INC. LASTED ANOTHER SEVEN YEARS, UNTIL THE HIDEOUS BRAIN-MELTING **BLAZE** STIMULANT CAUSED A WAVE OF BRAIN DEATHS, AND THE COMPANY'S LEADER BECAME A WANTED MAN.

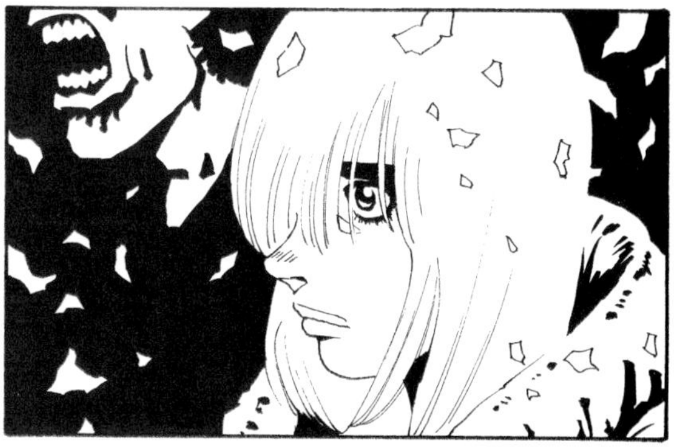

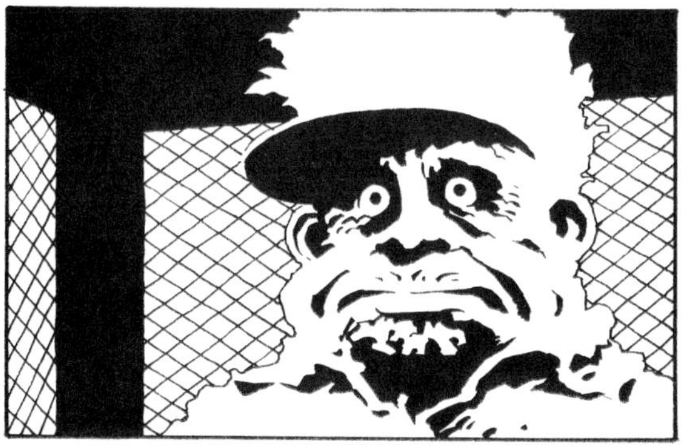

DRAGUNOV CONTINUED PLAYING MOTORBALL WITH ANOTHER TEAM AFTER THE END OF SPANDAU. HE WON 206 OUT OF 288 EVENTS UNTIL THE SIDE EFFECTS OF HIS ACCEL OVERUSE FORCED HIM INTO RETIREMENT.

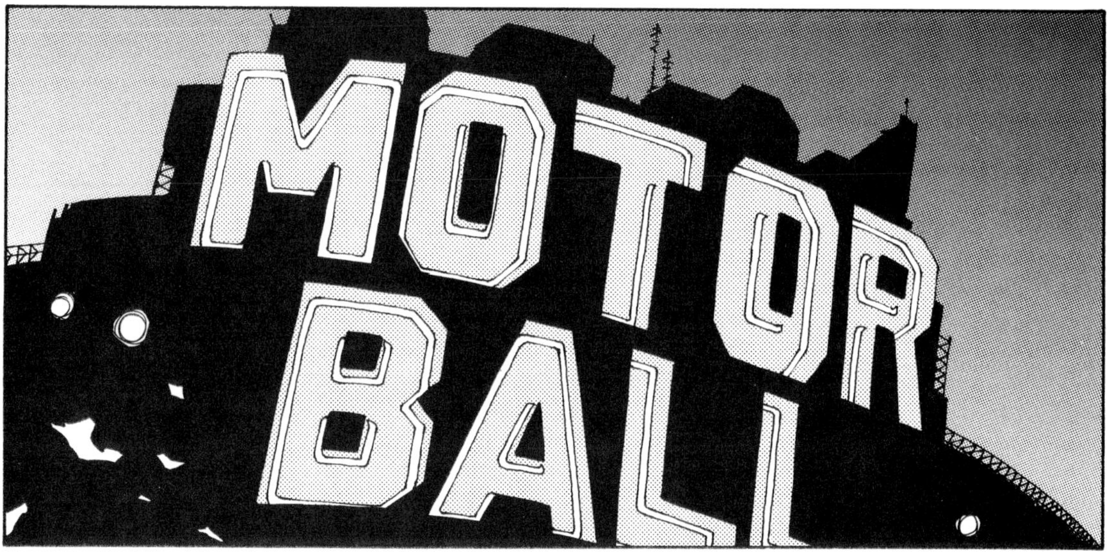
MOTOR
BALL

SNEV WAS NEVER SEEN AGAIN.

Translation Notes

Substantist, page 276

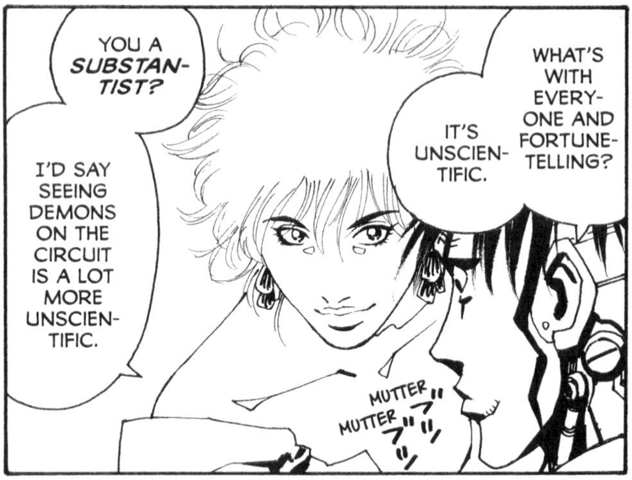
WHAT'S WITH EVERY-ONE AND FORTUNE-TELLING?
IT'S UNSCIENTIFIC.
MUTTER MUTTER
YOU A *SUBSTANTIST?*
I'D SAY SEEING DEMONS ON THE CIRCUIT IS A LOT MORE UNSCIENTIFIC.

An invention of the world of Battle Angel Alita that is presented as a contemporary religion at the time of the setting. In actuality it's a cheeky homophone of the Japanese word for "Buddhism" (bukkyô) that replaces the character for "Buddha" with "substance" or "matter."
(See Volume 1 for more information.)

Yukito Kishiro Speaks
An interview with Kodansha Comics

February 2018

KC: More than most manga, the original *Alita* series told short, self-contained stories in each volume, but they all led to a larger story about Alita and who she would become over the course of the manga. What made you decide to go with this approach on the first series, and why did you move away from it when Alita returned in *Last Order*?

YK: There are two reasons. The first is a reflection of the magazine in which it was published. *Battle Angel Alita* was published in Shueisha's *Business Jump*, which is targeted at 30-something, office-working men. It was necessary to make sure that even readers without an interest in science fiction could enjoy it. My idea was to modularize the story, constructing it in roughly volume-sized chunks to keep the length down. That way, it was easy to follow even if you only picked it up partway through.

My second reason was in case the series got canceled. Nowadays, it's fairly common to see SF/fantasy stories set in another world in Japanese comics, but at the time, in the late 1980s to early 1990s, there were many obstacles preventing a new artist with no track record from drawing pure sci-fi in a major manga magazine. There was another publisher that was so adamantly against the idea of a science fiction series that they refused me out of hand. Given this sort of headwind, I wanted to be ready to adapt in case the series was canceled prematurely.

ゴゴーーン
ゴゴーーーン
ゴゴーーーン
ガラ
ガラ
ガラガラ
ガランガラン

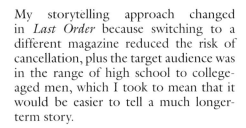

My storytelling approach changed in *Last Order* because switching to a different magazine reduced the risk of cancellation, plus the target audience was in the range of high school to college-aged men, which I took to mean that it would be easier to tell a much longer-term story.

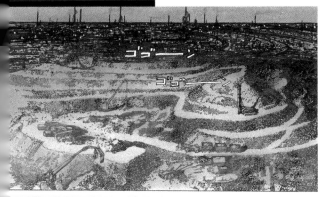

KC: I've heard that you ended *Alita* originally because you were ill. Is that true? If not, what prompted you to end it, and why did you want to return to it later?

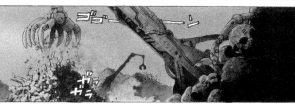

YK: The reason I ended the original *Alita* run was work-related interpersonal trouble causing me considerable stress. I decided it wasn't possible for me to continue on with the series at that point. I didn't see a doctor about this, so I suppose I might've been sick in some diagnosable way. All I know is that I was feeling fairly neurotic in general. The sound of rain was enough to drive me crazy, and I would tremble with fear just from looking at a blank sheet of paper. I didn't want to do it, but it was clear that the series had to be ended at that point.

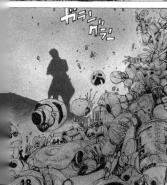

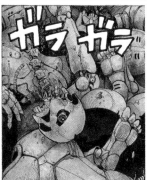

For the next few years, I worked bit by bit to get back to a healthy state, and that was when I started drawing *Last Order*, hoping to develop the "outer space arc" I'd been looking forward to telling.

KC: In "Ashen Victor," the side story included in this volume, you used a very different art style. Were you inspired by the work of Frank Miller, as has been speculated? Are there any other international comics artists who have inspired your work on *Alita*?

YK: At the time, I was just blown away by Frank Miller's *Sin City*. So there's a lot of Frank Miller's and Taiyo Matsumoto's influence in *Ashen Victor*. Some artists from overseas that have influenced me are Jean "Moebius" Giraud, Enki Bilal, Simon Bisley, Geof Darrow, and Jim Lee, among others.

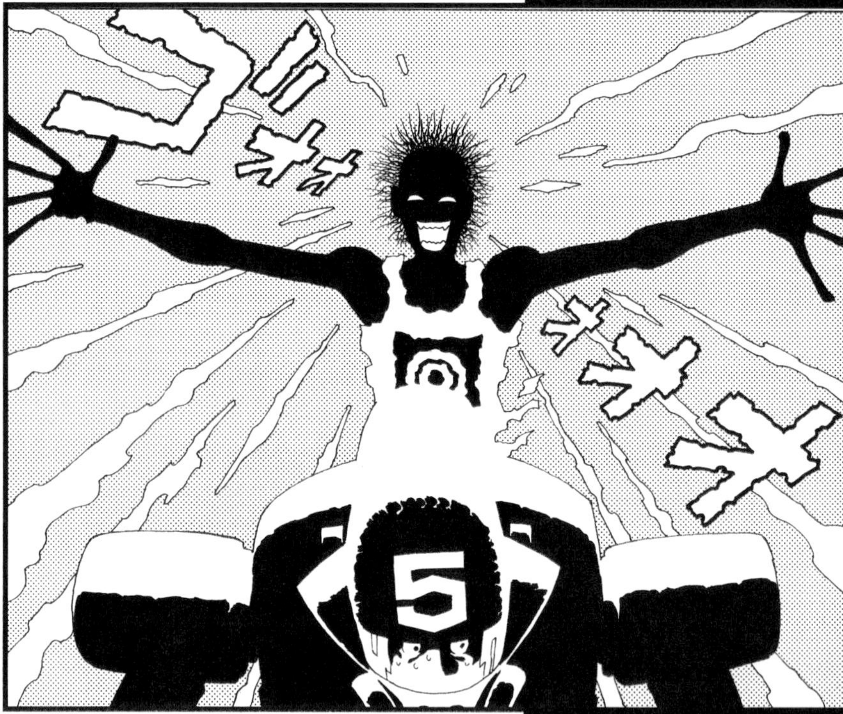

A panel from Ashen Victor.

KC: I've heard that James Cameron and Robert Rodriguez have worked closely with you to create the new movie. what has that process been like? How closely does the movie follow the books?

YK: I wouldn't say I'm "working closely" with them. In August 2016, Jon Landau visited Japan, and I was given a Japanese translation of the movie script. If you can trust the word of the guy who created the story in the first place, it's really good! But I haven't requested any changes or corrections of any kind to the script I saw.

In January 2017, I visited the set in Austin and got to meet Robert Rodriguez and members of the movie staff. I really felt a strong enthusiasm and respect for the source material from them. So I put my full trust in them to make the movie as they see fit, and I'm looking forward to the film as any other viewer would. There are parts of the movie that deviate from the details of the original work, but the core of the story – its "soul," if you will – is quite intact. Please don't worry.

KC: Though *Alita* was rooted in the cyberpunk movement of the 1990s, the story has remained fresh and relevant over 20 years later. Why do you think that is? What is it about the story that makes it so universally accepted and acclaimed?

YK: I think it's because humanity is central to the theme of *Battle Angel Alita*. There's a universality to questions like, "What is humanity?" or

"How do humans relate to other people?" or "How do individuals reach a compromise with the greater world?" such that there's always something that connects to the reader, no matter the era or the culture.

KC: The characters appear to be a wide variety of nationalities, and later in the story we discover that the Scrapyard is located in the former United States. What made you decide to take that approach instead of making the characters and setting Japanese?

YK: If the story had been set in future Japan, I would've introduce plenty of Japanese people, but that's not the world of *Alita*. Putting aside the fact that the setting makes it impossible otherwise, I intentionally chose to depict a diverse, universal, foreign vibe for the story. I wanted to draw something that was clearly "not here."

KC: If fans could only take away one thing from the experience of watching Rodriguez's *Alita: Battle Angel*, what do you hope it will be?

YK: I can only say so much, as I haven't seen the finished film yet. But as the creator of the original story, I think I would be most satisfied if fans of the series forgot all they knew, dove into the world that the movie depicted, went on Alita's adventure with her, and when the credits rolled, thought, "Ahh, that was great!"

KC: Language plays a big role in your depiction of the future. The Scrapyard has signs in Korean and Chinese, and there's a very heavy German presence on Mars and in its martial arts, like panzerkunst. Where did the inspiration for this come from? And why does German play such an important role on *Battle Angel Alita*'s Mars?

YK: The speech and text of foreign languages is exciting to me. They're mystical and mysterious, like some kind of exotic magic. At the bookstore, I'll go to the bilingual dictionary section and buy dictionaries of any foreign language I don't have yet. I'd love to use even more in my manga, like from countries in Southeast Asia or Africa, but I can't just half-ass it, so unfortunately, I can only stick to those languages I can get dictionaries for.

As for why I use German on Mars, the most direct reason for this is that when I started the series in 1990, the only non-English dictionary I had was for German. Why did I have a German dictionary? Years ago, I was obsessed with plastic models of tanks, and my favorites were the German WWII tanks. My enthusiasm for German weapons led me to buy a dictionary so I could look up the terminology. Mars is also the symbol of war, so it just seemed to fit.

KC: You've said before that the creation of Desty Nova was influenced by a variety of sources, such as Victor Frankenstein, Mozart's peculiar laugh in the film Amadeus, and even his name coming from a Blue Oyster Cult song. Are there any other characters that were created in this way? What is your process for developing characters?

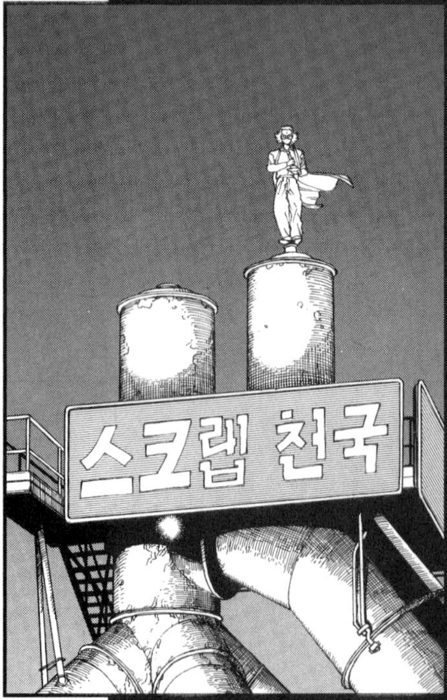
스크랩 천국

YK: Roughly speaking, there are three primary ways I construct my characters. First are the characters who are born to fill a particular need or role within the story. I tend to start my stories with the themes and plot first, so most of my characters fall into this category. Second are characters that come about because I want to draw them, regardless of what the story says. Alita, Desty Nova, Figure Four, Koyomi, Sechs, Caerula, Zekka, and more recently, Erica and Baron Muster fall into this category. Third are characters who ended up being more entertaining than I accounted for, and go on to support stories of their own, such as Zapan, Toji, and Rakan.

It's hard to go into further detail on the second and third types, as they come about for a variety of reasons, so I'll only go into my process when it comes to the first type, characters who are created to fill a crucial role in the story. In the plotting stage, they're nothing more than symbols (Character A, Character B) designed to play a specific part, which is very inorganic and flat. They're not really manga characters at this point.

So first, I decide on a name. This is not a rigorous process by any means; it's usually from some book I read or music I listened to recently. Sometimes I just open the dictionary until I find a random word I like. At the moment, I've got a handy reference book of "Names Around the World" that I often peruse for ideas.

Next, I do a few passes at visual designs in a sketchbook. By putting these vague ideas of characters into physical form, they become more solidified, and I start getting more ideas about what to do with them. Then I put them into a rough draft where they have dialogue and emotions to play with.

Until that point, I'm playing the part of the creator, thinking about them from a bird's-eye view, but in the draft of a chapter, I'm finally getting into that character's head and seeing things from their perspective. Sometimes I spend panels drawing things that have nothing to do with that character's role in the story. That makes them more alive, more actual people than just props or puppets to achieve a certain story effect.

KC: There are a few scenes in the original series that use popular music to great effect (for example, Kaos's performance of Alan Parson Project's "Inside Looking Out"). What role does music play in your creation process? Also, what songs would you put on the ultimate soundtrack for the *Battle Angel Alita* series?

YK: When I was still studying, I had a hard time wrapping my head around the way that manga is actually organized and constructed. Music taught me a whole lot about composition, which I was able to use in manga.

Music helps stir powerful emotions, and I've always tried to depict those feelings through stories. Music helps support me when the creative process gets difficult. I've got an iPod in the studio with over 8,700 songs on it that I'm constantly playing. (This isn't my entire collection, though. I've also got over two thousand CDs.)

As far as an ultimate *Alita* soundtrack goes, it would be too difficult to put together a 100-track playlist, so I'll pass on that one.

KC: You were an early adopter of digital art tools in the creation of your manga, but these days it's rare to see manga artists who work without digital assistance such as 3D models and tracing digital photos. How has your use of digital art tools changed over the years, and how do you feel about the use of digital tools in manga these days?

YK: If anything, my style is old-fashioned now. I haven't changed my production process in about 20 years. (I draw the art on paper, scan it, and finish in Photoshop.) Sometimes it causes problems, like when the old applications and plugins I use mean I can't upgrade my Macintosh to the latest OS. I'm actually mulling over whether I should buy an art tablet right now. In fact, for the past year I've been heading back toward a more analog style. (Spraying ink on the paper, for example.)

"Music helps stir powerful emotions, and I've always tried to depict those feelings through stories."

From what I hear, young artists these days won't use paper at all. They draw on a tablet and use a comics-drawing program called ClipStudio to finish up their manga. I can't go fully digital for my own circumstantial reasons, but I think if your finished manga is good, it doesn't matter how you created it. Tools are meant to be used.

KC: In 1990, when *Alita* debuted, you envisioned a world where cyberization was commonplace. Today, robots are widespread in industrial applications, and prosthetic limbs of the type you envisioned are on the verge of becoming reality. Meanwhile, how we interact with technology has changed rapidly. If you were creating the setting of *Battle Angel Alita* today, is there anything you would do differently, knowing what you know now?

YK: I was completely taken by surprise by the appearance and rapid spread of cellphones and smartphones. However, *Alita* is set in a world that's cut off from our own, so I don't think it would really work to put our present-day information technology into that setting.

KC: The idea of cyborg martial arts blends a long human tradition with imaginative, fictional technology. Are you a practitioner of any real martial arts? Have you used yourself or people you know as models for some of your fight scenes?

YK: I don't practice any martial arts. I'm just a nerd who likes to read about it and collect information.

KC: You've said before that parts of yourself end up in some of your characters when they're being developed, but I also noticed that in your profile on your website, you said that the *yokai* (traditional Japanese ghost) that you'd like to become is a *dorotabo* [one-eyed, three-fingered ghosts of vengeful farmers whose fields have been left fallow after their deaths], which happens to be a minor character in the 8th Volume of *Battle Angel Alita*. Could you tell us about why you like the *dorotabo* and what part of you resembles that *yokai*? Also, what character in *Battle Angel Alita* is closest to who you are as a person now?

YK: Me saying that I wanted to be a *dorotabo* was a bit of black humor on my part. I don't actually think of him as an ideal in any way.

The closest *Alita* character to me would be the engineer Umba from the Motorball story arc.

KC: There's a tendency for artists to see their earlier works in an unflattering light, but looking back on the original *Battle Angel Alita* series, what are you most proud of? And as an artist, what personal victories have you accomplished since you began *Battle Angel Alita*?

YK: The proudest I've ever been of the *Alita* series is when I hear fans tell me, "Reading this manga changed my life."

When I started *Battle Angel Alita* in Shueisha's *Business Jump* in 1990, I was 23 years old, just some ignorant kid with hardly any life experience, only a foolhardy determination to draw something great. I had no idea if I was going to succeed or fail. I'm remembering singing Gamma Ray's *Heading for Tomorrow* album while my brother and I spent an all-nighter finishing up the complete draft of the very first chapter before its deadline.

While it was running in *Business Jump*, I didn't know if *Alita* meant anything to the people who read it or not. When the series ended in 1995, all of a sudden I got a huge bag full of fan mail, and I'd barely received any until that point. I was stunned that there were this many fans of the series.

After I got onto the Internet in 1997, I got fan email from overseas readers, which helped me realize that *Alita* had transcended language and cultural barriers to be read and beloved by people all over the world. It was a phenomenal joy to find out that great Hollywood directors like James Cameron and Robert Rodriguez were fans of the series, too. I can't even put into words what it means to me that the dream cooked up by a 23-year-old kid from Japan 28 years ago is now going down in Hollywood history as *Alita: Battle Angel*.

Thank you to Yukito Kishiro for taking the time to answer our questions and for creating the wondrous and inspiring world of Battle Angel Alita, *and thank you to Dallas Middaugh for his assistance with this interview.*

"The proudest I've ever been of the Alita series is when I hear fans tell me, 'Reading this manga changed my life'."

The interview below was conducted by Stéphane Beaujean, art director of the Angoulême International Comics Festival, and was first published in French in the magazine Kaboom, issue No. 17 (November 2016-January 2017).

Beaujean: You've been carrying on with the *Battle Angel Alita* story for nearly 30 years now, which I'm sure hasn't always been easy. How does it feel to be heading into the final arc of the story at last?

Kishiro: As a matter of fact, even in the original *Alita* series, I had the idea for a space-based arc of the story. But due to several circumstances, that series had to be ended prematurely, which was disappointing to me. I was in bad shape mentally and physically for a while, until I eventually started *Battle Angel Alita: Last Order* in a new magazine called Ultra Jump. I started that one with the intention of expanding on that original idea, but it ballooned into something much longer. It grew in the telling. The Mars story I'm telling now [in *Battle Angel Alita: Mars Chronicle*] was originally supposed to be part of *Last Order*, but I ended up switching publishers in the middle, and it was getting long in the tooth, so it seemed better for a number of reasons to just end *Last Order* and move on to a new subtitled series for a fresh start. But it was all part of a rough plan I've had since the beginning.

Beaujean: From what I've read in old interviews, from around 1990 or so, you clearly had a firm vision for the roots of the Alita character, and it seems like you're writing with an idea already of how you ultimately want to end the story. Is that accurate?

Kishiro: I don't have all the fine details planned out, but I have had a general vision of how I'd like it to go, which hasn't changed much over the years. But I don't want it all fixed in place ahead of time, such that I strangle my own story and run out of ideas. Instead, I have the big picture decided, with everything below that open to improvisation, which allows me to add new ideas to it whenever I come up with them.

...THAN
'UT YOU
HROUGH
O MUCH
ADNESS.

I WOULD RATHER GIVE UP MY LIFE...

Beaujean: So, at the start, you had a vague idea for the ending without the fine details planned out. But do you have a firmer game plan for the ending at this point in time? Or is there still some haziness to the idea?

Kishiro: Actually, it's going to take a few years yet to get there, so the ending is still open and not fixed in place.

Beaujean: You mentioned that you'll still be drawing for years. The art has changed quite a bit from the start of the story to now. Was that a natural process, or did it come about intentionally, in pursuit of some kind of aesthetic idea?

Kishiro: It's both. But when I look at my old art, it's so terrible that it makes me want to die. (Laughs.)

Beaujean: That's not true at all! But if there is an intentional element that you're driving toward, what is it? What are you trying to achieve, artistically?

Kishiro: Well, there's line strength, for example. In the old *Alita*, I wasn't used to working with pens yet, and I couldn't fully control the width of my lines. I would try to draw a thick line and couldn't do it, or try to draw a fine line and fail at that. But by the time I got to *Last Order*, I had conquered that problem and learned how to draw the thickness I wanted. But then the problem was that when I drew fine lines, they ended up looking too weak when they were shrunk down to the size of the graphic novel. [Editor's note: In Japan, manga is first serialized in magazines at a larger size, then released in smaller paperback format.] But after a whole bunch of experimentation over the years, I'm now drawing almost all my primary linework in *Mars Chronicle* with a fude pen [brush pen].

Beaujean: Oh, a fude pen.

Kishiro: When I want to do fine detail, I'll use a more typical nib pen, like a G-pen. But using the fude pen allows me to get nice and thick. You have the magazine that's nice and big, then the art then gets shrunk down for the tankôbon [trade paperback], so stuff that looks bold at first gets a lot more delicate and might lose its visual impact somewhat. To counteract that, and to make my process more efficient, I use a fude pen as my main tool.

Beaujean: You started using digital tools at a time when most Japanese artists hadn't yet tried them out.

Kishiro: Right.

Beaujean: It would seem that you were very careful in adding in those new tools. I got the sense that you enjoyed doing digital work. Is that true?

Kishiro: I would say so. The first time I did a black-and-white piece digitally was an *Alita* side story called "Supersonic Fingers."* That was around 1996 or '97.

I actually had a bit of a research and testing period. Nowadays, this is common knowledge: When you print a monochrome image put together in Photoshop, the anti-aliasing causes the lines to get thicker. You can overcome this with high-resolution offset printing, but in the color printing we use for manga in Japan, it comes out thick and rough. After experimenting with ways to fix this, I realized that the best way to counteract the lack of anti-aliasing was to use the highest printing resolution possible, which at the time was 300dpi.

Beaujean: Three hundred?

Kishiro: That's on the low side now, but at the time I had to do a number of test printings without anti-aliasing, trying to keep the lines from getting too fine, making the patterns look like hand-pasted screentones, until I had a finished product. Basically, I'm a tech geek who loves trying out new stuff, so it's fun to experiment with things like that.

Beaujean: You mentioned being a tech geek. There are strong scientific elements in the setting of *Alita*, and strong political elements as well. Did you include these things in the story because of personal interest, or because you thought such things were necessary to build this sort of cyberpunk story?

Kishiro: Umm, the political stuff?

Beaujean: Scientific.

Kishiro: I like science. I mean, you have to work with it when you draw science fiction, and, obviously, I include some junk science as well, but I try not to let it get out of control, beyond a certain boundary.

Beaujean: Well, to be more specific, you've covered nanotechnology, transhumanism, pollution, excessive waste... all of these issues that weren't as prominent at the time, but are more important now. Are these things you brought to the story out of your own interests and sensibilities?

Kishiro: The things you just mentioned are probably about the original *Alita*, like the relationship between the Scrapyard and Zalem. The thing is, *Alita* didn't just pop into existence out of nowhere. There was a lot of trial and error involved to get it to that point. I'd produced a number of failures before it. Stories where the protagonist was a cyborg, for example. They were never published, more like... I guess you'd call them storyboards? Where me and an editor talked it over and I sketched out rough material, never inked or anything like that. Hundreds of pages of this stuff. So, during a few years of this trial and error, I made two short stories that had the Gunnm ("Gun Dream") name, but the setting was completely different from the actual Gunnm (*Battle Angel Alita*) series. It was just typical cyborg action stuff, like a C-movie.

Then I got the offer to do a series, but even I knew this wouldn't cut it. I liked the idea of a cyborg character who kicks a lot of ass, but I knew the world probably had to match that character better. Maybe this is just a typical archetype, but basically I was thinking it over in bed, and I just got this vague image of Zalem, a city in the clouds with an orbital elevator, and a mountain of scrap on the ground beneath it, all in a big interlocking system. I felt like, "This is it!" And that was the genesis of the *Alita* that everyone knows now. And along with that came the whole system of leeching, discarding and reusing resources, how cyborgs would live in this world – all of that was in the vision. Even the city in the sky, I knew that it was going to be suspended from an orbital elevator, not just floating there with anti-gravity powers. It was all there in the original vision.

Beaujean: There's a very strong class hierarchy in this world. In the interview that I mentioned earlier from around 1993, you actually said you might be somewhat of an anarchist. Does that have any connection to this story construction? Did you want to have class warfare be a theme?

Kishiro: Well, I was quite young then. I started *Alita* when I was 23, so it was a very long time ago. I was a bit of a firebrand back then...

Beaujean: Reading the original *Alita* series, there's a lot of action and killing, which seems like a metaphor for social dominance. Into that comes a hero, who brings this faint hope that the social hierarchy can be destroyed.

Kishiro: That's right, there was an element of that from the start. But I did have the premonition that if I made it more of a political warfare story, I'd probably fall flat on my face. I don't think it would've worked out.

Beaujean: In a sense, I feel like you're giving us your answer to the question of what life is through the lens of the character Alita. It seems like you're saying humanity isn't just consciousness, but experience and memories. Would you say that's right?

Kishiro: In the original *Alita* and then *Last Order*, it's revealed that Alita was sort of converted into a robotic exterior, but after that point there's nothing organic about her. Physically, she's essentially an android. Then you get into a question of soul – is Alita just the same as an android? – and I kind of think that's not the case, and the story is moving in that direction, but this is up to the reader to interpret, really. I'm just trying to put my character through a bunch of hardships, wondering how she'll react and what will happen as a result.

Beaujean: So has Alita lost all of her memories at the start? And if she has no memory – in other words, no humanity – it would seem that Alita's journey is the search for it. Is she undergoing all of these trials and tribulations and finding panzerkunst is the only way she can seize that kernel of her memory? Or is she seeking something larger than that?

Kishiro: Well, that's something I'll be drawing in the manga ahead.

Beaujean: I feel like you often depict people who are living in worlds that have been fundamentally destroyed. It's that way for Alita, and in the short story "Homecoming,"* the character Kenta is kind of lost in time, waiting for a message from a friend. Alita fights to profess her own humanity. It's kind of sad, and feels like there aren't any reasons for these situations that don't involve despair. Does this reflect your own view on life? Or is it completely invented for the sake of your stories?

Kishiro: That might be right. The fact that I subconsciously select elements like that probably says something about me. Looking back at my childhood memories, I was raised in a place outside of the big city, where they just bulldozed the forests into flat, empty land as far as I could see. There weren't many other children my age, so I basically lived like a feral child, running around through the trees catching bugs and playing in rusted out cars and things. As I grew older, I started to understand things I didn't as a child. I could tell that Japan was a really peaceful place, and yet there were contradictions I couldn't place or explain.

By the time I was in high school, I was smart enough to study history, where I learned that not that long in the past, Japan had fought a big war and lost, and that this brought democracy to the nation, and we've gone along with that since then. But the old values were clashing with the new values, and you had the student movement, which was ultimately defeated, and they ended up being the ones who created the anime that people like me grew up watching. People like Mamoru Oshii took the experience of losing in the protest movement and worked out their trauma through anime. And we were raised on those stories. I was stunned.

Then I found out that the natural sights I'd seen when growing up were caused in the time of Prime Minister Kakuei Tanaka, when they had a project to redevelop the Japanese archipelago, cultivating the entire nation and building more train tracks and highways. And I just happened to be born in one of the places that they bulldozed clean. So I always lived with this knowledge in the back of my head that there had been something there once, but it had been destroyed, and we were living there in the aftermath of that process.

When the '80s and *Mad Max* came around, I remember thinking, "This is it. This is where I grew up." So when I was in elementary school and I drew manga in my little sketch notebook, I was already making stories about post-civilization worlds, places where there's nothing, but there used to be a culture at one time, and it all got sent back to the Stone Age, where life is cheap and you have to fight to survive, just like in *Mad Max*. I was drawing that kind of stuff back in grade school.

Beaujean: In middle school?

Kishiro: No, before that, around 1974, so it would have been elementary school. Because of that environment, I suppose there's always been a resistance within me to a perfectly-arranged civil society. It makes me uncomfortable.

Beaujean: So in your oldest memories as a child, there were still forests, but then they got razed to the ground?

Kishiro: No...

Beaujean: Or were they already cut down by that time?

Kishiro: That's right. I was born in Tokyo, but I have no memory of it. My parents moved us out of Tokyo to a place called Kashiwa when I was about a year old. Now Kashiwa is packed with housing and development, but at the time, it was on the prefectural border and there were like two or three houses there. I think there used to be woods there, but they cut them down, then bulldozed the land, and we just had whatever grass grew, and water pooled up in what was left. There used to be nature there, but it had already been destroyed by the time I found it.

Beaujean: I suppose that might tie into the concept of memory.

Kishiro: Perhaps.

Beaujean: I wanted to ask about Dr. Nova. He appears to be the polar opposite of Alita. Was he created to be a balancing force against her?

Kishiro: I don't really remember why I created him. But it's a cyborg story, so it seems natural to have a scientist who creates other cyborgs with superhuman powers that Alita has to fight, with that mad scientist blood running in his veins. I bet that's how I came up with him.

Beaujean: After all of the twists and turns in the story, he seems to be her arch-enemy, in a way.

Kishiro: Well, a lot has happened, and they were temporarily allies for a bit, so he's not really her greatest enemy, but as I said earlier, a lot of what I do in the story is to present Alita with various challenges and tribulations to see what she'll do and how she'll answer. If there's any character who represents that process, it's Nova. He puts her through various challenges, and sometimes helps, but he's usually antagonistic and sends powerful foes after her, sometimes just by coincidence. It's not that he's there to make evil, but that he is drawn to fate as a concept. It's no coincidence that his topic of research is karma. He's ultimately trying to conquer fate, which controls humanity, even bad fate. However, ultimately his actions only create bad things, which comes back to haunt him in a way. That's the way it's constructed in the story.

Beaujean: So he represents you?

Kishiro: I hear that comment a lot.

Beaujean: I guess that answer suggests you wouldn't agree, but I was reminded of what you said about yourself as an author earlier. Perhaps it's as the stand-in for the author that he does experiments on people because he wants to see how they'll evolve in response.

Kishiro: I suppose that's right.

Beaujean: At the end of *Last Order*, Nova removes all the human parts from Alita. Basically, he leaves no physical matter left, so that she exists only as memory, or information. Was this a necessary conclusion for story purposes, or do you really believe that humanity can be defined without matter, just as memory or information or ones and zeros?

Kishiro: That wasn't a belief I held. It was more of a question: As a cyborg, what parts of your body can you turn into machinery before you're not human anymore? Nobody would think of you as a machine if you replaced an arm or a leg, but let's say your whole body, everything except your brain, was replaced with machinery. You'd look indistinguishable from a robot. Are you still human or not? In Zalem, they told Alita she wasn't human. You could have that argument. But the conclusion of the original *Alita* series was that as long as your brain was biological, you were human.

In *Last Order* I took that further, asking what if you replaced more and more and more. The Zalemites were biological bodies with their brains on computer chips, for example. Are they human? If so, then Alita with her mechanical body could still be considered human if you also put her brain on a chip, right? So I did that in the story. It was torturous for Alita, but ultimately she recovered and prevailed, which suggests that even in this state, she's still human. Then that raises the question of if she can be happy or not. At the end of *Last Order*, the Alita who gets restored from her biological brain reunites with Figure Four and finds human happiness, but the Alita with the brain chip is still wandering the wilderness looking for happiness. And now I'm drawing what happens after that point.

Beaujean: We don't have much time left, so I'd like to switch to the topic of your influences. You mentioned Mamoru Oshii earlier; are there any other artists who have influenced you...

Kishiro: Actually, I wouldn't say Mamoru Oshii...

Beaujean: Oh, not him, then...

Kishiro: I've been influenced by many artists. It's been different people at different times. For example... Yoshikazu Yasuhiko, the character designer of *Gundam*, was an influence on my character art. Before that, just about anyone active in the '70s was an influence on me, but when I was in high school and started drawing serious manga with normal human characters, I was influenced by Yoshikazu Yasuhiko first. After that, there were a bunch... I was influenced by Tetsuo Hara of *Fist of the North Star*, and Rumiko Takahashi of *Urusei Yatsura*. I really couldn't count them all.

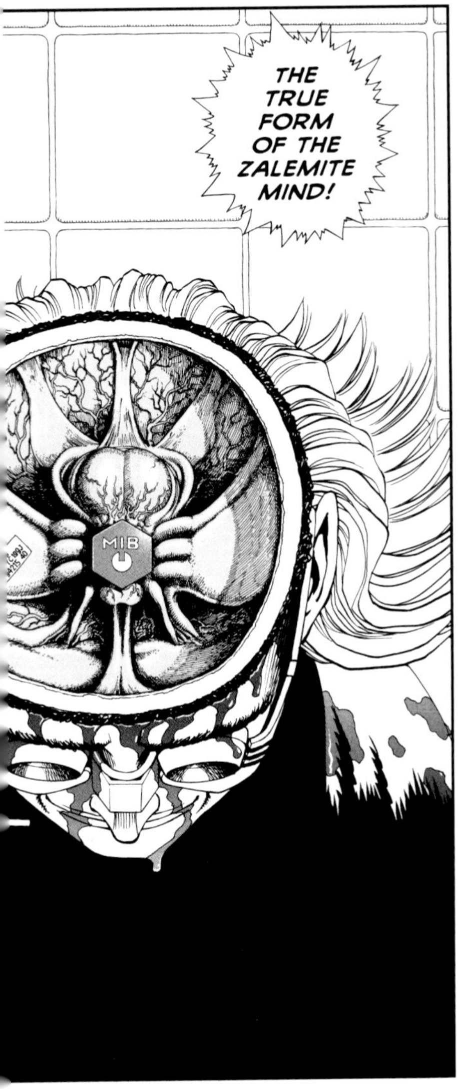
THE TRUE FORM OF THE ZALEMITE MIND!
MIB

Beaujean: Was there any experience that helped you jump from drawing manga for fun to drawing it professionally?

Kishiro: As I mentioned earlier, I was always drawing manga as a kid in my notebook. But actually, I wanted to be a movie director. *Star Wars* came out in Japan when I was in sixth grade, and I thought it was the coolest thing. I really wanted to direct movies, but then I learned about the state of the Japanese movie industry. By seventh grade, I'd already realized that I'd have to get hired by a company and work there until they finally let me direct a movie at age 50. So I gave up on that.

As far as hobbies go, I loved plastic models in middle school. It was right in the middle of the Gundam plastic model explosion, and I'd been collecting and building them since just before that. I liked building diorama sets, too. We'd go to a special import shop in Tokyo to get models of Star Destroyers or the Enterprise from *Star Trek*, stuff that cost thousands of yen, so I could put them together. I start to wonder if there was a way I could make a living with plastic models. There was a magazine, Hobby Japan, at the time, which is still around today. I would read that and wonder, well, nowadays you have modelers for figures, but there was none of that at the time. But I thought, maybe I could be a writer for Hobby Japan... and then I realized that was probably not going to happen.

So around tenth grade, I really started to think about my future prospects. My father was a tile layer for construction projects – he set down the tiles. I was his first son, so I always helped out, and it was assumed that I would take over the business. I respected my dad and always told him I'd continue in his footsteps, and that made him happy. But by high school, I wasn't satisfied with that anymore. I had those options I mentioned, but movie director and plastic models were out, so that left manga.

When I was in tenth grade there was a story about someone winning a manga contest at age 17, which blew my mind, and made me want to try it for myself. But I didn't tell my parents, because I was too scared. I knew I couldn't convince them unless I won some kind of award to show them I had what it would take. So I started drawing very hard with the intention of winning an award by my high school graduation. I told myself I needed to draw a thousand pages, and by the fall of my last year of school, I won an award from Shogakukan, and I still couldn't tell my dad I wanted to draw manga. After that I went to a vocational school and when I came back, I said I wanted to be a manga artist. And yes, he was pissed. For a time, I was practically disowned from the family. It was a big deal.

Beaujean: What kind of vocational school was it?

Kishiro: It was a design school called Tokyo Designer Gakuin.

Beaujean: A design school.

Kishiro: There were no manga classes back then, but they did have an animation class. I couldn't take that because I was on a scholarship from the newspaper company. I could only choose commercial design or technical design. I chose commercial, but in the end I only attended for one semester. I just acted like a big shot.

Beaujean: In old interviews, you said you'd be delighted to get a movie offer. Are you still happy about it now that it's happening? What sort of Alita do you suppose we'll see in the film? Personally, I can't imagine that a movie will provide something more than the Alita that's already on paper. I'd like to get your opinion on this.

Kishiro: Well, it's been quite a long wait. I'm very excited that it's finally coming together. Hmm, what should we expect...? When I met James Cameron, I said it was fine if he changed things. As long as it was independently good as a movie, I didn't mind if it was different from the original. Let me think...

Beaujean: I don't remember very well, but I believe that in an interview, you said that in a movie, you'd finally get to see the Alita you envisioned.

Kishiro: Well, it's not up to me to make it. (Laughs.) I'm the creator of the story, and I signed off on the contract, but I can't throw my weight around. So I basically said they can make it how they want. If I was making this myself, I'd put more thought into it, but all I really want is for them to do well and not let the fans down.

Beaujean: We're out of time. Do you mind if we ask one more? If this is too personal, feel free not to answer. You've been "with" Alita for 22 years now. What does she mean to you? She must be a personification of something, I feel. Is she your lover, or your child? Have you ever thought of her as a symbol in that manner?

Kishiro: I draw her hoping to infuse her with the best parts that don't really exist in me. But a goody-two-shoes isn't that fun to watch, so she's also got a violent side that I don't really have, either. Hmm. I guess I wouldn't say that I feel like she's my daughter or anything like that.

Beaujean: So she's like the good and bad parts that you yourself don't have.

Kishiro: Yes. In a rather distorted form.

Beaujean: Presented in a distorted form. Thank you very much. That's all. Thank you again.

Kishiro: Thank you.

Published in the United States by Kodansha Comics,
an imprint of Kodansha USA Publishing, LLC, New York.

Publication rights for this English edition arranged through Kodansha Ltd., Tokyo.

First published in Japan in 2013 and 2014 by Kodansha Ltd., Tokyo, as
Gunnm, volume 9 and Haisha.

ISBN 978-1-63236-602-3

Printed in China.

www.kodanshacomics.com

9 8 7 6 5 4 3 2 1

Translation: Stephen Paul
Lettering: Scott O. Brown
Editing: Ajani Oloye
Kodansha Comics edition cover design: Phil Balsman